THE
CIGARETTE
CENTURY

THE
CIGARETTE
CENTURY

The Rise, Fall, and
Deadly Persistence of the Product
That Defined America

A L L A N   M .   B R A N D T

BASIC
B
BOOKS

A Member of the Perseus Books Group
New York

Designed by Brent Wilcox
Set in 10.75 point Adobe Caslon

Library of Congress Cataloging-in-Publication Data
Brandt, Allan, M.
  The cigarette century: the rise, fall and deadly persistence of the product
that defined America / Allan M. Brandt.
     p.   cm.
  Includes bibliographical references and index.
  ISBN-13: 978-0-465-07047-3 (alk. paper)
  ISBN-10: 0-465-07047-7 (alk. paper)
    1. Tobacco industry—United States—History—20th century.
  2. Smoking—United States—History—20th century.   3. Smoking—
  Health aspects.   I. Title.
  HD9130.8.U5B72   2006
  338.4'767970973—dc22
                                                         2006029005

10 9 8 7 6 5 4 3 2 1

For Shelly,
Daniel and Jacob

CONTENTS

To the Princess, it was an enigma why anyone would smoke, yet the answer seems simple enough when we station ourselves at that profound interface of nature and culture formed when people take something from the natural world and incorporate it into their bodies.

Three of the four elements are shared by all creatures, but fire was a gift to humans alone. Smoking cigarettes is as intimate as we can become with fire without immediate excruciation. Every smoker is an embodiment of Prometheus, stealing fire from the gods and bringing it on back home. We smoke to capture the power of the sun, to pacify Hell, to identify with the primordial spark, to feed on the marrow of the volcano. It's not the tobacco we're after but the fire. When we smoke, we are performing a version of the fire dance, a ritual as ancient as lightning.

Does that mean that chain smokers are religious fanatics? You must admit there's a similarity.

The lung of the smoker is a naked virgin thrown as a sacrifice into the godfire.

TOM ROBBINS, *STILL LIFE WITH WOODPECKER*, 1980

Introduction
The Camel Man and Me

I N 1961, WHEN I was seven years old, my parents took me to New York City for the first time. In this, my introduction to the city's many sights and attractions, nothing elicited my attention and fascination more than the famous Camel billboard looming above Times Square. The Camel Man blew endless perfect smoke rings into the neon-lit night sky. I was quite simply amazed. The sheer size of the display, the wafting of the smoke, and the commercial tumult left me in a state of awe. Certainly I was already aware from my parents' warnings that smoking was "bad for you." Perhaps this threat was yet another reason why the Camel sign held my attention in ways that the art at the Metropolitan Museum could not. Someday maybe I would blow giant smoke rings. Not.

The Camel Man had gone into operation to great fanfare just days after Pearl Harbor, on December 11, 1941. The brainchild of billboard designer extraordinaire Douglas Leigh, the sign was located above the Hotel Claridge at Forty-Fourth Street and Broadway. At the time of its construction, the billboard cost some $35,000, and Reynolds paid nearly $10,000 a month to rent the space from Leigh. He designed the sign and invented the steam machine that would metronomically expel fifteen rings per minute, each two feet in diameter. Among other accomplishments, Leigh would also design in Times Square a steaming coffee cup for an A&P billboard and a block-long waterfall on a Pepsi-Cola billboard, as well as the lights that topped the Empire State Building. Widely recognized as the greatest billboard impresario of the twentieth century, Leigh rejected the common term *billboard*; he was constructing *spectaculars*.[1] At seven, I could attest to Leigh's success.

Here, at the crossroads of the world, the Camel billboard signified the triumph of the cigarette in the mid-twentieth century as well as the success of modern American marketing and commerce. In 1941, cigarette use was on a steeply rising trajectory, a behavior with almost universal acceptance and appeal. The Camel Man, confidently blowing his perfect rings into the Great White Way, marked just how far the cigarette had come in a relatively short span of time. At this American center of sales, shows, and sex, the Camel Man performed for the multitudes below. During the war, he was typically found in uniform (Navy, Army, Marines). Even when the Times Square lights went down in a blackout during the war, he continued to smoke.[2] He returned to civilian life following the war, often appearing in boating garb. During my visit in 1961, he appeared in uniform again, this time as a football player. No doubt, such powerful male icons had particular appeal to seven-year-old boys.

The Camel Man had earned his dominating view of Times Square through determination, hard work, and brilliant innovation in marketing and promotion. As recently as 1900, the cigarette had been a stigmatized and little-used product constituting a small minority of the tobacco consumed in the United States. Its rise to cultural dominance by mid-century marked a remarkable historical shift that brought together developments in business organization and consumer behavior as well as deeper changes in the morals and mores of American society. The movement of the cigarette from the periphery of cultural practice to its center encompassed critical innovations in production technologies, advertising, design, and social behaviors. The tobacco industry both utilized and helped to foment deeper changes in the culture that served to promote cigarette use. The ability of the industry to both read and shape the emergence of these new cultural forces was striking, and it distinguishes the cigarette as the prototypical—indeed emblematic—product of the century. The cigarette came to be a central symbol of attractiveness, beauty, and power. This transformation engaged social values about pleasure, leisure, sexuality, and gender.

But the cigarette's iconic position in the consumer culture represents only one prong of its historical significance. Indeed, there are few elements of American life in the last century that examining the cigarette leaves unexposed. It seems striking that a product of such little utility, ephemeral in its very nature, could be such an encompassing vehicle for understanding the past. But the cigarette permeates twentieth-century America as smoke fills an enclosed room. There are few, if any, central aspects of American society that are truly smoke-free in the last century. This book centers attention on how the cigarette deeply penetrated American culture. We have witnessed the remarkable success of smoking as a social convention, as well as its ignominious demise. These shifts in cultural meanings and practices have profoundly altered patterns of human health and disease through the twentieth century. As a result, this book attempts to link meaning to materiality. The cigarette fundamentally demonstrates the historical interplay of culture, biology, and disease. As we now know, the rise of the cigarette was sustained not only by convention and personal psychology, but by the powerfully addictive properties of the nicotine in tobacco. The Camel Man was the ultimate chain-smoker.

As I followed his circular exhalations into the night sky, medical science had only recently, in the previous decades, attained a fundamental determination of the often deadly harms smoking posed for health. The cigarette had drawn fire from critics ever since its popular introduction in the nineteenth century, with many of those opposed to smoking having voiced important health concerns. The medical literature of the late nineteenth and early twentieth centuries is replete with testimony to the multiple perils of tobacco. Nonetheless, the cigarette had largely trumped these objections by the 1930s as it became ubiquitous. Smoking came to be considered a behavior of medical discretion, an issue requiring the clinical judgment of physicians treating patients who might exhibit the telltale symptoms of immoderate use, smoker's cough, or smoker's heart.

A steep rise in lung cancer—a disease virtually unknown at the turn of the twentieth century—had, however, ominously followed in the wake of the rise of the cigarette. In the early 1950s, the relationship of these two trends would be explicitly and scientifically linked. When I visited with the Camel Man in 1961, substantial scientific investigations had concluded that smoking caused lung cancer and other serious disease. Although medical concerns had percolated as the cigarette rose to prominence, it had been difficult to achieve this scientific knowledge. Physicians and public health officials had long debated the impact of smoking on health and the best methods to assess its risks. Even though the relationship of cigarettes to disease is today perhaps the epiphenomenal fact of modern medicine, demonstrating this connection required a fundamental transformation in medical ways of knowing in the mid-twentieth century.

Research into the harms of cigarette smoking in the 1940s and 1950s generated breakthroughs in modern epidemiological thought, as well as technical innovations upon which subsequent medical knowledge would firmly rest. Although many clinicians had concluded that smoking could cause disease and death based on their experiences with patients, individual doctors lacked the capacity to demonstrate conclusively this connection in the 1940s. The historical application of innovative methods of causal inference is inextricably tied to proving the harms of smoking. At the core of this narrative are critical questions about the processes by which new scientific knowledge is ultimately achieved. All the while, the tobacco industry worked diligently to disrupt the course of this scientific investigation. The industry's strategic campaign to obscure and confuse the ongoing scientific enterprise would significantly impede public acceptance and understanding of these important findings. Fundamental questions about knowing, and about *how* we know, are illuminated by examining the obstacles that medical science and the public confronted as cigarettes came to be indicted as a powerful cause of serious disease and death.

In January 1966, two years after the historic news conference held by Surgeon General Luther Terry announcing—unequivocally and with the government's seal of approval—that cigarette smoking in fact causes lung cancer, the Camel Man quit smoking; the billboard came down. When R.J. Reynolds announced that "the longest running hit on Broadway" would be dismantled, its advertising agency, the William Esty Company, denied any connection to the rising public concerns about the impact of cigarettes on health.[3] Yet another example of a disingenuous industry denial; at that time, the industry continued to insist vigorously that there was "no proof" that cigarettes were harmful. Despite the pathbreaking scientific research demonstrating the hazards of smoking, the industry continued to argue for the next three decades that the evidence indicting smoking was neither scientific nor convincing.

The debate about smoking and its regulation would turn explicitly to the political arena in the years following the release of the surgeon general's report. The history of efforts to regulate the cigarette—and their relative ineffectiveness—demonstrated the power of the industry to disrupt public health, just as it had disrupted science. If the tobacco industry did not invent special interest lobbying, they raised it to a new art form in the establishment of the Tobacco Institute in 1958. Each time Congress took up the question of tobacco and public health, proposed regulations were either fully dismantled or had the not-so-ironic impact of actually favoring Big Tobacco. Following the surgeon general's findings that smoking caused lung cancer, the first required warning labels simply proclaimed: "Caution: Cigarette Smoking May Be Hazardous to Your Health." Attempts to develop public health approaches to reduce the prevalence of smoking were stymied in Congress repeatedly. Although public anxieties about the cigarette rose in the immediate aftermath of the report, by the time the Camel Man abandoned Broadway in 1966, Americans were again smoking in record numbers. Nearly half of all adults were regular smokers in the years before 1970.[4]

Not only did the tobacco industry effectively thwart tobacco regulation, they also shaped the public meanings of smoking to their benefit. Even as the health risks of smoking came to be more widely recognized and understood, it was still possible to argue that to smoke or not to smoke was simply an issue of personal agency. According to this logic (strongly endorsed by the industry): once apprised of the risks (with labels on every package beginning in 1966), the "decision" should be left to the individual. Antitobacco efforts faltered for at least two reasons. First, they could not compete effectively with the massive resources of the industry. And second, deep cultural sentiment (encouraged and sustained by the industry) viewed tobacco regulation as offensively paternalistic.[5] After all, wasn't smoking a matter of individual choice? In the great marketplace of ideas and products that constituted American consumerism, individuals could and should make their own decisions about smoking. The companies successfully utilized a deeply traditional American cultural norm that held individuals uniquely responsible for their health. As the knowledge of smoking's harms came to be widely disseminated, rather than drawing attention to the actions of the industry, many came to agree that individuals should either quit or bear the consequences. To hold the industry responsible for such individual failings seemed to violate core American values of individual agency and responsibility. Powerful American images of independence and autonomy came to be reflected in cigarette promotion and advertising.

Philip Morris, for example, sought to link the Marlboro Man—an invention of the mid-1950s—with the lone cowboy and the myth of the frontier. Tobacco regulation faltered on the shoals of American individualism, with its consequent hostility to governmental paternalism.

When public health advocates failed to breech the well-fortified ramparts of Washington politics, they soon looked to open up new fronts in the tobacco wars where grassroots guerillas might have greater success. At some distance from K Street where lobbyists held court at the Tobacco Institute, antitobacco forces deployed new evidence of the harms of passive smoking to considerable success. In this way, they began to reshape the politics of regulation. The growing evidence that smoke harmed nonsmokers, who did not "assume" the risks of smoking, began to erode traditional arguments. If Americans had high tolerance for "assumed" risks, they had low—to no—tolerance for unwanted "exposure."

Still, having lost most battles in the halls of Congress, antitobacco leaders also soon opened a new front in the courtroom. The tobacco companies had at first defended against such suits, claiming that there was no compelling scientific evidence of smoking's harmful impact. And while they never quite abandoned this argument, as time went by they increasingly relied on the assertion that individuals who smoked must take responsibility for their own "decision" to smoke—that smoking was the preeminent "voluntary" health risk. The fundamental question adjudicated in litigation was: who is responsible for the harms of smoking? In a rising tide of litigation, as individuals came forward to sue the industry for the harms they incurred as a result of smoking in a rising tide of litigation, the industry would assert the plaintiff's individual responsibility. From the 1950s, when the first litigation was brought, until the late 1980s, this argument consistently trumped the claims of smokers. By the early 1990s, the industry had never paid a cent in litigation, a record that they widely publicized as a means of discouraging prospective plaintiffs and their lawyers.

By the 1980s and 1990s, however, these arguments had begun to wear thin. And a series of forces radically destabilized the industry. American smokers had begun to give up their cigarettes in record numbers as the cigarette underwent a cultural transformation. In an age of considerable skepticism about the ability to change behaviors in the name of health, Americans quit smoking in record numbers. On the twenty-fifth anniversary of the first surgeon general's report, the current surgeon general, C. Everett Koop, announced that as a result of reductions in tobacco use and lower rates of initiation among children and teenagers, over 750,000 lives had been saved.[6] By the early 1990s, smoking rates—spurred by powerful shifts in the social meaning of cigarette use—would dip in the United States to approximately 25 percent, the lowest rates since the 1920s.

These changes in smoking prevalence did not go unnoticed within the tobacco industry. At R.J. Reynolds, for example, it became clear that their most popular brands, Winston and Salem, principally appealed to older smokers, those between forty-five and sixty, a market segment in decline from both quitting and deaths. R.J. Reynolds, evaluating these portentous changes, came to the decision to reinvest in the Camel brand, which had fared especially poorly in the years following the disappearance of the Camel Man from Times Square. As one R.J. Reynolds executive explained, young smokers, between the ages of fourteen and twenty-four "represent tomorrow's cigarette business."[7] As part of their new campaign, a Camel billboard returned to Times Square to much fanfare in June 1989, now in the form of a 37.5-foot-high cartoon camel named Joe, rendered in green, blue, and white neon. Joe rivaled the Camel Man in the deployment of high-tech promotion. The new sign would cost R.J. Reynolds more than $1.6 million to design and erect, and nearly $45,000 per month to operate. "The billboard will make an even bigger impact than the original smoking Camel billboard, which was a Times Square landmark for many years,"[8] explained one R.J. Reynolds executive. The Joe Camel billboard, R.J. Reynolds proudly explained, required 8.5 miles of wiring and more than a mile and a half of neon.[9]

This billboard was only one especially extravagant facet of a much broader campaign using the Joe Camel cartoon figure. Joe promised to meet R.J. Reynolds's objective of "youthening" the brand. From its inception, the new campaign drew intense fire from the increasingly well-organized antitobacco movement. It was no surprise that the offensive launched by R.J. Reynolds in the Joe Camel campaign immediately provoked defensive maneuvers by tobacco control advocates and public health officials. Both his cartoon image and the tone of the ads easily pointed to kid appeal. The antitobacco campaign, since its inception, had focused on preventing children from taking up smoking. R.J. Reynolds, no doubt, understood that Joe would be the center of a vocal protest. And they devised a clear strategy to respond to critics of the campaign. Cartoons, they suggested, promoted many products from household cleaners (Mr. Clean) to motels (Garfield). Did the Jolly Green Giant convince youngsters to purchase green vegetables? According to industry apologists, no one could claim that these promotions were directed principally at children. For executives with experience in the tobacco wars, responding to critics marked a challenge to be met rather than a moral or ethical dilemma restricting action.[10]

Sophisticated critics within the antitobacco movement understood that simply claiming that Joe appealed to kids would be inadequate in any successful attack on the industry. These activists duly recognized the importance of translating public assumptions about the goals of the Joe Camel campaign into research findings. Just as researchers in the 1940s and 1950s had sought to causally link cigarettes and disease, researchers in the early 1990s sought to causally link advertising with the use of cigarettes among underage children. Soon a series of studies designed to evaluate the appeal and impact of the Camel campaign on young smokers appeared in the influential *Journal of the American Medical Association* (*JAMA*). Publication in *JAMA* promised widespread media attention of several investigations designed to assess the impact of the campaign. In these studies, researchers sought to attack a series of traditional tobacco-advertising defenses. Since the 1950s, tobacco companies had insisted that advertising was designed merely to encourage patrons to maintain (or switch) brands, not to seek new smokers; that tobacco ads did not increase the overall use of tobacco products; and that tobacco promotion did not encourage the initiation of smoking among children and adolescents. One of the studies compared the recognition of Joe Camel among high school students and adults. Not surprisingly, the students were more likely to have seen Joe, associate him with R.J. Reynolds, and have a positive evaluation of his pitch. This same article concluded that Camel's share of the underage market had gone from 0.5 percent to 32.8 percent since the inception of the campaign. According to this report, the illegal cigarette market accounted for $476 million in the United States each year.[11]

Even more damning, however, was another study reported in this same *JAMA* issue that found that among children between the ages of three and six, Joe's recognition rate approached that of Mickey Mouse. Dr. Paul

Fischer, a pediatrician at the Medical College of Georgia, devised a study in which children were asked to pair cards representing popular advertising logos and figures with their products. This study galvanized the media and generated new outrage among the public. It rates as one of the most influential studies in the history of the modern tobacco wars.[12] R.J. Reynolds's marketing entered a new phase of intensive scrutiny and calls for regulation. Even if R.J. Reynolds continued to declare that it had no interest in underage smokers, this research into the recognition and appeal of Joe Camel worked to subvert such claims. Further, the study revealed a critical aspect of tobacco advertising: it was not specifically directed at teens about to try cigarettes for the first time; its appeals went much younger. One could easily conclude from such a study that R.J. Reynolds was eager to create appeals for tobacco that would hold a sympathetic audience from very young ages. Although the authors of these articles had strong advocacy positions in the tobacco wars, their publication in peer-reviewed *JAMA* had the desired effect of turning their critiques of the Joe Camel campaign into medico-scientific data. R.J. Reynolds's denials and defenses inevitably appeared self-interested in this context. And it became much more difficult for the company to claim that smokers were responsible for "choosing" to smoke.

The very prominence of Joe Camel and the aggressiveness of his campaign in the face of such vocal criticism led to the demise of the latest R.J. Reynolds's Times Square spectacular. In August 1994, after sustaining much calumny, Joe finally relinquished his spot high above the Marriot Marquis. R.J. Reynolds spokesperson Peggy Carter insisted that the decision to dismantle the billboard was unrelated to antismoking advocates' pointed criticism (echoing R.J. Reynolds's denials when the Camel Man came down in 1966). Describing the decision to erect the billboard in the late 1980s as part of R.J. Reynolds's "marketing strategies developed . . . to reposition the brand's image among adult smokers," she insisted, "the board did the job we wanted it to do, and now it's time to move on."[13] In large measure, R.J. Reynolds could put Joe out to pasture, having accomplished the critical goal of rehabilitating the brand and, more importantly, regaining market share among new initiates to the cigarette. In 1986, Camel had less than 3 percent of the underage market; by 1993, it had at least 13 percent.[14] Although R.J. Reynolds had succeeded in increasing its market share, the blows to the already tarnished image of the tobacco industry were significant. The Times Square Joe Camel billboard was not only a blight on R.J. Reynolds's reputation, it also appears to have made cigarette billboards vulnerable to regulation more generally. Ultimately, the industry would, under pressure from activists and litigation, pull all outdoor advertising in 1999. And so ended—once and for all—the cigarette billboard.[15]

Joe had, in part, exposed the complex risk-reward structure of the tobacco industry late in the twentieth century. The camel had succeeded in building market share in a critical segment, but he exposed the previously invulnerable tobacco industry to new legal attack.[16] In late 1991, after the publication and publicity associated with the *JAMA* articles, Janet Mangini, a family law attorney in San Francisco, decided to sue R.J. Reynolds for targeting minors. "When I read press reports about the *JAMA* articles, I was stunned," explained Mangini. "I mean, Mickey Mouse is a pretty important character and to think that six-year-olds find Joe Camel just as popular, well, I was outraged."[17] Soon assisted by additional counsel, Mangini's suit focused on the targeting of minors and the general duty not to engage in advertising against public policy. Mangini asked for the court to issue an injunction to bar the campaign in California; a corrective ad campaign to be paid for by R.J. Reynolds and supervised by the court; and the refund of all monies earned from the Camel campaign to be used for court-supervised charitable and research activities.[18] As the case neared trial in the fall of 1997, R.J. Reynolds agreed to settle the suit by pulling the Camel campaign in California, releasing a spate of previously confidential industry documents detailing the plans for the campaign, and paying $10 million for antismoking activities in California.[19]

The Mangini case demonstrated an important and increasingly significant vulnerability for the tobacco industry: the newly effective and creative use of litigation by antitobacco advocates. Such legal maneuvering took place in a radically altered social and cultural context in which the activities of the industry had now come under intensive public scrutiny. The Mangini settlement also resulted in the exposure of the planning and execution of the Joe Camel campaign to unprecedented public review by the court-mandated release of previously confidential documents. These records revealed the central goals and approach of R.J. Reynolds to youth smoking. Revelation of secret documents through litigation became a key strategy among tobacco control activists eager to encourage public outrage toward a hypocritical industry. Litigation forced the industry to reveal its most intimate corporate strategies in the tobacco wars.

This book is based significantly on the wide range of documentation that emerged in the context of such litigation. When I first began investigating the history of cigarette smoking, I quickly realized there would be a remarkable range of documentary evidence to sustain this work. The medical literature on tobacco alone had come to fill shelves in medical libraries; a vast popular literature in magazines and newspapers would assist in tracing changing social norms and values regarding smoking; and the large number of advertisements offered additional primary material for evaluation and analysis. Even before the governmental evaluations of smoking and health in the 1950s and 1960s, public health officials had explored the relationship of tobacco and disease, archiving large caches of additional documents for future researchers. As I made my initial research forays, I quickly came to understand that the wide diversity of historical materials would make this project both exciting and daunting. But there was one important exception: I knew I would be unlikely to gain access to materials revealing the internal dynamics of the tobacco industry. The tobacco companies were already facing challenges in the courts, and in the court of public opinion, regarding the rectitude of their business practices and their ongoing denials of the harms of smoking. As a result, I assumed my investigation would center on public meanings, behaviors, and debates about smoking rather than on industry strategy and activity. Nonetheless, in 1986 I paid a visit to the Tobacco Institute, having read about their extensive library and historical collections. Quickly and without fanfare, I was politely shown the door. I do remember, however, being impressed by the prominence of ashtrays throughout their offices. Thus, I began my work with the expectation that the inner sanctums of the tobacco industry would not be part of my investigation. I was both disappointed and a bit relieved. There was plenty to do without industry materials. The availability of materials limits every historical inquiry, and this study would be no exception.

At the time of my brief field trip to the Tobacco Institute, I could never have anticipated that in the next decade I would have access to millions of pages of internal and confidential industry correspondence, reports, and memoranda. Now, rather than staring up at the Camel Man, I can examine his personal papers—the very contracts, plans, and letters that made him a reality. The "discovery" process in the tobacco litigation, coupled with the revolution of the Internet, makes this access possible. I can now sit in my office, downloading thousands of pages of documents evaluating the industry's approach to the science and politics of marketing cigarettes. The industry strategy of avoiding liability by vetting internal materials and policies with legal counsel to claim attorney-client privilege ultimately backfired in the 1990s in the course of litigation. It is one of the great ironies of modern corporate history that we have come to know more about the internal operations of the tobacco industry than perhaps any other American big business in the last century. The tobacco industry fought diligently in many instances to keep these confidential documents from public scrutiny. Today, there are over 40 million pages of tobacco documents, searchable and downloadable, online. The story of how these materials became available through whistle-blowers and the legal process of discovery constitutes yet another central aspect of the history of tobacco. Following the revelations of these documents, the social standing of the industry—once an icon of American entrepreneurialism—sunk to new depths.

The cigarette century reveals the drama of historical change, the transformation of smoking, its meanings, and impacts. Today, we talk of the stink of cigarettes penetrating clothes and hair, not to mention the disgust engendered by nicotine-stained fingers and teeth. There was a time, not so long ago, when people thought cigarette smoke was fragrant. This book seeks to account for the meaning and pace of such radical transformations. Now, when smoking is so fundamentally contested and often publicly deplored, it may be difficult to remember that time when it signified beauty, glamour, and attraction; when being an executive at a tobacco company commanded status rather than shame. Sometimes, watching Humphrey Bogart and Lauren Bacall light up in *To Have and Have Not*, we return to a time when smoking held allure and people smoked everywhere and at anytime.

Today, living in a society in which cigarette smoking has become so culturally marginal and stigmatized, it may be difficult to recover that time in which it played such a prominent and popular role in the rise of a consumer age. Today, when it is so clear that smoking constitutes a momentous risk to health, it may be difficult to recover that time in which these harms were the subject of debate, confusion, and obfuscation. The strategy of this account is to layer temporally those forces that serve to explain the changing dynamics of tobacco use and the development of a massive pandemic in the twentieth century. It is in this very method of integrating historical inquiry—which is typically isolated by field and approach—that I believe we may learn the most not only about smoking, its meanings, and its material impact on the health of individuals and populations, but also deeper changes in culture and society. Ultimately, historical exploration of the cigarette reveals the advantages of problem-centered histories that call for disrupting some of the traditional boundaries of disciplinary inquiry. By examining cigarette smoking in the context of culture, science, politics, and law, critical elements of American society in the last century emerge. Without resorting to a set of fantastical counterfactuals, it is clear that the history of tobacco might well have followed different routes and taken decidedly different turns. Following the cigarette through the century offers a fundamental opportunity to evaluate the contingent nature of historical change.

The fall of the cigarette that marks the second half of the twentieth century may only be considered provisional at best. More than one in five American adults still smoke regularly, and today tobacco still kills more than 435,000 U.S. citizens each year (more than HIV, alcohol, illicit drugs, suicide, and homicide *combined*). Former Surgeon General C. Everett Koop, eager to translate these numbers for greater public impact, repeatedly explained that tobacco deaths equaled three 747s crashing daily for a year, with no survivors. But smokers don't die such sudden and traumatic deaths—they die, typically in hospitals, slowly, one at a time; often after extended illness and suffering; and now often ashamed, convinced that they have sown their own fate. It is the precise character of the slow risks involved that, in part, have impinged on more aggressive public health interventions. Among the questions at the heart of this book is the examination of those particular social processes by which a culture constitutes and assesses the risks of life—and death.

The numbers of deaths in the United States, however, are dwarfed by those now occurring around the world. And while many American smokers have tried to quit with some success, smoking has been on a steep increase, especially in poorer nations. As the tobacco companies lost ground in the developed world they aggressively sought new smokers in developing nations. The final section of the book explores the historical process— currently underway—in which cigarette consumption and its consequent burden of disease are transferred to the developing world. The imposition of this burden, along with its social and ethical implications, casts a shadow of genuinely enormous proportions over the coming century. It is now projected that in the course of the twenty-first century, one billion people across the globe will die of tobacco-related diseases. This figure represents a ten-fold increase over the deaths associated with the cigarette in the last century.[20] And these deaths are intricately linked to the social processes of redefining the cigarette in the United States over the last three decades. Originating in the flora of the Western Hemisphere, tobacco has come in modernity to wreak havoc on the health of nations across the globe. In this respect, it is a sobering tale, as many histories are. As medicine and science achieved new mastery over disease and human suffering during the last century, so too have we produced new, powerful vectors of disease and death, and developed techniques for spreading them widely among populations across the globe.

Even in 1961, as a seven-year-old, I knew that smoking was dangerous. In this sense, the billboard presented a paradox that I surely could not have articulated at that time. How could something so great, so remarkable, so public, be promoting something that I had already learned was so profoundly bad? The "badness" of smoking was constituted by more than its effect on health. Embedded in the cigarette were the complex historical meanings of rebellion and idleness, independence and attraction. All kids were told smoking was bad—and was only for adults—which created, in part, its impressive appeal. And this appeal was anything but "natural." It was the studied and meticulous invention of an industry that would come to understand—and exploit—critical aspects of motivation, psychology, and human biology. This book marks my attempt to resolve a child's paradox—a paradox of pandemic proportion.

The Cigarette Century looks both inward and outward at the cigarette. It uses the cigarette to explore central aspects of American culture. But it also hopes to utilize this cultural investigation to better understand strategies to reduce the massive pandemic we now understand cigarette smoking to produce. Our ability to control this pandemic will no doubt require new insights from the realms of both science and culture, and new strategies from law and politics. This book ultimately rests on a premise at the core of historical practice and method, that the past may offer particular insight into contemporary policy and cultural change. Understanding the cigarette century will provide no simple answer to the potential health catastrophe we face. But understanding more deeply the meaning and significance of the history of cigarette smoking in modern life may well provide us with a modicum of insight into how best to limit, if not control, the global harms of smoking.

I

CULTURE

My company is up against a stone wall. It can't compete with Bull Durham. Something has to be done and that quick. I am going into the cigarette business.[1]

BUCK DUKE, CA. 1882

You must have a cigarette. A cigarette is the perfect type of a perfect pleasure. It is exquisite, and it leaves one unsatisfied. What more can you want?[2]

OSCAR WILDE, 1891

CHAPTER 1

Pro Bono Publico

BEFORE THE CIGARETTE, there was tobacco. The centrality of tobacco within American culture is remarkable both for its longevity and for the elasticity of its products and meanings. By the time the modern cigarette was invented, in the last decades of the nineteenth century, tobacco had long been deeply insinuated into the American economy and culture. The cigarette would quickly become the vehicle for a dramatic transformation of traditional tobacco culture.

The tobacco plant was domesticated and cultivated by natives of the Americas long before Columbus, and it would remain a staple of the twentieth-century industrial economy. Tobacco would play a central role in the behaviors, rituals, and social activities of modern Americans, just as it had for centuries. Tobacco links us to our premodern roots, but only with the modern emergence of the cigarette do we witness its most powerful and transformative aspects. The cigarette would provide the essential vehicle for tobacco's transition from plantation crop to consumer product and vastly expand the market for tobacco in the twentieth century.

The genus *Nicotiana* most likely had its origins in South America and spread northward in prehistoric times. Although a number of species grew naturally, Europeans, on their arrival, found natives cultivating both tabacum and rusticum, depending on climate and soil.[3] But unlike every other major crop the natives cultivated, tobacco's purpose was not nutritional. According to many accounts, tobacco played a critical role in their religious and healing practices. Due to its high nicotine content, as well as the manner in which it was used, this early tobacco could produce hallucinogenic experiences.[4]

Early European explorers of the Americas noted natives' use of tobacco with considerable interest. They reported that tobacco use varied widely in purpose and meaning, serving a wide range of spiritual, social, and medical purposes.[5] In addition to smoking dried tobacco in the form of cigars, chiefs engaged in ritual blowing, in which they would blow smoke at the heads and faces of the tribe members. Early observers of Amerindian cultures also documented pipes and other implements to inhale tobacco smoke. There is evidence that tobacco was also chewed and inhaled through snuff. The European explorers—who conducted their own "experiments" with the herb—also reported its physiological effects. A critical element of native cosmologic ritual and practice, tobacco impressively altered the psychic state of its users. It could cause dizziness, perspiration, weakness, and fainting. Small doses acted as a stimulant, and large doses acted as a tranquilizer. Although its advocates disagreed about its administration and effects, many agreed on its profound medicinal advantages, and they integrated tobacco into their various religious and medical pharmacopoeias.[6]

In Europe, the characteristics of tobacco underwent comprehensive investigation. Jean Nicot, the king of France's consul, sent tobacco from Portugal to Paris in 1560; the alkaloid common to the many varieties of leaf, identified and isolated in the early nineteenth century, was named in his honor.[7] The scientific elucidation of this substance was a classic problem for early nineteenth-century German botanical chemists. These researchers delineated nicotine's unusually toxic properties: in *pure* form—colorless, strongly alkaline, and volatile—even the amount in a typical cigar would be lethal. Most forms of tobacco use, such as smoking through pipes and cigars, snuff, and chew, clearly diluted nicotine's impact but nonetheless created significant physiologic effects.[8]

Almost as soon as they "discovered" it, Europeans went from observing tobacco's use to commanding its growth and sale. Among the profound effects of contact between Amerindians and Europeans was the way in which tobacco became very quickly a European commodity.[9] Within a century of Columbus's first voyage across the Atlantic, tobacco would be grown on disparate continents across the globe. It found its way to Africa, India, and the Far East, grafting into indigenous agrarian ecologies as well as cultural systems of healing and belief.[10] In the intricate traffic of peoples, flora, fauna, and microbes, crisscrossing the Atlantic in both directions, tobacco held a prized place, solidifying the notion that the resources of the "new" world would justify settlement and that new resources, products, and practices would transform the "old" world and its culture. Although the health implications of this traffic were widely noted from the earliest contact, it would have been impossible to predict that tobacco would produce a pandemic three centuries later. In the unprecedented success of this crop, the seeds of the modern burden of disease were sown.[11]

Early colonists quickly displaced natives in the cultivation of tobacco.[12] Virginia and Maryland colonists exported a tobacco crop beginning in the early seventeenth century. Its use drew deep and consistent attack. In 1604, King James I offered a "counterblaste to tobacco," concluding its use to be "a custom loathsome to the eye, hateful to the nose, harmful to the brain, dangerous to the lung . . . ."[13] This would not be the last time such warnings went unheeded. Demand in England was nothing short of remarkable. By 1670, it was reported that a half of the adult male population in England smoked tobacco daily. By the end of the seventeenth century, the English were consuming more than two pounds per person each year, generally for "medicinal" purposes.[14] Principally smoked with clay pipes produced in London, tobacco grew markedly cheaper in the early eighteenth century as production in the colonies rose precipitously.[15]

The demands of tobacco cultivation shaped the character of colonists. Tobacco growing required a complex combination of intensive labor and good judgment. "The tobacco grower," wrote the anthropologist Fernando Ortiz, "has to tend his tobacco . . . leaf by leaf," and the outcome defined his status.[16] Individual moral character, honor, and reputation came to be inextricably linked to the quality of the leaf.[17] In colonial Virginia, the beginning of the process of cultivating tobacco commenced shortly after Christmas with the sowing of seed. By late April, seedlings were transplanted from beds to main fields; at that time, tobacco leaves would be approximately the size of a dollar. Successful transplantation required good fortune and keen judgment: soaking rains were needed to make it possible to safely remove the seedlings, and planters had to carefully assess the young plant's viability. During the summer, hoeing and weeding were crucial. Upon the appearance of eight to twelve leaves, the top of the plant was removed to prevent flowering, and secondary shoots were removed later as well. These processes of "topping" and removing "suckers" had to be precisely enacted. In September, tobacco was cut; again, timing was critical. Immature leaf was impossible to cure properly, but the farmer who waited too long risked a ruinous frost.[18]

Tobacco farming did not end at the harvest. Some of the most complex tasks came after the broad green leaves were removed from their stalks. The quality of the product would ultimately rest on the intricate processes of drying and curing the leaf. Curing itself could destroy a successful crop. The tobacco was hung in curing barns, where the product to be shipped could be neither too moist—thus certain to rot in transit—nor too dry. Curing required evaluating the climate and the fire used to dry the leaves. It was not unusual to lose both the harvest and the barn to the flame. Following curing, the tobacco was quickly stripped of the stalk from which it had hung and compressed into hogsheads, which, when filled, weighed about 1,000 pounds. Compressing the leaves into the wooden drum, known as "prizing," took up much of the fall. The hogsheads were often not shipped until the new crop was sown and growing, the entire cycle taking fifteen months.[19]

Tobacco became an integral part of the colonial Tidewater culture. Far more than just a crop, it defined the widest range of regional values, labor systems and practices, and the character of the calendar itself. Life was organized around the idiosyncrasies of "making a crop."[20] Tobacco created a boom economy in the Chesapeake and Tidewater; as the historian Edmund Morgan explained, it "took the place of gold."[21] It offered the potential to get rich quick and often diverted attention and resources from the commitments necessary to create a stable community. Even after tobacco prices fell in the early eighteenth century, it remained the most profitable of crops.

The success of growing tobacco depended not on land—but on labor.[22] The labor-intensive aspects of tobacco cultivation had dramatic implications for the colonies. With prices of the commodity falling and land cheap, increasing one's revenues became a matter of finding enough workers. During the seventeenth century, indentured servants met these needs.

According to some estimates, one-third of all English immigrants to America came because of the tobacco trade.[23] The very success of tobacco, however, turned many of these men into yeoman planters seeking their own servants. As profits fell, and cultivated acreage grew, the difficulty of recruiting new servants intensified. African slaves were the fateful answer. The shift from white, indentured servants to black slaves began in the second half of the seventeenth century, and by 1700, blacks made up a majority of the unfree labor force.[24]

To an impressive degree, it was tobacco—and its particular quality and characteristics as a crop—that organized the politics and culture of southern colonies. With tobacco at the very center of commerce and growth, the terms of trade and the large Tidewater plantation owners' rising indebtedness sowed the seeds of colonial rebellion. For those who grew tobacco during the eighteenth century, debt was strongly tied to their emergent political ideology and commitment to independence. It threatened to corrupt deeply held values; it brought the planters' moral and political worlds to a crisis.[25] The Tidewater's peculiar economy helped to create a relatively rare historical conjunction: elites with a powerful bent toward rebellion and revolution.[26]

By the late seventeenth century, tobacco production had emerged in two principal forms: the large plantation supported by slave labor and the small independent farms of modest acreage worked largely by their owners. Tobacco growing moved west with the expansion of settlement in the eighteenth century, generally in the form of small, family-run farms. Slavery followed as farms grew. In the decades following American independence, the rapid westward expansion of tobacco farming ultimately affected what type of plants were cultivated. The character of the harvest varied significantly with soil and climate. The rich soil of the Tidewater produced the dark aromatic tobacco that had spread across Europe and the globe.[27] As cultivation expanded into North Carolina and Kentucky, the poor soil gave the leaf from these regions a unique yellow hue and light flavor. This variety, called bright tobacco, became increasingly popular in the antebellum era, first as a wrapper for plug tobacco and later for chew itself.[28]

Another type of tobacco took hold in the new areas as well. The burley leaf, grown west of the Appalachians, grew in popularity among plug users before the Civil War. Plug tobacco producers added licorice, sugar, rum, and honey, as well as other sweeteners, in secret proprietary mixes, such as D. A. Patterson's wildly successful Lucky Strike. White burley, first grown in Ohio, Kentucky, and Indiana, was distinguished from its botanical ancestors by its light color, a greenish-yellow leaf with a milky stalk and stem. The introduction of white burley tobacco in the middle of the nineteenth century would mark a critical historical precursor to the emergence of the cigarette some decades later. A "dry" tobacco, it resisted rot and mildew, was easier to harvest, and could be air-cured. Lower in natural sugars than its botanic rivals, white burley quickly absorbed the flavorings that would become vogue in chewing and pipe tobacco, and ultimately cigarettes.[29]

One other development turned out to be critical to the ultimate triumph of the cigarette as a commodity of mass consumption. The open flames of wood and charcoal used in curing were well known to impart particular flavors to tobacco. But open fires were unpredictable and hard to control. In some instances, they led to overly dry or even burned leaves—or the curing barn could go up in flames. By mid-century, tobacco growers and manufacturers began experimenting with flue-curing—large furnaces with iron piping that could produce the necessary heat under more controlled conditions. Flue-curing became widespread after the Civil War.[30]

Flue-curing proved especially effective at turning tobacco a bright "lemon yellow" color. Many commented on the mildness of this tobacco and its particular suitability for cigarettes. But what they could not have known is that this process also subtly changed the chemistry of the leaf to make it slightly acidic rather than alkaline. The mildness of bright tobacco, processed in this way, promoted inhalation. Smokers soon found that they could take cigarette smoke deep into their lungs, rather than holding the smoke principally in their mouths as they did with pipes and cigars. In this way—as we now know—nicotine absorbs rapidly into the bloodstream; some seven seconds later, it reaches the brain. Nicotine addiction was born in the serendipitous marriage of bright tobacco and flue-curing. This physiological process would create a mass industry and a consequent epidemic of tobacco-related diseases.[31]

By the nineteenth century, then, tobacco and its products were deeply embedded in the new nation's social experience—in its commerce, its labor, its leisure, and its social ritual—all before the cigarette became the dominant form of consumption. Tobacco was not only an export; Americans' use of tobacco was widespread and cut across geographic, cultural, and class boundaries. When Charles Dickens traveled around the United States in 1842, he was struck by ever-present tobacco chew; he labeled Washington, DC, the "head-quarters of tobacco-tinctured saliva." In "all the public places of America," he observed, everyone accepted this "filthy custom." That Dickens found this remarkable shows that tobacco chewing was not only widespread, but a distinctively American form of tobacco use.[32] Though less prevalent than tobacco plug, cigars and pipes held significant shares of the market as well. All three forms were popular among the educated, urban, and well-to-do. Cigar smoking became a powerful symbol of social authority and power, its use soon ritualized in portraiture and politics.[33]

Although tobacco was important as an agricultural crop and consumer product, by the mid-nineteenth century, there was little hint that the cigarette would ever become an important vehicle for its use. The few cigarettes that were smoked before the Civil War were deemed a curiosity, a cheap commodity for the urban young who could not afford more appropriate forms. The shift from chew, snuff, pipes, and cigars would constitute a profound change in the production and consumption of tobacco. It would bring radical changes in business organization and industry, as well as deep cultural transformations in a consumer-driven economy.

The first successful cigarette entrepreneur, James Buchanan Duke (also known as Buck), had a capacious, even global vision for his industry, and he possessed both the vision and the energy to implement this plan. He led the radical consolidation of the industry, introduced new technologies of production and consumption, and advocated the notion that the tobacco market would know neither cultural nor geographic boundaries.

Cigarettes have existed for centuries. The earliest ones were probably wrapped in a cornhusk; tobacco consumers in early seventeenth-century

Spain replaced the husk with a fine paper that burned evenly when rolled around crushed tobacco. The cigarette spread first to other European countries, then Mexico, and ultimately to the United States. Manufacture of cigarettes in the United States began during the Civil War, but the product failed to attract much of a following until 1869, when the New York firm of F.S. Kinney brought experienced workers from Europe to instruct their American employees in the technique of hand rolling. By experimenting with tobacco blends and emphasizing the use of bright tobacco, Kinney came up with Sweet Caporals, which soon became popular in East Coast cities as a faddish and somewhat low-class alternative to more respectable forms.[34]

The economic depression of 1873 apparently spurred sales of cigarettes, however, because they were relatively inexpensive. By the middle of the decade, the firm of Allen & Ginter was offering Richmond Straight Cuts and Pet Cigarettes featuring Virginia Gold Leaf tobacco. Lewis Ginter, who successfully brought together blends of bright and burley, came to dominate the early cigarette business through his combination of tobacco knowledge and marketing savvy. Other tobacco concerns were soon attracted to cigarette production. Goodwin & Company, in New York City, produced Old Judge and Welcome; William S. Kimball, in Rochester, emphasized Turkish blends in his brands, Three Kings and Vanity Fair.[35] Even with these new brands, however, in 1900, cigarettes still made up less than 2 percent of the thriving tobacco market, dominated by chew, cigars, and pipes.[36]

W. Duke Sons & Company, based in Durham, North Carolina, began producing cigarettes in 1879. At first, their future dominance of the trade was far from certain. With a tedious and labor-intensive production process, cigarettes held little attraction to a firm like Duke, which produced mostly chew and smoking tobacco. Following the Civil War, Washington Duke and his sons rebuilt his failing company producing a bright leaf chewing tobacco under the name *Pro Bono Publico*. His son Buck soon took over the business and focused on competing with the leading brand of chew, the heavily promoted Bull Durham.[37]

James Duke almost single-handedly invented the modern cigarette. Duke had a genuine affinity for the new modes of industry that would come to dominate American business enterprise, and he had little patience for the staid practices of his competitors, which he would soon render obsolete. Aggressive and untethered, he brought together the technological, business, and marketing innovations that would define the coming new age of consumption.

Duke employed only ten cigarette rollers in 1882 but soon added fifty more. At that time, Allen & Ginter, the leading U.S. manufacturer, employed approximately 450 women to roll cigarettes in its Richmond factory. Taking advantage of a strike at a New York City cigarette producer, Duke solicited another 125 experienced rollers to move to Durham in 1883, offering to pay moving expenses and a wage of $2.00 per twelve-hour day, the highest in the industry. As demand for cigarettes continued to rise, Duke's operation grew with it. He greatly expanded his labor force of rollers by hiring young women, whose work was closely inspected for consistency and quality.[38] By 1885, he had over 700 cigarette hand rollers in two factories, one in Durham and one in New York.[39]

There were many attempts to replace these laborers with automated cigarette-rolling machines. But bringing tobacco filler and paper together with speed and precision proved extremely difficult, and despite several machines patented during the 1870s, hand rolling remained the only process reliable enough for commercial cigarettes. Most companies remained firmly committed to it. The breakthrough came when James Bonsack, a Virginia inventor, introduced a rolling machine he designed in 1881. Using processes transferred from his father's woolen mill, Bonsack's machine neatly fed compressed tobacco onto a paper ribbon that—upon being rolled into a tube—was precisely cut to cigarette-sized lengths. This one-ton contraption required three human attendants, but it produced over 200 cigarettes every minute, almost as many as a skilled hand roller could produce in an hour.[40]

Although James Bonsack's name rarely appears in the history of technology next to those of his contemporaries Alexander Graham Bell, Thomas Edison, or the Wright brothers, his machine, like theirs, formed the foundation of a major American industry. Each of these inventions would profoundly alter American life in the next century. Unlike the telephone, the incandescent light, or the airplane, the cigarette was not a new invention. The Bonsack machine constituted a classic example of what has been called innovation through emulation. It attempted to replicate the handmade process by packing tobacco, rolling paper around it, and precisely cutting the cigarette.[41]

With this new technology, the fledgling cigarette industry acquired the potential for unprecedented growth. At the time of the machine's introduction, four manufacturers—Allen & Ginter from Richmond, Virginia; William S. Kimball & Company from Rochester, New York; Kinney Tobacco from New York City; and Goodwin & Company, also from New York City—produced about 80 percent of the nation's cigarettes. Each of these companies, recognizing the advantages of mechanization, invested in rolling machinery. Allen & Ginter even offered a prize to any inventor who could produce a successful prototype. But given the persistent quality-control problems, there was concern among manufacturers that consumers would reject machine-made cigarettes and insist on a handmade product.

By early 1882, Bonsack, with the assistance of his father, brother, and brother-in-law, set up the Bonsack Machine Company. Their machine reduced the cost of rolling cigarettes by half. The Bonsack Machine Company rented its machines to cigarette producers, supplied an operator with the apparatus, and charged a royalty on sales of about $.30 per thousand. Manufacturers agreed to a minimum of $200 in royalties per machine.[42]

Allen & Ginter ordered a Bonsack machine but soon rejected it, eager to save the prize money they had offered. The first Bonsack prototype met an inauspicious end when the train taking it to New York caught fire en route. Although Bonsack successfully delivered a new machine, Allen & Ginter remained concerned about how customers would regard a machine-made product. Their rejection was more than a lost opportunity in the annals of industry; fear of mass production was a key factor separating the Victorian business culture from that of modern industrial firms like James Duke's.[43]

It was Bonsack's deal with Duke that secured his machine's dominance within the early cigarette industry.[44] Duke countered his competitors' concerns about mechanization by publicly declaring it an advantage, explicitly announcing on new packaging that the contents were machine-produced.[45] The efficiency and consistency of machines, he claimed, were superior to traditional craftwork. The cigarette—quintessentially a modern product—would soon be produced exclusively by modern machinery under Duke's lead. Moreover, Duke was well aware of the advantages of reducing his reliance on wage labor.

Unlike his competitors, who were more deeply committed to the historical traditions of tobacco commerce, Duke thrived on the battle; he had neither the taste nor the time for the customs of a gentleman's trade. It was precisely this independence from traditional products and practices that opened the way for his innovative and aggressive empire-building. Duke was first a salesman and entrepreneur, and tobacco was but a product. By 1884, while his competitors were still hesitating, Duke had installed two Bonsack machines in his Durham factory. A year later, after experimenting to improve the machines' performance, Duke signed a secret contract in which he agreed that he would produce all his cigarettes with the Bonsack machine; in return, Bonsack reduced Duke's royalties to $.20 per thousand. Duke and Bonsack soon reached a further agreement guaranteeing Duke a 25 percent discount on royalties against all other manufacturers. Also, Duke shrewdly hired one of Bonsack's disgruntled mechanics, William Thomas O'Brien, to operate his machines, assuring fewer breakdowns than his competition.[46] By June 1886, O'Brien was meticulously maintaining ten machines. Duke placed a heavy emphasis on efficiency and continuous production. The lessons he learned in developing the mass production of cigarettes he would soon apply more broadly to industrial organization.

By becoming Bonsack's premier customer, Duke secured essential control over its technology and turned Bonsack's patent into a powerful competitive advantage. It was increasingly common for inventors to relinquish their patents to corporations. Duke understood that control of the Bonsack patent—through his secret, discounted licensing agreement—was a critical lever in dominating the cigarette trade. His deal with Bonsack reflected an important change in the character of the patent system, from a legal mechanism protecting independent inventors to one that would protect large and powerful corporations.[47] In a letter to the president of the Bonsack Company in 1889, Duke would insist that his early and complete commitment to Bonsack more than justified such discounts. "I say openly if it had not been for us to-day," he claimed, "the Bonsack machine would be a smouldering wreck."[48] Duke would periodically assist Bonsack in the protection of his patent, recognizing that upstart inventors with new machines could threaten his advantage. He also periodically threatened Bonsack with lawsuits for violating their agreements.

The cigarette-rolling machine appealed to Duke as a mechanism of efficient mass production but also as a means to end his labor problems. He faced continued shortages of workers, as well as unrest and disgruntlement over wages. The installation of Bonsack's machines at the Duke factory was an unwelcome sight to his employees. For Duke, it marked a new form of control over the vicissitudes of human capital. With the installation of the machines, the hand rollers Duke had brought from New York now mostly returned, often to the cigar trade.

Cigar production did not quickly embrace machinery. As an older, bigger, and more successful industry, its workers led in the fight for unionization. These unions now fought with considerable success against the introduction of machines that would replace their workers. Further, the cigar industry, consisting of many small local firms, rarely commanded the necessary capital to invest in such technological improvements. This contrast between the cigar and the cigarette would soon represent the historical shifts typified by the twentieth century.[49]

Other technological innovations also made the success of the cigarette possible. Flue-curing helped create a raw product especially suited for cigarettes.[50] Also, the "short smoke" of the cigarette, unlike other forms of tobacco consumption, was dependent on the "quick light." As consumption increased in the 1880s and 1890s and the size of a pack doubled from ten to twenty, a safe and convenient mode of ignition became crucial to smokers. Although the first matchbook was invented in the 1890s, a truly safe match, free of toxic phosphorous, would not emerge until the early twentieth century. But once combined with the free matchbooks—covered with advertising—it gave smokers the implement needed to make the cigarette ubiquitous.[51]

The Bonsack machine and its successful application marked a transformative event in the rise of the cigarette. The machine shifted production from a traditional artisan-based shop and reorganized it to emphasize stan-

dardization, system, and control—key values in the culture of modern technology.[52] The Bonsack machine assured new economies of scale and speed
of production as well as long production runs. It mandated radical reorganization of virtually every other aspect of cigarette production, from the
purchase of leaf (to assure adequate volume) to retail sales. Many of Duke's
later innovations sought to address the imbalance the Bonsack machine
created between his ability to mass produce cigarettes and his ability to
market them. The overcapacity inherent in the mass production of the cigarette marked a characteristic problem of industrialization. Duke would
play a leading role in creating a corporate structure capable of turning this
problem into profits.

Duke understood that the solution to overcapacity involved the aggressive
solicitation of new smokers. The revolution in production required an
equally significant revolution in consumption.[53] Without the "invention" of
modern advertising, Duke could not have efficiently utilized the machinery
of production. At the same time that Duke committed his company to the
new technology, he also committed it to new techniques of intensive marketing and promotion. It was the articulation of this critical pathway from
production to consumption that would ultimately create the modern cigarette industry.[54] Duke was first a salesman with deep competitive instincts,
but he also understood the essentials of risk-taking and change. Promoting
a product, particularly one difficult to distinguish from one's competitors,
required the creation of new incentives.

Promotion, Duke insisted, would drive consumption. At the same time
that Duke was working to have the Bonsack machine perfected, he was in-
stalling a print shop in his Durham factory that would employ new color
lithography techniques. His marketing campaigns centered on premiums,
coupons, and collecting cards, freely distributed with each pack of Cameo,
Cross Cut, or Duke's Best. Illustrating themes of sports, adventure, Civil
War generals, fashion, and beauty, these cards varied from the educational
(flags and stamps of foreign countries) to the exotic (actresses wearing the
costumes of foreign countries). He encouraged patrons to collect complete
sets. Sets of "actresses," usually not fully clothed, were especially popular

with the boys and young men who constituted Duke's main market. Although Washington Duke objected to such "lascivious photos," his son,
knowing the impact on sales, expanded advertising budgets dramatically,
forcing his competitors to follow suit.[55] This commodity-connected collecting was a lasting innovation that continues today with baseball cards
and Pokémon. Duke had discovered important incentives for smoking in
the cultural rituals of youth.[56]

From its inception, the cigarette targeted the uninitiated; young people, for whom it was the first form of tobacco consumption, were the primary constituency. According to the *New York Times,* tobacco dealers like
Duke used premiums to "entice boys to excessive cigarette smoking."
"Every possible device has been employed to interest the juvenile mind,
notably the lithograph album." Youngsters seeking these picture books
"clamor[ed] for the reward of self-inflicted injury. . . . many a boy under
12 years is striving for the entire collection, which necessitates the consumption of nearly 12,000 cigarettes. He will become demoralized, and
possibly dishonest to accomplish his purpose."[57] But Duke and his competitors now understood that the future of the cigarette rested in the
nimble consuming hands of American youth. So began the long tradition
of explicitly advertising to children.

Using cigarette cards and other techniques, Duke parlayed a growing
advertising budget into dominance of the cigarette trade. One journalist in
1907 described him as "always an aggressive advertiser, devising new and
startling methods which dismayed his competitors . . . always willing to
spend in advertising a proportion of his profits which seemed appalling to
more conservative manufacturers."[58] The cigarette industry would set unprecedented ratios of promotion costs in relation to sales.[59] In 1889, for instance, Duke's American Tobacco spent $800,000 on advertising, compared
to sales of $4 million to $4.5 million.[60] In this respect—as in others—
Duke anticipated central elements of twentieth-century marketing, not
only of the cigarette, but of numerous other goods in a burgeoning consumer culture. Novelty and innovation became characteristic elements of
cigarette marketing. In 1884, Duke purchased 400,000 chairs emblazoned
with advertisements for his products that he freely distributed to retailers.
Soon, billboards and buildings throughout the states carried cigarette ads,
studding urban and rural landscapes with towering promotions. Not only

did such expenditures help recruit new smokers, high promotion costs quickly became an important barrier to new firms introducing competitive products.[61]

§

Duke also believed that, to reach its massive potential, the mechanized cigarette required a new system of industrial organization. The construction of the tobacco trust at the turn of the century—as well as the rise of a vertically integrated industry—would mark a central innovation in the history of industrial capital. Historians of American business and enterprise often point to the tobacco industry to demonstrate this important watershed in American economic and social history. These last decades of the nineteenth century saw intensive efforts on the part of businesses to use consolidation to gain control over the vagaries of production and markets. Just as Duke had instituted critical technological and marketing innovations, he now turned to radical organizational initiatives to disarm his competitors and build a massive industry. It is this organizational vision that ultimately earned him a place in the pantheon of American business leaders.[62]

Duke began to express interest in purchasing his competitors as early as 1887. His first entreaties were met with a measure of derision; Duke had yet to achieve dominance in a highly competitive industry, and few took him seriously. But by 1889, he was spending unprecedented sums to advertise his products, as well as aggressively lowering their price. His pricing policies helped him achieve his ultimate goal of moving his principal competitors (who did not know of his advantageous arrangements with the Bonsack Company) toward consolidation into a trust.[63] In part because the cigarette was so difficult to differentiate and so ephemeral, it was (and would remain) more sensitive to general price trends than many other products. Duke came to see powerful advantages in consolidation and monopoly: the ability to avoid price competition would be crucial to the ultimate success of the industry and the cigarette. He pursued increasingly thin profit margins in order to bring competitors into the fold.

In January 1890, Duke forced the other four major producers to join a consortium named the American Tobacco Company, under his leadership. Duke explained in retrospect that he felt that:

. . . in selling our business to the American Tobacco Co. in connection
with the other manufacturers we would get a good organization of people who would be of assistance in conducting the business, and then besides that I expected to make a profit by it because you can handle to
better advantage a large business than a small business.[64]

The newly formed American Tobacco Company was capitalized at $25
million; American Tobacco and Allen & Ginter each received $7.5 million
in stock; Kinney received $5 million; and W.S. Kimball & Company and
Goodwin and Company split the final $5 million. With Duke at its helm,
American Tobacco could immediately claim 90 percent of all cigarette sales
in the United States. The "Tobacco Trust," as it quickly became known,
had established a virtual monopoly—five fierce competitors joined under
Duke's organizational iron will. In the last years of the nineteenth century,
the Tobacco Trust aggressively acquired independent firms, closing their
plants and consolidating machinery, inventory, and products.[65]

The development of such trusts, most powerfully symbolized by John D.
Rockefeller's Standard Oil Trust, marked concerted efforts on the part of
industrialists to limit competition and the vagaries of the markets. But they
also offended powerful political and cultural sensitivities about the values
of competition, markets, and economic opportunity. Duke would insist
that such structures were simply devised to rationalize the complex tasks of
production and marketing. As he secured virtually absolute control over the
cigarette market, prices to consumers actually fell due to new economies of
scale and production. But in a political culture with a deep historical an-
tipathy to monopoly and "restraint of trade," such trusts would not escape
the attention of legislators and the courts. Their social and economic impact would become perhaps the central debate in the American polity at
the turn of the twentieth century.

The Tobacco Trust facilitated Duke's aggressive program of consolidation
and integration of the industry. Once it was set up, Duke fought with the
other owners over his plans to control plug, smoking, and snuff tobacco as
well. He developed a series of departments, each charged with selling its

particular form: cigarettes, smoking tobacco, small cigars, and others. Salesmen for each department competed for customers from the same retailers. Duke saw this decentralization as beneficial to the Tobacco Trust. It reflected his view that no one—not even Duke himself—could predict what form future tobacco consumption would take.

The trust realized impressive economies of scale. Duke and his competitors had been single-function enterprises, concerned only with making and selling the end product.[66] Growing and processing of tobacco on the front end and retail distribution on the back end were left to independent entrepreneurs. Duke was the first to take steps—even prior to the Bonsack machine—to establish a fully integrated industry. He now radically reordered the entire business to assure continuity and managerial control.

With the consolidation enabled by the Tobacco Trust, whole manufacturing was concentrated in large plants, and the industry developed an extensive buying operation under what became known as the Leaf Department. An even more extensive sales department eagerly sought the command of new markets. All were committed to high volume "throughput," from agriculture through production to sales.[67] The Tobacco Trust also brought to an end most competitive bidding at the famed tobacco auctions. Farmers were forced to take American Tobacco's offer as the Tobacco Trust came to dominate all purchasing.[68]

By creating selling and distribution offices in key cities, Duke developed a national network to market and distribute his products. He staffed each office with a manager, a salesman who would focus on the city, and another salesman who would service surrounding towns. These quickly became the basis of a national sales force. Together, these three departments—audit (which oversaw accounting and cost control), leaf, and retail markets—assured the movement of cured tobacco from warehouse to factory to sales. Individuals with specific expertise headed each department. The audit department, for example, introduced innovative accounting procedures that would later be utilized by many other industries.[69] The success of Duke's enterprise, which became a model for other industries, rested on salaried executives who could assure the efficient functioning of their aspect of the business as well as tight coordination with other departments and activities—in short, he invented the middle manager. These middle managers were a critical component of the emergence of a new middle-class culture. The social constituencies that would form the basis of the consumer culture now worked inside the tobacco industry.[70]

Just as Duke worked to get the bugs out of the Bonsack machine and assure continuous production, he now sought to eliminate inefficiencies and uncertainties inherent in vertical integration. If the last years of the nineteenth century have been aptly described as a "search for order," nowhere was this clearer than in the radical reorganization of big business.[71] And no one was a more inventive practitioner of corporate rationality than Duke. Vertical coordination assured that factories operated at full capacity. Further, it promised consistency of quality and timeliness of shipping and sales, crucial in an age prior to packaging, when the shelf life of tobacco products was short.

Duke's vertical consolidation sought to eliminate middlemen at every level. Wholesalers, jobbers, and others not only cut profits, they created inefficiencies. According to Duke, if something was part of the process of producing cigarettes, it must be done within the company structure. The complexities of legal relationships and liabilities in fashioning mergers and acquisitions soon prompted him to add a legal department to assure in-house counsel. Finally, he understood the utility of locating his central office in New York City, the capital of rising national commerce. With this move, Duke overtly recognized that ready access to capital was more crucial to building an international business than proximity to growers or processors. Tobacco was a crop; American Tobacco was a corporation.

Duke had never been regional in his business aspirations, nor would he stop at national boundaries. Even before the formation of the Tobacco Trust, Duke insisted that "the world is now our market for our product."[72] In the early 1880s, he sent one of his senior colleagues, Richard Wright, around the world in search of new markets for his tobacco products. In the context of extending the Tobacco Trust, he now eagerly sought to take over expanding world markets. He established subsidiaries in Canada and Australia, and then turned his attention to Japan and China. In response to high tariffs on American products in Japan, Duke purchased a controlling interest in Murai Brothers, a Japanese firm.[73] Soon, American Tobacco developed extensive interests in China as well.

In 1901, Duke traveled to Great Britain in yet a further attempt to expand the global reach of the Tobacco Trust. He purchased Ogden's Limited, one of the major British tobacco companies, and embarked on a full-scale trade war with the recently constituted Imperial Tobacco. By now, well versed in such combat, Duke soon turned his adversary into a partner. Duke and Imperial created British American Tobacco in a "global agreement" in which Duke controlled two-thirds of its stock and Imperial one-third; both sides agreed not to threaten each others' domestic markets. With this agreement in hand, American Tobacco had worldwide dominance of the tobacco markets well within its grasp. Again, yet another of the critical structural elements of tobacco production and sales in the new century was effectively realized.[74]

But the Tobacco Trust's focus was not solely on cigarettes. In spite of the phenomenal success of the cigarette following the introduction of the potent combination of mechanization and aggressive sales promotion, as late as 1904, cigarettes still constituted only approximately 5 percent of the American market in tobacco products. Few observers at the time could have predicted that this somewhat idiosyncratic product would soon become so embedded in the cultural life of the new century. This unpredictability explains Duke's obsession with bringing all tobacco products under the Tobacco Trust's control. The consuming public was fickle, and regardless of fad, he wished to control the product of the moment. "We wanted to have a full variety . . . of the different styles of tobacco. . . . If one style [of tobacco product] went out of fashion we would have another style ready for the public to take up." It was his aggressive move to consolidate all tobacco under his aegis that ultimately made the Trust so vulnerable to regulation and judicial dissolution. For all of Duke's business brilliance, he never trusted the potential of his most modern product.[75]

Duke's only failure came when he attempted to integrate the cigar industry into his increasingly extensive fold. Cigars, he found, fit poorly with his system of mechanization, standardization, and national marketing; cigarettes would come to be defined by uniformity and mass production; cigars could not be easily mass-produced. Production of cigars would remain labor intensive, skilled work; they continued to be distributed in small quantities to specialized dealers. This distinction in consumption patterns defines a key difference between the nineteenth and twentieth centuries.[76]

The cigar represented tobacco consumption of the past, and the cigarette heralded the future. For Duke, who had transformed his father's plug business into a multinational giant, it was all just tobacco. His aggressive moves to incorporate the full range of tobacco products would ultimately bring him into conflict with the federal government.[77]

The financial success of the Tobacco Trust was nothing short of spectacular. From the original capitalization of $25 million in 1890, assets grew to $350 million by 1910. As economist Richard Tennant put it, "the fruits of monopoly were enjoyed."[78] Every $1,000 invested in 1890 (held without reinvestment of dividends) brought in a profit of $35,000 by 1908.[79] Moreover, the trust succeeded in precluding new entries into the market.

The formation of the Tobacco Trust in 1890 was part of a national industrial merger movement. The growth of giant corporations inspired a combination of awe and loathing. The Tobacco Trust—and ongoing issues of industrial collusion and competition—reflected a deep ambivalence within the American polity between appreciating the decided advantages of big business and recognizing its costs to innovation and entrepreneurship.[80] For a nation with deep commitments to a free market, monopolies threatened higher prices and the end of innovation.[81] Perhaps if the tobacco monopoly had been the only one, public and political concern would have been more muted. But Rockefeller's oil trust (which Duke so admired) and numerous others in railroads, copper, lumber, and other crucial industries created intense concerns about the concentration of capital.[82]

Trusts aroused political and cultural anxieties about the character of big business and the American economy. As corporations sought control over the variables of the market—especially in a time of periodic and intense economic downturns—Congress and the courts sought to limit the consolidation of corporate power. The central point was not the regulation of products like the cigarette, but rather the very structure and arrangements of corporate capitalism. Generally, the courts, especially the Supreme Court, found in favor of promoting competition. Although the Court was loathe to dictate corporate structure, it did—utilizing the Interstate Commerce Clause of the constitution—assert authority over how such organizations promoted or inhibited the movement of goods from state to state.

The American Tobacco Trust and the Sherman Antitrust Act were both created in 1890, one by an industrial mastermind, the other by Congress. It would be almost two decades, however, before they would collide. By the time the Department of Justice indicted American Tobacco in violation of the Sherman Act in 1907, the combination controlled not only 80 to 90 percent of the cigarette trade, but also 75 to 85 percent of all other forms of tobacco use—everything except the recalcitrant cigar business. Duke not only brought all tobacco products into the combination, he added companies producing licorice paste for flavorings and tin foil for packaging. Under President Theodore Roosevelt, the Bureau of Corporations documented the actions and activities of the Trust in excruciating detail. When the Department of Justice undertook antitrust litigation against American Tobacco, it was one of the three largest companies in the United States. The other two were Standard Oil and U.S. Steel.[83]

In 1908, the Department of Justice filed a suit in equity against the American Tobacco Company, alleging violation of the Sherman Antitrust Act. Some sixty-five companies and twenty-nine individuals, led by Duke, were named in the suit. Under Roosevelt's watchful eye, the government insisted on the dismemberment of the trust. The federal court in which the case was initially heard found American Tobacco guilty of violating the antitrust statute but it exempted United Cigar Stores, British American Tobacco, and Imperial from prosecution. American Tobacco was banned from interstate trade pending the restoration of "competitive conditions." Both sides appealed to the Supreme Court.

In May 1911, the Supreme Court found the American Tobacco Company to be in violation of the Sherman Antitrust Act and ordered the company dissolved. On the same day, using similar logic, it issued its decision breaking up the Standard Oil Trust. Both decisions rested squarely on the newly instantiated principle of what the Court called "the rule of reason." Given the vague language of the statute, the Court would now assert the government's regulatory authority over the excesses of trust building. The decision closely narrated the construction of the trust:

> The history of the combination is so replete with the doing of acts which it was the obvious purpose of the statute to forbid, so demonstrative of

the existence from the beginning of a purpose to acquire dominion and control over the tobacco trade . . . by methods devised in order to monopolize the trade by driving competitors out of business.

The Court described the Trust as "ruthless" in its design. As Chief Justice Edward Douglas White explained:

We think the conclusion of wrongful purpose and illegal combination is overwhelmingly established by the following considerations [including] the gradual absorption of control over all the elements essential to the successful manufacture of tobacco products, and placing such control in the hands of seemingly independent corporations serving as perpetual barriers to the entry of others into tobacco trade.[84]

According to the Court, the facts spoke for themselves: American Tobacco deliberately sought and secured a monopoly. As a result, it had to be dissolved. It was on this basis that White asserted—in the face of a vague antitrust statute—the "rule of reason" in which the Supreme Court claimed, without clear precedent, the federal government's regulatory authority over the new economy.[85]

Untangling what Duke had knotted together proved no simple matter. Prior companies and production processes had become intertwined. At the time of the breakup, a single department managed the leaf purchases for the entire organization. Each concern produced brands previously owned by other companies. Plants had been assigned specific products without regard for previous ownership.

Over the eight months following the decision, American Tobacco officials, the Attorney General, and the circuit court judges negotiated a complex plan for the dissolution of the Trust. The settlement was meant to assure competition among the five newly constituted companies—each received factories, distribution and storage facilities, and name brands. But given the size and complexity of the business, there existed "insuperable obstacles to the creation of perfect competitive conditions" no matter how the industry was restructured. There simply was no going back.[86]

It was one thing to identify monopolistic practices and activities in restraint of trade, and quite another to figure out how to return the tobacco industry to some form of regulated competition. Even those who applauded the breakup of American Tobacco soon found themselves critics of the negotiated decree restructuring the industry. This would not be the last time that the tobacco industry would successfully turn a regulatory intervention to its own advantage.

Even with dissolution of the Trust, open market competition never really returned to the tobacco trade. Barriers to entry remained firmly in place, obstructing new competitors from entering the market. The decree ending the Tobacco Trust was also subject to criticism and public rancor. Assistant Attorney General Jim McReynolds, the chief prosecutor of the case, called the settlement "a subterfuge fit only for the scrapheap."[87] The major players in the Tobacco Trust escaped with the lion's share of assets and the potential to dominate key aspects of the tobacco market, especially cigarettes.

According to Louis Brandeis, who closely followed the case and was among the nation's most distinguished observers of the new economy, American Tobacco was divided into "three parts to be owned by the same persons in the same proportions and to be controlled by the same individuals who the Supreme Court held to have combined in violation of the [anti-trust] law." He went on:

> It is inconceivable that even a decision rendered by able and upright judges can make the American people believe that such a "disintegration" will restore "honest" competition.

It was, according to Brandeis, "An illegal trust legalized."[88]

Nonetheless, the antitrust laws would be the principal tools for tobacco regulation through much of the twentieth century. Subsequent modifications, such as the Clayton Antitrust Act and the creation of the Federal Trade Commission (FTC), both passed by Congress in 1914, failed to resolve the tensions between the public good and the character of big business any better than the Sherman Act did.

Dissolving the monopoly merely put an oligopoly in its place. Assets of the conglomerate were parceled back to four new firms: the American Tobacco Company, Liggett & Myers, R.J. Reynolds, and P. Lorillard, all of which would prosper to varying degrees throughout the twentieth century.

Only one company not on the corporate map at the time of this rearrangement—Philip Morris—would ultimately share in the dramatic industrial growth of tobacco in the twentieth century. Many popular brands with considerable local appeal—produced by members of the Tobacco Trust—disappeared after the breakup as each of the large companies came to focus on a single brand.

In the immediate aftermath of the dissolution of the Tobacco Trust, observers noted no apparent decline in the prices of tobacco products. What did occur—as we will see—was a major intensification of advertising and promotion in the cigarette industry. In this sense, the modern cigarette emerged from the ashes of the Tobacco Trust. The tobacco oligopoly would return to a highly combative and sometimes competitive mode. But the major firms continued to recognize—even as they vied for market share and higher profits—their collective best interests. Three decades later, in 1941, the companies would again be found in violation of the Sherman Act, this time on charges of price-fixing.[89] The residuum of collusion born of the Trust never entirely disappeared.

By 1911, certain key characteristics of cigarette consumption had been clearly established. Many of these attributes, though considered unusual at the time, went hand-in-hand with aggressive promotion to youth. Short, narrow, and wrapped in paper, the cigarette presented a unique contrast to more traditional forms of tobacco consumption. The brief encounter with tobacco it afforded seemed both insubstantial and unnatural. But it had already revealed qualities that would account for both its remarkable popularity and its dire impact. It demonstrated the critical link between mass production and mass consumption. Its highly addictive properties assured that once one became a smoker, one very likely remained a smoker. And the intense competition among manufacturers, as well as their intimate collusion, foretold a product of impressive potential and a vast multinational industry. Even in the late decades of the nineteenth century, the tobacco industry recognized the cigarette's global possibilities.

The modern market in tobacco would nonetheless differ from that of the nineteenth century in important ways. Duke never completely understood that the cigarette would dominate the tobacco industry. After the breakup of the trust, he showed little interest in the cigarette, soon retiring from active management of the American Tobacco Company to go into the

electrical power business. Duke and others thought the strong rise in cigarette smoking was another fad in tobacco's long history. With some thirteen billion cigarettes produced in 1912, he reasoned, the market was near
saturation.[90] By 1930, the still-expanding market would demand 119 billion.[91] What Duke failed to take in was that this product, which he had
done so much to invent, was only in the earliest stage of its modern development. A corporate visionary, Duke anticipated and shaped major shifts
in business organization and practice, and in cultural practice as well. But
in the way that time and culture bind historical vision, he could not fully
see what his own boundless ambitions wrought.

The boy who smokes cigarettes need not be anxious about his future, he has none.[1]

DAVID STARR JORDAN, 1915

I never smoked a cigarette until I was nine.

H. L. MENCKEN, DATE UNKNOWN

I'd walk a mile for a Camel.[2]

MARTIN FRANCES REDDINGTON, 1919
R.J. REYNOLDS EXECUTIVE

CHAPTER 2

Tobacco as Much as Bullets

W HEN THE STATE of Washington made the sale of cigarettes illegal in 1893, many legislators supportive of the law
cited their disapproval of the business practices of the trusts.
As one reporter explained, "This powerful combine which has secured control of the manufacture of all the leading brands of smoking tobacco and of
nearly all cigarettes in the United States has been grinding the merchants
and retailers to such an extent that they are glad to see it get a dose of its
own medicine." Retailers described feeling squeezed by the tobacco industry: "I'm glad the bill has passed. I am tired of getting off my stool 250
times a day to sell a five cent package of cigarettes and then making only
ten cents on the whole lot."[3]

But opposition to the cigarette was not grounded only in antagonism
to trusts. The radical popularization of tobacco in this "perverse" form
was contested as a moral and cultural offense. For some late nineteenth-
century reformers, the cigarette represented many of the evils already associated with alcohol: wastefulness, indulgence, a poison harmful to self and
others. As the movement to prohibit the manufacture and sale of alcohol
drew increased attention and support in the last decade of the nineteenth
century, temperance literature increasingly made reference to the rise in
popularity of tobacco, especially in its new and most devious form, the
cigarette.[4] Cigarette smoking was widely seen as a "dirty habit"—a dis-
reputable form of tobacco consumption typically practiced by disrep-
utable men (and boys). Temperance reformers drew no distinction

between tobacco and alcohol: in their view, immorality led to bad health and unhealthful living to immoral life.[5]

The cigarette's offense to the moral sensibilities of late nineteenth-century American society was deep-seated. Since the earliest days of the colonies, Americans had expressed ambivalence about the acquisition of worldly goods and their impact on character. Economic success and its material trappings invited moral failure. If the Puritan rigors of self-abnegation and austerity were relaxed in the eighteenth and early nineteenth centuries, leisure itself continued to be regarded with considerable doubt. For Victorian sensibilities, pleasure, idleness, and material waste constituted important threats to personal character and social rectitude. The very nature of character building emphasized thrift, discipline, and industry. Personal wealth, though an important goal, held the subversions of indulgence and decline. As religious strictures loosened, many Americans regarded these seductions with ever-heightening concern.[6] Even as the engines of consumption began to rev up in the mid-nineteenth century, social critics were quick to point out that satisfaction and salvation would not be found in the glittering marketplace of goods.[7]

As the growing popularity of the cigarette threatened to shatter aspects of these increasingly endangered values, their guardians would mount an all-or-nothing defense of the realm. The antitobacco movement was steeped in hostility to the seismic cultural alterations that the cigarette represented. The consumption of tobacco—particularly in this popular new form—quickly came to symbolize a basic moral and cultural crisis in the nation. "The anti-tobacco crusade is a moral one, just as was the struggle for temperance," wrote the social reformer Vida Milholland. "It is a fight to free our beloved nation from a form of mental slavery, to which she is submitting, as long as she permits the poisoned drug, tobacco, to spread its fumes, like a pall over the land."[8] An 1884 *New York Times* editorial stated the national crisis in no uncertain terms: "The decadence of Spain began when the Spaniards adopted cigarettes, and if this pernicious practice obtains among adult Americans the ruin of the Republic is close at hand."[9]

Attacks on the cigarette drew on traditional temperance rhetoric to generate a new reform agenda. In the early 1890s, Lucy Page Gaston, a Woman's Christian Temperance Union worker and journalist, emerged as the national leader of a growing antitobacco movement. Traveling throughout the Midwest, she administered the New Life Pledge to boys and girls in which they promised to abstain from alcohol and tobacco. Thousands took the pledge, and Gaston soon turned her full attention—and ire—to the cigarette. A founder of the Chicago Anti-Cigarette League in 1899, she brought together local efforts to form the National Anti-Cigarette League, which claimed some 300,000 members by 1901.[10] As superintendent of the League, she combined grassroots activities with political lobbying to abolish smoking through legislation.

Many states had already banned the sale of cigarettes to minors. By 1900, North Dakota, Iowa, and Tennessee had enacted prohibitions on the sale of cigarettes altogether. As dozens of states debated such laws, rumors flew that Tobacco Trust representatives were liberally dispensing bribes among state legislators to fight the restrictions. Despite such efforts, Kansas, Minnesota, South Dakota, and Washington had all passed prohibition measures by 1909. As these bans went into effect, however, sales nationwide of cigarettes soared.

Gaston's anticigarette coalition drew together a typical menagerie of Progressive-Era reformers: old-time temperance advocates, self-fashioned modern critics of waste in an age of efficiency, social reformers who perceived a link between tobacco and delinquency, physician reformers anxious about the health implications of smoking, and eugenicists who believed cigarette use was associated with degeneracy. Henry Ford became a prominent and vigorous supporter of the crusade. In 1916, he published a widely circulated compendium of antitobacco materials under the title *The Case Against the Little White Slaver* and vowed not to hire smokers:

> Boys who smoke cigarettes we do not care to keep in our employ. In the future we will not hire anyone whom we know to be addicted to this habit. . . . We made a study of the effect upon the morals and efficiency of men in our employ addicted to this habit and found that cigarette smokers were loose in their morals, very apt to be untruthful . . . [11]

Ford recruited Detroit baseball star Ty Cobb to the campaign. Cobb's assessment was similarly condemnatory:

> Cigarette smoking stupefies the brain, saps vitality, undermines one's health, and lessens the moral fiber of the man. No boy who hopes to be

successful in any line can afford to contract a habit that is so detrimental to his physical and moral development.[12]

For Ford, Cobb, and their compatriots in the anticigarette movement, smoking was a profound moral failing and a sign of other social and characterological flaws.

The purported association with juvenile delinquency particularly aroused critics. In 1915, Leo W. Marsden, the officer in charge of the Police Juvenile Bureau of Los Angeles, concluded that smoking among young boys must be causally linked to crime. "By keeping an exhaustive record of such matters," explained Marsden, "I find that over ninety per cent of the boys under twenty-one years of age who are arrested or brought to my office are cigaret smokers." He found these boys to be "stunted in growth and under-developed in mind."[13] Such a view was not at all uncommon. At the heart of such conclusions stood an ongoing question: did smoking lead to physical and moral decline? Or did it simply attract misfits and weaklings?

As cigarette use increased in the first decades of the twentieth century, antitobacco activists and their medical supporters eagerly devised "cures" for individuals who had succumbed to the habit. In Los Angeles, the city sponsored a popular "anti-cigaret clinic" that drew a "veritable mob" of men, women, and children seeking treatment for their tobacco addictions. Such clinics, using a variety of medications, mouthwashes, and throat swabs, proved popular in many cities. Apparently, these prescriptions, like the silver nitrate solution administered at a Chicago clinic by Dr. D. H. Kress, made cigarette smoking thoroughly unpalatable.[14] "The taste will grow more repulsive by tomorrow," the physician assured his patients.[15] Gaston vigorously supported such interventions, hoping to deter cigarette use before it became habitual. "We are opening [Dr. Kress's] clinic," she explained, "because we are convinced that there are thousands . . . in Chicago who would rid themselves of the vice if they had the opportunity."[16] In Hoboken, New Jersey, at a similar clinic, boys were turned away when the supply of silver nitrate gave out.[17]

Charles B. Towns was a central figure in developing treatments to help smokers quit. He claimed that cigarette smoking was "the greatest vice devastating humanity today" because of the "mental, moral and physical deterioration" it caused.[18] Like many of his colleagues, Towns also was active in developing alcohol and opium treatment facilities. In 1901, he opened the Charles B. Towns Hospital in New York City, earning much praise from the medical community for his treatments. Rather than concentrating on his patients' moral failings, Towns focused on detoxification and criticized many of the antidotes touted by others.[19]

Other opponents of smoking insisted that the cigarette polluted the public environment. Unlike cigars and pipes, typically used in parlors and drawing rooms, the cigarette quickly became a public accessory, smoked in the widest array of settings. Just as their successors would do in the late twentieth century, many now called for restrictions on smoking in public places in the name of the rights of nonsmokers. "In all fairness, is it not reasonable to demand that some limitation be placed upon the indulgence of this habit?" asked New York attorney and anticigarette crusader Twyman Abbott. Public smoking, he claimed, was worse than alcohol because of the toxic fumes left behind. He urged that dining rooms, railways, and public buildings provide adequate accommodations for nonsmokers.[20]

In 1910, Dr. Charles Pease, an antismoking advocate in New York City, founded the Non-Smokers Protective League in order to lobby for bans on smoking in public places.[21] "The relaxed regulations which allow smoking in almost all public places, such as hotel dining rooms and theatres, inconvenience sufficiently those to whom smoking is generally offensive," noted the *New York Times* in 1913. The *Times* opposed a petition to create smoking cars in public subways.[22] Nonsmokers complained bitterly about the new veil of smoke in restaurants: "Smoking is now general in restaurants, and a non-smoker can seldom take a meal without the sickening fumes of tobacco puffed by a man who has a profound disregard for the rights and comforts of others."[23] A decade later, as health reformer John Harvey Kellogg noted, "Smoking has become so nearly universal among men, the few non-smokers are practically ignored and their rights trampled upon."[24]

In the balance of "rights," smokers made their claims as well. In New York City, smokers petitioned for the repeal of a law forbidding cigarettes on the rear platforms of streetcars. Tobacco dealers apparently supported these efforts.[25] Other smoking activists lobbied for smoking cars on the state railways and elevated cars.[26] The very process of claiming public space for smoking marked a critical element in the rise of the cigarette. And those who voiced their disapproval of cigarettes also revealed how prevalent cigarettes had become.

The antitobacco movement marked the intensification of a fundamental conflict in values between the Victorian and the modern. What critics of the cigarette often miscalculated was an ongoing social process by which this form of tobacco use displaced other, more traditional modes. The cigarette stood on a cultural cusp. By one set of arguments, its failings mirrored those of alcohol, yet by another, it was radically distinct from alcohol and its many related social pathologies. Just as alcohol seemed a poor fit for the exigencies of an urban industrial society, so too did the other forms of tobacco use, which declined precipitously in the face of the triumph of the cigarette. "Plug tobacco," noted Richard Tennant, "which was the chief form of nicotine dispensation in the mid-nineteenth century, is messy and socially disagreeable at the best, and in city life it is nearly intolerable."[27] The spittoon soon became an antique. The cigarette, produced by the very techniques of the modern era, fit the demands of its time.

§

The use of cigarettes within the military became a crucial battleground. On the one hand, the military represented conventional nineteenth-century views of discipline, morality, and health as well as the conviction that the state had the essential responsibility of protecting "manhood" from vice and decay. The cigarette, like alcohol, was often seen as undermining the control essential to military discipline. Delinquent boys with cigarettes hanging from their mouths did not project a desirable image of military decorum. On the other hand, tobacco had long been seen as an important element of the military experience. As military officials debated the increasing ubiquity of cigarettes in their units, soldiers vigorously defended their presence.

In 1907, Surgeon General Presley Marion Rixey of the Navy recommended that sailors under the age of twenty-one be prohibited from smoking. Enlisted men were quick to protest. An underage recruit explained:

If this cigarette recommendation is made the rule and such a thing is ordered, it's going to put us young fellows who like them on the beam. It's all right to talk about your cigars and your pipes, but cigarettes are cigarettes, and when you once get to liking the little sticks there's nothing that can take their place. Then don't forget that life on the ocean, with none of your women folks or girl friends around to break the monotony, is a lot different from life ashore, and I tell you those dreamsticks help you to pass away many a dreary and homesick hour.[28]

By the time the United States entered World War I, opposition to smoking in the military was increasingly restrained.[29] The campaign against tobacco, which had played on dominant chords of late nineteenth-century culture, now appeared prudish and out of tune with the moment. In the face of war's bloodshed, the traditional notions that a prohibition on tobacco protected the troops from moral harm and health risks seemed frivolous. Ideas like deferred gratification and self-discipline were eviscerated by the violence of combat. "The men who for us have so long breathed the battle-smoke are to be defended from the dangers of tobacco smoke," noted one critic of the anticigarette campaign. "We might as well discuss the perils of gluttony in a famine as those of nicotine on a battlefield."[30]

The moral threat of the cigarette suddenly seemed tame and anachronistic, and smoking seemed positively safe compared to the profound violence confronting the men overseas. The heroes of the American Expeditionary Forces (AEF) could hardly be viewed as delinquent and degenerate for smoking. When General Pershing was asked what the nation could do to assist in the war, he issued his famous plea to the home front: "You ask me what we need to win this war. I answer tobacco, as much as bullets."[31] Soon the very groups, such as the YMCA, that had stood at the center of cigarette opposition found themselves eagerly distributing them near the front and basking in the popularity of this largesse. Few transformations in our culture are so vividly clear as the shift from the bitter opposition to cigarette smoking voiced by the YMCA before the war and its enthusiasm for distributing cigarettes during the war. Many YMCA workers returned from their outposts in France as dedicated smokers.[32]

Despite these volunteer efforts, cigarettes were often in short supply and sold to the troops at a premium. Reports circulated widely that the YMCA and Salvation Army canteens were making a profit selling cigarettes to the troops. Soldiers complained that the YMCA, a major supplier, often charged fifteen cents a pack—the same price as in the United States. Dr. John R. Mott, general secretary of the YMCA, denied that the organization was making any money on tobacco and insisted that in many instances, especially at the front, tobacco and coffee were distributed for free.[33] Although soldiers could purchase packs of eight at the military commissaries, these were often inaccessible.[34]

The collection and distribution of cigarettes became a way for those on the home front to demonstrate their support for, and solidarity with, the boys in France. Volunteers organized smoke funds to collect donations to assure that the troops had adequate supplies of cigarettes. The "Sun Fund" amassed 137 million cigarettes in a two-month period. "Tobacco may not be a necessary of life, in the ordinary sense of that term," explained the *New York Times,* "but certainly it lightens the inevitable hardships of war as nothing else can do."[35] The National Cigarette Service Committee collected the names of soldiers without families to make sure they received cigarettes. Volunteers prepared packages for shipment to the troops under the auspices of groups such as the Army Girls Transport Tobacco Fund.[36]

Getting the donated cigarettes to the boys on the front, however, proved difficult. The *New York Times* reported: "We know there are hundreds of patriotic American societies, clubs, and individuals raising funds for smoke comforts for our soldiers. They know the difficulties they are encountering in getting these smoke comforts to our boys 'over there.'"[37] In May 1918, the War Department agreed to assume the responsibility of equitable distribution, issuing tobacco rations. "A wave of joy swept through the American Army today," noted the *New York Times.* "This step has been long hoped for by the soldiers and recommended by all officers from corporal to General Pershing."[38] The tobacco ration was set at four-tenths of an ounce per day (with papers) or four ready-made cigarettes. At the height of the tobacco shortage, the government decided to take the entire output of Bull Durham for distribution to the troops.[39] For those back home, denied their cigarettes, the *Times* suggested, "There is a remedy! Enlist and all will be well!"[40]

Opponents of the cigarette now appeared petty and vindictive. As one opinion piece from 1919 stated:

As for the poor fellows lying mangled in shell holes or in field and evacuation hospitals, with life slowly ebbing away from a body soon to become dreamless dust—who would be heartless enough to "prohibit" this last and only solace.[41]

Writing in retrospect, one commentator described the effect of the war on attitudes toward cigarettes: "Five million men, physically the flower of American manhood, were invited into a maelstrom of hardship, deprivation, danger and destruction. Smokers and non-smokers alike were collected and thrown haphazard into the field. Some young non-smokers witnessed husky, healthy and hard-boiled cigarette smokers. Cigar and pipe smokers with a grudge against the 'fags' found their prejudice slipping away. The general tendency was aided by the exigencies of the new and strange existence. . . . [T]he last vestiges of opprobrium that public understanding had not already removed were dissolved in the training camps and trenches."[42] The war radically reconfigured Victorian notions of risk and danger. The risks of smoking could only be known in context, and in this setting they looked very minor indeed.

Amidst the deprivations of war, cigarettes were high on the list of "realizable desires."[43] The camaraderie of war came to be symbolized in the sharing of a cigarette, a new commodity of morale. Finding a cigarette for a wounded soldier was an act of tender generosity in the "brotherhood of the front."[44] Supporting such acts was a matter of patriotism: Bull Durham tobacco came out with the slogan, "When our boys light up, the Huns will light out."[45] As one commentator explained:

> The difference between the old army and the new was strikingly illustrated by the difference in their choice of tobacco. The soldier of the old army was most strongly addicted to the use of that unlovely article known as "plug"—thereby giving steady employment to the spittoon-makers. The men of our new armies, however, expressed an overwhelming preference for the cigarette. Thus does tobacco gauge the progress of civilization.[46]

Cigarettes were the "modern" tobacco for this "modern war."

World War I would mark a critical watershed in establishing the cigarette as a dominant product of modern consumer culture. Rather than interrupting the rise of the consumer culture, the Great War accelerated it. In retrospect, promotion and patterns of use among servicemen during the war confirmed that the cigarette would not be, as Duke had feared, a mere fad. Promotional efforts, tightly tied to wartime patriotism and morale, proved impressively successful in transforming a popular, if marginal, product and behavior into a cultural idiom. Moreover, the wartime smoking experience would demonstrate a central aspect of cigarette smoking: it is a behavior that is powerfully reinforcing, both biologically and psychologically. Soldiers returned home committed to the cigarette.

§

The rise in popularity during the war had been preceded by an intensification in promotion. In the aftermath of the dissolution of the American Tobacco Trust in 1911, advertising budgets skyrocketed as each company fought for its share of a growing cigarette market.[47] One year prior to the breakup, the U.S. Commission of Corporations estimated total tobacco advertising expenditures at around $13 million, with cigarettes accounting for approximately one-third. Two years after dissolution, cigarette advertising alone would account for $13 million. As other forms of tobacco consumption declined in the years before World War I, demand for cigarettes rose dramatically. Although the new market for cigarettes cannot be ascribed only to increased advertising, corporate promotion was certainly effective in both channeling tobacco use to the cigarette *and* recruiting those previously uninitiated to tobacco. Even though cigarette makers emphasized differences in the production and taste of their respective products, they realized that they were at the mercy of the subjectivity of "taste." And that taste depended as much on the consumer culture as on the blend of tobacco.

The "Coming of the Camel" campaign, sponsored by the Reynolds Tobacco Company, marked the first signs of what was to follow. Reynolds had never acceded to participation in the Tobacco Trust, and although Duke eventually acquired two-thirds of the company's outstanding stock, its founder and president, R. J. Reynolds, refused to cooperate and even worked to promote the legal case against the Trust. When the Trust was broken, he resolved to crush Duke. "Watch me and see if I don't give Buck Duke hell," he reportedly announced upon hearing of the Supreme Court decision.[48] Whereas Reynolds's primary market had been plug, in the waning days of the Trust he introduced a new cigarette, Red Kamel. The brand failed, but Reynolds liked the name, and in 1913 he brought out a new cigarette, now simply called Camels. A tobacco connoisseur, Reynolds combined bright, white burley with a sprig of Turkish tobacco to produce a "blended" cigarette, with a mild taste that closely resembled more costly options. Priced at ten cents a pack, it competed well with more expensive brands and still turned a profit given its use of cheaper domestic tobaccos.[49] The apparent mildness of Camels was developed to create mass appeal. To help distinguish it from its competition, Reynolds offered no promotions. "Smokers realize that the value is in the cigarettes and do not expect promotions or coupons," he explained.[50] Against Duke's earlier advertising devoted to these now traditional promotional devices, Reynolds went modern.

Reynolds committed unprecedented advertising money to promote this single product, creating a national campaign to make the Camel cigarette a truly national brand. In 1914, newspapers throughout the country ran ads several days in succession that announced simply, "The Camels are coming." These were followed by a second wave of ads proclaiming, "TO-MORROW there'll be more in this town than all of Asia and Africa combined." Creating such expectations—and their fulfillment—would become a central technique of modern consumer advertising. The third ad portraying the Camel cigarette package read "Camel cigarettes ARE HERE." This advertising campaign—and here the term *campaign* appropriately reflects the strategic technique—met with unprecedented success.

Between its introduction in 1913 and 1915, Camel became the first truly national cigarette brand. By the end of the war, it had climbed to the top of sales. With market share determining what brands of cigarettes the government bought for soldiers during the war, Camel, now accounting for over one-third of the U.S. cigarette market, received a significant boost.[51] By 1918, with Camel holding such a significant part of the overall cigarette market, that massive promotion was no longer required, Reynolds cut his advertising budget. Camel was soon joined by two other competitive national brands, the handiwork of the other two dominant companies after the breakup of the Trust, American Tobacco and Liggett & Myers. Each also came to rely on an intensive advertising campaign similar to Reynolds' Camel campaign. By the mid–1920s, the three firms commanded over 80 percent of the cigarette market, each with a single brand: R.J. Reynolds's Camel, Liggett & Myers's Chesterfield, and the American Tobacco Company's Lucky Strike. Each brand would become a national icon for its corporate parent.[52]

The rise of national brands of cigarettes was but one indication of the cultural transformation occurring in the early twentieth century. The consumer culture in which the cigarette became so prominent and popular marked the construction of the first truly national, secular culture in American history. The localism and regionalism that characterized the "island communities" of the nineteenth century gave way to a fully nationalized cultural ideal that diluted local economies, values, and practices.[53] Small-scale production, regional distribution, and local clienteles were all on the way out. With a national culture came national products. Tobacco traversed this sea change through the cigarette. Moreover, such national commodities drew together, at every cash register, the country's diverse ethnic, regional, and social groups. Rich, poor, black, white, German, Indian, Jewish, or Chinese, you could always smoke a Camel.[54]

Closely tied to the twentieth century's new norms and beliefs was the cultural dominance of youth. If the Eighteenth Amendment, prohibiting alcohol, was the nineteenth century's last stand, the triumph of the cigarette marked the impressive social and cultural shifts that would characterize the new century. When T. S. Eliot described "Cousin Nancy" in 1917, he captured this transformation.

> *Miss Nancy Ellicott smoked*
> *And danced all the modern dances;*
> *And her aunts were not quite sure*
> *How they felt about it,*
> *But they knew it was modern.*[55]

Through the 1920s, as the cigarette became an increasingly omnipresent prop in the culture of youth, smoking stood as a prominent symbol in the fires that burned between generations.

The cigarette soon came to play an important role in the rituals of adolescent identity. For many adolescents eager to leave childhood behind, the cigarette signified adult status. Even as smoking became phenomenally popular in the 1920s and 1930s, it caused increasing concern for parents, who now had the burden of policing this behavior among their offspring, often while practicing it themselves. Many parents noted that the fact that they smoked incited intergenerational conflict. Adolescent boys came under intense peer pressure to smoke; "to refrain from smoking," noted one author, "would be the same as joining the 'sissy' group of boys."[56] Impressively, just as smoking became a marker of masculinity, it simultaneously became a symbol of beauty, glamour, and sexuality for women.

Many would link cigarettes with a new sexual accessibility among adolescent women, a marker of independence and autonomy. Following the war, young men and women smoked together with impunity. For women, the cigarette was part of a syndrome of rebellion that typically included cosmetics, dancing, and sexual experimentation. "The coarsening effect upon young womanhood through the smoking of cigarettes, through the exposure of nakedness in public appearance, of overpainting the face and lips, and of petting parties, are everywhere apparent," noted the *Buffalo Evening Post*. "It may be true that women have the same right as men to drink and smoke and indulge habits peculiar to masculinity, but that means the lowering of the standards of womanhood to the level of the men."[57]

Even as strident opponents of the cigarette lost favor, attitudes toward women and young smokers ranged from ambivalent to disapproving. While states debated comprehensive restrictions on smoking, local governments instituted their own. In 1904, Jennie Lasher was sentenced to thirty days in jail in New York under a new state law for endangering the morals of her children by smoking in their presence.[58] The New York City Board of Aldermen unanimously passed an ordinance in January 1908 restricting public smoking among women. Public establishments permitting women to smoke could lose their licenses.[59] Katie Mulcahey was arrested under the law and fined $5. "I've got as much right to smoke as you have," she told the magistrate. "I never heard of this new law, and I don't want to hear about it. No man shall dictate to me." After defaulting on the fine, she was taken to a cell.[60] Mayor George Brinton McClellan, Jr., had actually vetoed the ordinance, but it had been incorrectly posted by a court clerk. Mulcahey was soon freed.[61]

The fact that the antismoking movement centered so forcefully on smoking among women and children ultimately undercut its legitimacy. As notions of women's equality grew and women campaigned for political recognition, arguments against their smoking seemed like a dusty artifact of Victorian moral beliefs of female separateness and vulnerability. Smoking bans directed at women offended their newly honed sensibilities. Such opposition was perhaps as effective a motivation for women to smoke as any advertisement. And there is overwhelming evidence that women were experimenting with the cigarette long before the industry would explicitly acknowledge this in its own advertising and promotion.[62]

Apparently, not all the cigarettes shipped to France during the war were used by the troops. As A. E. Hamilton explained, the gender boundaries associated with smoking dissolved in the war:

> But since 1914, when nurses and you lassies joined Tommy and Dough-boy in a smoke, this line has begun to melt away, until the picture of the flapper without her cigarette has become like a picture of [Vice President] Charles G. Dawes without his pipe.[63]

Women workers on the home front, housed in government dormitories, also smoked like their brothers-in-arms—notwithstanding some protests. "If Congress admits that women have a right to vote," explained one working woman, "I'd like to see them stop us from smoking. If a woman wants to smoke, she'll smoke."[64]

Cigarette smoking among young women was often viewed by critics as the first step down a slippery path of moral decline that led to drinking, petting, and "other" sexual behavior. The cigarette, they suggested, was a marker of sexual accessibility and rebellion from familial and social conventions. Antitobacco rhetoric inevitably backfired among young women especially. According to *Good Housekeeping*, "girls begin smoking to demonstrate that they are strictly modern and up-to-date in their views and habits of life."[65]

As the nation attempted to "return to normalcy," the growing popularity of the cigarette antagonized antitobacco groups that viewed it as the next symbol of an amoral modernity. The war necessitated a critical hiatus in the anticigarette movement (while it created many new smokers), but activists eagerly saw the armistice as the moment to reinvigorate their efforts. Buoyed by the victory of national prohibition with the passage of the Eighteenth Amendment, anticigarette activists returned to their trenches. Evangelist Billy Sunday reportedly proclaimed, "Prohibition is won, now, for tobacco." "The time when the suggestion of tobacco prohibition could be laughed at has passed," wrote the *New York World* in 1920. "It is a definite possibility and unless vigorously met, it will become a real probability. The same forces that imposed prohibition on an unwilling nation are behind the antitobacco movement."[66] The WCTU widely distributed a new pamphlet, *Nicotine Next*, outlining the rationale for the attack on smoking.

State campaigns to limit the use and sale of cigarettes reemerged after the war. In 1921, after much public debate, Utah banned "the giving away, sale, exchange or barter of cigarettes," as well as the advertising of cigarettes and public smoking. The anticigarette bill's supporters, who included the WCTU and temperance advocates, and representatives of Brigham Young University, offered a series of objections to the cigarette. In particular, they emphasized the dangers, both moral and medical, to women and children. Senator Edward Southwick, the bill's author, quoted Surgeon General Hugh S. Cumming that "if American women generally contract the habit, as reports now indicate they are doing, the entire American nation will suffer. The physical tone of the whole nation will be lowered. This is one of the most evil influences in American life today . . . The habit harms a woman more than it does a man."[67] Another supporter of the legislation noted that "the fingers of our girls are being varnished with the stains of those harmful little instruments of destruction."[68] Just as earlier opponents of the cigarette had done, Senator Southwick argued that the use of the cigarette violated the liberties of nonsmokers, offended moral sensibilities, and polluted public space. "We cannot bring our wives and daughters to the city," he wrote, "and cannot come along without encountering tobacco smoke everywhere that saturates our clothing, and nauseates us. Personal liberty! Ours is as inviolate, or should be, as theirs."[69]

Increasingly aggressive and prominent advertising also drew the ire of activists. The belief that tobacco interests sought new customers among women and children was frequently voiced: "It is not . . . those who have acquired the cigaret habit," Southwick noted, "but new material and victims, that this advertising seeks to find."[70] For antitobacco campaigners, the 300 percent increase in cigarette sales over the previous decade could only be attributed to the nefarious power of advertising. One legislator described an ad portraying Santa Claus smoking a cigarette as "a desecration of the child's faith, if not blasphemy." Southwick argued that "skilled advertising causes the boy to think he will never be a man until he smokes cigarettes." Senator Reed Smoot of Utah took the floor of the Senate to argue that the aggressive promotion of cigarettes through the 1920s encouraged widespread "cigarette addiction."

> Not since the days when public opinion rose in its might and smote the dangerous drug traffic, not since the days when the vendor of harmful nostrums was swept from our streets, has this country witnessed such an orgy of buncombe, quackery, and downright falsehood and fraud as now marks the current campaign promoted by certain cigarette manufacturers to create a vast woman and child market for the use of their product.[71]

"The cigarette campaign," concluded Smoot, "is a libel—a great libel—upon American business ethics."

Those in favor of maintaining the legality of cigarette smoking frequently centered their counterarguments on more pragmatic grounds. Bills like Utah's restricting the sale of cigarettes, they argued, were difficult to enforce and promoted black markets. American Legion posts, with many members fresh from their experiences in the war, composed declarations opposing the Utah bill or offered satirical critiques advocating a ban on "all things pleasurable." Other critics of the legislation argued that its supporters' ties to the Mormon Church were indicative of a minority attempting to impose a religious belief upon the majority. They condemned the bill as "incapable of enforcement, unjust in its deprivation of inalienable personal liberty and as perverting the basic principles of the constitution in attempting to force the masses to act in accord with the whims and peculiar views of certain groups."[72]

By 1922, sixteen states had either banned or restricted the sale or promotion of cigarettes. But virtually all these laws proved short-lived. Passed with publicity and fanfare, they were quickly repealed after brief periods of erratic and weak enforcement. Increasingly, opposition to the cigarette proved out of step with cultural and political expectations, which made its restriction seem ironically intemperate in the new postwar national climate. By the 1920s, it was one thing to criticize smoking, quite another to enlist government to police its use. Much as Lucy Page Gaston and her colleagues tried to focus moral outrage on the cigarette, the emerging urban industrial culture found it decidedly unthreatening, even for women. Indeed, many now recounted its impressive and reassuring assets. The days of serious restrictions on tobacco use were numbered (at least for the moment). Antitobacco statutes marked the last stand of Victorian moral strictures that could not long survive in the modern consumer culture with its new norms regarding pleasure, sexuality, and spending.[73]

Still, concerns about smoking persisted. Progressive leaders, disturbed by the sharp increase in tobacco consumption during the war, formed a distinguished Committee to Study the Tobacco Problem in 1918. The Committee comprised a diverse group of noted academicians, clinicians, and social reformers, including William Osler, Irving Fisher, Henry Ford, and John Harvey Kellogg. Attempting to strike a moderate tone, they neither condemned tobacco from a moral perspective nor approved its use. Instead, consistent with the Progressive ethos, they focused on its economic impact and its ancillary costs to society. One study commissioned by the Committee argued that, despite some popular beliefs, tobacco did not contribute to "mental efficiency."[74]

Most notably, the Committee sought—notwithstanding its strong antitobacco bias—to disassociate itself from the moralistic tone of the prohibition crusade. This new model of antitobacco activity accepted the basic rubric of the consumer age; by investigating and publicizing the harmful effects of cigarettes, the committee's members believed they could have an important impact on behavior. They would soon come to understand, however, that the clout of the industry, new techniques of promotion, and the particular addictive attributes of the product overmatched them. The rise of the cigarette could not be impeded by Progressive reason.

Many now argued that cigarettes were the ideal product for the modern age, offering pleasure, solace, and relief from the stresses of contemporary life. Whereas temperance reformers had presented alcohol and tobacco as related threats, tobacco advocates and consumers eagerly dissociated their product from alcohol. As the *Literary Digest* noted: "Because it promotes contentment, tobacco becomes a blessing to those who use it properly. Tobacco is not associated with excesses as liquor is. A man might smoke too many cigars, it is true, but then even the most zealous anti-tobacco agitator wouldn't expect the smoker to go home and 'beat up' his family. The purchase of a can of smoking tobacco seldom leads to arrest for disorderly conduct. In most cases, indulgence in tobacco makes one calmer and more peacefully inclined."[75] "Tobacco would-be prohibitionists," noted the *New York Times,* "have a case not a hundredth part as good as they had against alcohol . . . To call tobacco a 'demon' would be such an obvious and wild exaggeration of its real demerits that those who did it simply would be laughed at."[76]

As a commentator in 1919 argued:

> Who ever heard of a man committing murder or rape or felonious assault while under the influence of—tobacco?
>
> Who ever heard of a man's children going without shoes because he spent all his money on—tobacco?
>
> Who ever heard of a woman's ruin made possible because she had been plied with—tobacco?[77]

With Prohibition having made alcohol less accessible, tobacco assumed many of the elements of sociability and leisure that had historically rested primarily on alcohol. Observers of the social scene remarked on how cigarettes were employed to "break the ice" in social encounters. Some argued that the cigarette was the new stimulant of the modern age, the perfect drug for an urban-industrial society. By the mid-1920s, Gaston's highhanded moral fervor had become the focus of satirical barbs. Sinclair Lewis, in his novel *Arrowsmith,* poked fun at "the anti-nicotine lady from Chicago" who injected ground-up cigarette paper into laboratory mice at a health fair only to incur the wrath of "an anti-vivisection lady, also from Chicago."[78] No doubt, the times had changed; the cigarette had come to play an increasingly important role in the day-to-day manners of the consumer culture. In the face of rising consumption, Gaston's apocalyptic claims for cigarette use now seemed to reveal more about her and her social movement than about the product she so bitterly detested.

Opposition continued through the 1920s in the face of the cigarette's rising popularity, but antitobacco proposals failed. Instead, state legislatures debated new approaches to limiting the use of tobacco. Many of these proposals would be debated again later in the twentieth century: in Illinois a bill called for restrictions on ads pitched to youth; Idaho debated bans on billboards and radio advertising. Senator Smoot urged that cigarettes come under the regulatory aegis of the Food and Drug Acts. Although opponents of smoking would continue to raise objections, the success of the cigarette made antitobacco rhetoric increasingly peripheral. Those states in which successful prohibitions had been legislated found them widely disobeyed and unenforced; the statutes, ironically, now symbolized the triumph of the cigarette.

§

But while the cigarette had gained a national foothold overall, social acceptance of women smokers did not proceed apace. Even though women's consumption had increased, disapproving commentaries still abounded. As *Good Housekeeping* explained in 1929:

> The odor of stale tobacco does not add to a girl's charm, neither do nicotine-stained fingers, nor will the repulsive affections of the mouth and throat which sometimes afflict smokers.[79]

Women, critics warned, were especially susceptible to the harms of smoking because of the peculiar biological vulnerabilities of the "weaker" sex.

> Tobacco will do to girls and to women all that it does to boys and do it harder. One of the worst things that tobacco does is shake nervous systems, and the nerves of women are less able to stand abuse than those of men.[80]

For those opposed to the cigarette, the increase in women smoking constituted a growing moral crisis that was sharpened by the practice's particular sexual meanings. One parent asserted that it was not cigarette smokers per se that alarmed her, but the social context and meanings of the behavior. Though perfectly content for her children to smoke, she nonetheless suggested that "if [my daughter] smokes as part of a petting party in a car parked out along the ocean or in the woods—then I have a problem, but that problem is not smoking."[81]

Among the young, proper women who attended college in the 1920s, the use of cigarettes became an important issue. The ritual of setting and breaking of rules in some ways resembled the experience of soldiers before World War I. At elite women's colleges, where issues of political and social equality between men and women were the subject of intense debate, conventions and regulations about female smoking came into occasionally vigorous dispute. Smoking bans on campus arose only as earlier social conventions were tested. In one typical example, at Wellesley College, the first rules against smoking were issued in 1918; first offenders lost privileges for six weeks, and further violations could lead to expulsion. Such limits not surprisingly generated dissent. "Violations of the no smoking rule rose to a climax when all the occupants of one Quadrangle dormitory were 'campused' [i.e., not allowed off campus] for the rest of the year."[82]

In 1922, the *New York Times* reported that two Wellesley students had been forced to leave school for refusing to relinquish their cigarettes. "The college does not permit of the development of the new woman," explained freshman Billie Burse to the *New York Times*. "To advance a girl must dare, and again dare, and dare forever more. The faculty frowns on our knickers; then they frown on our ideas; and now, having found our cigarettes, they're frowning again."[83] Although the story was later exposed as a ruse, it nonetheless drew widespread attention to the rising intransigence among young women toward no-smoking policies.

Despite student protests, the faculty upheld the ban, noting that "to sanction smoking is contrary to the spirit and traditions of the college." Wellesley students apparently evaded the rules that forbade students smoking within the towns of Wellesley and Natick, by walking to the town line to smoke. "Needless to say," explained a history of the college, "this custom was not popular with the faculty nor with the neighboring citizens to whom long rows of girls perched on their walls and puffing industriously was not a pleasant sight."[84] Disciplinary measures for violations of smoking regulations varied from college to college. At Bucknell University, forty-four women who admitted to smoking in their rooms were restricted from having dates for the next six months. The ruling caused the cancellation of an upcoming dance.[85]

One college administrator suggested that as long as women smoked in their rooms, there would be no consequence. But public smoking—an open declaration of autonomy—invited discipline. Even so, once the Lucky Strikes were out of the box, they could not be put back in. Women at colleges and universities quickly became committed to the important meanings the cigarette conveyed about them.[86] College rules forbidding smoking and drinking were routinely violated and soon deemed unenforceable. Smoking became a "choice" and a powerful symbol of breaking with convention. The importance of "personal style, preference, and taste," provided critical opportunities for defining the new, pluralistic mores that would characterize twentieth-century American culture.

By the mid-1920s the faculty at Wellesley had reconsidered their opposition to smoking and opened Alumnae Hall for students' use. In 1925, Bryn Mawr College also opened smoking rooms to its students, officially recognizing what "everyone" knew: bans on women smoking would inevitably fail because they reflected assumptions about gender, sociability, and sexuality that were in rapid decline. By this time, forbidding the cigarette was largely a lost cause.[87] Marion Edwards Park, Bryn Mawr's president, explained that "the experience of every college head is that an unenforceable regulation leads to the formation of secret practises which glorify the supposed evil and tend to weaken other disciplines."[88] Vassar and other women's colleges soon followed suit, relaxing restrictions on campus. Other institutions, however, dug in to maintain convention by affirming new prohibitions against women smoking. The Dean of Women at Northwestern University insisted that any girl caught smoking—at school or elsewhere—would be dismissed immediately. "Smoke and Leave School," announced another dean to her women students.[89] But such rules gave off the musty smell of a previous century's moral order. By the end of the 1920s, even the thrill in the rebelliousness of smoking was lost, as women's smoking became increasingly conventional.

By the late 1930s, most surveys at women's colleges confirmed that a majority of students were smokers.[90] "Most persons regard the question not so much as one of right or wrong as one of good taste and bad taste," explained one newspaper.[91] The earlier conflicts about the right to smoke at these institutions reflected the rich symbolic politics of young women in the 1920s. But like so much else, these conflicts did not last into the new decade.

If the cigarette proved a divisive element in the struggle over political and social equality between the sexes, it was principally women who contested the new patterns of behavior, and their principal concern was the link between smoking and promiscuity. Groups such as the International Anti-Tobacco League lobbied filmmakers not to portray women smoking except as "the accompaniment of discreditable character."[92] Other women's groups, responding to reports of smoking among teenage girls, often encouraged young women to pledge abstinence from tobacco along with jazz dancing and petting.[93]

The tobacco industry watched the debate about women smoking with obvious interest and concern. Early in the 1920s, explicit solicitation of women smokers had drawn the hostility of antismoking groups and the threat of regulation. Intimations that cigarette producers coveted the women's market drew supporters to the antitobacco campaign. "The manufacturers have started an insidious campaign to create women smokers," noted an advertising agent in 1919.[94] "This situation is a challenge to every right-thinking man." The author suggested such activity would inevitably strengthen the antitobacco crusade. Citing ads for smaller brands like Helmar and Murad showing women smoking, he argued:

When the "Antis" begin to wind up and put all they have on the ball, the cigarette people will wish they had stuck to the adult male market or had not tried to take in too much territory.

The *Christian Century* warned:

Such advertising is inexcusable; it illustrates how far men will go toward undermining the health of a growing generation in order to add to their profits.[95]

For opponents of the cigarette, the solicitation of women smokers marked the willingness of big business to cast aside propriety and morals for profits. "If the cigarette companies are not to 'get' the girls," wrote Allan Benson in *Good Housekeeping* in 1929, "there must be swift and effective interference with their power to tempt them. Particularly the use of radio for the carrying to young women of cigarette propaganda should be stopped. Parents who do not want their daughters to be cigarette fiends should be able to have a radio in their homes without feeling that they are opening their homes to a flood of insidious cigarette propaganda."[96] But as parents quickly learned, it was impossible to keep the floods contained. The recruitment of women smokers proceeded apace and by the mid-1920s, the outrage over this strategy had mostly dissipated in the face of changes in conventions about women generally and smoking in particular.

Women who smoked reported that they felt more sociable doing so. By presenting smoking as daring and irreverent, the cigarette attracted women who were eager to test the boundaries of public mores. They crowded powder rooms and restrooms seeking fellow smokers. Dressing rooms on trains were often filled with smoke. "The Women smokers are bringing about a new democracy of the road," wrote Marguerite E. Harrison in 1922. "There is growing demand for women's smoking compartments. The feminine traveling public wants a place in which to lounge and smoke just as much as the male contingent."[97] In 1922, the Globe Theatre in New York City, recognizing such demands, created a smoking lounge for women theatergoers.

Women also smoked in mixed company, exposing to criticism not just their manners but their skill. It was often suggested that they did not understand how to smoke correctly. A hotel manager explained: "They don't really know what to do with the smoke. Neither do they know how to hold their cigarettes properly. They make a mess of the whole performance."[98] Still, it was increasingly accepted that men and women—even if they smoked in particular ways—could politely do so together.[99]

The triumph of the cigarette did not occur by serendipity. Even as smoking seemed to fit with a modern consumer age, the very development of consumption was carefully and artfully constructed by powerful corporations with extensive resources. Beginning with the establishment of national brands in the years before the Great War, the tobacco industry would continue to develop marketing and promotion techniques that would later become commonplace in the age of consumption.[100] Certainly the industry would position itself as an advocate of "choice" in the marketplace, but even more significantly it would purposely move to reorient the culture on behalf of its product.

The ongoing attacks on the cigarette paradoxically made it a powerful symbol of modernity and burnished its appeal. "The more violently it has been attacked," noted one observer, "the more popular it has become."[101] Try though they might to limit the popularity of what they considered a vile and unhealthy product, they could not stop the cigarette from becoming phenomenally popular, deeply embedded in social interactions, and the basis of an enormously successful and powerful business enterprise. The cigarette century had arrived.

There are some women's clubs in this city which encourage cigarette smoking by their members. . . . I consider such demoralization a blot on our city's fair name. I think this club should declare itself officially opposed to the increase of such a crime. I think we should discourage in every way persons who attempt to corrupt our civilization.[1]

MRS. ALFRED ARTHUR BROOKS, 1908
GOTHAM CLUB LEAP YEAR MUSICALE
WALDORF ASTORIA, NEW YORK CITY

A formidable barrier between the sexes had broken down. The custom of separating them after formal dinners, for example, still lingered, but as an empty rite. Hosts who laid in a stock of cigars for their male guests often found them untouched; the men in the dining-room were smoking the very same brands of cigarettes that the ladies consumed in the living room.[2]

FREDERICK LEWIS ALLEN, 1931
ONLY YESTERDAY

CHAPTER 3

Engineering Consent

C IGARETTE SMOKING quickly became an implement for divining those sensitive and complex cultural idioms of gender and sexuality, autonomy and agency, in a new age of consumer motivation and design. The tobacco industry clearly realized that women made up half its potential market. While in no way given to gender exclusions in attracting new patrons, the industry was nonetheless aware that by targeting women it entered contested cultural terrain. Advertisers and marketers recognized that if smoking was to become a truly mass behavior, they would need to shape this territory. They seized on early debates about the meaning of smoking for women as opportunities. That smoking appealed to women before the onset of targeted advertising does not reduce the significance of tobacco industry efforts to recruit women smokers.[3]

Even though social conventions had restricted advertisers from explicitly pitching the cigarette to women before the late 1920s, many tobacco ads indirectly sought women smokers through images that emphasized the sociability and allure of the cigarette. Women frequently appeared in tobacco ads in rapt attendance to an attractive and powerful smoking male. By the late 1920s, advertisers' concerns about convention and mores had succumbed to widespread recognition of the vast female market for cigarettes. Their ads still offended some moral sensibilities. A new subscriber to the *Century* wrote in 1928, "I was surprised, chagrined, and disappointed that your high-class magazine cooperates with the tobacco industry in the endeavor to make women smoke."[4] But such objections carried less and less weight against the advertising revenue to be had from tobacco. Women had become fair game for the cigarette's increasingly sophisticated marketers.

Within the tobacco industry, the battle lines in advertising combat were already clearly demarcated by the end of the Great War. In the face of R.J. Reynolds's success with Camel, American Tobacco launched its own offensive, introducing a new cigarette brand, Lucky Strike, in 1916. The company's president, George Washington Hill, committed unprecedented resources to Lucky Strike's promotion, spending more than $100 million on advertising in the brand's first decade.[5]

If Hill did not invent the hard sell, he nonetheless drove it to new heights. Selling Lucky Strikes became his obsession. Packages dangled on strings in the windows of his Rolls Royce, which had the Lucky Strike logo emblazoned on its taillights. Hill named his pet dachshunds Lucky and Strike and grew tobacco in the garden of his Hudson River estate. Even Albert Lasker, his adman, found Hill's excesses were notable: "The only purpose in life to him was to wake up, to eat, and to sleep so that he'd have strength to sell more Lucky Strikes. . . . It was just a religious crusade with him—which made it very difficult to work with a man so narrow-minded on a thing which was all out of focus."[6]

American Tobacco lore says that in 1916, after observing the manufacturing process at the company's Brooklyn factory, Hill emerged with the slogan "They're Toasted." He was convinced he had discovered, in the heat of the factory where he had witnessed the drying, flavoring, and mixing of the tobacco, the thing that would make Lucky Strike the number one cigarette. Advertising theory at the time asserted that consumers required a "reason why" to spur their purchase.[7] Now, Hill was convinced he had one. He explained:

> The Burley tobacco is toasted; makes the taste delicious. You know how toasting improves the flavor of bread. And it's the same with tobacco exactly.[8]

The "toasting" process, he argued, made Luckies a superior and safer product. "This extensive campaign grows out of the increased demand for cigarettes from which harmful elements have been removed. Improvements in the manufacture of cigarettes now make it possible by the application of heat in the toasting process, to eliminate from the tobacco those impurities which heretofore have been a source of irritation to the smoker's throat."[9] By emphasizing "impurities" and "irritation," Hill offered a quasi-medical, therapeutic rationale for his brand. This was not the last time the company would use health claims on behalf of its product.[10]

Even as Hill shaped and promoted this rationale, he understood that toasting, taste, and tobacco would not, by themselves, increase sales. Over the years, he added new elements to the pitch. The "Reach for a Lucky" campaign was the most important of these permutations. Lasting for the better part of a decade, it was among the most successful—and controversial—in the history of modern advertising. "Reach for a Lucky" was the handiwork of Albert Lasker, who joined Chicago's Lord & Thomas Agency at the age of eighteen. He quickly rose to become president and owner of the firm by 1903. Known for his dynamism and aggressiveness in marketing both the agency and its clients, as well as his "cannonball copy," Lasker was first credited with introducing the "Reason Why" campaigns in 1904. Lucky Strike, at the time the largest account in advertising history, accounted for more than 25 percent of his firm's billing of $40 million in 1929.[11] In a collaboration of titans, Lasker and Hill were each certain that he alone was in control.

One evening in 1925, as the Laskers dined at Chicago's Tip Top Inn, Flora Warner Lasker lit up a cigarette. The headwaiter asked her to put it out. The incident led Albert Lasker to reconsider the character of tobacco advertising, which up to that time walked gingerly around social convention, especially concerning women smoking. Lasker and Hill were both eager to advertise directly to women. Recognizing that by the mid-1920s smoking among women was increasingly commonplace, they now devised plans to make Lucky Strike the cigarette of choice among this vast, largely unclaimed market.

In what would become a typical sequence for advertising campaigns, emphasis on the brand itself gave way to offering consumers a particular rationale for action. This rationale could vary from "They're toasted" to the somewhat more subtle claims that a brand helps in dieting, to the fact that tobacco men choose these cigarettes over competitors.[12] Lasker sought to offer a "reason why" to women smokers. Having developed, earlier in the decade, the campaign that broke through the convention and taboo surrounding sanitary napkins,[13] Lasker was now convinced that testimonials from prominent women would be equally effective in discrediting social mores against women smoking. He seized on a new slogan, "Reach for a Lucky Instead of a Sweet," a pointed rephrasing of Lydia Pinkham's turn-of-the-century slogan for her highly popular patent medicine: "Reach for a Vegetable." A 1928 ad featuring aviator Amelia Earhart proclaimed that Lucky Strikes were the cigarettes carried on the "Friendship" when she crossed the Atlantic. This was followed by "For a Slender Figure—Reach for a Lucky Instead of a Sweet."[14]

As one commentator explained, "It was a swell slogan as slogans go. It was easy to say. It tempted the great sweet-eating American public to think of cigarettes every time it opened its mouth. And it could be elaborated upon and supported by all sorts of pseudo-scientific and frightfully convincing arguments in its favor."[15] The "Reach for a Lucky" campaign ingeniously brought together several goals.[16] First, it was aimed directly at women. By suggesting Luckies could help women assume "the modern form," it associated the cigarette with contemporary trends in beauty, fashion, and changing women's roles. Second, the use of testimonials offered important opportunities for new smokers to identify with prominent individuals. In using these public assertions by "public" women going on record as smokers, the Lucky Strike campaign took advantage of the "cult of personality" that emerged in the 1920s as a force in advertising.[17] American Tobacco collected an eclectic range of public figures, both men and women, in constructing its campaign: opera stars and athletes, businessmen and socialites. The choice of spokespersons involved a combination of authority and association: figures of note offering personal testimony to the use of the product, and the ability of consumers to "associate" themselves with such figures. Identification proved to be a crucial element in the fine structure of consumer culture.[18]

The testimonials drew controversy, but it was controversy that Hill assessed as central to the success of the campaign. The advertising industry expressed concern that paid testimonials tested the legitimacy of advertising. Were prominent figures bought off by companies simply trading on their names? Did they really use the product they endorsed? An early Lucky Strike ad soliciting women smokers featured European opera star

Madame Ernestine Schumann-Heink; she later denounced the campaign as a hoax. The October 1927 issue of *Liberty* magazine contained eleven different ads for a wide variety of products, all endorsed by movie star Constance Talmadge.[19] The newly discovered phenomenon of overexposure revealed a critical problem with the use of celebrities. Talmadge nonetheless joined the long list of prominent individuals endorsing Lucky Strikes. "Light a Lucky and you'll never miss sweets that make you fat," she explained in an ad in the early 1930s.[20]

By pushing hard against the margins of legitimate advertising, Hill came to be widely perceived as a threat to the emerging authority of the advertising enterprise. Just as, in the late twentieth century, the industry feared the long-term impact of Joe Camel, in the 1920s advertisers were concerned that extravagant claims, paid testimonials, and aggressive competitiveness threatened to draw public attention to the process rather than the product. When a Lucky Strike ad asserted that cigarettes had improved a ship's crew's performance during a rescue at sea, *Printers' Ink,* the advertising trade publication, objected in an editorial. In a poll, the editors asked "Do you believe that the use of purchased testimonials is good for advertising in general?" Although 54 respondents replied that it was, a resounding 843 respondents said "No."[21] Failure to assert internal norms, it was feared, would lead to demands for stronger regulation of advertising.

Along with pointedly targeting women, the very notion of "Reach for a Lucky Instead of a Sweet" committed the company to a new marketing aggressiveness. Whereas advertisers had generally avoided going head to head with competitors and alternative products, the "Reach for a Lucky" campaign, with its emphasis on "Instead," proposed the cigarette as the modern alternative to candy. This direct attack outraged the candy industry. One chain of New York candy stores advertised:

> Do not let anyone tell you that a cigarette takes the place of a piece of candy. The cigarette will inflame your tonsils, poison with nicotine every organ of your body, and dry up your blood—nails in your coffin.[22]

The National Confectioners Association established a defense committee, which threatened Hill with legal action and a full-scale response. The candy manufacturers also hired Dr. Herman Bundesen, who had served as health commissioner for the city of Chicago, to prepare a pamphlet on the "importance of candy as food."[23] Restaurant owners soon joined the confectioners in the attack on the Lucky Strike campaign, calling it "insidious, immoral and outrageous propaganda." "For all the billions spent to advertise cigarettes," noted one observer of the battle, "the anti-sweet campaign looks like the first attempt to *create* consumers instead of merely tossing consumers from brand to brand."[24]

Some critics drew particular attention to the idea that the campaign was specifically designed to appeal to youngsters. The goal of the ads, they warned, was to "transform the school girls, the growing boys and the youth of the country into confirmed cigarette addicts, regardless of established medical and health findings." Joseph Berger, president of the United Restaurant Owner's Association, concluded ominously that "a more flagrant assault against public welfare has never been witnessed in the United States."[25] A commentator in the trade journal *Advertising and Selling* warned that "while the American Tobacco Company may laugh at the idea of the Better Business Bureau and the Federal Trade Commission as censors of its advertising, it can least of all companies, hardly afford the imputation that it is seeking to recruit an army of first smokers out of young boys and girls who are, of course, notably the chief consumers of candy."[26]

The hyperbole on both sides strained public credulity. In retrospect, the high-profile dispute looks like a strategy. Attention and controversy are dynamic elements in any advertising campaign, and Hill may have intended to provoke an outraged response. In any case, the "Reach for a Lucky" campaign ultimately drew the attention of the Federal Trade Commission.[27] Hill was ordered to relinquish all dietary claims for Luckies and to stop purchasing testimonials. But these modest interdictions did little to quiet the fevered pitch of tobacco advertising.

Other advertisers insecure about the status of their trade, looked to the boorish Hill with disdain. His extravagant claims for Lucky Strike, his eagerness for attention and controversy, and his monumental ego offended even Lasker; but Hill offered the painful reminder that in the relationship of agency to client, the client was always right—especially a client with a budget the size of American Tobacco's. And much to the chagrin of critics, sales of Lucky Strikes soared in response to the bombast. By 1931, in the midst of sharp criticism, Lucky Strike was the leading brand of cigarette. Vulgarity had its rewards.[28]

Hill no doubt delighted in the protests and threats of the candy industry. Ads defending candy (such as "You can get thin comfortably 'on candy,'" sponsored by the National Confectioners Association) were precisely the type of attention Hill relished.[29] These reactions showed that his ads had effectively tied cigarettes to pleasure, dieting, and the "modern figure," and demonstrated that controversy and aggressive advertising, rather than reducing public confidence and trust in a product, could create interest, attention, and sales.

Attacks on advertising as a manipulative evil tended to sound shrill to the public. Were ads so powerful, and men and women so easily flim-flammed? The public insisted that it could assess extravagant claims dispassionately; advertisements, many argued, were but a new form of theater. The advertisers thought otherwise. In 1928, American Tobacco spent $7,000,000 to advertise Lucky Strikes, second only to General Motors. More than twenty other companies spent more than $1,000,000 on advertising campaigns, all incorporating many of the characteristics of the Lucky Strike campaign.[30]

Political figures and policy makers approved of the creation of demand for its positive effect on the country's economy. As President Calvin Coolidge explained in his 1926 speech to the International Advertising Association, "Mass production is only possible where there is mass demand. Mass demand has been created almost entirely through advertising." With the sale of goods increasing by 400 percent between 1900 and 1925, at a time when the population increased only by 50 percent, the great expansion of consumer culture clearly indicated more than simple population growth.[31]

The rise of aggressive national marketing, and the powerful techniques of advertising and promotion it utilized, raised important questions about the character of the consumer culture.[32] How powerful was advertising in its ability to bend consumer behavior? What if such power came to be used to support antisocial ends? The rise of national advertising raised new doubts about manipulation and behavior in a mass society. And the cigarette, as a popular icon of the consumer culture built on the edifice of mass marketing, only intensified these questions.

But even as many worried about their manipulative power, advertisers developed and refined their field. Lord & Thomas, Lasker's agency, used a shrewdly self-promotional pamphlet in 1911 to urge the "professionalization" of advertising. Seeking to explain the rise of agencies and clients alike, it emphasized advertising's power to change action:

> No vocation with such far-reaching control over the minds of millions is yet so poorly *appreciated*, in proportion to its limitless capacity for good or evil.
>
> - To compel a definite *Action* on the part of millions he has never seen—
> - To cause minds of these millions to work, in accord, upon an *impulse* which he transmits, via type, and sway them inexorably toward the goal he elects—
> - To determine in advance that, through his will and skill, they shall make a concerted movement, toward a purpose of purchase they never previously contemplated, in direct response to his printed word—
>
> *That* is the mission, privilege and power of the modern advertising man who can live up to his opportunities.[33]

Portraying the agency as an "altruistic" force spurring industry and consumer into relationships of social value, Lord & Thomas now argued, with considerable self-interest, that *advertised* products protect consumers.

> The manufacturer who trademarks and extensively advertises an article thereby *proves his own faith* in *the merit of the article,* and practically puts up a *bond* to vouch for it.
>   All this means that a manufacturer who sells *unadvertised* and *unbranded* goods can quietly take out of *quality* or quantity enough to compensate him for advance in his costs, to maintain a liberal profit.

The grandiosity of such claims led to concerns about the possible abuse of advertising.

By the 1920s, it was common to define selling as a science. Advertisers and their critics believed the processes of motivating consumer behavior rested on techniques that could be rationally articulated and reproduced. During the Great War, new attention was directed to motivation, public opinion, and the rational manipulation of mass behavior, and the admen believed they could apply this knowledge in peacetime as well. Their confidence was indeed staggering. As Walter Dill Scott, a founder of the field of advertising psychology, wrote:

> Every competent writer of advertisements understands the importance of psychological principles for his work. All students of the subject are aware that their work must conform to the laws of mental action so far as these are known or can be determined.[34]

Psychologists catalogued a wide range of drives and desires, ranging from hunger and thirst to sexuality and beauty, that individuals could "satisfy" in the marketplace of consumer goods. The advertiser's role was to identify particular products with specific forms of gratification.

When advertisers for Chesterfields noted bluntly in the 1920s "They Satisfy," they explicitly subscribed to this psychology of needs. Whereas earlier models of markets focused on the interrelationship between supply and demand, modern advertising in the consumer culture emphasized the creation of both need and desire. The cigarette in particular suggested to many observers that demand could be fashioned and shaped by the techniques of advertising. For example, an analyst writing in *Advertising and Selling* in 1936 explained the basis of tobacco advertising this way:

> You know a large part of the public really doesn't know what it wants. Our big task in recent years has been to dig up new likes or dislikes which we think might strike the public's fancy, and sell them to the public. We have dealt with diet, weight, coughs, mildness, quality of tobacco, nerves, toasting tobacco, youthful inspirations and a host of other subjects. The public must be given ideas as to what it *should* like, and it is quite surprising sometimes how the public is sold on what might look, in sales conference, like the brainchild of a demented person. The

old sales bywords "know your customer's needs" have been remolded to "know what your customer should need and then educate him on those needs."[35]

The targeting of woman by cigarette advertisers provides a prime example of this creation of needs. If women were perceived as the arbiters of morality in late nineteenth-century American culture, now they were seen as the principal force in the ethos of consumption.[36] As one advertising psychologist explained, "The advertiser, especially the one using large space consistently, has within his power not only to affect temporarily, but to mold permanently, the thought and attitude he wants his particular public to have with reference to the relative importance of style and beauty and such other factors as he may choose to play up by means of advertising."[37] Beginning with Lucky Strike's "Reach" campaign, cigarette ads targeted to women made explicit appeals to both style and beauty. As a symbol of both attributes, the cigarette became deeply embedded in the politics of gender in the 1920s and 1930s. Smoking for women, in this crucial phase of successful recruitment, became part and parcel of the good life as conceived by the American consumer culture and explicitly represented in advertising campaigns. The effectiveness of these campaigns was heightened and reinforced by public relations efforts to create a positive environment for the new images. Together, the ad campaigns and the PR promoted a product and a behavior that now possessed specific and appealing social meanings of glamour, beauty, autonomy, and equality.

The vehicle for the sale of American Tobacco remained the same for women as for men: a single, national brand with malleable, targeted images. Observers of the consumer culture looked to the cigarette as the principal exemplar of the rise of national brands. "The habitual smoker," noted *Printers' Ink* in 1941, "buys brands rather than cigarettes and it is the advertising that has built up this prestige in the consumers' eyes for a particular product."[38] This was especially important because the cigarette was largely an undifferentiated product. Certainly, cigarettes varied in tobacco blend, production, and taste, but it was through advertising and marketing that brands came to be distinguished. "There can be little doubt that if Reynolds, Liggett & Myers, or American had to give up either their secret formulas or their brand names, they would keep the brand names," noted *Fortune* in 1936.[39] In no other industry was the importance of brand so heralded.

Observers of the new consumer watched this process of branding with considerable interest. A frequently repeated experiment asked blindfolded smokers to identify their regular brand. Smokers confidently asserted their ability to do this, but they invariably failed at high rates.[40] In 1928, early consumer advocate Stuart Chase reported:

> Another [subject], while smoking a Camel, which he had named a Lucky Strike, said that Luckies never hurt his throat, but "go down easy and smooth, " whereas Camels are "terrible and stick in one's throat."[41]

By the 1940s, more intensive investigation confirmed the similarity of all brands. *Reader's Digest,* eager to separate "fact and fiction" in cigarette advertising, commissioned a research laboratory to investigate the "objective" differences among the major brands. A "smoking robot" collected samples of nicotine and tars as well as other data. *Reader's Digest* concluded that "the differences between brands are, practically speaking, small" and that "it makes no earthly difference which of the leading cigarettes you buy."[42]

These kinds of experiments, repeated through the 1920s, 1930s, and 1940s, came to be viewed as demonstrating the power of image over substance, and promotion over quality. The cigarette came to epitomize this crucial aspect of the consumer culture, in which advertisers manipulated meaning and experience, creating needs and consumer loyalties. As one critic lamented: "Has there been in all history so colossal a standardizing process—such a vast demonstration of the sheeplike qualities of the human race as in the spread of the tobacco habit? Has not this increase in the use of cigarets been brought about through the expenditure of millions of dollars of advertising through the hired misuse of psychology, art, writing, printing, and radio; through the degradation of newspapers and magazines?"[43] Brand differentiation—and the rise of the cigarette—was viewed by critics as representative of a new and dangerous element: the artificial creation of desire for purposes of profit.

The central importance of brand differentiation, which came to be deeply embedded in the consumer culture, was that it marked not only "differences" in products but differences in consumers as well. Brand choice became an indicator of status and judgment, an assertion of the consumer's individuality. For critics of the consumer culture, cigarette brands and their aggressive promotion were a primary example of the "invention" of choice. A standardized product was used to promote "individualism." The paradox of asserting one's individuality through "market choice" was not lost on contemporary observers. The cigarette in its marketing and advertising walked the fine line so characteristic of the consumer culture between demanding conformity and the assertion of individuality. "The constant struggle within the individual to be different and at the same time to conform manifests itself in convention and custom, style and fashion, and their more extreme forms known as fads and crazes," noted one advertising expert. "This shifting of the conformity, non-conformity attitude forms the basis of a larger proportion of our class advertising."[44]

Although it is impossible, at this distance, to adequately reconstruct the subtle differences in the meanings of particular brands to smokers in the 1920s and 1930s, we can nevertheless recognize the importance of such differences and the process by which they were constructed. Brand choice—and loyalty—conferred status in what one historian has called "the drama of consumer desire."[45]

§

George Washington Hill, among others, understood that mass advertising was but one side of the marketing coin. Effective marketing required the deployment of a wide range of complementary techniques, from public relations to corporate design. Advertising had to be sensitive to cultural norms and desires, but the culture was changing. Could it be *intentionally* changed? Could the "fit" between product and patron be consciously altered? In pursuing this objective, Hill enlisted the efforts of Edward Bernays. A nephew of Sigmund Freud, born in Vienna in 1891, Bernays came to the United States with his family a year later. After graduating from Cornell, he went to work for the Committee on Public Information during World War I, where he developed both his communication skills and his theory of propaganda.[46] Following the war, Bernays embraced the new psychology and the new corporate order, eagerly offering the techniques of mass opinion to corporate clients. Unlike his predecessors in the "science" of public opinion, he did not see his role as an "educator." Rather, Bernays looked to exploit the insights of psychology to shape mass behavior and values.

Just as the cigarette emerged from World War I as a central element in the culture, so too did public relations. Bernays quickly fashioned himself into the first "counsel on public relations," offering his services to a wide range of industries in the United States and abroad. As the new field's chief advocate and publicist, he came to define public relations as the science of the "group mind" and "herd reaction." A central element of Bernays's approach was the use of media, particularly what he called the "created event." As he explained in 1923, "The counsel on public relations not only knows what news value is, but knowing it, he is in a position to *make news happen*."[47] The staging of public events, produced to draw news coverage, marked a central element of the "counsel's" corporate responsibility. Bernays eagerly pointed out that generating news incurred no advertising costs and was also free of the taint of self-interest and manipulation already being questioned within the advertising industry.[48]

The manipulation of public opinion, values, and beliefs would, in the 1920s, become a dominant aspect of the consumer culture. It was at this time that blurring the line between advertising and the news became a critically important technique in marketing products of all kinds. Bernays prized the power of the news media precisely because it hid the interests of the industry. He understood that his behind-the-scenes machinations—typically conducted surreptitiously on behalf of clients—could easily disturb the delicate trust on which the consumer culture rested. To prevent clients from becoming "unsocial or otherwise harmful," he argued, the counsel of public relations must play a central role in guiding corporate policy. He devised a set of functions for modern PR sharply distinguished from those of publicist and press agent; yet even Bernays's ingenuity and ego could not make this distinction permanent.[49]

Bernays's work on behalf of American Tobacco illustrates this approach to promotion. In 1929, he outlined the structure of a proposed PR arm for American Tobacco. The "Tobacco Information Service Bureau," he suggested, would provide news releases and information in an array of media and "provide a certain scientific background for what the Bureau may from time to time say from a scientific standpoint." This Bureau should develop strong relations with the press, placing articles that would ultimately favor the interest of American Tobacco. Examples of stories, he suggested, might be "INTERNAL REVENUE STATISTICS ON TOBACCO INTER-PRETED," or "DOCTORS SAY CIGARETTES REDUCE NUMBER OF BACTERIA IN YOUR MOUTH." This "educational work" would help to overcome the criticism Hill's campaigns attracted, as well as defray ongoing concerns about the health effects of smoking.

Bernays also traded ideas with Hill to "increase good-will and sales" for Lucky Strikes. He suggested, for example, planting photos and news articles linking cigarettes, women, beauty, and a range of smoking accessories.

> Feature story for fashion editors on importance of cigarette cases and holders to smartly dressed women as part of their ensemble. This with photographs. Propaganda to be injected into the story regarding toasting.[50]

A year earlier, Hill's first assignment for Bernays had been to assist in the campaign for soliciting women smokers. Hill reportedly explained, "It will be like opening a new gold mine right in our front yard." According to Bernays, "Hill became obsessed by the prospect of winning over the large potential female market for Luckies."[51] Lasker's "Reach for a Lucky Instead of a Sweet" campaign was then in production; Hill and Bernays set out to exploit the pitch's impact. With women's fashions moving to a new emphasis on slimness, Lucky Strike ads proclaimed their product as a tool for beauty and physical attraction. Bernays sought to enlist the fashion industry, sending out hundreds of Parisian *haute couture* photos of slender models to magazines and newspapers. To strengthen his case, he solicited medical writings on the deleterious impact of sugar on the human body and then used the media to broadcast the findings.

He understood his role as working behind the scenes to create support for the more overt marketing upon which public attention and opinion would form. On behalf of the "Reach for a Lucky" campaign, Bernays—without ever noting his relationship with American Tobacco—sponsored a conference on the evolution of the modern ideal of beauty. Artists at this meeting insisted that the "slim woman [is] the ideal American type."

Another tool that Bernays employed was the survey—quick and dirty polls of social attitudes or practices. In his hands, the survey was not an instrument to measure public opinion but a technique for shaping it. Surveying department store managers, he again found support for the Lucky Strike campaigns' emphasis on the modern figure. "According to this survey" announced a Bernays press release, "the slender, modish saleswoman is in demand and can earn more for herself and her employer than her heavier sisters."[52]

Bernays also helped shape public reaction to American Tobacco's attack on "sweets." When the campaign elicited protest and the threat of legal action from confectioners, he sought to portray such competition as in consumers' interest and to define the battle between American Tobacco and the candy industry as characteristic of an important and timely shift in American economic life. He eagerly sponsored "news" articles, and then, if they served the company's interest, had them widely reprinted and distributed. Articles by chemists, agricultural experts, and physicians were solicited to underscore the themes of ongoing advertising campaigns. Physician Clarence Lieb, for example, recruited to write in support of the "moderation" campaign, explained his position in language that echoed American Tobacco ad copy:

> It may also be said that in every form of our complex civilization, whether in work or play, in social life, in eating and other forms of indulgence, particularly in eating between meals, excess seems to have become the rule instead of the exception and the thought of moderation is like a small voice crying in the wilderness.[53]

For Bernays, expertise was but a commodity for the PR expert to purchase and exploit. His efforts on behalf of recruiting women smokers provided a laboratory for his theory.

In 1929, Hill sought even more aggressive interventions in the market. As Bernays recounted, "Hill called me in. 'How can we get women to smoke on the street? They're smoking indoors. But damn it, if they spend half the time outdoors and we can get 'em to smoke outdoors, we'll damn near double our female market. Do something. Act!'"[54] So Bernays set out to identify and destroy the taboos associated with public smoking for women. He enlisted the advice of noted New York psychoanalyst A. A. Brill, who explained, "Some women regard cigarettes as symbols of freedom. Smoking is a sublimation of oral eroticism; holding a cigarette in the mouth excites the oral zone. It is perfectly normal for women to want to smoke cigarettes."[55] As Freud's nephew, Bernays was sympathetic to the notion that such insight could be used to modify patterns of consumption and the use of cigarettes. As Brill suggested, "Today the emancipation of women has suppressed many of their feminine desires. More women now do the same work as men do. Many women bear no children; those who do bear have fewer children. Feminine traits are masked. Cigarettes, which are equated with men, become torches of freedom."[56]

Bernays seized on this notion of "torches of freedom" as his weapon against the traditional taboos against women smoking in public. In a publicity stunt of genuine historical significance, he recruited debutantes to march in the 1929 New York City Easter parade brandishing their "torches of freedom." The staging of the event was carefully thought out, as Bernays's notes reveal:

OBJECT

To increase the consumption of cigarettes by women and to gain publicity for Lucky Strikes. Specifically, pictures of women smoking to appear in papers on Easter Monday and in newsreels. In reading matter, stories that for the first time women have smoked openly on the street. These will take care of themselves, as legitimate news, if the staging is rightly done.

The women would be carefully chosen: "Discretion must be used in their selection . . . while they should be good looking, they should not look too model-y." Bernays called for a meeting with the women on Good Friday when they could be "given their final instructions" and "furnished with Lucky Strikes." He even went so far as to provide his own photographer "to guard against the possibility that the news photographers do not get good pictures."[57]

In planning and organizing this event, Bernays remained behind the scenes, following a central tenet of his approach to public relations. For a man of his colossal ego, this, no doubt, must have been quite a struggle.

Nonetheless, he eagerly arranged this event, fed news to the media, and conducted surveys, all of which maintained his own and his clients' anonymity. Invitations to march in the Easter Parade came from feminist Ruth Hale:

Women!
Light another torch of freedom!
Fight another sex taboo!

The young women marched down Fifth Avenue puffing Lucky Strikes, effectively uniting the symbol of the emancipated flapper with that of the committed suffragist. Newspapers widely reported their exploit, touching off a national debate.[58] Bernays eagerly expected protests: "These should be watched for and answered in the same papers." The stunt reinvigorated the controversies of the past decade, and used them to advance Bernays's marketing campaign. While women's clubs decried the fall of the proscription on public smoking, feminists hailed the change in social convention. Reports of women smoking "on the street" came from cities and towns across the nation. "Age-old customs, I learned," wrote Bernays, "could be broken down by a dramatic appeal, disseminated by the network of media."[59] He prized the fact that he had "secretly" instigated news and controversy on behalf of his client's marketing interests.

In 1934, Bernays intervened once again in American Tobacco's efforts to promote smoking among women. Apparently concerned that women shunned Luckies because the green packaging clashed with current fashions, Hill urged Bernays to change the fashion. Bernays wrote, "That was the beginning of a fascinating six-month activity for me—to make green *the* fashionable color."[60] He developed an eclectic and far-reaching strategy, sponsoring fund-raising balls in which invitees agreed to wear green gowns, and a "Green Fashion Fall" luncheon to promote the color within the fashion industry, at which experts discussed the artistic and psychological meaning of *green*. Bernays later explained, "I had wondered at the alacrity with which scientists, academicians and professional men participated in events of this kind. I learned they welcomed the opportunity to discuss their favorite subject and enjoyed the resultant publicity. In an age of communication, their own effectiveness often depended on public visibility."[61] The consumer age was predicated, Bernays discovered, on providing a forum for voices that would do an industry's bidding.

Bernays understood early on that these new cultural media were not like advertising, in which interest is overtly and even crudely on display. He preferred the implicit qualities of other cultural forces. For example, Bernays quickly realized the importance of encouraging the use of cigarettes in film. Long before "product placement" became a core element of marketing (widely deployed by the tobacco and other industries), Bernays recognized the power of film to shape consumer expectations. In an anonymous essay prepared for directors and producers, Bernays reviewed the range of dramatic meanings the cigarette could convey. "Cigarettes have become chief actors in the silent drama or the talkie, for a great deal can be said with a cigarette which would ordinarily require a great many words to express," he noted.[62]

> There is many a psychological need for a cigarette in the movies. The bashful hero lights a cigarette, the better to gain a hold of himself in this trying interview with his future father-in-law. The villain smokes hasty puffs to hide his nervousness or to ease his conscience. But perhaps the most dramatic scenes are those where the cigarette is not smoked. How much can be expressed by the habitual smoker, when he is too perturbed to smoke! The gambler in the Casino, who has staked his last thousand on one card, and has lost—his cigarette falls unlighted from his trembling hands, and tells us worlds of chagrin. The deceived husband, deserted by the heartless wife, reaches for a cigarette, but lets the package drop, to signify his utter loss, his absolute defeat. The enraged crook, who feels that his pal has double-crossed him, viciously crumbles his cigarette in his fingers, as if it were the body and soul of his once trusted comrade, on whom he is wreaking vengeance. . . .
>
> Everything from the gayest comedy, to the most sinister tragedy can be expressed by a cigarette, in the hands or mouth of a skillful actor.

By the 1930s, the cigarette, with Bernays's help, became an important prop in movies, used to invest characters and scenes with a range of meanings.[63] Even a cursory review of the great films of the 1930s and 1940s confirms just how central the cigarette had become in the social idioms of everyday life. Films both reflected and reified cultural norms at the same time that they created styles and fads.

At mid-century, *Atlantic Monthly* catalogued the wide range of affect and emotion that could be served on screen or stage by the cigarette as a prop. The litany closely resembled what Bernays offered nearly two decades earlier. Cigarettes could easily demonstrate self-confidence or shyness, anxiety or surprise. To demonstrate anxiety, the authors suggested, "Take quick and frequent puffs at cigarette, while moving briskly round stage or set. Discard a half-finished cigarette and straightaway light another." To reveal "acute distress" actors were advised to "crush out a half-smoked cigarette with awful finality." Shyness could be portrayed by fumbling with a cigarette and matches. Finally, "passion in the raw" could be exhibited as follows: "Put two cigarettes in mouth at same time. Light both, then, with possessive air, hand one of them to adored." This was exactly how Paul Heinreid, in the 1942 blockbuster *Now Voyager*, "consummated" his romance with Bette Davis.[64] And, of course, couples calmly smoking in bed had become a surefire indicator of just-finished sex.

Still, to suggest that George Washington Hill and Edward Bernays were solely and wickedly responsible for turning women into smokers would be to misrepresent the history of the era. Given the range of economic and social forces eroding prohibitions on female smoking, as well as the remarkable rise of cigarette consumption in the first decades of the twentieth century, it was inevitable that women would be tapped as an important constituency for the product. Hill and Bernays—and their competition—shaped and promoted the cigarette's status as the symbol of the independent feminist and the bold, glamorous flapper. The cigarette revealed the power of the technique of investing a commodity with cultural meaning in order to motivate consumption. It was this ability to recognize, shape—*and exploit*—cultural change that lay at the heart of successful consumer motivation.

As a master of mass motivation Bernays understood that it was crucially important for the individual to fully believe in his or her own free choice and agency. This may be why he regarded advertising with some skepticism. In its overtly mass appeal, it could erode the confidence of what he called "consent," the belief in reflective and rational individual choice. A phrase he coined, "engineering of consent," brilliantly captures the stance of public relations toward the consumer culture. With the term *engineering* Bernays specified the instrumental precision with which he aspired to operate; in *consent* he implied that, ultimately, individual autonomy persisted despite the power of corporate manipulation. "Engineering of consent" was sharply ironic. It suggested that the *illusion* of agency was a critical component of the consumer culture and a central element of the promotion of cigarette smoking.

§

Raymond Loewy's redesign of the Lucky Strike package for Hill illustrates a complementary element to the rise of national advertising and public relations. The field of industrial design ranged from the architecture of machinery and objects to the development of logos and corporate symbols. The cigarette—in this case, its packaging—reflected the importance of design in organizing the new consumer consciousness and in constructing the meaning of products. A few years after Hill and Bernays worked to popularize the green in Lucky Strike packaging, Hill tried a new tack. He turned to Loewy, an acclaimed designer known for eviscerating Victorian sensibilities with a new aesthetic of spare, clean designs that connoted efficiency and modernity. Loewy had transformed the look of everything from Coca-Cola bottles to the Shell Oil logo to Studebaker cars.

In 1941, still concerned that green—despite Bernays's efforts—alienated women, Hill hired Loewy to reconfigure the package of Lucky Strikes. According to Loewy, the two men bet $50,000 on the effectiveness of the new design, a bet that Loewy reportedly collected. He later explained that any change in the design of an established product was risky. "It must not destroy the identity of the package established at the cost of millions of dollars, as in the case of Luckies."[65] Loewy made the package white, believing that this change would convey "freshness of content and immaculate manufacturing."[66] His other major intervention was to place the dominant red target on both sides of the package. In the past, the target had appeared only on the front; now both sides became the front. As Loewy explained, "Thus, a package lying flat on a desk, a wrapper discarded, would inevitably display the brand name . . . the Lucky Strike target has been displayed twenty-five billion times at no additional cost to the American Tobacco

Company." It was one thing, however, to redesign the package and quite another to rationalize it to the consumer. Hill would never admit his package needed "freshening." World War II presented an opportunity to explain the change in the Lucky Strike package in terms of patriotism and morale. American Tobacco claimed that the green dye used was now required by the War Office for camouflage. The marketing shift was announced with the slogan, "Lucky Strike Green Has Gone to War."

Hill had successfully engaged three giant figures in the establishment of twentieth-century consumer culture: Lasker, Bernays, and Loewy. In these three individuals and their work on behalf of Lucky Strikes, we may see the core elements of the cigarette's rise to prominence. A relatively undifferentiated product, it traded on identities fashioned not through any intrinsic qualities but through advertising, public relations, and design. With these techniques, the rise of the cigarette closely followed the articulation of a mass consumption culture.

Aggressive tactics, clever ad copy and packaging, and innovations in marketing were in no way limited to Hill and American Tobacco. The intense competition among the Big Three—Lucky Strike, Chesterfield, and Camel—elicited the creative and combative energies of a burgeoning advertising industry. By the early 1930s, the major tobacco companies had all enlisted professional marketing experts and were spending unprecedented sums on advertising.

At first, R.J. Reynolds continued to rely on traditional slogans to promote Camel: "No Better Cigarette Is Made." But as Lucky Strike sales soared from 1927 to 1931, their success came at the expense of Camel, whose sales fell from 45 percent of the national market to 28 percent. In March 1930, Reynolds retaliated, investing $300,000 in newspaper ads in that month alone, attempting to take Hill on directly: "Turning the light of Truth on false and misleading statements in recent cigarette advertising."[67] Hill apparently responded, "If you throw a stone into a pack of dogs, you can tell which one is hit by the way he barks."[68]

Feeling a need to find a new, more effective approach, in 1931 Reynolds dismissed N.W. Ayer, its advertising agency since the inception of Camel, and eventually turned to William C. Esty, who devised what he called a

campaign of "whizz and whoozle." [69] *Fortune* magazine explained this operation as "the whatever-it-takes in an advertising plug. The thing with
power to transform wheel horses into sprinters, loaders into spendthrifts,
and sales curves into rockets."[70] Esty went head-to-head with Hill's Lucky
Strike bluster. The slogan "It's Fun to Be Fooled" draped ridicule on Hill's
pseudo-scientific claims for "toasting" by subtly exposing it as a chicanery.
Esty's copy then turned back to the theme of "costlier tobaccos," music to
the ears of R.J. Reynolds's executives. By winning the Reynolds account,
Esty established himself as a major presence in what had quickly become
a major industry all by itself. In his first five years of service to R.J.
Reynolds, his firm's standard 15 percent of advertising expenditures netted
$9,800,000.[71]

Reynolds was concerned that Camel had become known as "a truck-
drivers' cigarette," in large measure because the company had failed to aggressively solicit the growing middle-class women's market. Esty suggested
modifying the pack. Bowman Gray and his fellow executives at Reynolds
quickly rejected this proposal as sacrilege so Esty instead developed a series
of campaigns that successfully touched a nerve in American culture. Taking a page out of Lasker and Hill's playbook, Esty aggressively sought testimonials from prominent society figures, sports heroes, and stars of stage
and screen. These he adroitly combined with "man on the street" testimonials and cartoons. This interplay of the famous and the mundane struck a
powerful chord in the midst of the Great Depression. No matter one's financial status, cigarette brands could be shared.

National brands marked yet another critical aspect of the full-scale
emergence of the consumer culture: namely, the democratization of goods.
In the depths of the Great Depression, cigarettes were held out as a truly
national product, one that crossed the wide boundaries of class, gender,
race, and ethnicity. Unlike many other products whose sales were limited to
particular social strata, the cigarette was seen by industry and advertisers
alike as a symbol of "choice" for all. If the United States was hardly a class-
less society, at least national brands appealed across such distinctions.[72]
Cigarettes—relatively inexpensive and increasingly ubiquitous—symbolized the democracy of the marketplace, the notion that luxury and leisure
would be accessible across the boundaries of ethnicity and class. "The price

of one's favorite brand," wrote the *American Mercury* in 1925, "is no longer an indication of the means at one's command or the circle in which one moves. More often than otherwise, the banker and his bootblack agree in their preferences. The cigarette, in truth, has become the most democratic commodity in common use."[73] Here was a product and a behavior with genuinely mass appeal, through which the distance between Hoboken and Hollywood could be easily traversed.

At the height of the Great Depression, advertisements pictured America's social elites ensconced in the most expensive restaurants smoking popular brands. Rather than creating the association, for example, of Camels with "the rich," such ads were a source of popular identification; any woman could smoke the same brand as Mrs. William Hollingsworth, pictured at the Victor Hugo Restaurant in Beverly Hills, California. The appeal of such ads depended on an industry strategy of unifying the cigarette market around a few national brands. This was not entirely voluntary: attempts to develop a high-end luxury market segment had generally failed or had mixed results. Smoking was decidedly independent of status, and brands became a source of commonality in the face of material disparity. According to a survey reported in *Fortune* in 1936, among both whites and African-Americans regular smoking had risen to well over 40 percent of the population.[74]

Esty's next major campaign, inspired by an article in *Science* in 1934 indicating that smoking increased sugar in the blood, promised that Camel smokers would "Get a Lift." Other research, on smoking among diabetics, seemed to confirm this finding, noting that nicotine stimulates the adrenals; adrenaline causes the release of sugar. One of the scientists who had conducted the study was appalled to see the resulting claims in Esty's copy. But the quibbles of scientists did not concern Esty. Reynolds prepared a form letter for those who inquired about the ad:

> The effect continues for approximately half an hour, when the percentage of blood sugar again goes back to the previous level. However, the smoking of another Camel will again increase the blood sugar concentration.[75]

(Clearly, the company understood the importance of assuring readers that any effects were transitory.)

By the mid-1930s, the Big Three had reached near parity; this had the effect of intensifying advertising expenditures, each company eager to maintain and expand its clientele through marketing combat. Any brand's dominance was ephemeral. The aggressiveness of Lucky Strike in the early 1930s now seemed dated as consumers were attracted to Chesterfield's more conservative copy.[76] Observers watched the race among the Big Three cigarettes like stocks and horses. Explanations of success and failure were plentiful in part because it was so difficult to gauge the impact of any particular sales strategy. All that seemed to matter was the aggressiveness of the budget. Whoever invested most heavily in ads appeared to reap the rewards. By 1930, tobacco advertising led all other commodities with the possible exception of automobiles; here, then, was an industry in which product and pitch had become both inseparable and indistinguishable.[77] The medium was the message.

The combat often turned nasty. Competitive ads not-so-subtly attacked opposing brands; a Lucky Strike ad read "You Wouldn't Eat Raw Meat. Why Smoke Raw Tobacco?" Reynolds shot back with an ad announcing "The Stench of a Contemptible Slander Is Repulsive Even to the Nostrils of a Buzzard." Reynolds claimed that individuals on the American Tobacco payroll were spreading false rumors about hygiene in the Camel factories and offered rewards for the culprits' identification and arrest.[78] In 1936, a "whispering campaign"—probably started by individuals hired by local sales representatives—spread the rumor that the makers of Chesterfield (Liggett & Myers) had fired all their Jewish employees. The company offered $1,000 rewards for information about those spreading the rumor.[79]

But even as these companies competed fiercely in what became widely known as the "tobacco wars," they also found good reason to cooperate. Their common interest in the cigarette's success probably led to a certain restraint and the tacit acceptance of some ground rules. Despite the bitterness of the ad campaigns—their cost and vitriol—cigarette prices remained absolutely consistent across brands.[80] The scent of antitrust violation would draw the renewed interest of the Department of Justice.[81]

During the 1930s and 1940s, growth was phenomenal and brand loyalty only in an early phase. In each successive year, new smokers constituted an impressive market. As these three companies continued to compete and conspire together, they also continued to enjoy great financial success. In the years following the 1929 stock market crash, many industries succumbed to the global depression. Not so for cigarettes. As one business writer concluded, "People, it seemed, must smoke cigarettes, as well as eat, in good times and bad." He deemed cigarettes a "depression-proof" industry.[82] Certainly, the addictive properties of nicotine helped sustain demand. The impressive stability of this market was widely recognized. "Cigarettes, a product of habitual use, and not likely to be discarded even in times of reduced income; accordingly they have a relatively steady demand," explained Neil H. Borden, professor of advertising at Harvard Business School.[83] Although the tobacco companies would not be made to face the issue publicly for another half-century, the cigarette's addictive properties were already widely noted.

While the dominating sales of the Big Three—American's Lucky Strike, Reynolds's Camel, and Liggett & Myers's Chesterfield—led *Fortune* to conclude that "launching a new cigarette is like picking a number at roulette," the Depression spawned a variety of "cheapies"[84]: ten-cent cigarettes, roll-your-own, and other niche products. In the early years of the Great Depression, brands like Stephano Brothers' Marvels, Brown & Williamson's Wings, Axton Fischer's Twenty Grand, and Pinkerton Tobacco's Sunshines cut substantially into the Big Three, reaching more than 20 percent of the market in the early years of the Depression. By collectively reducing the wholesale prices, however, the major brands ultimately recouped their patrons, and the percentage of the market buying "cheapies" dropped quickly to 6.4 percent by May 1933.[85]

Smaller tobacco companies—in eclipse since the breakup of the Trust—tried throughout the 1920s to exploit the remarkable new market for cigarettes, and Lorillard was the most successful. After becoming president of P. Lorillard in 1924, Benjamin Belt mimicked Hill himself in generating public attention for his new brand Old Gold. During the "Reach for a Lucky" campaign, Old Gold sought to engage the debate with copy like this: "Eat a chocolate. Light an Old Gold. And enjoy both! Two fine and healthful treats." Philip W. Lennen of Lennen and Mitchell, Lorillard's advertising agency, came up with the slogan "Not a Cough in a Carload," which subtly recognized the persistent health concerns associated with smoking. This successful campaign was the first to use comic strips in national advertising. Lennen followed up with a series of innovations: blindfold tests, double cellophane wrapping, and ultimately prize contests offering Old Gold smokers who solved a puzzle the chance to win thousands of dollars, pushing the limits of postal regulations and lottery laws. Although Old Gold held just a 7 percent market share, by the early 1930s it nevertheless achieved wide recognition as the fourth leading brand.[86]

By 1937, the company was offering contestants an unprecedented first prize of $100,000, helping sales to climb by more than 70 percent over the previous year. Some two million people returned answers to the puzzle (accompanied by 90 million Old Gold wrappers). According to one report, Mrs. George Washington Hill, Jr., daughter-in-law to the chief, played avidly. Entrants apparently devoted an average of eighty hours to answering the puzzle's ninety questions. The sale of tip sheets became a big business in itself. The reference room of the New York Public Library was reportedly a center of activity for Old Gold "contesticians." "When a firm like Lorillard offers in all seriousness a first prize of $100,000 . . . and 2,000,000 Americans think their chances at it are worth eighty hours of hard work, the time has come to inquire whether Lorillard or the American public is screwy," *Fortune* grumbled.[87] Lorillard concluded that if it could hold on to only a quarter of those individuals who switched to Old Gold during the contest, the game would pay off. And it did; the Big Three became the Big Four.[88]

The Old Gold contests—inhabiting the thin margins of hard work, hope, and chance—offered a fantasy of riches and mobility. They also marked a new notion of participation in the "game" of consumption. Following Old Gold's lead, Americans would collect box tops for generations to follow, and sweepstakes would remain a big—and largely unregulated—business. Contests, though widely identified as mere hype, nonetheless drew consumers. The lottery tied to a product became a pervasive aspect of consumer fantasy in the twentieth century—yet another example of tobacco industry innovation.

As new advertising media became available, the industry quickly seized these promotional opportunities. During the 1930s, the tobacco companies became among the most prolific advertisers on commercial radio. American Tobacco developed the legendary musical variety show, *Your Hit Pa-*

rade, which premiered on NBC radio in April 1935 but ultimately moved to CBS, where it remained until 1947. Featuring popular singers and musical performers, the show—dominated by Hill—offered a weekly ranking of hit songs based on a national survey, the precursor of the "top forty." Lord & Thomas prominently centered attention on the weekly announcement of the "number one" song in the nation, as well as on Lucky Strike cigarettes. Beginning in 1950, the show made the transition to television, where the industry would begin to invest lavishly in the production of spot commercials and product placement.[89]

§

Yet another company also joined the ranks of the Big Three. In 1933, Philip Morris entered the cigarette market with its namesake brand Philip Morris, and, to the surprise of many, the cigarette took off. Having emerged as an independent entity from the corporate debris of the old Trust, Philip Morris and its predecessors had introduced some fifty different cigarette brands to little acclaim. The company's best-known product was a premium brand introduced in 1927 specifically for women—the first to explicitly do so—known as Marlboro, a twenty-cent cigarette with a small but loyal following.

Philip Morris cigarettes found quick popularity after their introduction in 1933, largely on the basis of a claimed innovation, a new casing (applied to retain moisture) called diethylene glycol. After sponsoring a series of investigations, Philip Morris made extravagant medical claims that its product was less irritating than its competitors'. The company worked diligently to bring its research to the attention of the medical profession, advertising heavily in medical journals and often providing free cigarettes to receptive physicians. The company's ads for the general public advised readers to "Ask Your Doctor about a Light Smoke." In a campaign worthy of Bernays himself, the company worked diligently to make Philip Morris the cigarette of the American medical profession during a period of simmering concern about the product's health effects. As a *Fortune* writer explained:

> The object of all this propaganda is not only to make doctors smoke Philip Morris cigarettes, thus setting an example for impressionable patients, but also to implant the findings [about diethylene glycol] so

strongly in the medical mind that the doctors will actually advise their coughing, rheumy, and fur-tongued patients to switch to Philip Morris on the ground that they are less irritating.[90]

In addition to the promise of a milder, less irritating cigarette, Philip Morris ads featured "the best bellhop in New York City." Johnny Roventini, soon renamed Johnnie Morris, was a forty-three-inch tall dwarf who could be heard throughout the country broadcasting the slogan "Call for Philip Morris." His smiling countenance was plastered on posters, billboards, and ads everywhere. Traveling across the country liberally disbursing free cigarettes, Johnnie was an unabashed success. "He will go . . . wherever his dwarfhood, his voice, and his free cigarette will win him the eyes, ears, and lungs of a crowd," cooed *Fortune,* assigning the campaign to the "harmless nonsense (as against reason-why) school of advertising."[91] Johnnie earned $20,000 a year for his efforts, and Philip Morris insured him for $100,000 against growing an inch. During this period of Philip Morris's meteoric rise, the company went beyond advertising to promote its product in the Bernays manner, paying college students to distribute the brand to friends.[92]

By the end of the 1930s, the success of Old Gold and Philip Morris had reconfigured the industry. But it had now reached its plateau; while Philip Morris and Lorillard achieved big-time status, no others did. The Big Five of 1950 would—in various incarnations—remain the major producers of cigarettes in the United States for the rest of the century.

§

By the 1930s, it became eminently clear that cigarettes would dominate all other forms of tobacco consumption. American Tobacco produced some five hundred tobacco products—plug, pipe tobacco, and cigars as well as cigarettes—yet a single cigarette brand, Lucky Strike, accounted for 75 percent of the company's sales in that decade and 65 percent of its profits.[93] Similarly, Camel accounted for more than 75 percent of R.J. Reynolds's profits in 1938, selling some 45 billion cigarettes. In 1916, the tobacco industry rolled out 25 billion cigarettes, astounding corporate observers at the time; by 1943, the number had grown to 255 billion. By 1950, the industry was getting more than 90 percent of all revenues from cigarettes.

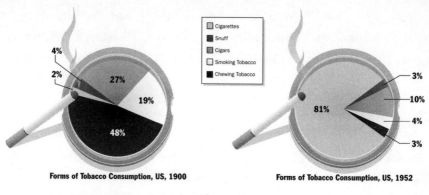

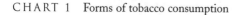

Forms of Tobacco Consumption, US, 1900   **Forms of Tobacco Consumption, US, 1952**

Source: Robert K. Heimann, *Tobacco and Americans* (New York: McGraw, 1960).

CHART 1   Forms of tobacco consumption

Not only had cigarettes displaced all other forms of tobacco use; total consumption of tobacco increased dramatically in the first half of the twentieth century. In 1880, at the time of the inception of the modern cigarette, approximately 250 million pounds of tobacco were consumed annually. By the early 1950s, Americans consumed more than 1.5 billion pounds, a five-fold increase. Cigarettes accounted for this rise almost completely, while all other forms of tobacco use either remained stable or fell. By 1950, each cigarette smoker consumed more than seven pounds of tobacco yearly, cigar smokers less than one pound. Cigarette consumption had increased from approximately fifty cigarettes per adult per year in 1880, to nearly five hundred by 1920. Over the next decade, consumption would double to nearly one thousand, and by the start of World War II, it would double yet again. At mid-century, Americans smoked over 350 billion cigarettes a year.

Such massive growth had powerful implications for the economy as a whole. Cigarettes accounted for 1.4 percent of the gross national product and a remarkable 3.5 percent of all consumer spending on nondurable goods. The cigarette reverberated throughout the American economy. Tobacco was the fourth largest cash crop in the nation, and in Connecticut, Maryland, North Carolina, and Virginia, it ranked first.[94]

"The cigarette horizon still has a virtual unlimited ceiling," crowed *Printers' Ink*, proudly mixing its metaphors in 1941. "The rate of expansion will be largely influenced by the ingenuity and merchandising ability of the manufacturers."[95] If the cigarette was deeply insinuated into

American culture by the middle of the century, it had also become central to the modern nation's industrial economy. This was a remarkable story given that as late as 1920, it was unclear that the cigarette was much more than another fad in the two-and-a-half century commercial history of tobacco. By mid-century, its triumph was complete.

§

By the end of the 1920s, the cigarette had accrued a remarkably elastic set of meanings. Though nearly ubiquitous and overwhelmingly sold in just three brands, it was often regarded as a marker of independence and autonomy. Smoking was associated with sexual attractiveness, physical beauty, and leisure. For men, it could connote virility, strength, and mental acuity. When used by women, the same product—even the same brand—could be deployed to invoke feminine beauty as well as social and political equality. Amid the social rigidities of urban industrial culture, the cigarette was favorably associated with pleasure and satisfaction. When surveyed, smokers overwhelmingly cited "sociability" as an essential attraction of the cigarette. The cigarette had assumed meanings previously associated with alcohol, fostering social encounters. A majority also noted the pleasing fragrance (a reminder that responses to smell are historically contingent). Only 5 percent cited taste as one of the cigarette's pleasures.[96]

Unlike most other consumer goods, the cigarette also caused a radical change in social behavior. American society had to learn how to smoke. Cigarette smoking became integrated into the social and cultural mores of both work and leisure until it had crossed traditional boundaries of tobacco use. Whereas smoking of cigars and pipes had been a largely private activity, the cigarette came to be brandished publicly, first by men and then by women. Restaurants, theaters, railways, and other public institutions all had to accommodate this new product and behavior.

The cigarette also fit the "modern" culture emerging in the first decades of the twentieth century. It was frequently cited as respite and solace in an increasingly bureaucratized and industrialized world. Certainly this quality was noted during World War I, when soldiers employed cigarettes to relieve the anxiety and boredom of war. But they were seen no less as an antidote to the frenetic pace of urban-industrial society. As early as 1889, the *New York Times*—an early critic of the cigarette—explained:

Whatever its merits and demerits, one thing is certain—namely, that there is an ever increasing subjection to the influence of this narcotic, whose soothing powers are requisitioned to counteract the evil effects of the worry, overpressure and exhaustion which characterize the age in which we live.[97]

This theme would echo through the first half of the twentieth century. The quiet of a short smoke were promoted as particularly well suited to the pressures of a driven culture.

Since smokers could light up quickly in factories and offices, on buses and trolleys, the monotony of modern work was now punctuated and calibrated by the length of a break needed to smoke a cigarette. That the cigarette could be used anywhere—and anytime—was an attribute widely noted by its advertisers. The time to light up, their ads proclaimed, is "Now." As the boundaries of where and when to smoke eroded through the 1920s and 1930s, the cigarette was rapidly diffused into the shops, stores, restaurants, and transport that made up the new consumer world.

The process by which the cigarette came to "fit" within the parameters of American culture was anything but "natural" or serendipitous. Product and culture were brought into conformity by specific and often purposeful economic and social forces, a process that required "adjustment" of traditional boundaries and social expectations as well as the deployment of new techniques that structured both product and market. It is perhaps its remarkable range of meanings—and their successful definition and construction through advertising and promotion—that makes the cigarette such a powerful symbol of the consumer culture.

Adjusting the message to meet the moment tested the creativity and ingenuity of the cigarette's promoters. Advertisers quickly picked up and utilized the cigarette's "functions": it "soothed the nerves," "aided digestion," encouraged a good diet, provided a "lift," and was "your best friend." Advertisers promised relief from "jangled nerves" and special respite from the frenetic rhythms of the urban society. "Build yourself a CAMEL SMOKE SCREEN," counseled one ad, "We claim with good evidence to back us that a cool cloud of CAMEL smoke is a practically perfect protective smokescreen. Outside the charmed circle of its mellow fragrance, troubles and worries and sundry bothers hover baffled. Within, all is peace, pleasure, content."[98]

Another strategy was to emphasize the taste of the advertiser's particular brand: blends of tobacco and flavorings were closely guarded secrets. Taste possessed double meanings, both crucial to the success of the cigarette. When tobacco ads touted their brand's superior taste, they suggested much more than the experience of the individual smoker; they not so subtly implied that smokers of their brand publicly demonstrated "better taste." This demonstration was a public act of great significance; although the idea of "conspicuous consumption" is usually applied to homes and cars, the cigarette—as advertised—offered important opportunities for a form of conspicuous consumption that crossed the lines of social class. Marketers both drove and responded to these tastes. If the cigarette signaled new values concerning pleasure, it was not simply a mark of easing Victorian strictures. Increasingly, pleasure would come to be associated with satisfying needs through the very process of consumption. The tobacco industry had created a product that could be virtually all things to all people; a product with such an impressive elasticity of meanings that it came to be defined by its promotion more than by any innate characteristic. Business writers, social critics, and cultural observers could all agree as early as the 1930s that the cigarette had emerged as perhaps the central icon of the new consumer culture.

At mid-century, "the cult of the cigarette," concluded Walter B. Hayward in the New York Times, "has spread over the world. Demand is strong, supply is short and prices are high in many countries."[99] During World War II, marketers had yet again adjusted to historical contingencies, using the product as a symbol of support for the military effort. In the years immediately after the war, cigarettes were used as currency in occupied Germany, and black markets for tobacco flourished in Europe.[100]

But with all its astonishing success, its array of social and political meanings, and the most determined efforts of its advertisers and promoters, the cigarette could never entirely conceal its dark side. Many argued that it was a frequent cause of ill health. Through mid-century, claims and counterclaims about the dangers and benefits of smoking to health were left unresolved while consumption continued its meteoric rise. But try though the industry might to allay concerns, belief in the dangers of the cigarette could not be dispelled.

Even as the consumer culture triumphed, criticism remained—not only of the cigarette but the cultural norms in which it came to be affixed—often drawing upon deep, traditional American values emphasizing restraint and deferred gratification. Deeply embedded within the culture of consumption was a profound ambivalence about the nature of agency, individuality, and risk. Later in the century, as the health risks of smoking became fully explicit, this ambivalence would resurface in powerful ways.

II

SCIENCE

*Men and Women with irritation of the nose and throat
due to smoking were instructed to change to Philip
Morris Cigarettes. Then day after day, each doctor kept
a record of each case. The final results, published in authoritative medical journals, proved conclusively that
when smokers changed to Philip Morris, every case of
irritation cleared completely or definitely improved.*[1]

PHILIP MORRIS ADVERTISEMENT, 1937

*Yes, the T-Zone is your own critical laboratory for any
cigarette. That's where you learn by actual smoking
experience the particular cigarette that suits you best.*

*For your taste and your throat are individual to you.
Only your taste and throat can decide which cigarette
tastes best to you . . . and how it affects your throat.*

*Try Camels. See how your taste responds to the rich
full flavor of Camel's choice, properly aged tobaccos. See
how your throat reacts to the delightfully cool mildness
of Camels.*[2]

CAMEL ADVERTISEMENT, 1947

*Smoking is not the devilish habit it has often been ac-
cused of being, but I know of no condition in which the
persistence in it has ever done the slightest good, but I
do know of a vast number of records which conclusively
prove that smoking has done harm. Most people are
more or less aware of this in a general way, but continue to smoke. . . .*[3]

M. F. ASHLEY MONTAGU, 1942

CHAPTER 4

More Doctors Smoke Camels

A T THE 1947 AMA convention in Atlantic City, doctors formed long lines to get free cigarettes. The Philip Morris display at the convention explained the advantages of diethylene glycol as a hygroscopic agent, insisting it was the healthiest cigarette. Just down the boardwalk, R.J. Reynolds proudly announced that more doctors chose Camels than any other brand.[4] These claims of comparative health advantage marked an implicit recognition of ongoing concerns about tobacco and serious disease. At the very moment that these doctors queued up to get their free twenty-cent packs, researchers in the United Kingdom and the United States were beginning the studies that would demonstrate the causal relationship between smoking and lung cancer.

The year before, R.J. Reynolds had initiated a major new advertising campaign for Camels centered on the memorable slogan "More Doctors Smoke Camels than Any Other Cigarette." This phrase would be the mainstay of Camel's advertising for the next six years. Offering glowing portrayals of physicians in both medical journals and popular magazines, the ads exploited the respected and romantic image the medical profession had achieved in American society.[5] The first ad was prefaced with the bold statement "Every doctor in private practice was asked." This brought immediacy to the slogan by linking the general depiction of doctors to each consumer's own physician. Admirable, forthright physicians, including the reader's own, had "named their choice," and that choice, the ad proclaimed, was Camels.

Besides providing images of professional trustworthiness and dedication, the "More Doctors" campaign also exploited popular faith in modern
medicine. One ad referred to the "amazing strides in medical science [that]
have added years to life expectancy," and urged readers to "thank medical
science for that. Thank your doctor and thousands like him . . . toiling
ceaselessly . . . that you and yours may enjoy a longer, better life."[6] Life-
saving scientific discovery was linked, through the magic of advertising, to
Camel-smoking doctors.

In retrospect, these ads are a powerful reminder of both the character of
emerging public concerns about the health effects of smoking and the cultural authority of physicians and medicine. In the 1930s and 1940s, smoking was the norm for both men and women in the United States—including
a majority of physicians.[7] At the same time, however, tobacco companies
were concerned about rising anxiety over the cigarette's risks to health. The
physician was an evocative, reassuring figure to include in their advertisements—and their clinical authority allayed fears about cigarettes' safety.
R.J. Reynolds's "More Doctors" campaign was the capstone of a strategy liberally used from the 1930s to the early 1950s, in which tobacco companies
competed to portray their cigarettes as the most healthy while utilizing
physicians to counteract any fears of serious health risks. At the same time,
the tobacco industry attempted to sustain, for as long as possible, the verdict
that the links between smoking and disease were "unproven."

§

One of the most important "discoveries" of the last century was to demonstrate scientifically that cigarette smoking *causes* serious disease and death.
From our contemporary vantage point, simple logic suggests that the dramatic rise in cigarette smoking must be correlated with the finding in 1946
that lung cancer cases had tripled over the previous three decades.[8] But this
seemingly obvious epidemiological conclusion was delayed by decades of
medical and public debate, largely fueled by the tobacco industry. As a result, this knowledge—this *fact*—was not easily accepted.

Medical concern about the health effects of tobacco dates back to its
earliest use, long before the rise of the cigarette. The first research, conducted in the eighteenth century, centered on nicotine and its impact. The
longstanding knowledge that, in its purified form, a drop of nicotine could

kill helped sustain the antagonisms of the nineteenth-century antitobacco movement. In the early twentieth century, activists circulated news accounts of a baby who died from swallowing a cigar. A few years later, reports circulated that cattle straying into a tobacco field died from "chewing the weed."[9] As cigarettes grew in popularity, they were viewed as a particular danger especially because, critics warned, they were so easily overused. Unlike pipes and cigars, cigarettes could be smoked anytime, anywhere, offering new opportunities for "intoxication." In 1887, the *New York Tribune* reported the sudden death of Russell H. Kuevals, a medical student at the elite College of Physicians and Surgeons and "a constant and excessive smoker," who apparently "was killed by cigarettes." An autopsy revealed that "the poison had so destroyed [the heart's] action that it was unable to do its duty."[10] The *New York Times* published similar stories of young men carried away on a bed of smoke, poisoned by nicotine.[11]

Such concerns led early researchers to explore the chemical composition of tobacco smoke. Their studies typically found carbonic acid and "a series of elements which, with almost no exception, are poisonous": nicotine, hydronic acid, carbon monoxide, and pyridine.[12] Additionally, physicians often associated inhalation with carbon monoxide poisoning. A number of reports linked inhalation to "a decreased or decreasing supply of normal blood,"[13] which, in turn, led to a number of conditions typically associated with cigarette smoking: anemia, lack of growth, and loss of energy. "The smoker carries his furnace between his lips and breathes the same kind of gas that the coal-stove produces when its combustion is not perfect," noted *Harper's Weekly* in 1912. "If he does not poison himself with nicotine . . . he poisons himself with oxide of carbon."[14]

Beneath these physiological observations about the bodily impact of tobacco ran deeper anxieties about the moral implications of cigarette smoking. It would have been uncharacteristic of the times to make a sharp distinction between physical and moral harms. The relationship between smoking and health received considerable attention, in part, because it apparently confirmed contemporary moral assumptions. Smoking—defined as an act of dubious morals—*must* lead to disease. For antitobacco crusaders, such as Lucy Page Gaston, physicians were crucial allies confirming through medical diagnosis what common sense dictated. Dr. D. H. Kress, the well-known anticigarette crusader, expressed orthodox reformist views when he suggested the powerful sympathy between physical health and morality. "There exists a very intimate relation between a man's physical habits and what he is morally," explained Kress. "Possibly there exists a physical cause for every immoral act and crime committed."[15] According to Kress, nicotine was a narcotic poison acting on both the brain and the heart. Smokers developed an addictive craving; constant use would lead to physical decline. "The liver, kidneys, and other vital organs," he claimed, "whose work it is to keep the blood freed from poisons, wear out prematurely."[16]

Other physicians moved just as easily from making clinical assessments of smoking's bodily harms to expressing moral qualms about the impact of smoking on character, mores, and responsibility. Attacks on smoking did not differentiate such concerns; therefore, the question of "proof"—as we would later know it—had no explicit meaning in this context. Critics of the cigarette enjoyed considerable flexibility in assessing smoking's harms. As one writer explained, "smoking is very likely to stunt something, most probably the mind, or perhaps the body only, or sometimes both mind and body."[17] One way or another, dire effects would take hold. Physicians and researchers followed tobacco's moral opponents to evaluate the health effects of smoking on those deemed most vulnerable to its harms. In its focus on the harms of smoking for children and adolescents, college students, and women, medical science was clearly responding to social forces. These were precisely the groups of greatest concern to opponents of cigarette smoking. This interplay of social forces and medical "opinion" drew on deep historical roots.[18]

Moral considerations were practically indistinguishable from concerns about the health effects of cigarette smoking. Did smoking cause degeneracy? Or was it simply that degenerates liked to smoke? This question, posed in a wide variety of forms for a breathtaking range of negative effects, succumbed to no easy answers. Was the cigarette but a signal of "relaxation of self control," poor scholarship, and other signs of moral laxity, or could the problems of youth be attributed to smoking itself?[19] In the face of such unanswerable conundrums, moral presumptions about smoking frequently surfaced to dominate debate. It would take nearly half a century to disentangle these moral assumptions from medical research on smoking. This conflation of the medical and moral would serve as a significant obstacle (among many) to establishing the evidentiary basis of the harms of smoking.

By the mid-1920s, medical opinion on the health impact of the cigarette had become sharply split. "If one asks of a librarian for works on tobacco," observed Dr. Robert Abbe, "he will probably ask you, 'For or against?'"[20] Still, some points of consensus emerged from this debate. Many concluded that smoking could be harmful to some susceptible individuals; "excessive" smoking—often poorly defined—came to be judged as dangerous; and smoking was deemed harmful to children and adolescents.

Antitobacco vitriol often utilized the cultural authority of science and medicine. As the eugenics movement gathered momentum, it drew the cigarette into its vortex. Many physicians argued that the deleterious consequences of the cigarette fell disproportionately on the young during key phases of development. "It becomes plain that any insidious narcotic poison which exerts its chief effects upon the respiratory function and the motor nerve cells of the spinal cord and brain, can not fail to be disastrous to the young," explained one concerned doctor. He went on, in a tone not untypical of such critiques, to call the desire to smoke an "unhealthy appetite" and "one of the potent causes of the physical, mental and moral degeneracy that is fast filling our jails with criminals, our almshouses with paupers, and our asylums with the imbecile and insane."[21] Although it is easy to dismiss such attacks as moralistic pseudoscience, they were representative of medical positions of the time, and held with deep conviction.

Physician-eugenicists tied cigarettes to patterns of hereditary degeneracy. According to Dr. L. Pierce Clark, neurologist at Manhattan State Hospital, tobacco caused degeneracy by inducing chronic poisonous congestion of the brain, the spinal cord, and nerves.[22] Other observers found that the onset of the "cigarette habit" had dire implications for mental and physical development. Charles B. Towns, the well-known activist and expert on tobacco, described the effects of nerve damage as physical ("insomnia" and "lowered vitality") and moral ("desire to avoid responsibility and to travel the road of least resistance") and asserted a 15 percent difference in "general efficiency" between smokers and nonsmokers.[23] Boys who smoked were labeled "physical and mental dwarfs" typically unable to progress beyond eighth grade.[24] Such accounts often depicted the cigarette as the first step on the road to decline and failure. While there might be other contributing factors, one researcher warned, "smoking is likely to put a boy in such a condition that other and worse habits will be taken up, largely on account of a weakened moral stamina."[25] Tobacco became the preeminent "gateway drug" leading its patrons to lives of decay and degradation.

Looking back at this question from a time in which rigid barriers have been constructed in an attempt—not universally successful—to differentiate between medicine and morality, one is struck by the same concerns expressed by both physicians and health crusaders. The attack on smoking as both unhealthful and immoral often placed critics of tobacco on unsteady turf, for their claims often contradicted reality. Some smokers were excellent athletes, others were tall and healthy, and others were noted for their literary skills and sharp intellect. Dr. J. W. Seaver, physical director of the Yale gymnasium, claimed that "'high stand men' at Yale do not smoke," but *Harper's Weekly* noted that "a large majority of the leading men in New York—judges, politicians, merchants, bankers, lawyers, doctors—smoke tobacco. And some of the ablest ministers do the like, though perhaps not a majority of them."[26]

And yet the axiom that good living and good health go hand in hand persisted. Critics often cited college studies demonstrating the sorry impact of the cigarette on students. According to one such study conducted by Seaver, nonsmoking seniors at Yale were 20 percent taller than smokers, were 23 percent heavier, possessed 66 percent more lung capacity, and were superior students.[27] A poll of high school and college coaches overwhelmingly confirmed their belief that cigarettes were harmful for athletes. The coaches believed not only that smoking retarded physical development and hindered performance, but that nonsmokers were more cooperative and easier to discipline.[28]

Such studies generally lacked rigor and were subject to many kinds of bias. Research on college smoking, for example, often produced confounding findings. One investigation at Columbia University found that smokers tended to be more successful athletes.[29] A typical study of the impact of cigarette smoking on college students, conducted at Antioch College, showed no discernible effects on pulse rate, lung capacity, or blood pressure. Nonetheless, researchers did find a dramatic impact on the quality of school work: more than 62 percent of heavy smokers failed to maintain required grades. According to many of the college-based studies, smoking "devitalized ambition." This, one researcher speculated, might be explained by "deterioration of nervous tissue" leading to "lower mental output."[30]

But causal relationships remained unclear. "School records indicate," explained the *American Journal of Public Health* in 1923, "that when a pupil begins to use tobacco his intellectual work is apt to decline. While this is not always true the relationship between the use of tobacco and low scholarship is so frequent and well marked as to warrant the belief that we have cause and effect exemplified."[31] Another researcher complained that "our methods of getting the cumulative results are less exact, owing to the objection to subjecting sufficient numbers of human beings to the use of tobacco for sufficient periods of time under proper control."[32]

In the end, even the most carefully collected data inevitably demonstrated the researcher's *a priori* assumptions: smoking was a peril. Such findings, *Good Housekeeping* suggested, should shift the debate about smoking and youth away from questions of "personal liberty." "Doesn't a college enter into a compact with society to do its utmost to make real men and real women of the boys and girls who are sent to it?" the magazine huffed. "Why permit any one accepted to fall into habits that almost inevitably lower scholarship and either result in dismissal or an inferior quality of finished product?"[33] Unlike many journals reporting similar findings, *Good Housekeeping* took its social responsibilities seriously, refusing to accept tobacco ads.[34]

As they began to see the weakness of mere moral anecdotes, researchers increasingly applied statistical techniques. By the late 1920s, their investigations had become more sophisticated.[35] A particularly detailed and impressive assessment of a group of smokers and nonsmokers was done with University of Minnesota students in the late 1920s by Dr. H. S. Diehl. Determined to conduct a truly scientific study, free of the bias that typically characterized the tobacco debate, Diehl found no significant differences between the two groups, dispelling longstanding concerns about the impact of smoking on development. Nonetheless, he noted that students at college had only recently taken up smoking: "[In] persons of 19 years of age the habit has not been practiced sufficiently long for degenerative effects, if there are any, to have proceeded very far."[36] This was a prophetic insight that pointed out a critical obstacle in demonstrating the harms of tobacco: the long latency period between the start of smoking and the onset of disease.

Early critics of the cigarette focused their attention on the impact on boys and adolescent men, but as women took up smoking, medical investigation quickly followed. The opposition to women smoking drew strong medical allies. Physicians prominently joined the antitobacco campaigns, and many pointed to particular harms associated with smoking for women.

Their warnings typically emphasized the vulnerabilities of the "weaker sex." Dr. Samuel Lambert, a prominent New York physician, explained:

> Intemperate smoking causes nervousness and may lead to something worse. . . . Women who use cigarettes cannot be temperate. At best it is a horrible weed and should be let alone. It fouls the breath and makes woman unwomanly.

"Women smoke nervously," agreed Dr. Samuel A. Brown, dean of Bellevue Hospital. "They cannot smoke moderately." The cigarette became a symbol for the loss of feminine control as well as for the changing roles of women in the early twentieth century.[37]

Critics often revealed powerful gender expectations as they elucidated the particular degenerative effects of cigarettes on women. As Charles B. Towns explained in 1916, "It degrades everything in a woman that is worth while," making "the lovely, devoted, clean wife and mother . . . negligent of all her womanly duties and responsibilities."[38] Early opposition to women smoking was connected to broader concerns about eugenics, degeneration, and motherhood.[39] The cigarette became another example of the perceived failure of white, middle-class women to act responsibly as "mothers of the race."[40] In this respect, the rise of women smoking marked a deeper erosion of the traditional separate spheres of gender. One physician considered it fortunate that women who smoked failed to reproduce, explaining, "No more pitiful sight on earth could possibly be imagined than the spectacle of some mother who is a cigarette smoker bringing into the world a poor, pitiful physically and mentally defective child." [41]

The prominent Michigan physician and surgeon Bertha Van Hoosen argued that smoking had particularly dire consequence for prospective mothers. "Motherhood and tobacco," she wrote, "are as antagonistic as water and fire. Motherhood is the greatest thing in life; in fact the essence of all life and the perpetuation of life. Motherhood is too complex to tamper with tobacco or any other drug-forming habit."[42] Some medical critics noted that nicotine could lead to spontaneous abortions. Others claimed that nicotine was present in amniotic fluid and breast milk.[43] Already concerned about declining birth rates among white, middle-class women, physicians now suggested that smoking "may have a deleterious effect upon female fecundity."[44]

By the 1930s, such eugenic hyperbole gave way to studies of the impact of smoking on fertility and lactation. Systematic assessment of smoking's effect on breast milk began by the late 1920s. One group of researchers concluded that nicotine suppressed secretion of breast milk in several animals, but that "they had never observed any diminution in the secretion of milk, or any effect on the child, that could be attributed to the smoking of cigarettes by the [human] mother." Nonetheless, hospitals began to prohibit smoking immediately after labor.[45] Another study, conducted in the early 1940s, concluded that although nicotine could be found in both the breast milk and urine of nursing mothers, milk production was affected little. The researchers hypothesized that the mother's tolerance of nicotine might moderate its effect on infants and lactation.[46]

The relation of nicotine to lactation again raised questions of causality. Did anxiety cause insufficient production of milk (anxious women tended to smoke more), or was nicotine the culprit? "It is not my belief that the effect of nicotine is the sole or even the chief factor involved in diminished lactation," explained one doctor. "Usually it is the nervous, excitable woman who, whether a smoker or abstained, has a deficient milk output. . . . There is insufficient evidence to conclude that the one is cause, the other effect. . . . One is sorely tempted to conclude that excessive smoking does influence milk production adversely," this investigator concluded. But unambiguous data was hard to come by. Some individuals would take a few shallow puffs of a cigarette and discard it, or not inhale at all. Others inhaled deeply all the way to the end. Further, the different brands' nicotine content varied considerably. "These and other factors," explained this physician, "make it extremely difficult to formulate safe and sane standards."[47]

Like much smoking research, these studies often reached no definitive conclusion. Given the repeated inability to *prove* that cigarettes constituted a clear danger to mother and child, clinical recommendations typically reverted to the default position: mothers who smoked should practice moderation. But prospective mothers, more of whom smoked, sought more reassurance than this. *Hygeia,* the AMA's magazine for the general public, concluded in 1934 that "smoking by mothers is in all probability, not an important factor" in infant mortality.[48] Many physicians preferred—given the uncertainty of the data—to be risk averse in their recommendations to women patients. "Until we can prove that excessive cigarette smoking is not harmful in pregnancy" argued one doctor, "we should caution against it."[49] Nonetheless, many smokers dismissed such warnings.

Not every piece of commentary was loaded with assumptions about women, their social roles, and biological dispositions. Dr. S. Josephine Baker, a public health leader in New York, found no reason to assume that cigarettes posed a special risk for women. She considered smoking "more an individual than a race or sex problem."[50] "I have been unable to trace any valid reason for the prevailing impression that the health of women is more seriously affected by smoking than is the case with men," she noted in the *Ladies' Home Journal*.[51] Harvey Wiley, who directed the earliest federal investigations of the harms of smoking, offered no disagreement. "Women have just as much right to smoke cigarettes as men," he wrote in 1928. But he added, with considerable prescience, "They are likely to suffer the same penalty as men. . . . I am inclined to believe that cancer . . . will increase among women exactly in proportion to the number that acquire the smoking habit."[52] Wiley anticipated a conclusion that would take nearly a quarter century to categorically demonstrate.

By the 1920s, moral claims against the cigarette began to diminish in the face of the product's popularity. As the percentage of regular smokers grew, it became increasingly clear that not all of them would suffer the cigarette's purported harms. Too many smokers used tobacco without any apparent consequences to sustain the reformers' claims of incipient moral and physical decay. As the *New Republic* wryly noted, "Moderate cigarette smoking can scarcely be considered disastrous, as many octogenarians or nonagenarians will testify."[53]

The very popularity of the cigarette typically was cited as medical reassurance. How could the cigarette be dangerous if so many millions of Americans used it regularly without any apparent consequences? "Any substance so widely and commonly used as the cigarette cannot be as dangerous and deleterious as the propaganda of the more fanatical 'no-tobacco' advocates might lead one to infer," argued Emil Bogen, a tobacco researcher.[54]

Conventional medical wisdom settled on the idea of smoking in "moderation." Although many agreed that excessive smoking could be harmful, moderate smoking was now deemed medically acceptable. By 1929, *Hygeia* declared that "The general opinion of those who have studied the subject is that a person in sound health may bear what are for him moderate doses without injury."[55] But the actual distinction between "moderate" and "excessive" smoking was rarely defined. This was, no doubt, partly the result of problems of self-reporting, and the wide disparities in precisely how cigarettes were consumed.

Physicians increasingly viewed cigarette smoking as a behavior "tolerated" by most individuals and embraced by the public. It remained dangerous only for *some* people. As one physician summed it up in 1920:

> There are some individuals who cannot use tobacco, there are some who should not use it, there are some who use it to excess and who suffer in consequence. There is on the other hand a large army of moderate tobacco users, who indulge for years without appreciably bad physical effect and good mental effect.[56]

This approach protected the often contested sphere of clinical authority; it was a matter of professional discretion to identify individuals who should reduce or eliminate smoking. Individual variation became the theater of clinical judgment: some smokers seemed completely unaffected by their habit; others appeared particularly sensitive to the complex constituents of cigarette smoke. It was precisely the exercise of such discernment that distinguished physicians and made their recommendations authoritative and important. The historic aphorism, "Ask your doctor," was predicated on these individual judgments.[57]

According to a number of accounts, physicians—having prominently joined the ranks of inveterate smokers—lost interest in the connection between smoking and disease after 1930. But in reality, clinical medicine claimed the issue as a matter for individual assessment. During this era, there was a strong tendency to avoid causal hypotheses in matters so clearly complex. There was—and would remain—a powerful notion that risk is variable and, thus, most appropriately evaluated and monitored at the individual, clinical level. As cigarette smoking became increasingly popular, medicine offered no new insight into how best to evaluate such variability other than after the fact. If and when an individual developed symptoms, a physician might appropriately advise restricting or eliminating tobacco. This approach kept cigarette use firmly outside the sphere of public health.

Through the first half of the twentieth century, it proved impossible to categorically substantiate the claims of the harmfulness of smoking. "It is only too true that in matters affecting human behavior, as well as in many studies that are carefully made and aim to be truly scientific, there is too great a tendency to assume that because two factors exist side by side one is necessarily either the cause or the effect of the other," explained the unusually clear-headed S. Josephine Baker. "It may truly be that smoking lowers academic grading but it may be equally true that lowered mental status is the factor that leads to habitual smoking."[58]

Many observers noted the difficulty of "impartiality." "A large amount of partly scientific or pseudo-scientific work has been done," commented the noted psychologist William H. Burnham of Clark University, "and not even much of the painstaking experimentation of scientific men has sufficiently considered the mental factors involved." In a careful assessment of the available studies, Burnham concluded that "as regards causal relations the evidence justifies no sweeping assertions." He concluded nonetheless that "moral, social, and economic considerations, perhaps, quite as much as hygiene, should determine the desirability or undesirability of the use of tobacco. . . . In the words of the older moralists, how far is it desirable to become the slave of a habit?"[59] No behavior so deeply entwined with social and cultural mores could ever be evaluated exclusively on a scientific metric.

As the cigarette triumphed over its moral opponents, questions about its health effects would nonetheless persist. After 1930, researchers investigating the health effects of smoking took care to isolate their claims from moral concerns. The status and legitimacy of their work now would depend on its reproducibility and its independence from Victorian prescriptions for health and good living. This did not mean that scientific investigation shook off all vestiges of moral and cultural assumptions. "Objective science" could offer powerful prescriptions of its own—but they would now be sustained by a new, historically specific logic premised on new forms of scientific investigation and argumentation.[60] Any evaluation of the harms of smoking—to be persuasive and authoritative—would henceforth require an approach dissociated from traditional moral rhetoric. But this was no simple process.

During these years, theories of carcinogenesis tended to focus on hereditary vulnerabilities. Chronic diseases, in general, were attributed to multiple causes, from genetic predispositions to environmental and behavioral exposures. This underscored the "clinical" approach to smoking. Perhaps, some argued, individuals with a personal or familial history of cancer should avoid cigarettes. Diseases of rising frequency like cancer, heart disease, and stroke were also typically labeled degenerative diseases of the aging organism, often revealed by the rise of life expectancy.

Even in the early twentieth century, physicians catalogued a wide range of chronic diseases that they associated with smoking. By the 1930s and 1940s, clinical anecdote carried considerable authority with physicians, who carefully recorded their observations of the effects of tobacco upon their patients.[61] Many investigations focused on the cigarette's impact on the heart and circulation.[62] "Tobacco heart," a well-known syndrome, included arrhythmias, angina, and sometimes cardiac arrest.[63] Physicians also commonly attributed oral cancers to smoking, especially among cigar and pipe smokers.[64]

Additionally, by the early 1940s, investigation into the physiologic effects of smoking had grown in sophistication. Doctors at the Mayo Clinic, for example, conducted a detailed series of studies concerning the impact of cigarettes on circulation under controlled experimental conditions. New diagnostic tests were applied to evaluate blood pressure, basal metabolism, and electrocardiographic changes. New standards of experimental design required investigators to reduce confounding variables and bias. Using these new methods, researchers found evidence that smoking constricts the blood vessels—an effect they attributed to nicotine. They also concluded that smoking increased basal metabolism, as well as heart rate and blood pressure. And yet the clinical significance of these findings remained unclear. The researchers suggested that patients with coronary artery disease or high blood pressure should abstain, but "when the heart is healthy, no harm is likely to result from smoking."[65] Smoking might exacerbate a "preexisting" condition or "weakness," but it was not seen as *causing* disease.

By the 1940s, researchers were using animal models to assess tobacco's effects. Experimenting with rats, pharmacologists concluded that repeated dosing with nicotine led to tolerance.[66] Other researchers demonstrated that continued nicotine ingestion by rats led to a disruption in the "estrus" cycle and aberrations in growth and development.[67] Scientists experimented with new techniques to expose rats to cigarette smoke. In a 1940 study of pregnant rats, the authors found that exposure to smoke lowered birth weight and otherwise hindered growth and development; nonetheless, they noted, "individual variation is much in evidence."[68] While some rats apparently suffered harm, others "receiving the same treatment as the rest, stood the exposure to tobacco products with no apparent detriment." They easily made the comparison with humans: "Likewise there are women who smoke continually and rather heavily and yet they and their offspring remain in what appears to be perfect health."[69]

An Argentinean scientist, A. H. Roffo, developed techniques in the 1930s for distilling the residues in burning tobacco. Employing the relatively new technology of chemical spectroscopy to identify the constituents in these tobacco "tars," Roffo discovered the presence of polycyclic aromatic hydrocarbons, well-known carcinogens. Applying these distillates to rabbits, Roffo, a vigorous critic of cigarette smoking, was able to produce tumors, confirming his hypothesis that the tars were carcinogenic. Nonetheless, observers would continue to question the applicability of these findings to humans.[70]

The jump from animal models to humans raised a host of scientific problems. In experiments on rats, for example, it proved especially difficult to develop a means for estimating equivalent doses for exposure to cigarette smoke and nicotine. "Under no circumstances should it be assumed that chronic effects of nicotine in the human subject are similar to acute effects of nicotine in animals," lectured one researcher. "To date [1948] there have been no animal experiments which fully simulate smoking by the human being. Hence, no analogy can be drawn from the experimental data at hand."[71]

§

Thus, there remained a significant gap between ongoing assessments of the risks of smoking—based principally on case studies, animal experiments, and laboratory research—and the ability to categorically demonstrate these risks. It was one thing to suggest that smoking might harm susceptible individuals, and quite another to claim that it *caused* serious disease. The elusiveness of this causal link confounded investigators. The problem involved some of the deepest issues in science: how do we know? Are there alternative ways of knowing? What constitutes proof?[72]

During the first half of the twentieth century, historical strategies of investigation and explanation within medicine had been marginalized by the elegant experimental cogency of the laboratory. But the question of smoking and disease was being raised not in a laboratory but in a complex environment shaped by powerful interests. What did it mean to identify the cause of disease? No longer would it suffice to explain that a disease appeared to be airborne or waterborne, contagious or constitutional. No longer was it adequate to associate patterns of disease by socioeconomic status, climate, or geography. According to many investigators, proving causation now required the identification of a "specific" mechanism under laboratory conditions. This approach had been highly successful in identifying the causes of infection; from the 1880s to 1910, over thirty "causal organisms" were found for specific diseases utilizing the famous postulates set forth by German physician and researcher Robert Koch in 1884. The very meaning of the term *cause* had been revolutionized.[73]

Koch's four postulates, in which a specific organism could be (a) identified, (b) isolated, (c) grown in culture, and (d) utilized to induce disease, now served as the fundamental basis for determining causality in instances of infection. The tradition of environmental and behavioral investigation that had once characterized the search for "cause" was now deemed by many researchers to be primitive and imprecise. The center of action had shifted to the laboratory. The "field" was now beneath the lens of the microscope.[74]

When they were first formulated, Koch's postulates had offered an important model for understanding causality. But their limitations became apparent almost immediately. Even Koch cautioned against their uniform and rigid application. For example, he failed to satisfy all the postulates for important diseases like cholera and typhoid, even though the causal organisms were isolated in the laboratory. The late nineteenth century witnessed several important scientific critiques of the postulates, especially since it was clearly understood that many who became infected with a microorganism nonetheless remained healthy. Such cases clearly demonstrated that the one-to-one relationship between cause and disease was not absolute. Other factors had to be involved in pathogenesis. Koch found that while he himself was infected with the tubercle bacillus, he had no signs whatsoever of the disease of tuberculosis.[75]

Early in the twentieth century, it also became clear that the postulates often could not be satisfied for other infections, especially those caused by viruses. As a result, there was an extensive medical literature on the limitations of the postulates and the need to modify them. Many scientists argued that it would be unscientific to let a commitment to the postulates inhibit medical and scientific advances. Finally, it was widely accepted that chronic diseases called for alternative approaches to investigating and understanding causality. Since these diseases were so obviously multicausal, involving not only specific agents but the attributes of the host and the environment as well, the postulates were a weak and limited approach to understanding them. Most physicians and researchers grasped these distinctions quite well. By mid-century the notion that the postulates constituted a "gold standard" for determining causality in both infectious and chronic diseases no longer reflected the status of the postulates or the history of their application in twentieth-century medical science.[76]

Nonetheless, mechanism became something of a fetish in the modern medical sciences. The municipal laboratory became the new focus of public health. Even when researchers identified environmental or behavioral risks, they now generally focused on the mechanism of disease. The whole notion of statistical inference was marginalized as research came to center on the cellular level. In this respect, exposure to a carcinogen was often equated with exposure to an infectious organism. Identifying the health risks of a particular behavior like smoking fit this model poorly. The length of time before the disease developed was protracted (and equated to an "incubation period"); in addition, the large number of intervening variables confounded the emerging notion of specific causality. Everyone "exposed" did not get the disease, and most did not; and some who were not exposed, did. Also, there was broad cultural discomfort with notions of comparative risk assessment. How dangerous was the cigarette? How did this danger rate vis-a-vis other risks? Finally, medical theory offered few persuasive models for understanding systemic and chronic diseases; the anomalies of cigarette smoking did not fit the reductionist biomedical model's ideal of specific causality.

In this context, traditional epidemiological methods of inference based on close observation of patterns of disease—central to nineteenth-century medical thought—fell into disrepute. In the first decades of the twentieth century, epidemiology—eager to associate its work with the cutting-edge findings of the bacteriologic revolution—focused attention on the identification of infectious microbes in the community. In this respect, the cultural barriers to determining the harms of cigarette smoking actually grew. The precise mechanics of the postulates made other, more abstract historical approaches to causality—like statistical inference—seem outmoded.

§

The risks posed by cigarettes were especially difficult to assess. Early in the twentieth century, when so many Americans began smoking, the most significant health effects had yet to develop. Early studies often failed to find clear evidence of serious pathologies and, thus, had the ironic effect of exonerating the cigarette. By the late 1930s, the long-standing hypothesis that smoking caused disease remained only a hypothesis. Both cause and effect appeared so imprecisely defined that pinpointing a relationship between them might prove impossible. Smoking was a complex behavior, by its nature difficult to study, confounded by human variability. Some individuals could smoke for a lifetime with apparently no ill effects.

Researchers also committed the tactical error of studying smoking's effects in young people, in whom the consequences were difficult, if not impossible, to discern. Time would show that the risk of smoking increases with exposure. During the first decades of the twentieth century, when most cigarette users were young and had only recently taken up the habit, the most serious health impacts had yet to result. But it was this generation who would ultimately provide the crucial data substantiating the relationship between smoking and disease.

Despite the many obstacles to investigation, suspicions about the health impact of cigarettes persisted, especially as long-term smokers accumulated. Summarizing medical opinion in 1937, Dr. James J. Walsh noted that cigarette smoking was making once-rare ailments fairly common.[77] "I am deeply persuaded," he wrote, "that we are now reaching the limit that nature can stand of the various harmful substances inevitably associated with excessive cigarette smoke." Walsh's observation centered attention on a critical insight: that it could take many years, even decades, for smoking to cause disease. Again, the relatively short latencies associated with infections had directed researchers away from studying long-term, cumulative exposures.

The causal conundrum of smoking and disease could be "solved" only by a truly significant increase in disease. This certainly occurred with lung cancer. Not until the 1940s would the full health implications of the mass consumption of cigarettes become statistically visible. Many of the health effects of smoking simply did not appear on the radar screen of epidemiologic surveillance until the 1940s. But by then, many had already concluded that cigarette use posed little or no risk.

Moreover, it took a dramatic epidemiologic transition—the decline of infectious disease as a dominant cause of mortality—to make the harms of cigarette smoking fully explicit. In the first half of the twentieth century, the most significant causes of death shifted from infectious diseases, such as tuberculosis and pneumonia, to chronic diseases like cancer and heart disease. This shift was accompanied by an impressive increase in life expectancy. In 1900, life expectancy at birth for men in the United States was approximately forty-eight; by 1970, it approached seventy and would continue to climb for the remainder of the century. Other developed countries enjoyed similar increases: in France, expected longevity for men improved from forty-five in 1900 to sixty-nine in 1972, in England and Wales from fifty-two in 1910 to sixty-nine in 1970.[78] The shift in patterns of disease and the increase in life expectancies made new risks possible— and ultimately *visible*.

Even so, the "visibility" of the harms of smoking required new strategies for observation and assessment. By the 1940s, discussion of the consequences of cigarette smoking had shifted from individual clinical "tolerance" and the perceived effects on growth and development to the possibility of cancer and premature death. But even this transition demanded new technical capacities. Was the apparent increase in cancer and heart disease attributable to the dramatic rise of cigarette smoking? Or were these diseases simply more prominent because individuals now survived longer rather than succumbing to infection earlier in life? Or perhaps, as some argued, the apparent rise in rates of lung cancer was an artifact of new technical abilities to clearly diagnose diseases previously invisible to both medical science and public health.[79]

There was, of course, a long historical tradition of investigating disease in populations. Researchers throughout the ages had engaged in the systematic process of developing hypotheses about the causes of diseases and testing them against clinical observations of the trajectory of disease and individual patients' specific medical histories and exposure. A strong historical lineage connected James Lind's investigation into the causes of scurvy; John Snow's remarkable demonstration that cholera in London was waterborne; and Joseph Goldberger's illuminating experiments proving that pellagra was a diet-deficiency disease.[80] These and many other examples are evidence of a powerful tradition that predated the germ theory; nonetheless, such investigations of medical causality had important limitations.

Researchers investigating the relationship of smoking to disease would draw upon and expand this traditional approach. Proponents of the "new epidemiology" that flowered at mid-century saw their discipline as a strategy for resolving causal questions that could not be answered through clinical observation or laboratory experiment. Although some scientists saw such approaches as "soft" compared to the precision and replicability of the laboratory, it had become clear that many fundamental questions about causality simply would not succumb to either standard experimental methods or clinical observation.

New, more sophisticated approaches to the epidemiology of cancer began to emerge by the 1920s. In particular, it became increasingly clear that focusing only on those who had cancer was inadequate; any full investigation would require "controls"—matched individuals free of disease. "We feel that any study of the habits of individuals with cancer," explained Herbert L. Lombard and Carl R. Doering of the Massachusetts Department of Public Health in a 1928 article in the *New England Journal of Medicine*, "is of little value without a similar study of individuals without cancer."[81] They collected a cohort of more than two hundred cancer patients and a similar number of healthy controls, matched for age, economic status, and race. By organizing their study in this way, Lombard and Doering demonstrated that cancer was not contagious and that it was not associated with poor housing or, as some had suggested, with constipation.

Although Lombard and Doering did not focus specifically on smoking and cancer, they did examine the relationship of "heavy smoking" to disease in the study population, finding a 27 percent increase in overall rates of cancer among the smokers. This increase, they concluded, was "highly significant which suggests that heavy smoking has some relation to cancer in general."[82] Still, sharply aware of the limitations of their study, the authors advocated more systematic assessments:

> Although we realize that the figures in this study are too small and incomplete for significant conclusions to be drawn, they are represented to show the methods used in order that others may conduct similar studies. We feel that other independent samples collected in a like manner would do much to either prove or disprove our findings.[83]

But sustained attempts to use statistical inference and epidemiological investigation to explicate the relationship of smoking and health would not come for another two decades.

§

By the 1930s, the relationship of smoking to cancer was a topic of unresolved debate. It was the life insurance industry, which like the tobacco corporations grew by leaps and bounds in the first half of the twentieth century, that took the lead in understanding the effects of smoking on health.[84] Insurance companies had a vested interest in prevention, behavioral aspects of health, and social and environmental influences on patterns of disease. With the ongoing decline in the authority and resources of public health agencies, expertise on the health of populations—bringing together statistical, epidemiologic, and demographic data—was often most prominently found within the insurance industry. Health experts, such as Louis Dublin, statistician at Metropolitan Life Insurance Company, Edgar Sydenstricker of the U.S. Public Health Service, and Frederick Hoffman, a statistician at Prudential, made these subjects their primary focus.[85]

Hoffman, in particular, took the lead in investigating the rising prevalence of cancer and its relationship to environmental conditions, offering a comprehensive analysis of the evidence for smoking as a cause of cancer in 1931.[86] Already well-known for his comprehensive *San Francisco Cancer Survey,* published annually from 1924 to 1934, Hoffman was well aware of the methodological dilemmas inherent in any attempt to determine the impact of smoking on health.[87] Did smoking *cause* serious disease, especially cancer? Hoffman noted that it was one thing to determine that cancer patients might have a tendency to be smokers, quite another to obtain thorough, reliable data about their smoking practices. What did it mean, for example, to call someone a "heavy" or "moderate" smoker? Many smokers used pipes or cigars as well as cigarettes. Did this affect their risk of disease? And it was difficult to ascertain how long and with what regularity an individual had smoked. All these questions made systematic evaluation of the impact of smoking especially difficult. Like all researchers attempting to tie behavior to disease patterns, Hoffman found himself confronting the limits of smokers' own testimony. In 1930, when he conducted his surveys, a sixty-five-year-old man with oral cancer might well have smoked since youth, but if his smoking patterns followed historical trends, he most likely began with pipes and cigars, only to shift later to cigarettes. Even if he accurately recalled exactly when he took up cigarettes, this typical pattern made it even more difficult to draw causal inferences with any confidence.

Hoffman nonetheless noted the impressive rise in cases of lung cancer in the United States during the first two decades of the twentieth century. In 1915, the rate stood at 0.7 per 1,000; it rose to 1.1 per 1,000 in 1920, 1.6 in 1924, and 1.9 in 1926. Although some observers attributed the increase to improved diagnosis, Hoffman disagreed. "I am strongly inclined to think that the increase is directly connected with the much wider spread of cigarette smoking habits," he noted, "including the inhaling of smoke which must enter the lungs to a considerable extent in many cases."[88] Finally, he realized that "the injurious effects of tobacco smoking in their relation to cancer probably require quite a long period of time to become noticeable."[89]

Yet Hoffman was not prepared to recommend abstinence. Rather, he invoked moderation, the watchword of Progressive hygiene. "Moderation in smoking," he concluded, "commenced in adult life and carried on with reasonable safeguards is, in all probability, free from serious danger . . ."[90] If this were not so, he reasoned, given the dramatic rise in cigarette smoking, one would likely have seen an equally dramatic "increase in cancers of the specific organs and parts most affected by smoking habits," such as the mouth and lip.[91] The obstacles to a more definitive assessment of the relationship of smoking to lung cancer—and other diseases—would remain largely intact until mid-century.

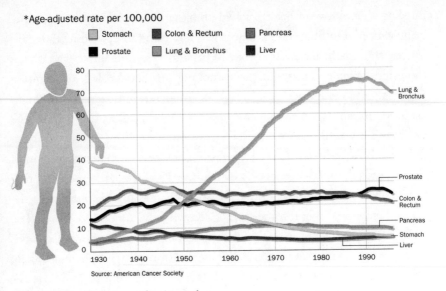

*Age-adjusted rate per 100,000

Legend: Stomach | Colon & Rectum | Pancreas | Prostate | Lung & Bronchus | Liver

Source: American Cancer Society

CHART 2   Cancer rates by site, males

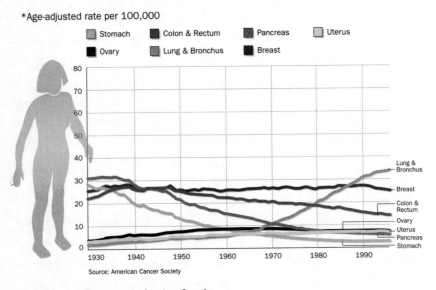

*Age-adjusted rate per 100,000

Legend: Stomach | Colon & Rectum | Pancreas | Uterus | Ovary | Lung & Bronchus | Breast

Source: American Cancer Society

CHART 3   Cancer rates by site, females

In 1938, Raymond Pearl, the eminent Johns Hopkins biologist and population geneticist, examined the relationship of tobacco use to longevity. Unlike everyone who studied the health impact of smoking before him, Pearl went for the bottom line: was tobacco use correlated with a shortened life span? Using the data collected in his Family History Records of nearly 7,000 white males, he concluded that "the smoking of tobacco was statistically associated with the impairment of life duration, and the amount of this impairment increased as the habitual amount of smoking increased."[92] His findings anticipated a dose-response relationship; the greater the sustained exposure, the shorter anticipated life expectancy. Pearl refused to speculate as to why this might be so. But he did point out that the use of pharmacologically active agents for pleasure—despite potential harms—was a longstanding historical tradition.

> There are undoubtedly great numbers of human beings who would continue the habitual use of a particular material they liked, even though it were absolutely and beyond any question or argument proved to be somewhat deleterious to them.[93]

Although Pearl's study might have strong statistical implications for life insurers, its meaning for individual smokers remained less clear. Did smoking lead to specific diseases that resulted in premature death? Or was it possible that less-healthy individuals might be predisposed to smoke? Were some individuals particularly vulnerable to the effects of the cigarette? Pearl's study did not directly address these questions.

Others, however, now suggested that such questions could be addressed through more systematic comparisons of smokers to nonsmokers. One such study, excerpted in the *Journal of the American Medical Association,* came from Germany. Franz Hermann Müller, a physician from the University of Cologne's Pathological Institute, identified 96 individuals who had died of lung cancer. Of these individuals, he was able to determine that only three had been nonsmokers; about one-third smoked moderately. Müller's study was important in that he had compared smokers to a control group who had died of other causes.[94] Statistical observations like Pearl and Müller's sustained concerns about the impact of smoking through the 1930s.

§

Those who treated diseases of the lung saw smoking as a daily issue. Chest surgeons like Alton Ochsner in New Orleans and Richard Overholt in Boston drew attention in the 1930s with their observations that patients with advanced lung malignancies typically had smoked. Ochsner prohibited his staff from smoking and became known as a vigorous antitobacco advocate. He and colleague Michael DeBakey, assessing the increase in cases of primary carcinoma of the lung, concluded:

> In our opinion the increase in smoking with the universal custom of inhaling is probably a responsible factor, as the inhaled smoke, constantly repeated over a long period of time, undoubtedly is a source of chronic irritation to the bronchial mucosa.[95]

According to most prevailing explanations of carcinogenesis, irritation played a crucial role in instigating the development of tumors, though exactly how was not known.

But this statement powerfully revealed the limits of clinical observation, a hallmark of medical science and investigation. There was no indication that DeBakey and Ochsner systematically collected information on their patients' smoking patterns. They possessed no method for turning clinical observations, however acute, from causal hypothesis into fact. Evarts Graham, a prominent surgeon at Barnes Hospital in St. Louis, who had trained Ochsner, told him, "Yes there is a parallel between the sale of cigarettes and lung cancer, but there is also a parallel between the sale of silk stockings and cancer of the lung."[96] The observations of thoracic surgeons like Overholt and Ochsner left the underlying causal hypothesis unresolved.[97]

These clinical observations of the impact of smoking are, in retrospect, quite impressive. Almost all the risks that would later come to be attributed to smoking had been well documented by clinicians in the first decades of the century. Even the risks of passive exposure to cigarette smoke had been well articulated.[98] Yet physicians and researchers could not move from such clinical observations to more powerful and generalizable assessments of the relationship of smoking to disease. Surgeons like Ochsner might well be convinced that tobacco had *caused* their patients' malignancies, but their observations could never settle the larger questions of cause and effect.

But standard experimental methods exported from the laboratory could not settle the question either. Not only would it be impossible to design the requisite experiment—randomizing children into groups of smokers and controls—it was widely recognized that such an approach would also be unethical.[99] As Evarts Graham humorously explained in a 1954 commentary that appeared in the *Lancet:*

> One must grant that indeed no absolute proof has been offered. But what sort of proof is called for? To satisfy the most obdurate of the diehards it would be necessary to take the following steps:
>
> 1. Secure some human volunteers willing to have a bronchus painted with cigarette tar, perhaps through a bronchial fistula.
> 2. The experiment must be carried on for at least twenty or twenty-five years.
> 3. The subjects must spend the whole period in air conditioned quarters, never leaving them even for an hour or so, in order that there may be no contamination by a polluted atmosphere.
> 4. At the end of the twenty-five years they must submit to an operation or an autopsy to determine the result of the experiment.
>
> I will say to those who wish to volunteer for such an experiment, "please form a queue to the right; no crowding please."[100]

By the 1940s, several innovative and suggestive studies offered impressive support for the theory of cigarettes as a cause of disease. And yet, these studies did not constitute "proof" in its scientific, medical, and social definition. Nor did they have any significant effect on consumption, medical views of the cigarette, or policy. They served as little more than scientific footnotes in an ongoing debate about the impact of smoking. Their implication for doctors and patients remained far from clear. Many physicians noted that medical studies of the health effects of smoking produced ambiguous and often contradictory findings. Although the moral opprobrium directed at the cigarette had dissipated, it left behind a substantial but quiet medical uncertainty. In this state of uncertainty, doctors and the public would be forced to confront a new epidemic: lung cancer.

If the evidence incriminated only an article of diet, such as spinach, for example, probably nearly everybody would accept it as conclusive. I have never encountered any non-smoker who makes light of the evidence or is skeptical of the association between excessive cigarette smoking and lung cancer.[1]

EVARTS A. GRAHAM, 1954

Medical literature has numerous examples of such fallacious conclusions which have been proved to be wrong in the light of subsequent experience. This whole question of cause and effect deducted on a statistical basis is subject to the greatest fallacies. One way I like to emphasize it is to say that simply because one finds bull frogs after a rain does not mean that it rained bullfrogs.[2]

MAX CUTLER, 1954

Perhaps it is never possible to prove with absolute certainty that a naturally occurring event was the product of a specified set of naturally occurring conditions. However, such can often be established beyond reasonable doubt. In human affairs, important decisions must necessarily be based upon the preponderance of evidence.[3]

E. CUYLER HAMMOND, 1955

CHAPTER 5

The Causal Conundrum

IN 1933, AT BARNES Hospital in St. Louis, Dr. Evarts Graham performed the first successful pneumonectomy—total removal of a cancerous lung. The procedure he devised required significant innovations in surgical technique and offered the best available treatment for bronchogenic carcinoma, well known to be uniformly fatal. Following his triumphant announcement of the procedure at the annual meeting of the American Association for Thoracic Surgery, pneumonectomy became the treatment of choice for lung cancers that had yet to spread to other organs. Graham's professional reputation soared.[4]

Despite his extensive experience treating individuals with cancers of the lung, Graham had greeted Alton Ochsner's theory about the relationship of such cancers to smoking with a mix of skepticism and derision. A heavy smoker who had suffered no apparent ill effects, he believed that if Ochsner's ideas were correct, surgeons would more typically see tumors in both lobes. Given that cancers were typically found in but one lobe, Graham reasoned, smoking was unlikely to be the cause. Why, when the smoke obviously entered both lobes, would only one be affected?[5]

Despite these views, or perhaps because of them, Graham was sympathetic when a third-year medical student at Washington University, Ernst Wynder, approached him in 1947 to collaborate on a study of the relationship of smoking to lung cancer. Graham was eager to resolve the lurking suspicions that by then had surrounded the cigarette for more than a decade. Wynder had spent the previous summer on his own initiative in

131

New York collecting data from some 146 lung cancer patients about their smoking practices. Impressed by this student's independence and fortitude, Graham agreed to participate. Even more importantly, he contacted the American Cancer Society (ACS), where he had a number of influential colleagues, to obtain modest funding for the work.[6] Wynder threw himself into the investigation, pulling the senior surgeon along with him.

Wynder quickly became something of a shoe-leather epidemiologist, traveling widely to interview lung cancer patients about their smoking histories and other toxic exposures. Wynder and Graham collected extensive data on 604 such patients, located at hospitals across the United States. Their approach to the question of whether cigarette smoking caused lung cancer was rooted in the historical tradition of the anecdotal collection of cases, well known to surgeons who would report successive surgeries to demonstrate their effectiveness. But following a practice that was growing increasingly common in clinical research, they also decided to apply rudimentary statistical techniques to their evaluations.[7]

Unlike earlier researchers, who had separated smokers into crude categories of "moderate" and "heavy," Wynder and Graham devised categories that carefully reflected levels of smoking over a twenty-year period, rating smokers in five groups from "light" to "chain." They arranged for histological examination of cells from lung tissue in each case to confirm the cancer diagnosis.[8] Cases of lung cancer without a history of tobacco use proved exceedingly rare, and in these instances Wynder often uncovered exposures to other inhaled carcinogens, such as gasoline fumes or insecticides.[9] Wynder and Graham also attended to a number of the questions that had previously confounded investigators. They evaluated the types of tobacco their subjects used, noting that cigarettes were more frequently inhaled and used more heavily than pipes and cigars.

Notably, Wynder and Graham established a control group of cancer-free individuals in hospitals for systematic comparison to their lung cancer patients. Interviewers carefully inquired about the smoking patterns of this group using the exact same questionnaire for lung cancer patients. "Two objects were realized by this control group," they explained. "One was to learn of possible exposures to exogenous irritants of a large group of patients without cancer of the lung and the other to test the validity of the interviews made of those who knew the suspected diagnosis in a given case in advance."[10] Wynder and Graham assumed that the age distribution in the study group and control groups were comparable, and made adjustments where appropriate. They were eager that their findings stand up to statistical scrutiny.

At the *Journal of the American Medical Association* (*JAMA*), editor Lester King reportedly greeted the resulting paper with considerable suspicion. He was eventually convinced of its merits by Morton Levin, a physician and epidemiologist at the State Institute for the Study of Malignant Diseases in New York, who noted that the paper's statistical approach emerged from the historical tradition of case study and observation.[11] *JAMA* published the paper on May 27, 1950.

Wynder and Graham reported that lung cancer could occur among nonsmokers and that heavy smokers did not necessarily develop cancer. Therefore, they reasoned, "smoking cannot be the only etiologic factor in the induction of disease." Nonetheless, "the temptation is strong to incriminate excessive smoking, and in particular cigarette smoking, over a long period as at least one important factor in the striking increase of bronchogenic carcinoma. . . ."[12] They offered four reasons to support this conclusion. First, it was very unusual to find lung cancer among nonsmokers. Second, among patients with lung cancer, cigarette use tended to be high. Third, the distribution of lung cancer among men and women matched the ratio of smoking patterns by gender. Finally, "the enormous increase in the sale of cigarettes in this country approximately parallels the increase in bronchogenic carcinoma."[13]

Wynder, idealistic and ambitious, was impressed and excited by the potential significance of his findings and saw them—correctly—as his chance to make a mark in medicine. "The data are most impressive," he enthused in a letter to Graham. "Our final paper will ring forth startling as well as decisive news indeed. It lies within our hands to lower considerably the incidence of one of the major cancers."[14] He had become so focused on completing the study that he apparently neglected his medical school work.[15]

Born in Germany in 1922 to Jewish parents, Wynder had escaped with them from Nazi rule, arriving in the United States in 1938. He worked his way through New York University selling newspapers and waiting tables. During the war, he attained citizenship and entered the Army. His knowledge of German led to his assignment in a psychological warfare unit monitoring German newscasts. Following the war, Wynder followed his father into medicine, enrolling at Washington University School of Medicine. In Graham, he found a mentor eager to foster his strengths.[16]

As the results of their study began to come in, Graham wrote to Ochsner, acknowledging that "I may need to eat humble pie."[17] Soon, Graham and Ochsner would become steadfast allies in their conviction that smoking was an important cause of lung cancer. With a push from his student, Graham employed the tools of epidemiology to transcend the limits of his own clinical observations. He would be forever associated as a key player in this path-breaking finding.

§

As Wynder traveled around the United States, visiting hospitals and collecting data, two distinguished medical statisticians in Great Britain had independently embarked on a parallel study. Under the auspices of the British Medical Research Council (MRC), which had recently become a unit of the newly created National Health Service (NHS), A. Bradford Hill and Richard Doll began in 1947 to study the rising incidence of lung cancer. As they both noted, there was no easy way to account for the notable rise of diseases, such as lung cancer. On both sides of the Atlantic, the selection of this disease as an area for investigation reflected rising concern about the chronic systemic diseases of later life in the face of demographic changes clearly recognized at mid-century. Among the central tasks of the NHS would be to monitor and prevent chronic diseases, which had over the course of the twentieth century become increasingly prominent causes of morbidity and mortality. While Wynder and Graham initiated their study of the disease from a clinical perspective, their English counterparts worked within an epidemiological tradition deeply rooted in the investigation of vital statistics and population health.[18]

Doll and Hill recognized that certain questions of great medical and public significance simply would not readily succumb to clinical evaluation and laboratory experiments. Nonetheless, the timeliness and importance of determining the factors leading to cancers warranted immediate attention. As a result, they joined together to utilize a sophisticated set of statistical and medical skills that they had developed independently over the previous decades to implement a rigorous investigation of the relationship of smoking to cancer.

It had been expected that Hill, like his father before him, would pursue medical training and practice. But as a pilot in the Royal Navy Air Service in World War I, he contracted tuberculosis and was "sent home to die." Defying the probabilities, Hill survived, but a medical career was now out of the question. Major Greenwood, the leading medical statistician in Great Britain and a friend of Hill's father, recommended he pursue a correspondence degree in economics. This Hill accomplished while still bedridden. As his recovery proceeded, Greenwood arranged for him to undertake a field investigation of the reasons for high mortality rates in rural Essex. While conducting this study, Hill continued his education under Greenwood's watchful eye; he also attended a course on statistics at University College taught by Karl Pearson, the noted mathematician and eugenicist.[19]

In 1923, Hill was hired by the MRC to study occupational disease. While at the MRC, Hill lectured at the London School of Hygiene and Tropical Medicine on medical statistics and its applications. These lectures were published in the *Lancet* in 1937; collected in book form, they provided the basis for the epidemiologic techniques that would become the center of Hill's subsequent investigations.[20] The articles emphasized the need to make appropriate comparisons, to avoid bias, and to understand the role of chance—all principles central to modern epidemiologic methods. Hill urged the medical profession to apply new forms of scientific deduction and quantification in their assessment of medical practices and patterns of disease.[21] Rather than dismissing clinical knowledge as anecdotal and idiosyncratic, Hill sought to develop systematic strategies for utilizing and assessing hard-won clinical observation. This work was a key element in the effort to place medicine, public health, and therapeutics on a new evidentiary foundation.[22]

After World War II, Hill championed the utility of medical statistics for the evaluation of new treatments—following the pioneering work of the British statistician and geneticist R. A. Fisher, whose work in agricultural experimentation had been a great influence. One of Hill's innovations was the first randomized, double-blind clinical trial, designed to reduce investigator bias in the evaluation of clinical outcomes. Attempting to assess the effectiveness of streptomycin in treating infectious tuberculosis, Hill divided patients with TB into two groups: one received streptomycin, the other a placebo. Neither researcher nor subject was informed about who was getting the drug—hence the term *double-blind*. As a result, evaluations of the drug's efficacy would not be shaped by prior knowledge, expectations, or unknown biases. This method, which drew on Fisher's agricultural experimentation in genetics, became a critical new tool for evaluating medical treatments.[23] Hill would apply elements of this same framework to investigating the relationship of smoking to disease.

Doll's career was also dramatically influenced by tuberculosis. He had shown great promise in mathematics as a student but followed his father into medicine. Although eager to find ways to employ his interest in research and quantification, Doll struggled to find a situation in medicine that would demand these skills. During World War II, he contracted TB and had to have a kidney removed. Following his military discharge in 1945, at the age of thirty-two, Doll became involved in a study with Dr. Avery Jones at Central Middlesex Hospital on occupational factors in peptic ulcers. His meticulous survey, funded by the MRC, came to the attention of Bradford Hill just as he was about to begin his investigation of the causes of the rise of lung cancer. Hill asked Doll to join him at the MRC in January 1948. Together, they made a formidable partnership in the evolution of modern epidemiology. The young research assistant quickly became a full collaborator on the project.[24]

Hill sought to adapt his new type of clinical trial to investigations where randomization was not possible, specifically cigarette smoking. Obviously he and Doll could not divide individuals into two groups, apply the intervention (in this case the cigarette), and later evaluate the impact on a double-blind basis. The period of exposure necessary to produce disease (probably twenty years) was far too long, there could be no placebo control group, and most significantly, since such a study would randomly subject individuals to unknown and possibly serious harms, it was clearly unethical. So Hill and Doll worked to develop a strategy that would follow—to the degree possible—the methodological rigors of randomization: how could one systematically design and implement observational studies in populations that invoked the strategies of an experimental "trial"?

The answer, they concluded, was to turn the randomized trial back-to-front. Instead of a "prospective" study—in which the subjects were randomly divided into two groups, and half of them subjected to some clinical treatment—Doll and Hill would run a "retrospective" study, taking a group of lung cancer patients and pairing each one with a carefully matched but healthy control, in order to analyze the differences in the two groups' long-term behavior. Doll and Hill were therefore eager to bring quantitative rigor to the medical and scientific assessment of both the causes of disease and the effectiveness of treatment. In this respect, they saw no fundamental tensions between the randomized clinical trial and the retrospective (case-control) study, which they devised in 1948 to determine the causes of lung cancer. Both types of designs—prospective and retrospective—rested on a foundation of statistical inference and the systematic collection and evaluation of data. And both relied on carefully structured observations of specific variables, clinical interventions, and "risk factors." Mathematically, researchers could treat the risk factor—cigarette smoking, poor diet, or any behavioral or social variable—as if it were an intervention, such as a new drug or a surgical procedure. Researchers could then compare those exposed to the specific risk factor to controls who had not received the "intervention."[25]

Like Graham, Doll and Hill began their investigation with considerable skepticism about smoking's influence on lung cancer. In their first list of factors that might account for the disease, the rise of the cigarette appeared as but one of several possibilities. Doll believed the introduction of the automobile, the widespread expansion of paved roads, and the consequent changes in air quality would emerge as the most important factors. As he later reflected:

> Motor cars . . . were a new factor and if I had had to put money on anything at the time, I should have put it on motor exhausts or possibly the tarring of roads. Because of course the whole road system in the country had changed with the advent of the motor car, and we knew . . . that the tar that was put on roads contained many carcinogens.[26]

In contrast, "cigarette smoking was such a normal thing and had been for such a long time that it was difficult to think it could be associated with any disease."[27]

But as their data began to accrue in late 1948 and early 1949, it became clear to Doll and Hill that cigarettes were the crucial factor in the rise of lung cancer. Hill later recounted:

As I went through and checked the diagnoses I saw that patient after patient in the "lung cancer" group who was regarded as a non-smoker turned out not to have lung cancer; whereas, in those who were heavy smokers the diagnoses seldom had to be changed. . . . This was a striking finding and quickly drew our attention to the importance of smoking.[28]

Even without any sophisticated statistical analysis, the findings were impressive: among the 647 lung cancer patients entered into Doll and Hill's study, all 647 smoked cigarettes. When Doll computed the p value for statistical significance, it turned out to be 0.00000064! In other words, the possibility that this was a "chance" finding was less than one in a million. Among those who smoked more heavily, lung cancer was correspondingly more prevalent, confirming the dose-response effect noted a decade earlier by Raymond Pearl.[29]

The comparison of lung cancer patients to carefully matched controls was central to Doll and Hill's investigation. During the 1920s and 1930s, control groups had become a key feature of clinical trials, a way to eliminate possible bias on the part of the researcher by providing rigorous comparisons. Now Doll and Hill's quasi-experimental studies employed controls as well.[30] The two men understood that their conclusions rested fundamentally on explicit comparisons: lung cancer patients to other patients (similar in every other way); smokers to nonsmokers (similar in every other way). The systematic use of such comparisons constituted a critical analytic tool of modern epidemiology, and indeed, of all medical knowledge.

Another key aspect of this study was its analysis of the different rates of lung cancer in men and women. These variations, Doll and Hill suggested, were not due to any inherent sex difference but instead reflected historical patterns of cigarette consumption. "Although increasing numbers of women are now beginning to smoke," they wrote, "the great majority of women now of cancer age have either never smoked or have only recently started to do so." Few women had lung cancer in 1948 because relatively few had been smoking long enough. Implicit in this conclusion was the stark prediction—soon to be realized—that rates of lung cancer among women would rise significantly in the second half of the twentieth century.[31]

Contemporary assessments of the Doll and Hill and Wynder and Graham studies often drew attention to the potential for bias—on the part of both patients and investigators—in a retrospective study. Patients might recount their histories inaccurately, or they might tend to overestimate or underestimate their exposure to cigarette smoke. Interviewers, too, might have preconceived assumptions. Those who were eager to substantiate the smoking-cancer link might unconsciously or consciously skew their questions. Although Doll and Hill hoped to keep the patients' diagnoses hidden from their interviewers, this had proven impossible in practice. The two researchers were highly aware of such opportunities for bias: "Serious consideration must therefore be given to the possibility of interviewers' bias affecting the results (by the interviewers tending to scale up the smoking habits of the lung-carcinoma cases)."[32] Doll carefully checked the diagnoses of each patient entered into the study; additionally, he obtained histologies and information about the part of the lung in which the tumor had originated.

Sharply aware that their data and conclusions could be critiqued based on these personal histories, Doll and Hill assessed their reliability by reinterviewing a group of controls six months later. They found only small changes, concluding that the original interviews were "reliable enough to indicate general trends and to substantiate material differences between groups."[33] They understood the importance of recording detailed smoking histories from their respondents. "It was necessary to define," they wrote, "what was meant by a smoker," a category that did not include "the woman who took one cigarette annually after her Christmas dinner."[34] Doll entered the data by hand into columns in a record book and added the columns. He later commented, "The whole thing was done with a nineteenth-century clerical technique."[35] This systematic collection and analysis of data harkened back to the historic epidemiologic assessments of figures like John Snow investigating cholera in mid-nineteenth-century London.

Although the findings were striking, Doll and Hill understood that it would be easy to dismiss them—as the tobacco industry would repeatedly try to do—as "merely" statistical. So they meticulously described the criteria they applied before any "association" between smoking and lung cancer could be identified as a genuine causal relationship. The problem with epidemiological studies was the potential that some bias or some unanticipated variable might obscure an alternative explanation for the apparent causal relationship. This is why critics of these studies frequently warned that a statistical "association" should not be assumed to be a conclusive demonstration of a *cause*. No one was more aware of these problems than Doll and Hill. Every apparent limitation of their work was clearly articulated, addressed in detail, and rebutted.

Even aside from its groundbreaking results, this study was important for its explicit commitment to investigatory science, hypothesis testing, and experimental method. Doll and Hill worked to eliminate the possibility of bias in the selection of patients and controls, as well as in reporting and recording their histories; they emphasized the significance of a clear temporal relationship between exposure and the subsequent development of disease; and they sought to rule out any other factors that might distinguish controls from patients with disease. This explicit search for, and elimination of, possible "confounders" was a critical step toward their conclusion. Further, they insisted on carefully addressing all possible alternative explanations for their findings. Was there some other explanation that could plausibly account for the same data? "Consideration," they wrote,

> has been given to the possibility that the results could have been produced by the selection of an unsuitable group of control patients, by patients with respiratory disease exaggerating their smoking habits, or by bias on the part of the interviewers. Reasons are given for excluding all these possibilities, and it is concluded that smoking is an important factor in the cause of carcinoma of the lung.[36]

Doll and Hill's first paper on smoking and lung cancer appeared in September 1950 in the *British Medical Journal*, four months after Wynder and Graham's article in *JAMA*. Although Doll and Hill regretted not publishing first (they had held off, at the suggestion of MRC Secretary Harold Himsworth, to collect more data from patients outside London), their paper differed from their American counterparts in ways that would ultimately be of great significance. While they understood the importance of their conclusion, they had a complementary commitment to demonstrating the power of epidemiologic methods in investigating causal questions in medicine and public health.[37]

Both Doll and Hill would spend their careers applying these methods to tobacco and other risk factors, but also working to demonstrate their utility for addressing questions poorly suited to laboratory investigation. They sought to identify a scientific approach that could be used to investigate disease *in situ*, especially in instances where laboratory experimentation and clinical observation were so significantly limited in determining causality and outcome. The framework they sought to develop was specifically designed to address the inherent limitations of these other forms of knowing.

The issue of causal criteria would be debated for decades. Absent some clearly articulated physical mechanism, was a statistical argument sufficient to prove that A *causes* B? Although their criteria would be refined and expanded, Doll and Hill brilliantly and explicitly outlined the basis for a systematic epidemiological approach to determining causality in noninfectious chronic disease. In this sense, modern epidemiology was constructed around the problem of determining the harms of smoking.[38]

Although observers would later debate the "priority" of the Doll/Hill and Wynder/Graham investigations, such discussions obscured the fact that priority in epidemiology was not like physics or chemistry. No single study can be definitive. Given the complex variables being assessed, a conclusive judgment on cigarettes as a cause of disease would require the accumulation of many studies both similar in design yet distinctive from each other. No single study could conclusively demonstrate a causal relationship between smoking and cancer.

Following Doll and Hill and Wynder and Graham, a number of investigations reported strongly consistent findings.[39] There now seemed little doubt that among patients with lung cancer, there was a disproportionate number of heavy smokers (and few nonsmokers). "We would never have said, on the case control study alone," explained Doll, "that cigarette smoking was a cause of carcinoma of the lung." The move from an "association" to a causal relationship was made only in light of the consistency of a wide range of evidence. For example, Doll and Hill collected international data to see if there was any country where smoking had been prevalent for a long time, but that had a low incidence of lung cancer. None existed. In countries where the cigarette was not introduced until late, lung cancer was uncommon. Additionally, they found, risk of disease was lower among light smokers worldwide.[40]

Although the many researchers now entering the field would assert a healthy competitiveness, their combined work formed an important collaboration-in-kind. Researchers conducting retrospective studies on cigarette smoking and lung cancer, using a variety of methods and populations, consistently replicated and validated the most important findings.[41] As more studies accrued, so too did medical and public confidence in the conclusion. This aggregative process marked a significant difference in scientific epistemology from the traditional notions of individual investigators "making" scientific "discoveries." In epidemiology, discovery and proof were iterative, as no specific experimental situation could be precisely replicated. Researchers now sought to take advantage of this variability; "consistency" across multiple studies would become another criterion for defining causality.

Retrospective studies, such as those reported by Doll and Hill and Wynder and Graham, were subject to extensive criticism from those who understood their methods, and from many who did not. Some dismissed the findings as but a figment of statistical manipulation (although little highly sophisticated statistical analysis was actually applied). Others focused on suspicion of bias. Both patients and interviewers, they suggested, might overestimate smoking, skewing the results.

One of the most strident critics of the new epidemiological studies came from the world of statistics. Joseph Berkson continually raised questions about possible bias in the selection of individuals in the respective epidemiological investigations. Berkson had trained in medicine at Johns Hopkins where he also received a doctorate in statistics. After serving as a fellow in physiology at the Mayo Clinic in 1931, he joined the Statistics Division there. In 1934, he was named head of Biometry and Medical Statistics at the Mayo Clinic, a post he would hold for more than thirty years. Berkson found himself drawn to controversy and cherished his identity as a skeptic of the emerging consensus about lung cancer and smoking. According to Berkson, the fact that a number of the retrospective studies had used hospitalized patients as subjects and volunteers as interviewers were confounding factors. This critique was repeatedly addressed and rebutted by the epidemiologists. Berkson was also suspicious because cigarette smoking seemed not only to cause more cases of lung cancer but higher mortality from multiple causes. When such investigation "turns out to indicate that smoking causes or provokes a whole gamut of diseases, inevitably it raises the suspicion that something is amiss." But smoking *was* eventually linked to many different diseases. Berkson's *a priori* commitment to specificity (one cause, one disease) led him to erroneously dismiss significant findings. Despite numerous answers to his critiques, he never relented in his skepticism.[42]

Another vocal critic of the lung cancer findings was Sir Ronald Fisher, the leading biometrician and geneticist in Great Britain during the first half of the twentieth century and a man deeply committed to bringing statistical analysis to genetics and agricultural experimentation. His 1925 book, *Statistical Methods for Research Workers,* quickly became a classic, leading to academic appointments at University College London and Cambridge University. Fisher's critiques were similar to Berkson's. The ethical impossibility of conducting a randomized experiment led him to question the results of the epidemiological studies. As a believer in genetic notions of cancer causality, Fisher speculated that there was some constitutional factor that led individuals both to become smokers and to get lung cancer, even though smoking and lung cancer might not be causally related. Doll and Hill repeatedly rebutted this theory, returning to the critical question of how to account for the rise in lung cancers during the twentieth century if the disease was simply "constitutional."[43]

While Fisher and Berkson raised important questions, their critiques were no match for the overwhelming evidence of repeated studies. Nonetheless, the industry broadcast and rebroadcast these attacks and ultimately hired both Fisher and Berkson as paid consultants. Although both men identified themselves as "independent" skeptics, they brought both *a priori* assumptions and, later, conflicts of interest to their unremitting critiques.[44]

In 1951, Wynder wrote to his mentor Graham about the ongoing attacks by Fisher and Berkson:

> It seems strange that after the British paper there should still be statisticians who find serious doubt in our findings in regard to errors of memory that patients may have. Our critics seem not to note that similar errors of memory would apply to our controlled population. . . . I am glad to report that the statistical powers . . . at the National Cancer Institute have been all on our side since we were so thoroughly confirmed by the Doll and Hill paper.[45]

Doll and Hill understood—as did their American colleagues—that these studies demanded additional, confirmatory investigations using other methods. The language in these reports varied from observing an "association" between cancer and cigarettes to claiming "causality." Doll and Hill concluded that additional investigations of patients with lung cancer would not resolve the ongoing doubts about this relationship. "Further retrospective studies of the same kind would seem to us unlikely to advance our knowledge materially or to throw any new light upon the nature of the association," they wrote in 1954.[46] They began designing additional studies that would employ different research strategies to confirm and sustain their earlier findings. To counter the charge of bias that had been leveled against their earlier studies, in 1951 they initiated a major prospective study to follow health outcomes among healthy smokers paired with nonsmoking controls. They sent 60,000 questionnaires to British physicians about their smoking practices and got back some 40,000 replies. Doll and Hill chose doctors for their study for a number of reasons. First, they wanted to attract the attention of the medical profession. Second, they expected that physicians might offer more accurate replies to their questionnaires. And most importantly, they knew that all physicians were registered by the government, facilitating identification and follow-up.

They followed this group *forward*, noting deaths through the Registrars-General Office in the United Kingdom. The prospective study demonstrated Doll and Hill's experimental approach to epidemiology. By gathering two groups similar in every respect except for their smoking behaviors, they had created an experiment—in effect, a randomized trial in which the "intervention" was cigarette use rather than a therapeutic agent. Now they awaited the effects of the intervention. As the data came in, it proved fully consistent with their previous research: they found an impressive excess of deaths among the doctors who smoked. Strikingly, heavy smokers had death rates 24 times higher than nonsmokers.[47]

In a preliminary report on the study, published in the *British Medical Journal* in 1954, they remarked

> We thought it necessary, in view of the nature of our results, to lay these preliminary data before the survivors of the 40,000 men and women who made them possible.[48]

Impressing these survivors was central to legitimating both their findings and their methods: if the medical profession was convinced, it would persuade individual doctors to advise patients against smoking and also provide authority to the new epidemiological methods of inquiry.

In the United States, statisticians E. Cuyler Hammond and Daniel Horn simultaneously conducted a similar prospective study under the auspices of the American Cancer Society. The antismoking advocate Alton Ochsner had become president of the ACS, and he now pressed the organization for a more systematic assessment of changing rates of cancer mortality. For this work, the ACS turned to Hammond, who had received his doctorate at the Johns Hopkins School of Hygiene and Public Health, where he had come under the influence of Wade Hampton Frost, Lowell Reed, and Raymond Pearl, dominant figures in pre-war epidemiology and medical statistics. In 1946, he went to the American Cancer Society to lead its Department of Statistical Research. Hammond had been among the most vociferous critics of Wynder and Graham's initial retrospective study. In December 1950, a frustrated Evarts Graham called Hammond a "two for a nickel guy" who had "done everything [he] could to obstruct this work."[49]

Now, however, Hammond and Horn, a psychologist with training in statistics, worked to design a trial free of the potential limitations of retrospective studies. They focused on two primary ways to reduce bias: a prospective design, like that used in Doll and Hill's physician study, and perhaps more significantly, the largest study population anyone had yet assembled. Over nearly four years, Hammond and Horn followed a sample of 200,000 men between the ages of fifty and sixty. During this period, 12,000 died. Not only was lung cancer a far more prevalent cause of death among those who smoked (twenty-four times more common than among nonsmokers), so too was heart and circulatory disease.[50]

Even though Hammond had been dismissive of the retrospective studies, as his prospective data came in he grew increasingly convinced of the causal relationship. "All the evidence collected to date," he wrote to Graham in 1954, "certainly points strongly to the conclusion that cigarette smoking does increase the probability of developing lung cancer."[51] That September, Graham wrote to Ochsner concerning Hammond's change of heart:

I am very happy that Hammond has completely reversed himself from the position which he took in 1950 when he told me that our work was no good and that if he had anything to do with it we would not get a nickle [sic] for any renewal of our work.[52]

Hammond was also increasingly attuned to other serious health consequences. "I am strongly suspicious," he noted, "that cigarette smoking increases the death rate from causes other than lung cancer."[53] When the study was published, Hammond and Horn had added cardiovascular disease to the short but growing list of the cigarette's harms. "Tobacco heart" reappeared in modern form, confirmed by these substantial epidemiological investigations.[54]

Hammond's investigation also addressed two questions that had been raised by Doll and Hill's study. He showed that the risks of smoking did not vary between urban and rural areas, and that even light smokers incurred higher risk of disease and death than nonsmokers.[55] With these findings, Hammond countered the frequent arguments of skeptics that environmental confounders, such as air pollution, were more important than cigarettes in causing cancer and that only "excessive" smokers were at risk.

Doll would later praise Hammond's study for introducing much larger data pools and showing the wide range of maladies associated with smoking, far more than had been anticipated. Hammond's data demonstrated that smoking might be responsible for up to 40 percent of mortality among smokers. Although the retrospective studies had focused on lung cancer (by starting with lung cancer patients), the prospective studies offered the important opportunity of identifying a wide range of other potential health outcomes among smokers.

Hammond subsequently pointed out that the relationship between smoking and disease could be found only in a particular historical and social context:

> We are concerned here with a restricted set of conditions—human populations where death from infectious and parasitic diseases is uncommon and where violence and accidents account for a relatively small proportion of all deaths. It is only in such populations that a remarkable degree of association has been found between death rates and amount of cigarette smoking.[56]

Hammond offered an important rationale for the discovery of the harms of smoking. Only in developed nations that had experienced a decline in infectious disease and possessed the affluence of a consumer culture would the harms of smoking become fully visible.[57]

While Doll and Hill moved to employ additional epidemiological strategies to confirm their initial findings, Wynder and Graham tried to uncover the biology of carcinogenesis through animal studies.[58] Wynder reasoned that such studies, if successful, would be an important step in confirming the cancer-tobacco link. He and Graham believed that the crucial question was now centered on what came to be called the "biological plausibility" of the causal claim. In the same year that they reported their epidemiological findings, they initiated a study in which they painted mice with condensed tars from tobacco smoke. Wynder, accompanied by Graham's assistant Adele Croninger, traveled to Bar Harbor, Maine, to visit the renowned Roscoe B. Jackson Memorial Laboratory, founded in 1929 by geneticist C. C. Little, to learn about techniques of experimentation on purebred mice. Even after Wynder had gone to Washington, DC, to do his internship at Georgetown University and then on to the Sloan-Kettering Institute in New York, Graham and Croninger continued painting mice with the chemical tars distilled from tobacco smoke.

After a year, 44 percent of the mice thus treated had developed cancers. Wynder found benzopyrenes, arsenic, and other carcinogens in the tars but could not determine which chemical specifically caused the animals' cancers. "It remains to be seen whether removing a small percentage of the tar will decrease the carcinogenic activity of this material," he wrote. "The answer to this question cannot be given until such time as we know what the active carcinogenic component of tobacco tar really is."[59]

Even so, Wynder and Graham's studies on mice offered critical support to the emerging epidemiological studies. Applying tobacco tars to laboratory animals had been attempted in the past, with similar results.[60] But in the context of the epidemiological data, these findings took on new importance. No longer could skeptics—whether within the industry or within science—claim that the evidence linking smoking to disease was "merely" statistical; Wynder and Graham had given the connection the crucial quality of biological plausibility. The production of tumors in lab animals offered a powerful indicator that something in cigarette smoke could account for the epidemiological findings.

Although some researchers had difficulty replicating these experiments—there was confusion about dosing, length of observation, and the character of the evolving tumors—the wide recognition of the existence of carcinogens in tobacco nonetheless provided critical scientific support for the conclusion that smoking did cause cancer. The first published account of the Wynder, Graham, and Croninger mouse experiments appeared in the December 1953 issue of *Cancer Research*.[61] The paper galvanized medical and public attention.

By early 1954, many physicians, scientists, and public health professionals were convinced of the hazards of smoking. Graham would proclaim that "those who have ventured to express doubt on the significance of our findings can almost be counted on the fingers of one's two hands."[62] Following the publication of the prospective studies by Doll and Hill and Hammond and Horn a year later, Wynder wrote to Graham, "It is interesting to see how the circle is beginning to close."[63] He had a right to feel vindicated. Noting Hammond's early skepticism, Wynder wrote that "one can relish in the thought that one's original stand has been accepted."[64] Graham, for his part, expressed resentment that Hammond's findings—which he saw as merely confirming his own—had generated so much attention and praise.[65] But Graham perhaps underestimated that there were two simultaneous processes at work: the validation of the causal relationship of lung cancer to smoking *and* the legitimation of epidemiology as a tool of medical science. Clinical medicine remained antagonistic to quantitative analysis.[66]

By the mid-1950s, researchers employing a range of approaches had substantially advanced medical and scientific knowledge of the harms of cigarette use. Collectively, they had reached a conclusion of signal importance about the relationship of smoking to lung cancer. This conclusion emerged from three distinct but related domains of medical knowledge: clinical observations, population studies, and laboratory experiments. The questions associated with cigarettes as a cause of disease illuminated the relative strengths and weaknesses of these approaches to medical knowledge as well as important connections among them. Demonstrating that smoking caused disease ultimately required important insights integrating clinical, epidemiological, and laboratory investigations.

As we have seen, clinical observations concerning the possible harms of cigarette use proved crucial to investigations like Ochsner's and DeBakey's, but they alone could not resolve the hypothesis they helped to generate. Physicians, healers, and other health care providers on the front lines may observe symptoms, make diagnoses, offer therapeutics, and draw conclusions about what causes disease. Often, physicians have related particular patterns of disease to the environment, noting that some environments appear to be comparatively healthy while others seem to foment disease. They have also drawn attention to the role of particular behaviors in the development of disease—including nutrition and diet, exercise, and the use of stimulants. And they have long known that individuals vary in their innate resistance to diseases. Physicians have often written up specific cases from which they drew conclusions about health and disease, and about prevention and causality.

But the difficulty of making reliable generalizations from such observations had historically been a crucial limitation of clinical knowledge. Given the well-recognized variation among patients, how could a physician be sure that other individuals would respond in similar ways to "causes"? Without rigorous statistical methods developed for epidemiological research, they could not. As Bradford Hill would explain, it was the very nature of variability that required additional modes of investigation. How else could medicine reach broad conclusions beyond the observation that every patient is indeed different? "Far, therefore, from arguing that the statistical approach is impossible in the face of human variability," he explained, "we should realize that it is because of variability that it is often essential."[67]

The epidemiologists whose work proved so central in demonstrating the harms of tobacco use drew on a deep historical legacy of exploring the causes of disease. In the centuries before the ascendance of the laboratory and the microscope, careful observations of patients, populations, and their behavior and environments, sustained by the collection and evaluation of vital statistics, had been central to understanding causality. This tradition's crucial contributions included the association between poor health and poverty studied by Edwin Chadwick in Great Britain and Lemuel Shattuck in the United States, and the remarkable efforts by John Snow and William Farr to assess the causes of epidemic cholera during the nineteenth century.[68]

The breakthroughs of the germ theory, most sharply articulated by Louis Pasteur and Robert Koch during the last decades of the nineteenth century, disrupted this approach to the investigation of disease. Their research situated the laboratory, rather than the clinic, at the top of the epistemological hierarchy of medical knowledge. Even more importantly, the identification of specific organisms as necessarily related to specific diseases radically reconfigured assumptions about the nature of disease causality. Following his discovery of the tubercle bacillus in 1882, Koch's conclusion that a specific pathogen was invariably associated with a specific infectious disease would radically reorient medical thought and practice concerning disease causality. Although the power of his postulates and their experimental elegance transformed the biological sciences, their reductionist assumptions soon became handicaps in the effort to understand other kinds of disease.[69]

As infectious diseases gave way to chronic systemic diseases like heart disease and cancer as causes of death in developed nations over the first half of the twentieth century, these handicaps grew more significant. A model that assumed a simple, straight path from cause to disease lacked sufficient explanatory power. From tracking microbes and their impact on the cellular level, investigators would now come to investigate risks and their impact on population health.[70] The investigations into the harms associated with tobacco would be crucial in this transformation of medical ways of knowing.

Such changes do not arise without conflict. Among the many appeals of laboratory experimentation was that it appeared to replace probability with something approaching "proof"—and by precisely identifying the cause of a disease, it also held out the promise of certain cure. By mid-century, with penicillin and other antibiotic drugs newly on the scene, this promise looked close to being fulfilled. Scientists who were steeped in the values of the laboratory, with deep intellectual and cultural commitments to controlled experimentation, often voiced skepticism about field investigations dependent on the collection and assessment of statistics drawn from populations. As a means of data collection, the patient interview was woefully imprecise when compared to the carefully designed experiments of the laboratory. For those in search of a "definitive" demonstrative experiment, notions of probabilistic, quantitative findings were anathema. Many researchers now pointed out, however, that much in medicine and science could not necessarily be confirmed in the laboratory. "In short," concluded statistician Jerome Cornfield of the National Institutes of Health,

> if we insist on direct experimental demonstration on humans there are many widely held beliefs that must be regarded as without solid foundation. . . . The truth of the matter appears to be that medical knowledge (and one suspects, many other kinds as well) has always advanced by a combination of many different kinds of observation, some controlled,

and some uncontrolled, some directly and some only tangentially relevant to the problems at hand. Although some methods of observation and analysis are clearly to be preferred to others when a choice is possible, there are no magical methods that invariably lead to the right answer. If we cannot specify exactly what has been learned in medicine from the study of statistical associations, we can at least say that we could not have accumulated the knowledge we have without them.[71]

Epidemiological findings like those of Doll and Hill would come under attack from scientists unilaterally committed to experimental laboratory investigation. But the lab offered no way of resolving the question of smoking's harms. Even if scientists could have decided on the most appropriate animal model for the investigation of smoking, the production of disease in animals could not perfectly replicate pathogenesis in humans. In the end, resolving the lung cancer–smoking relationship would require a new and more sophisticated understanding of the very character of medical knowledge.

Even those advocating laboratory science must have understood that such observations only could be preliminary. As British physician George White Pickering explained, "Any work which seeks to elucidate the cause of disease, the mechanism of disease, the cure of disease, or the prevention of disease, must begin and end with observations on man, whatever the intermediate steps may be."[72] In the case of smoking and lung cancer, Hill argued, the ultimate answers could never come from the laboratory:

> Yet in this particular problem what experiment can one make? We may subject mice, or other laboratory animals, to such an atmosphere of tobacco smoke that they can—like the old man in the fairy story—neither sleep nor slumber; they can neither breed nor eat. And lung cancers may or may not develop to a significant degree. What then? We may have thus strengthened the evidence, we may even have narrowed the search, but we must, I believe, invariably return to man for the final proof or proofs.[73]

Rather than seeing the multiple ways of acquiring new knowledge as being at odds, Hill viewed them as complementary. Each approach would have particular advantages depending on the particular hypothesis and the possibilities for its evaluation.

There are of course no grounds for antagonism between experiment and observation. The former, indeed, depends on observation but of a type that has the good fortune to be controlled at the experimenter's will. In the world of public health and preventive medicine each will—or should—constantly react beneficially upon the other. Observation in the field suggests experiment; the experiment leads back to more, and better defined, observation. . . . However tangled the skein of causation one must, at least at first, try to unravel it in vivo.[74]

This is what Hill's mentor, Major Greenwood, called "the permeation of statistical research with experimental spirit."[75]

Critics of the epidemiological method could not see this clearly. But there had never been, as some would later claim, a single gold standard of disease causality. That the biomedical paradigm of single cause and single disease was a chimera was well understood by even its most vigorous advocates. And medical knowledge was always provisional and contingent. Just as drugs deemed "effective" do not work in every case, so too a cause of disease does not always result in disease. As Richard Doll would later explain, the epidemiologists had identified *a* cause of lung cancer (and other diseases), not *the* cause.[76]

Some historians have suggested that modern epidemiological techniques were radically innovative and untried at the time.[77] But this underestimates their deeper historical traditions, as well as the experimental basis of much of modern epidemiological technique. Certainly, the epidemiologists understood the necessity of controlling variables and limiting opportunities for bias—but it had also been shown that there were ample opportunities for these problems to intrude in laboratory investigations.[78]

A great deal was at stake in the debates about tobacco and health in the 1950s. Epidemiologists and statisticians often pointed to the limitations of laboratory investigation for sorting out complex multiple causes of disease, even as they imported experimental techniques into their work. Physicians working in clinical settings noted that laboratory and epidemiological findings alike often failed to conform to their observations of patients and their symptoms, even as those pursuing laboratory and epidemiological investigations disparaged clinical observation as "anecdotal."

The question that troubled the entire medical community in the 1950s was what constituted adequate knowledge to act in the various realms of medicine, public health, business, and politics. No one doubted that it would be valuable to understand the most basic mechanisms of carcinogenesis. But neither would anyone in public health or medicine presume that all knowledge short of defining those mechanisms was inadequate or suspect. Medical and public health interventions had often been pursued with great benefit before causal mechanisms were known. John Snow's heroic studies of cholera never identified the underlying organism, yet brought fundamental changes in urban infrastructure. The history of medicine is filled with examples of partial knowledge being used to reduce disease. Unlike some other domains of knowledge, the pragmatic demands of human health place a clock on investigation. The cost of acting must be balanced against the cost of not acting.

The development of systematic knowledge about the harms of cigarette use illuminates the complex character of medical science in the mid-twentieth century. Typically, the debate about cigarettes and lung cancer is portrayed as a battle between laboratory and statistical science. But this is largely a particular historical construction offered by some of the protagonists in the debate, most notably the tobacco industry. It is an example of how powerful economic and industrial interests would deploy their resources to influence, delay, and disrupt normative scientific processes.

§

By the mid-1950s, clinicians and researchers were largely convinced of the connection between cigarettes and cancer. In early 1955, the chair of the pathology department at the University of Michigan, Carl Weller, offered a comprehensive assessment of the evidence. As someone whose work depended on the visualization of disease-related changes in cell and tissue, Weller, like many pathologists, had previously been highly skeptical that smoking was a cause of lung cancer. "I early subscribed to the then prevailing opinion that protoplasm was relatively stable and the chromosomes particularly so," he explained in his book, *Causal Factors in Cancers of the Lung*. Most pathologists had tended to accept the notion that rates of cancer, including lung cancer, varied little over time. "The rate of the incidence of cancer in any organ was considered to be a fairly constant function," he wrote, "not readily influenced by environment, although numerous occupational carcinomas of the skin had been demonstrated." Weller therefore concluded that the reports of rising rates of lung cancer were probably spurious. "I joined others in attempting to explain it by the aging of the population, by the advent of radiography, by clinical awareness, and by better diagnostic methods in general." Ultimately, however, "these explanations proved inadequate and it was necessary to admit that some recently acquired feature of our way of life was very rapidly changing the incidence of pulmonary cancer."[79] The increase of the disease was real.

Weller undertook a systematic review of all the studies to date as well as the criticisms. In *Causal Factors in Cancers of the Lung* he described his shift of perspective. "I have searched the literature for other reasonable explanations or for recognizable fallacies. I have found none of importance." He concluded: "As of today, I must agree with many of the specialists in statistical analysis and in the endemiology of cancer, that this association has been established."[80] Weller understood the significance of this conclusion: it was now incumbent upon the medical profession to address the problem of smoking. "What is the next step?" he asked. "When will it be not only proper but requisite that the medical profession take cognizance?" Citing the long delay between English surgeon Percivall Pott's recognition of the high rates of scrotal cancers among chimney sweeps and the eventual identification of carcinogens in soot, Weller urged immediate action. "May we show the same practical sense as our forefathers," he wrote, "and not look for direct proofs which are out of reach before we transmit experience into practical measures."[81]

As physicians and scientists critically assessed what by now amounted to dozens of reports, they typically arrived at similar positions. The medical and scientific director of the American Cancer Society, Charles Cameron, followed the same path as Weller. The ACS presented itself as a voluntary health agency dedicated to funding research and public education regarding cancer prevention and treatment, and since the 1930s it had emphasized education to encourage early diagnosis and treatment. This agenda, based on highly touted medical technology, such as X-rays and surgery, had received strong support from both the medical profession and powerful donors. For ACS executives like Cameron, the findings about tobacco came as a mixed blessing. On one hand, it was valuable to know that smoking might lead to cancer. On the other hand, the news demanded a significant reorientation of the agency's strategy and put it in the center of a potentially vicious contest between business and public health. Most importantly, the ACS did not want to take any position that might be deemed as usurping physicians' professional prerogatives.

In early 1952, for example, Cameron invited Evarts Graham to write an article on lung cancer for a book to be published by the ACS for the lay public. Graham accepted and, not surprisingly, emphasized the causal relationship between smoking and disease. Cameron wrote to request revisions in the manuscript:

> Could I ask you to redo this piece with emphasis on the need for frequent X-ray examinations of the chest. . . . I really think this would be of greater value than the emphasis on smoking which is the theme of the present article. I have no objection, of course, to your mentioning it but feel that the space given it should be decreased in favor of references to early diagnosis.[82]

Yet a few years later, Cameron had become convinced that smoking constituted a major cause of cancer, and he brought the ACS along with him. In 1956, in an article for the *Atlantic Monthly* entitled "Lung Cancer and Smoking: What We Really Know," he wrote:

> Although the complicity of the cigarette in the present prevalence of cancer of the lung has not been proved to the satisfaction of everyone, yet the weight of the evidence against it is so serious as to demand of stewards of the public welfare that they make the evidence known to all. . . . There is in some quarters an unbecoming skepticism of statistics in general and of these remarkably consistent results in particular. By some—a diminishing band, as I see it—the findings are rejected because there is not "laboratory proof."[83]

But this standard, Cameron argued, was both unrealistic and unprecedented. "What is the nature of the proof which is demanded to establish the cancer-causing effect of cigarette smoking? If it is that smoke or another tobacco product must be shown to cause cancer of the lung under conditions of experimental control using living human subjects, then I hope the experiment will never be undertaken. No standards of proof in the entire world of research demand as much as that."

While still not prepared to "hold that smoking causes cancer of the lung," Cameron nonetheless joined the growing medical consensus, concluding: "If the degree of association which has been established between cancer of the lung and smoking were shown to exist between cancer of the lung and say, eating spinach, no one would raise a hand against the proscription of spinach in the national diet."[84] The time had now arrived, he wrote, to act on this knowledge.

By the mid-1950s, other astute observers of clinical medicine had come to agree. Assessing the evidence in September 1953, Joseph Garland, editor of the *New England Journal of Medicine,* noted that the most recent Doll and Hill publication (their prospective study) "yielded evidence of an association between cigarette smoking and lung cancer so strong as to be considered proof within the everyday meaning of the word." Garland continued, "If similar data had incriminated a food contaminant that was not habit forming and was not supported by the advertising of a financial empire, there is little doubt that effective counter measures would have followed quickly." He concluded, "The situation affords unusual opportunities for the vast tobacco interests to support impartial researches into the effects that their products may have on human health." Leading figures in medical science now argued that the evidence was clear, convincing, and scientifically persuasive, and that physicians and public health officials had a responsibility to warn their patients and the public. They reasoned that medical knowledge incorporates social responsibility and that the findings about lung cancer and smoking had reached a level of significance and certainty that triggered these professional commitments.

Many physicians, as they came to know and accept these findings, began to quit smoking. According to a study done in Massachusetts, nearly 52 percent of physicians reported being regular smokers in 1954, with over 30 percent smoking at least a pack a day. Just five years later, only 39 percent were regular smokers, and only 18 percent went through a pack or more per day.[85] Evarts Graham attributed much of the remaining skepticism to the fact that many in the medical profession were smokers themselves. "Unfortunately," he wrote in 1954,

> it has not been universally accepted and there are still many cigarette addicts among the medical profession who demand absolute proof. . . . The obstinacy of many of them in refusing to accept the existing evidence

compels me to conclude that it is their own addiction to this drug habit which blinds them. They have eyes to see but they see not because of their unwillingness or inability to give up smoking. . . . I have never encountered any non-smoker who makes light of the evidence or is skeptical of the association between excessive smoking and lung cancer.[86]

It is important to recognize just how popular smoking was at mid-century. The findings implicating smoking as a cause of disease and death were an indictment of an enormously popular behavior, difficult to moderate. This, Graham argued, constituted an important and powerful bias in the evaluation of the data.

Survey research conducted by the ACS confirmed Graham's perspective. Physicians who were heavy smokers were among the most skeptical of the research findings linking tobacco use to lung cancer. In 1955, Cameron, Horn, and David Kipnis surveyed members of the American Board of Thoracic Surgery, the American Board of Pathology, and the American Association for Cancer Research. Among those polled, 55 percent agreed with the statement that heavy smoking may lead to lung cancer; 32 percent expressed uncertainty; while only 5 percent disagreed. But among those surveyed who smoked a pack or more each day, only 31 percent agreed that "Heavy smoking may lead to lung cancer." Among nonsmokers, the figure was more than 65 percent.[87]

Faced with his own research findings, Graham had quit smoking, so he well understood the difficulty of withdrawing from nicotine. But his five decades of exposure to tobacco smoke would now confirm in the most personal and intimate way what his and Wynder's research had so clearly demonstrated. In 1957, he wrote to his friend and colleague Alton Ochsner, "Perhaps you have heard that I have recently been a patient in the Barnes Hospital because of a bilateral bronchiogenic carcinoma which sneaked up on me like a thief in the night."[88] Ochsner, deeply shaken by the news, wrote back, "Thank you for your letter . . . which simply crushed me. It is a perfectly horrible thing to think that you have bronchiogenic carcinoma, a condition for which you have done so much."[89] Two weeks later, Graham died, a victim of the very disease that had been the center of his professional life. In the end, he became yet one more data point in the lethal history of smoking.

As a result of several statistical surveys, the idea has arisen that there is a causal relationship between ZEPHYR and tobacco smoking, particularly cigarette smoking. Various hypotheses have been propounded, from time to time, as explanations of this conception. The two which seem most important at the present time are:

(i) Tobacco smoke contains a substance or substances which may cause ZEPHYR

(ii) Substances which can cause ZEPHYR are inhaled from the atmosphere, e.g. in the form of soot.[1]

BRITISH AMERICAN TOBACCO, 1957

I just don't believe it. People are hearing the same old story, and the record is getting scratched.[2]

BOWMAN GRAY, JR., 1960
CEO, R.J. REYNOLDS

Members of the Research Department have studied in detail cigarette smoke composition. Some of these findings have been published. However, much data remains unpublished because they are concerned with carcinogens and carcinogenic compounds. This raises an interesting question about the former compounds. If a tobacco company pled "Not guilty" or "Not proven" to the charge that cigarette smoke (or one of its constituents) is an etiological factor in the causation of lung cancer or some other disease, can the company justifiably assume the position that publication of data . . . should be withheld because such data might affect adversely the company's economic status when the company has already implied in its plea that no such etiologic effect exists?[3]

ALAN RODGMAN, 1962
RESEARCH SCIENTIST, R.J. REYNOLDS

CHAPTER 6

Constructing Controversy

THE IDENTIFICATION OF cigarette smoking as a cause of
serious disease shook the tobacco industry to its core. For decades,
tobacco companies had developed strategies for dealing with concerns about the health impact of smoking. From ads promising mildness to
claims like "More Doctors Smoke Camels," the companies had repeatedly
sought to calm smokers' medical anxieties. Such competitive claims were
yet another vehicle to promote individual brands.

By the early 1950s, however, it was abundantly clear that the evidence
implicating cigarette smoking as a risk to health was now of a different
order. First, the link between smoking and disease was categorical, outside
the realm of individual clinical judgment. Although physicians might advise individual smokers to "cut down," no one could offer assurance that
any level of smoking was safe. Second, the cigarette was tied to the most
feared disease of mid-century: cancer.[4] Earlier concerns about cough or
scratchy throat gave way to the ominous medical data indicating that the
"habit" could kill. No major industry had ever faced such a fundamental
threat to its future.

In this unprecedented crisis, the company executives came to recognize that traditional approaches to promotion and marketing had to
change radically. The new scientific evidence would require a collective
response if the industry was to survive. Unsubstantiated health claims
proffered for individual brands would merely call attention to the problems with the cigarette, and they were sure to draw intense medical and

scientific scrutiny if not regulatory intervention. In the early 1950s, despite decades of concerns about the health impacts of smoking, the industry possessed almost no internal capacity to assess the new scientific evidence. The research departments in each company were focused on product design and modification—small changes to enhance "mildness" or vary taste. Having brilliantly mastered the meaning and character of their product for more than half a century, the tobacco companies found that they had begun to lose control of the very cultural processes that they had so effectively utilized in creating the modern cigarette. Try though it might—often with some considerable success—the tobacco industry would never again unequivocally control the meaning of the cigarette. The scientific findings of the 1950s constituted a sea change in the history of smoking. Industry executives found themselves in uncharted waters, and the boat was leaking.

They responded with a new and unprecedented public relations strategy. Its goal was to produce and sustain scientific skepticism and controversy in order to disrupt the emerging consensus on the harms of cigarette smoking. This strategy required intrusions into scientific process and procedure.[5] The production of uncertainty in the face of the developing scientific knowledge required resources and skill. The industry worked to assure that vigorous debate would be prominently trumpeted in the public media. So long as there appeared to be doubt, so long as the industry could assert "not proven," smokers would have a crucial rationale to continue, and new smokers would have a rationale to begin. Equally important, the industry would have cover to resist regulation of its product and the basis of a defense against new legal liabilities. The future of the cigarette would now depend on the successful production of a scientific controversy.

Reports in the medical literature rarely drew public notice, but given the huge popularity of cigarette smoking—which had grown by 1950 to some 2,500 cigarettes per person each year—journalists now reported the results of the new studies to an increasingly anxious public. One article, in particular, by journalist Roy Norr, touched off widespread concern.[6] Appearing first in the *Christian Herald* in October 1952, the article translated the Wynder and Graham findings into ominous layperson prose, noting that "what gives grave concern to public health leaders is that the increase in lung cancer mortality shows a suspicious parallel to the enormous increase in cigarette consumption."[7] The piece drew little attention until it was reprinted two months later in *Reader's Digest*, the most widely circulated periodical at the time, under the title "Cancer by the Carton."

Other prominent magazines and newspapers followed with related scientific findings. *Time* reported on the Wynder, Graham, and Croninger mouse-painting studies in an article entitled "Beyond Any Doubt" in November 1953. The article quoted Graham as saying that the experiments "show conclusively" that a substance in cigarette smoke could produce cancer. "This is no longer merely a possibility," Graham concluded. "Our experiments have proved it beyond any doubt." *Time* noted that rates of lung cancer in the United States had quadrupled for men and doubled for women since 1933.

Following this spate of publicity, the nature and meaning of cigarette smoking, so carefully constructed over the last half-century, would never be the same. After decades of successfully manipulating the media regarding the cigarette, the industry now found that it had lost its mastery of the public perception of its product. The wide coverage of successive medical findings generated intense pressure for the industry to respond. Alton Ochsner told *Time:*

> If the tobacco people are smart—as I am sure they are because they have been enormously successful—they will support research to find out what the cancer-producing substance is, and then take steps to remove it.

Graham concurred, noting, "It is certainly the moral obligation and common sense on the part of the manufacturers to support research."[8]

In late 1953, the tobacco industry began to draw its wagons together. As the evidence of the harms of smoking accrued, the tobacco industry first attempted to continue its aggressive and reassuring marketing.[9] One approach was to simply deny the problem. The entertainer Arthur Godfrey— who promoted Chesterfields on television—touted studies that he claimed exonerated Chesterfields from the rising health concerns. In early 1953,

Godfrey announced during his weekly variety show, "I smoke two or three packs of these things every day. I feel pretty good. I don't know, I never did believe they did any harm, and now, we've got the proof." Godfrey went on to explain the Liggett & Myers research program:

> This doctor and specialist and some of his assistants, have been conducting experiments for 8 months, and they—people had been smoking Chesterfields for 10 years, some of 'em, and they smoked Chesterfields and nothing but Chesterfields for the last 8 months—it's a little more than that now, and they have discovered that to date, he can't find any adverse effects in the nose, the sinus, the ears or throat, or wherever else you smoke 'em.[10]

R.J. Reynolds ran similar campaigns, urging smokers to take a thirty-day test for Camels' mildness. In the July 1949 issues of several local and national medical journals, Reynolds ran an ad asking "How mild can a cigarette be?" In answering this question, the ad juxtaposed a "Doctors Report" illustrated with a physician, cigarette in hand and head-mirror strapped around his brow, and a "Smokers Report," illustrated with smiling Sylvia MacNeill, secretary. Physicians, the ad explained, had concluded after scientific investigation that there was "not one single case of throat irritation" from smoking Camel cigarettes. "Noted throat specialists" had conducted "weekly examinations" of patients in making this determination.[11]

The ad went beyond medical authority, however, to assert that smokers didn't even have to take their physicians' word for it. They could take their "own personal 30-day test," as Sylvia MacNeill had done. She concluded that she "knew" that "Camels are the mildest, best-tasting cigarette I ever smoked." Ads in popular magazines took this theme even further; for example, Elana O'Brian, real estate broker, gushed that "I don't need my doctor's report to know Camels are mild." The ad showed six other smokers, from various walks of life, under the heading "thousands more agree!"[12] In another example, Anne Jeffreys, a stage and screen star, insisted, "The test was fun and it was *sensible!*" Still other ads called on Camel smokers to "*Prove it yourself!*" and even offered a money-back guarantee for dissatisfied customers.[13] These ads attempted to subvert the emerging population-based epidemiologic findings by appealing to smokers' individual judgment.

But in the face of those findings, such claims were now seen as drawing attention to the problem—in particular, the attention of government and consumer agencies. In February 1953, the national Better Business Bureau wrote to Liggett & Myers:

> Although cigarette advertising, as such, has been widely and justly criticized in recent years, we believe that your current advertising represents a particularly flagrant disregard of the public interest. Your advertising will not only deceive some members of the public to the detriment of their health but it will, in addition, tend to impair the integrity of advertising and lessen public confidence in it. . . . Godfrey's free translations of the carefully worded copy theme clearly assure any listener that smoking Chesterfields is harmless. If one as close to the advertiser could draw such inferences from the copy theme, it is apparent that others may likewise be misled.[14]

Despite these critiques, Chesterfield and Camel ads (as well as others) continued during these years to attempt to quiet rising public concerns about the health impact of smoking. Decades later, the health warranties clearly implied in these ads would come back to haunt the industry in litigation. Cigarette apologist Arthur Godfrey died of emphysema in 1983, after surviving removal of the cancerous part of a lung in 1959.[15]

§

The pressure on company executives to respond rose with each new public report. Would the industry rely on its extensive advertising and public relations expertise, or would the companies collaborate and participate in the ongoing scientific assessments? Recognizing that bold claims for specific brands would not resolve the crisis and might in fact heighten popular concerns, the industry began to explore other options. In particular, it was becoming clear that it required a strategy for addressing the new peer-reviewed medical findings appearing in important medical journals. The crisis revealed the severe limitations of the companies' own research programs. Many researchers now advocated that the industry give funds to the National Research Council, the American Cancer Society, or the National Cancer Institute to investigate—intensively and independently—the relationship of smoking to disease. Ultimately, it was argued, the industry would need a detailed knowledge of the problems with the product if they were to be fixed.

The tobacco company CEOs tended at first to view the new findings as "attacks" by a small group of misguided researchers. As studies were reported in the popular press, they felt compelled to come to the defense of their product and the integrity of their companies. In November 1953, American Tobacco President Paul Hahn took the offensive against "loose talk" about the now widely reported scientific findings. In a press release issued by the company, he wrote that "with all the research being conducted in the field, no one has yet proved that lung cancer in any human being is directly traceable to tobacco or to its products in any form." He noted that American Tobacco was supporting independent scientific research (through the Damon Runyon Fund of the ACS), and concluded that "we are confident that long-range, impartial investigation and other objective research will confirm the view that neither tobacco nor its products contribute to the incidence of lung cancer."[16]

There was no scientific basis for such optimism, nor had the companies conducted research into the question. To the contrary, emerging independent research now cast an ominous shadow over the cigarette's future. Hahn nevertheless understood the need to respond to public fears. He explained:

> Believing as we do that cigarette smoking is not injurious to health, I feel that a statement of reassurance to the public should be made. What the public wants to know about is whether it is true that smoking has been proved to contribute to the incidence of lung cancer. The fact, of course, is that it has not been so proved.[17]

As Hahn's statement made clear, "proof" and how it was constituted became the critical issue. The industry would soon make explicit its approach to seizing the ambiguities in this question.

Hahn realized that such statements of reassurance—denying that cigarettes were harmful—would have little value if there was not a full-scale, industry-wide commitment to addressing the rising tide of medical and public concern about its product. The new findings demanded a new strategy of collaboration. Common interests now displaced the tobacco companies' long history of rivalry. If any company sought to use health concerns against a competitor, the entire industry could descend in a downward spiral. He therefore called for an unprecedented meeting of the CEOs of the major companies to develop a unified public relations strategy in response to the new scientific evidence implicating cigarette use as a cause of cancer. When the executives met together at the Plaza Hotel on December 14, 1953, in New York City, it marked the first time since 1939 that the group had come together.[18] Concerns that working together would invite another antitrust investigation following their 1941 conviction for price-fixing were now overwhelmed by the mounting crisis over the emerging scientific findings.

§

T. V. Hartnett, president of Brown & Williamson, summarized the problem in an internal memorandum following the initial meeting. "Excessive care," he warned, "must be used at this time in the methods we use to counteract these claims. . . . The problem is to challenge these findings ethically and effectively without rancor—to win friends rather than create enemies." Hartnett went on to outline the two approaches that would dominate the industry's strategy:

> Cancer research, while certainly getting our every support, can be *only half an answer.* . . . The other side of the coin is *public relations.* . . . [which] is basically a selling tool and the most astute selling may well be needed to get the industry out of this hole. It isn't exaggeration that no public relations expert has ever been handed so real and yet so *delicate* a multi-million dollar problem. . . . Finally, one of the roughest hurdles which must be anticipated is how to handle significantly negative research results, if, as, and when they develop.[19]

The next day, representatives of the tobacco companies met with John W. Hill, president of the public relations firm Hill & Knowlton. Hill had already had a series of talks with tobacco executives and had started his staff on evaluating strategies for addressing what all agreed was a monumental public relations crisis. The industry executives now agreed to retain Hill & Knowlton to help shape their response.[20]

By the time Hill & Knowlton took on the tobacco industry in 1953, it was already the most influential public relations firm in the United States, with a client list that included the steel, oil, and aircraft industries. John W. Hill had cultivated close relationships with executives in these fields since the 1930s. And his firm had also worked with the liquor and chemical industries, areas where the health risks of products had emerged as issues in the past. He shared his clients' strong opposition to government intrusion into business. "The role of public relations in the opinion forming process is to communicate information and viewpoints on behalf of causes and organizations," Hill later wrote. "The objective is to inform public opinion and win its favor."[21] He had quit smoking in the early 1940s for health reasons, but such concerns would not affect his work on behalf of his tobacco clients.[22] For Hill, the tobacco industry had a public relations problem that his firm could effectively manage.

The tobacco industry had successfully used public relations since the 1920s to shape the meanings and cultural contexts of tobacco use. It was not surprising that in a moment of crisis, the industry would again deploy public relations as the antidote. But now these techniques were used not to change mores and social convention, but to distort and deny important scientific data. In the winter of 1953–54, the industry crossed a legal and moral line by entangling itself in the manipulation of fundamental scientific processes. There would be no easy route back to legitimacy.

Hill immediately recognized that the principal public relations approach of the industry would require strict collaborative action. Even as the companies continued to vie for market share among their respective brands, it was imperative that their in-house public relations offices present a united front in the critical domain of health and science. Hill & Knowlton's operatives expressed particular skepticism about the role of advertising in addressing the industry's crisis. "Some bright boy from Madison Avenue," one staffer noted, could "spoil the confidence building."[23] Hill's skepticism concerning advertising reflected two central insights. The public confidence the industry sought could not be achieved through advertising, which was self-interested by definition. Second, it would be crucial for the industry to assert its authority over the scientific domain; science had the distinct advantage of its reputation for *disinterestedness*.[24]

Hill's work for the industry marked the most significant public relations interventions on its behalf since those of Edward Bernays. The two men shared a skepticism about the role of advertising in influencing the public perceptions of tobacco. To those deeply schooled in public relations, advertising ran the risk of exposing corporate self-interest. Good public relations relied on the scrupulous behind-the-scenes management of media. As Bernays had demonstrated in the 1920s and 1930s, the best PR work left no fingerprints.

Hill and his colleagues set to work to review a full range of approaches open to them. Dismissing as shortsighted the idea of mounting personal attacks on researchers or simply issuing blanket assurances of safety, they concluded instead that seizing control of the science of tobacco and health would be as important as seizing control of the media. It would be crucial to identify scientists who expressed skepticism about the link between cigarettes and cancer, those critical of statistical methods, and especially those who had offered alternative hypotheses for the cause of cancer. Hill set his staff to identifying the most vocal and visible skeptics. These people would be central to the development of an industry scientific program in step with its larger public relations goals. Hill understood that simply *denying* the harms of smoking would alienate the public. His strategy for ending the "hysteria" was to insist that there were "two sides." Just as Bernays had worked to engineer consent, so Hill would engineer "controversy." This strategy—invented by Hill in the context of his work for the tobacco industry—would ultimately become the cornerstone of a large range of efforts to distort scientific process in the second half of the twentieth century.

Individual tobacco companies had sought to compile information that cast doubt on the smoking–cancer connection even before Hill & Knowlton got involved. A. Grant Clarke, an Esty advertising employee on loan to R.J. Reynolds, announced to other industry executives in November 1953 that the company had formed a "Bureau of Scientific Information" to "combat the propaganda which is being directed at the tobacco industry."[25] At the same time, American Tobacco began to collect the public statements of scientists who had expressed skepticism about the research findings indicting tobacco. The company's public relations counsel, Tommy Ross, understood that it would be critical to create questions about the reliability of the new findings and to attack the notion that these studies constituted "proof" of the relationship of smoking to cancer.[26] The resulting "White Paper" was a compendium of statements by physicians and scientists who questioned the cigarette–lung cancer link. When Hill & Knowlton started to shape and implement its PR strategy, the White Paper became fundamental to those efforts.

Following the December 15 meeting that formally brought Hill & Knowlton into the picture, its executives spent the next two weeks meeting with various industry staff. During this time, Hill & Knowlton operated in full crisis mode. Executives and staff cancelled all holiday plans as they worked to frame and implement a full-scale campaign on behalf of the industry.[27] They apparently made no independent attempt to assess the state of medical knowledge; nor did they seek informed evaluations from independent scientists. Their role was limited to serving the public relations goal of their client.

During these meetings, both Hill & Knowlton staffers and tobacco executives continued to voice the conviction that the industry's entire future was threatened by the medical and scientific findings linking cigarette smoking to lung cancer and the consequent widespread public anxieties about smoking and health. "Because of the serious nature of the attack on cigarettes and the vast publicity given them in the daily press and in magazines of the widest circulation, a hysteria of fear appears to be developing throughout the country," Hill wrote in an internal memo. "There is no evidence that this adverse publicity is abating or will soon abate." According to his media intelligence, at least four additional major periodicals (*Look Magazine*, *Cosmopolitan*, *Woman's Home Companion*, and *Pageant*) were currently planning articles on smoking and health.[28]

It was apparently Hill who hit on the idea of creating an industry-sponsored research entity. Ultimately, he concluded, the best public relations approach was for the industry to become a major sponsor of medical research. This tactic offered several crucial advantages. The call for new research implied that existing studies were inadequate or flawed. It made clear there was "more to know," and it made the industry seem a committed participant in the scientific enterprise rather than a detractor. The industry had, as noted, supported some individual research in recent years, but Hill's proposal offered the potential of a research program that would both be *controlled* by the industry yet promoted as *independent.* This was a public relations masterstroke. Hill understood that simply giving money to scientists offered little opportunity to shape the public relations environment. The very nature of controlling and managing information in public relations stood in marked contrast to the scientific notion of unfettered new knowledge. Hill and his clients had no interest in answering a scientific question; their goal was to maintain vigorous control over the research program, to utilize "science" in the service of public relations. After tobacco executives proposed forming a "Cigarette Information Committee" dedicated to defending smoking against the medical findings, Hill argued aggressively for adding research to the committee's title and agenda. "It is believed," he wrote, "that the word 'Research' is needed in the name to give weight and added credence to the Committee's statements." Hill understood that his clients should be viewed as "embracing" science rather than dismissing it.

Hill also advised the industry that continued competitive assertions about the health benefits of particular brands would be devastating. Instead, the industry needed a collective research initiative to demonstrate its shared concern for the public. Rather than using health research to create competitive products as they had been doing, the companies needed to express—above all else—their commitment to public well-being. Hill believed that the competitive fervor over health claims had harmed the industry's credibility. No one would look for serious information about health from an industry that was making unsubstantiated claims about its product.

The future of the industry would reflect its acceptance of this essential principle. From December 1953 forward, the tobacco companies would present a unified front on smoking and health; more than five decades of strategic and explicit collusion would follow.[29] The industry pursued its strategy despite worries about recurring antitrust claims. Although its lawyers would later claim that the government was informed of and approved the Plaza Hotel meeting on December 14, it is worth noting that U.S. Assistant Attorney General Stanley Barnes advised that the industry support independent research by a third party. As Hill & Knowlton operative Carl

Thompson explained, Judge Barnes told him that an independent approach "might be smarter," both "to eliminate the question of getting involved in anti-trust difficulties" and "to lend authenticity to the case."[30] But the need to control the scientific message took precedence. By the time Thompson spoke to Barnes, the companies were already fully committed to the establishment of the Tobacco Industry Research Committee, an organization that would be shaped by Hill & Knowlton to serve the industry's collective interests.

Hill carefully outlined the plans for a research program before a single scientist was consulted. The utility of such a strategy was its apparent commitment to "objective" science and its search for the "truth." As Carl Thompson argued, "A flamboyant campaign against the anti-smoking propagandists would unquestionably alienate much of the support of the moderates in both scientific and lay publics." [31] Instead, tobacco companies had to respect the moral valence of science in American culture at mid-century. If science now threatened the industry, the industry must "secure" science.

The companies' first public action, under the direction of Hill & Knowlton, was to produce a public statement of their collective intentions. In the last weeks of 1953, Hill & Knowlton drafted "A Frank Statement to Cigarette Smokers" that sought to establish the industry as reliable, responsible, and fully committed to the public's interest. The "Frank Statement," as it would come to be known, brilliantly represented Hill's essential strategy. It announced:

> We accept an interest in people's health as a basic responsibility, paramount to every other consideration in our business.
> We believe the products we make are not injurious to health.
> We always have and always will cooperate closely with those whose task it is to safeguard the public health.[32]

The Frank Statement was a triumph of modern PR. It reassured smokers by promising them that the industry was absolutely committed to their good health.

The statement went on to announce the creation of the collaborative research entity, the Tobacco Industry Research Committee (TIRC):

We are pledging aid and assistance to the research effort into all phases of tobacco use and health. This joint financial aid will of course be in addition to what is already being contributed by individual companies.[33]

Such reassurances became characteristic even as the scientific evidence indicting cigarettes grew in strength, sophistication, and professional acceptance. The Frank Statement represented the industry as serious, authoritative, and judicious—committed without exception to the public's well-being. If there is a problem, it implied, the cigarette manufacturers would solve it, expeditiously and scientifically. The industry had seized the controversy and made it its own. In retrospect, it is especially impressive that less than three weeks after the initial Plaza Hotel meetings, Hill & Knowlton had not only devised a major new strategic approach, but announced it to the media. Signed by the top executives from the major tobacco manufacturers (except for Liggett & Myers), several smaller companies, and growers, the Frank Statement appeared on January 4, 1954, as an advertisement in 448 newspapers in 258 cities. This advertisement and the establishment of the TIRC, the industry hoped, would calm the crisis. Hill & Knowlton executive E. C. Read urged restraint in the days following the announcement, noting that there was "far more danger of fanning the flames by making too many statements. . . . Now that one good statement is out from the committee, I believe the controversy should be given every chance to die a natural death."[34]

The Frank Statement depicted an enlightened industry eager to fulfill its responsibilities to its patrons and the public. With obvious satisfaction, Hill & Knowlton staffers noted that editorials embraced the industry line as presented in the announcement. Through the meticulous interventions of Hill & Knowlton with editors, writers, and scientists, the Frank Statement received broad support in the public media. The *Cleveland News* saw the industry as "wisely answering the challenge of medicine" and exclaimed: "Good for the industry!"[35] Leslie Gould in the *New York Journal-American* opined that "The tobacco industry has taken a proper step in finding out if there is any truth or not in the recent scares about cigarette smoking and lung cancer."[36] And the *Jersey Journal* called the formation of the TIRC "a brave approach to a fundamental problem . . . with a keen sense of public service as well."[37]

If the tobacco companies had but followed their own explicit commitments, the history of the cigarette might be distinctly different. But at the moment the Frank Statement was released, the industry had yet to take even the first step toward creating a research program.

§
3

Many of the researchers who had spent the last years demonstrating the harms of smoking now anticipated that the companies would seriously invest in scientific research. John Hill understood that nothing would quiet the immediate storm like the notion of the need for *more* research—and the availability of new funding. Even as the findings mounted, Hill realized that the very culture of the scientific community compelled it to focus on the limitations of the research and the remaining uncertainties. The fact that science valued knowledge and honored skepticism opened a critical space for this campaign strategy.

Some researchers were receptive to industry funding of their work. In late 1953, Ernst Wynder continued to hope that the industry might support independent tobacco research through programs, such as the Damon Runyon Fund.[38] Others, including Evarts Graham, Wynder's senior collaborator, doubted that the tobacco companies would provide funds for truly independent research; Graham cautioned Wynder on the matter, insisting "we must preserve our independence" and emphasizing "I should not like to enter into any agreement with any tobacco company to carry out research that might be colored a little by financial contribution."[39] Following the public announcement of the TIRC, Ochsner wrote to Graham. "Have any of the tobacco people offered to finance some of your research?" he asked. "I am in hope that they might finance some of ours, but I am afraid they will not, because I think they are accusing us of being prejudiced."[40] Ochsner naively believed that the TIRC might develop a program to explicitly address the health risks of smoking.

But the TIRC, from its inception, was dominated by its public relations goals. Ochsner's hopes for funding support faded as the TIRC's research agenda quickly became clear. "Of course, the critical areas of investigation, as every research scientist knows, have to do with the problem of how to make smoking a less lethal agent in lung cancer incidence and a less deadly killer in heart disease," he noted. "Yet it is precisely these areas that apparently have been declared out of bounds for the industry's research committee."[41] Industry assessments confirm Ochsner's view. As one internal industry evaluation would conclude a decade later, "most of the TIRC research has been of a broad, basic nature not designed to specifically test the anti-cigarette theory."[42] From the outset, Hill & Knowlton exerted extensive influence over the industry's collaborative research program. The TIRC administrative offices were even located at Hill & Knowlton.

W. T. Hoyt, executive director of the TIRC, came to the position with no scientific experience whatsoever. Before joining Hill & Knowlton, he sold advertising for the *Saturday Evening Post*. At Hill & Knowlton, where he began work in 1951, he had run the Scrap Mobilization Committee for the Iron and Steel Industry. Now in early 1954, he assumed a dominant role in the day-to-day operations of the tobacco industry research program. Carl Thompson described how the PR firm had "loaned" Hoyt to the tobacco industry because he was "a proved administrator and organizer."[43] Ultimately, Hoyt would become a full-time employee, remaining integral to the TIRC until he retired in 1984.[44]

Tobacco company leaders also played important roles in the organization. In the early months of operation, Paul Hahn of American Tobacco and Parker McComas of Philip Morris served as its acting chairs. The first full-time chairman of TIRC was Timothy Hartnett, the retired CEO of Brown & Williamson. The press release announcing his appointment explained:

> It is an obligation of the Tobacco Industry Research Committee at this time to remind the public of these essential points:
>
> 1. There is no conclusive scientific proof of a link between smoking and cancer.
>
> 2. Medical research points to many possible causes of cancer . . . .
>
> 5. The millions of people who derive pleasure and satisfaction from smoking can be reassured that every scientific means will be used to get all the facts as soon as possible.[45]

Hartnett and his successors would reiterate this message for the next forty years.

Hill & Knowlton executives and industry scientists also carried out the search for the scientific director of the TIRC. They carefully sought out a leader who was skeptical of the emerging medical consensus. A three-man Industrial Technical Committee—H. R. Hanmer, research director at American Tobacco; Irwin Tucker, director of research at Brown & Williamson; and A. Grant Clarke, a William Esty advertising executive and director of the Medical Relations Division at R.J. Reynolds—followed an ambitious itinerary in search of a leader. Not just anyone could fill such an important and complex position.

As this threesome made their rounds conducting interviews, they paid especially close attention to the candidates' smoking habits. Leon Jacobson, they noted, "is a heavy smoker." He was ultimately invited to join the Scientific Advisory Board (SAB). Lawrence Kimpton, chancellor at the University of Chicago, also smoked. Lowell Coggeshall, the dean of the Division of Biological Sciences at Chicago, they observed with some disappointment, did not. Coggeshall advocated giving the funds to an independent organization, a suggestion heard from many. After interviewing Clayton Loosli, who explained he had lost his taste for tobacco, Hanmer explained, "We gathered the impression . . . that he thinks there is a definite connection between smoking and lung cancer, based on the statistical association which has been established." The search committee concluded that they "did not feel that Dr. Loosli was acceptable."[46] Dr. R. Harrison Rigdon, pathologist from University of Texas Medical Branch, advised the group "to shift the burden of guilt to smog, smoke, and automobile exhaust and other forms of air pollution," a strategy that had already been widely noted by the Hill & Knowlton crew.[47]

Finding a scientist of stature willing to serve as scientific director proved no easy task. In a culture that prized independence and autonomy, taking a high-salaried job with an industry-supported research entity was viewed with suspicion. Most of the candidates insisted they could be considered only if they could maintain their current academic affiliations. Such an arrangement was fine with Hill & Knowlton, which remained eager to oversee the day-to-day operations of the Tobacco Industry Research Committee.

After failing to recruit three distinguished scientists, including Harold Stewart (the NCI's chief pathologist) and McKeen Cattell (head of pharmacology at Cornell University), the industry decided to construct the

SAB first, offering positions to nine scientists (seven accepted).[48] They then offered the position of scientific director of the TIRC to biologist Clarence Cook Little, who had already agreed in early 1954 to serve on the SAB and had been elected its chair.[49] In this appointment, Hill and his clients found precisely what they hoped for: the ultimate skeptic concerning the harms of smoking. As one Hill & Knowlton operative noted, "Little filled the bill perfectly."[50] He now emerged as the industry's leading spokesman on the science of tobacco and health, a position he would hold for the next two decades. Gregarious, charming, combative, and arrogant, he was a seasoned fund-raiser and much-sought public speaker. His view of the relationship between smoking and disease would never change: there was "no proof" that smoking caused lung cancer or, for that matter, any other health problems.

By the time Little joined the TIRC in early 1954, he had already publicly declared his skepticism concerning the link between smoking and cancer. "If smoke in the lungs were a sure-fire cause of cancer," he explained, "we'd all have had it long ago."[51] No doubt, such a statement enhanced Little's candidacy for director. He explained at the press conference announcing his appointment that "I am an ultraconservative about cause and effect relationships."[52] Confidential reports of a TIRC meeting make Little's agenda explicit:

> He [Little] declared that both he and the members of the board were aware of the attacks which had been made on tobacco for over 200 years, and wished to build a foundation of research sufficiently strong to arrest continuing or future attacks.[53]

Such an approach was central to Hill & Knowlton's overall PR strategy.

Little's personal commitments and *a priori* assumptions about cancer causality made him the ideal proponent of the industry's singular goal of maintaining a "controversy" regarding smoking and health. His scientific beliefs about cancer corresponded directly to his belief in the importance of heredity for understanding the causes of disease. From his earliest scientific training, Little had been deeply committed to hereditarian notions of cancer and society. In 1936, as president of the American Birth Control League, he decried the "ill-advised and unsound policies of economic relief employed in the country," which he maintained would only lead to the further propagation of the unfit, and he offered gratitude to "the gentlemen who rule Italy, Japan, and Germany for demonstrating that a program of stimulating population is a program of war."[54] Little's eugenic science was closely tied to his politics. "Our political and sociological premise in America is based on the false premise that all persons are born free and equal. This is an absolute absurdity," he wrote in 1936. "We must segregate men according to their standing."[55] Little also became a founding director of the National Society for the Legalization of Euthanasia and the Race Betterment Congress. He vigorously defended compulsory sterilization, urging the expansion of legislation mandating such policies. "When a sink is stopped up," he wrote, "we shut off the faucet. We favor legislation to restrict the reproduction of the misfit. We should treat them as kindly and as humanely as is possible, but we must segregate them so that they do not perpetuate their kind."[56]

Such views—not uncommon throughout the first half of the twentieth century—provide insight into Little's deep commitment to hereditarian causes of cancer. Cancer, he believed, resided in an individual's genetic lineage. It was self-evident that most systemic, noninfectious diseases originated *in* the body and were fundamentally subject to genetic predisposition. If smoking "appeared" to cause disease, this was but an artifact of an intrinsic constitutional vulnerability. Environment and behavior could mask these internal causes but did not themselves "cause" disease. Moreover, following eugenic theory, social and behavioral interventions were at odds with evolutionary schema. The lung cancer–smoking connection threatened to topple Little's rigidly held world view of biology, disease, and society.

Born in Boston in 1888, Little attended Harvard, where he earned a doctorate in science in 1914 while studying with noted geneticists W. E. Castle and later Edward Tyzzer. His earliest work focused on the genetics of mouse colors, but he soon turned his attention to susceptibility and resistance to cancers. His work was an important precursor to fundamental discoveries on the genetics of transplant immunology. Among his most important scientific discoveries was the murine mammary tumor virus. He also pioneered the use of strains of inbred mice for genetic research.[57]

Along with his research, Little assumed administrative roles that would increasingly become central in his career. After receiving his doctorate, Little joined the Harvard faculty, where he was appointed secretary to the Corporation, a notable administrative post. Then, following Army service in the World War I, he spent three years at the Cold Spring Harbor Laboratory, where he quickly rose to assistant director. As a result of Little's obvious administrative skill, he was offered the presidency of the University of Maine in 1922 at the age of thirty-three. At that time, he was the youngest college president in the United States. Although Little's identity as a scientist had been well established by his important laboratory findings, his scientific research would now come to be secondary as he emerged as a leading academic and scientific administrator. However, this work was not without controversy. At the University of Maine, Little quickly became embroiled in an intense conflict with Governor Percival Baxter over funding issues. He left after only three years to take the presidency of the University of Michigan. By now, he had come to be widely known for his vigor, energy, outspokenness, and arrogance.

At Ann Arbor, Little's reputation for conflict and combativeness was soon enhanced. His public advocacy of eugenics, birth control, and sex education apparently outraged the regents and the faculty.[58] And his support for prohibition of alcohol in fraternities alienated students. Little would denounce the impact of automobiles, coeducation, and liquor on campus as "splendid centres of hypocrisy" in American higher education. He also expressed his skepticism of the professoriate, noting "I know that of some of the most distinguished loafing in America is being done by American faculties in the universities."[59] Little tendered his resignation in January 1929, after having served for less than five years. At the time of his resignation, it had also become widely known that his first marriage of eighteen years was ending in divorce and that he had become romantically involved with a student. In the course of his presidency, he had alienated the regents, the faculty, and polite society.[60]

Little, however, had no shortage of ideas and energy, and he moved quickly to take on two other prominent positions. First, in 1929, he became managing director of the American Society for the Control of Cancer (ASCC), a part-time position. That same year, he founded the Roscoe B. Jackson Memorial Laboratory in Bar Harbor, Maine.[61] The lab was named in memory of a principal donor, the president of Hudson Motors, who Little had come to know in Michigan and from vacationing in Bar Harbor for many years. Financial support also came from Edsel Ford, Richard Webber, and George B. Dorr, all of whom summered on Mt. Desert Island in Maine.[62] Under Little's spirited leadership, activities at the lab grew quickly. By 1933, Little, who had become widely known for developing strains of inbred mice for research, began to support the work of the lab by selling inbred mice to other research institutions in the United States and abroad. This program reflected to a considerable degree the central personal aspects of its founder. Little was both lab scientist and entrepreneur, administrator, and advocate.[63]

At the ASCC, Little helped to establish the Women's Field Army, an educational and fund-raising campaign staffed by volunteers that urged early detection, treatment, and more scientific research. Together with newly appointed publicity director Clifton Read, Little successfully enhanced the visibility of the organization through the 1930s into the 1940s. Little's simultaneous roles at ASCC and the Jackson Lab established him as a leading figure in the emerging program to establish a national cancer policy. U. S. Surgeon General Thomas Parran appointed him to the National Advisory Cancer Council at the time that Congress created the National Cancer Institute in 1937. In these contexts, Little became a powerful advocate of more funding for basic science investigation.[64]

He also gained real prestige in the field with his combined work maintaining the Jackson Laboratory and directing the ASCC. In 1950, he received the American Cancer Society's annual award for "distinguished service in cancer control." Dr. Alton Ochsner, then-president of the ACS, presented it to him, calling him a scientist with "unprecedented vision." In accepting the award, Little stressed his firm—and telling—belief that the "discovery of a 'cause' or a 'cure' for cancer will be made by an individual working alone and not by a team of scientists working on a project."[65]

Given Little's position as a "leading man of science," his appointment to scientific director of the TIRC came to be widely praised initially. But his work on behalf of the TIRC would bear all the marks of his personal history as geneticist and eugenicist. As TIRC's scientific director, Little repeatedly centered attention on the so-called constitutional hypothesis, other environmental risks, and the need for more research:

Too little is known about many factors, including why people smoke or what kind of people become particularly heavy smokers.

The problem of causation of any type of cancer is complex and difficult to analyze. All research on this so-called constitutional disease is, and must be, painstaking and time consuming. There is not known today any simple or quick way to answer the question of whether any one factor has a role in causing human lung cancer.

Despite all the attention given to smoking as an accused factor in human lung cancer, no one has established that cigarette smoke, or any one of its known constituents, is cancer-causing to man.[66]

While Little favored basic science investigations into the mechanism of disease, often utilizing animal models, he never confronted the critical issue of the relationship of translating such research from the laboratory to humans. Little, whose own work had rested so fundamentally on animal research, now often found himself dismissing animal studies as irrelevant to questions of human disease.

Other cancer researchers reacted to Little's appointment as scientific director of the TIRC with surprise and distaste. "You may be surprised to know that Dr. C. C. Little was willing to become the chairman of that Committee," noted Evarts Graham in a 1956 letter to Hill. "It seems astonishing to me that a man of his eminence in the field of cancer and genetics would condescend to take a position like that."[67] Graham went on to express his frustration with Little's persistent skepticism in the face of mounting evidence. "Isn't the evidence at hand sufficient to convince anybody with an open mind?" asked Graham. When the TIRC announced its first set of grants almost two years earlier in November 1954, Ochsner—already clearly disillusioned with Little after praising him so highly four years earlier—called the TIRC program, "a tapeworm research into the physical and chemical composition of tobacco." According to Ochsner, the industry "sought to postpone a day of reckoning for the irresponsible advertising and sale of its products."[68]

In Little the industry identified a leader with a distinguished scientific pedigree. But perhaps even more importantly, Little brought to his work on behalf of the industry considerable experience with, and attraction to, combat and controversy. Throughout Little's career, he had become involved in a series of contests. In this respect, he seemed to relish a new public role in which he would be the lightning rod. Little, the inveterate contrarian, re-discovered the public limelight at this late point in his career.

Was Little disingenuous in his skepticism? Did he dissemble on behalf of his employer? The evidence on this question remains indeterminate. What we do know is that Little, by self-proclamation deeply committed to science and rationality, lost all capacity to evaluate his own biases as he as-sessed the question. Fiercely independent throughout his career, he failed to see how effectively he had come to do the industry's bidding; he failed to comprehend the corrosive social and psychological mechanisms of con-flicts of interest. Colleagues and friends came to question his judgment and rectitude: he had sold his science to industry. His starting salary in 1954, publicly announced, was $20,000 for the part-time position ($134,800 in 2006 dollars). No doubt Little's opinions on tobacco science were subject to financial conflicts, but it seems equally apparent that Little prized the no-tion of his own intellectual independence in the face of attack. After all, this had been the story of his life. In Little's view, he was defending science against emotion and hysteria; the integrity of objective experimentalism against the forces of moralism and ignorance.

Little's role in prolonging the cigarette controversy, which was a central part of the TIRC's public message, offers an important opportunity to ex-plore the sociology of scientific skepticism. In examining the debates about the health risks of smoking in the 1950s, it is crucial to put the var-ious protagonists into specific social and intellectual contexts. Did partic-ular investigators and commentators bring existing assumptions to their assessment of the causal relationship between smoking and disease? What was the nature of their *a priori* assumptions about the harms of cigarette smoking? And how did they shape the character of ongoing debates about methodology and findings? As a geneticist who had devoted his lifetime to exploring genetic links to cancers utilizing laboratory experiments, Lit-tle had few inherent sympathies to the approaches taken in the early epi-demiological investigations that were the linchpin to demonstrating that cigarette smoking caused lung cancer. Not only was he inclined not to trust these methods, he had a prevailing view of carcinogenesis that ran counter to the notion that cancers were caused by behavioral and environmental factors. As a result, Little steadfastly refused to acknowledge the growing evidence, repeatedly confirmed, that smoking was a cause of lung cancer. Little was not a physician, and perhaps this explains, in part, his ongoing demand to locate causality exclusively in the laboratory, as well as his apparent lack of concern regarding the medical questions involved.

Little also had a deep commitment to an increasingly anachronistic view of scientific discovery and innovation. His belief that the conundrum of cancer would eventually be solved by an individual scientist working alone harkened back to an image of Louis Pasteur or Robert Koch toiling long hours in their laboratories, unlocking the secrets of the microbes. But contemporary scientific investigation—as was so often true in the past—was both collaborative and iterative, rarely the work of a single scientist experimenting in isolation and rarely yielding definitive answers in a single stroke. Moreover, to solve multicausal questions, such as those associated with systemic and chronic diseases, would require the integration of methods and approaches across the biomedical sciences.

Little was convinced that the support of the industry for independent research marked an unprecedented boon to American science. In a 1956 guest editorial for the journal *Cancer Research,* Little explained:

> If those of us on the Board have the wisdom and vision to plan creatively, we may be able to justify this confidence placed in us. If we do justify it, the tobacco industry will have made its greatest contribution of service to mankind and may well establish a precedent or pattern which other industries will follow.
>
> Should this occur, the stability and development of basic research in a democracy will be assured on a foundation of nonpolitical support, unselfish and idealistic in concept and execution.[69]

It was essentially this perspective that shaped Little's approach to the question of cigarettes and disease. Given Little's personal rigidities and conceit, no epidemiological findings could possibly unsettle such deeply held convictions. Little had no respect for clinical and field observations. He brought these unbending views to his work for the industry and structured its research program accordingly.

A related question would be the significance of his role working on behalf of the tobacco industry. Once Little became the scientific director of the TIRC, he demonstrated a complete unwillingness to be swayed from the positions he took in 1954. No new evidence ever convinced him of the relationship of smoking to disease. In his role with the TIRC, Little now had an important conflict of interest to open scientific and medical inquiry into the health impact of cigarettes. And he worked concertedly to direct the scientific program of the TIRC away from the most important immediate questions of the harms of smoking.

Little and his Hill & Knowlton colleagues constructed a basic science research program into aspects of carcinogenesis that had little or no potential to resolve the question that the TIRC had promised the American public would be at the center of attention: do cigarettes cause disease? Little became the industry's primary spokesman for obscuring this question. The sharp disjuncture between the research agenda of the TIRC and the commitment to resolving the controversy about smoking and health is a major indicator of the essential PR goals of the TIRC. In the end, the TIRC was designed to direct attention away from the questions of immediate concern to the American public and American medicine: the health effects of smoking.

Little certainly brought *a priori* scientific and medical assumptions to his position, as well as conflicts of interest, but these were sustained by certain traits of personality. Throughout his career, Little had manifested a certain rigidity and combativeness that were now deployed to great effect on behalf of the tobacco industry. Certainly, skepticism is a valued attribute in scientific debate and controversy, but so too can it inhibit the production and legitimation of new and valuable knowledge. Just as it would be incorrect to simply view Little's skepticism as a function of his remuneration from the industry, it would be inaccurate to view it simply as representing rationality and objectivity. Little's skepticism reflected a deeply held worldview about genetics, society, and scientific investigation, perspectives that ultimately distorted the rationality and science of an individual who explicitly prized rationality and science.

Little would consistently maintain his public position on the scientific evidence and would repeatedly deny that there were any known carcinogens in tobacco tars (this despite clear industry knowledge to the contrary).

At the same time that he attacked the substantial scientific evidence indicating the harms of smoking, he had no compunction about offering unsubstantiated claims about the health benefits of cigarette use based on personal anecdote and social observation: "It is very well-known, for example, that tobacco has relaxed a great many people. It is a very good therapy for a great many nervous people."[70]

§

By 1960, largely through the efforts of Hill & Knowlton and the TIRC, the tobacco industry had succeeded in creating a "cigarette controversy" within the American media. The very idea that cigarettes caused lung cancer had come to be vigorously contested by the companies, and the emerging scientific consensus of 1953 had by 1960 given way to widespread debate—even as new peer-reviewed findings repeatedly confirmed the causal link between smoking and disease. We cannot know what trajectory science and public health would have taken without the tobacco companies' deliberate and studied interventions. But we can evaluate their impact.

Given that a number of scientists—even some epidemiologists—were skeptical of the smoking-cancer link, several historians have recently claimed that the "cigarette controversy" was real.[71] By this, they apparently mean that there were substantive areas of scientific debate, *independent* of the actions of the companies to denigrate the emerging evidence. There is no question that there was a real controversy about tobacco. But it is important to evaluate the range of interests that were engaged in this controversy: What were its causes? What forces contributed to its resolution? And what interests contributed to its continuation?

To understand the nature of the controversy, it is critical to examine the trajectory of research, evidence, and skepticism as it developed through the 1950s. Many of the prominent cigarette researchers began their investigations with considerable skepticism—including important figures like Evarts Graham, A. Bradford Hill, Richard Doll, and E. Cuyler Hammond. But by 1953, most of them had modified their positions in the face of new and convincing scientific research. For instance, Hammond doubted the link between smoking and lung cancer when only retrospective findings were available; but in July 1954, when the preliminary results of his prospective study had come in, he stated publicly, "In my opinion, it is now well established that cigarette smoking causes an increase in death rates from primary cancer of the lung."[72] To suggest, as the industry consistently did, that through the 1950s and 1960s eminent scientists equally and independently lined up on both sides of a "controversy" about the harms of smoking is to grossly misrepresent the historical record.[73]

Moreover, the nature of scientific skepticism to tobacco research evolved during the 1950s. Early in the decade, many physicians and scientists were unfamiliar with statistical and quantitative methods of research. These subjects were barely touched on in medical schools, and quantitative evaluations were not the routine feature of medical journal articles that they later became. This unfamiliarity led some to reject certain kinds of research as "merely" statistical. Many of these physicians and scientists had been trained in an era when the superiority of laboratory investigation over other forms of inquiry was an unquestioned assumption. The unique status and authority of the laboratory made some scientists and physicians skeptical of any knowledge produced by other means. Certainly, there were important epistemological questions about the character of scientific inference at stake. Still other skeptics brought *a priori* assumptions to their assessment of the evidence. Someone like Little, for example, who was deeply committed to the hypothesis that cancer was a genetic disease, would be skeptical of the suggestion that a particular behavior, such as smoking, might cause lung cancer. Such deeply held *a priori* assumptions often shape scientific controversies. Yet other scientists and physicians were swayed by personal psychological and sociological factors. They were concerned with defending their turf (the primacy of the laboratory) or were smokers themselves who did not want to accept the idea that their own behaviors put them at risk.

The industry was aggressively solicitous in identifying and supporting skeptics. They were invited to join the Scientific Advisory Board of the TIRC; they and their home institutions were provided with research grants; their views were sought and broadcast widely. In this way, the tobacco industry managed to sustain the widespread perception of an active and highly contested scientific controversy into the 1960s despite overwhelming evidence and scientific consensus that smoking caused serious disease. According the TIRC, many independent and responsible scientists continued to voice opposition to these findings. In reality, over the course of the decade, such views were increasingly marginal and limited to those with financial ties to the TIRC. One central question for the evaluation of skepticism is "what evidence would be convincing?" One sign that open-minded doubt has turned intractable is the answer: "I cannot say."

But skepticism does not indicate that there is not consensus. With each passing year, skepticism concerning the relationship of smoking and cancer was increasingly dominated by industry resources and activity. Doubt was no longer a matter of culture or training, but the carefully crafted center-piece of an industry effort to sow confusion and heighten debate through explicit attempts to disrupt the process of normative science. The TIRC marks one of the most intensive efforts by an industry to derail indepen-dent science.

The process of coming to understand the coherence, accuracy, and sig-nificance of the findings on smoking and lung cancer is illustrated by the manner in which the various scientists at the NCI considered the question. By 1957, Joseph Heller, NCI's director, would make clear that consensus existed among the scientists there, but the arrival at that consensus was a complicated process. Some NCI researchers, like Wilhelm Hueper, worried that acceptance of the cigarette hypothesis would deflect attention from other potential carcinogens, such as occupational toxins and environmental pollutants.[74] Most of the remaining handful of prominent pathologists and laboratory investigators at NCI and elsewhere who resisted the consensus found support for their views in the tobacco industry PR campaigns.

§

According to the Hill & Knowlton design, the Tobacco Industry Research Committee consisted of a Scientific Advisory Board with a scientific direc-tor as well as an administrative staff. The SAB was to evaluate research proposals and make decisions about funding, which it did in regular meet-ings. The initial slate of seven respected senior scientists was chosen by the industry. Their appointment lent credence to the industry's contention that it planned to seriously examine the question of tobacco and health. The SAB had a number of distinguished members in the forty-plus years of its existence.

Although the independence of the SAB was widely publicized, the SAB's work was directed by the full-time staff of the TIRC, specifically

W. T. Hoyt and, after November 1954, Assistant Scientific Director Robert Hockett, a sugar chemist. Both men exercised considerable authority over grantees and day-to-day practices. Numerous Hill & Knowlton executives also spent a great deal of time attending TIRC meetings and drafting TIRC PR initiatives.[75] Strikingly absent from the initial list of SAB members was any statistician, and although by the summer of 1954 they had found one willing to join, the TIRC never sponsored statistical or epidemiological investigations. It supported some research exploring alternative hypotheses of carcinogenesis, but little direct research on cigarettes and disease. Most of its resources were devoted to exploring alternative theories of the origins of cancer, centering on genetic factors and environmental risks.

Most sponsored projects had nothing to do with smoking but were concerned with basic questions in immunology, genetics, cell biology, pharmacology, and virology. In 1954, its first year of operation, the TIRC budget approached $1 million—almost all of which went to Hill & Knowlton, media ads, and administrative costs. Funding for the grants program increased substantially in later years, reaching $800,000 by 1963.

Under Little's leadership, the SAB settled into a program of funding research principally on the basic science of cancer, with little or no relevance to the critical questions associated with the medical risks of smoking. This focus apparently suited all concerned. It was certainly ideal from a public relations standpoint since unrelated research would not condemn cigarettes. SAB members could assert that they were offering valuable resources, yet distance themselves from the specific question of the harms of tobacco and thus avoid accusations of bias; SAB members frequently told the TIRC staff that they did not wish to be associated with the TIRC's public statements. They were generally skeptical or agnostic concerning the harms of smoking but felt that their direct association with TIRC statements asserting "no proof" would make them appear prejudiced and partisan.

In February 1958, a number of members of the Scientific Advisory Board communicated that they were "disturbed by a misunderstanding of the relationship between the TIRC and the SAB." Several board members expressed concern about the public statements of the TIRC. Physiologist Julius Comroe apparently threatened to resign because he and other members of the SAB had been placed in the "awkward position of unwittingly endorsing everything that the TIRC said." Leon Jacobson echoed this worry and, according to the minutes of the meeting, explained that "he did not wish to be linked with any of the statements made by the TIRC." Although the founding members of the SAB would steadfastly defend their independence from the industry, the reality is that under the Hill & Knowlton plan, they had been manipulated for effective PR, a fact they periodically acknowledged with some bitterness.[76]

By steering funds away from the effects of tobacco toward basic science in cancer, they avoided the implication that they served industry interests. SAB members were frequently in a position to secure funding from the industry to support the work of colleagues and associates, as well as other research at their home institutions. Such arrangements gave them considerable influence and clearly sustained their loyalty to the TIRC.

The TIRC never developed an approach to carcinogenesis and tobacco that could resolve the question of the harms induced by cigarette smoking. At the same time that they demanded experimental evidence, the TIRC refused to acknowledge that new results came not only from additional observational studies, but from pathological and experimental findings. Pathologist Oscar Auerbach's research, for example, was especially notable because it demonstrated the characteristic precancerous changes in lung tissue among smokers. Auerbach's study, published in 1957 in the *New England Journal of Medicine,* involved autopsies on 30,000 deceased patients with confirmed smoking histories. To ensure against bias, microscopists were kept ignorant of these histories. Auerbach concluded in his paper that

> These findings are fully consistent with the hypothesis that inhalants of one sort or another are important factors in the causation of bronchogenic carcinoma.
>
> The findings are also fully consistent with the theory that cigarette smoking is an important factor in the causation of bronchogenic carcinoma.[77]

In light of such studies, to claim that the evidence for a causal relationship between smoking and lung cancer was based exclusively on statistical data—as the tobacco industry would repeatedly insist—was to fundamentally misrepresent the emerging scientific knowledge.

By mid-1956, the industry found itself in yet another public relations dilemma. The utility of the TIRC lay in its commitment to "objective" science and the search for the "truth," but the SAB had expressed "strong opposition" to being drawn directly into the PR campaign. Little found himself caught between his handlers at Hill & Knowlton and his scientific colleagues on the SAB. Eventually, given the SAB's discomfort with Little's prominent public role in denying any proof of tobacco's harms, Little relinquished his title of chairman of the SAB while remaining a member and scientific director of the TIRC. Hill & Knowlton and the TIRC staff worked to maintain the image of the SAB as impartial and scientific while still calling on Little to make statements in the media.[78]

Hill, in turn, was under increasing pressure from his industry clients to deliver a definitive statement that cigarettes posed no risk. Tobacco executives repeatedly asked for a more aggressive public relations campaign than the measured approached Hill & Knowlton had engineered. They expressed frustration with the TIRC approach to staying above the fray: Philip Morris President McComas wrote to Hartnett in July 1957 that "the very substantial part of the money which Philip Morris has contributed to TIRC for public relations has been wasted." Threatening to withhold further funding unless the organization took the "offensive against its detractors," McComas insisted that "The SAB will only be consulted on publicity activities which have to do directly with the SAB or its projects."[79] The SAB became increasingly isolated from the more ambitious PR activities of the TIRC even as it was invoked as proof that the tobacco industry was honoring its commitment to scientific research.

By the 1970s, the status of the TIRC (now renamed the Council for Tobacco Research or CTR) as a public relations enterprise had become clear to almost everyone. In 1972, Earl Newsom & Company, a public relations firm, evaluated the content of the CTR (and earlier, the TIRC) Annual Reports for the industry:

> From a public relations point-of-view, if from no other, it would seem that the Council should continue to receive support from its members, particularly in these times of mounting consumerism. . . .

More specifically, we get the impression that when the use of laboratory animals indicates that the findings are favorable, or at least not unfavorable, to the use of tobacco, then the covering report either makes a positive statement about the use of animals or no statement whatever. On the other hand, when the findings from any particular project indicate that tobacco use may be contributing to a discernible and unhealthy change in laboratory animals, then we get, in the covering report, mention of the limitations imposed by the use of animals. . . .

Whenever possible the reports pointedly refer to "some who would" say smoking is dangerous, based on any given test, as scientific crackpots. When possible, Dr. Little qualifies the results of animal tests that tend to be critical, but emphasizes them when they do not find evidence of carcinoma, implying that smoking is harmless. The aim of his summations, much too apparently, seems to be to protect smoking. . . .

More recent annual reports show decreasing editorial comment. This may be the result of accumulating evidence, in the Council studies as elsewhere, which shows some of the deleterious effects of heavy smoking.[80]

In 1974, Alexander Spears, then director of research and development at Lorillard (he became CEO and chairman in 1995), confirmed this assessment:

Historically, the joint industry funded smoking and health research programs have not been selected against specific scientific goals, but rather for various purposes such as public relations, political relations, position for litigation, etc. Thus, it seems obvious that reviews of such programs for scientific relevance and merit in the smoking and health field are not likely to produce high ratings. In general, these programs have provided some buffer to the public and political attack of the industry, as well as background for litigious strategy.[81]

§

At the same time that Hill and his colleagues were establishing the Tobacco Industry Research Committee, they worked aggressively to reshape the media environment. Hill & Knowlton's public relations strategy relied on intensive contact with authors, editors, scientists, and "opinion makers." Hill understood that the success of any public relations strategy was highly dependent on face-to-face interpersonal relations with important media outlets. Each time the TIRC issued a press release, the Hill & Knowlton organization had initiated "personal contact." The firm systematically documented the courtship of newspapers and magazines where it could urge "balance and fairness" to the industry. Hill & Knowlton staff, for instance, assisted Donald Cooley in preparing an article entitled "Smoke Without Fear" for the July 1954 issue of *True Magazine* and then distributed more than 350,000 reprints to journalists throughout the country. "If you are a man or woman who smokes, relax and enjoy it," Cooley advised. "If you have tried to give up smoking a dozen times and failed, quit trying."[82]

As Scientific Director of the TIRC, C. C. Little was integrally involved with Hill & Knowlton's media strategy. By the 1960s even Little's allies in the industry complained that his constant refrain of "no proof" increasingly lacked credibility and that he had outlived his utility to the industry. But he was undeterred, insisting that the relationship between smoking and disease remained an "open question." "If anything," he maintained, "the pure biological evidence is pointing away from, not toward, the causal hypothesis."[83] It was one thing to voice such a view in the early 1950s, quite another by the end of decade. Some accounts of the controversy fail to adequately calibrate the character of change over the course of the decade. Little was unshakable in his commitments, and he thrived as a combatant. These qualities stood him in good stead with his employers, and his position of "skepticism" was sustained and broadcast by his handlers at Hill & Knowlton.

Given his role as the industry's most preeminent spokesman on science and health, Hill & Knowlton worked to burnish his reputation. For instance, Dick Darrow of Hill & Knowlton directed his staff in 1955 to focus "stature-building attention on Dr. Little and his own work."[84] Little's value lay in his status as a prominent scientist, his historical role in cancer research, and his past leadership of the American Society for the Control of Cancer. As the politics of tobacco became more intense in the late 1950s, Hill & Knowlton was careful to protect Little in this sphere. Carl Thompson wrote to Hill explaining, "Dr. Little should not be brought too much into discussion of direct [political] action." Little's crucial role would be his insistence on scientific uncertainty and his perennial calls for more research.

Moreover, the executives at Hill & Knowlton understood the value of Little's insistence on his independence. Although he frequently asserted to the press that "I am my boss," in reality he closely followed the script prepared by Hill & Knowlton. And when he was perceived early on as not sufficiently making the case for "two sides" to the tobacco question, he heard directly from John Hill.[85] "All the industry has any right to ask or expect now is for the public to understand that the case has not been proven and that there are 'two sides,'" Hill wrote.[86] And Little used his allies on the SAB to attack new scientific findings. In one instance, he asked William Rienhoff, a member of the SAB, to respond to the publication of Alton Ochsner's 1954 book, *Smoking and Cancer*, with the following statement: "Doctors Ochsner and Graham . . . have long been recognized as the foremost and most vociferous medical, anti-tobacco propagandists." Rienhoff readily complied.[87]

Hill & Knowlton operatives made Little available to editors, journalists, and others in the media. Most of these people, lacking much scientific sophistication, eagerly portrayed both sides of the "controversy." The controversy, after all, made it a story.[88] Little's statements, shrewdly broadcast by Hill & Knowlton staff, were part of a much broader effort. The other branch of the TIRC, beyond its carefully orchestrated scientific research, was the construction and implementation of a consistent industry-wide public relations message. TIRC representatives frequently issued statements during this period explaining: "[TIRC's] purpose is solely to obtain new information and to advance human knowledge in every possible phase of the tobacco and health relationship."[89] But such statements misrepresented the preeminent public relations origins and functions of the program. While publicly repeating its research focus, tobacco executives knew that the TIRC was primarily a public relations vehicle. In April 1955, W. T. Hoyt, executive secretary of the TIRC, explained the relationship of PR and research in the TIRC's program:

> Essentially, the major purposes of the TIRC are Research and Public Relations. Our job is to maintain a balance between the two, and to continue to build soundly so that at all times Research and Public Relations

complement each other. In that way we intend to assume the mantle of leadership and, ultimately, to create a condition where the public will look to the TIRC for answers rather than to others.[90]

The White Paper issued in April 1954 was the primary vehicle of the TIRC's early media strategy. Formally entitled *A Scientific Perspective on the Cigarette Controversy*, it comprised eighteen pages of quotations from physicians and scientists casting doubt on the link between smoking and lung cancer. Over 200,000 copies were distributed to the medical community and to the general media.[91] The White Paper catalogued the widest range of criticism and skepticism, including that of scientists from the National Cancer Institute and elsewhere. Its arguments would be deployed by industry interests for the next half-century. For example, according to Max Cutler, a cancer surgeon and TIRC favorite—"simply because one finds bullfrogs after a rain does not mean that it rained bullfrogs."[92] The recurrent theme of calling for more research was loudly sounded in the White Paper, as were claims that scientific reports of cigarettes' harms promoted public hysteria.

Not everyone was enthusiastic. Joseph Garland, editor of the *New England Journal of Medicine*, commented:

> Many persons recently received a brochure entitled "A Scientific Perspective on the Cigarette Controversy" emanating from the Tobacco Industry Research Committee. The title is pretentious, for the publication seems rather a series of testimonials than a scientific study.[93]

He went on to discuss the White Paper's dangers to the public's health:

> If there is no place for the missionary who has prejudged the issue of smoking and found too simply that "smoking causes cancer," so too there is no place in this arena for the glossing over of the suspected hazard—and it is considered real—by the presentation of carefully selected evidence.[94]

Despite Garland's concerns, the White Paper, like the Frank Statement, garnered a great deal of praise in the public media, which Hill & Knowlton carefully documented.[95]

As new scientific findings emerged, the TIRC deployed the quotations and themes gathered in the White Paper. Each time a new finding implicating smoking as a cause of disease was announced, the TIRC would respond, contacting prominent journalists and news outlets to offer their critiques. Journalists, eager to provide "both sides of the story," typically offered equal time for Little and his peers to rebut substantive investigations of smoking's harms. Hill and his assistants lobbied editors and journalists for "fairness" and "balance" in covering the "controversy." Controversy was precisely the outcome Hill & Knowlton sought. Through the auspices of Hill & Knowlton, the TIRC had access to figures like Joseph Garland, Henry Luce, Arthur Sulzberger, and Edward R. Murrow, which helped ensure that tobacco's "side of the story" was well represented in their coverage.

In mid–1955, Murrow devoted two consecutive broadcasts of his CBS television news documentary *See It Now* to the tobacco controversy. The show offered interviews with both Little and Wynder, as well as other industry representatives, scientists, and officials. Hill & Knowlton got precisely what they had hoped for, an ambiguous conclusion noting that more scientific research would be needed to settle the question and that the industry was fully committed to this process. Hill would not leave this outcome to chance. He arranged a meeting with Murrow, his producer Fred Friendly, and writer/researcher Arthur D. Morse prior to the production of the broadcast. Hill also contacted his friend Art Hall, director of public relations at Alcoa, the corporate sponsor of the broadcast. Hall assured him that the program would be a "balanced one." Hill wrote confidently to Hartnett that Friendly "believes that if anyone gets a break in the program it would be the tobacco industry."[96] As virtually all American television viewers of the 1950s knew, Murrow was a chain smoker, often consuming sixty to seventy cigarettes a day. He would smoke throughout his live broadcasts. A decade later, he would succumb to lung cancer, just after turning fifty-seven.[97]

In 1962, Carl Thompson, who had worked the tobacco accounts for Hill & Knowlton since their inception in 1953, compared this work to an iceberg in which only one-ninth was visible: the most important work of public relations was accomplished out of public view, yet powerfully shaped the information environment on tobacco and health. The firm's well-oiled machinery, fueled with the resources of the tobacco industry, rivaled the Bonsack machine for efficient productivity. Hill & Knowlton offered skeptics, information, research, and even copy to an eager media. A twenty-four-point list entitled "Special Assistance to Press, Radio, Magazine and Others" related many instances when "personal contacts" with editors and reporters had modified stories to the industry's benefit. In one instance,

> [t]wo editorials widely used in "home town" dailies and weeklies through-out the country were prepared for and then distributed by the U.S. Press Association. These were "The Same Old Culprit" and "Truth Makes a Slow Crop." Over 100 clippings of these have already been received.[98]

In their entreaties for fairness to the industry, the firm's staffers repeated several key themes. First, they would note that the industry completely understood its important public responsibilities. Second, the industry was deeply committed to investigating all the scientific questions relevant to resolving the "controversy." Third, they urged skepticism regarding the "statistical studies." And fourth, they offered the media a long list of "independent" skeptics to consult to assure balance in their presentations. The primary independent skeptic was the TIRC's Little.

Given the press's penchant for controversy and its often naive notion of balance, these appeals were remarkably successful. Hill & Knowlton expertly broadcast the arguments (typically not based on substantive research of any kind) of a small group of skeptics as if their positions represented a dominant perspective on the medical science of the cigarette. The press, in response, dealt with scientific debate as if it were the same as a political debate. In one telling example, Dwight MacDonald, a *New Yorker* reporter, wrote to American Tobacco Company President Paul Hahn while researching an article on cigarettes and science in late 1953. Hill & Knowlton, anticipating that MacDonald's piece would be "a blast at the industry," sent him a list of "over 100 eminent cancer experts" who had expressed doubts about the relationship between lung cancer and smoking. They reported that as of July 1954 he had apparently abandoned the piece. No article on tobacco by MacDonald ever appeared in the *New Yorker*.[99]

Another strategy deployed throughout the 1950s was to learn about new scientific findings and consensus reports, and to be ready to attack when they were released. The agency took pride in its extensive network of scientific informants. At its headquarters in New York, the TIRC developed a large, systematically cross-referenced library on all things tobacco-related. As Carl Thompson explained:

> One policy that we have long followed is to let no major unwarranted attack go unanswered. And that we would make every effort to have an answer in the same day—not the next day or the next edition. This calls for knowing what is going to come out both in publications and in meetings.[100]

In many instances, the TIRC offered a rebuttal of new findings even before they had become available. They could be so nimble because they aggressively solicited a small group of doubters and broadcast their misgivings as if they were based on rigorous and systematic research. So long as skepticism survived (and of course it would) the industry possessed the basis for their aggressive defense.

The Hill & Knowlton offices were adept at taking a single dissenter and assuring widespread media coverage of his views. They were particularly proud, for example, of the intensive reporting they secured for Wilhelm Hueper's paper at the Sixth International Cancer Congress in Sao Paulo, Brazil, in 1954. Hoyt noted how "copies of Hueper's paper were (quote) made available (end quote) to the New York press." Even independent skeptics like Hueper were eager to have the attention that Hill & Knowlton could bring them. Any finding potentially calling into question the smoking-disease link, no matter how tangential or insignificant, was heralded and sent on to the media. As Hoyt later explained:

> Len Zahn has often been the Daniel in the Lions Den. As the man on the spot at a meeting where an adverse attack is being made, Len goes right into the press room with the T.I.R.C. answer and sees that the correspondents working on the stories have our side to go right into their first stories. This takes some doing. And it takes good contacts with the science writers.[101]

The public impression of scientific and medical uncertainty that resulted was a crucial element in maintaining the market of current smokers as well as recruiting new ones.[102] Industry literature, for example, frequently pointed to the fact that nonsmokers could also develop lung cancer. Therefore, they argued, how could one attribute lung cancer to cigarette smoking? But none of the researchers who had found a relationship between smoking and lung cancer even suggested such a one-to-one correspondence. And medical science had long ago accepted notions of cause which assumed that not every exposure to a causal agent resulted in disease.[103]

Hill also emphasized the need for "editorial and statistical research in all phases of the cigarette problem to be carried on through public relations counsel."[104] By this he meant that the industry should survey public opinion about smoking as a cause of disease. In a subsequent memo he explained: "1. it should attempt to evaluate what has been the degree of penetration in the public mind of the cancer scare; 2. it is impossible to develop an intelligent public relations activity without a more decided knowledge of public attitudes than is now in hand."[105] Such "research" could then be offered to the media. Hill suggested articles on "What are the smoking habits of long-lived distinguished public leaders?" and "What are the human ills erroneously attributed to tobacco over the centuries?"[106]

§

One critical aspect of the public relations program was to influence the medical profession. Physicians stood at a critical juncture in the chain of authority regarding the health effects of smoking and so required special attention. As a result, Hill & Knowlton developed particular approaches to targeting clinicians. The TIRC (and later the Tobacco Institute) distributed the periodical *Tobacco and Health* free to doctors and dentists. The January/February 1958 issue declared:

> Continuing scientific research lends support to the position that too many unknowns exist today concerning lung cancer to warrant conclusions placing a major causative role on cigarette smoking, according to the 1957 Report of the Scientific Director of the Tobacco Industry Research Committee.[107]

Human cancers, the "journal" constantly asserted, were complex processes, difficult to study, difficult to understand. With a circulation of over 500,000, *Tobacco and Health* was an important vehicle for sustaining doubt among physicians, who would in turn influence the views of patients. As Carl Thompson explained in 1962:

> [I]t goes to all doctors and dentists in the country and, believe me, not all of them like to get it. However, we know that a good many of them pay attention to it or else we wouldn't have so many complaining letters— as well as the more receptive kind. We have concluded that even if TOBACCO AND HEALTH aggravates a doctor, its very presence re- minds him that there are other aspects to the lung cancer problem and the smoking and health question. . . . We don't try to kid ourselves that all doctors are aware of the publication or that many of them even open it or see it. However, the checks that we have made, both by personal in- terview and post card surveys, indicate that it does get attention to a rather surprising degree.[108]

The publication was also widely disseminated to legislators, journalists, and others.

The mantra "not enough research" would echo throughout the 1950s and beyond. In 1958, four years after the original statement, the TIRC drafted "Another Frank Statement to Smokers." Scientific investigation had progressed greatly in these intervening years, but the tobacco industry's position remained constant:

> [A] substantial number of doctors and scientists of high professional standing and repute have, after investigation, publicly challenged the va- lidity of these broad charges against tobacco. . . . The cause of cancer re- mains as much a mystery as ever."[109]

Hill & Knowlton was still making a "mystery" in the face of increasingly compelling medical research.[110]

In 1962, Hoyt restated this line, now honed for nearly a decade: "The T.I.R.C. position is . . . a fairly simple one. We don't know the answers. We don't know what causes lung cancer. Tobacco has not been absolved but neither has it been found guilty, in whole or part. We must continue research." This position had served the industry well. For smokers and would-be smokers, uncertainty offered a powerful rationale to start or keep using cigarettes. Second, the "we don't know" approach offered legal protection. The industry had subtly backed away from assurances of "safety" that could constitute grounds for accusations of negligence. Third, the approach bought the industry critically needed time to combat regulation and, if it chose, to investigate the production of "safer" products. Finally, "we don't know" offered those engaged in the production and sales of tobacco an important moral defense of their own actions. This need for denial would become, in the second half of the twentieth century, a crucial element in the promotion of a life-threatening product.

By 1962, after nearly a decade of work, Hill & Knowlton was eager to be able to explicitly demonstrate the impact of their interventions on their client's behalf.

> Now—can we, from this experience, answer this fundamental public relations question: Is such preparation and effort for simultaneous comment on attacks on your client worth the effort it requires?
>
> We say the answer is unequivocally yes!
>
> Proof? Well, how do you prove it?
>
> From time to time, man-on-the-street interviews ask about the smoking question. In almost every one of these, there will be a quotation that is almost an exact paraphrase of some statement issued for the tobacco accounts.[111]

Hill & Knowlton had successfully produced uncertainty in the face of a powerful scientific consensus. So long as this uncertainty could be maintained, so long as the industry could claim "not proven," it would be positioned to fight any attempts to assert the regulatory authority of public health.

⚜

Even as the tobacco industry carried out its massive effort to sustain and amplify scientific skepticism during the 1950s, its own researchers were confirming and adding to the evidence showing the connection between lung cancer and cigarette smoking. Internal assessments of the potentially carcinogenic characteristics of cigarette smoke stand in sharp contrast to the companies' public statements. In February 1953, Claude Teague, an R.J. Reynolds research scientist, closely reviewed epidemiologic studies and animal studies and concluded:

> The increased incidence of cancer of the lung in men which has occurred during the last half century is probably due to new or increased contact with carcinogenic stimuli. The closely parallel increase in cigarette smoking has led to the suspicion that tobacco smoking is an important etiologic factor in the induction of primary cancer of the lung. Studies of clinical data tend to confirm the relationship between heavy and prolonged tobacco smoking and incidence of cancer of the lung.
>
> . . . There appears to be a growing suspicion, or even acceptance, among medical men and cancer researchers that the parallel increase in cigarette consumption and incidence of cancer of the respiratory system is more than coincidence.[112]

Despite such candid internal assessments, company executives continued to offer blanket reassurances to consumers and stockholders.[113]

At the same time that the Frank Statement was asserting that "there is no proof that cigarette smoking is one of the causes [of cancer]," the industry documented a large number of known carcinogens in its product. Although the industry (except for Liggett & Myers) insisted that it did no in-house research on smoking and health, it conducted a number of studies on the constituents found in tobacco smoke. In-house researchers also tried to replicate Wynder's experiments painting mice with tar condensates, and some were successful.[114]

Alan Rodgman, another scientist at R.J. Reynolds, drew conclusions similar to Teague's several years later. Rodgman, who had trained at the University of Toronto in the distinguished lab of Frederick Banting, wrote an extensive paper, "The Analysis of Cigarette Smoke Condensate," based on experiments done at R.J. Reynolds using standard Camel cigarettes. He explained:

In view of this data, it is logical to assume that the carcinogenic activity of cigarette smoke condensate is due to the presence of one or more carcinogenic polycyclic aromatic hydrocarbons.[115]

Rodgman proposed that the company try to develop technologies to filter out these substances. When R.J. Reynolds President E. A. Darr learned of this research, he was "somewhat perturbed" that one of his scientists had found benzopyrene in cigarette smoke.[116] Rodgman's findings were clear:

Since it is now well-established that cigarette smoke does contain several polycyclic aromatic hydrocarbons, and considering the potential and actual carcinogenic activity of a number of these compounds, a method of either complete removal or almost complete removal of these compounds from smoke is required.[117]

But accomplishing this would prove no simple matter. Rodgman, eager to get on with the research, expressed frustration that so-called biological work was to be left to the TIRC, which did nothing. In 1959, in a summary of his work to date, he reported "some thirty-odd polycyclic hydrocarbons," eight found to be carcinogenic in mice.[118]

Some industry scientists not only acknowledged carcinogens in cigarettes but advocated more intensive research into decreasing the health risks of cigarettes.[119] One strategy they considered was to identify all the constituents in tobacco smoke, single out any carcinogens, and develop the technical capacity to remove them. As one Philip Morris scientist explained in a memo to company executives:

Moreover, because it is not only good business but is our duty to our customers and stockholders, we are dedicated to going beyond any efforts of TIRC, ACS or any other organization. Our objective is to determine all chemical constituents of smoke, and to develop means of removing any which are considered harmful.[120]

This strategy, however, entailed risks the companies were unwilling to take. The removal of certain constituents from the smoke was an admission that tobacco might be harmful. This seemed too great a liability, es-

The legendary Camel sign at Times Square blew fifteen smoke rings per minute. Douglas Leigh, the giant of twentieth-century billboard production and promotion, designed the sign, which quickly became a New York City landmark following its premier in late 1941. Outdoor advertising was a mainstay of tobacco promotion throughout the century. I visited the Camel sign in 1961, in my first visit to New York City. Its run on Broadway lasted until 1966.

James "Buck" Duke became the principal force in moving the tobacco industry from chew, snuff, and cigars into the cigarette trade. At the same time, he consolidated the Tobacco Trust into a corporate monolith at the turn of the twentieth century.

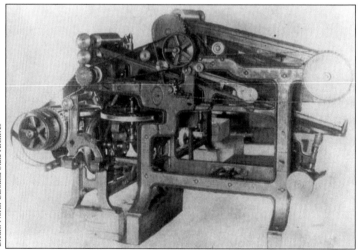

The Bonsack Machine, introduced in 1882, could produce some 100,000 cigarettes per day. It displaced the labor-intensive craft work of hand rolling and standardized a mass-consumption product. Duke's mechanics worked to modify and improve the Bonsack prototype. Pictured above is a re-engineered version from 1892.

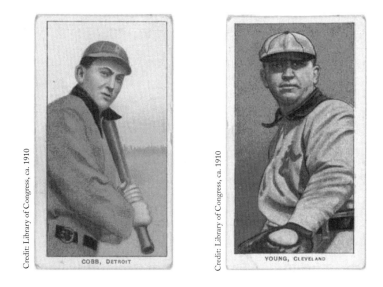

COBB, DETROIT

YOUNG, CLEVELAND

The tobacco industry began to insert collecting cards into packages in the 1880s in order to stiffen paper wrappers. More importantly, the industry understood what would appeal to boys, the principal target of promotions for collecting and trading. Card collecting tapped into a powerful dynamic in the initiation of new smokers.

MISS BATCHELOR

NINA FARRINGTON

The first Camel cigarette campaign of 1915 announced the arrival of national brands. Devised by the N.W. Ayer Agency, the campaign created considerable anticipation and interest.

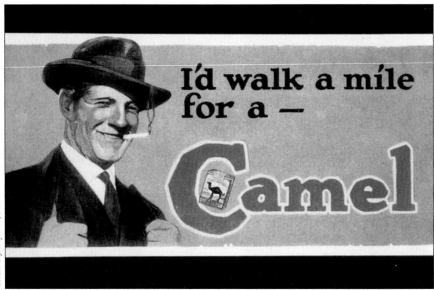

By 1920, one of the most resilient advertising slogans of the century adorned ads for the nation's most popular brand.

Credit: *Life* magazine, June 1935

By the mid-1930s, as this *Life* magazine cover indicates, social prohibitions on women smokers had been overwhelmed by a potent combination of industry public relations and promotion grounded in feminism and cultural change.

Credit: Liggett and Myers, 1926

In the years before tobacco companies considered it culturally viable to advertise directly to women, they offered more subtle and suggestive notions to would-be women smokers. Initiated in 1926 this Chesterfield advertising slogan reportedly led to a 40 percent increase in sales.

These ads, drawn by well-known pinup artist John La Gatta, make explicit the sexual allure that the companies sought to associate with their product. "Everybody's doing it!" noted the ad below. "Do you inhale? Of course you do!"

The "Reach for a Lucky Instead of a Sweet" campaign touched off a major controversy in the late 1920s. Not only did the candy industry rise in protest, but a number of critics suggested that American Tobacco was using these ads to solicit youngsters. CEO George Washington Hill utilized the public relations skills of Edward Bernays to sustain both the campaign and the controversy that helped to make Lucky Strike the most popular brand. The association of smoking and weight loss would be repeatedly used as a marketing promotion throughout the century.

By the early 1930s, advertisements portraying physicians suggested underlying public concerns about the health impacts of smoking. Tobacco companies competed to reassure smokers that their particular brands relieved any symptoms associated with cigarette use, from "irritation" to "coughing" to "scratchy throat."

In the combat of tobacco advertising of the 1930s, the William Esty Agency offered the idea that "it's fun to be fooled"—taking a direct shot at Hill's claims about "toasting."

American Tobacco told its fashionable women smokers to "Ask your Doctor About a Light Smoke."

During the 1930s, cigarettes were often promoted with explicit therapeutic rationales or health assurances. According to some ads, they could provide "a lift" or "stimulate digestion." In this characteristic ad, prominent professional athletes, including Lou Gehrig and Dizzy Dean, claimed that "Camels don't get your wind."

This ad, which appeared at the height of the Great Depression, showed a party of Camel smokers at the Victor Hugo Restaurant in Beverly Hills. It featured the endorsement of Mrs. William Hollingsworth Jr., who explained "Camels stimulate my taste, aid digestion." National brands promoted the "democratization" of goods. Claire Huntington, an "efficient stenographer," is also pictured in the ad.

The cigarette became an ever-present prop in portraiture, film, and popular culture. Marlene Dietrich (right) poses in the 1930s. Humphrey Bogart (below), is shown in a still from *The Maltese Falcon*, 1941.

Smoking in movies both recognized
and promoted the centrality of the
cigarette in contemporary culture, a fact
not lost on an industry that thoroughly
understood the power of this medium.
The use of cigarettes in film conveyed
powerful symbolic meanings about
characters and relationships.

Right, Frederic March and Joan
Bennett in *Trade Winds*, 1938.

Below, Paul Henreid and Bette Davis
in *Now, Voyager*, 1942.

Dana Andrews and Joan Fontaine in *Beyond a Reasonable Doubt*, 1956.

Faye Dunaway and Warren Beatty in *Bonnie and Clyde*, 1967.

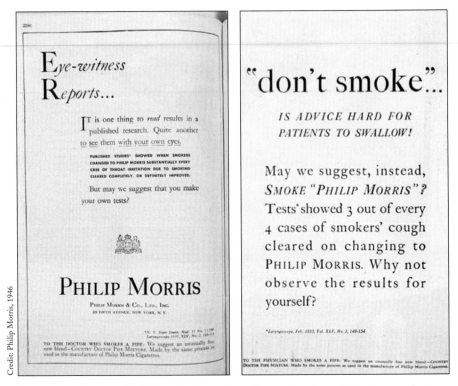

As concerns about the health implications of smoking persisted—and then increased—in the 1930s and 1940s, advertising explicitly addressed these anxieties. Companies initially saw competitive opportunities in such concerns. The ads reproduced here appeared in medical journals. Claiming that Philip Morris cigarettes did not cause the common symptoms associated with smoking, they urged physicians to recommend the brand to their patients.

R.J. Reynolds fixed on the likely notion that smokers would be attracted to the brand that their physicians chose, and that physicians would advocate for a brand that lionized the medical profession. These prominent ads of the late 1940s, pitched at both doctors and the general public, subtly sought to subvert emerging statistical and epidemiological knowledge by inviting doctors and patients to "make your own test."

The "More Doctors" campaign was apparently based on the work of A. Grant Clarke, a William Esty ad executive, on loan to R.J. Reynolds to establish a Medical Relations Division. Clarke would distribute free packs of Camels at medical conventions; pollsters from an "independent research organization" would then be sent to ask the physicians what brand of cigarettes they were carrying.

pecially since, despite the hype of filters, no clear technology for their removal had emerged.

Helmut Wakeham joined Philip Morris as a research chemist in 1958 and became director of research and development in 1960. Wakeham, who introduced the use of gas chromatography for assessing the constituents in tobacco smoke, would champion, within the company, the development of a "medically acceptable" cigarette that would be free of the now well-documented carcinogens. He wrote numerous internal memoranda that acknowledged the cancer-causing effects of cigarette smoke. In a memo dated September 22, 1959, for instance, he wrote: "One of the main reasons people smoke is to experience the physiological effects of nicotine on the human system. Nicotine, to the best of present knowledge, does not produce cancer. Hence, in theory one could achieve the major advantage of smoking without the hazard of cancer. But nicotine in tobacco smoke is present in the tar phase."[121] Wakeham became committed to solving this dilemma.

In a 1961 proposal to investigate the possibilities of reducing carcinogens in smoke, Wakeham listed fifteen carcinogens and twenty-four cocarcinogens, or "tumor promoters," in cigarette smoke. He also cited the belief that "cardiovascular ailments that may arise from smoking are due to the physiological effects of nicotine," noting, in particular, nicotine's "[s]pecific effects on the adrenal medulla, causing it to discharge epinephrine, a hormone which accelerates the heartbeat, contracts the peripheral blood vessels, and raises the blood pressure." Wakeham also remarked that of the more than four hundred gas and particulate compounds in cigarette smoke, including those specifically recognized as carcinogens, some 84 percent could be found in sidestream, or secondhand, smoke. He concluded:

Low irritation and *low nicotine* cigarettes for commercial exploitation will be developed in the course of our present R & D program during the next two to five years with an expenditure of not more than 25% of the R & D budgets during this period.

A medically acceptable low-carcinogen cigarette may be possible. Its development would require:

TIME

MONEY

UNFALTERING DETERMINATION[122]

At the same time that industry researchers, such as Rodgman and Wakeham, were detailing carcinogenic substances in cigarettes and potential strategies for their removal, the TIRC put out a press release explaining: "Chemical tests have not found any substance in tobacco smoke known to cause human cancer or in concentrations sufficient to account for reported skin cancer in animals."[123] The industry would aggressively exploit public desire for a safe product while simultaneously denying any adverse health effects of smoking.

§

In 1958, three scientists—Herbert Bentley from Imperial Tobacco, David Felton from British American Tobacco, and W. W. Reid from Carreras—representing the Tobacco Manufacturers Standing Committee, the British counterpart to the TIRC, visited the United States to assess the status of industry-related science. They met with research directors of major tobacco companies, the Scientific Advisory Board of the TIRC, and its Industry Technical Committee, as well as other experts in tobacco and disease in the academy and government. They noted that there was virtual consensus among industry researchers that cigarettes played a role in human cancers.

> With one exception (H.S.N. Greene) the individuals whom we met believed that smoking causes lung cancer if by "causation" we mean any chain of events which leads finally to lung cancer and which involves smoking as an indispensable link. In the U.S.A. only Berkson, apparently, is now prepared to doubt the statistical evidence and his reasoning is nowhere thought to be sound. . . .

Having interviewed prominent scientists at universities, the NIH and within the industry, the visitors went on to summarize these scientists' comments regarding the TIRC:

> In their opinion, T.I.R.C. has done little if anything constructive, the constantly re-iterated "not proven" statements in the face of mounting contrary evidence has thoroughly discredited T.I.R.C., and the S.A.B. of T.I.R.C. is supporting almost without exception projects which are not related directly to smoking and lung cancer. Liggetts [sic] felt that the

problem was sufficiently serious to justify large-scale investment by the Company directly in experimental research on smoke and cancer, accepting privately that a strong case against tobacco had been made out and avoiding any public comment until their own research had provided something concrete to offer. . . .

These British industry scientists believed that a clear consensus on causality had emerged:

> The majority of individuals whom we met accepted that beyond all reasonable doubt cigarette smoke most probably acts as a direct though very weak carcinogen on the human lung. The opinion was given that in view of its chemical composition it would indeed be surprising if cigarette smoke were *not* carcinogenic. This undoubtedly represents the majority but by no means the unanimous opinion of scientists in U.S.A. These individuals advised us that although it is not possible to predict unambiguously the effect of any substance on man from its effect on experimental animals the generally successful use of animals in other fields as a model for man fully justifies their use in our problem.[124]

This document is important because it reflects the candid assessment of industry officials and scientists. It depicts a broad consensus about tobacco as a carcinogen even among industry researchers, a consensus the industry repeatedly denied publicly through its comprehensive public relations operations. Further, the document shows how marginal individual skeptics like Berkson and Greene had become by 1958.

In 1961, Hill & Knowlton celebrated its successes on behalf of its tobacco client. The total number of cigarettes sold annually had risen from 369 billion in 1954, the company's first full year of service to the industry, to 488 billion. Per capita consumption had risen from 3,344 a year in 1954 to 4,025 in 1961, the highest ever. "From a business standpoint," Hill & Knowlton crowed, "the tobacco industry has weathered this latest spate of health attacks on its products."[125] In less than a decade, the industry had been stabilized and was thriving. As Joseph Lelyveld concluded in the *New*

York Times, "Surprisingly, the furor over smoking and health failed to send the industry into a slump. Instead, it sent it into an upheaval that has resulted in unforeseen growth and profits." He went on to quote an unnamed American Cancer Society official who claimed, "When the tobacco companies say they're eager to find out the truth, they want you to think the truth isn't known. . . . They want to be able to call it a controversy."[126] TIRC, under Hill & Knowlton's guidance, had turned tobacco science into yet one more political controversy on which people of good will could differ. So long as it could maintain this "liberal" notion of scientific knowledge, the industry remained free to aggressively promote tobacco without regulation or liability. This explains, in part, why the industry would tenaciously cling to the notion of controversy.

By the early 1960s—in spite of categorical research findings indicating the harms of smoking—a significant "controversy" had arisen over the validity and meaning of these findings. Indeed, given the widespread acceptance of the conclusion, especially among those who had analyzed and evaluated the research most closely, the persistence of debate about the harms of smoking is a striking demonstration of the powerful impact of the tobacco industry's public relations campaign. The industry insistence, at the direction of Hill & Knowlton, on the notion of "no proof" and the need for "more research" was an inspired manipulation of the natural tendencies within science to encourage skepticism and seek more complete answers to important questions.

Hill & Knowlton had served its tobacco clients with commitment and fidelity, and with great success. But the firm had also taken its clients across a critical moral barrier that would have two important impacts on American society. Trust in science, confidence in the media, and the responsibility of the corporate enterprise were all substantially harmed by Hill & Knowlton's efforts on behalf of the tobacco industry. By making science fair game in the battle of public relations, the tobacco industry set a destructive precedent that would affect future debate on subjects ranging from global warming to intelligent design. And by insinuating itself so significantly in the practice of journalism, Hill & Knowlton would compromise the legitimacy and authority of the very instruments upon which they depended. The tobacco industry's PR campaign permanently changed both science and public culture. It changed the character of public knowledge in dangerous new ways. So long as Hill & Knowlton and the tobacco industry could cling to their particular forms of denial and reshape them into a proactive public relations program, the industry had bought not only critical time, but a new generation of smokers.

Hill & Knowlton could point to many successes on behalf of the industry. In June 1961, the *New England Journal of Medicine* published an exchange between Ernst Wynder and C. C. Little. Regardless of what was written, the very existence of such an exchange was a victory for the industry. The authors in their respective articles laid out their well-worn positions. Wynder reviewed, yet again, the substantive evidence demonstrating conclusively that smoking posed a serious and lethal risk to human health. He explained:

> I know of no other chronic disease that has been studied epidemiologically and statistically in such detail and with such uniform results as smoking and lung cancer. The tobacco industry would like to give the impression that scientific evidence is divided on this issue. I do not consider this to be the fact. . . . A number of reputable scientists have testified that they do not believe smoking to be a cause of cancer of the lung, but few of them have done research on the subject under discussion. It is true in virtually any field of human endeavor that one finds people who will take an opposing view to any proposed evidence. This was true in the days of Semmelweiss, as well as in the days of Pasteur, and in previous centuries just as it is true today.[127]

The persistence of a few skeptics without direct research experience in the field, Wynder argued, should not detract from the overwhelming scientific consensus concerning the relationship of smoking and disease. In his conclusion, he let his frustration with such critics show:

> Of those who will not accept existing evidence, I should like to know what evidence would be acceptable. If one criticizes epidemiology for being statistical, if one criticizes animal research for being unrelated to the human problem and if one criticizes chemical identification of carcinogens as not have any bearing to human disease, I should like to ask if there is a form of evidence that would be accepted as being conclusive.

If it were humanly possible we would at once set up a study that could yield such evidence. If it is humanly impossible, it is not a constructive kind of suggestion that would advance scientific knowledge.[128]

In his response, not surprisingly, Little refused to answer Wynder's question.

To expect, as Dr. Wynder and some others do, that those still unconvinced should state the exact and specific evidence that would "convince" them is being completely unrealistic. If one could define such specific evidence the problem would be already solved.[129]

As he had so often done, Little reiterated "that much more research in depth is needed before definitive answers will be available." He concluded:

Lung cancer, indeed all cancer, is a *challenge,* an *unsolved problem.* Its etiology will probably long be an *open question.* As such, greater co-operation and exchange of ideas among experimenters, statisticians and clinicians are the goals to be focused on and to be attained.[130]

Along with these two articles, the *New England Journal* ran an editorial written by Joseph Garland entitled "The Great Debate." "Both authors," Garland wrote, "are dedicated, sincere proponents of their points of view, each upholding what he believes to be the truth and nothing but the truth, each ready to admit that the whole truth has not yet been revealed to aspiring man."[131] In the end, Garland left the question to the individual judgment of physicians and the public:

Each individual must choose his own course, whether to woo the lady nicotine or abjure the filthy weed, while the search for truth continues.[132]

Such an ecumenical conclusion was precisely what Hill & Knowlton and the industry sought. Garland's conclusion reads as if it had been written at least a decade earlier, prior to the publication of extensive peer-reviewed studies from epidemiology, pathology, and laboratory investigation. He had reached far more definitive conclusions about the harms of smoking as early as 1953, when he wrote that the previous year's scientific results from Doll and Hill had provided "an association between cigarette smoking and lung cancer so strong as to be considered proof within the everyday meaning of the word."[133]

One can only conclude from the dispassionate tenor of Garland's 1961 editorial, placing the harms of smoking back into the domain of doubt, that the tobacco industry had gotten its money's worth from Hill & Knowlton.

III

POLITICS

No reasonable person should dispute that cigarette smoking is a serious health hazard.[1]

SURGEON GENERAL
LUTHER TERRY, 1964

In the meantime (we say) here is our triple, or quadruple or quintuple filter, capable of removing whatever constituent of smoke is currently suspect while delivering full flavor—and incidentally—a nice jolt of nicotine. . . . And if we are the first to be able to make and sustain that claim, what price Kent?[2]

ADDISON YEAMAN, 1963
GENERAL COUNSEL AND
VICE PRESIDENT,
BROWN & WILLIAMSON

We believe there is no connection or we wouldn't be in the business.[3]

JAMES C. BOWLING, 1963
PHILIP MORRIS

Doubt is our product, since it is the best means of competing with the "body of fact" that exists in the mind of the general public.[4]

BROWN & WILLIAMSON, 1969

CHAPTER 7

The Surgeon General Has Determined

IN THE FACE OF THE "continuing controversy" over the health effects of cigarettes—widely and loudly broadcast to an expanding media by the TIRC—researchers and public health representatives tried to make the public aware of the actual state of scientific knowledge. They expressed growing exasperation at the toxic combination of industry denials and reassuring claims for new filtered cigarettes—which radically distorted popular understanding of the harms of smoking. The industry, meanwhile, well understood that its carefully maintained posture of scientific uncertainty provided a shield against new regulatory initiatives.

In 1960, most public health policies still centered on the control of infection. From compulsory vaccination to new mechanisms of case reporting and tracking, the major interventions of public health had focused on the use of state police powers to limit communicable diseases.[5] But by mid-century, systemic chronic diseases had overtaken infection as the major causes of death, and public health officials were forced to adjust their priorities. The control of "noncommunicable" diseases posed a new and entirely different set of problems. The identification of the cigarette as a cause of serious disease marks a critical turning point in the history of public health.[6]

Many public health officials, though committed to the notion that smoking caused disease, were nonetheless unsure of how to approach the problem. Was it the province of public health to regulate personal behaviors,

211

especially those deemed of little risk to others? For behavioral risks, such as smoking, the role and authority of public health officials had yet to be defined. Throughout the twentieth century, the state's responsibilities in disease detection, prevention, and health promotion had centered on the notion of communicability. Thus, the state was charged with the identification of infectious organisms, contact tracing of infected individuals, and, when appropriate, the detention or quarantine of those who might pose risks to the wider public.[7] These activities and the boundaries of public health, had, in general, been scrupulously policed by the medical profession to assure that all aspects of clinical care (and remuneration) remained the hallowed prerogative of physicians.

Now, however, the uneasy relationship between public health and medicine would receive new scrutiny. Tobacco explicitly raised the question about the role of public health officials in addressing important health risks. Many within public health were reluctant to enter the exclusive turf of clinical medicine by addressing matters of individual behavior.[8] But as the importance of cigarettes as a cause of illness and death became increasingly apparent, these officials began to recognize that like it or not, smoking was already a public health issue. In 1956, at the urging of U.S. Surgeon General Leroy Burney, a study group on smoking and health was organized by the American Cancer Society, the American Heart Association, the National Cancer Institute, and the National Heart Institute. This group met regularly to assess the scientific evidence relating to tobacco and health. The group noted that sixteen studies had been conducted in five countries, all showing a statistical association between smoking and lung cancer. Collectively, these studies demonstrated that

- lung cancer occurs five to fifteen times more frequently among smokers than nonsmokers
- on a lifetime basis, one of every ten men who smoke more than two packs a day will die of lung cancer
- cessation reduces the probability of developing lung cancer[9]

These epidemiological findings were supported by animal studies in which malignant neoplasms had been produced by tobacco smoke condensates. Further, human pathological and histological studies added evidence to strengthen the "concept of causal relationship." "Thus," the authors explained, "every morphologic stage of carcinogenesis, as it is understood at present, has been observed and related to the smoking habit." All three domains of scientific and medical knowledge now confirmed the epidemiological findings of the early 1950s. The significance of the data was powerful:

> The sum total of scientific evidence establishes beyond reasonable doubt that cigarette smoking is a causative factor in the rapidly increasing incidence of human epidermoid carcinoma of the lung.

The authors went on to call for a public health response to these findings: "The evidence of a cause-effect relationship is adequate for considering the initiation of public health measures." Although "additional research is needed to clarify many details and to aid in the most effective development of a program of lung cancer control," they felt that public health initiatives did not have to wait for this supplemental work to be completed.[10] They explicitly addressed the relationship of scientific knowledge to public health action. After these conclusions were published, Surgeon General Burney released a statement on behalf of the Public Health Service (PHS) that "there is increasing evidence that excessive cigarette smoking is one of the factors which can cause lung cancer."[11]

But Burney and his colleagues soon questioned whether such statements were sufficient, especially when they were so vigorously contested by the powerful combination of tobacco public relations and marketing. What could the Public Health Service, with its limited authority and limited budget, do to reduce disease associated with smoking? It could provide a systematic and definitive assessment of the evidence. And it could challenge the disinformation campaign waged by the industry. Given ongoing public confusion and the widespread uncertainty among physicians about what to tell their patients, the PHS began evaluating its role in addressing the harms of smoking. Though relatively weak, the PHS could still command the expertise to strike a blow against science-by-public relations.

Certainly, it was within the purview of public health to assess medical and scientific evidence and make these evaluations available to the public. But Burney's review raised essential questions about what additional steps might be taken. Burney's staff was characteristically sensitive about the implications of moving public health into the realm of advocating changes in personal risk behaviors. If public health were viewed as usurping medicine's traditional role of counseling patients about how to avoid disease, it could easily incur the wrath of well-oiled and well-heeled organizations like the American Medical Association. Moreover, the very idea of risk reduction, simply because it was a new development in health care, was contested terrain in the long-standing divide between public health and medicine.[12]

At a February 1956 meeting to plan the PHS policy regarding the tobacco findings, two views emerged. Most of the surgeon general's staff concluded that it was time to "get this message out," especially to schoolchildren. Chief assistant to the surgeon general, James Watt, however, expressed concern that the PHS should avoid "a missionary statement . . . designed to influence personal habits." Lewis Robbins, a physician in the PHS with responsibility for relations with the medical profession, shared some of Watt's concerns. According to Robbins, "Public health should never take a position which gets ahead of the medical profession." To the PHS, the boundary between clinical care and public health was something to be very closely watched. Among other reasons, their modest funding was dependent on a Congress heavily lobbied and supported by the representatives of organized medicine. Robbins estimated that only half of all practicing physicians had become convinced of the relationship between smoking and cancer. As a result, he concluded that the surgeon general should work to influence the "scientific community through appropriate channels."[13] These anxieties led a weak and uncertain public health community to conceive only a limited notion of its role in one of the biggest health issues of the century.

As a result, consensus panels about the harms of smoking proliferated, each offering state-of-the-art assessments of the evidence. In January 1959, yet another distinguished group of cancer researchers, led by statistician Jerome Cornfield of the National Cancer Institute, offered a substantive review of the accruing evidence linking cigarettes to lung cancer. Cornfield and colleagues also noted that the persistent "debate" about the science was driven by the tobacco industry:

> It would be desirable to have a set of findings on the subject of smoking and
> lung cancer so clear-cut and unequivocal that they were self-interpreting.

The findings now available on tobacco, as in most other fields of science, particularly biologic science, do not meet this ideal. Nevertheless, if the findings had been made on a new agent, to which hundreds of millions of adults were not already addicted, and on one which did not support a large industry, skilled in the arts of mass persuasion, the evidence for the hazardous nature of the agent would generally be regarded as beyond dispute.[14]

Just as the tobacco industry in the late nineteenth century had developed the technology for the mass production of cigarettes, so now it had developed techniques for the mass production of controversy and doubt. The industry insisted on scientific criteria that it knew full well could not be attained then, or ever—when it was still willing to admit such criteria at all. C. C. Little, as we saw, explicitly refused to do so. As Cornfield explained, despite the impressive data—not only from epidemiology but from laboratory and clinical science—bringing the controversy to resolution would prove no easy matter.

To confront the doubt fomented by the industry, Cornfield's group carefully considered the range of alternative hypotheses to account for the significant rise in cases of lung cancer. They scrupulously read the standard critiques offered by skeptics, such as Joseph Berkson and Ronald Fisher, knocking down each question in turn. Their conclusions went even further than the 1957 report initiated by Surgeon General Burney. "The consistency of all the epidemiologic and experimental evidence," they wrote, "also supports the conclusion of a causal relationship with cigarette smoking. . . ."[15] Like the 1957 study group, these authors felt an imperative for action, stressing that the available findings were "sufficient for planning and activating public health measures."[16]

Following the Cornfield article, Surgeon General Burney offered yet another comprehensive assessment. He revisited the epidemiologic data as well as the animal and pathological investigations, and came to the following categorical conclusion, published as the official "Statement of the Public Health Service":

The Public Health Service believes that the following statements are justified by studies to date [1959]:

The weight of the evidence at present implicates smoking as the primary etiological factor in the increased incidence of lung cancer.

> Cigarette smoking particularly is associated with an increased chance
> of developing lung cancer. . . .[17]

In Burney's view, the evidence of cigarette smoking's harms was overwhelming and certainly worthy of government attention. Nonetheless, the
TIRC continued to disparage such consensus statements. TIRC Scientific
Director Little asserted, "scientific evidence is accumulating that conflicts
with, or fails to support, the tobacco-smoking theories of lung cancer."[18]

Burney was especially disappointed by the response at *JAMA*. An editorial, actually drafted in the surgeon general's office with some modifications, shaded Burney's message, much to his chagrin. "A number of
authorities who have examined the same evidence cited by Dr. Burney do
not agree with his conclusions," argued John Talbott, editor of *JAMA*.[19]
Not surprisingly, *JAMA* offered a defense of clinical authority, emphasizing
the role of the physician as guide and counselor:

> Neither the proponents nor the opponents of the smoking theory have
> sufficient evidence to warrant the assumption of an all-or-none au-
> thoritative position. Until definitive studies are forthcoming, the physi-
> cian can fulfill his responsibility by watching the situation closely,
> keeping au courant of the facts, and advising his patients on his ap-
> praisal of those facts.[20]

§

Even as the industry attempted to obscure scientific results on cigarettes
and lung cancer, government agencies had begun to recognize and publi-
cize the cigarette's harms. American scientists and public health officials
who were convinced by the evidence were joined by colleagues in other nations. Between 1957 and 1962, the Medical Research Council of Great
Britain, the Royal College of Physicians, the World Health Organization,
and public health officials in the Netherlands and Norway publicly acknowledged that cigarette smoking caused lung cancer.[21] The British Royal
College of Physicians, after a two-year investigation, stated, "Diseases associated with smoking now cause so many deaths that they present one of
the most challenging opportunities for preventive medicine today."[22] The
report concluded:

The strong statistical association between smoking, especially of cigarettes, and lung cancer is most simply explained on a causal basis. . . . The conclusion that smoking is an important cause of lung cancer implies that if the habit ceased, the death rate from lung cancer would eventually fall to a fraction, perhaps to one fifth or even, among men, to one tenth of the present level. Since the present annual number of deaths attributed to lung cancer before the age of retirement is some 12,000 . . . a large amount of premature shortening of life is at issue.[23]

The Royal College of Physicians clearly recognized that lives were at stake. Repeatedly, independent critical evaluation of the scientific findings that cigarettes caused lung cancer reached the same conclusion.

The Royal College of Physicians' report marked a crucial step in the legitimation of the link between cigarettes and disease.[24] E. Cuyler Hammond, director of the statistical research section of the American Cancer Society, wrote the preface to the American edition. He noted the esteem in which the Royal College was held and pointed out that "the reader is asked to accept nothing on faith." The huge amount of scientific research presented in the report, Hammond explained, provided "evidence from which [readers] can draw their own conclusions concerning the effects of cigarette smoking."[25]

That such statements had to be repeated so many times reflected the power and resources the tobacco industry committed to the production of uncertainty in the face of knowledge. Each new research report implicating tobacco as a cause of disease elicited a denial that any conclusive proof had been found. Typical of such volleys was Little's response to Burney's statement of 1957:

The Scientific Advisory Board questions the existence of sufficient definitive evidence to establish a simple cause-and-effect explanation of the complex problem of lung cancer.[26]

Such language—typical of TIRC statements—reflected the careful wordsmithery of the experts at Hill & Knowlton. Burney had not claimed that the evidence was "definitive" nor that the relationship of smoking and lung cancer was "simple." Nor would he have disagreed that the problem of lung cancer was "complex." But such equivocations did not alter the fact that smoking constituted a demonstrated health risk of great significance.

§

News accounts of new medical findings were generally accompanied by a statement from the TIRC insisting that "nothing new" had been found and that the studies were "merely" statistical. The TIRC was very effective in mobilizing a relatively small group of skeptics and amplifying their views as if they were equal in numbers and significance to the broad scientific consensus. But these skeptics, and the tobacco industry that trumpeted their views, produced no new research.

These persistent industry denials helped to generate a major innovation in medicine and public health: the consensus report. To a degree, unprecedented in the history of medicine, thorough and objective statements reviewing the findings gained increasing significance to medical and public health groups wishing to acknowledge resolution in the face of the widespread perception of an ongoing scientific "controversy." The development of consensus reports would have long-range implications for establishing public health knowledge, clinical guidelines, and what would eventually come to be known as evidence-based medicine.[27] Consensus reports typically seek to systematically and critically evaluate data and come to a conclusion about its medical and public health significance. They ask what is known and what is the best practice. In the case of smoking, the government found itself responsible for adjudicating a scientific dispute while the industry sought to maintain the notion that adjudication was the domain of individual clinicians, smokers, and would-be smokers. Irresolution was crucial to the industry's interest; uncertainty the basis of its future livelihood.

The best efforts of the voluntary health organizations, the surgeon general, and other public agencies failed to bring closure to this carefully constructed controversy. This situation, in which powerful corporate interests both shaped and clouded a crucial scientific debate, ultimately compelled the surgeon general and the federal government to take unprecedented action. An independent and definitive assessment of the scientific evidence could not be achieved without state intervention. A question that had arisen in doctor's offices and clinics found its ultimate resolution in conference rooms in Washington. With medicine and public health now buffeted by powerful economic and political forces of commerce, the federal government found it necessary to develop new capacities for the disinterested and independent evaluation of data.

By the 1960s, pressure was building for the U.S. Public Health Service to take some concerted action against smoking. The voluntary health agencies, including the American Lung Association and the American Heart Association, proposed in June 1961 that President Kennedy appoint a commission to "study the widespread implications of the tobacco problem."[28] Kennedy declined to respond, apparently to avoid alienating southern congressional delegations. There was little corresponding enthusiasm in Congress when Senator Maurine Neuberger (D-Oregon) proposed legislation also calling for a commission. By the spring of 1962 it looked like the issue might be tabled, when Kennedy was asked about the health controversy during a nationally televised press conference. His halting response revealed his surprise:

> The—that matter is sensitive enough and the stock market is in sufficient difficulty without my giving you an answer which is not based on complete information, which I don't have, and therefore perhaps we could— I'd be glad to respond to that question in more detail next week.[29]

Two weeks later, Kennedy's surgeon general, Luther Terry, announced that he would establish a committee to fully investigate the ongoing questions of smoking and health.[30] A native of Alabama, Terry had come to the surgeon general's office after a long career in the PHS, including most recently eleven years at the National Heart Institute.[31]

To offer a rigorous and systematic assessment of the health implications of smoking, the Terry committee had to provide a full and open inquiry among independent scientists and medical experts. Terry's staff created a list of candidates for the advisory committee consisting of some 150 individuals representing fields ranging from pulmonary medicine to statistics, cardiology to epidemiology. The PHS then circulated the list to the American Cancer Society, the American Heart Association, National Tuberculosis Association, American Medical Association, and the Tobacco Institute, the tobacco industry's PR arm.[32] Each group had the right to eliminate any name, without any reason cited. Terry also eliminated individuals who had already published on the issue or had taken a public position.

Not surprisingly, this procedure drew objections. Congressman Clark MacGregor wrote to Terry, "It has been suggested that several members of the commission were appointed on the basis of tobacco industry recommendations. If so, this would immediately suggest a conflict of interest destructive to the necessary unbiased study and recommendations of the commission."[33] But the selection process was actually a mark of Terry's political savvy. Having anticipated that the industry would seek to discredit any findings that suggested the harms of tobacco, he and his advisors had preempted any chance that the report might be attacked on the basis of the committee's membership. The group was scrupulously made up of five smokers and five nonsmokers.[34] Photos of the committee meeting at the National Library of Medicine show a smoke-filled room with a conference table littered with ashtrays.[35] The constitution of the committee demonstrated Terry's commitment to reaching a genuine and definitive consensus.

The TIRC monitored the selection process carefully. Peter Hamill, a young commissioned officer in the PHS who served as staff director of the committee, maintained consistent contact with the industry representatives, frequently consulting with Robert Hockett, associate scientific director of the TIRC, about the prospective appointees. According to Hockett, Hamill promised him that "one of our nominees, and probably two, will be on the commission."[36] Two committee members, chemist Louis Fieser, who had consulted with Arthur D. Little on its tobacco industry projects, and pharmacologist Maurice Seevers were widely perceived as sympathetic to the industry.[37]

Prospective committee members were also reviewed by Stanley Temko, the industry's counsel for the Tobacco Institute, who shared them with Ed Jacob, an attorney who directed the "Special Projects" arm of the TIRC, as well as the ubiquitous Clarence Cook Little. They shot down the nomination of University of Chicago pathologist Clayton Loosli because they understood that "he has become a nonsmoker." After Little consulted with Jacob and George Allen, president of the Tobacco Institute, they agreed that they would not object to William Cochran and Stanhope Bayne-Jones, but would oppose Esmond Long because of his association with the American Cancer Society.[38] No one turned down an invitation to serve on the committee, indicating to Terry "that these scientists were convinced of the importance of the subject and of the complete support of the Public Health Service."[39]

The committee drew on the varied disciplinary strengths of its members. Walter J. Burdette was a prominent surgeon and chair of the surgery department at the University of Utah; John B. Hickam was chair of internal medicine at the University of Indiana; Charles LeMaistre was a pulmonary specialist and director of the chest program at Parkland Hospital in Dallas. The pathologists joining the committee were Emmanuel Farber, chair of pathology at the University of Pittsburgh, and Jacob Furth from Columbia, an expert on the biology of cancer; and Maurice Seevers, a noted toxicologist who chaired the University of Michigan pharmacology department. Louis Fieser of Harvard University was an eminent organic chemist. Completing the committee were Bayne-Jones, a bacteriologist, former head of New York Hospital and dean of Yale Medical School; Leonard M. Schuman, epidemiologist at the University of Minnesota; and Cochran, a Harvard University mathematician with expertise in statistical methods. By appointing this distinguished group, Terry assured that the advisory committee would be protected from charges of bias. The committee possessed a full range of experts, with no single discipline dominant.[40] Moreover, the methodological diversity of the committee reflected the understanding that determinations of causality required a range of medical and scientific perspectives.

The charge Terry set for the committee was one stage of a two-part process. The assignment of the advisory committee was to arrive at a clinical judgment—to determine the "nature and magnitude of the health effects of smoking."[41] As one public health official explained, "What do we (that is, the Surgeon General of the United States Public Health Service) advise our Patient, the American public, about smoking?"[42] These findings would be followed by phase II, proposals for remedial action. This separation into two phases kept the committee away from the political morass that circled around the tobacco question. Terry astutely recognized that the advisory committee could speak with authority only about the scientific and medical issues; he would leave the policy questions to the politicians. This is not to suggest that the report was not a political document. Its main purpose was to provide sufficient medical authority to generate new public policies.[43]

What Terry sought—and ultimately got—was a political document that was scientifically unimpeachable. Without it, the regulatory agencies and the Congress would lack the basis, in the face of industry-generated "controversy," to create powerful public health policies relating to smoking and health. But while the committee was working, the PHS continued to express frequent concerns about its role and authority in relation to the medical profession. Bayne-Jones would somewhat defensively point out that the report made no attempt "to advise anybody to [do] anything."[44] The job of the committee (on behalf of the PHS) was to answer a single, strictly empirical question: is smoking harmful? That they were able to do so was a major accomplishment, bringing to an end the notion that there remained a persistent, unresolved scientific controversy.

§

At its first meeting, in November 1962, the committee decided that it would base its assessment on a comprehensive review of the now considerable existing data; new research would greatly delay the announcement of any conclusions, and given more than a decade of substantial peer-reviewed science, there was already exhaustive data on which to make such a judgment. Over the next year, the committee met eight more times. In between these meetings, both committee members and staff worked concertedly to review, critique, and synthesize the formidable volume of scientific work on tobacco.

William Cochran proved to be the committee's central figure, subtly negotiating and leading members through the complex statistical arguments concerning causality. He wrote the pivotal chapter on statistics in the final report and made crucial contributions to the chapter on "Criteria for Judgment." He also collected all the prospective findings that had been reported in the literature and integrated their analyses. In this way, he was able to assure their consistency and at the same time test their significance. In doing this large-scale integration, Cochran helped to develop the essential underpinnings of what would come to be called meta-analysis in statistics and epidemiology. The whole was greater than the sum of its parts; the results of numerous studies possessed far more statistical and analytic power than any single study.[45] Not only had each new study confirmed earlier findings, the collective data, as Cochran conclusively demonstrated, was especially robust.

Burdette initially drafted the chapter on lung cancer, but after members of the committee objected that he had not done justice to the epidemiological findings, the chapter had to be completely rewritten. Burdette apparently considered resigning but was persuaded by his fellow members to stay on. The loss of any committee member during the process would have shattered the necessary unanimity. The chapter that appeared in the report contained sections written by Burdette as well as Schuman and others. As a result, the committee's work rested on the complex interpersonal and intellectual process of disciplinary respect, trust, and negotiation. Bayne-Jones, the senior member of the committee and a seasoned administrator and negotiator, had to use all of his considerable military and administrative experience to ensure that the process led to scientific consensus.

Given the diversity of scientific training and temperament, tensions within the group were a constant. Farber, a pathologist, apparently worried about the use of the term *cause*. A strict constructionist whose work was dependent on visualizing pathology, he nonetheless came to be convinced that smoking could legitimately be called a *cause* of lung cancer. The ultimate agreement that the language of *causality* was not only appropriate but crucial, fundamentally shaped the committee's final report. Bayne-Jones later explained that the members had concluded that the "monomorphic conceptions of Koch and others [to determine causality] were too strict" to accommodate the multiple causes of complex diseases.

Louis Fieser, the distinguished Harvard organic chemist, smoked throughout the meetings, up to four packs a day. Committee members warned him to cut down while they sifted through hundreds of studies demonstrating the serious harms of smoking. He didn't, even though he signed on to the committee's conclusions. With this evidence of the effects of nicotine before his eyes, Maurice Seevers, the committee's expert in pharmacology, still refused to accept the idea that smoking was addictive by current standard definitions. He conceded that it was habit-forming and smokers might experience withdrawal. But the prevailing definitions of addiction centered on the social impacts of drug use. Since it was widely perceived that cigarettes had no "social pathologies" like alcohol, marijuana, or heroin, the committee followed Seevers's lead. The addictiveness of smoking would ultimately be the subject of the surgeon general's report of 1988, which documented the addictive properties of nicotine.

During the year the committee was at work, the prominent skeptic Joseph Berkson wrote repeatedly to Cochran, pointing to what he saw as fundamental flaws in the statistical arguments. Cochran offered a sympathetic ear but nonetheless moved the committee forward. To assure that the group fully reviewed Berkson's position, Cochran invited him to prepare a written statement summarizing his critique. Cochran and colleagues carefully reviewed this statement and ultimately dismissed it. By 1963, Berkson's critiques had been repeatedly rebutted. Berkson would soon join the last remaining hard-core skeptics on the tobacco industry payroll, where he became a paid consultant.[46] While no one questioned his sincerity, it had become clear that his doubt was impervious to evidence.

For the seventy million regular smokers in the United States, the report of the committee's findings confirmed their worst fears. It told them that the death rate from lung cancer was 1,000 percent higher among men who smoked cigarettes than among nonsmokers. The report also found chronic bronchitis and emphysema to be of far greater incidence among smokers, and it found that rates of coronary artery disease, the leading cause of death in the United States, were 70 percent higher among smokers. In short, cigarette smokers placed themselves at much higher risk of serious disease than did nonsmokers.[47]

§

The tobacco industry and its TIRC had no intention of waiting passively for the Surgeon General's Advisory Committee to report its assessment. Rather, they worked assiduously to attempt to shape the process and conclusions. In the first instance, they had sought, wherever possible, to influence the selection of the committee members. Once the Committee was selected and its staff appointed by the PHS, the industry generously offered the services of the TIRC for consultation and research support. In his contacts with committee members and staff, Little reiterated that he hoped the final report would direct attention to ongoing gaps in scientific knowledge.[48] Throughout 1963, Little and his assistants at TIRC, Robert Hockett and William Hoyt, had frequent correspondence and meetings with the committee's medical coordinator, Peter Hamill, who eagerly sought their counsel and advice.

Hamill's job was to coordinate the collection of the data and the organization of the inquiry. Little wrote at one point that "I feel that he really would appreciate our taking a more active part behind the scenes."[49] In November 1962, as the work of the committee was getting underway, Hamill wrote to Little expressing his hope that the TIRC would play an important role. "I am very optimistic about the services which you can render this study," Hamill said. "In the ensuing months I will undoubtedly be taking from you much more than I will be giving, but I hope you will not be offended by having your brains picked."[50] He called the TIRC to invite Little and Hockett to attend the committee meetings as observers. His superiors quickly nixed this idea, and Hamill called to correct the "mistake."[51]

As Hamill took on the nearly monumental task of administering the work of the committee, he demonstrated little understanding of the previous decade of scientific and political combat. Further, he did not seem to have grasped the complexities of assuring an unbiased and objective process. As the study was commencing, for example, he met with Charles Kensler, who had worked on the Liggett contracts at Arthur D. Little for nearly a decade. Afterwards, Hamill urged that the PHS hire ADL as a consultant on statistics.[52]

Following a visit with C. C. Little, Hamill also wrote Assistant Surgeon General James Hundley, liaison to the advisory committee, urging him to permit Little to consult with the committee. "Dr. Little and his staff did not appear to be desperately trying to protect tobacco or to create jobs for themselves," he argued, and "they seemed overwhelmingly pleased with our activities and seemed most desirous to help in any way possible." All but overwhelmed with the committee's workload, and strikingly naive about the TIRC, Hamill failed to see Little's generous offers of help as attempts to gain influence.

Hamill was no doubt eager to assure the industry representatives that they would get a fair shake from the committee. He admired Little as a "great man of science," and Little reciprocated by offering a room at the Harvard Club whenever Hamill might be visiting New York on committee business. This offer Hamill gladly accepted. After meeting with Little at the TIRC offices in New York in 1963, Hamill wrote a note to the files explaining: "My impression of Dr. Little is that he is one of the most estimable men I have ever met. For the past four years I've heard rumors that he was the soul of integrity, and also that he had been one of the true giants in the biological sciences, but that he was nearing his dotage and was a mere figurehead in the TIRC . . . my impression was that the first two items were entirely correct but the last two items were not quite accurate."[53] As the report was nearing completion, Hamill was placed on medical leave, relieved by the more experienced and appropriately detached Eugene H. Guthrie, who guided the committee through the complex discussions and debates leading to its unanimous conclusions. According to Bayne-Jones, Hamill had suffered a breakdown under the weight of work and anxiety.[54] Hamill later denied this.[55] Nonetheless, after August 1963, he was no longer involved in the work of the committee.

Following the release of the report, Hamill would pay yet another ill-advised visit to Little at the TIRC headquarters in New York. According to Little, Hamill "expressed real disappointment in the quality of the Report" and told him that "he does not believe in any specific effect of tobacco in causation of the various diseases." Little concluded, "I have a strong feeling that this is a man of whom we probably can and should make use."[56]

The committee understood that there had been a long-running debate within the medical sciences over the term *cause*. Was a cause both *necessary* and *sufficient* to result in disease? Might there be something that sometimes causes disease? Could a factor be a *cause* if it was neither necessary nor sufficient? Might there be other factors? As we have seen, these questions were not new. But the resolution of the question—do cigarettes cause disease?—demanded that the committee articulate its methodological and epistemological criteria for arriving at a definitive answer. As a result, the Surgeon General's Advisory Committee worked to define the specific approaches utilized to reach a causal conclusion. By mid-century, it had become clear that population-based investigations would be critical to the understanding of systemic and chronic diseases. The Surgeon General's Advisory Committee came to understand the complex interdisciplinary process of determining the causes of chronic disease.

William Cochran took the lead in organizing and drafting the report's most critical chapter, "Criteria for Judgment," which laid out the justification for its causal conclusions. What did it mean to say, for example, that cigarettes *caused* lung cancer? How should *cause* be distinguished from *associated with*, *a factor*, or *determinant*? The report sought to clarify this issue at the outset, noting that "the word 'cause' is the one in general usage in connection with matters considered in this study, and it is capable of conveying the notion of a significant, effectual, relationship between an agent and an associated disorder or disease in the host." But the committee understood the problem with stating simply that smoking causes cancer.

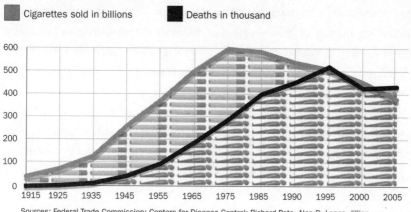

Sources: Federal Trade Commission; Centers for Disease Control; Richard Peto, Alan D. Lopez, Jillian Boreham, Michael Thun, and Clark Heath Jr., *Mortality from Smoking in Developed Countries,* 1950-2000 (Oxford: Oxford University Press, 1994).

CHART 4   Cigarettes sold and tobacco-related deaths in the United States, 1915–2005

Many individuals could smoke heavily throughout their lives and yet not develop lung cancer, just as many individuals might become infected with the tubercle bacillus but never develop tuberculosis. Therefore, they acknowledged the complexity of causal processes in medical science:

> It should be said at once, however, that no member of this Committee used the word "cause" in an absolute sense in the area of this study. Although various disciplines and fields of scientific knowledge were represented among the membership, all members shared a common conception of the multiple etiology of biological processes. No member was so naive as to insist upon mono-etiology in pathological processes or in vital phenomena.[57]

Yet the members of the committee did not wish to give too much ground. After all, the critical question, from a public health perspective, was whether smoking increases an individual's chance of developing a potentially life-threatening disease. Therefore, they concluded:

> Granted that these complexities were recognized, it is to be noted clearly that the Committee's considered decision to use the words "a cause" or "a major cause" or "a significant cause," or "a causal association" in certain conclusions about smoking and health affirms their conviction.[58]

The tobacco industry would consistently argue for an esoteric and unobtainable definition of *cause*—one that would have eliminated the known *causes* of many diseases—but the Surgeon General's Advisory Committee understood that the public's health was at stake. In the medical sciences, cause always required inference.

The committee established a clear set of criteria to evaluate the significance of a statistical association. Recognizing that inference requires judgment, the committee sought to define this process specifically, outlining five particular conditions for judging causal relations:

Consistency of the Association. Comparable results are found utilizing a wide range of methods and data.

Strength of the Association. The cause and effect has a dose response, the greater the exposure, the more likely the effect.

Specificity of Association. The effect is typically and powerfully associated with the cause. (90 percent of all lung cancers were found to occur among smokers.)

Temporal Relationship of Associated Variables. The cause must precede the effect.

Coherence of the Association. There must be an overall logic to the cause-and-effect relationship.[59] The report, for example, demonstrated that the epidemiological findings made sense in light of the animal experiments and knowledge of the pathology of cancer.

Through these five principles, the assessment of causality became part of a consistent and rational scientific explanation. These criteria are now the basic orthodoxy for integrating quantitative techniques with other data to make a causal inference regarding disease. Although the criteria themselves had been used in the past, they had never been so systematically and categorically articulated.[60]

As committee member Leonard Schuman later explained in an interview, what struck the committee was the "consistency of the findings" on lung cancer. Over the thirty case-controlled studies the committee examined, "the strength of the associations" was undeniable, "regardless of the methodology, regardless of the controls, regardless of the characteristics of the case samples . . . the outcome was the same."[61] The surgeon general's report effectively ended any remaining medical and scientific uncertainty concerning the harmfulness of smoking. Their conclusion did not mean that important scientific questions about tobacco no longer needed examination, but the *essential* question, systematically and thoroughly investigated for more than a decade, had been definitively resolved. The core skeptics—now almost exclusively tied to the industry—had been marginalized and delegitimated. At the press conference announcing the committee's findings, Terry was asked whether he would now advise a patient to stop smoking. His answer was an unequivocal "yes."[62]

Those committee members who smoked were now confronted with their conclusions. Terry, another cigarette smoker, had switched to a pipe just weeks before the 1964 report was released. He explained, "I became increasingly more convinced that cigarettes were not good for me and frankly that I was not setting a good example for the American youth and the American public."[63] Schuman, who had also continued to smoke during the work of the committee, followed Terry's example and announced that he had smoked his last cigarette. In spite of the findings, as well as the urgings of his fellow committee members and the entreaties of his wife and daughter, Cochran relied on his own statistical analysis to support his decision to continue smoking. Having smoked for a long time, he could not become a statistical nonsmoker, only a former smoker. Quitting now, he reasoned, would reduce his chances of succumbing to lung cancer from 40 percent higher than a nonsmoker's to 24 percent. "I think the comfort of my cigarettes is worth that 16 percent chance," he explained. He nonetheless conceded that he would probably cut down, and he noted that "I certainly intend to see that my children never start."[64]

In the year following the release of the report, Fieser, the heaviest smoker on the committee, was diagnosed with lung cancer. Following the removal of a lung, he wrote to his former colleagues, "You may recall that although fully convinced by the evidence, I continued heavy smoking throughout the deliberations of our committee and invoked all the usual excuses. . . . My case seems to me more convincing than any statistics."[65] Suffering as well from emphysema, heart disease, and bronchitis, all linked in the report to smoking, Fieser now relinquished his cigarettes once and for all. He wrote to Cochran, urging him to quit as well. "I recommend total nonsmoking, for it certainly makes you feel better," Fieser told his Harvard colleague. "I have not smoked since August 27th and do not find abstinence particularly painful."[66] Disease and looming mortality fractured denial with a power that the most intimate acquaintance with the data could not match.

§

For the industry, the report offered an opportunity to change course by beginning to warn its patrons about the risks of using its product. Instead, the industry chose to maintain the strategy it had adopted in 1953: insist that there is no proof that tobacco causes disease; disparage and attack all studies indicating such a relationship; support basic research on cancer largely unrelated to the hypothesis that smoking and cancer are linked; and support research on alternative theories of carcinogenesis. These four principles would continue to guide the industry, which was now firmly under the control of its legal counsel.

Although the Surgeon General's Advisory Committee cited a wide range of evidence beyond statistical and epidemiological findings, critics—especially those representing the tobacco industry—continued to portray the causal link as but a mathematical aberration. Given the definitive findings of the surgeon general's report, the cigarette companies were forced to redouble their efforts to maintain the smoke screen of "scientific controversy" and "uncertainty." They quickly developed a policy, determined by their legal staffs, to neither deny nor confirm the findings. In public, they continued to insist on the need for more research; the "merely statistical" nature of the surgeon general's conclusion; and their eagerness for their customers to "keep an open mind." They agreed to emphasize the "much" that was not known and to maintain that experimental evidence to demonstrate causality was still lacking. Little yet again offered his now traditional perspective:

> After ten years, the fact remains that knowledge is insufficient either to provide adequate proof of any hypothesis or to define the basic mechanisms of health and disease with which we are concerned. It is true now as it was in 1954 that continued research in all areas where knowledge is deficient offers the best hope for the future.[67]

And thanks to Little and the TIRC, prominent news sources would continue to report the "controversy."[68] The industry had constructed a standard of "proof" that it knew could never be met. This was not a clash of scientific epistemologies or research methods; it was a calculated PR approach, brilliantly conceived and executed for inventing controversy. Sustaining the product in the face of overwhelming knowledge of its dire harms called not for more science but for a public marketing strategy.

Tobacco researchers often expressed frustration with the industry's self-interested construction of "proof." Wynder noted that calls for experimental evidence negated the potential for any conclusion: "If you doubt statistics . . . you have already cut off every possible road to coming to an answer to the problem before you even start it."[69] Others reached similar conclusions. As A. Bradford Hill explained in 1965:

> All scientific work is incomplete—whether it be observational or experimental. All scientific work is liable to be upset or modified by advancing knowledge. That does not confer upon us a freedom to ignore the knowledge we already have, or to postpone action that it appears to demand at a given time.
>
> Who knows, asked Robert Browning, but the world may end tonight? True, but on available evidence, most of us make ready to commute on the 8:30 the next day.[70]

The authoritative voice of the Surgeon General's Advisory Committee and the subsequent surgeon general's reports left the industry with little room to maneuver. Little's repeated insistence on scientific uncertainty was wearing thin. In the face of the surgeon general's report, the decade-long strategy of denial and distortion of the medical evidence would receive new scrutiny within the industry.[71]

§

Industry researchers and executives tacitly acknowledged the scientific consensus even before the release of the first surgeon general's report. Even though their public position remained unchanged, industry executives internally expressed great concern about the government's report. It constituted the most significant crisis for tobacco companies since 1953, when they created the TIRC. With its key defenses in disarray following the report's release, the TIRC sought to construct a response. Its first act was to change its name. The TIRC now became the Council for Tobacco Research (CTR). At the same time it broke its tie of more than a decade with Hill & Knowlton, which continued to maintain the Tobacco Institute account. At the TIRC meeting in which the name change was approved, tobacco executives urged Little to take the offensive in critiquing the report. Little outlined what he saw to be the chief problems in the review, centering attention on issues of measurement (inhalation, whole smoke versus condensates, and socioeconomic differences in lung cancer rates), and he was encouraged to raise these issues with Terry and the PHS. Bowman Gray of R.J. Reynolds, as he had done in the past, urged a more aggressive response to the "attack" of the surgeon general. Rather than using the TIRC and the Scientific Advisory Board to promote "more research," he argued for a sustained counteroffensive. According to the minutes of the meeting, Edwin P. Finch, president of Brown & Williamson, chided the TIRC leadership and "expressed disgust . . . at the fat-assed attitude of Hartnett and company"—which, according to American Tobacco executive Robert Heimann, "had gone on for ten years."[72]

Others, however, questioned the decade-old industry approach of maintaining "controversy." A number of analysts now concluded that this formulation could only alienate the public and weaken the industry's credibility. After more than a decade of denial and obfuscation, the report offered the industry an opportunity to set a new course, to accept the risks of its product, intensify its research into modifying these risks, and sharply reconfigure its promotion and marketing. These alternative strategies received significant comment and analysis within the inner circles of tobacco executives and scientists.

A number of industry leaders recognized that in light of the overwhelming accrual of scientific and medical studies of smoking's harms, the strategy created by Hill & Knowlton in 1953 had become exceedingly threadbare. It was a new era, and the sale and marketing of cigarettes demanded new thinking. In July 1963, Brown & Williamson's chief counsel, Addison Yeaman, offered this confidential assessment:

Whatever qualifications we may assert to minimize the impact of the Report, we must face the fact that a responsible and qualified group of previously non-committed scientists and medical authorities have spoken. One would suppose we would not repeat Dr. Little's oft reiterated "not proven." One would hope the industry would act affirmatively and not merely react defensively.

In calling for an active response, Yeaman asked that other tobacco industry executives accept that the cigarette had been categorically shown to be a serious risk to health:

Certainly one would hope to prove there is no etiological factor in smoke but the odds are greatly against success in that effort.[73]

He proposed a wholly new approach:

I suggest that for the new research effort we enlist the cooperation of the Surgeon General, the Public Health Service, the American Cancer Society, the American Heart Association, American Medical Association and any and all other responsible health agencies or medical or scientific associations concerned with the question of tobacco and health. The new effort should be conducted by a new organization lavishly financed, autonomous, self perpetuating, and uncontrolled save that its efforts be confined to the single problem of the relation of tobacco to human health.[74]

The TIRC, given its history, would *not* be in a good position to perform this task. Yeaman acknowledged that since its inception, the TIRC had principally acted as a public relations unit:

The TIRC cannot, in my opinion, provide the vehicle for such research. It was conceived as a public relations gesture and (however undefiled the Scientific Advisory Board and its grants may be) it has functioned as a public relations operation. Moreover its organization, certainly in its present form, does not allow the breadth of research—cancer, emphysema, cardiovascular disorders, etc.—essential to the protection of the tobacco industry.[75]

This proposal never came to pass. Denial of the relationship between smoking and disease had been deemed a crucial element of the industry's

234 THE CIGARETTE CENTURY

legal defense against liability litigation, and any shift in this position was viewed as potentially enhancing the litigation risk. Yeaman soon assumed the helm of the TIRC (now CTR) and never changed its course. The organization continued to argue that there was still a controversy and continued to fund research unrelated to the question of smoking and health. The central problem with the industry's position—and cover-ups in general—is that there is no easy exit strategy. Having steadfastly denied the harms of smoking in the face of scientific data for a decade, the industry lawyers saw no alternative but to continue.

Still, the position of insisting on a "continuing controversy" had itself become a source of internal controversy. In 1967, an R.J. Reynolds executive, J. S. Dowdell, noted that "the industry has little, if any, positive evidence" to refute the findings that cigarettes cause disease.[76] After more than a decade of TIRC research, no evidence to contradict the knowledge of smoking's harm had been produced. In 1968, William Kloepfer, Jr., vice president of public relations for the Tobacco Institute, wrote to Earle Clements, the institute's president, to say that that the industry's consistent denial of harm and risk might now be untenable:

> Our basic position in the cigarette controversy is subject to the charge, and may be subject to a finding, that we are making false or misleading statements to promote the sale of cigarettes.[77]

There was much to be said for Kloepfer's assessment. The industry's very efforts to limit its legal liabilities were augmenting those liabilities.

Helmut Wakeham, the director of research and development at Philip Morris, advocated a similar shift in strategy starting in 1970. In May of that year, he wrote to Clements expressing doubts about the industry approach in the aftermath of the report. He cautioned, "I think we have spent too much time and energy being 'negative' on the subject of smoking and health, undermining our public image," and went on to warn that the industry's focus on controversy could have contradictory elements:

> Our medical research support efforts through C.T.R. and A.M.A. have been confusing and contradictory in the public eye because we have on the one hand proclaimed these endeavors to be aimed at "finding the

truth about smoking and health" and at the same time denied the existence of a problem.

According to Wakeham, this inconsistency cost the industry credibility in all its public pronouncements. "I am, therefore, advocating emphasis on the positive aspects of smoking both in research and in public relations," he explained.

Nobody believes we are interested in the truth on this subject; and the fact that a multibillion dollar industry has put up 30 million dollars for this over a ten-year period cannot be impressive to a public which at the same time is told we spend upwards of 300 million dollars in one year on advertising.[78]

In December 1970, Wakeham wrote to Philip Morris President Joseph Cullman III, suggesting that the industry change its tack. "It might be appropriate to comment on the question: what kind of CTR program is best for the industry?" Wakeham noted.

It has been stated that CTR is a program to find out the "truth about smoking and health." What is true to one is false to another. CTR and the Industry have frequently denied what others find as "truth." Let's face it. We are interested in evidence which we believe denies the allegation that cigarette smoking causes disease.

Wakeham suggested what he called "Option B":

Use the CTR program as a means of establishing expert scientific witnesses who will testify on behalf of the Industry in legislative halls, in litigations, at scientific meetings, and before the press and public.[79]

This is precisely what the CTR was already doing under the Special Projects programs that began in 1966.[80]

Under the rubric of special projects, the CTR could exert greater influence and control over research than was the case with research selected for funding under the grants program of the SAB. Perhaps the most notorious known case was that of pathologist Freddy Homburger, whose Cambridge-based Microbiological Associates had been retained to conduct experiments on hamsters exposed to smoke. Homburger and his colleagues found precancerous lesions similar to earlier research conducted by pathologist Oscar Auerbach on beagles. But when he submitted the draft paper to CTR, Hockett raised a series of objections, requesting that he substitute medical euphemisms to describe the characteristic malignant lesions; Hockett advised that he use the term *pseudoepithieliomatous hyperplasia*. When Homburger refused, he was notified that CTR would no longer fund his work. Further, they enlisted publicist Leonard Zahn (formerly of Hill & Knowlton) to attempt to discredit him. Such cases were in all likelihood unusual; researchers doing contract work for CTR, as well as those funded through the SAB, understood that the future of their support depended on not rocking the boat of Big Tobacco. For the most part, CTR research steered clear of experiments and studies that might elucidate the relationship of cigarettes and disease.[81]

A number of other observers also noted that the industry would require fundamentally new strategies to sustain the cigarette business. George Weissman of Philip Morris concluded that "at some point, reflecting the same seriousness with which we met the Report, we must in the near future provide some answers which will give smokers a psychological crutch and a self-rationale to continue smoking."[82]

§

Despite internal debate, the cigarette manufacturers continued to collude in a PR approach that claimed that the evidence against their product was wholly inadequate and that attempts to regulate their product were unnecessary and inappropriate given the "continuing controversy." Executives insisted publicly that there remained an "open question" and "ongoing controversy" about the harms attributed to their product. In a 1968 memo on industry communications with doctors and dentists, sent to William Kloepfer of the Tobacco Institute, Carl Thompson, who had worked on the tobacco account at Hill & Knowlton since 1953, underscored the industry's commitment to denial:

The most important type of story is that which casts doubt on the cause and effect theory of disease and smoking. . . . Thus, the headline should strongly call out the point—Controversy! Other factors! Unknowns![83]

As many company executives anticipated, the surgeon general's report greatly weakened this defense strategy. While the industry refused to abandon its commitment to "uncertainty," its focus would shift. It would now contend that the (*alleged*) risks of smoking must be borne exclusively by the smoker. Even as it insisted that the harms of smoking were unproven, the industry would argue that those same harms were well-known to smokers, who accepted them rationally and knowingly. This new strategy would prove essential to the marketing, promotion, and especially the defense of tobacco in the decades ahead.

§

Following the release of the report in January 1964 and the resulting banner headlines throughout the country, it was widely assumed that Americans would give up tobacco. After a fine year in 1963, cigarette sales fell some 15 to 20 percent in the first half of 1964. By 1965, however, the industry had rebounded, reporting record sales, per capita consumption of 4,318 cigarettes, and the highest profits in its history. By 1973, tobacco consumption had not declined appreciably from 1964 levels.[84] Reports of the demise of Big Tobacco had been premature.

Nonetheless, the surgeon general's report was a pivotal document in the history of public health. In making such a powerful and definitive statement, the report created a new realm of action for public health officials. As political scientist A. Lee Fritschler pointed out in his analysis of smoking and federal policy making, the surgeon general's office provided the "combination of legitimacy and exposure" necessary to making smoking's harms an unquestioned fact. The PHS distributed 350,000 copies of the report within a year after its release, including one to every medical student in the country. It also planned to post a brief summary of the report in 50,000 pharmacies by January 1965.[85] But the surgeon general's office possessed few resources to mount any significant public health programs. Nonetheless, the report did create an authority that surgeons general have been eager to use ever since. The report became the model for thirty subsequent reports on smoking and its harms, which have been influential in shaping the policy of tobacco regulation.[86] The report's format became a model for reports on numerous other health concerns as well.

Ultimately, the Surgeon General's Advisory Committee and its report opened a new era of what might be called procedural science. The substantive authority and impact of the report rested fundamentally on the integrity and independence of the *process* of reaching its conclusions. Resolving controversies in science, medicine, and public health—especially in areas where there were powerful vested interests—would increasingly require the integration of scientific data from a wide range of experiments, studies, and clinical observations. This would, in turn, require a collaborative process of critical evaluation to reach a state-of-the-art conclusion and recommendation for action. These recommendations could range from clinical interventions to policy innovations in public health to the assertion of regulatory authority.

The production of the report created the essential protocol for procedural science. The participants must be deemed free of conflicts of interest, the process had to be essentially transparent, and the conclusion, to be received as authoritative, must ultimately rest on the collective expertise, status, and independence of those reviewing and negotiating over the available data. This is why, in subsequent decades, conflict of interest emerged as such a critical element in medical and public health science. Unannounced and undisclosed conflicts threaten the legitimate basis of procedural science and its impact on the integrity of clinical medicine and public health policy. Policies regarding conflict of interest came to be more sharply articulated and mandated.[87] This approach stood in sharp contrast to the explicit conflicts of interest in industry-sponsored research.

Procedural science calls for reaching consensus across diverse disciplines and perspectives, using multiple scientific methodologies. The search for agreement and consensus is crucial to this process. Participants are not required to relinquish disciplinary claims or approaches but to reach agreement within a diversity of methods and *a priori* claims. Finally, procedural science requires wide dissemination of clinically and socially important knowledge.

The Surgeon General's Advisory Committee created the operational model for procedural science in adjudicating conflicts in which powerful economic and political interests might unduly influence medical practice and public policy. Given the resources which the industry had brought to bear to sustain the notion of a scientific controversy, it was crucial for the government to develop a process to evaluate carefully and critically the available evidence and seek a consensual conclusion. Only with this type of unassailable evaluation could the government adequately inform the public and legislate programs for health promotion and disease prevention.

To a reader of the report many decades later, the depth of the review, the importance of the analysis of causality, and the momentous conclusions are reflected on every page. In the dry prose of federal bureaucracy and modern science, the report succeeded—by its application of the principles of procedural science—in settling for good the question of the lethal harms of cigarette smoking. In an age in which powerful corporate interests threaten to overwhelm the integrity of science, procedural science offers a powerful counterweight.

Following the release of the report, the surgeon general's office and the federal government would assert new authority and responsibility for the most important health issues of our time. In this sense, the report can be seen as yet another example of the expansion of the federal government's regulatory powers during the Kennedy and Johnson administrations.[88] By setting out to determine the true relationship between cigarettes and disease, the government accepted new authority for science and health in the consumer culture. Inherent in the report, therefore, were powerful notions of the possibility of the liberal state. In the future, from tobacco to HIV, the American public and even the international community would look to the surgeon general for scientifically validated public health policies. The 1964 report remains a signal contribution not only to the history of the cigarette but to the history of public health.

The Surgeon General is entitled to draw his own con-
clusions. He is treading on questionable ground, how-
ever, when he begins to impose these opinions on the
public, without *acknowledging the fact that this mat-*
ter is in controversy among scientists.[1]

SENATOR SAM J. ERVIN, JR., 1965

In the six years that have elapsed since the Surgeon
General's massive report on Smoking and Health, the
total number of Americans who have died of cigarette-
induced lung cancer is approximately ten times the
number of deaths caused in August, 1945, by the drop-
ping of the atomic bomb on Hiroshima.

Can it possibly be true that the lethal effects of even
ten Hiroshimas, in the form of these then silent holo-
causts in our very midst cannot move the Food and Drug
Administration to act to warn and protect the American
people against the perpetuation of this horror?[2]

THOMAS WHITESIDE, 1971

CHAPTER 8

Congress:
The Best Filter Yet

AMONG THE CONCLUSIONS of the 1964 surgeon general's report was that smoking constituted a hazard requiring "remedial action." Although Luther Terry had proposed a "second phase" of investigation by the Public Health Service into what that action should be, it was already clear when the report was released that this assessment would take place in other venues. As Stanhope Bayne-Jones, the most politically seasoned member of the committee, later explained:

Phase II led, of course, into economic and legal considerations of great magnitude. What would be done would affect the industries, affect part of the national economy, affect international relationships, possibly disturb labor relationships as well as laboring individuals. It was so important from a governmental standpoint that I doubt whether any clear notion of ever undertaking phase II through this mechanism was envisioned under the Public Health Service.[3]

The very success of the advisory committee had depended on its isolation from such questions. Terry astutely recognized that the committee could only speak with authority about the scientific and medical nature of the health risks of smoking; the policy questions would be decided by a process far different from the procedural science conducted by his committee. Its main purpose

241

was to provide scientific and medical authority to generate new public policies on tobacco. The committee sat at the boundary between knowledge and politics but derived its legitimacy and influence by not treading across it.

If Terry's committee had been distinguished by its disinterested adherence to facts as determined by scientific research, the next phase would be remarkable for aggressive political combat. The need to decide what should be done about the risks of smoking—now that they had been so clearly determined—created a radical new era in the history of the cigarette and, for that matter, the history of regulatory politics. Although the tobacco industry would maintain its ten-year-old strategy of scientific denial and rhetorical skepticism, the battle turned sharply away from science and into the domain of public policy. What should the state do when a popular product is demonstrated to cause such significant harm to health?

The historical evolution of the cigarette offered few precedents for regulatory intervention. The "fiasco" of Prohibition would be repeatedly cited— especially by the tobacco industry—as supporting a hands-off approach. The industry argued that the government had no regulatory burden: since "everyone" was now aware of the "controversy" over the "alleged" harms of smoking, it would be paternalistic and counterproductive to regulate the promotion and sale of cigarettes.[4] But there were many available options between the extremes of no action and outright prohibition, ranging from education to radical restrictions on the marketing and public use of cigarettes.

Tobacco products were still virtually unregulated, an increasingly exceptional status at mid-century. Throughout the economy, the regulation of new products for safety had become a prominent feature of the emerging consumer culture. But the cigarette had fallen through this tightening net. As food and drug regulation was created in 1906 and stiffened in 1938, tobacco products were viewed within the Food and Drug Administration as neither food nor drug and, thus, outside the agency's mandate.[5] The industry successfully avoided any requirements for reporting ingredients or evaluating the safety of the product. There was virtually no governmental oversight of the manufacturing process. Given the overwhelming task of assuring the safety of food and drugs, it was small wonder that the FDA avoided adding tobacco to its mandate, even as concerns about the health impact of smoking were rising.

The first regulatory proposals following the 1964 surgeon general's report centered on advertising and packaging. The growing public recognition of the harms of smoking had brought cigarette promotion under close scrutiny. In a time when many saw advertising's purpose as mainly informational—educating consumers to make rational choices among competing products—cigarette ads were widely viewed as motivational and perhaps too persuasive.[6] They had so stretched the notion of "information" that they were frequently offered as key examples of excess in modern consumer marketing.[7] Now that the product was deemed harmful—even deadly—the manipulation of consumer desire could no longer be ignored. Should tobacco advertisements and packaging be required to apprise consumers of the risks the surgeon general's committee had now so explicitly specified?

Unsure that either the industry or consumers were to be trusted, advocates of tobacco regulation looked to the federal government to adjudicate these tensions at the intersection of culture and public health. The Federal Trade Commission, the agency charged with maintaining standards of truth in advertising, was the governmental branch to address this task. The FTC had investigated tobacco ad campaigns as early as the 1930s, focusing mainly on ads that promised particular health benefits of smoking. These ads had often been found by the federal agency to be misleading, prompting officials to issue orders for the companies to "cease and desist" from such claims. This process was both time-consuming and costly. Certainly, the industry considered such interventions a nuisance, but the very purpose of these campaigns was to test the boundaries of what was permissible in a fluid market.[8] If an ad campaign came under FTC scrutiny, it could be modified or abandoned for an even bolder alternative.[9]

Throughout the 1950s, tobacco companies continued to circumvent advertising regulation, presenting a variety of claims about the salutary health effects of particular brands, downplaying health concerns, and attempting to reassure consumers with images of healthy, attractive smokers. As we have seen, several prominent campaigns—most notably, R.J. Reynolds's "More Doctors Smoke Camels"—prominently featured doctors in an effort to reassure smokers about rising medical concerns.

In 1955, in the face of the emerging epidemiological findings, the FTC issued voluntary guidelines that urged cigarette makers to avoid unsubstantiated or ambiguous claims about the tar and nicotine content of particular brands.[10] Such claims were all but meaningless because there was no uniform technique for measuring this content and no approach to assessing how cigarettes were smoked in practice. Yet they could have a powerful influence over smokers worried about their health.

Beyond listing tar and nicotine content, tobacco companies had been altering their product in response to public concerns about the cigarette's health effects. The most durable and popular of these changes was the introduction of new filter cigarettes. Even as manufacturers—at John Hill's insistence—abandoned the use of doctors and other health claims in their advertising, they began to market filters and promote apparent reductions in tar and nicotine with bold fanfare. Kent's "Micronite" filter, which in its original form contained asbestos, assured consumers that "your voice of wisdom says SMOKE KENT." Liggett & Myers proclaimed that its new filter was "just what the doctor ordered." Viceroys promised "Double-Barreled Health Protection." Menthol cigarettes were also promoted aggressively during this period, drawing upon traditional therapeutic associations with cough and cold remedies.[11] Salem, combining both innovations, announced that its mentholated filter cigarette marked the "First Truly New Smoking Advance in over 40 Years!"

By 1954, filters made up approximately 10 percent of the cigarette market. The number would approach 90 percent by the mid-1970s. At the same time that the tobacco industry continued to insist there was no credible scientific evidence of the harmfulness of smoking, it nonetheless undertook major campaigns to develop and market cigarettes whose main selling point was that they kept harmful substances out of smokers' lungs. The industry understood that in the face of the mounting scientific evidence, smokers needed many kinds of reassurance. It might come in the notion that there was a "controversy" about whether or not smoking was dangerous; or it might come in the notion that filters effectively eliminated those dangers.

It became clear early on, given the media prominence of concerns about smoking and lung cancer, that filters were a critical new marketing tool. Yet industry researchers always knew that filters projected an image of safety, rather than a reality. In December 1953, as Hill & Knowlton took the public relations helm, chemist Claude Teague filed a "disclosure of invention" with the directors of his research laboratory at R.J. Reynolds. Teague had found that varying the pH in test filters led to changes in their color upon smoking. "I have observed, and believe it to be generally true," he wrote, "that the cigarette smoking public attaches great significance to visual examination of the filter material in filter tip cigarettes after smoking the cigarettes. A before and after smoking visual comparison is usually made and if the filter tip material, after smoking is darkened, the tip is automatically judged to be effective." Teague, therefore, recommended altering the pH to ensure that filters darkened upon smoking. He concluded, "While the use of such color change material would probably have little or no effect on the actual efficiency of the filter tip material, the advertising and sales advantages are obvious."[12] As Myron Johnston and W. L. Dunn of Philip Morris would later note, "the illusion of filtration is as important as the fact of filtration."[13]

By introducing a range of filtered products and explicitly claiming that they reduced tar and nicotine, the industry promoted the notion that its product not only could be successfully modified but had been. This approach—meticulously designed and implemented—proved remarkably successful.[14] It appealed to the hopes of smokers eager to maintain a highly addictive behavior and embraced the allure, in a technological age, of a technological fix.[15] If and when a harmful substance was identified in cigarette smoke, the companies promised, they would simply remove it. "Well, obviously, a filter takes out certain tar and nicotine. I don't think the industry admits that there are any bad elements. If there are bad elements, through our laboratories, through the surgeon general, through the AMA, through acts of God, and luck, we hope we may find them, and if they are found they will be removed, but at this point we don't know," explained Hugh Cullman, president of the Tobacco Merchants Association and director of Philip Morris.[16] Tobacco Institute President James Richards noted that "the production and marketing of filter cigarets are matters of individual company competitive business. Anyone familiar with the tobacco industry knows that tobacco manufacturers constantly compete to make products to please customers."[17] The rise of filters simply followed "consumer preferences." It had nothing to do with consumer fears of a threat the companies would not admit existed.

The competitive introduction of new brands in the late 1950s and early 1960s, often called the "tar derby," produced claim and counterclaim among the tobacco companies and eventually drew the attention of Congress and federal regulators.[18] Questions of public interest and regulation rose to the fore. What was actually being filtered out? Could it be measured? Did filters really reduce the harms of smoking? How and why were the manufacturers modifying their product, and how were they assessing these changes?

In 1957, Minnesota Congressman John A. Blatnik, chairman of the Legal and Monetary Affairs Subcommittee of the House Government Operations Committee, held hearings on filtered cigarettes to investigate whether the FTC was properly policing cigarette advertising. Witnesses told the committee that filtered cigarettes typically delivered tar and nicotine content similar to (in some cases greater than) unfiltered brands, and that companies had often increased levels of tar and nicotine as they introduced filters. This despite advertisements with lines like "Just what the doctor ordered!" Blatnik, a regular smoker, halved his smoking following the hearings.[19] The *Report of the Hearings* concluded that "the cigarette manufacturers have deceived the American public through their advertising of cigarettes."[20] Shortly after the hearings ended, Blatnik reflected that "much of current cigarette advertising is misleading the public into thinking that it is getting a protection which really isn't there. And the principal device that is used is the filter tip."[21] Following the hearings, the notion of warning labels on cigarettes began to attract proponents. At the very least, it was now argued, the industry should be required to alert consumers to the "potential" risks associated with their product.[22]

The only representative from the industry to appear before the committee was none other than the industry's perennial spokesman, C. C. Little, who claimed that he did *not* represent the industry but rather the "independent" committee. He insisted he had no knowledge whatsoever of the science of filters. A "man of science," Little had no patience for the committee and its questions, which he deemed irrelevant. Since cigarettes had not been demonstrated to pose risks to smokers, he asked, why even address the question of filters? The popular interest in filters was the fault of the American Cancer Society, which he accused of alarming the American public unnecessarily.[23] *Time* found it "surprising" that Little had claimed to know nothing about filters one way or the other.[24] Little wrote to Editor-in-Chief Henry Luce, protesting the coverage. He explained, "It's not really 'surprising' . . . that industry problems such as filters are and will remain outside [the TIRC's] field unless and until there is scientific evidence of something that needs to be fil-

tered. Such evidence does not exist today."[25] Luce, amused by Little's defensiveness, shot back a rejoinder: "A witness so distinguished as yourself who
voluntarily takes the stand and professes innocence of—and indifference
to—the subject in question, becomes, I believe, an object of legitimate surprise to any thoughtful reporter." He reviewed the publications of the TIRC,
taking issue with Little's claim that "cigarette filters [are] irrelevant to the research program," and noting: "One other point in your letter, which was not
in your testimony in such concise terms, is quite striking. I refer to your statement that there is no scientific evidence that *anything* needs to be filtered
from cigarettes. Too bad that quote couldn't have been in *Time*'s story."[26]

§

Even though tobacco companies aggressively marketed filtered cigarettes,
they refused to acknowledge that cigarettes were harmful. Crucial to avoiding regulatory interventions was the campaign for scientific "controversy" developed with such skill by Hill & Knowlton. The industry therefore insisted
on an agnostic position. Regulatory action on tobacco during the 1950s
foundered on the shoals of the widely promoted "uncertainties" of the harms
of the cigarette not fully legitimated until the 1964 surgeon general's report.
In this respect, the TIRC public relations activities had the additional function of diverting public health and other potential regulatory action. If the
harms of smoking were "unknown"—as the industry so persistently and publicly claimed—the potential for political action was decidedly limited.

Following the Blatnik hearings, the limits of the FTC to regulate tobacco advertising became explicit. The Food, Drug, and Cosmetic Act of
1938 had provided the FTC with additional authority—including the
right to obtain court injunctions—to regulate the claims on food, pharmaceuticals and medical devices, and cosmetics, but with tobacco outside this
mandate, the FTC claims were constrained. While the 1955 rules had forbidden advertisements featuring unvalidated figures on tar and nicotine
content, ultimately the FTC would ban the publication of these numbers
irrespective of their apparent validation. In 1960, the FTC issued new rules
in an attempt to address widespread concern that the "tar derby" had created the impression among the public that lower numbers meant a safer
product. According to the FTC, tar or nicotine levels were unsubstantiated
"health claims" that now must be eliminated from all tobacco promotion.[27]

According to FTC Chair Earl W. Kintner, the claims about tar and nicotine content "were confusing to the public and possibly misleading," given that there were no uniform testing methods and no proof "of the advantage to the smoker." He encouraged the companies to end the "tar derby." To demonstrate that a company had a "safer" cigarette would require the companies to acknowledge precisely what they refused to: that there were serious problems with the product. Kintner was pleased that the industry had apparently agreed on a voluntary basis to eliminate the questionable tar and nicotine data. FTC monitors, however, found that despite the February 1, 1960, deadline, some ads continued to make excessive claims. On behalf of Brown & Williamson, for example, a television announcer proclaimed that Viceroy "does the best filtering job in the world."[28]

To have any hope of implementing effective regulation, the FTC needed a definitive scientific statement. The surgeon general's 1964 report provided it. With this confirmation of the harms of smoking, it was now widely perceived within the FTC that their regulatory authority over the packaging and marketing of cigarettes could, at last, be sustained. As the surgeon general's committee had gone about its business, so too had an eager FTC. If, as Terry's panel had so authoritatively concluded, smoking *causes* lung cancer and other serious diseases, then specific approaches to regulatory action would be appropriate. On the day the report was released, the FTC announced that it would move "promptly"—and within its authority—to address the regulatory needs inherent in the findings.[29]

Now under the direction of Kennedy appointee Paul Rand Dixon, the FTC moved with what one commentator called "lightning speed for a federal agency" to consolidate its regulatory authority over tobacco in the wake of the surgeon general's report.[30] In the week following the release of the report, it unveiled a new set of proposed rules requiring warnings on all packs and all advertisements and called for public hearings to review the proposed labels. While this action drew support from public health groups and the voluntary health organizations, such as the American Cancer Society, the industry and its allies in Congress began preparing their defense.[31] There was already in place a strong contingent of legislators from tobacco-growing states ready to oppose any measures that might negatively impact the industry and the tobacco farmers. The proposed FTC regulations also illuminated critical tensions within the federal bureaucracy. The U.S. Department of Agriculture—which administered the tobacco price support program for farmers—weighed in heavily against any health warnings on packages.[32] The USDA had longstanding ties to tobacco farmers, their congressional representatives, and the industry. The department clearly understood that their future congressional support was dependent on sustaining these alliances. The industry quickly became expert in assisting the tobacco farming community in their opposition to regulation.[33]

The industry found another strong ally in organized medicine. Concerns about pending health legislation and other potential professional regulations led the American Medical Association (AMA) to resist taking any position on the harms of smoking.[34] Following the release of the surgeon general's report, the tobacco industry offered the AMA's Education Research Fund an initial grant of $10 million to conduct further research.[35] This contribution led to the view, heartily endorsed in the industry, that "more research" was needed. The AMA was eager not to alienate those tobacco-state congressmen and senators whose votes would be needed in their efforts to defeat Medicare and Medicaid. When the FTC proposed warning labels, Dr. F. J. L. Blasingame, chief executive of the AMA, wrote that they were "likely to be ignored"; instead, he explained, "it is our opinion that the answer that will do most to protect the public health lies not in labeling . . . but in research." In a letter published in *JAMA*, Blasingame explained:

> More than 90 million persons in the United States use tobacco in some form; and, of these, 72 million use cigarettes. Long standing social customs and practices are established in the use of tobacco; the economic lives of tobacco growers, processors, and merchants are entwined in the industry; and local, state, and federal governments are the recipients of and dependent upon many millions of dollars of tax revenue. For these reasons, it is most appropriate that a subject of this magnitude, regarding the labeling and advertising of tobacco, be controlled by the Congress of the United States in the form of enacted legislation, if any, rather than promulgated administrative regulations.[36]

Journalists Drew Pearson and Jack Anderson would call the AMA–tobacco industry connection, "the weirdest lobbying alliance in legislative history. . . . The doctors were more concerned about Medicare, which they fancied as a threat to their fees, than about the threat to the nation's lungs."[37]

In March 1964, the FTC held hearings in which the full range of industry and public health interests were heard, and on June 27, it issued new trade regulation rules.[38] The FTC contended that given the surgeon general's findings, tobacco companies would be engaging in "an unfair or deceptive act" (explicitly following the FTC's statutory mandate) if they did not disclose on both packages and in ads: "Caution: cigarette smoking is dangerous to health and may cause death from cancer and other diseases."[39] According to its ruling, such warnings would be uniformly required as of January 1, 1965. After decades of sporadic, weak attempts to police tobacco advertising campaign by campaign, the FTC had thrown down the regulatory gauntlet.

§

The companies answered with a meticulously prepared set of counter-maneuvers. Since the late 1950s, the industry had been building the Tobacco Institute into a considerable force for political lobbying, in order to address a growing concern among the company CEOs that the TIRC was not mounting a vigorous and effective response to the ongoing "attacks" on their product. As R.J. Reynolds President E. A. Darr explained in a 1957 letter to his counterpart Paul Hahn at American Tobacco:

> It now appears . . . that the tobacco industry should go on the offensive in bringing the truth about cigarette smoking to the public. The only way to destroy a lie is to correct it with the truth. . . . Certainly, no one can question the necessity of our going on the offensive without delay."[40]

John Hill advised the establishment of another unit, separate from the TIRC, that would explicitly act as a trade association for the industry's growing political and PR needs. After all, the TIRC had been explicitly developed to sustain claims of independence, commitment to science, and pursuit of the "truth" about tobacco. Its credibility and influence rested on the perception of restraint and a narrow scientific mission. As Carl Thompson of Hill & Knowlton explained in a confidential memo, "A flamboyant campaign against the anti-smoking propagandists would unquestionably alienate much of the support of the moderates in both scientific and lay publics." Moreover, the scientists whom Hill & Knowlton had recruited to serve on the TIRC's Scientific Advisory Board had expressed repeated concerns about the board's independence and their personal credibility among scientific peers. Thompson urged that TIRC stay the course.[41] In the words of an industry attorney, "the creation of a separate organization for public information was hit upon as a way of keeping Little inviolate and untainted in his ivory tower while giving a new group a little more freedom of action in the public relations field."[42]

This approach would protect the PR "capital" invested in the TIRC while creating an unencumbered unit that could conduct both political lobbying and a more aggressive brand of public relations. Freed of the constraint of the TIRC's "scientific mission," Hill & Knowlton worked to create a state-of-the-art political and PR operation to address the regulatory initiatives on the horizon in the wake of the Blatnik hearings. After its founding in 1958, the Tobacco Institute quickly emerged as one of Washington's most powerful and effective political lobbies. Just as the industry had made critical innovations in advertising and public relations, so now it pioneered new and aggressive approaches to managing its regulatory and political environment.

In 1964, utilizing a combination of skills, resources, and Washington insiders, the Tobacco Institute assiduously prepared for the political fights that would follow in the wake of the surgeon general's report. The institute anticipated that the ground on which the tobacco wars were fought would shift from the scientific realm to the political. Certainly, these battles would engage scientific questions, but Congress, not the medical journals, would be the new primary site of conflict. It was terrain that greatly favored the tobacco industry.

§

In September and October 1964, Sir Philip J. Rogers and Geoffrey F. Todd, senior officials of the British Tobacco Research Council, conducted a comprehensive tour of the American tobacco industry, meeting with the heads of the major companies, the research directors, and the legal teams formulating tobacco policy. In a confidential report filed upon their return to Great Britain, the two men offered a candid analysis of the policy dilemmas now facing the American companies following the release of the surgeon general's report.

According to Rogers and Todd, the crucial factor shaping industry policy in the United States was the fear of litigation. Political and regulatory

strategy was principally set by legal counsel, who scrupulously guarded tobacco companies from liability risk. In this respect, the regulatory environment in the United States differed from that facing the industry in Britain,
where litigation against the companies was not considered a serious risk. By
1964, over thirty lawsuits accusing the industry of negligence and other
malfeasance had been filed in American courts. Though most had been
dismissed or dropped, the risks associated with liability litigation were considered potentially disastrous. "In consequence of the importance of the
lawsuits, the main power in the smoking and health situation undoubtedly
rests with the lawyers," Rogers and Todd wrote.[43]

> The leadership in the U.S. smoking and health situation therefore lies with
> the powerful Policy Committee of senior lawyers advising the industry, and
> their policy, very understandably, in effect is "don't take any chances." It is
> a situation that does not encourage constructive or bold approaches to
> smoking and health problems, and it also means that the Policy Commit-
> tee of lawyers exercises close control over all aspects of the problems.[44]

Following the surgeon general's report, even as some industry executives
(including some lawyers) offered proposals for modifying the decade-old
"not proven" claim, the Policy Committee strongly resisted any deviation
from this traditional position, which it deemed crucial to the effective defense against liability actions. The committee feared that any discussion of
modifying the product or openly researching its biologically active properties—as was being done in the United Kingdom—could be viewed in the
courts as an "implied admission" that the manufacturer *knew* the product was
harmful.[45] Any move away from an "agnostic" public posture could lead to
high-risk litigation. Even as the industry's insistence on a "continuing controversy" became increasingly untenable from a scientific and public relations
perspective, the companies remained wedded to it for legal reasons. This
dilemma would shape tobacco politics right into the twenty-first century.

§

The Policy Committee began as a group of industry lawyers who met to plot
the industry's response to the expected regulatory effort. In late 1963, as the
Surgeon General's Advisory Committee was finishing its report, the com-

mittee met almost daily, mapping strategies to deflect any potential regulatory initiatives, especially those that required warning labels on packages and advertisements. Evaluating every possible contingency, they drafted testimony, offered questions and statements to sympathetic legislators, and prepared witnesses for legislative hearings.[46] Chaired by R.J. Reynolds's Henry Ramm, the group included attorneys Addison Yeaman from Brown & Williamson, Fred Haas from Liggett & Myers, and Cy Hetsko from American Tobacco, as well as representatives from Lorillard and Philip Morris. "This Committee is extremely powerful; it determines the high policy of the industry on all smoking or health matters—research and public relations matters, for example, as well as legal matters—and it reports directly to the presidents," explained the two industry representatives from Great Britain.[47]

The industry understood that the situation demanded unity. Even as companies competed sharply for market share and pushed the boundaries of health claims, they were committed to presenting a seamless front on science, policy, and law. In a February 1964 meeting, the executives agreed to appoint a single spokesman to respond to the FTC regulators. "Counsel were in agreement that if representatives of individual companies were to make a presentation to the FTC, they might be faced with embarrassing questions as to particular advertising and that conflicting statements as to the proposed Trade Regulation Rules might be voiced." As a result they agreed to rely on attorney Thomas Austern of Covington & Burling to speak for them all. He "would be best able to 'field' these questions, to plead ignorance to ads, etc."[48]

§

The industry lawyers understood, even before the release of the Terry report, that the writing was on the wall, if not yet on the package. It was inevitable that some form of warning labels would soon be required. With the FTC rules pending and laws regulating the promotion of cigarettes being proposed in up to twenty state legislatures, the tobacco industry brilliantly reversed field. The most effective strategy for derailing proposed FTC regulations, they now determined, would be to *seek* congressional oversight. If the industry could not avoid government action, it could ensure that the action was taken in their preferred venue: the U.S. Congress. "An Act of Congress is essential to the industry" concluded the British observers in their confidential memo.[49] Not only did the industry have "friends" in Congress, especially—but not exclusively—from tobacco growing states, industry lawyers and lobbyists recognized that Congress would be eager to protect its own authority against an activist regulatory agency. Therefore "[t]he Policy Committee was directed to propose a form of bill for Congressional action which would *preempt* the field."[50] The industry would achieve this preemption by acceding to a package label while precluding any warning in advertisements. The "concession" on a package label, the lawyers reasoned, might offer leverage in avoiding other pernicious intrusions into tobacco marketing and promotion.

Preemption had multiple meanings. The term had its origin in the Constitution, where federal statutes were deemed to *preempt* those of states and localities. Among the reasons the industry called for congressional legislation was the potential nightmare of diverse rules and controls among the fifty states. In a traditional application of Article VI of the U.S. Constitution, the industry sought legislation that would explicitly preempt any state and local regulations about labeling and advertising in favor of a congressionally mandated—and heavily lobbied—federal act.

Beyond this technical constitutional sense, the bill drafted by the industry also sought to preempt the regulatory authority of the FTC as well as any possible initiatives on the part of the other regulatory agencies, such as the Federal Communications Commission (FCC). The legislation *was* aggressively regulatory in this one respect: it clipped the wings of the FTC, which was legally *banned* from taking regulatory actions against tobacco for four years. In this sense, it marked an unprecedented attack on the federal regulatory structure of consumer protection.[51]

At the same time, the bill was also designed to preempt what had become the industry's single greatest concern: namely, tort litigation. Among the many advantages of legislation requiring a label was that it allowed the industry to insist—in court if necessary—that claims against the companies for negligence and deception were now moot. Every smoker would be repeatedly warned that "smoking may be hazardous to your health." The legislation would substantially assist in the industry's principal legal argument that smokers knowingly *assumed* whatever risks might be associated with the product.[52] Even those who sought to gain a regulatory foothold on the industry slipped into the language of assumption of risk. Warren

Magnuson, chairman of the Senate Commerce Committee and one of the bill's sponsors, explained, "this warning will . . . serve notice upon all who read it that they smoke at their own risk."[53] In the historic language of Edward Bernays, the industry had reengineered consumer consent to assume the risks associated with a dangerous and sometimes deadly product, and moreover had accomplished this even while denying that the product posed a risk. Most importantly, the industry had heightened social and cultural expectations of individual responsibility that would be crucial to its future.

§

With the lawyers' committee's version of the bill in hand, the industry unleashed its newly invigorated Tobacco Institute on the back halls of Congress. Earle Clements, a former governor, U.S. congressman, and senator from Kentucky, masterminded the industry's legislative strategy.[54] Clements, having learned the legislative dance from the master of American politics—he had served as majority whip and lieutenant to Lyndon Johnson when Johnson was senate majority leader—brought a unique combination of political experience and powerful connections to the industry's agenda.[55] He had been instrumental in engineering the Democrats' Senate majority in 1958 and had many legislators in his debt.[56] After Johnson's landslide victory in the 1964 presidential election, Lady Bird Johnson hired Clements's daughter as her appointments secretary.[57] In short, Clements was in thick with Johnson. When Johnson, who had quit smoking in 1955 following a massive heart attack, sent his proposals for public health programs to Congress in 1965, smoking was not on the list.[58] Clements enlisted Oren Harris, chairman of the House Interstate Commerce Committee, to help slow FTC attempts to place a label on cigarette packages. Harris held hearings on cigarette regulation before the FTC announced its labeling initiative in June 1964.[59] In the intensive lobbying that would be required to secure the industry's version of the bill, Clements was ably assisted by Abe Fortas, Washington attorney and power broker, whose firm had been central in devising tobacco-industry strategy. Fortas, who worked the phone lines in the legislative campaign, would soon be named by Johnson to the Supreme Court. Big Tobacco had friends in the highest places.[60]

Although the Policy Committee was worried that southern congressmen might oppose federal preemption of state authority (the battles over civil rights made federal authority and states' rights a big issue in 1964), the lawyers nonetheless concluded that "this did not appear to be a cause of great concern because of the important position of the industry in Southern States and the difference between what we have in mind and civil rights legislation."[61] There was already in place a strong contingent of legislators from tobacco-growing states ready to support any measures deemed beneficial to their local constituents of farmers and businesses.

The Federal Cigarette Labeling and Advertising Act emerged from Congress bearing the fingerprints of the tobacco industry and its remarkably able, if heavy handed, lobby. If the bill read as if it might have been written by the industry, this was because in large measure it had been. The proposed FTC warning label had been watered down to read: "Caution: Cigarette Smoking May Be Hazardous to Your Health." Indeed, such ambiguity—"may be"—made it a warning in name only, all but officially retracting the findings of the surgeon general's committee. The FTC protested this language but had no power to change it. "The Commission is convinced that the present cautionary statement on cigarette packages . . . cannot compete with the forces that promote cigarette smoking."[62] At the hearings before the Senate Commerce Committee, the industry orchestrated the testimony of some thirty-eight scientists, most of whom had received funds from the TIRC, the Tobacco Institute, or the law firms. Issues of science, proof, and knowledge were repeatedly raised by questioners and witnesses alike, as if the surgeon general had never studied or issued a report on precisely such questions. But given the powerful political interests at stake, the senators were unwilling to take the surgeon general's word at face value. Committee Chairman Warren Magnuson, under considerable pressure from Fortas and other industry representatives, eventually acceded to the weaker wording of the House bill as well as other important concessions, such as leaving the label's placement to the companies' discretion. The bill also explicitly prohibited any regulation of tobacco advertising for four years.[63]

§

The Federal Cigarette Labeling and Advertising Act of 1965 (FCLAA) is a classic demonstration of how efforts to regulate can be turned 180 degrees—given enormous clout in Congress and a successful strategy, implemented with great tactical skill and military precision. The chief beneficiary of

FCLAA—despite public proclamations to the contrary—was the tobacco industry. The legislation also provides a powerful reminder of the heterogeneity of federal policy making. As much as the act marked congressional recognition of growing concern about the public health impact of tobacco, it also gave a sharp rebuke to the FTC. When the authority of an "independent" regulatory agency came up against congressional interests, the agency could be easily eclipsed. John Blatnik was one of eight congressmen and senators in 1965 who wrote to President Johnson urging him to veto the bill. In their letter, they voiced the concern that though packaged as a public health intervention, the law "protects only the cigarette industry." In particular, they pointed to the prohibition on FTC requirements for health warnings in ads for four years. "This delay is inexcusable," they wrote.[64]

According to Michael Pertschuk, who was a young staff member of the Senate Commerce Committee in 1965 and was principally responsible for moving the bill through Congress, this first major attempt at cigarette regulation "ended up a sorry piece of tobacco knavery."[65] He later wrote, "[W]hat tobacco wanted, tobacco got."[66] This conclusion does not require any deep historical perspective. At the time of the passage of the act, a number of observers pointed out with considerable despair how this so-called consumer legislation brazenly advanced the interests of the industry it purported to regulate. Although Magnuson publicly called it "a forthright and historic step toward the responsible protection of the nation's citizens," the *New York Times* labeled it "a shocking piece of special interest legislation" that "protect[s] the economic health of the tobacco industry by freeing it of proper regulation."[67] Journalist Elizabeth Drew wrote, "It is an unabashed act to protect private industry from government regulation."[68]

Although cigarette sales slipped in the immediate aftermath of the surgeon general's report, by June 1964 they had rebounded. "Tobacco products pass across sales counters more frequently than anything except money," wrote one commentator.[69] By 1966, cigarette sales had reached all time highs. In June 1967, the FTC could find "virtually no evidence that the warning statement on cigarette packages has had any significant effect."[70]

FCLAA marks one of American history's most impressive examples of the power of special interests to shape congressional action. Even as the industry offered minor concessions in subsequent legislation, analysts would repeatedly note the historical importance of the act in protecting the industry from more effective regulation and costly litigation.[71] The federal labeling law would be modified twice by Congress, both times to make changes in the label's wording. The Public Health Cigarette Smoking Act of 1969, passed after more than a year of testimony and debate, mandated that beginning in 1971 all packages would announce: "Warning: The Surgeon General Has Determined That Cigarette Smoking Is Dangerous To Your Health."[72] And in 1984, Congress passed the Comprehensive Smoking Prevention Education Act, creating the four rotating labels that still adorn U.S. packages more than two decades later. On Capitol Hill, the ability of public health forces to spirit this bill through was widely seen as marking an erosion in the strength of the tobacco lobby, but the labels apparently did little to reduce smoking.[73] Certainly, the structure of Congress and the disarray of the public health community contributed to this outcome. But FCLAA clearly shows that the industry possessed a systematic strategy and a capacity to further its interests irrespective of the public good.

Before 1964, it had been widely perceived that the state bore essential responsibility to regulate market forces and interests that could be socially harmful. The early failures to regulate tobacco demonstrated the limits of this ideal. In the face of a report sponsored by the federal government categorically identifying cigarettes as a dire risk to health and a cause of serious disease, the industry had successfully secured a major piece of federal legislation that protected it from further regulation, tort litigation, and other serious corporate risks. It was a turnabout that shocked public health advocates and other observers of the political scene. In the future, many corporations would look to the tobacco industry with awe and admiration as a model for how best to utilize legislation and regulation in their own interests.

§

Even as the industry acceded to labeling, it worked diligently to avoid any regulation of its advertising. Since advertising had been such a prominent and attractive spur to tobacco use throughout the century, it was not surprising that antitobacco forces concentrated on developing new restrictions. In April 1964, with a range of FTC and statutory actions pending, the industry announced a program of "self-regulation" of its advertising. The companies offered a well-worn approach to federal oversight by promising to regulate themselves as good and responsible corporate citizens.[74] The Cigarette Advertising Code, designed by the industry's legal team, promised to ban all cigarette advertising aimed at those under twenty-one; to ban all unproven health claims; and to ban the "virility" theme. It also assured that models under twenty-five years of age would not be used in tobacco ads, nor would testimonials by entertainers or athletes be allowed. Finally, the code prohibited ads depicting smoking as "essential to social prominence, distinction, success, or sexual attraction."[75]

The companies agreed to fines of up to $100,000 for a violation of the code. Infractions would be policed exclusively by the code's administrator, who would be appointed by the industry. In June 1965, the Tobacco Institute announced that former New Jersey Governor Robert B. Meyner had agreed to serve as administrator. Although Meyner vowed to enforce an exacting standard, no fines were issued during his tenure.[76]

The industry and its advocates trumpeted the Cigarette Advertising Code as an enlightened and effective innovation. During congressional hearings on the renewal of FCLAA in 1969, Vincent Wasilewski, the president of the National Association of Broadcasters (NAB), testified that tobacco ads (which had cleared the voluntary standards of the industry) were also subject to systematic evaluation and regulation by the Code Authority, the broadcast industry's own voluntary review board. According to Wasilewski, the code had performed admirably in assuring that tobacco ads met the high standards of *both* the tobacco and the broadcast industries. This testimony was vigorously contested, however, by Warren Braren, one of the earliest whistle-blowers in the tobacco conflict, who came forward to argue that the broadcasters' policy had had virtually no effect on the tobacco industry's commercials. Braren had been head of the Code Authority's New York office and was principal author of a 1966 report that documented a wide range of questionable practices and depictions among tobacco industry ads including "encouragement to smoke, the good life, nature settings, popularity and filter representations."[77] Braren concluded that current cigarette commercials "cannot help but have an intrinsic youth appeal."[78]

According to Braren, when confronted by data indicating that the tobacco industry was ignoring the code, the NAB had done nothing for fear of losing the immense revenues coming from tobacco advertising. Apparently Clair R. McCullough, chairman of the code board, had found Braren's critiques "too rigid" and offered the criterion "when in doubt, okay."[79] Braren testified that a network vice president who was a member of the code board had told the Code Authority "to stay clear of cigarette advertising for fear that any action would lead to forcing all cigarette advertising off television."[80] Industry cooperation with the code had been "token," according to Braren, and eventually the Code Authority had virtually stopped trying to monitor and regulate tobacco ads. "The NAB strategy," he concluded, "has been to avoid meaningful self-regulatory action as long as the possibility exists that Congress will enact legislation favorable to the broadcasting and tobacco industries."[81]

Braren was outraged that the NAB, with its voluntary Code Authority as the watchdog for tobacco ads, had simply become a rubber stamp for the financial interests of the broadcasting industry. "The broadcast industry has had ample opportunity to demonstrate its willingness and ability to enact a truly responsible and meaningful program to self-regulate broadcast cigarette advertising," he said. "Congress gave broadcasters this opportunity in 1965. The NAB and the Code Authority have failed in this public trust." Prior to his testimony, Braren had been fired by the Code Authority, and in openly hostile questioning, the industry's congressional allies sought to portray him as a disgruntled former employee. Braren's testimony was an embarrassment to both the broadcasters and the tobacco companies, who had maintained that they were participating in a scrupulous program of self-regulation.[82]

The debate about controls on tobacco ads illuminated the complex set of interests and power that would prove to be important obstacles in bringing tobacco under any particular regulatory regime. The roots of tobacco had deeply penetrated the economic and financial structures of American industry, media, and politics. As a result, the tobacco industry could exercise its considerable economic influence to dilute, if not defeat, regulatory initiatives. As the broadcasters demonstrated, in the political sphere, the industry demonstrated an impressive ability to co-opt allies.

Despite the two industries' assurances, it soon became clear to those monitoring tobacco ads that the Cigarette Advertising Code was having little impact; whenever the companies found it intrusive, they simply ignored it. In any case, the restrictions themselves were so vague and underspecified that they would have been all but impossible to implement. "That's the reason no one is really worried about the code," explained an advertiser in 1966. "They can't stop us from showing good-looking people doing good-looking things."[83] And although baseball heroes like Phil Rizzuto and Bobby Thompson lost their endorsements, there remained myriad and subtle ways to promote the product under the new "rules." As one advertising agent explained:

> We're not trying to sell cigarettes, we're selling a way of life, an exclusive club which has its own song, its own passwords, and a membership of millions. You say, "Come on over to the L&M side." You talk about "Marlboro Country"; and you form an in-group of "Us Viceroy Smokers" and create an image of the swinging people who smoke your brand. We're saying, "Look attractive, feel at ease, smoke Burpos with that filter of straw or that carcinogenic taste, and you'll never again be lonely."[84]

Some advertisers, in an exercise of conscience, refused to use their skills to recruit smokers. In 1964, as the discussion of advertising restrictions and labeling heated up, David Ogilvy, the chairman of Ogilvy, Benson & Mather, announced that his agency would not accept cigarette accounts.[85] He called cigarette commercials "disgraceful . . . villainy."[86]

The Cigarette Advertising Code and the threat of further regulation offered a powerful reminder to industry and advertisers alike that the cigarette had always conflated product and meaning. With little else to distinguish them, brands had always been a mechanism of self-identity. Now, given a more complex legal and regulatory environment, advertisers would demonstrate their full range of creative skills in circumventing the (relatively innocuous) restrictions. In 1970, the industry abandoned the code. The three companies that still claimed to follow it decided to stop submitting their ads for review. The code had served its purpose—it had bought the industry some time as it fought FTC efforts to mandate a warning label in advertisements—but the pretense was no longer worth the money or the trouble.[87]

§

As we have seen, the industry had prosecuted a two-front offensive in the emerging tobacco wars. While deploying considerable resources on obscuring and denying the emerging scientific data, including the surgeon general's report, the industry also worked to convince the public that important changes to its product, especially the introduction of filters, had now solved the nonexistent problem. These two approaches—despite the obvious inconsistencies—went hand in hand. As conditions on the science front deteriorated, the "promise" of "effective" filtration rose in significance. Health concerns created new marketing opportunities.

One indication of how seriously the industry understood its dilemma was the intensive commitment, starting in the early 1950s, to produce new filtered brands or to modify and reposition established ones. At the very time that industry executives gathered in New York in late 1953, their companies were gearing up to produce new brands. Such was the case for Marlboros, which over the next two decades would transform Philip Morris from the smallest of the six major manufacturers to a global behemoth. Marlboro was not a new brand. Since the early 1930s, it had been established as an elite women's brand with "ivory tips."[88] The transformation of Marlboro from a luxury women's cigarette to a macho smoke is a testament to the sophistication of the mass marketing and promotion techniques largely invented by the tobacco industry early in the twentieth century. Some would have thought it impossible to so radically remake an existing brand (especially with Marlboro's effeminate filter), but George Weissman of Philip Morris brought together a diverse team of consultants, public opinion experts, and marketers to manage and manipulate the transition.

In the tobacco trade, package and product were inextricably linked. Weissman soon contracted with Molins, a British company, to produce a new "crush proof" cardboard flip-top box, a radical innovation in cigarette packaging. A new filter was developed with technical assistance from Benson and Hedges, which Philip Morris had recently acquired. But even with its cellulose acetate filter, tar and nicotine levels of the new Marlboro were nearly as high as the earlier unfiltered version.[89] The design firm of Fran Gianninoto & Associates, following consultation with color experts, came up with the now legendary red and white packaging. In the long and impressive history of cigarette packaging and design, the new Marlboro package would become the preeminent success of the twentieth century. Few other products have enjoyed such a longstanding design triumph.[90]

With prototype of product and package in hand, Weissman turned to Leo Burnett to devise an appropriate advertising campaign. Offered the task of reinventing Marlboros to make them the leading filtered cigarette, Burnett explained to the executives at Philip Morris that he sought to give the brand a "personality and a reason for being" that would sustain it in a difficult and competitive market. Burnett, who had fathered the Jolly Green Giant, was based not on Madison Avenue but in Chicago. It was characteristic of his less-is-more approach that the Marlboro campaign was straightforward and avoided the high-pitched claims of typical filter brand ads.

Burnett offered a counterintuitive approach. He argued against promotional themes that emphasized the safety and effectiveness of the filter, noting that "people who have 'fears' resent being reminded of these 'fears.'"[91] Marlboro advertising would explicitly avoid discussing filtration. It would not discuss anything. In a major breakthrough, not just for cigarettes but for advertising generally, Burnett's Marlboro ads would dispense with copy almost entirely and instead convey message and meaning exclusively through image. The Marlboro campaign would brilliantly navigate the tension between offering reassurance without fracturing denial.

Burnett was especially eager to find a way to displace public perceptions of filters as unmanly. Research conducted for Philip Morris by Elmo Roper, Burnett explained, "shows that many people think of filter cigarettes as a woman's smoke." This was a particular vulnerability for Marlboro in view of its lineage. "Our own talks with smokers indicate that many people who know the old ivory-tipped Marlboro regard it as a fancy smoke for dudes and women," he observed. "This is not the *personality* we want for the New Marlboro, which must appeal to the mass market."[92] As a result, the original Marlboro campaign, beginning in 1954, featured men's men (and "the men women like") as Marlboro smokers. Sea captains, athletes, gunsmiths, and cowboys all appeared in the early ads, all sporting wrist tattoos.[93] It would take nearly a decade before the campaign gelled into its ultimate iconic form. The cowboy took the reins of the Marlboro campaign, displacing the other macho men, in 1962. Pared with the triumphant musical theme from Elmer Bernstein's *Magnificent Seven* (whose rights were quickly purchased from United Artists), the new ad literally trumpeted "Marlboro Country."

> For a man's flavor come to Marlboro Country. My Country. Its big, open, makes a smoker feel ten feet tall. . . . This is my cigarette, Marlboro. It's like this country, has spirit . . . .
> Come to where the flavor is, come to Marlboro Country.[94]

More than three decades after it was banned from television and radio ads, children of the 1960s can sing the Marlboro jingle on cue.

Burnett's goal was to tap into certain very basic human desires and fantasies. Reviewing the conceptualization of the campaign, he wrote, "This sounds as though Dr. Freud were on our Plans Board."[95] The Marlboro cowboy suggested a mythic time, not only before the bureaucratization and urbanization of the twentieth century, but a time of *simple* pleasures, before the mid-century discovery that smoking brought risk and disease. Marlboro Country promised control and autonomy in a world where these were slipping away. What was so remarkable about the brand and its promotion was its precise timing and symbolism. Just as the Marlboro Man had the fortitude to face down the elements, so too would he face down anxiety about the risks of smoking. Rarely, if ever, had marketing so brilliantly combined American values, traditions, and symbols with a promotional message. The campaign created a visual shorthand for the motivation for, and meaning of, smoking in an age of technology, science, risk, and disease. It offered images rich in denial and escapism, in reassurance and immortality. The Marlboro cowboy would find an enduring place at the American campfire.[96]

§

Amid its repeated political and promotional victories, the industry did make serious missteps in the sphere of public relations. A prime example was the Tobacco Institute's 1967 contract with advertising entrepreneur Rosser Reeves. A former head of Ted Bates & Co. notorious for his hard-sell campaigns, Reeves apparently promised a major new effort to "re-establish the smoking and health controversy."[97] Advertising insiders suggested that the campaign would insist that smoking was for informed adults and that the industry strongly opposed smoking among youth.[98]

In January 1968, *True Magazine* published an article by Stanley Frank entitled "To Smoke or Not to Smoke—That Is Still the Question."[99] The article recycled the now desiccated scientific critiques—all effectively rebutted—that the industry had been trotting out since the early 1950s. Reeves's public relations firm, Tiderock Corporation, arranged for more than one million reprints, with some 600,000 to be sent to physicians and other professionals; the piece was also heralded in newspaper ads. All this was done with no attribution to its generous sponsor, the Tobacco Institute, which had contracted with Reeves for $500,000.[100] These tactics, of course, were not new. Hill & Knowlton had placed a piece—remarkably similar in its arguments and evidence—in *True Magazine* in 1954.[101] But times had changed, and in 1968, the industry's reliance on such unscrupulous techniques of journalistic influence drew sustained criticism just as it faced renewed regulatory interest in Congress.

Warren Magnuson, who had sent the piece to Surgeon General William Stewart for review, explained on the floor of the Senate that

> it brings into the most serious question the article's accuracy, impartiality and integrity. . . . These articles . . . are not what they seem to be. And I agree with Dr. Stewart that this is a questionable exercise in high-powered public relations [that] may, if it achieves its apparent objectives, add to the disease and death our population caused by smoking.[102]

Not only did the exposure of such activities damage the companies in the media and in the political sphere, it pointed to the central dilemma at the heart of industry strategy. Any industry-generated attempts to contest the science would not only seem self-interested, but might make the companies even more vulnerable to litigation and ongoing charges of negligence and fraud.

During the 1950s, Hill & Knowlton stood ready to challenge every new scientific finding implicating tobacco as a cause of disease. Following the surgeon general's report, however, PR counsel understood that "TIRC had spoken far too much in the past, and this had merely stimulated adverse medical comment." As the Tobacco Institute replaced the TIRC as the industry's public relations arm, there was a notable decrease in public efforts to rebut scientific findings. According to some reports, Hill & Knowlton had come to recommend a revision of their original strategy.[103] They now understood that straining public credulity would ultimately threaten the industry's well-being. But the lawyers were now in control, and litigation anxiety powerfully shaped ongoing tobacco strategy.

Certainly, it was a basic premise of public relations theory—since the time of Bernays—that effective PR could shape public opinion in powerful ways. But by the late 1960s, the harms of smoking were no longer a matter of *opinion*. An astute public relations strategy would need to take account of this reality. To the lawyers in charge, however, such a shift was deemed impossible and risk prone. As Rogers and Todd noted during their 1964 visit, "Hill & Knowlton have been sidetracked; they have little to do and know little of what is going on. They have not seen a President of a company for a long time and are now responsible to the Policy Committee of the Lawyers."[104] New public relations strategies, though often vetted internally, were rejected by the lawyers with phrases like "implied admissions" and "assumed warranties." With legal concerns trumping public relations, the Hill & Knowlton team began to voice frustration with its marginal status. In April 1968, the company resigned from the Tobacco Institute, ending a nearly fifteen-year run of directing the tobacco industry's public relations effort. Hill & Knowlton's departure marked the end of an era in the century of the cigarette. Even as the industry clung to the strategy Hill had devised in 1953, it was losing credibility.

§

The Federal Cigarette Labeling and Advertising Act had not totally cut out the FTC: that agency was tasked with monitoring the effectiveness of labeling and the ongoing impact of advertising and promotion. The FTC's first assessments in 1967 found the industry's voluntary code a severe disappointment. Although the companies had promised to ban "any representation with respect to health" in ads promoting filters, the FTC concluded that "whether the filter advertisements . . . constitute representations with respect to health and well-being can best be judged by the following: 44 percent of the public and 57 percent of filter cigarette smokers believe that filters reduce the health risks of smoking."[105] Perhaps more ominously, the FTC found that advertising was still significantly pitched to youth. "Self-regulation by the industry has proved to be ineffectual. Cigarette commercials continue to appeal to youth and continue to blot out any consciousness of the health hazards. . . ."[106] As a result, the FTC contended, the notion of informed "choice" was obliterated:

> To allow the American people, and especially teen-agers, the opportunity
> to make an informed and deliberate choice of whether or not to start
> smoking, they must be freed from constant exposure to such one-sided
> blandishments and told the whole story.[107]

By 1981, the FTC would conclude that the warning labels then appearing on packages and advertisements had been ineffective. Even when they were read, the warnings left important gaps in knowledge about the risks of smoking. Research had shown, moreover, that fewer than 3 percent of adults "even read the warnings."[108] They concluded that the warnings were "overexposed" and "worn out."[109] The FTC was forced to concede that the warnings it had vigorously sought a decade earlier had significant limitations in communicating the health risks of smoking. *Consumer Reports*, which typically avoided any taint of partisanship or political advocacy, now saw that the cigarette issue raised unprecedented questions for consumer protection.

> In an age when some of the most creative men and women in the country spend their talents devising ingenious ways to make smoking attractive, we must confess a certain pessimism about the countervailing power of sober sentences on the side of the cigarette package or even of "education" conducted on anything less than the scale and style of cigarette advertising itself.[110]

It was an ironic statement coming from this magazine, which had been created as a kind of antidote to commercial marketing in a consumer age.[111] The editors acknowledged the impotence of education in the face of regulatory failure and the powerful engines of promotion, and conceded the limitations of their own model of a consumers' democracy in which reliable information would protect citizens from dangerous or useless products.

§

The time had come for public health to employ the same tools of marketing and public relations that had served the tobacco companies so well. One upstart found a chink in the tobacco industry's armor. John F. Banzhaf III, a young New York lawyer, in 1967 asked the Federal Communications Commission to apply the "fairness doctrine," which required broadcasters to give equal time to opposing views on controversial topics, to cigarettes. Banzhaf contended that the blanket of tobacco ads merited "equal time" for antitobacco messages. "I was concerned about the use of the public airwaves to seduce young people into taking up smoking without any attempt to tell them the other side of the story on television and radio," Banzhaf later wrote. "It looked as though the fairness doctrine offered a legal loophole that might allow me a large output for a small amount of input."[112]

Banzhaf initially wrote to WCBS-TV in New York asking for free time to present the public health perspective on smoking. When this was summarily denied, as anticipated, Banzhaf filed a petition with the FCC, noting the response from the station. In June 1967, the FCC ruled in Banzhaf's favor, requiring broadcasters currently airing tobacco ads to provide time to citizens seeking to present the hazards of smoking. According to the FCC ruling, "the repeated and continuous broadcasts of the advertisements may be a contributing factor to the adoption of a habit which may lead to untimely death." As a result, broadcasters had a responsibility "to devote a significant amount of time to informing [their] listeners of the other side with the matter—that however enjoyable smoking may be, it represents a habit which may cause or contribute to the earlier death of the user." "The simple fact" is "that the public interest means nothing if it does not include such a responsibility."[113] Although the FCC did not grant "equal time," it did mandate a ratio of approximately three cigarette commercials to one antismoking announcement.[114]

This ruling was based on the assessment that smoking was a matter of sufficient controversy and public significance to trigger the statutory provisions requiring free time. During the next three years, public health messages offered by the voluntary health agencies received millions of dollars of "free" airplay. Until these antitobacco spots began to air, the companies had treated most regulatory initiatives as opportunities to dismiss public health as a trivial nuisance. Banzhaf's single-handed intervention, however, created a worrisome situation, a hairline fracture in the industry's dominant control of the structures of bureaucracy and regulation. Banzhaf monitored the stations' compliance with the order, forcing stations to add more tobacco-control commercials if they fell short of the required ratio.[115]

The Banzhaf initiative unsettled the antitobacco status quo. The American Cancer Society had relied on sympathetic broadcasters to periodically air its public service announcements seeking donations, and its leaders apparently worried about alienating the networks. But as the FCC took up the fight, the ACS came to see opportunities. For the first time, public health engaged some of the strategies and techniques that had been invented on behalf of the tobacco companies a half-century earlier. The advertising firm of Lord, Geller, Federico & Partners set to work producing commercials on behalf of the society, donating time and resources. Richard Lord, the president of the company, had written copy for Kents, Parliaments, and Newports at both Young & Rubicam and Benton & Bowles and knew how cigarettes were marketed.[116] The free airtime was put to good use. According to Thomas Whiteside, a reporter for the *New Yorker,* these antismoking ads "seemed to have the capacity of acting upon the existing crowd of cigarette commercials like antibodies grappling with some bacterial swarm."[117]

"Have you ever thought what happens when you smoke a cigarette?" asked a man holding up a cigarette in an American Cancer Society spot. "We have." Public health advocates were eager to see smoking finally tied to its consequences—the very reality that tobacco ads so studiously sought to deflect. The new public service announcements demonstrated for the first time how Madison Avenue savvy and ingenuity could be turned against Big Tobacco. William Talman, the television actor who, in the role of Hamilton Burger, had made a career out of losing case after case to Perry Mason, was now dying of lung cancer and bravely offered his services for an antitobacco spot:

> "I have lung cancer. Take some advice about smoking and losing from someone who's been doing both for years. If you don't smoke, don't start. If you do smoke, quit. Don't be a loser."

Talman died before his message was broadcast.[118]

This ad and others had a noticeable impact on rates of smoking. In 1967, per capita consumption declined, as it would in each of the four years in which the equal time ads appeared. During this period, national cigarette consumption fell by 1 percent despite a 6.6 percent increase in population.[119] Banzhaf had discovered a set of tactics that public health forces would adopt as crucial to their efforts. First, his approach was indirect. Rather than argue for new ways of regulating the industry, he had used existing rules to shift the contested terrain to an entity independent of the industry, in this case the broadcasting networks. Second, Banzhaf demonstrated that the courts might provide a more sympathetic venue for public health advocacy than the legislature. The courts were not subject to the powerful political lobbying the industry had perfected. Finally, he had shown how strategic advocacy could use the resources of others to seek regulatory victories. In the FCC, Banzhaf had found a new ally whose authority he could employ toward a nascent public health campaign.

Now deeply involved in the legal battle, Banzhaf left his New York law firm to form Action on Smoking and Health (ASH), one of the first dedicated antitobacco advocacy organizations. ASH was free of the complex constituencies that prevented groups like the American Cancer Society from engaging in hand-to-hand combat with the industry. Banzhaf issued press releases calling himself "the Ralph Nader of the tobacco industry" and quickly showed his talent for riling not only the industry but his antitobacco allies. He took a teaching position at George Washington University Law School, where he decorated his office with photographs and clippings covering his own activities.[120]

The industry, caught off guard, explored strategies for negating these attacks. Ross R. Millhiser, president of Philip Morris, suggested that the industry might threaten to make the networks or individual stations "prove the accuracy of their unregulated anti-cigarette commercials." He suggested that the "possibility of suit liability" might restrain such ads and sought to make the anticigarette commercials "more balanced." Each antitobacco ad, he said, should be made to carry a disclaimer: "Caution: Cigarette smoking may be injurious to your health—or it may not be."

Millhiser also suggested suing the ad agencies making the public service announcements, arguing, "We feel the charges are untrue, unsubstantiated, irresponsible, etc."[121] But such proposals merely showed the denial and defensiveness now ruling the industry's internal culture. After more than two decades of overwhelming scientific evidence, some industry executives still clung to the belief that cigarettes would ultimately be exonerated. In such proposals, tobacco executives exposed their central vulnerability in prosecuting the tobacco wars: a set of entrenched views that increasingly strained public credibility.

In February 1969, the FCC issued a public notice that it would seek a ban on all broadcast cigarette advertising. Like the FTC, the FCC had been restricted from any regulation of the tobacco industry until the FCLAA moratorium expired on June 30, 1969. The FCC announcement put both the industry and Congress on notice that the agency was preparing to reenter the regulatory fray.[122] The industry claimed that banning all broadcast ads would violate its First Amendment rights to free speech. To this the FCC responded:

> The issue is thus whether the First Amendment protects the advertising of a product as to which there is a most substantial showing that it is the main cause of lung cancer, the most important cause of emphysema and chronic bronchitis. We do not believe so.[123]

Even as the industry fought the FCC, it again offered concessions in exchange for an alternative advantage. The genius of this strategy was that the proposed concession (like package labeling in 1965) actually provided considerable advantage to the industry. With effective and frequent anti-tobacco messages appearing in prime time—and having apparently significant impacts on consumption—the industry reevaluated its commitment to constitutional rights. Banning tobacco from the airwaves would also end the equal-time advertisements, an outcome that started to have considerable appeal. In 1969, the industry once again acceded to regulation.

In July, Joseph F. Cullman III, president of Philip Morris, told the Consumer Subcommittee of the Senate Commerce Committee that the tobacco industry would voluntarily end all television advertising. In return, he requested that the industry be spared any potential antitrust legislation.[124] Cullman's offer surprised Congress as well as his allies in the broadcasting industry. His announcement preempted an emerging plan that would have gradually eliminated broadcast advertising. By the time the companies agreed to the ban, they clearly understood that it was neither a catastrophe for the industry nor a triumph for the tobacco-control advocates; Great Britain had banned television ads in 1965 to little effect, and Denmark, France, Italy, Norway, Sweden, and Switzerland all had tight restrictions on broadcast ads—and high rates of smoking.[125] On January 1, 1971, America heard its last tobacco jingle. The year before the ban, tobacco companies were the biggest advertisers on television, spending some $230 million a year and buying 8 percent of all advertising time.[126]

The broadcast ban, like FCLAA, served a number of industry interests. First, the end of cigarette commercials also ended broadcasters' obligations to provide free time for public service announcements. Within weeks, the antitobacco ads had all but disappeared. Second, the prohibition on broadcast advertising seriously limited the opportunities for any company to introduce new brands, or more crucially, for new companies to gain entry into the market. Finally, there were obvious cost savings in the elimination of this most expensive form of promotion.[127]

§

The broadcast ad ban did lead to important shifts in cigarette marketing. Companies invested much more significantly in point-of-sale promotion and what would commonly come to be called "brand stretching." The "Marlboro Country Store" sold products with the Marlboro logo, often turning their patrons into walking advertisements. Sponsorship of sporting events, especially auto racing, also became increasingly prominent. The Public Health Cigarette Smoking Act, which codified the voluntary ban, was also a bonanza for the print media. In the first year of the ban, *Life* magazine nearly doubled its pages of cigarette ads. Journalist Thomas Whiteside, who had closely followed the Banzhaf intervention, was outraged to see the print media take up where broadcasters left off. "How can any publisher—anyone—*make money* out of selling advertisements for a product that is known to cause death on a disastrous scale year after year?"[128] According to Whiteside, *Time* and *Newsweek* also more than doubled their cigarette ads.[129] Having watched the passage of the ad ban with considerable optimism, Whiteside was disgusted that the companies worked so diligently to maintain and expand their market. A mere broadcast ban, he wrote, was "insufficient to restrain the tobacco industry from what can only be regarded—considering what is known about the relationship of smoking and various diseases—as near slaughter on a massive scale."[130] Whiteside's moral indignation marked an important shift in journalistic coverage of tobacco. Even as regulatory initiatives lagged, social and cultural attitudes about the cigarette and its producers were shifting.

With the "concession" of the broadcast ban, the industry moved ahead to block any warnings in advertising. The 1969 act extended the preemption on FTC labeling requirements for ads to at least July 1, 1972,[131] and required that the FTC give Congress six months' notice of any intention to issue regulations. In 1972, the FTC finally achieved its goal of requiring a warning label on all advertising. By the time these cautions appeared (in small type), however, they had lost all impact. What had seemed like an initiative of real significance when it was first proposed in 1964, was now an ineffective disclaimer whose main effect was to protect the industry from liability. The "warnings" had little impact on consumption.

§

In an age of growing political debate about consumer protection, the tobacco industry had devised a remarkably effective campaign to assure that it could successfully market a product of demonstrably great risk. The Tobacco Institute and its able lobbyists saw to it that cigarettes were explicitly excluded from series of important consumer legislation, including the Fair Labeling and Packaging Act of 1966, the Controlled Substances Act of 1970, and the Consumer Product Safety Act of 1972. Unlike the Federal Cigarette Labeling and Advertising Act, these bills often received little public scrutiny, but the Tobacco Institute closely monitored their design and passage to assure the explicit exclusion of its product.

Such approaches to negating regulation, however, did not go completely unnoticed. In 1974, Senator Frank E. Moss, a Utah Democrat, and the American Public Health Association submitted a petition to the Consumer Product Safety Commission (CPSC) asking that it ban cigarettes containing twenty-two or more milligrams of tar. (There were twenty-seven such brands, making up more than 15 percent of the current market.) This request was based on the provisions of the 1960 Federal Hazardous Substances Act. In their request, they noted that despite the labeling requirement, both cigarette sales and lung cancer had increased since 1965. When the petition was rejected by the CPSC by a vote of 3–2, Moss moved forward to file the request with the federal district court. In April 1975, Judge Oliver Gasch ruled that the CPSC had the right to ban the interstate shipping of high-tar cigarettes. In his opinion, Gasch noted that the hazards of cigarettes were not known in 1960, when the legislation was written. Although his ruling did not compel the CPSC to ban these cigarettes, the commission was ordered to consider whether some cigarettes were so high in tar that no warning could "sufficiently protect the public, so these cigarettes should be banned from interstate commerce."[132]

The CPSC—eager to avoid the burdens of bringing cigarettes under its mandate—sought (with the able support of the Tobacco Institute) to have Congress pass an amendment that would explicitly exclude tobacco from its regulatory mandate. As columnist Colman McCarthy wrote in the *Washington Post:*

> Two questions can be asked. Is the Commission trying to avoid the issue because it knows that if anything was going to be done against the menace of cigarettes it would have been done long ago, and thus why waste effort on a cause hopelessly lost? Or is the commission about to sink into the mediocrity that characterizes so many other regulatory agencies, and be content to issue tough standards for hazardous playpens and tricycles while ducking an issue in which, according to Senator Moss, "hundreds of thousands of lives are at stake"?[133]

As McCarthy had noted, the CPSC's desire to avoid having anything to do with tobacco products was not an anomaly. The regulatory agencies and their administrators understood that tobacco regulation would easily test the limits of their already limited authority. Asking mice to regulate the boa did not appear to serve the mice's political interests. And after all, if Congress sought more control over tobacco, it should make its wishes known through legislation. The Tobacco Institute strongly encouraged such thinking. As the industry repeatedly insisted, Congress—where the industry could best exert its influence—was the only appropriate venue for any regulatory initiative. And so, rather than appeal the court's ruling, the tobacco industry sought relief directly from Congress. By the mid-1970s, the well-oiled lobbying machinery preferred new legislation overturning the decision to the vagaries of another judicial proceeding. In October 1975, Congress passed HR 6844, the CPSC Amendments Bill, specifically excluding tobacco products from the jurisdiction of the CPSC.[134] President Gerald Ford signed the bill into law without fanfare.

While the industry decried the rise of burdensome regulation, the reality was that tobacco was all but exempt from government oversight. One of the most dangerous products in the history of American consumer culture was all but immune to the growing federal regulatory apparatus. Just as the FTC had been rebuked in 1964, so one could now add the FDA, the

CPSC, the Occupational Health and Safety Administration, and a host of other agencies with the potential authority to regulate tobacco.

§

Given his deep southwestern roots and his aggressive legislative agenda, Lyndon Johnson was leery to risk alienating tobacco state congressmen and senators by advocating public health interventions. He did order, however, the establishment of a task force to address the growing lung cancer problem in light of the surgeon general's report. Among the group's first actions was the creation of a new initiative at the National Institutes of Health to bring together scientists from the government and the tobacco industry to explore the feasibility of a "less-hazardous cigarette." Ernst Wynder, after publishing his early and critically important work in the 1950s on the epidemiology of smoking, had turned his attention to attempting to identify the biologically active components in smoke.[135] Wynder became convinced that it would be possible to remove these agents, thereby making smoking safer, if not risk free. In 1968, he convinced the head of the National Cancer Institute (NCI), Kenneth Endicott, who had attempted without success to quit smoking, to set up a study group to conduct research on possibly safer products. Between 1968 and 1978 a committee known as the Tobacco Working Group brought together industry and NCI scientists to explore low-yield filtered cigarettes. Prominent industry scientists, including Helmut Wakeham, Alexander Spears, and Murray Senkus, agreed to serve. The industry was both eager to be involved in such a public collaboration, while at the same time publicly insisting that they knew of nothing that made current cigarettes "unsafe." The industry refused to offer up its own data on tobacco smoke, filtration, and tar yields.[136]

In 1978, the whole enterprise collapsed when Gio Gori, the director of the TWG and the deputy director of the NCI's Smoking and Health Program, claimed in the *Journal of the American Medical Association* and the public media that one could avoid a critical threshold of risk of disease by choosing several low-tar brands. The *Washington Post*, for example, reported, "Some Cigarettes Now 'Tolerable,' Doctor Says." But the data for Gori's claim was sketchy at best, and there remained no certain way to determine how cigarettes were smoked in practice.[137] Soon Secretary of Health, Education, and

Welfare Joseph Califano and Surgeon General Julius Richmond would move to close down the Tobacco Working Group. Richmond would note in his massive 1979 surgeon general's report which reviewed the "overwhelming" data on the harms of smoking that had been generated in the fifteen years since the first report, that "there can be no final assessment of the public health benefits of our present search for less hazardous cigarettes."[138] And Califano explained that "there is no such thing as a safe cigarette." Gori eventually decamped to become a paid consultant for the industry.[139]

§

During the two decades following the publication of the 1964 surgeon general's report, the "remedial measures" forecast by Luther Terry never did materialize. The Tobacco Institute, on behalf of the companies, assembled an impressive record of derailing attempts to bring tobacco under any regulatory mandates whatsoever. As the *Wall Street Journal* noted in 1972, the Tobacco Institute had developed a unique reputation for "turning a series of imminent disasters into near victories."[140] As William Kloepfer, senior vice president of Tobacco Institute, explained, the "tobacco industry believes in informed consumer response as opposed to government consumer coercion."[141]

The defeat of regulatory initiatives reflected the many ways in which tobacco money fueled the American economy. The industry had many friends to call upon to help it fight off public health legislation. Its strong base of tobacco-state congressmen and senators, often vested with important committee assignments and chairmanships, were only the beginning. Lobbyists for the advertising industry, antitaxation coalitions, and even civil liberties groups were among the strange bedfellows generated by tobacco politics.[142] Within this matrix of allies, the industry quickly learned how best to exert power in a sympathetic Congress.

The notion that regulation serves the needs of the regulated is often identified as "paradoxical," but it has deep historical roots.[143] It was anything but a paradox to those who meticulously mapped and executed the tobacco industry's strategy in the gradual accumulation of battles that was coming to be known as the tobacco wars. Just as the cigarette both illuminated and shaped major transformations in culture and science, so now it marked critical shifts in the nature of American politics. Although special interests and their influence had a long history in shaping the legislative process, the tobacco industry broke new ground in its ability to upend regulatory efforts. The Tobacco Institute, in concert with elite corporate law firms, ran circles around the poorly financed and weakly organized public health advocates.

The two most significant acts of federal tobacco regulation promulgated by Congress in the second half of the twentieth century—labeling and the ad ban—had, upon inspection, proven to be little more than special interest legislation protecting the very actions they were meant to inhibit. Moreover, through the Tobacco Institute, the industry had a mechanism to ensure that its strategy was implemented systematically. Thus, the industry could score repeated victories in spite of an overwhelming scientific judgment justifying new restrictions on the promotion and marketing of its product.[144]

Wars typically feature combat between at least two opposing forces, though they may be wholly unequal in strength, skill, or resources. In these early years of the tobacco wars, however, it was sometimes difficult even to identify any coherent public health force to resist Big Tobacco. While the tobacco industry plotted a centralized strategy in their corporate board rooms, legal conference rooms, and in the offices of the Tobacco Institute, public health advocates were poorly organized and diverse. They lacked the capacity for an integrated strategy and commanded few resources to counter the industry's planning and implementation. As a result, the tobacco industry was often able to determine on what terrain it would seek engagement. Congress was an especially congenial venue in which to do battle. Spending liberally in support of political campaigns, the Tobacco Institute had easy access to the levers of congressional power and authority.[145]

The legislation that emerged from Congress during this period testifies to the masterful preparation and strategic command of the tobacco industry. Given the disparity in resources between the companies and public health interests, these outcomes are not surprising. But even in these early decades of the war, the industry showed vulnerabilities that a gathering force of public health advocates would later exploit. Even as tobacco scored wins in specific conflicts, it was growing apparent that antitobacco forces would not leave the field uncontested for long.

Do you mind if I smoke?

Why, no . . . Do you mind if I fart?

   It's one of my bad habits. I quit once for a year, you know, but I gained a lot of weight. It's hard to quit. You know, after sex I really have the urge to light one up.[1]

STEVE MARTIN, 1977

If children don't like to be in a smoky room, they'll leave.[2]

CHARLES HARPER, 1996
CEO, R.J. REYNOLDS

CHAPTER 9

Your Cigarette Is Killing Me

B Y THE MID-TWENTIETH century, smoking had become almost a required practice, and the norms of etiquette reflected its prominence. Emily Post, the doyenne of manners experts, turned her attention in 1940 to those who continued to object to cigarette use: "those who do not smoke cannot live apart, and when they come in contact with smokers, it is scarcely fair that the few should be allowed to prohibit the many from the pursuit of their comforts and their pleasure."[3] Although making exceptions for visitors to a sickroom or a bride with a veil on, Post felt that smoking was appropriate in almost all settings, something to be not only tolerated by nonsmokers, but accommodated and admired.

As Post's advice made clear, the cigarette's triumph rested fundamentally on its public nature. By the middle of the century, cigarettes had become a ubiquitous prop in a full set of highly ritualized social interactions. From coffee breaks to the college seminar room, from bars and restaurants to boardrooms and bedrooms, the cigarette was a constant presence. With the able guidance of the growing tobacco industry, the early twentieth-century prohibitions on public smoking had been dismantled. The industry had well understood that the commercial success of the cigarette depended on its public associations with leisure and pleasure, for men and women alike, across all socioeconomic and ethnic groups.

Beginning in the 1960s and 1970s, the acceptability of smoking would come under increasingly aggressive attack from public health activists and grassroots groups. This new front in the tobacco wars would reveal how a popular product, along with a behavior with positive meanings and associations, could be quickly and radically transformed. If the meanings of smoking were, as we have seen, elastic, they were by definition vulnerable to change. In the decades following the first surgeon general's report, the tobacco industry would lose control of the very meaning-making processes that they had all but perfected early in the century.

There was a powerful irony in this transformation, since by the early 1970s it appeared that the tobacco industry had emerged from two decades of catastrophic news in remarkably good shape. Despite the emergence of conclusive scientific evidence that cigarette use caused serious disease, debility, and death, cigarettes remained remarkably popular and virtually free of public regulation. Even with warning labels on the packaging and a ban on broadcast advertising—both measures initially opposed by the industry—cigarette sales and profits remained impressively robust. Per capita consumption in 1974 was virtually the same as it had been a decade earlier, approximately 4,100 cigarettes per year.[4] And it appeared that the regulatory initiatives of the previous decade had reached their limits. Through an impressive combination of public relations, product modification (filters), political hardball, and outright misrepresentation, the industry had managed to fight off regulation and litigation, invent new approaches to promoting its product, and generally secure its ongoing success and stability.

Widely shared libertarian attitudes about both the role of the state and the behavior of individuals constrained the future of campaigns against tobacco. The American individualist credo, "It's my body and I'll do what I please," cast a net over further antismoking initiatives. Unlike other industrial nations, most of which had developed national health insurance systems, the United States retained a strong disposition to hold individuals strictly accountable for their behaviors.[5] American culture held that citizens must take responsibility for their own health, including making sensible decisions about risk and behavior based on the available information. Now that every cigarette package had a warning label, it was assumed that smokers were fully capable of taking responsibility for their own behavior.[6] Moreover, there existed a deep and abiding skepticism, if not overt hostility, to paternalistic interventions on behalf of health.

The tobacco companies and the Tobacco Institute had aggressively and effectively presented the case for smoking as a *voluntary* risk.[7] According to this view, there was a "debate" about the risks of smoking, and Americans had been fully informed of the arguments on both sides. They should now be permitted to make up their own minds about whether to smoke or not. This line of reasoning raised the question of whether cigarette smoking any longer constituted a risk to *public* health at all. Since the risks incurred were entirely to the individual, the authority to regulate and restrict smoking should rest there too.

The industry and its political allies frequently invoked Big Brother or the Prohibition debacle to point out how paternalistic government interventions offended the basic American values of independence, autonomy, and the right to take risks. Dictating other people's behavior, even in the name of health, was portrayed as un-American. It was one thing, for example, to educate the public about seat-belt use, and quite another to *require* Americans to buckle up. Once Big Brother entered your car, he would inevitably follow you into your home. These ominous themes began to characterize the discussions of further regulation of cigarettes in the early 1970s. Consenting adults, the argument went, had been informed of the cigarette "debate" and should now be left alone. Spurred by the well-oiled tobacco interests, critics proudly decried the "health and safety fascists" telling Americans how to live and sapping their sense of individual responsibility.[8] Cigarette smoking had become the quintessential voluntary health risk.

§

But what if the risks were not purely individual? What if smoke from cigarettes harmed nonsmokers? If this were true, the very same arguments in defense of smoking could be turned on their head. Beginning in the 1970s, a new set of grassroots antismoking groups would begin to explore this assumption. Cigarette smoke as an environmental toxin would become the basis for a radical shift in the tobacco wars. Risks to nonsmokers would emerge as a critical problem for the companies and lead to a more stringent regulatory environment.

Nothing spurred the effectiveness of this new anticigarette movement so powerfully as the recognition of the so-called "innocent victim" of "secondhand smoke." The old ambivalence about preaching to smokers about their individual behavior disappeared; now one could talk about the impact their self-destructiveness had on others. The identification of "innocent victims"—typically nonsmoking women married to smokers, or children with smoking mothers—radically reconfigured the moral calculus of cigarette smoking in the United States.[9]

If Americans have been highly tolerant of risks assumed by individuals, they have been aggressively intolerant of risks imposed on others. If there were innocent victims of cigarette smoke, then smokers became guilty of imposing risk, disease, and even death on unsuspecting women and children.[10] As a *New York Times* editor explained in 1978:

> Non-smokers who breathe the air in smoke-filled rooms are in a sense engaging in 'involuntary smoking' . . . much of this out pouring also lands in the lungs of innocent bystanders.[11]

It is ironic that the impact of smoking on nonsmokers, rather than on smokers themselves, is what finally transformed the regulation and cultural perception of the cigarette. Even as the industry asserted in the aftermath of labeling that smokers were now well-informed of the "alleged" risks of smoking and thus could make their own decisions, nonsmokers were seen as being *subjected* to the smoke of those decision makers. These innocent victims heightened the state's interest in controlling behaviors previously viewed as outside its purview.[12]

§

The first efforts to address the harm smoking caused to nonsmokers had a simple logic. If, as the surgeon general had concluded in 1964, smoking causes serious disease, how could ambient smoke, both from the burning cigarette and from the lungs of the smoker, not do the same? Though the industry would try mightily to reassure the nonsmoking public on this point, it would never manage to disrupt this commonsense view, which rested squarely on the authoritative assessment of the first surgeon general's report.[13] Nonetheless, the precise nature and severity of the harms of secondhand smoke were not so easily determined.

The smoke produced by cigarettes was labeled with a range of terms, each with different social and cultural implications. *Environmental tobacco smoke (ETS)* invited public concern about cigarette use as promoting an environmental hazard.[14] *Passive smoking* contrasted with *active smoking; secondhand smoke* contained the ominous implication that someone else had used it first; *involuntary smoking* assumed that the practice of smoking was indeed a *voluntary* act. These terms reinforced each other in mobilizing this new campaign against public smoking.[15]

The growing concerns about air pollution from factories and automobiles soon extended to tobacco smoke as well. As early as 1967, Philip H. Abelson, the editor of *Science,* implicated cigarette smoke as an important and potentially dangerous element in air pollution, especially in combination with other pollutants. Abelson noted that while the diseases incurred by smokers might be considered their personal responsibility, the impact of smoking on the environment also endangered nonsmokers, who had accepted no such responsibility:

The principal effects of smoking are borne by the smokers themselves. They pay for their habit with chronic disease and shortened life. Involved are the individual's decision and his life. However, when the individual smokes in a poorly ventilated space in the presence of others, he infringes on the rights of others and becomes a serious contributor to air pollution.[16]

His editorial marks an early instance of how the rise of rights-based arguments in the context of scientific analysis would begin to reframe the smoking debate.

The following year, Frederic Speer, an allergist writing in *Archives of Environmental Health,* noted that "the effect of tobacco smoke on nonsmokers has received very little attention."[17] It was not surprising that an allergist would be interested in this question. For the better part of the twentieth century, people who had bad reactions to cigarette smoke were deemed to be suffering an allergic reaction. Calling sensitivity to cigarette smoke an allergy defined these reactions as idiosyncratic to a small group of affected individuals. Speer investigated the responses of exposure to smoke in both "allergic" and "nonallergic" subjects and found that smoke caused reactions in both groups, suggesting that the irritation many experienced might not be allergic at all. Noting how common exposure to smoke was and how intense it might be, he raised

the possibility that heavy exposure of the nonsmoker may lead to the serious diseases which afflict smokers. It cannot be denied that such exposure might have such grave results, but the answer to this question must
await studies similar in complexity to those used in studying the effect of
tobacco smokers.[18]

But the scientific investigation of secondhand smoke would prove no
simple matter. Although the new research would employ the same epidemiological and statistical techniques, honed in the 1950s, that demonstrated the risks of smoking for smokers, investigators faced a new set of
research obstacles. With any environmental toxin, measuring a small exposure or a small effect is more difficult than measuring a large one. It was already known that cigarette smoke could cause lung cancer in smokers, but
little research had been done on the harms smoke might cause at lower
doses. Symptoms among nonsmokers exposed to smoke ranged from eye,
nose, and throat irritation to coughing, sore throats, and sneezing to the
potential for cancers and serious respiratory and heart disorders. There was
no unexposed population to serve as a basis for comparison, as nonsmokers
had done for smokers, and no clear way to reliably identify groups with dif-
fering exposures. Given the widespread use of cigarettes, almost everyone
breathed in some smoke, some inhaled significant amounts, and many people's exposures could change unpredictably. As they had done when determining the risks to smokers a generation earlier, epidemiologists would
assess the harms of smoke for nonsmokers by a range of different methods.

These studies often took years, even decades, to complete. One of the
first major studies to be reported came from a longitudinal investigation
that had been underway in Japan since 1965 but was not reported until
1981. Epidemiologist Takeshi Hirayama of the Tokyo National Cancer
Center Research Institute had been studying the impact of factors, such as
alcohol use, occupation, and marital status on health in over 250,000 adults
over forty years of age. Having already collected substantial data on smoking in this population, he now measured the rates of lung cancer among the
nonsmoking wives of smoking husbands in his study. Hirayama found that
wives of smokers and ex-smokers had a substantially increased risk of developing lung cancer and that these risks were significantly related to dose.
The greater the consumption of cigarettes by the husband, the higher the

wife's risk. Women whose husbands smoked fourteen cigarettes a day had a 40 percent greater chance of developing cancer than those whose husbands did not smoke at all. If a husband smoked a pack or more a day, the difference rose to 90 percent.[19]

At the same time that Hirayama was exploring the impact of second-hand smoke among Japanese couples, epidemiologist Dimitrios Trichopoulos and colleagues were conducting a case control study in Athens. Trichopoulos identified fifty-one women with confirmed diagnoses of lung cancer admitted to Greek hospitals between September 1978 and June 1980. He then matched this group to a control of 163 women who did not have cancer. Eliminating the women who smoked from his analysis, he found significantly higher rates of lung cancer among nonsmoking wives of smoking husbands. It was not by chance that these two early and important studies of the risks of passive smoking were conducted in Japan and in Greece. Both were countries where very few women smoked, offering what Trichopoulos called an "unusual opportunity to investigate this issue."[20] He noted that high rates of smoking among both men and women in other populations would "confound and conceal the lesser effects of passive smoking."[21]

In the United States, James Repace, a physicist, and Alfred H. Lowey, a theoretical chemist, were employing a different approach. Drawing upon new technology as well as sophisticated new theoretical models, Repace and Lowey conducted a study of the effects of tobacco smoke on indoor air quality. They developed a model for estimating the "respirable suspended particles" (RSPs) from cigarette smoke in enclosed environments and then measured actual levels of smoke in bars, restaurants, bowling alleys, and other sites using a small handheld device called a piezobalance. The resulting article, which appeared in *Science* in 1980 following that journal's usual extensive peer review process, explicitly compared these familiar environments to the vicinities of coke ovens and other heavily polluted sites, noting that ETS exceeded legal levels for carcinogens by 250 to 1,000 times. "Under the practical range of ventilation conditions and building occupation densities," Repace wrote, "the RSP levels generated by smokers overwhelm the effects of ventilation and inflict significant air pollution burdens on the public." Better ventilation was unlikely to solve the problem, he contended, "Indoor air is a resource whose quality should be maintained at a high level. Smoking indoors may be incompatible with this goal."[22] Repace described "the RSP burdens from ambient tobacco smoke" as "so large that they must be incorporated explicitly in future epidemiological assessments of the relation between particulate levels and morbidity and mortality." His conclusions underscored the risks to the nonsmokers:

> Clearly, indoor air pollution from tobacco smoke presents a serious risk to the health of nonsmokers. Since this risk is involuntary, it deserves as much attention as outdoor air pollution.

Repace's research offered scientific confirmation of his personal experience as a sufferer of childhood asthma, exposed to smoke by his father, who died of lung cancer at fifty-nine.[23] Soon employed at the EPA, he would help make indoor air quality a significant aspect of the agency's regulatory efforts. These studies would mark the early recognition of the built environment as posing important health risks.

In 1981, a National Academy of Sciences committee on indoor air pollutants directed specific attention to the impact of tobacco smoke, urging that "public policy should clearly articulate that involuntary exposure to tobacco smoke ought to be minimal or avoided where possible."[24] By the late 1980s, many additional studies of the harms caused by secondhand smoke had cleared the bar of peer review in medical and scientific journals.[25] These studies would be subjected to intense scrutiny and attack by those representing the tobacco interests and from some independent scientists as well.

§

Even before scientific evidence of the harms of secondhand smoke emerged, tobacco-control advocacy groups and grassroots organizations began calling for restrictions on smoking in public places. In the early 1970s, John Banzhaf III and his small public interest group, ASH, which had so effectively challenged tobacco ads on the airwaves, turned their attention to the impact of smoking on nonsmokers. Banzhaf urged nonsmokers to stand up for their rights and to tell smokers, "Please put your cigarette out; the smoke is killing me."[26] He noted ominously (if speculatively) that "a non-smoker may actually be forced against his will to breathe almost as much carbon monoxide, tar, and nicotine as the active smoker sitting next to him."[27] Implicit in this tactic was a new line of attack on smokers themselves, whom antitobacco advocates would portray as selfishly disregarding the health and well-being of nonsmokers. "It's time we made them stop taking such liberties with our health and comfort,"[28] Banzhaf argued. He began petitioning the federal government to establish nonsmoking sections on planes and public transport, and in the workplace.

Such campaigns offered new opportunities for public health activists who had been stymied in their attempts to secure effective federal regulation in Congress, where the tobacco lobby held sway.[29] New grassroots organizations, typically modeled on environmental groups, began to solicit activist volunteers to advocate for the rights of nonsmokers. They were influenced as well by the examples of the civil rights and antiwar movements. Organizations like Group Against Smoking and Pollution (GASP), founded in 1971 by Clara Gouin, developed small groups of volunteers committed to local action. Their constituents generally had two things in common. Many, including Gouin, had lost family members and loved ones to lung cancer and other diseases. Gouin's father had died of lung cancer at fifty-seven, and she attributed his death to smoking. Others joined the group primarily because of their own sensitivities to smoke from allergies, asthma, and other respiratory diseases. Soon, Gouin's small cohort was printing flyers and buttons, sending out a newsletter—the *Ventilator*—to local lung associations, and offering advice to new local chapters. By 1974, the newsletter claimed fifty-six local chapters, each pushing forward the agenda that "non-smokers have rights, too."[30] Framing the question as a rights issue drew on the powerful antecedents of the civil rights movement and offered an important justification for state action in response to the libertarian perspectives that had traditionally dominated the politics of smoking. GASP's local chapters quickly moved from seeking to define the problem of secondhand exposures to aggressively seeking local and state ordinances regulating smoking in offices, public buildings, and restaurants.[31] They successfully called for special sections for nonsmokers in restaurants and other public spaces. Some restaurants were easily persuaded, before any legislation was passed, to set up small nonsmoking sections, which expanded as they proved popular with patrons.

The fight for tobacco control ordinances demonstrated the possibilities of grassroots public health advocacy. Single-issue advocacy groups were in a far better position to take up the fight than the traditional voluntary health organizations like the American Cancer Society and the American Heart Association. The latter had complex constituencies and philanthropic and educational missions that led to an inherent conservatism; they sought to avoid political controversy that could alienate not only smokers, but donors from tobacco-growing states.[32] The new organizations reveled in controversy, deliberately seeking media attention to sustain their cause.

The principal message of these local efforts appealed to the public's disdain for involuntary exposures to tobacco smoke. In 1966, Betty Carnes, an ornithologist whose son had died of lung cancer, had founded Arizonans Concerned About Smoking, one of the first nonsmokers' rights groups established in the United States. She and her colleagues sent off thousands of "Thank you for not smoking" signs and lobbied state legislatures for new regulations. Carnes was quick to point out that a majority of the state population did not smoke; in lobbying for the bill, she surveyed legislators to find who might be nonsmoking supporters. Arizona, with a large number of individuals with respiratory ailments, proved to be a strong base to generate popular support for the legislation. In 1973, after two years of intensive campaigning by Carnes and her group, Arizona became the first state in the nation to pass a law restricting smoking in public places—banning it in elevators, theaters, museums, libraries, and buses, and establishing assigned smoking areas in government buildings, health care facilities, and other public spaces. The law was soon amended to include restrooms, doctors' offices, and school buildings. Skeletal in its approach, it provided no funding to the Health Department to oversee compliance.[33] Even without a commitment of funds, such legislation demonstrated the political feasibility and popularity of antismoking measures. Activists and legislators soon found that even unenforced regulations had high levels of compliance. The fact that such legislation typically required no new funds gave it a significant political advantage over costly public health initiatives.

In 1975, Minnesota became the first state in the nation to pass a comprehensive Clean Indoor Air Act, banning smoking in most public offices, stores, and banks. A former state senator, Edward Brandt, had helped to found the local chapter of the Association for Non-Smokers' Rights

(ANR) in early 1973.[34] ANR surveyed restaurants in the Twin Cities to see how many offered nonsmoking areas. Although many of the restaurants expressed interest in providing such accommodations, few were doing so. In 1974, after much grassroots campaigning and rising public interest, Representative Phyllis Kahn introduced the bill, designed to "protect the public health, comfort and environment by prohibiting smoking in public places and at public meetings except in designated smoking areas."[35] Smoking in all public places was forbidden unless specifically allowed, and restaurants had to set aside at least 30 percent of their seats for nonsmokers. Penalties for violating the act ranged from warning citations to $100 fines.[36]

With the tobacco industry's lobbying being focused in Washington, these early bills came in under its radar. But as the industry geared up to resist state and local legislation, it became increasingly difficult to move smoking regulation bills through legislatures. In 1978, for example, some fifty-four bills were proposed, but only six resulted in legislation, and none contained major limits on public smoking like those in the Minnesota Act.[37] A decade later, when the Minnesota legislature sought to create a major campaign to reduce smoking, the industry was well prepared to dismantle the proposed bill through aggressive lobbying and opposition.

In 1978, a referendum in California, Proposition 5, which would have led to statewide restrictions on smoking, went down in defeat after the tobacco industry spent some $6.5 million to kill it. This loss, however, helped to galvanize the state's emerging nonsmokers' rights movement. After a second statewide campaign failed in 1980, activists shifted their focus to local municipalities, where the tobacco industry had considerably more difficulty in exercising political clout. In 1983, for example, San Francisco enacted broad restrictions on public smoking. Even against the industry's significant efforts to prevent such regulations, by 1981 thirty-six states had some form of restriction on smoking versus just five a decade earlier. Further, 20 percent of firms had issued workplace rules restricting smoking, and litigation often supported protections for nonsmokers in the workplace.[38]

Increasingly, employers realized the potential liabilities of *not* providing smoke-free workplaces. A report prepared by a consultant to *Fortune* 500 companies explained:

There is a growing body of court cases and legal opinions that indicate (1) employees have a right under federal law to sue for a smoke-free work environment, (2) employers must be prepared to bear some responsibility for the discomfort, pain, and illness caused to employees by smoke in the workplace, and (3) employers are within their rights in banning smoking in the workplace or in hiring only non-smokers.[39]

By the mid-1980s, most large corporations—and many smaller businesses—had developed explicit smoking policies with no prompting from the government. Boeing Company, with some 90,000 employees, announced a total ban and sponsored free smoking-cessation programs for its workers.[40] The elimination of smoking in the workplace offered several advantages: lower health care costs, fewer absences, and reduced cleaning services. What had been unimaginable ten years earlier now became commonplace as offices mandated their own "local" rules. Surveys of smoke-free companies demonstrated that overall tobacco consumption decreased even outside the workplace.[41] But perhaps most significantly, the very notion of smoking as a normative behavior was now in decline.

Closely monitoring these new restrictions, the tobacco industry regarded the debate about public smoking as a powerful threat to its future. In many ways, the issue had taken tobacco executives by surprise. But in tracking the changing social attitudes toward cigarette smoking in public, they soon came to appreciate the role that secondhand smoke would play in their future. Notably, the Roper Organization, which conducted a survey for the Tobacco Institute in 1978, warned that "once smoking becomes widely thought of as a public health hazard . . . the justification for legal measures against cigarette sales and use has been established. . . . What the smoker does to himself may be his business, but what the smoker does to the non-smoker is quite a different matter."[42] Roper's assessment emphasized that "more people say they would vote for than against a political candidate who takes a position favoring a ban on smoking in public places."[43]

Nearly six out of ten believe that smoking is hazardous to the non-smoker's health, up sharply over the last four years. More than two-thirds of non-smokers believe it and nearly one-half of all smokers believe it. This we see as the most dangerous development to the viability of the tobacco industry that has yet occurred.[44]

Given the industry's recent history, this was no small judgment, but it was not an overstatement. This movement in public opinion, resting on a changing knowledge base regarding smoking and its perils, now radically reoriented the personal and public meanings of tobacco—and with it, the image of the industry.

Roper presented the industry with a "balance sheet" of assets and liabilities in public attitudes toward smoking. The liabilities were serious and mounting. Of particular concern, the report noted, was the fact that a majority now believed that it was "probably hazardous to be around people who smoke even if they are not smoking themselves." There was growing interest in segregating smokers from nonsmokers in public spaces. This loss of confidence in the cigarette and its social legitimacy would compromise the companies' ability to respond to regulatory and other challenges. Even smokers were ambivalent about cigarettes, with two-thirds expressing a desire to quit. Finally, the Roper survey indicated that the tobacco companies' credibility had significantly deteriorated and that "favorable attitudes toward the industry are at their lowest ebb." According to the report, "a steadily increasing majority of Americans" now believed that the companies knew smoking was harmful despite their ongoing denials.[45] The survey ominously predicted:

As the anti-smoking forces succeed in their efforts to convince non-smokers that their health is at stake too, the pressure for segregated facilities will change from a ripple to a tide. . . .[46]

And the threat did not stop there:

If segregated facilities do not accomplish the anti-smoking forces' desire of making segregated smoking so untenable that smokers will give it up, the next step could be an outright ban.[47]

Roper, ever helpful, offered some scientific advice:

The strategic and long run antidote to the passive smoking issue is, as we see it, developing and widely publicizing clear-cut, credible medical evidence that passive smoking is not harmful to the non-smoker's health.[48]

This approach was in the grand Hill & Knowlton tradition. It both denied the current state of science and suggested that the industry could simply obtain—at will—the desired findings. Roper's suggestion closely mirrored John Hill's counsel in 1953: if you don't like the prevailing science, get your own.

§

As the industry renewed its strategy of attacking the developing science on passive smoking, the federal government sought to evaluate the emerging data. As early as 1971, Surgeon General Jesse Steinfeld had directed attention to the impact of smoke on nonsmokers, telling the Interagency Committee on Smoking and Health, "Nonsmokers have as much right to clean air and wholesome air as smokers have to their so-called right to smoke, which I would redefine as a 'right to pollute.' It is high time to ban smoking from all confined public places such as restaurants, theaters, airplanes, trains and buses. It is time that we interpret the Bill of Rights for the Nonsmoker as well as the smoker."[49] But Steinfeld offered no new data to back this proposal. The first surgeon general's report to explicitly raise the possibility of harm from passive smoke appeared in 1972.[50] Subsequent reports—focusing on cancer in 1979 and chronic obstructive lung disease in 1984—devoted somewhat more attention to the risk of harm to nonsmokers but generally noted a lack of conclusive data. In 1986, two major reports on the issue appeared, one from Surgeon General Koop, the other from the independent National Academy of Sciences (NAS).[51] The NAS report, comprehensively reviewing the scientific studies, found that children of smokers were twice as likely to suffer from respiratory infections, bronchitis, and pneumonia than children whose parents did not smoke. Though vigorously contested by the tobacco industry, these reports, utilizing the strategies of procedural science, tipped the balance in the debate. The effect of cigarette smoke on nonsmokers was transformed from an annoyance into a verifiable, quantifiable health risk.

Surgeon General Koop's report confirmed the findings of the NAS and went on to suggest that simply segregating smokers in the same workplace might reduce, but not eliminate, the risks to nonsmokers. "The right of the smoker to smoke stops at the point where his or her smoking increases the disease risk in those occupying the same environment," explained the surgeon general. "The data contained in this report lead me to conclude that the simplest, least expensive and most effective way to accomplish this protection is to establish a smoke-free work-site."[52] Koop clearly intended to spur new regulatory efforts at the local and the federal levels.

These reports distinguished between the two sources of environmental tobacco smoke. "Mainstream smoke" was the aerosol mixture inhaled from the cigarette by the smoker, filtered in the lungs, and exhaled into the environment. This smoke mixed with the "sidestream smoke" released directly from the burning end of the cigarette. Both types of smoke were found to contain oxides of nitrogen, nicotine, carbon monoxide, and a number of known carcinogens. "Sidestream smoke" had a higher concentration of carbon monoxide and constituted approximately 85 percent of the nonsmoker's intake.[53] By this time, smoke inhaled by nonsmokers had become a familiar enough concept to acquire an acronym: ETS.

Determining the number of deaths attributable to ETS was critical to the impact of these reports at the policy level. The National Academy of Sciences study estimated that ETS caused between 2,500 and 8,400 lung cancer deaths per year in the United States. Surgeon General Koop placed the number at approximately 3,000.[54] These numbers, seized by the media, transformed complex statistical calculations—odds ratios, relative risks, issues of statistical significance, and complex debates about validity and inference—into a basic social truth: passive smoking causes cancer and, ultimately, deaths. Secondhand smoke posed risks not only to vulnerable individuals—those with respiratory and other diseases—but to healthy adults and children as well. The NAS and Koop reports had converted the nuisance of secondhand smoke into a validated *risk*.

§

The tobacco companies now updated and intensified their well-tested methods of attacking both scientific procedures and the findings. The industry eagerly sought to link scientific assessments of secondhand smoke to other environmental toxins, especially those about which there was considerable scientific uncertainty. In December 1987, the Executive Committee of the Tobacco Institute discussed a proposal for an industry-based Center for Indoor Air Research, with the understanding that a primary goal would be "to expand interest beyond the misplaced emphasis solely on environmental smoke." Again, this "expansion" was a familiar strategy to industry executives, who had long insisted that the Tobacco Industry Research Committee maintain a broad focus on disease instead of investigating the risks of smoking.[55] As one planning memo suggested:

> Strategy:
> 1. Mobilize all scientific studies of indoor air quality (i.e., radon, wood stoves, gas stoves, formaldehyde, asbestos, etc.) into a general indictment of the air we breathe indoors. Use a scientific front—especially some liberal Nader group.
> 2. Use this material to fuel PR offensive on poor indoor air quality.[56]

This type of diversionary science would be an essential tool in combating the reports of secondhand risk.

The companies reasoned that since few scientists wished to be associated with the industry, they should establish a grant-making institute like the Council for Tobacco Research.[57] Founded in March 1988 by Philip Morris, R.J. Reynolds, and Lorillard, the Center for Indoor Air Research (CIAR) was designed to provide counterarguments against the emerging regulatory efforts. The bulk of its peer-reviewed science was unrelated to environmental tobacco smoke and served to divert attention from smoking as a pollutant by centering attention on other indoor air toxins. "To date," explained William Murray, vice chairman of the board of Philip Morris, "our principal defense has been the position . . . that there are many other things to blame for poor indoor air quality, and tobacco smoke is only a small part of the problem." He urged that "we must find stronger arguments to support our position on ETS."[58] The research on ETS that CIAR did sponsor, usually funded through a "special review" process, typically confirmed industry positions. In a review of more than one hundred scientific review articles about ETS that appeared between 1980 and 1995, researchers found that 37 percent concluded that ETS was not a risk to human health. Three-quarters of these articles were authored by scientists with ties to the tobacco industry, many through CIAR.[59]

Many epidemiologists, statisticians, tobacco company publicists, and antitobacco activists vigorously debated the quality and significance of the findings regarding the health impact of passive smoking. Arguing from what they called a perspective of objective science, some pro-tobacco forces suggested that the process of determining the risks of passive smoking had been perverted by an aggressive antitobacco movement offering rhetoric rather than research.[60] Dr. Philip Witorsch, a lung specialist at George Washington University Medical School, told a *Washington Post* reporter that the contribution of ETS to air pollution was "minimal" and "insufficient to produce a pathophysiological effect." Witorsch's work had been sponsored by the industry-funded Indoor Air Pollution Advisory Group. Such conflicts of interest eroded the authority of these claims.[61] The industry would continue to assert—as it had done for the harms of direct smoking—that passive smoke posed "no proven harm or risk whatsoever."[62] In a press release, the Tobacco Institute protested the Koop report, noting that "the continued propagation of unfounded claims that tobacco compromises—even slightly—the health of nonsmokers will only intensify the current climate of emotionalism and impede the progress of scientific integrity. . . . Most alarmingly, scientific integrity and academic freedom face a serious threat from political pressures being applied by government health officials and otherwise principled scientists."[63] Such statements now only confirmed how profoundly out of touch the tobacco industry had become. By the mid-1980s, as Roper had indicated, few people looked to the tobacco industry as a crusader for scientific integrity.

Changes in the broader culture worked against the companies' efforts. First, it was no longer possible, as it had been in the 1950s, to denigrate epidemiology and statistics. These elements of medical science had grown to be trusted influences on both public opinion and policy making. Second, the industry's own loss of credibility—a product of its "skepticism" of scientific findings about the harms of smoking—made the media and the public unwilling to accept industry attacks as scientifically legitimate. The industry would increasingly have to seek third parties and front groups to represent its position even though this, too, was already a familiar gambit. Finally, American society had become far more health-conscious since the 1960s—and more risk averse. The 1980s and 1990s were simply not a good time to urge consumers to tolerate low-dose risks.[64] To the contrary,

American society became committed both culturally and politically to the identification and removal of even small risks.

The relationship of the epidemiologic and toxicologic data to regulatory politics is best understood as a complex dialectical process. Given that no scientific study is ever final—there is always *some* uncertainty—the question always comes down to what level of risk merits what level of intervention. Thus, the social process of identifying and regulating risk, though ultimately resting on scientific discourse, was powerfully influenced by a range of social and moral factors that mobilized the public health and antitobacco movement. Determining the risks of secondhand smoke was not like evaluating the causal relationship between smoking and disease for smokers themselves. In a society deeply concerned about imposed risks, how conclusive did the data about ETS need to be? In an atmosphere of rising concern about environmental contaminants and especially carcinogens, how long would local governments and businesses wait to regulate public smoking, especially in instances where they might possess liability?[65] How good did the data need to be when many businesses perceived that regulating smoking could bring significant cost savings, and when social conventions were already moving quickly to stigmatize smokers as irrational, dirty, and self-destructive? How persuasive did the data on passive smoking need to be, when the harms that were identified were typically inflicted on "nonconsenting, innocent victims"? Early regulatory initiatives drove the research agenda. In turn, research results—though preliminary—drove the regulatory process. The surgeon general's 1986 report and the NAS report added legitimacy to a social movement and regulatory agenda that already possessed considerable momentum.

In the case of passive smoke, risk and nuisance were deeply entangled. Even those who questioned the scientific data indicating the measurable risks of secondhand smoke found it hard to assert that smoking could not be restricted simply because nonsmokers found it to be irritating and bothersome. As the tobacco industry and its patrons came to learn, there was no inalienable right to smoke in public. The very practice of public smoking. which the industry had worked so assiduously to secure in the early part of the twentieth century, was a contingent cultural norm that was now decidedly reversed by a combination of cultural, scientific, and political factors. The public did not need "proof" that passive smoke could cause lung cancer to decide that it wanted smoke-free workplaces, restaurants, and transportation. The cigarette had little standing in a health-conscious culture, increasingly skeptical of an industry whose self-interest had long since been exposed.

§

By the late 1980s, the tobacco companies recognized that secondhand smoke posed a potentially life-threatening risk—to the industry. As John Rupp, a lawyer at Covington & Burling working on tobacco accounts, put it, "we are in deep shit." Rupp was speaking at a 1987 conference for Philip Morris's Project Down Under, organized to devise new strategies to address the threat.[66] Attendees continued to hope for ways to upend the research implicating secondhand smoke as a serious health risk. Minutes from the meeting reported, "A scientific battle was lost with the Surgeon General's '86 Report. Is there any way of showing the Surgeon General is wrong?"[67] Even as the gathered executives recognized that they were losing the battle of public perceptions, they understood that they still had considerable advantages in resources and power. One theme discussed at the conference was "Make It Hurt." "Let pols know down side of anti activity," noted the conference minutes. "To do this, we take on vulnerable candidate, beat him/her, let people know we did it."[68]

At a brainstorming session, the Philip Morris executives came up with more than one hundred "solutions to the problem." These ranged from "create a bigger monster (AIDS)" to "undermine Koop et al."[69] Even as they agreed to attack the science of passive risk, those gathered understood the essential dilemma in constructing their defense: "We've got to get people on the street, but we are constrained because we can't say it's 'safe.'"[70] Notes from the meeting concluded, "ETS issue will have devastating effect on sales" and predicted that "we are just at the *beginning* of impact of ETS issue."[71]

Industry executives and lawyers at the meeting, aware that their adversaries in the tobacco wars had again successfully seized the science, complained that "what created [negative] perceptions is *their* science."[72] Nonetheless, the industry sought to regain control of this aspect of the debate. Regarding risks to smokers, the industry had come to rely on proclamations of "not proven." With ETS, they understood that promoting scientific uncertainty was unlikely to stem the growing demand for regulatory action. Individual smokers might well decide to continue if the risks were "not proven." But such a stance was a weak and meaningless promise to nonsmokers, on whom such risks (even if small and uncertain) were *imposed*. Even internal industry reviews apparently confirmed the risks.[73] At the same time, throughout the debates about ETS, the industry continued to deny that direct smoking had been proven harmful to smokers, while carefully avoiding any definitive assurances to the contrary. Locked into this position by ongoing fears of litigation, the industry had lost much of its scientific credibility. Now, executives worried that contesting the harms of secondhand smoke too strongly could be perceived as an acknowledgment that smoking was dangerous for smokers. "Pervasive fear," noted the conference minutes, "that if you fight too hard on ETS, it means conceding the primary issue."[74]

§

In the fight against public restrictions on smoking, the companies worked to initiate and support grassroots campaigns on behalf of "smokers' rights."[75] The tobacco industry was quick to point to such restrictions as "an intrusion into the businessman's and the individual's rights."[76] "Our concern," explained Walker Merryman of the Tobacco Institute, "is what this portends for society and business, for governmental bodies to be regulating public behavior." He explicitly evoked images of the civil rights movement. "It is dangerous when you try to paint our members as social pariahs and to make 60 to 80 million smoking Americans second class citizens. We already sit in the back of the plane and the bus."[77]

In an effort to recruit smokers to defend their rights, the industry eagerly sought to portray restrictions on smoking as the beginning of a massive government intrusion into citizens' personal behavior. Stanley S. Scott, vice president and director of corporate affairs for Philip Morris, offered an ominous vision of the slippery slope ahead:

The basic freedoms of more than 50 million American smokers are at risk today. Tomorrow, who knows what personal behavior will become socially unacceptable, subject to restrictive laws and public ridicule? . . . Could travel by private car make the social engineers' hot list because it is less safe than public transit? Could ice cream, cake and cookies become socially unacceptable because their consumption causes obesity? What about sky-diving, mountain climbing, skiing and contact sports? How far will we allow this to spread?

Scott sought to place smokers' rights in the hallowed tradition of American social movements to secure basic freedoms:

> The question all Americans must ask themselves is: can a nation that has struggled so valiantly to eliminate bias based on race, religion and sex afford to allow a fresh set of categories to encourage new forms of hostility between large groups of citizens? . . . After all, discrimination is discrimination, no matter what it is based on.[78]

Cigarettes now came wrapped in the First Amendment. Philip Morris sponsored a nationwide essay contest on free speech, publishing the winning entries in a volume called *American Voices*.[79] This contest did not go unnoticed by the other side in the tobacco wars. In a striking example of antitobacco guerilla tactics, a small group known as Doctors Ought to Care, founded by activist physician Alan Blum, sponsored a competing contest on the question "Are tobacco company executives criminally liable for the deaths, diseases, and fires that their products cause?" Although Blum could not match the industry's resources to advertise his contest, he nonetheless drew media attention for spoofing the companies' campaign.[80]

In the tobacco wars, it was now hand-to-hand combat. Each new incursion was met with a counteroffensive. Philip Morris decided, for example, to mount a campaign in response to the American Cancer Society's Great American Smokeout, an annual educational effort in which smokers were encouraged to quit. So the company offered a Great American Smoker's Kit, complete with a lapel pin and a sign to hang on a doorknob announcing, "Great American Smoker at work." "We hope you will find the Great American Smoker's Kit useful and enjoyable," explained the accompanying pamphlet. "We understand the kinds of pressures you may face from friends and coworkers. Their efforts are well-meaning, but they can be intrusive and some may even be aggressive." The pamphlet concluded, "Above all, if you've chosen to smoke, help them understand it is your right to choose."[81] Philip Morris also offered a Bill of Rights for smoking:

> As a smoker, I am entitled to certain inalienable rights, among them:
>
> > The right to the pursuit of happiness;

The right to choose to smoke;

The right to enjoy a traditional American custom;

The right to be treated courteously;

The right to accommodation in the workplace;

The right to accommodation in public places;

The right to unrestricted access to commercial information about products;

The right to purchase products without excessive taxation;

The right to freedom from unnecessary government intrusion.[82]

Along with other companies, Philip Morris helped fund the National Smokers' Alliance (NSA), a "grassroots" organization created with the assistance of the PR firm Burson-Marsteller to advocate smokers' rights and oppose smoking restrictions. Claiming some three million members, NSA sought to promote a pro-smoking agenda "unlinked" to the industry. But it soon became clear that NSA was a front for industry interests.[83]

Although the industry never generated a true popular coalition of smokers eager to come to its defense, it did successfully exploit themes of personal freedoms in its efforts to fight more restrictive state and local legislation. For example, civil liberties groups and labor unions—hardly traditional allies—supported antidiscrimination provisions to protect workers who smoked during nonbusiness hours.[84] Generating enthusiasm for smokers' rights proved difficult when the vast majority of smokers were already deeply ambivalent about their own habit. Most polls indicated that most smokers *wanted* to quit.[85] "Smokers are not easily allied. They are defensive, and many would like to quit," noted an industry assessment.[86] They were hardly likely to insist on smoking as an "inalienable" right.

Try though the companies might to stir a popular rebellion against restrictions on cigarette smoking, smokers never really warmed to the campaign. Even as the industry sent its patrons into battle in defense of the right to smoke, smokers themselves, increasingly stigmatized and socially marginalized, went AWOL. The antismoking campaign had scrupulously avoided a Prohibition-like stance. The real contest centered on *where* one could smoke, not on smoking per se. Efforts by the tobacco companies to generate sympathy for their aggrieved constituents by claiming the language of rights—most baldly visible in Philip Morris's promotion of the two-hundredth anniversary of the Bill of Rights—came across as but a new form of postmodern humor.[87] The thinly veiled self-interest of the industry and its historic hypocrisy on the health issue left it little room to maneuver.[88]

§

The industry understood how important it was historically that smoking be accepted as a public behavior. Early in the twentieth century, it had been critical to secure the notion that men and women would prominently smoke in public. This was a crucial element of the highly positive social meanings that the cigarette would acquire in the first half of the twentieth century. In those days, opposition to public smoking had centered on questions of gender equality and morals. Now, the practice was under attack again, but on decidedly different grounds.

Internal documents reveal the extensive planning and resources devoted to the industry's effort to keep smoking a legitimate activity.[89] In 1985, the president of the Tobacco Institute outlined the industry's strategy concerning environmental tobacco smoke, explaining that the industry would act "to redefine [the issue], to broaden it, to demonstrate . . . that we are contributing to the solution rather than to the problem."[90] This strategy quickly took tangible form. During the first four months of 1986, tobacco PR representatives lobbied representatives of 1,500 companies, 14 chambers of commerce, the National Restaurant Association, and 13 state restaurant groups, running seminars concerning workplace smoking policies.[91] To keep smoking in the realm of socially acceptable behavior, the industry focused on manners, insisting that conflicts could be dealt with through "mutual respect" and "accommodation."[92] Any tensions engendered by smoking could be resolved by a polite tolerance of others' needs. Smokers and nonsmokers could amicably negotiate the use of public space. Such tobacco industry rhetoric became well established by the mid-1980s.

In the early 1990s, Philip Morris undertook a new campaign for what it called "The Accommodation Program." Advertisements for the program argued that negotiation, manners, and mutual respect were a better means of regulation than "outright bans." "The rights of one group should not supersede the rights of the other," one ad explained. Another advocated "common courtesy and mutual respect . . . to work things out." The company produced materials for business owners, restaurants, hotels, and bars to advise them on voluntary policies to assure protected space for smokers and non-smokers alike. "The program works because it respects the rights and wishes of both groups," Philip Morris explained, "So both get what they want." An ad for a similar campaign, R.J. Reynolds's Project Breakthrough, noted, "There are ways for smokers and non-smokers to co-exist." "Together, we can work it out," the ad promised. Project Breakthrough also suggested that the ultimate goal of the new regulatory environment was prohibition. One ad featured a nonsmoker who explained, "The smell of cigarette smoke annoys me. But not as much as the government telling me what to do." The industry repeatedly sought to link restrictions on public smoking to a conservative political argument about overreaching government.

Even Emily Post would have had difficulty negotiating this cultural territory. As the tide shifted to favor smoke-free public space, the United States' new etiquette maven, Judith Martin (a.k.a. Miss Manners), frequently encountered what she identified as discourtesies among the nonsmokers. "Miss Manners is not a smoker herself," Martin wrote, "but she has noted that foul emissions from non-smokers are hazardous to the public welfare. . . . The idea that health-conscious righteousness justifies rudeness is a repulsive one."[93] She found that the whole smoking issue, much to her professional chagrin, had degenerated into conflict and acrimony. "Miss Manners is hard put to say who is behaving worse: those who insist upon offending other people with their smoke or those who insist that only rudeness and humiliation toward smokers will clear the air."[94] In 1985, Martin threw up her hands, exclaiming, "The issue of smoking has inspired such widespread unacceptable manners in both smokers and nonsmokers for so long that Miss Manners would be relieved to have regulation of smoking made a matter of law, as many people are suggesting. She is more than ready to turn her attention to more complicated problems."[95] The very fact that smoking had passed from a matter of etiquette to a regulatory issue was an impressive victory for anti-smoking advocates. "Society has changed on this issue," Martin would later conclude, "and smoking is no longer considered to be a standard liberty."[96]

Individuals, who a decade earlier would not have dreamed of asking a smoker to stop, now became emboldened. With the sudden flowering of "No Smoking" signs, the nonsmoker was deputized as an agent of the state. Smoking in such areas now constituted an infraction; asking a smoker to stop was a far less aggressive act than it had been in the past. Further, smokers themselves viewed violation of the new norms as inviting personal embarrassment, if not overt hostility. They came to internalize a new set of ethics about public smoking, just as nonsmokers developed new and heightened sensitivities to smoke. Peer pressure and social conformity—critical aspects of the cigarette's popularity earlier in the century—now weighed heavily against it. The most basic assumptions about where and when it was appropriate to smoke had been reconfigured. As a result, the very meaning—even the "pleasure"—of cigarettes began a downward spiral.[97] Try though the industry might to create some cultural space for the smoker through smokers' rights campaigns and the insistence on accommodation through manners, by the 1990s smokers in the United States literally had no place to hide.

Airplanes, the epitome of enclosed spaces, became the focus of considerable debate. Most of the new initiatives to restrict smoking had occurred at the local and state level, but air travel remained under federal jurisdiction. In the battle maps of the tobacco wars, antismoking advocates looked on the federal government, especially Congress, as enemy-occupied territory. Calls for smoking bans on airlines date back to 1969, when consumer advocate Ralph Nader first asked the Federal Aviation Agency to eliminate smoking on flights. Many individual consumers also complained to airlines. In 1971, United became the first carrier to develop segregated seating for smokers and nonsmokers, with other carriers soon following.[98] Two years later, the Civil Aeronautics Board (CAB) made nonsmoking sections a federal requirement. Banzhaf successfully petitioned the CAB in 1976 to ban cigar and pipe smoking on planes. GASP established a Non-Smokers Travel Club for members eager to avoid exposure to smoke in their travels.[99]

But the airline industry and public commentators did not quickly jump on the smoke-free bandwagon. In a 1977 editorial criticizing a federal proposal to limit the number of smoking seats on all planes, the *Washington Post* claimed, "The CAB should tell anti-smoking groups to back off. It's reasonable to make smokers sit in the back of the plane. But it isn't the airlines' business, or the government's, to decide how many passengers should be allowed to smoke."[100] Even after nonsmoking sections were required on all U.S. airlines, the carriers (and the tobacco companies) by no means accepted smoking bans. The airline industry claimed it should be free to decide how to accommodate passengers without outside interference. Airline executives worried that federal policies would put them at a competitive disadvantage internationally, that effectively separating smoking and nonsmoking sections would prove costly and difficult, and that these policies would create extra work for their in-flight personnel.[101]

The creation of separate smoking sections, moreover, did little to improve air quality in the cabin. Smokers often selected nonsmoking seats but would then congregate in the back of the plane to smoke. As one reader put it in an outraged letter to the editor of the *New York Times* in 1983, "Why is smoking permitted at all on airplanes? There appears to be no effective way to section off the fuselage so that non-smokers can be adequately protected from drifting smoke. . . . Health and safety benefits will far outweigh the inconvenience suffered by temporarily deprived smokers."[102] Passengers seated near the smoking section frequently filed complaints. One critic suggested that "a smoking section on an airplane . . . is like having a peeing section in a swimming pool."[103] Airlines found no easy way to accommodate both smokers and nonsmokers, especially since nonsmokers felt increasingly entitled to demand smoke-free space.

The issue of smoking on airplanes brought together several strands of the rising concerns about cigarette use as a health risk, a nuisance, and an occupational hazard. While it was sometimes difficult for nonsmoking passengers to justify their demands for a smoke-free flight on the basis of risks to health (given short exposures), such was not true of flight attendants, whose work required repeated exposure to smoke-filled cabins. They became leading advocates for more aggressive regulation of smoking on flights. Joyce Hagen, a flight attendant, explained, "While we wait for someone to take the lead on this, we are breathing this carcinogen for hours at a time every time we fly."[104] Still, despite flight attendants' rising concerns and increasing public opposition to smoking on flights, bans did not quickly follow. As late as 1984, the U.S. tobacco industry joined forces with the airline industry to help defeat a proposed CAB smoking ban on short flights. The CAB's chairman, Dan McKinnon, explained at the time, "Philosophically, I think nonsmokers have rights, but it comes into market conflict with practicalities and the realities of life."[105]

The National Academy of Sciences issued a report in 1986 that evaluated the risks posed by smoking on airplanes. Since aircraft ventilation systems, the committee found, were not capable of meeting the standards required in other public spaces, "cabin air ventilation is in violation of the building codes for most other indoor environments." The report pointed out that the group most significantly affected by smoke on airplanes was flight attendants, whose exposure was estimated to be the same as living with a pack-a-day smoker. Thomas Chalmers, president emeritus of Mount Sinai Medical Center, who chaired the study, explained that the group of eleven experts had concluded that smoking should be banned on all commercial flights in the United States.[106] With the other NAS and surgeon general's reports on environmental smoke appearing in 1986 as well, the scientific basis for federal regulations of airlines was increasingly secure.

In the fierce battle that ensued, public sentiment and the tobacco control lobby won out over the tobacco interests. GASP chapters and ANSR mobilized their considerable constituencies on behalf of a ban on smoking on all flights two hours or less. They secured the support of the AMA, the American Heart Association, the American Lung Association, and Koop himself, among others. The legislation, sponsored by Congressman Richard Durbin, passed in the House by the narrow margin of 198–193, after the tobacco and the airline industries lobbied vigorously to kill it; in the Senate, the vote was 84–10. "People choose to smoke, but there is no choice about breathing," said conservative Republican Senator Orrin Hatch of Utah, a supporter of the legislation. In fighting the ban, the industry sought to foment grassroots protest among smokers. "People who smoke cigarettes have a right to," noted Senator Jesse Helms of North Carolina (also a conservative Republican), "but they are going to have no choice."[107] "I doubt the studies show you anybody dying on an airplane from smoking." added Democratic Senator Ernest F. Hollings from South Carolina. "The Indians were smoking when we got here."[108] The smoking ban on flights of two hours or less went into effect in 1988. At that time, Northwest Airlines announced a total ban on smoking on all its flights and heavily advertised the new policy. When such restrictions proved popular with a majority of passengers, the airlines dropped their opposition. A year later, legislation was introduced to ban smoking on all domestic flights. Although the Tobacco Institute argued it was "unnecessary, unfair, and unwarranted," this legislation passed easily in 1990.[109]

The popularity of airline bans reinforced the broader cultural changes already underway. Each new restriction brought dire warnings of civil unrest and nicotine fits, but the reality was that smoking bans were often celebrated by nonsmokers and smokers alike. Planes were both cleaner and safer from fire risk—advantages shared by all. Smokers found, sometimes to their surprise, that they could do without their cigarettes. It was a message that the tobacco industry had sought to hide. Today, it is sometimes hard to remember that smoking on airplanes was once permitted.

In late 1992, after more than two years of evaluation and political wrangling, the Environmental Protection Agency (EPA) declared tobacco smoke a Class A human lung carcinogen. Unlike the earlier NAS and surgeon general's studies, this ruling had far-ranging policy implications, putting the Occupational Safety and Health Administration under pressure to ban smoking in the workplace nationwide. The industry and its allies in Congress had fought to delay or weaken the final report, which declared ETS responsible for approximately three thousand deaths from lung cancer each year among nonsmokers. The study suggested that 20 percent of all lung cancers among nonsmokers were due to ETS, making the risk about one in one thousand; higher than almost all chemicals regulated by the agency.[110]

The tobacco industry responded by criticizing the EPA for inadequate and poorly analyzed data. The Tobacco Institute called the study "another step in a long process characterized by a preference for political correctness over sound science."[111] Steven Parrish, senior vice president at Philip Morris, argued that the EPA was indirectly targeting smokers. "There is a mind-set that we want to discourage people from smoking," he explained, that made the EPA willing to "adjust the science to fit the policy."[112] Parrish's statement reflected a deliberate and sharply articulated strategy within the industry. As an internal memo from Philip Morris explained, "The growing perceptions about and animosity to EPA as an agency that is at least misguided and aggressive, at worst corrupt and controlled by environmental terrorists, offer one of the few avenues for inroads."[113] With the assistance of APCO Associates, a public relations firm, Philip Morris established a "sound science" coalition ostensibly dedicated to improving the quality of scientific discourse by rooting out "junk science." One aspect of this carefully calculated effort was a move to revise the standards of scientific proof so that the harms of secondhand smoke could never possibly satisfy them. C. C. Little's dogmatic assertions of "not proven" would no longer suffice: the industry realized that it could avoid new regulatory intervention only by redefining the science of risk. Following years of fighting epidemiologists, Philip Morris now initiated a campaign for "Good Epidemiological Practices," organized to "fix" epidemiology to serve the industry's interests by changing standards of proof. One objective of the program, an internal memo explained, was "to impede adverse legislation."[114]

By the late 1980s, as local ordinances spurred by grassroots public health campaigns proliferated, the tobacco industry returned to a strategy that had proved valuable and effective in the past. It sought state-level statutes that would preempt the profusion of local ordinances.[115] This approach offered a number of important advantages. The industry simply could not keep up with the hundreds of pending ordinances being introduced and enacted in such short order. As Roger Mozingo of R.J. Reynolds explained, "They can introduce a bill one day in Bridgeport, Connecticut, and the same bill will turn up two days later in Marin County, California."[116] By working at the state level, the industry could reduce the number of battlegrounds.

As the industry continued to lose credibility in the 1980s and early 1990s, preemption became an increasingly important political tool. By 1997, nearly thirty states had passed legislation that in one form or another preempted local jurisdiction over tobacco. The industry increasingly utilized legitimate antitobacco legislation as a "vehicle" for inserting preemptive clauses. Given that such bills often originated with public health advocates and their allies, the addition of preemption clauses sometimes had the effect of dividing the antitobacco coalitions, as they found themselves forced to decide whether to accept valuable public health interventions at the cost of conceding preemption of local controls.[117] These divisions nearly killed California's smoke-free workplace law as well as similar legislation in Pennsylvania, Florida, and Illinois.[118] Walker Merryman predicted that this strategy would ensure that "about 90 percent of legislation at the state level [adversely] affecting our industry will not be enacted."[119] In 1987, for example, as Pittsburgh, Philadelphia, and several other Pennsylvania towns moved toward enactment of local smoking restrictions, the state of Pennsylvania passed a clean air bill mandating weaker rules than those under consideration locally. The state act preempted the local governments' proposed rules. Mark Pertschuk of Americans for Non-Smokers Rights called the state legislation "a tobacco industry relief act."[120] At the behest of tobacco interests, several states passed smokers' rights laws that prohibited public regulation of smoking.[121] About half the states passed laws guaranteeing that smokers would not be discriminated against in hiring decisions. In lobbying for such legislation, the Tobacco Institute would bring forward restaurant associations, grocers, marketers, and retailers, as well as organized labor, farming groups, and other allies, to help dilute clean air standards. Even in an increasingly hostile cultural environment, the tobacco industry found strategies to sustain its product and its profits.

§

But the cigarette had reached a critical tipping point, and rates of smoking began a slow but persistent fall. In 1983, approximately one-third of all adults were regular smokers; three years later, the number had fallen to about 30 percent. This decline reinforced the notion that smoking was becoming an increasingly minority behavior. The recognition of this fact further emboldened nonsmokers to assert their rights over a minority perceived as inflicting the risks of their bad behavior on the majority.

At the same time, smoking became increasingly associated with lower educational and socioeconomic status. Data from the Centers for Disease Control showed smoking declining with levels of education: more than 40 percent of people who dropped out of high school were smokers, compared to 15 percent of those with college degrees. On seeing these numbers, University of Michigan economist Kenneth Warner remarked that "smoking-related diseases will increasingly become a class-based phenomenon."[122]

The cultural shift associated with secondhand smoke had tipped the balance in favor of quitting. Smokers reported increasing social pressures to quit, as well as declining pleasure from cigarettes. But the reductions in smoking followed patterns of education and class. Once loaded with positive meanings, the cigarette now carried the burdens of risk, pollution, and contamination. The product and its consumer had moved from the normative to the stigmatized.

309

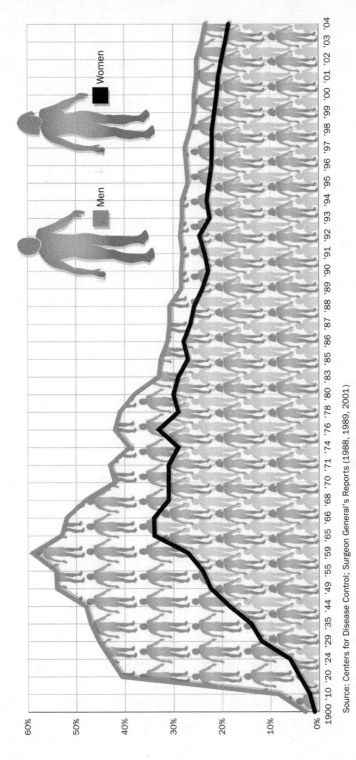

Source: Centers for Disease Control; Surgeon General's Reports (1988, 1989, 2001)

CHART 5   Male and female smoking prevalence, United States, 1900–2004

§

As the social acceptability of cigarette use fell precipitously, the tobacco companies redoubled their efforts in marketing and promotion, intensifying efforts to target new smokers, women, and ethnic minorities. Of particular note were new strategies across the industry to solicit African-American smokers. During the course of the twentieth century, African-Americans had generally begun smoking in large numbers later than whites, in part responding to advertising campaigns directed to them in the 1930s and 1940s. By the early 1960s, rates of smoking among blacks had become similar to those among whites. Among African-Americans there was a long-standing preference (frequently investigated and commented on within the tobacco industry) for menthol cigarettes. According to most assessments, patrons associated these brands—intensively advertised in black media—(Kool, Newport, and Salem) with less harsh, cooler, and medicinal tastes. Such preferences could perhaps also be linked to the use of menthol and other herbal remedies in African-American healing practices dating back to the colonies.[123]

As rates of smoking began to fall in the 1970s and early 1980s, the tobacco companies centered new attention on the African-American market.[124] Promotional campaigns were linked to efforts to secure stronger ties to the African-American community through philanthropic support of key institutions and charities. Philip Morris had been a trendsetter in corporate integration in the 1940s and 1950s, and it was the first tobacco company to promote African-Americans into sales and executive positions.[125] Along with its competitors, Philip Morris also became a major contributor to the NAACP, the National Urban League, and the United Negro College Fund. In 1988, the principal sponsors for the annual conference of the Congressional Black Caucus were Anheuser Busch, Philip Morris, R.J. Reynolds, Miller Brewing Company, and Coors. Observers of this trend drew attention to the companies' attempts to curry good will and political favor within the minority community. In an internal memorandum, Brown & Williamson explained its support for African-American philanthropies:

Obviously, care must be exercised not to "over-commercialize" the agreement or B&W's association with the NAACP. However, if managed with sensitivity, this association can be linked positively to the minority buying public. . . .

Clearly, the sole reason for B&W's interest in the black and Hispanic communities is the actual and potential sales of B&W products within these communities and the profitability of these sales.

. . . [T]his relatively small and often tightly knit community can work to B&W's marketing advantage, if exploited properly. Peer pressure plays a more important role in many phases of life in the minority community. Therefore, dominance of the market place and the community environment is necessary to successfully increase sales there.[126]

Corporate philanthropy and targeted promotion drew new advocates to the ranks of tobacco control. Increasingly, critics pointed out that tobacco billboards were concentrated in poorer urban neighborhoods, especially in African-American communities. "Every day when little children are on their way to school they get a message that the way to be happy and get ahead is to have a beer and smoke cigarettes," Representative John Lewis explained.[127] Philip Morris spokesman Steven Weiss quickly countered, "The argument that minorities are more susceptible to our advertising is at best reprehensible and at worst racist." Walker Merryman of the Tobacco Institute added that claims of targeting were "offensive" and "implied that blacks and other minorities are unable to make their own decisions as to whether or not to smoke, and that they do not have information to make their own decisions." A 1987 survey in St Louis showed that black neighborhoods had three times as many billboards as did white areas.[128]

In 1977, an R.J. Reynolds executive noting that their "business among Blacks is underdeveloped," suggested that "a project designed to develop a cigarette for Blacks may even be a viable business proposition."[129] With market share of its principal menthol cigarette, Salem, in decline, R.J. Reynolds decided to launch a new brand to compete with Lorillard's Newport in the black community. The result of these efforts was Uptown, designed specifically to appeal to urban, African-American smokers. R.J. Reynolds planned to promote the brand in packs of both ten and twenty with a gold and black logo. Ads sought to associate Uptown with the "good life" announcing "Uptown. The Place, The Taste."[130]

In Philadelphia, where the brand was test-marketed, R.J. Reynolds's announcement of Uptown touched off a grassroots protest that soon attracted national media attention. The introduction of Uptown, along with its marketing campaign, ignited a vigorous debate about smoking, the tobacco industry, and the African-American community. Ultimately, Secretary of Health and Human Services Louis Sullivan publicly called for the withdrawal of Uptown. "At a time when our people desperately need the message of health promotion, Uptown's message is more disease, more suffering, and more death," declared Sullivan.[131] R.J. Reynolds was forced to scrap the campaign and kill the brand. The company lost some $5 million to $7 million invested in the project and, even more significantly, considerable public credibility. "Much can be said about the Uptown cigarette debacle," concluded an internal R.J. Reynolds assessment.

> However, even an error of this magnitude can represent a positive thing if one can extract an important lesson to guide his future direction. . . . Had Blacks across various strata been asked to respond to this issue (a cigarette targeted specifically at Blacks), undoubtedly researchers would have discovered or been reminded of the fact that an underlying distrust exists among Blacks for institutions, governments, industries and companies controlled by whites. A white-owned tobacco company, targeting a cigarette to Blacks, a product widely accepted as harmful to one's health, would undoubtedly surface that inherent distrust inevitably described as 'institutional genocide.'[132]

In response, the industry eagerly sought to connect attacks on smoking as discriminatory and stigmatizing, forces well understood in the African-American community. But others suggested that targeting of minorities simply represented one more predatory strategy in the marketing of a deadly product. Further, they argued, the impact of funding black charitable institutions had blunted the political response of leaders in the African-American community. "To suggest that we are buying influential members of the community is an outrageous insult to the members of that community," argued Steven Weiss for Philip Morris. "Any of our funding of programs is no-strings-attached funding."[133] Some African-American leaders reacted defensively to the questions raised about the propriety of these gifts. "Implicit in this is the premise that Blacks are so naïve they will be persuaded to smoke by a billboard or an ad," contended Benjamin Hooks, executive director of NAACP. "This is an insidious form of paternalism. Blacks, like the rest of the populace, can make the choice of whether to smoke or not."[134] "The leaders of these organizations should have been fanatical in their opposition to smoking, which slaughters their membership," responded Bob Herbert in the *New York Times*. "Instead they lined up before the tobacco companies with their lips zipped and their hands out for their share of the industry's hush money."[135]

Looming over this debate were statistics showing that African-Americans suffer disproportionately from tobacco-related diseases. By 1990, some 45,000 deaths per year among African-Americans were associated with smoking. Black men reportedly had a 48 percent higher rate of lung cancer than white men and lost twice as many years of life to tobacco-related diseases. According to some studies, African-Americans had significant metabolic differences, perhaps genetic in origin, which led to an inability to detoxify NKK, a particularly toxic carcinogen in tobacco smoke.[136]

The debate about targeting minorities had the effect of drawing even more critical attention to the larger problem of marketing tobacco in an age of declining rates of smoking. The fall in consumption led companies to devise more aggressive and targeted marketing campaigns. These efforts, in turn, subjected the industry to growing social sanctions and political attack. Because of its tactics, the tobacco industry would come to be singled out as the preeminent example of corporate irresponsibility, greed, and the failure of business ethics.

§

The tobacco industry worked hard to maintain public acceptance for its customers. "The social acceptability issue will be the central battleground on which our case will be lost or won," an industry executive explained in 1979.[137] The industry worked to restore "first-class citizenship status to smokers." At the same time, however, it recognized that there were "immediate and awesome obstacles" to this task. As an R.J. Reynolds memo explained:

> First, it is going to be difficult to restore first-class citizenship status to smokers when an overwhelming percentage of the public believes smoking does indeed cause numerous dread and terminal diseases.

Second, although to a lesser degree, a still significant percentage of the public believes the smoker is harming the health of the nonsmoker in his presence. Public suicide and voluntary spreading of diseases to innocent victims are never going to be socially acceptable or regarded as a characteristic of first-class citizenship.[138]

"Increasingly," noted the memo, "the general public and its leaders are of the opinion that smoking is a messy, indulgent, down-scale, non-family oriented, non-fashionable habit—one that is increasingly a smaller part of contemporary lifestyles and increasingly alien to contemporary lifestyles and increasingly alien to contemporary aspirations."[139] As industry executives and consultants agreed, this decline in the social acceptability of the cigarette created a hostile new territory in which to market their product.

In the first half of the twentieth century, the cigarette's success depended on the industry's ability to create acceptance for a product that had long been disparaged, disdained, and stigmatized. As cigarette smoking became phenomenally popular, it came to be governed by complex notions of mores and manners. Where and when was it appropriate to smoke? Should men and women smoke in mixed company? Changes in such practices depended on subtle but powerful shifts in the cultural norms and meanings of cigarette use.

The American tobacco industry had worked persistently through its advertising and marketing to control these meanings so as to make smoking an appropriate public activity. The industry read and exploited the rise of a consumer culture, the standardization of products, and mass production to ensure that cigarettes and modern mores went hand-in-hand. But now, with the culture shifting the other way, it was critical to the industry that social conventions *against* public smoking be overturned. In 1926, Chesterfield, then the nation's number one cigarette, ran its famous advertisement in which a woman asks a man smoking nearby to "Blow Some My Way." From the perspective of the late twentieth century, this ad is a strikingly ironic indication of the radical shift in the nature of smoking and risk. At that time, it was still considered inappropriate to show women smoking in advertisements. But the ad clearly suggested the sexual allure of smoke, its intimacy, and its fragrance. The very idea of "blow some my way," by the 1990s, was associated with antagonism, risk, and environmental taint. Despite the companies' obvious ability to defend their political interests, especially at the state and federal levels, they were losing the cultural battle. And as their own analyses pointedly demonstrated, losses in the "culture wars" of tobacco could have dire implications for the industry's ongoing regulatory, business, and legal vulnerabilities.

Many observers in the media and among tobacco interests predicted a war between smokers and nonsmokers, but it never happened. As public restrictions on smoking became more aggressive in the 1980s and early 1990s, compliance remained remarkably high despite little or no official enforcement. Whether it was McDonald's going smoke-free, federal bans on airline smoking, or antismoking policies in corporate offices, regulations were generally respected. The thousands of smoking regulations enacted during this period were only a step ahead of changing social conventions, and they did not cause conflict so much as help legitimate the new norms.[140]

Thus, in the decades following the first surgeon general's report, both the smoker and the cigarette were transformed. What was fragrant became foul; what was attractive became repulsive; a public behavior became virtually private. The identification of the health risks of passive smoke was the main force behind this radical change. American smokers became pariahs in a powerful moral tale of risk and responsibility—objects of scorn and hostility clustered around the doorways of buildings. A cultural climate inhospitable to smoking had changed the very experience. Many smokers, given the limited and hostile space in which they could still smoke, gave it up.[141] The pleasure of smoking had proved to be historically contingent.

The tobacco companies observed these changes—and the corresponding regulations—with a mixture of anxiety, outrage, and denial. The cigarette would survive the assault, but the companies would never again unilaterally shape the public perception of their product. After nearly a century, they lost control of the cigarette's image. But this cultural reconfiguration of the smoker was something of a double-edged sword. In one important sense, it played into industry hands by asserting the individual agency and moral irresponsibility of the smoker, exonerating the industry from culpability. It often had the effect of making the smoker the object of condemnation, rather than the industry that had produced the cigarette. If the smoker was pariah, or criminal, it was easy to forget that it was the smoker who was the victim, inevitably suffering the double jeopardy of inhaling both active and passive smoke.

IV

LAW

In the past, we at R&D have said that we're not in the cigarette business, we're in the smoke business. It might be more pointed to observe that the cigarette is the vehicle of smoke, smoke is the vehicle of nicotine and nicotine is the agent of a pleasurable body response. . . . We are not suggesting that the effect of nicotine is responsible for the initiation of the habit. To the contrary. The first cigarette is a noxious experience. . . . To account for the fact that the beginning smoker will tolerate the unpleasantness we must invoke a psychosocial motive. Smoking a cigarette for the beginner is a symbolic act. The smoker is telling the world, "This is the kind of person I am." Surely, that there are many variations of the theme, "I am no longer my mother's child, I'm tough, I am an adventuress, I'm not square." Whatever the individual intent, the act of smoking remains a symbolic declaration of personal identity. . . . As the force from the psychological symbolism subsides, the pharmacological effect takes over to sustain the habit, augmented by the secondary gratifications.[1]

HELMUT WAKEHAM, 1969
VICE PRESIDENT OF RESEARCH AND
DEVELOPMENT, PHILIP MORRIS

Thus a tobacco product is, in essence, a vehicle for the delivery of nicotine, designed to deliver the nicotine in a generally acceptable and attractive form. Our industry is then based upon design, manufacture and sales of attractive dosage forms of nicotine which have more overall value, tangible or intangible, to the consumer than those of our competitors.[2]

CLAUDE TEAGUE, 1972
RESEARCH SCIENTIST, R.J. REYNOLDS

CHAPTER 10

Nicotine Is the Product

I N THE SPRING OF 1983, Marc Edell was an attorney in search of a client. He had come to the conclusion that the tobacco industry, after years of virtual immunity from liability, might now be vulnerable. Having previously defended an asbestos company in health litigation, he had grown well acquainted with pulmonary pathology and the risks of smoking. It was not uncommon in asbestos litigation for defendants to assert that injuries attributed to workplace risk had actually been caused by smoking. Edell reasoned that cigarettes represented the preeminent product of high risk with little or no compensatory benefit, making the tobacco industry uniquely vulnerable to liability. A New York chest surgeon referred him to fifty-eight-year-old Rose Cipollone of Little Ferry, New Jersey, who was then undergoing treatment for lung cancer. Edell filed a complaint on her behalf against four of the major tobacco companies on August 1, 1983.[3]

Since 1954, literally hundreds of similar cases had been brought, without a single victory for plaintiffs. Typically taken on a contingency basis by the plaintiff's attorneys, who would be compensated only should they recover damages, these cases had left plaintiffs without compensation and the attorneys with nothing but thousands of dollars in unremunerated legal hours and other court costs. A principal strategy of the companies had been to undertake legal maneuvers to maximize these costs. Edell had nonetheless persuaded his law firm, Porzio, Bromberg & Newman, to back the initiative. The obstacles to a successful case were high, but so were the payoffs if he should succeed. The culture of liability litigation had come to accept such calculations.[4]

The range of liability claims brought unsuccessfully against the tobacco companies since the mid-1950s included negligence, misrepresentation, and fraud (among other torts). Perhaps the most well-known case in the early phase of litigation against the tobacco companies was *Green v. American Tobacco*. Edwin Green had begun smoking Lucky Strikes around 1925 when he was sixteen years old. In the mid-1950s he developed lung cancer, and in 1957, as the health evidence implicating cigarettes grew, he filed a suit against American Tobacco for $1.5 million. The suit was continued by Green's family after he died in 1958.[5]

In all such suits, the industry mounted a vigorous, three-part defense. First, it presented experts, such as C. C. Little of the Tobacco Industry Research Committee (TIRC), who testified that it had not been proven that cigarettes cause lung cancer.[6] Many of these experts were directly employed by the TIRC or were dependent on it for research funding.[7] According to the argument they put forward, the plaintiffs could not claim that the consequences of smoking were "foreseeable" and that the companies had a legal responsibility to warn consumers and modify their product, because the cause of lung cancer remained in scientific doubt. Second, industry lawyers argued that no *specific* case of cancer could be conclusively linked to smoking. Given the complexities of pathological evaluation, there were always experts willing to disagree with any particular diagnosis. Third, the defense contended that the "controversy" regarding smoking and health was well-known and highly publicized; as a result, plaintiffs were well-informed of any "alleged" risks. They had personally accepted any risks that cigarettes *might* possess. Advertisements and other promotions were well understood by the public to be "puffery" and thus did not constitute an implied warranty of the product.[8] Plaintiffs who proceeded in spite of these arguments soon found themselves facing an even higher hurdle: a blizzard of briefs, motions, and other time-consuming and costly legal initiatives brought by the defendants.[9]

As was typical in early tobacco litigation, the *Green* case had a complex procedural and legal history. After a number of appeals, it was remanded back to the U.S. District Court for the Southern District of Florida, where it had been originally tried. The exclusive issue confronting the jury, according to the judge's charge, was to determine if the plaintiff could prove that "the cigarettes were not reasonably fit or wholesome, as the case may be, for the use of the general public and for the use for which they were sold."[10] This would constitute "a breach of the implied warranty for fitness, which is imposed upon the manufacturer who sells cigarettes."[11] The jury ultimately returned a unanimous verdict for the defendants. Although it held that cigarettes do cause cancer, they were nonetheless "reasonably fit" for ordinary use. "Good tobacco" was not a defective product. The decision underscored the difficulties inherent in suing Big Tobacco.

§

The historical development of American tort law is predicated on the theory that it leads to greater safety of consumer goods. Since manufacturers are put at risk for the costs associated with the harms caused by faulty products, they have a strong incentive to modify them. Moreover, if they do not modify their products, companies are responsible for the excess social costs that ensue. Following World War II, this theory inspired a dramatic expansion of so-called strict liability torts. In these cases, courts do not need to evaluate whether or not a given company has acted negligently; manufacturers are simply deemed responsible for the harms generated by the product. Tort law became a tool for indirect regulatory policy; the full costs of the product would be borne by a company with appropriate incentives for safety and risk reduction.[12]

William Prosser, a law professor and attorney in Minnesota and one of the giants in the elucidation of tort theory and practice, described strict liability in 1941 as a means of "allocating a more or less inevitable loss to be charged against a complex and dangerous civilization, and [placing] liability upon the party best able to shoulder it."[13] Strict liability was "unburdened by notions of fault."[14] But while Prosser had been a prime mover for expanding strict liability, he was also the principal figure in assuring that tobacco, liquor, and pharmaceuticals did not face liability as "unreasonably dangerous" consumables. The American Law Institute's highly influential treatise on tort law, drafted by Prosser in 1965, declared:

> The article sold must be dangerous to an extent beyond that which would be contemplated by the ordinary consumer who purchases it, with the ordinary knowledge common to the community as to its characteristics. Good Whiskey is not unreasonably dangerous merely because it will make some people drunk, and is especially dangerous to alcoholics; but

bad whiskey, containing a dangerous amount of fusel oil, is unreasonably dangerous. Good tobacco is not unreasonably dangerous merely because the effects of smoking may be harmful; but tobacco containing something like marijuana may be unreasonably dangerous. Good butter is not unreasonably dangerous merely because, if such be the case, it deposits cholesterol in the arteries and leads to heart attacks; but bad butter, contaminated with poisonous fish oil, is unreasonably dangerous.[15]

It was this notion of "unreasonably dangerous" that guided the verdicts in *Green* and other early tobacco cases.[16] If the product was made as designed and as consumers expected, then one could argue that smokers "assume" the risks of their own behavior. Prosser's restatement of tort law was something of a "grandfather clause" for tobacco, exempting it from the emerging legal theories of strict liability. Since by the 1960s the harms of tobacco were deemed to be widely known and understood, the industry was found to be immune from claims that the product was "unreasonably" dangerous. The dramatic expansion of product liability in the 1960s and 1970s was ironically built on the exclusion of the single most dangerous product in the consumer culture. Plaintiffs seeking compensation for tobacco-related harms were forced to prove negligence, fraud, and other acts of industry perfidy. As a result, tobacco litigation would continue to center attention on fundamental issues of moral responsibility, personal guilt, and blame.[17]

After the first wave of litigation in the 1950s, potential plaintiffs faced even higher obstacles as the industry diligently worked to burnish the assumption-of-risk defense. The introduction of mandatory warning labels—despite their vague wording—had the effect of underscoring the notion: use at your own risk. David Hardy, a partner at Shook, Hardy & Bacon, the Kansas City law firm that fashioned the industry's principal defense strategies, explained that warning labels were among the industry's most important weapons against plaintiffs. "Once the purchaser is informed of a danger," Hardy argued, "the burden of any injuries incurred from that danger would shift to him."[18] The assumption-of-risk defense eventually preempted earlier industry claims that the harms of smoking were unforeseeable; these had been significantly eroded by many studies conducted in the 1950s and 1960s. Certainly, after the release of the surgeon general's report in 1964, it was no longer possible for the industry to seriously make this argument. It would now, ironically, use the emerging knowledge of the harms of smoking as its principal defense. If there was a risk, even though "unproven," it nonetheless must be the smoker's risk, since the smoker had been fully informed of the "controversy." The industry had secured the best of both worlds: a "warning" label that deterred few smokers but could nonetheless be invoked to defeat litigation. In a culture that emphasized individual responsibility, smokers would bear the blame for their willful risk-taking.[19]

The federally mandated warning label turned into a major triumph for tobacco defense teams. Attorney Richard Wegman compared lawsuits against the tobacco companies to a case in which a woman had (unsuccessfully) sued a candy company after she knowingly ate a worm-infested candy bar:

> The cigarette smoker of today is in much the same position, except that the facts in his situation are even more compelling. He is aware that medical evidence has clearly indicated cigarettes are the major cause of lung cancer. He is aware that even the moderate smoker substantially increases his risk of premature death. Nevertheless, he continues to smoke. The requirements for assumption of risk are all satisfied. It is difficult to imagine twelve reasonable men coming to any other conclusion.[20]

§

By the early 1980s, as product liability litigation came to be a common feature of American tort law, some legal analysts began to focus on the essential paradox that while tort law held American corporations to an increasingly high standard regarding the safety and toxicity of their products, the makers of cigarettes had never been successfully sued. Law professor Donald Garner, writing in 1980, noted that the tobacco industry had enjoyed "almost an imperial form of immunity," turning back nearly three hundred lawsuits since the mid-1950s without a single award to any plaintiff.[21] Marc Edell would later conclude that the "cigarette manufacturers in the United States have enjoyed an immunity from liability far beyond the wildest dreams of any manufacturers."[22] Tobacco companies had worked diligently to secure this immunity through aggressive legal strategies, regulatory politics, and cultural influence. Ever since persuasive scientific data implicating cigarettes as a cause of disease had begun to emerge, the threat of product liability had hung over the industry. As a result, legal counsel had come to dominate every aspect of the industry's strategic policy, from scientific research and product design to promotion, public relations, and the industry's approach to regulation.[23]

When Edell took on Cipollone's case, he was convinced that the important social and cultural shifts in public attitudes and knowledge about tobacco had created a "more receptive" legal climate to sue. In particular, he noted the accumulation of scientific and medical findings on both *causation* and *addiction*.[24] Companies could no longer claim, as they had for a generation, that the links between smoking and disease were "not proven." Straining credibility in this way was unlikely to inspire sympathy in a jury. Moreover, new scientific data demonstrating the addictiveness of nicotine undermined the notion of consumer "choice." Edell concluded as well that the tobacco industry was vulnerable under new risk-utility provisions of New Jersey state tort law, which held that risky products must provide important advantages to consumers. Cars might be dangerous, but they offered significant personal and social benefits. Given the well-documented dangers of smoking and the few, if any, benefits, he believed the product was highly vulnerable under these provisions. Rose Cipollone, he would argue, had been convinced through fundamental misrepresentations to use a highly dangerous product with minimal, if any, utility.

§

Cipollone's smoking history was typical of her generation. Born Rose De-Francesco in Queens, New York, in December 1925, at age sixteen she began smoking Chesterfields, then the third most popular brand behind Camel and Lucky Strike. Only two years earlier, DeFrancesco's father had died of a stroke that her mother attributed to his heavy smoking. But despite her mother's entreaties that smoking was not "ladylike," by the end of 1943 she was smoking a pack a day. In those days, there were many inducements for young girls taking up smoking. A typical Chesterfield ad from 1941 pictured a comely Ellen Drew, Chesterfield's Girl of the Month, waving a racing flag in her right hand and a cigarette in her left. "They Satisfy Millions," the ad declared. As we have seen, smoking was by this time highly popular and accepted among women as well as men. In 1940, some 15 to 20 percent of women smoked and 53 to 64 percent of men. By 1944, a Gallup poll reported that 48 percent of adult men and 36 percent of adult women smoked. Urban women, like Rose, were considerably more likely to smoke than rural women.[25]

In 1946, Rose DeFrancesco met Antonio Cipollone, and they were married a year later. He urged her to quit. Soon pregnant with their first child, Rose Cipollone made her first—unsuccessful—attempt to quit. Her husband apparently "begged her" to stop during the pregnancy. "I thought, oh, I'm going to be so good that I will not smoke and endanger the life of my child or myself," she explained in her deposition before the trial. Even in those years, before the studies by Doll and Hill or Graham and Wynder were published, Cipollone's worries were common. She cut down from a pack and a half a day, but continued to sneak cigarettes throughout her pregnancy.[26] Quitting or even cutting down, she discovered, was no easy matter.[27]

In 1955, as public concern grew following reports in the media linking lung cancer to cigarettes, Cipollone switched from Chesterfields to L&Ms, a new filter cigarette that Liggett & Myers was promoting as "Just What the Doctor Ordered." In her deposition, Cipollone said she made the switch because "they were talking about the filter tip and it was milder, and a miracle that would keep that stuff inside the trap, whatever."[28] L&M's "pure white Miracle Tip," the ads promised, offered "much more flavor" and "effective filtration." Over half of women smokers had switched to filters by 1958, as had 42 to 47 percent of men.[29]

In 1968, Cipollone changed brands again, this time to Philip Morris's new entry, Virginia Slims, designed exclusively for the women's market. The Virginia Slims campaign tied the brand to emerging feminist sentiment, spoofing early twentieth century strictures against women smoking. The Leo Burnett agency, which had also created the "Marlboro Man" campaign, described Virginia Slims as "the first cigarette for women only . . . designed slimmer for a woman's slimmer hands and lips . . . and packaged in a slim purse pack." Internal memoranda suggested that the new brand should be "aspirational." In establishing "brand personality" the agency sought to make "a brand that was feminine but was non-threatening. It was 'user friendly.'" Virginia Slims women were women who could make choices but had not lost their femininity. Advertisements for the brand featured fashionable young women and asserted, "You've Come a Long Way, Baby."[30] Cipollone explained that she "thought they were very glamorous . . . they were long, and it represented beautiful women." The models "really got to me."[31]

When Cipollone changed brands yet again, in 1972, it was for health reasons. Parliament, another Philip Morris product, offered a recessed filter resembling a cigarette holder. "I was starting to hear noises about smoking and tobacco and, you know, all that kind of thing that I didn't want to listen to, but I was listening to it," Cipollone said at her deposition.[32] "Most low-tar cigarettes are flush tipped," explained a Parliament advertisement. "So tar buildup is flat against your lips." Such ads were designed to appeal to smokers with concerns about the health impact of smoking. The ad announced that Parliaments were the "thoughtful choice in low-tar smoking."[33]

Cipollone made her final brand shift two years later, when she began smoking Lorillard's True cigarettes, introduced in 1966 as a "health conscious" brand. By this time, it was becoming more common for physicians to urge their patients to quit smoking or cut down. Cipollone's doctor apparently told her that if she was going to continue to smoke she should switch to True, which was highly touted—by Lorillard—as being low in tar and nicotine. She smoked this brand until 1982. "I figured they were better," she said.[34] True's advertisements focused on the growing segment of the market that was considering quitting. "I thought about all I'd read and said to myself, either to [sic] quit or smoke True," a woman in one advertisement explained. "I smoke True." Some True ads featured head-on shots of the plastic filter insert. True illustrates the subtleties of tobacco marketing in the age of scientific risk; it preserved market share by dissuading worried smokers from quitting.

Smokers of new filtered and "light" cigarettes soon found that they often smoked more to compensate for the reductions in nicotine that typically accompanied reductions in tar. Since the companies understood that addicted smokers would seek to sustain an anticipated dose of nicotine, they worked to develop cigarettes with "elasticity" of yield.

In other words, smokers like Cipollone, could select low-tar brands but achieve the same intake of nicotine by altering how the cigarette was smoked (or simply smoking more). Unfortunately, as most data came to show, low-tar and light cigarettes did not reduce the risks of smoking. But as the companies well understood, consumers believed that they had taken action to reduce their risks.[35]

The industry, in its defense, would use Cipollone's brand choices as evidence of her capability to make independent decisions. Its lawyers would repeatedly contend that she had made the deliberate and reasoned decision to continue smoking, and that she could have quit if she had so chosen. In a characteristic industry defense, they would assert that she had knowingly assumed the risks of smoking. Although she had tried to cut down after reading articles on smoking and health in the 1950s and 1960s, she had not succeeded. "Of course I didn't want to believe [that smoking caused lung cancer] because it was very hard to quit and I figured, ah, how true can it be if they strapped a monkey 24 hours to a machine. . . . I figured I'm not strapped to a machine and the government was there and there was no real proof, tobacco companies wouldn't do anything that was going to kill you."[36]

Just as Cipollone's smoking history mirrored that of so many others, so too did her medical history. During the mid-1960s she had developed a chronic "smoker's cough." By late in the decade, she experienced a series of health problems, including pleurisy, tachycardia, chest pain, and hypertension. A routine medical exam in 1981 turned up a spot on her right lung. Following a second chest X-ray, Cipollone had a partial lung resection with the biopsy indicating "atypical carcinoid of the lung." Even after this procedure, she continued to smoke, though now often in secret. Wheezing and coughing up bloody sputum, she went in for a bronchoscopy in May 1982, which revealed that the middle and lower lobes of her right lung were now affected. In anticipation of a second major surgery, Rose Cipollone finally smoked her last cigarette. The following month, the entire lung was removed. Her doctors removed a large adrenal mass a year later. When she met Edell in 1983, she was still undergoing treatment, including chemotherapy. But by June 1984, the cancer had spread and was now inoperable. Cipollone died on October 21, 1984, one of about 390,000 smokers in the United States who died of a smoking-related disease that year.[37] Her case, continued by her husband, would not go to trial for three more years.

Edell's complaint accused Liggett, Philip Morris, and Lorillard—the producers of Cipollone's five brands—of five separate torts. First, the product possessed a design defect: Edell would seek to show that the companies had researched and designed safer products but failed to put these safer designs on the market. Second, the manufacturers had failed to adequately inform consumers about the risks. Before labels were federally mandated, the companies had understood the dangers of smoking but failed to warn the public. Further, the ads and promotion had diluted the federal warnings. Third, the manufacturers had breached express warranty, especially through explicit health claims offered in their advertisements. Fourth, they had committed fraudulent misrepresentation through their efforts to neutralize the effects of the mandated warnings through promotion of their products and by failing to act on their own knowledge of the harms of smoking. Finally, through their actions to deprive the public of known medical and scientific data concerning the harms of smoking, the companies had conspired to commit fraud.[38]

In response, the companies first sought to have the entire case dismissed. They based this request on the 1966 Federal Cigarette Labeling and Advertising Act. The industry claimed that the act not only preempted the states from acting independently to regulate tobacco, it also preempted any state *litigation*. According to the industry lawyers, the warning labels on packages as of January 1, 1966, precluded any claims that the companies had concealed health risks; moreover, it could not be argued that advertising, promotion, and public relations had made the warnings less effective. According to the defense, the federal legislation excluded *all* suits after 1965; the industry was immune from litigation. "No matter how outrageous the conduct may be?" asked Judge H. Lee Sarokin, the New Jersey judge who would try the case. The defense attorney, Robert E. Northrip of Shook, Hardy & Bacon answered, "I think that is my position."[39]

After Sarokin ruled against the companies on the critical question of torts committed after 1965, his ruling was reversed by the Third Circuit Court of Appeals. The appeals court held that "the carefully drawn balance between the purposes of warning the public of the hazards of cigarette smoking and protecting the national economy would be upset by state law damages actions."[40] It remanded the case back to the district court, barring all claims regarding advertising, promotion, and public relations after January 1, 1966, when the labeling law went into effect. This radically limited the actionable claims in the case, but Edell and Cipollone decided to continue.

Sarokin, who seldom minced words, called the higher court's ruling "despicable." "It is inconceivable," he wrote, "that Congress intended to protect and insulate such intentionally misleading activities, but the Third Circuit has so declared and once again this court must follow that directive."[41] On this restricted basis, the case proceeded to trial. Sarokin allowed Edell to offer evidence that the companies had acted to undermine the label, but the "duty to warn" claim had been mooted by the appeals court. Other pretrial rulings further restricted the scope of claims against the companies. Sarokin would ultimately bar Edell from using the new risk-utility provisions of the New Jersey law.[42]

An additional pretrial ruling on "alternative design" further limited Edell's claims. He had initially presented evidence that Liggett had worked to develop a safer cigarette. This argument was important for two reasons. First, it established that the industry knew that its conventional product, even following the introduction of filters, was dangerous. Second, it showed that the industry had the capacity to produce a product with a safer design but chose not to. James Mold, a former research scientist at Liggett who had been central in the development of the experimental XA cigarette, proved to be one of the first tobacco industry whistle-blowers. In a video deposition played for the jurors, he testified that Liggett had suppressed the safer cigarette that he had worked to develop. "Whenever any problem came up in the project, the legal department would pounce . . . in an attempt to kill the project," Mold said, "and this happened time and time again." At a time when the industry was defending itself in court and in public by steadfastly denying the harms of its product, a safer cigarette threatened to destroy key defense strategies. A cigarette that used palladium, a heavy metal, to reduce carcinogens had been patented in 1977, but it was never marketed.[43]

§

Although he sharply restricted the case that Edell could present, Sarokin did offer one ruling that would give the Cipollone case a truly historical impact. Through a meticulous and relentless process of discovery, Edell had gained access to some 300,000 internal tobacco industry documents. He showed remarkable skill in this phase of the litigation. As an industry lawyer defending asbestos companies, he had learned specific techniques for making discovery requests, citing named individuals from specific departments. The magistrate overseeing the discovery process, Robert Cowan, had ruled that the companies must turn over pertinent materials in 1984, but that Edell was barred from releasing any of these materials to the public. In July 1985, Judge Sarokin ruled that plaintiff's counsel and the public had a constitutional "right to know what the tobacco companies knew and know about the risks of cigarette smoking and what it did or did not do with regard to that knowledge." Sarokin justified his ruling by arguing that future plaintiffs should not have to repeat the difficult and expensive process that Edell had initiated on behalf of his client. "The court cannot ignore the might and power of the tobacco industry and its ability to resist the individual claims asserted against it. . . . To require that each and every plaintiff go through the identical, long and expensive process would be ludicrous."[44]

The defense attorneys had claimed that the release of documents bearing "trade secrets" would harm their clients' competitive interests—one of the many tactics the industry would deploy to protect its records from public scrutiny. They appealed Sarokin's ruling to the Third Circuit, where they argued that if "taken out of context and left unexplained," the materials might lead to "embarrassment, oppression, and apparent incrimination."[45] The ruling was upheld.

The companies then appealed to the Supreme Court, which refused to hear the case, causing the first public disclosure of confidential industry documents. By permitting Sarokin's decision to stand, the Supreme Court opened a devastating crack in traditional industry defenses. The industry's defeat on this question created what eventually became a torrent of tobacco papers. Much of what we now know about the cigarette century was made possible by Sarokin's ruling on the documents in the Cipollone case, and the Supreme Court's (non)decision to let it stand. According to antitobacco activist attorney Richard Daynard, the Cipollone documents would "provide a firm foundation for future plaintiffs to build a convincing case of fraud and conspiracy against the tobacco industry." Daynard went on to note that these documents "may represent only the tip of the iceberg."[46] But they encouraged a wave of plaintiffs' lawyers to aggressively pursue discovery in future cases.[47]

The documents produced in *Cipollone* offered an unprecedented view of industry activity during the crucial period when the harms of smoking came to be determined. They showed that the industry's concerns about the carcinogenic effects of smoking dated back to at least the mid-1940s. A document recovered from 1946, written by Lorillard researcher H. B. Parmele, explained that "certain scientists and medical authorities have claimed for many years that the use of tobacco contributes to cancer development in susceptible people. Just enough evidence has been presented to justify the possibility of such a presumption."[48] Although Parmele felt it was impossible to make such claims with "absolute authority" (a reasonable position in 1946), he called for more research into the "compounds existing in cigarette smoke" and "carcinogenesis." Edell used this memorandum, presented in the testimony of his principal expert witness, physician and economist Jeffrey Harris, to argue that the companies had adequate knowledge from mid-century to apprise the public of the risks and to take action to modify their product. But the detailed timeline offered by Harris would show that instead, the industry publicly denied these risks through a sophisticated public relations program and an aggressive lobbying crusade, even while it confirmed the carcinogenic properties of tobacco smoke in its own laboratories.[49]

Harris's testimony illuminated the critical questions of what the industry knew, and when. A memo written by researchers at Arthur D. Little, contracted to do research for Liggett, explained in 1961:

1. There are biologically active materials present in cigarette tobacco. These are:
   a) cancer causing
   b) cancer promoting
   c) poisonous
   d) stimulating, pleasurable, and flavorful.[50]

Harris also cited a number of instances where Ernst Wynder's experiments using tobacco condensates to induce cancer in mice had been successfully replicated by industry scientists but never revealed. A 1955 document noted that a speaker at an industry conference, reporting on one such experiment, said he had been told by an official from a large maker of cigarette paper that "some people didn't want to be informed about what he had found." The official, Milton O. Schur of Ecusta Corporation, "mentioned one big manufacturer of cigarettes whose people . . . at a high level have said they didn't want to be told certain factual knowledge because they wanted to be in a position to say they didn't know about these things."[51] Harris said he believed the "high level" executives were from Lorillard.[52]

Harris would also claim that the companies had a "gentleman's agreement" not to conduct in-house biological research. This agreement, he testified, was mentioned in the first draft of a November 1968 appeal by Philip Morris scientists for increased funding, partly because other tobacco companies had been discovered violating the pact. A second draft, prepared by research chief Helmut Wakeham, deleted "gentleman's agreement" and substituted "previous arrangements within the tobacco industry." A third draft dropped that language too, remarking only that the request for more research money "may seem a radical departure from previous policy and practice."[53]

In a 1971 memo urging Philip Morris executives to expand their research capacity, Wakeham explained that the industry was "gradually emerging from the dark ages when it was not considered knowledgeable about the biological effect of smoke and its components. Maybe we learned from crises past that it is better to be informed about potential dangers than to be silenced by ignorance."[54] The tension between "knowing" the product and denying its harms would be a persistent conflict within the industry.

Beyond using memos, letters, and reports to demonstrate executives' awareness of the potential harms of the cigarette, Edell also sought to draw attention to the industry's reaction to the growing knowledge that cigarette smoking caused lung cancers—like the one that had led to his client's death. Among the incriminating internal documents now in Edell's hand was a 1972 assessment of industry strategy written by Frederick R. Panzer, a vice president of the Tobacco Institute. Panzer described their three-pronged "holding strategy" of:

> —creating doubt about the health charge without actually denying it
> —advocating the public's right to smoke . . .
> —encouraging objective scientific research
>
> *On the litigation front* for which the strategy was designed, it has been successful. While we have not lost a liability case, this is not because juries have rejected the anti-smoking arguments.
>
> *On the political front,* the strategy has helped make possible an orderly retreat. But it is fair to say that it has not stemmed the pressure for new legislation, despite the major concessions we have made.
>
> *On the public opinion front,* however, our situation has deteriorated and will continue to worsen. This erosion will have an adverse effect on other fronts, because here is where the beliefs, attitudes and actions of judges, juries, elected officials and government employees are formed.

Panzer's insightful memo made clear the industry's knowledge and strategy.[55]

Among the revelations in the cache of industry documents that Edell recovered were a series of memoranda and letters detailing the strategy behind the industry's scientific program of the Council for Tobacco Research. Now, for the first time, the internal documentation of the public relations emphasis of the origins and conduct of this program came to light. In particular, documents revealed that from the outset, industry legal counsel oversaw the program, assuring that research did not compromise their defense strategies. In 1966, CTR had established, under the guidance of its Committee of Counsel, a "special projects" program to undertake specific research projects and to prepare scientific witnesses for trials and congressional testimony. Special Projects offered the lawyers considerably more control to direct the research and to withhold negative findings. This program was overseen by Ed Jacob of the firm Jacob, Medinger, Finnegan & Hart. As one former R.J. Reynolds employee explained, "As soon as Mr. Jacob funded [a scientific study] it was a privileged communication and it couldn't come into court."[56]

In 1978, a group of industry attorneys and executives met in New York to review the status of the CTR. At the meeting, according to the minutes, Bill Shinn of Shook, Hardy & Bacon, offered a candid assessment of the history of the organization:

> CTR began as an organization called the Tobacco Industry Research Council [sic] (TIRC). It was set up as an industry shield in 1954. That was the year statistical accusations relating smoking to disease were leveled at the industry; litigation began; and the Wynder/Graham reports were issued. CTR has helped our legal counsel by giving advice and technical information, which was needed at court trials. CTR has supplied spokesmen for the industry at Congressional hearings.
>
> The monies spent at CTR provides a base for introduction of witnesses.
>
> Bill Shinn feels that "special projects" are the best way that monies are spent. On these projects, CTR has acted as a "front"; however, there are times when CTR has been reluctant to serve in that capacity and in rare instances they have refused to serve in that capacity.
>
> CTR began to lose their luster in the mid-60s and the tobacco industry looked around for more beneficial ways to spend their research dollars on

smoking and health. It was at this time that special projects were instituted at Washington University, Harvard University, and UCLA. Bill
Shinn noted that the industry received a major public relation "plus" when
monies were given to Harvard Medical School.[57]

As it had for decades, the industry would claim that CTR materials (and
documents like the minutes cited above) were subject to attorney-client
privilege.[58]

In addition to relying on these internal documents, Edell emphasized
the powerful advertising and promotional campaigns for the specific
brands that Cipollone had smoked in order to show the industry's strategy
to maintain smokers' denial and allegiance. Richard Pollay, a historian and
archivist who had collected and analyzed thousands of cigarette advertisements and campaigns, testified as an expert witness. Pollay showed that
health and safety had historically played an important part in tobacco advertising.[59] In Edell's argument, this constituted an express warranty implied in the hard sell of cigarettes.

§

Edell's case ultimately depended on his convincing the jury that Cipollone's
continued tobacco use was a result of her addiction to cigarettes and was,
therefore, anything *but* an informed and voluntary choice. At the trial,
Jerome H. Jaffe testified as an expert witness on addiction on behalf of
Cipollone. Jaffe, a psychiatrist who had served as "drug czar" in the Nixon
White House and was now director of the Addiction Research Center in
Baltimore, had interviewed Cipollone for more than an hour shortly before
her death. Noting that Cipollone had continued to smoke following removal of part of her right lung, Jaffe concluded that she was "heavily dependent" on nicotine. In defining drug dependence at the trial, he explained
that "physical dependence, social dependence or neuroadaptation is one element of a very complex relationship between the individual and history of
using a drug that causes the individual to lose a certain range of option as to
whether to continue to use the drug or not."[60] "Tobacco is a drug," he testified, "in the same way opium is a drug or marijuana."[61] Jaffe concluded that
Cipollone had a physical dependency and that attempts to reduce her consumption or to quit would lead to symptoms of withdrawal.[62] These could

include restlessness, anxiety, and increased appetite, all of which Cipollone experienced. "The withdrawal symptoms have a certain adversive quality," Jaffe explained. "They are things that you don't want to experience; the anger, the confusion, the depression, the irritability, the anxiety. That becomes another motive to continue to use the drug."[63] Cipollone had told Jaffe at their interview: "I didn't think about quitting because I didn't think I could bear it; I avoided all occasions that would lead me to think about stopping; I always made sure that the cigarettes were there; I would have extra food delivered just to have cigarettes delivered."[64] Cipollone confided that in the rare instances when she did run out of cigarettes, she would look in the trash for butts. Jaffe did not claim that Cipollone's tobacco dependence made it impossible for her to quit, but he did conclude that it would have made any such attempt extremely difficult.[65]

Another expert for the plaintiff, consumer psychologist Joel B. Cohen, offered a theory of cognitive dissonance to account for Cipollone's smoking. According to Cohen, Cipollone had minimized the findings linking smoking to disease to reduce the "dissonance" between her desire to continue smoking and her concerns about its impact. Cohen claimed that brand switching, especially to filters and light cigarettes, was one important mechanism by which dependent smokers dealt with their ambivalence about cigarette use.[66]

Rose Cipollone herself—now dead for over three years—was, in a sense, on trial. The outcome would turn on her behavior and how it was regarded by the jury. Edell vigorously sought to demonstrate that Cipollone was addicted and that the addictive properties of cigarettes had been well-known to the companies. The defendants emphasized that "Rose Cipollone was fully aware of the alleged risks of smoking before she began smoking and at all times thereafter." The industry insisted that smoking was purely a "personal choice," and so it had been for Cipollone.[67]

Addiction subverted this traditional industry position. And it disrupted the claim of "assumption of risk." As Edell argued, Cipollone did not knowingly "assume" the risks of addiction and cancer when she began smoking as a sixteen-year-old girl. The trial illuminated a long history of debates about addiction and nicotine. Even though the difficulty of quitting cigarettes had been widely recognized since the nineteenth century, there was considerable disagreement about whether this difficulty constituted an addiction. There were questions about the pharmacologic properties of nicotine as well as considerable medical and social uncertainty about the definition of addiction and its relationship to "habituation." The trial would reveal a deep cultural ambivalence about the meaning of "addiction."[68]

Meanwhile, the surgeon general's office, under the leadership of C. Everett Koop, was preparing a new surgeon general's report on nicotine addiction. Released to much fanfare and debate in May 1988—during the trial—the report offered three major conclusions. First, cigarettes were addicting. Second, nicotine was the drug causing addiction. And third, the pharmacologic and behavioral processes determining nicotine addiction "are similar to those that determine addiction to drugs such as heroin or cocaine." The explicit comparison to powerful, illicit drugs was a carefully considered strategy on Koop's part.[69] It generated intense media coverage of his report as well as intense controversy, stirred by the industry.

Koop's report focused on the science of addiction, as well as new findings about nicotine that had emerged since the first surgeon general's report was published in 1964. Research over the previous decades had demonstrated that tobacco use possessed the three characteristics of all addictive substances: dependence, tolerance, and withdrawal. Fundamental research into the pharmacokinetics and pharmacodynamics of nicotine demonstrated it to be clearly within the scientific rubric of addictive substances. This research, Koop explained, overturned the 1964 report's conclusion that cigarette smoking was "habituating" rather than "addicting."

The first surgeon general's report had sought to dispel concerns that nicotine led to addiction. It did, however, confirm that cigarettes could be habit-forming: "Smokers and users of tobacco in other forms usually develop some degree of dependence upon the practice, some to the point where significant emotional disturbances occur if they are deprived of its use." Still, the committee reached the comforting conclusion that the "evidence indicates this dependence to be psychogenic in origin." The committee drew a sharp distinction between "habituation" and "addiction," assuring the public that "the biological effects of tobacco, like coffee . . . are not comparable to those produced by morphine, alcohol, barbiturates, and many other potent addicting drugs." Following definitions promulgated by the World Health Organization, the 1964 report insisted that addiction was a more severe condition than habituation and indicated an underlying psychiatric disease. Addictions led to states of "periodic or chronic intoxication" and of "overpowering desire" to continue taking the drug and "to obtain it by any means." Further, addictive substances had a "detrimental effect on the individual and society." Habituation merely led to a "desire (but not a compulsion)" to continue using the drug and an absence of physical dependence. Most importantly, the detrimental impacts, "if any," fell primarily on the individual.[70]

Given the popularity of cigarette smoking at mid-century and its legitimacy in American culture, identifying smokers as having a psychiatric disorder must have seemed extreme to Terry's committee. They ultimately agreed to punt on the fundamental question of the nature of nicotine. In subsequent decades, as the meaning of smoking shifted and definitions of addiction became more rigorously systematized into disease models, nicotine would come to be incorporated into the medical and psychiatric nomenclature of addiction—a critical transformation that led, ultimately, to Surgeon General Koop's *Report on Nicotine Addiction*.[71] This shift had important implications for Cipollone in her suit.

If the goal of the 1964 report was to demonstrate categorically that smoking caused pathology, the next two decades' research established smoking as a pathology, an addiction to a powerful and dangerous drug. Increasingly, smoking was embedded in an emerging discourse of "substance abuse." Terry's distinction between habit and addiction did not survive the vigorous medical and scientific scrutiny of the cigarette.[72]

As the incentives for quitting rose sharply, many responded. Smoking rates among Americans declined steadily after 1964, from a high of over 40 percent to approximately 25 percent thirty years later. Over 40 million Americans successfully quit during these years.[73] Yet the very fact that so many Americans gave up their cigarettes suggested to some that it was less addictive than other drugs. Further, as the industry liked to point out, unlike most other addictive drugs, cigarettes did not impair judgment. This was a critical element of the companies' argument about personal responsibility. According to industry logic, Rose Cipollone, had she chosen to do so, could have joined the 40 million other Americans who had quit smoking over the previous three decades. Yet ironically, the more that smokers sought to quit, the more they came face to face with withdrawal and tobacco craving. It was the recognition of the harms of smoking that explicitly exposed its addictive properties.

§

As Marc Edell attempted to introduce the 1988 report into evidence, the industry subjected both it and Koop to withering criticism, mounting what it would call a "contradiction of common sense" defense against the claim that cigarettes were addictive. Charles O. Whitely of the Tobacco Institute said that the comparison of cigarette smoking to cocaine and heroin use "trivializes, and almost mocks, the serious narcotic and other hard drug problems faced by our country." Koop had deliberately sought to incorporate tobacco into the "drug problem." Major newspapers like the *Boston Globe* attacked what they perceived to be Koop's effort to include smoking in the drug abuse crisis of the 1980s:

> Smoking bears no resemblance to drug abuse or alcohol abuse. Smoking does not affect mental acuity, nor temporarily derange a person, nor produce so much as a lull in anyone's contact with reality.[74]

The industry also pointed to the large number of Americans who had now quit smoking as proof that nicotine was not addictive in any commonly used sense of the word. Walker Merryman of the TI commented:

> Well, I think it's very clear that, as the Surgeon General also told us, forty-three million people have quit smoking. And ninety-five percent of those who quit do so on their own. Now, if that's an addiction, then the definition of addiction has been stood on its head. There's nothing about smoking that interferes with an individual's ability to make a decision about whether or not to quit or continue, unlike truly addictive drugs, such as heroin or cocaine or other things which impair the individual's ability to make that decision.[75]

"I've not heard of anyone holding up a liquor store or mugging an old lady to get money to buy cigarettes," Merryman told the *Wall Street Journal*.[76]

Nonetheless, Judge Sarokin agreed to admit the Koop report into evidence. At the trial, Edell would go beyond simply proving the addictiveness of cigarette smoking: he would show that the tobacco companies had known the addictive properties of nicotine for decades. Despite their campaign to discredit the Koop report, the companies had been deeply involved in studying the scientific and behavioral effects of nicotine since at least the 1960s.

Edell used internal industry documents to show that the rise of medical evidence implicating cigarettes as a cause of lung cancer and other diseases had spurred the companies to conduct new research into the biochemistry of their product and its physiological effects. He also introduced memos in which tobacco lawyers who followed this research expressed concern about how the publication and discussion of such studies might make the industry vulnerable to litigation. In a 1983 legal memo produced by the law firm Shook, Hardy & Bacon evaluating research done by Philip Morris researchers Victor DeNoble and Paul Mele that demonstrated the "reinforcing properties of nicotine,"[77] the firm concluded that "their overall results are extremely unfavorable"[78] and that "research such as this strengthens the adverse case against nicotine as an addictive drug."[79]

Shook, Hardy & Bacon recommended that company scientists stop all research on the addictive properties of nicotine.

> Research engaged in, as well as some possibly under consideration, by Philip Morris, has undesirable and dangerous implications for litigation positions the industry takes in regard to smoking behavior. The pharmacological nature of the research implies strongly a view of the importance of nicotine. What is worse, research reports under Philip Morris' sponsorship contain claims of physiological tolerance to nicotine, as well as claims of unequivocal demonstrations of reinforcement by nicotine in animals. This kind of research is a major tool of our adversaries on the addiction issue; the irony is that industry-sponsored research is honing that tool. In the final analysis, the performing and publishing of nicotine research clearly seems ill-advised from a litigation point of view.[80]

During this same period, industry executives and scientists began to speculate more explicitly about ways to deliver nicotine without the risks of tar. R.J. Reynolds researcher Claude Teague made clear:

It should then be possible, using modifications of techniques developed by the pharmaceutical and other industries, to deliver that nicotine to the user in efficient, effective, attractive dosage form, accompanied by no "tar," gas phase, or other allegedly harmful substances.[81]

At the trial, Edell would introduce several internal documents that confirmed the industry's knowledge of the addictive properties of cigarettes. For example, expert witness Jeffrey Harris cited a memorandum from J. L. Charles, a Philip Morris researcher, noting that nicotine has "powerful" effects on the body and "may be the most important component of cigarette smoke." Charles had argued that "nicotine and an understanding of its properties are important to the continued well being of our cigarette business since [it] has been cited often as 'the reason for smoking'; he also noted that nicotine had effects on the "nervous system as well as influencing memory, learning, pain perception, response to stress and level of arousal."[82] A memo from Philip Morris researcher W. L. Dunn put it more boldly, describing a cigarette pack as "a storage container for a day's supply of nicotine," a cigarette as a "dispenser for a dose unit of nicotine," and "a puff of smoke" as a "vehicle of nicotine." He went on to say:

> The physiological effect [of smoking] serves as the primary incentive; all other incentives are secondary.
>   The majority of the conferees would go even further and accept the proposition that nicotine is the active constituent of cigarette smoke. Without nicotine, the argument goes, there would be no smoking.[83]

These documents and others, Edell contended, proved that Cipollone's smoking was not simply a matter of choice.

§

At trial the industry would also assert, as it had for decades, that it had yet to be demonstrated that smoking causes lung cancer. Nearly a quarter-century after the first surgeon general's report, the industry still took the position that the harms of smoking were "not proven." By the time of the trial, this claim was barely credible, and the defense lawyers downplayed it. They did, however, offer evidence that Cipollone's particular type of lung cancer was not typically associated with smoking. Sheldon Sommers, a pathologist, and longtime member of the Scientific Advisory Board of the CTR, and an experienced industry witness, testified, "It's my opinion that cigarette smoking has not been proved to be a cause of lung cancer." He added, however, that "it is a risk factor." This carefully parsed conclusion would become the industry's new "official" position in the years following the trial. At the same time, Sommers, who had examined the slides from Cipollone's right lung, concluded that her cancer, a type called atypical small cell lung cancer, was not caused by smoking.[84] In other words, even if smoking did cause some lung cancers, it did not cause Cipollone's.

The tobacco companies mounted a classic "plaintiff-conduct" defense. As one tobacco-industry lawyer explained, "people think there's something a little tawdry about deciding to smoke and then turning around and suing the tobacco companies."[85] Using this argument, even if cigarettes did cause Rose Cipollone's death, it was not the tobacco companies' responsibility. This defense was viewed within the industry as reducing the "strictness" of strict liability. A focus on the behavior of the plaintiff would direct attention away from the product and its dangers. Throughout the trial, attorneys repeatedly pointed to the evidence that Cipollone, by her own admission, understood the dangers of smoking and had knowingly and voluntarily exposed herself to the risks. The key issue, they stressed, was not the reality of these risks but whether Cipollone was duly aware of them. They contended that she was well-informed and had therefore "consented" in her *decision* to continue to smoke. The industry would consistently portray Cipollone as a smart, forceful, determined, and independent woman, capable of quitting or continuing to smoke at her own discretion.

This tactic gave the industry a powerful psychological advantage in their arguments before the jury. In American culture, the ability of individuals to take control over their behaviors and their health is the cornerstone of rational notions of personal responsibility. Edell was forced to assert that Cipollone was not in control. Not only did this view not comport with jurors' views of her—repeatedly offered by the defense—it also threatened a view of the world in which individuals can and should take action to secure their health. Blaming the tobacco companies disrupted this powerful cultural notion of individual control.

Edell sought to show that the mandated warning labels had been "drowned out" by the industry's aggressive advertising and promotion. The defense sought to rebut this argument by asserting that the "information environment" was saturated with warnings about the potential harms of smoking. Slang terms like *coffin nails* to describe cigarettes, which long predate the first surgeon general's report, showed that the public had been warned long before the congressionally mandated labels. Given such hostile terms and the wide media coverage of rising health concerns in the 1950s, the industry argued that it would have been impossible for Cipollone not to know the purported risks of using its product. Frederick C. Carstensen, a University of Connecticut economics professor who served as an expert witness for the defense, offered the opinion that "common knowledge" of the risks of smoking was widespread. He testified that the *Bergen County Record,* the local newspaper where Cipollone lived, had carried some 155 articles on the relationship of smoking and health in the five years prior to the mandated warning labels.[86]

Such testimony did not go uncontested. On cross-examination, Edell forced Carstensen to admit that the many articles he collected constituted less than 1 percent of all the stories printed in those years. Moreover, the articles that Carstensen cited as indicative of the "information environment" also contained industry denials concerning the link of cigarettes to disease. Carstensen, a political economist who had never previously researched tobacco issues, was also forced to admit that he had not investigated the impact of advertising, movies, and other instances where cigarettes were portrayed as "socially desirable" or glamorous within the "information environment." Nonetheless, the industry had effectively asserted that knowledge about the harms of tobacco was widespread for decades.

The next industry expert, Claude Martin of the University of Michigan School of Business, offered testimony supporting the industry claim that advertising's principal rationale was to encourage smokers to switch brands. According to Martin, advertising had little impact on decisions to take up smoking. Sarokin interceded, asking Martin, "If a cigarette manufacturer put out an ad showing an attractive young woman in a tennis outfit in a nice setting, or put an ad showing a funeral for that woman and said, smoking kills, you mean that second ad would not have an impact on the information environment?" Defense lawyers objected, calling the judge's interrogation "prejudicial."[87]

The star witness for the defense proved to be Joseph Cullman III, CEO of Philip Morris, who was actually called to testify by Edell. Even though Liggett & Myers was the company principally at risk (especially as trial claims came to center on the period before 1966, when Cipollone smoked Chesterfields and L&Ms), the defense team relied on the gregarious, energetic Cullman to rebut the allegations of industry malfeasance. Ironically, it was rising concern about the health impacts of smoking that had helped to turn Cullman's small boutique company, Benson and Hedges, into a target for acquisition by Philip Morris in the early 1950s. Benson and Hedges's principal brand, Parliament, had been introduced with a cotton filter in 1931. In the face of rising public anxieties about the health risks of smoking, Philip Morris bought Parliaments, the company's filter expertise, and the redoubtable Cullman. By the time of the Cipollone trial, he was widely credited with moving Philip Morris from a marginal spot in the constellation of major tobacco companies to the center of the tobacco universe. He had played a central role in the reconstruction of the Marlboro brand and had initiated major programs for international marketing and diversification of the company.[88]

Cullman proved to be a sophisticated and canny witness, insisting under sharp cross-examination from Marc Edell that the industry was sincere in its commitment to resolve the smoking and health issue. At the same time, however, he confirmed the industry's position that the link between smoking and lung cancer had never been proven. He brought to the witness stand years of experience in responding to such questions. On *Face the Nation* in 1971, Cullman told a national television audience, "I do not believe that cigarettes are hazardous to one's health." When asked by a reporter about studies linking smoking to low birth-weight babies, he notoriously answered, "Some women would prefer smaller babies." Cullman's public views had not changed much since 1971. At the Cipollone trial, he said, "There is still only a statistical association. It has never been proven. Very deep thinking medical men, I think, would concur in that."[89] It fell to Cullman to attempt to explain or rebut the incriminating documents that Edell had introduced into evidence. Confronted by documents showing knowledge of carcinogens and the results of addiction research within Philip

Morris, Cullman simply replied that he was "not aware" of the particular correspondence. These documents could not be made to disappear, but such a defense could perhaps undercut their generalizability.

§

At the end of Edell's presentation of his case, the industry again moved to have the case dismissed. This was denied. In a ruling that reflected his outrage and candor, Judge Sarokin offered a stinging rebuke to the companies. "A jury might reasonably conclude," he wrote,

> that defendants in particular, and the industry in general, intentionally and willfully ignored the known health consequences to consumers from the sale of their products; that their so-called investigation into the risks was not to find the truth and inform their consumers but merely an effort to determine if they could refute the adverse reports and maintain their sales. . . . [T]he evidence presented also permits the jury to find a tobacco industry conspiracy, vast in its scope, devious in its purpose and devastating in its results.[90]

Industry lawyers claimed that Sarokin's judgment (which did not go to the jury) was excessive and sought his removal. Nonetheless, he did dismiss the failure-to-warn claims against Philip Morris and Lorillard since Cipollone had not smoked these brands until after 1966, when the federally mandated warnings appeared on packages. He also dismissed the plaintiff's claim that the companies could have produced a safer cigarette, noting that Edell would have had to establish that Cipollone would have used such a product if it had been marketed, which could only be speculated.

§

Donald Cohn, representing Liggett & Myers, emphasized in his closing argument that Cipollone had smoked for pleasure, fully aware of the hazards. An "intelligent, strong-minded woman," she did not want anyone—including her husband—telling her to quit, according to Cohn, and "was in control of her life." Attacking plaintiff's claims of nicotine addiction, Cohn asserted "It's a free country. No one forces you to smoke." He argued that Liggett & Myers had no legal responsibility to warn smokers in the period before mandatory labeling since it was "well-known" that smoking carried risks. "We didn't conceal anything," he concluded. "We didn't misrepresent anything."[91]

The industry lawyers effectively tried to have it both ways. While denying that smoking was harmful, they nonetheless argued that, knowing of its harms, Cipollone should have quit. As attorney Peter Bleakley posited:

> If you accept that it is relevant that there is a statistical association between cigarette smoking and cancer, then you have to accept the evidence on the record of this case that Mrs. Cipollone could have reduced that risk, probably to the level of a nonsmoker, after fifteen years, but in any event very, very substantially by quitting.

Bleakley then reiterated a notion that Cohn and Northrip had already raised, telling the jury, "You are not the conscience of the community in this lawsuit. You are the judges of the facts in this lawsuit, and you apply the facts to the law that will be given to you by the Court, and your job is to decide whether Mr. Cipollone gets money. That is what this case is all about."[92]

There was a weekend between the defense's closing and his own, and Edell made good use of it. In a strong closing, he blasted the motives of tobacco manufacturers. "What you have seen in this case is an evil-minded conspiracy intended for one purpose and one purpose alone—profits on their part, deceit of the public on the other." He also tried to unravel the defense strategies. "If everybody knew all the way back here, in the 1930s, 1940s, if everybody knew [about the hazards of smoking], why weren't they doing research if everybody knew? On one hand they said there is not enough research. Not enough scientific research to warrant doing research, but, on the other hand, they say everybody knew. Do you want to know the truth of the matter? That is nothing more than a fabricated legal defense."[93]

The defense, Edell said, had deflected attention from the big picture and focused it on Cipollone. "They put Rose Cipollone on trial," he said. "She did something wrong. They argued to you freedom of choice. . . . If you don't know what your options are or risks are, it is not free and informed choice." He then turned the issue of choice on its head, arguing:

Well, the defendants had a choice, too. Theirs was an informed choice because they knew what the facts were, and they chose a carefully orchestrated strategy designed by public relations counsel, designed by lawyers. . . . It boggles the mind.

Edell's conclusion accused the companies of "outrageous misconduct." He argued that the companies had acted callously in the "sacrifice of the lives of their loyal customers for dollars. . . . [A]s the first jury ever to see the internal workings of this industry, [you] can say, 'That is it. We have had enough . . . this is not acceptable behavior.'" [94]

§

The case had been heard by eleven jurors, six of whom—three men and three women—were chosen by lottery to render the verdict. Each juror was presented with a seventy-two page charge written by Judge Sarokin, and twenty specific interrogatories. After six days of deliberations, the jurors returned to the courtroom. [95] In the end, they seemed unsympathetic to both sides. Despite having heard the most compelling evidence to date about the industry's activities, they held Cipollone to a high standard of personal responsibility. Edell's strategy for rebutting the traditional assumption-of-risk defense by depicting Cipollone as addicted to tobacco had not worked. The jury's decision reflected the deep social ambivalence about smokers and cigarettes in the late 1980s.

The jury did award $400,000 in damages to Antonio Cipollone—the first judgment against the tobacco companies after more than three hundred suits. But they sent mixed signals. Despite awarding damages to her husband, they also found that Rose Cipollone was principally responsible for her death from lung cancer and that the companies were not guilty of fraud and conspiracy to misrepresent the risks of smoking. Because the jury determined that Rose Cipollone was 80 percent at fault (based on their assessment of "personal choice"), recovery on the duty-to-warn claims was barred under New Jersey law. The award of $400,000 in damages stemmed from the jury's finding that Liggett should have warned consumers before 1966 and therefore had contributed to Cipollone's smoking, lung cancer, and death. Philip Morris and Lorillard were exonerated on the only remaining claims against them, conspiracy and fraud.

Both sides sought to hide their dismay and declare victory. Edell had been disappointed in the size of the judgment and especially the failure of the jury to find for Rose Cipollone on the issue of express warranty. He said the $400,000 was "fair and just for Tony." "But I was shocked," he added, "that they didn't give an award to Rose on the express warranty."[96] On the industry side, Cohn called it "basically a clear victory for the defendants," saying it sent a message "loud and clear that Americans have freedom of choice and are responsible for their actions." A lawyer for Lorillard and Philip Morris, Charles R. Wall, said, "We're disappointed with the damage award. But we're very happy to win on the two major issues of conspiracy and fraudulent misrepresentation. And I hardly think an award of $400,000 is going to cause any rush to the courthouses with new lawsuits."[97] Edell responded that "the only industry that could lose a $400,000 verdict and claim victory is the same industry that told you that it still hasn't been proven that cigarette smoking causes lung cancer."[98]

§

The verdict powerfully demonstrated the severe difficulties in bringing suit against tobacco companies. Edell had mounted the most compelling liability case in the history of tobacco litigation. He had gained unprecedented access to internal industry files and incriminating evidence of the companies' knowledge of the harmful and addictive nature of their product. But by the late 1980s, this may have seemed like old news to jurors, who ultimately held that Cipollone should have known better. Moreover, as the social acceptability of smoking declined, it had become more difficult to make a smoker into a sympathetic plaintiff. With Cipollone gone, the defendants had free reign to characterize her however they saw fit.

It may well have been Edell's insistence on Cipollone's addiction that ultimately alienated the jury. Portraying her as diminished or incompetent—as the addiction claim required—did not make her a more sympathetic litigant. And given that so many Americans had managed to stop smoking, claims of addiction were somehow less credible. The industry aggressively hammered home this point, reminding jurors of the multitudes of former smokers. There was simply no cultural reservoir of sympathy for an "addict."

Both sides, unhappy with the jury's findings, pursued the case on appeal. In 1990, the Third Circuit Court of Appeals threw out the verdict.[99] It set aside the $400,000 finding on the grounds that Sarokin's ruling that the plaintiffs did not need to demonstrate that Cipollone had specifically relied on the ads in question was in error. According to the appeals court, Liggett should have been able to question whether Cipollone had seen these ads and believed what they said. Once again, the industry could loudly repeat its claim—explicitly meant to discourage new plaintiffs and their lawyers— that it had never paid out a cent in liability actions. "We're very happy," exclaimed Cohn. "Now we're back where we should have been."[100]

But as one door closed, another opened. Several other aspects of the appeals court ruling actually cleared the way for future litigations. According to the court, plaintiffs could sue the companies on design claims regarding risk-utility, a claim Sarokin had dismissed. It would, the court asserted, be possible for a plaintiff to claim, for example, that prior to 1966 (when such claims were preempted by the labeling law) that a person was not aware of the harms of smoking. If a jury were to find that it was reasonable for a person to be unaware of the hazards, a company could be held liable for producing a product whose harms outweighed its benefits. This part of the decision led to new assertions of victory on the part of Edell and other plaintiffs' lawyers bringing tobacco suits. Edell explained, "I definitely lost the verdict, but I got a lot. I got back something that I really wanted to try."[101] The Third Circuit had concluded that Cipollone had "live claims" against the companies on the risk-utility question. But five days after this ruling, Antonio Cipollone died. His son eventually decided to continue the case.

Shortly after the Third Circuit decision, the New Jersey Supreme Court issued a ruling in another tobacco case brought by Edell, *Dewey v. Brown & Williamson*, that the mandatory labels on cigarette packages did not preempt liability claims from smokers and their families. In a decision that flew in the face of other state and federal rulings, the New Jersey court permitted Claire Dewey's action against the companies for responsibility in the death of her husband, who died at age forty-nine of lung cancer, to proceed. Even more significantly, the ruling served as a major push toward putting the question of preemption before the U.S. Supreme Court.

The federal and state courts were in obvious contradiction. Edell decided, on the basis of this conflict, to ask the Supreme Court to review, once and for all, the issue of preemption and tobacco litigation. The industry, eager to have the preemption doctrine enshrined, urged the high court to take the case as well.[102] A definitive positive ruling on preemption would give the industry critical immunity to fight off new cases. In March 1991, the Court agreed to hear the case, and in October, it was argued before the eight sitting justices (at the time, Clarence Thomas awaited confirmation). In early 1992, the Court asked to have the case reargued before the full Court. This request was widely viewed as an indication that the Court was split, perhaps four to four.[103] In this instance, noted constitutional scholar Laurence Tribe replaced Edell, who had argued the case the first time around. On the eve of the second round, the *New York Times* explained:

> The Cigarette Labeling and Advertising Act requires uniform national package warnings and provides that "no requirement or prohibition based on smoking or health shall be imposed: on manufacturers that properly label their packages." It says nothing about lawsuits. To read civil lawsuits into the law would require judicial rewriting by justices touted by Presidents Reagan and Bush as dedicated to "interpreting law, not making it."
>
> Normally the Court demands the clearest expression of intent to preempt state laws, of a Federal regulatory scheme so pervasive as to occupy the entire legal field. Tobacco makers never asked Congress for such clarity, yet they ask the Court to discover it now. In the name of federalism and judicial restraint, they should not be handed in court something they failed to win in the legislature.[104]

§

Just as the *Cipollone* verdict offered complex mixed messages about tobacco torts, so too would the Supreme Court. Its decision held that the federal legislation, in particular the Public Health Cigarette Smoking Act of 1969 (Cigarette Act), did preempt certain failure-to-warn claims against the industry. This meant—among other things—that all claims about the industry's responsibility to appropriately apprise smokers of the risk of smoking must focus on the period prior to 1969. With the aging of the population, this ruling radically restricted the pool of potential litigants. But even more importantly, it removed a central claim of most prospective plaintiffs, namely that the labels did not adequately represent what the tobacco industry knew about smoking.

At the same time, however, the Court found that other common-law claims asserted in the *Cipollone* case—conspiracy and fraud—had not been barred by the legislation and could be retried. Smokers had the right to recover damages if they could prove that the industry conspired to hide evidence of the harms of smoking, misrepresented these dangers to the public, and breached express warranties in ads and other statements.

The *Cipollone* decision confirmed the industry's prescience in 1964 when it reversed field to seek a warning label that would preempt state regulations. The majority opinion, written by Justice John Paul Stevens, defined more specifically what fell under the preemption scope of the federal legislation:

> The 1965 Act did not pre-empt state-law damages actions; the 1969 Act pre-empts petitioner's claims based on a failure to warn and the neutralization of federally mandated warnings to the extent that those claims rely on omissions or inclusions in respondents' advertising or promotions; the 1969 Act does not pre-empt petitioner's claims based on express warranty, intentional fraud and misrepresentation, or conspiracy.

In examining the legislative history of the 1969 Cigarette Act, the Court interpreted the phrase *imposed under state law* to expand the original 1965 legislation to now include common-law rules (that is, tort litigation), arguing that the "broader language" of the 1969 version extended that section's "preemptive reach." In the congressional debate on the bill in 1969, there had been no discussion of tort liability whatsoever.[105]

Although they voted with the majority, Justices Blackmun, Kennedy, and Souter signed a separate opinion, which argued that no damage claims were preempted by the act. The language of the 1969 Act, they said, did not make explicit Congress's intent to preempt state common-law damage actions. They disagreed, therefore, with the other four in the majority—Justices Stevens, Rehnquist, White, and O'Connor—who argued that failure-to-warn and fraudulent misrepresentation claims were preempted by the act.

A dissenting opinion, written by Justice Scalia and signed by Justice Thomas, argued that all claims should be preempted. This was surprising given that Scalia and Thomas were widely recognized for protecting the prerogatives of the states against encroachment by the federal government. Nonetheless, they read into the federal cigarette statute a preemption of tort liability claims that was nowhere in the text. By so boldly asserting federal preemption, Scalia and Thomas revealed a certain judicial activism.

As they had done throughout, both sides in the suit again claimed victory. Legal commentators pointed to the complex tensions, if not contradictions, at the basis of the unusual plurality decision. "*Cipollone* professed to give force to the heavy presumption against displacing state law in the face of congressional silence," explained a commentator in the *Harvard Law Review:*

> However, the *Cipollone* Court weakened this presumption, first by finding express preemption of inadequate labeling claims despite the failure of the 1969 Cigarette Act's preemption provision to mention common-law actions, and, second, by not limiting the ability of courts to consider implied preemption in the absence of expressly preemptive language.[106]

"When you look at the entire decision, it's good for us," explained Steven Parrish, vice president and general counsel of Philip Morris. Laurence Tribe responded, "If this is a victory for the smoking industry, I wonder what kind of nuclear meltdown it would take to make them admit defeat."[107]

The Court did leave the door ajar for suits against tobacco companies by not ruling out plaintiffs' claims of fraud and misrepresentation by the industry. Still, the legal basis for bringing individual claims against the industry had become more constricted. Moreover, the *Cipollone* litigation, which had cost Edell and his firm several million dollars to pursue—as the industry had intended—stood as a powerful disincentive to any lawyers considering a future suit. If Edell had not succeeded with a suit that looked so promising, the likelihood of a big victory, and consequent award, now appeared to have poorer odds than a roulette wheel. In the years immediately after the Third Circuit vacated the award to Cipollone, the filing of new litigation slowed to a trickle.[108]

At first, Edell was all for retrying the case on the basis of the Supreme Court's rulings. But any support within his firm for pursuing tobacco litigation had now all but disappeared. He soon withdrew, and the family—after more than nine years of litigation—decided to end the case. Edell then dropped his other pending tobacco cases. In each instance it was difficult, if not impossible, to find law firms that would step into such costly and risky litigation.[109]

Edell and his current firm, Budd Larner, Gross, Rosenbaum, Greenberg & Sade, had made unprecedented commitments in both time and money to suing the tobacco companies and had come up empty-handed after a cash outlay widely estimated to be near $10 million. Edell had spent more than 3,000 hours a year during the *Cipollone* trial; more than one hundred motions had been briefed. For him and his partners, taking on tobacco plaintiffs had proven to be a "bad business decision." One former partner at Budd Larner complained, "There was a direct relationship between what I had in my checkbook and Marc Edell."[110]

The industry pursued what Richard Daynard, a leading proponent and strategist of antitobacco litigation, called a "king of the mountain" strategy.[111] Industry lawyers used a wide range of procedural tactics designed to discourage the plaintiffs' bar. R.J. Reynolds attorney J. Michael Jordan explained:

> The aggressive posture we have taken regarding depositions and discovery in general continues to make these cases extremely burdensome and expensive for plaintiffs' lawyers . . . to paraphrase General Patton, the way we won all of these cases was not by spending all of [R.J. Reynolds's] money, but by making the other son of a bitch spend all his.[112]

Edell's brilliant challenge to the industry had taken nearly a decade of tenacious work and brought no reward. "Marc was sort of like Moses taking his people across the Red Sea, but not being able to go to the promised land," offered Daynard. "Other people will have to finish the job."[113]

§

The *Cipollone* case marked a critical transition in both the legal and social history of the cigarette in American life. For the first time, the courts—even including the Supreme Court—had emerged as a critical battle site in the tobacco wars. The industry had long feared the emergence of such aggressively contested litigation. Much of its strategy since the 1950s had centered on reducing the risks of unpredictable and financially devastating tort claims. In the courts, antitobacco advocates certainly had not found a level playing field; nonetheless they had found a field. The courts opened up a new and important venue for tobacco regulation and public health initiatives.

Tobacco litigation became a lightning rod for a larger public debate about the role of tort litigation in American society. For critics of the liability revolution, suits against the tobacco companies epitomized the excesses of tort claims, if not the ultimate perversion of the courts. According to such arguments—encouraged by the industry—tobacco litigation was an abuse of the legal system in several ways. First, it was a veiled attempt to secure through the courts regulatory legislation that Congress had never enacted. This marked a constitutionally inappropriate breach in the separation of powers. Second, the litigation created a radical expansion of torts that threatened to flood all industries with costly and spurious claims from consumers. Finally, tobacco liability was seen as a cultural failure: the refusal of individuals to take responsibility for their own willful actions. It was the height of moral hypocrisy, according to this view, for Rose Cipollone, and others like her, to try to hold the tobacco industry responsible for her illness and death after she had been repeatedly warned by both her husband and the surgeon general that smoking could kill her. Case closed.

These arguments did not go uncontested. Advocates for tobacco litigation believed they had at last found a forum to confront the deceptions and frauds perpetrated by the tobacco industry since the development of medical knowledge demonstrating the harms of smoking. Tobacco regulation had crashed and burned in Congress, where the tobacco lobby had proven itself so powerful and effective, but public health would finally have its day in court. Through the litigation process—and especially the discovery of internal industry documents—the companies' strategy of denial of the science and aggressive promotion of their product would finally be revealed. Judges and juries would then force the industry to pay its victims their due. If the legislatures were "captured," the judiciary would now charge tobacco's massive costs in health and well-being back to those who were truly responsible.

Liability would be the spur to corporate responsibility in a consumer age. Torts, these advocates asserted, were Big Tobacco's Achilles' heel. Liability cases had been the expressed nightmare of the companies since 1954, when the first case was filed. Now, after four decades, the companies would confront this nightmare in the light of day.

For Edell, the goals had been compensation for Rose Cipollone and her family for the wrongs committed by the industry and, not trivially, compensation for himself and his firm. He had taken huge risks and failed. But from the perspective of public health, there were critical victories that made the case a turning point in the history of tobacco litigation. Perhaps the most significant of these was the discovery of incriminating industry documents. Eager lawyers and antitobacco advocates were sure there were more where those came from.

Others were skeptical about what such suits would accomplish. Would a big settlement for the Cipollone family, had it occurred, have helped control smoking? Would it have led to a decline in tobacco-induced illness? These were important questions, but they overlooked the potential of liability to assign responsibility and contribute to new public health strategies. Even as Edell failed in *Cipollone*, he had demonstrated to antitobacco activists that the courts now offered a new venue of possibility in the ongoing tobacco wars. Following *Cipollone*, litigation would be the heavy cloud over the future of the industry.

§3

The battles in the courtroom illuminated deep faults in the American cultural geology. On one side of the culture wars, such cases were viewed as the ultimate abdication of personal responsibility. Individuals who had suffered because of their own willful self-indulgence now sought sympathy and compensation (often in the millions if not billions) from corporate America. Such suits were seen as marking the corrosion and the corruption of basic moral assumptions about risk, blame, and responsibility. The litigation represented the refusal of individuals to take responsibility for their folly and the perverse use of the system of justice.

Proponents of tobacco litigation, on the other hand, saw such cases as an opportunity to bring a greedy, unregulated industry to the bar of justice. For these people, the tobacco industry marked the worst excesses of American corporate capital. It was a business where profits had trumped all sense of citizenship or responsibility for the dire effects of their product. In this view, the courts offered the last recourse to victims of the frauds and deceptions perpetrated by a morally bankrupt industry.

In this deeply contested debate over the meaning and nature of agency, responsibility, and addiction, cigarettes hold a special place. They are a legal product, powerfully identified with the rise of the consumer culture, yet a remarkably dangerous one. When such products cause harm, how do we adjudicate responsibility? When the product turns out to have addictive properties, how does this change our perception of responsibility? Addiction has historically served the complex and even contradictory functions of relieving some individuals of responsibility for their actions and generating moral outrage. While many Americans have become convinced of the addictiveness of cigarettes—and increasingly understand the role of the companies in creating these addictions—there remains a strong disposition to continue to hold smokers accountable for their actions. While we insist medically and scientifically that addictions are diseases meriting support and treatment, we also insist that individuals must take responsibility for their plight if they are to be treated.

At stake in such debates about addiction are deep cultural norms and values about the nature of agency and the dynamics of social and personal control. On the one hand, we seem increasingly aware of the powerful corporate forces in modern societies that subtly and not so subtly shape opinion, behavior, and action, often in ways that do not conform to individual interests and health. Nonetheless, the need to believe that we can and must assert individual will over these forces is a characteristic element of contemporary American culture. Embedded in this tension lies both our hostility to the cigarette and those who produce it, and our ongoing skepticism and antagonism toward those who smoke.

We have looked at the data and the data that we have been able to see has all been statistical data that has not convinced me that smoking causes death.[1]

ANDREW TISCH, 1994
CEO, LORILLARD

Cigarette smoking is no more addictive than coffee, tea, or Twinkies.[2]

JAMES W. JOHNSTON, 1994
CEO, R.J. REYNOLDS

For decades, the tobacco companies have been exempt from the standards of responsibility and accountability that we apply to all other American corporations. Companies that sell aspirin, cars, and soda are all held to strict standards when they cause harm. We don't allow companies to sell goods that recklessly endanger consumers. We don't allow them to suppress evidence of dangers when harm occurs. We don't allow them to ignore science and good sense. And we demand that when problems occur, corporations and their senior executives be accountable to Congress and the public.[3]

CONGRESSMAN HENRY WAXMAN, 1994

Whatever the challenges, the industry cannot be left to peacefully reap billions of dollars in profits, totally unrepentant, and without thought to the pain caused in the process. For that remains its intent.[4]

DAVID KESSLER, 2001
FORMER FDA COMMISSIONER

CHAPTER 11

Mr. Butts Goes to Washington

THE TOBACCO INDUSTRY had dodged a bullet. In decades of litigation against the companies brought by individuals claiming fraud and deception, there had never been a case as long and powerfully argued as *Cipollone*. Yet in the face of this attack, the industry had largely sustained the argument for the individual smoker's assumption of risk. Edell had argued not only that cigarettes were addictive but that the companies knew about the effects of nicotine from their own research. Nonetheless, the jury deemed Rose Cipollone—addicted though she might be—principally responsible for her own death. The experts might split hairs over definitions of habit, habituation, addiction, and dependence, but it had been widely known for over a century that cigarettes were hard to quit. Yet as the industry kept repeating, millions had done so.

It was another thing entirely, however, to assert that the companies had deliberately taken steps to maintain the addictive nature of their product. This was precisely the claim that would be made beginning in 1994. A potent combination of investigations by journalists, Congress, and the Food and Drug Administration—as well as continued litigation—would be fueled by unprecedented whistle-blower revelations from within the industry. For the first time, scientists from within the secure laboratories of Big Tobacco would emerge to reveal the industry's sophisticated knowledge about the pharmacologic properties of cigarettes. To these accounts would be added a mountain of incriminating internal documents: memos, letters, and reports that the industry had scrupulously guarded from disclosure.

Already under severe stress, the companies would soon discover that the terrain of the tobacco wars had undergone a seismic shift. The public was about to get a look inside the complex machinery of cigarette research and development, as well as the public relations and political strategies that had guided the industry since the fateful days of late 1953. The firewall surrounding the tobacco industry's intricate scientific, legal, and trade secrets was about to come down. It was one of the great ironies that this industry, so protective of its prerogatives and so aggressive in defense of its secrets, would be so publicly exposed that we now know more about the history of the tobacco industry than any other business in the history of business. Indeed, this book would not have been possible without access to this archive.

§

In 1991, Walt Bogdanich, a Pulitzer Prize-winning reporter at the *Wall Street Journal,* was hired by ABC News to work for a broadcast newsmagazine then under development, to be known as *Day One.* Bogdanich, who had won his Pulitzer for a series of articles exposing unregulated medical laboratories, was in search of stories. Sidney Wolfe, the activist physician directing Ralph Nader's Public Citizen Health Research Group, referred him to Clifford Douglas, a longtime tobacco-control advocate and attorney who was then working for the American Cancer Society. After consulting with Douglas, Bogdanich decided to do a series of three eighteen-minute segments on nicotine. The first piece, "Secret Sickness," which aired in late 1993, was about "green tobacco sickness" a form of severe nicotine poisoning suffered by tobacco pickers after extended contact with the leaves. In producing this report, Bogdanich became increasingly knowledgeable about the chemistry and toxicology of nicotine.[5]

Douglas had been confidentially contacted by an informant from R.J. Reynolds, who soon came to be called "Deep Cough"—in a reference to Watergate informant "Deep Throat"—by Bogdanich's team at ABC. She agreed, somewhat reluctantly, to tell Bogdanich about the production process at R.J. Reynolds, becoming one of the first industry whistle-blowers to go public. Anchor Forrest Sawyer led off the segment, which aired on February 28, 1994, by explaining that "for nearly a year *Day One* has been investigating nicotine—the ingredient in cigarettes that keeps smokers addicted—and we've discovered that cigarette manufacturers had been carefully controlling levels of nicotine in cigarettes."[6] John Martin, the on-camera reporter of the piece, told viewers that *Day One* had "uncovered perhaps the tobacco industry's last best secret—how it artificially adds nicotine to cigarettes, to keep people smoking and boost profits." According to Martin, "The methods the cigarette companies use to precisely control the levels of nicotine is something that has never before been disclosed to consumers or the government."[7] He went on to quote from a Philip Morris document that had become available through the discovery process in *Cipollone:*

> Think of the cigarette pack as a storage container for a day's supply of nicotine.
> Think of the cigarette as a dispenser for a dose unit of nicotine.
> Think of a puff of smoke as the vehicle of nicotine.[8]

Deep Cough had described a process that had become standard throughout the tobacco industry. Part of cigarette production required separating the tobacco leaves from the stems. Once simply discarded, beginning in the 1940s and 1950s these stems and other scraps were recovered and used.[9] Through a process known as pulping, their soluble elements could be removed and then pressed into sheets to make thin rolls of "reconstituted leaf," which was then ground up and used in cigarettes along with natural tobacco leaf.[10] But this was not the only by-product. As the pulp was made into sheets, the rollers squeezed out a liquid, often called "tobacco liquor," that was rich in sugars and nicotine. Extract from this liquid was added back—often sprayed on—to the reconstituted leaf. According to Deep Cough, who appeared in silhouette with her voice disguised, tobacco liquor was purchased from the "flavor houses" that produced the complex recipes for adding taste to tobaccos. The *Day One* report showed a clip of tankers unloading barrels, purportedly of nicotine to be added to reconstituted leaf.

Following the recognition that tars were carcinogenic, the companies had made significant efforts to reduce their volume in cigarettes, typically by adding filters. Reduced tar, available in so-called "light" cigarettes, quickly became a critical aspect of cigarette promotion. But less tar also meant less nicotine. Within the industry, it was widely understood that nicotine was essential to the product, the key ingredient motivating "dependence." As Philip Morris nicotine expert William Dunn noted in 1972, "No one has ever become a smoker by smoking cigarettes without nicotine."[11] Thus, it became critical to the companies to produce a "light" cigarette with enough nicotine to sustain addiction. Otherwise demand for cigarettes would ultimately decline.

Bogdanich and his ABC colleagues now claimed that they had discovered the industry's "secret" of adding back nicotine into cigarettes. Bogdanich had a good ear for the explosive sound bite. His report showed Jack Henningfield, a leading addiction expert at the National Institute on Drug Abuse, calling cigarettes "the crack cocaine form of nicotine delivery." Cliff Douglas, who had helped coax a nervous Deep Cough to go on camera, added, "The public doesn't know the industry manipulates nicotine, takes it out, puts it back in, uses it as if it were sugar being put in candy." Confronted onscreen with the ABC findings, Democratic Congressman Mike Synar, a strong critic of the industry, said, "it disgusts me."

In the broadcast, Joseph deBethizy, a scientist at R.J. Reynolds, denied that nicotine was added to cigarettes. But when Bogdanich forced him to concede that it was technically possible to produce a nicotine-free product, deBethizy countered, "I think the real issue is that we, as a company, are providing a legal product to people who are looking for a pleasing sensory experience with mild pharmacology." Bogdanich saw this statement as the major admission of the piece. The industry had now acknowledged something it had always publicly denied: the addictive nature of the product, as well as its *intent* to manipulate these addictive qualities.

The February 28 report was followed a week later by another segment that focused on cigarette additives, which included thirteen substances banned in food. The list of some 700 ingredients, the report explained, was supplied to the government but kept as "trade secrets" unavailable to press and public. According to the report, it was uncertain if even the President of the United States could obtain this information.

The *Day One* reports—especially the Deep Cough segment—were blockbusters—a fact not lost on the industry, the FDA, and Congress. ABC soon received two coveted journalism awards for the broadcasts: the George Polk award, given by Long Island University, and a DuPont/Columbia University award. The broadcasts had demonstrated that the industry clearly understood the critical importance of nicotine in maintaining consumption and employed sophisticated technologies to monitor and control the tar and nicotine content of its product. At the same time, however, the report was vague about precisely how much nicotine was "added back" or where it came from. These uncertainties opened the door for industry attacks on the piece. They would insist that *Day One* had erred; no additional nicotine was added to their cigarettes. In any event, the old days of Hill & Knowlton glad-handing with the press to secure "balanced" reporting were now long over. The tobacco wars were about to intensify yet again.

Although the broadcast itself never used the term, the promotional trailer that ABC aired claimed that the tobacco industry was "spiking" cigarettes with nicotine. This would become the focal point of a massive legal battle between the industry and the network. Ultimately, ABC's choice of the word *spike* would be used by the industry in its efforts to discredit a critically important piece of investigative journalism. The day following the broadcast—day two—Philip Morris announced its intention to file a libel suit. The decision reflected the perception within the industry of the damage the report could cause if not rebutted. The industry's long-standing perception of being under siege began to take on some aspects of reality.

The *Day One* allegations caught the interest of the FDA and Congress. The broadcast itself specifically raised the question of federal regulation, and Bogdanich and his colleagues were well aware that David Kessler, the commissioner of the FDA, had already begun a major investigation aimed at regulating nicotine in cigarettes. Near the conclusion of the segment, former Surgeon General Everett Koop noted, "I would think that if I were the administrator of FDA and I learned that nicotine was being added to cigarettes to increase the amount of nicotine present that I would view that cigarette as a delivery device for the use of nicotine which is, under ordinary circumstances, a prescription drug. And I would think that demanded regulation."[12]

Indeed, Kessler, eager not to be scooped by ABC, had sent a letter to the Coalition on Smoking OR Health on February 25, explaining that the FDA had decided to consider bringing tobacco under its regulatory authority. In his letter, he raised the possibility of restrictions on nicotine as well as a ban on nicotine-containing cigarettes:

A strict application of these provisions could mean, ultimately, removal
from the market of tobacco products containing nicotine at levels that
cause or satisfy addiction. Only those tobacco products from which the
nicotine had been removed or, possibly, tobacco products approved by the
FDA for nicotine-replacement therapy would then remain on the market.

But he realized that serious regulation of nicotine content could have powerful implications for the 40 million American smokers:

Given the widespread use of cigarettes and the prevalence of nicotine addiction, such a regulatory action could have dramatic effects on our society. One must consider the possible effects of the loss of this source of
nicotine on the health of some people who are addicted to nicotine and
the possible need for a weaning period. It is also important to consider
the potential for a black market in nicotine-containing cigarettes.

He also emphasized the need to work closely with Congress to assure the
FDA's regulatory mandate:

We recognize that the regulation of cigarettes raises societal issues of
great complexity and magnitude. It is vital in this context that Congress
provide clear direction to the agency. We intend therefore to work with
Congress to resolve, once and for all, the regulatory status of cigarettes
under the Food, Drug, and Cosmetic Act.[13]

Kessler was scheduled to testify before Henry Waxman's Subcommittee
on Health and the Environment on March 25, 1994. The day before this
appearance, Philip Morris filed its libel suit against ABC and its owner,
Capital Cities, in Richmond, Virginia. Also named as defendants were
producer Bogdanich and reporter Martin. At a news conference, Murray
Bring, a senior vice president at Philip Morris asserted, "Philip Morris does
not in any way, shape or form spike its cigarettes with nicotine. These allegations are not true, and ABC knows they are not true." He went on to
claim that "nicotine in cigarettes is not a drug. It's a natural element found
in the plant itself." Philip Morris demanded $5 billion in compensatory
damages and an additional $5 billion in punitive damages, noting that the

"false and defamatory statements contained in the . . . broadcasts were made knowingly, recklessly and with malice."[14]

§

Kessler understood that before the FDA could invoke any regulatory authority over cigarettes, the public understanding of the product must be radically changed. This, in turn, demanded a careful investigation of precisely how the industry understood and utilized nicotine in its product. The *Day One* report had only hinted at a more complex story of industry research into the pharmacology of nicotine and the biochemistry of tobacco leaf. After more than a year of investigation into the tobacco industry, Kessler had concluded that FDA regulation could succeed only if he were able to show that the industry "intended" cigarettes to "affect the body," as specified in the statutory mandate of his agency. As long as smoking was considered a matter of individual choice, there would be no regulation. At the hearings, therefore, he centered attention on the nature of nicotine as a drug:

> The issue I will address today is simple: Whose choice is actually driving the demand for cigarettes in this country? Is it a choice by consumers to continue smoking? Or is it a choice by cigarette companies to maintain addictive levels of nicotine in their cigarettes?

Kessler suggested that a "picture is beginning to emerge" indicating that the companies manipulate nicotine levels to ensure cigarettes' addictive potential. He reviewed with the committee his research team's findings concerning a number of patents for enriching the nicotine content of tobacco plants. "The research undertaken by the cigarette industry," he noted, "is more and more resembling drug development."[15] He went on to make a critical point: while most cigarettes' tar and nicotine levels had declined significantly since the 1950s—as the industry would repeatedly claim—they had recently begun to climb again, even in low-tar cigarettes. This clearly indicated that the industry had the capacity and intention to maintain nicotine at addictive levels. Kessler would show—contrary to industry claims—that tar and nicotine did not "travel together."[16] He also asserted that the industry had done extensive research on self-administration of nicotine and then acted to suppress these findings. "In other words," Congressman Waxman asked, "the tobacco industry sponsored studies on their own where they found out that nicotine was addictive and before the public could know about it, they acted to suppress those studies?"[17]

§

R.J. Reynolds and Philip Morris had both experimented with product in-novations that revealed the fundamental legal and regulatory dilemmas fac-ing the industry. Reynolds spent some $68 million developing a "smokeless" cigarette that would deliver nicotine by heating rather than burning tobacco. This high-tech product was developed largely in response to rising concerns about sidestream smoke. If cigarette smoking could be accomplished without smoke, R.J. Reynolds's executives reasoned, they might stop or even reverse their product's fall from grace. Moreover, al-though they refused to say so explicitly, a nonburning product could not only spare nonsmokers the risk of secondhand smoke but, even more im-portantly, reduce the risks to smokers as well. R.J. Reynolds invested heav-ily in this new product, which it called Premier. But antitobacco advocates immediately claimed that what R.J. Reynolds was proposing was not a cig-arette at all but a "nicotine delivery device."[18] Even as tobacco-control ad-vocates insisted that the FDA should regulate it, the Premier "cigarette" was proving to be a $300 million mistake. In regions where it was test-marketed, consumers complained that the thing was hard to light (matches could not be used) and even worse, the smell was intolerable. Philip Mor-ris had a similar but less pricey disaster with Next, a de-nicotinized ciga-rette it test-marketed in 1989.[19] This product raised an important question: if nicotine could be readily extracted from cigarettes, why wasn't it, if not to keep smokers addicted?

These two new products were not only failures among smokers; they also directed the attention of public health officials and tobacco-control advocates to new regulatory possibilities. Moreover, they demonstrated a technical sophistication that the simple notion of tobacco rolled in paper had allowed the industry to mask for more than a generation. The tobacco companies had made a critical misstep that their opponents would relent-lessly exploit. Once again, the companies fell victim to a perennial prob-lem. Since they refused to acknowledge the problems with the product (disease and addiction), it was difficult for them to aggressively market and promote products that sought to address the very problems that could not be named.

§

Day One and David Kessler had fundamentally recast the debate about tobacco. The *Cipollone* verdict, despite Edell's best efforts, had hinged on Rose Cipollone and her "decision" to smoke and continue to smoke. Edell had tried to shift attention to the actions of the companies, but in the end he could not. Now, as journalists and government investigators began to focus on industry research and production, an altogether different narrative of smoking began to emerge: one of secret technologies, research laboratories precipitously closed down, and nicotine as a potent drug carefully added to a high-tech product to sustain a greedy industry's profits.

Kessler, cautious in his approach to Congress, explained that he was "seeking guidance" about how to proceed.

> Clearly, the possibility of FDA exerting jurisdiction over cigarettes raises many broader social issues for Congress to contemplate. It could lead to the possible removal of nicotine-containing cigarettes from the market, the limiting of the amount of nicotine in cigarettes to levels that are not addictive, or restricting access to them, unless the industry could show that nicotine-containing cigarettes are safe and effective.[20]

That such thoughts were voiced in such powerful venues constituted the gravest crisis for the tobacco industry since the first surgeon general's report was released three decades earlier. As it had done in 1964, the industry took the offensive, expressing outrage and indignation over the charges of nicotine manipulation and the addictiveness of smoking.

§

On April 14, 1994, the chief executives of the seven largest U.S. tobacco companies appeared before Waxman's subcommittee. They insisted that tobacco was not addictive and that their companies had taken no action to manipulate the levels of nicotine in cigarettes. "We do not do anything to hook smokers or keep them hooked," said James Johnston of R.J. Reynolds. "We no more manipulate nicotine in cigarettes than coffee makers manipulate caffeine."[21] This was an odd claim given that decaffeinated coffee products had been available for many years. The hearings, marked by abundant angry questions and hostile replies, were televised live on CNN and C-SPAN and covered widely in the print and broadcast media. Waxman put the executives on notice that the ground had shifted when he announced, in his opening remarks, that "this hearing marks the beginning of a new relationship between Congress and the tobacco companies. The old rules are out; the standards that apply to every other company are in."[22]

The tobacco executives had little interest in any new relationship; they fell back on the reliable tactics of the past, denial and naïveté. Each CEO testified in language that many commentators saw as rehearsed:[23]

> William Campbell, Philip Morris: "I believe nicotine is not addictive, yes."
>
> James Johnston, R.J. Reynolds: "Congressman, cigarettes and nicotine clearly do not meet the classic definitions of addiction. There is no intoxication."
>
> Joseph Taddeo, U.S. Tobacco: "I don't believe that nicotine or our products are addictive."
>
> Edward Horrigan, Liggett: "I believe nicotine is not addictive."
>
> Andrew Tisch, Lorillard: "I believe that nicotine is not addictive."
>
> Thomas Sandefur, Brown & Williamson: "I believe that nicotine is not addictive."
>
> Donald Johnston, American Tobacco: "And I, too, believe that nicotine is not addictive."

These denials outraged Waxman and some of his colleagues, and the heat of their indignation raised the temperature in the hearing room. Several of the CEOs then gave their views on the meaning of addiction. William Campbell of Philip Morris dismissed the supposed connection between cigarettes and addictive drugs: "I'm a smoker, and I'm not a drug addict, and basically I can function really in quite a normal way. My judgment's not impaired." James Johnston of R.J. Reynolds compared cigarettes to milk, sweets, and Twinkies. Waxman pounced on him for downplaying the harmfulness of cigarettes. "You and I both know that Twinkies don't kill

a single American," he charged. "The difference between cigarettes and . . .
the other products you mentioned is death."[24] The executives continued to
assert the industry's long-standing position concerning the harms of smoking. When asked if he knew that cigarettes caused cancer, Lorillard's Andrew Tisch replied, "I do not believe that." Johnston insisted that neither
he nor anyone else knew the death toll of tobacco since such numbers were
"generated by computers and are only statistical." When asked whether or
not smoking caused a series of specific diseases, he repeatedly insisted, "I
don't know." Waxman concluded by sharply admonishing him, "All of you
have a responsibility to say something more than you don't know. You have
a responsibility to know."[25]

Tactics that had reliably worked in the past had now all but expired. As
the studies accumulated over decades, it had become impossible for executives to claim, as they had always done, that they did not know or that more
research was needed. And although many Americans had succeeded in
quitting smoking, it had become clear that nicotine possessed all the mark-
ers of a powerfully addictive substance. This had been authoritatively documented in Surgeon General Koop's 1988 report.[26]

For the industry, the executives' suspect testimony—and the image of
them standing in a row, with their right hands raised—was an unprecedented media disaster. Newscasts and newspapers throughout the country
led with accounts of the tobacco CEOs' professed ignorance about the
dangers of their product. Editorialists and columnists across the political
spectrum had a field day submitting reviews of Waxman's political theater.
"Good thing no one asked those tobacco executives whether they think the
world is round or flat," commented the *Baltimore Sun*.[27] A *New York Times*
editorial noted, "It was a shameful day for American business, even though
we are wearily familiar with the obfuscations employed by the defenders of
an industry responsible for the deaths of nearly half a million Americans
every year."[28]

John Hill had understood in 1953 that the strategy he had helped mastermind would one day stop working; now the day had arrived. Tactics that
were effective just a decade earlier were now dated and radically out of
touch with science and, more importantly, with the public's increasingly sophisticated view of tobacco and its purveyors. Nonetheless, they remained
wedded to denial. Any serious concessions on the health issue and on the

question of addiction would, according to the industry's legal counsel, open the floodgates of litigation that they had so successfully bolted shut. It was one thing to have a PR problem, quite another to be saddled with billions of dollars in litigation risk.

As a shrewd bit of media theatrics, the Waxman hearings had their desired effect. They exposed the industry's tired old deceits and fueled the public indignation needed to forge the political will that would, in turn, yield legislative and regulatory action. Lining up the tobacco executives to deny, under oath, any knowledge of the harms of smoking had exposed their hypocrisy and self-interest to the glare of sound-bite politics. Further, Waxman's hearings played to a deep popular anger about corporate dishonesty and greed. While the tobacco companies would continue to insist that cigarette use was a matter of individual choice, opponents like Waxman were eager to expose an industry knowingly valuing its own profits over the public's health. He described the industry as the "evil empire," a metaphor now frequently heard in public discussions of tobacco. After April 1994, the tobacco industry would be redefined as outside the boundaries of American corporate culture, a rogue industry. One year later, every one of the CEOs who appeared before Waxman's committee had resigned or been replaced. The public humiliation of the hearings had not gone unnoticed in the Big Tobacco boardrooms.

Waxman, armed with the FDA's research findings as well as his own sources, expressed outrage at the CEOs' stonewalling. "The tobacco companies have lied to us . . . and it is a criminal offense to try to mislead Congress," he warned.[29] In the hearings, he had set a trap for the CEOs. Following the April 14 hearings, Waxman's colleague, Massachusetts Democrat Marty Meehan, would request that the Department of Justice (DOJ) begin an investigation of possible perjury on the part of the company executives. In December 1994, Meehan sent a 111-page prosecution memorandum to Attorney General Janet Reno, urging her to appoint a grand jury to investigate possible criminal conduct on the part of the industry. Although the request had originated from the suspicion that the CEOs had lied in their testimony in April, Meehan now suggested that there was new evidence that the companies, their executives, and perhaps even their lawyers had violated federal laws over more than three decades. "The enormity of the harm perpetrated by tobacco companies and their agents on American consumers is difficult to comprehend," Meehan wrote. "It is apparent, however, that the crimes alleged here, committed over decades have contributed profoundly to the serious illness and early death experienced by tens of millions of Americans, as well as to literally trillions of dollars in health care costs and lost productivity borne by the economy of this nation and the individual states."[30] Among these alleged crimes were perjury, mail fraud, false advertising, deception of the public, deception of federal agencies, and deception of Congress. Meehan also suggested that the DOJ explore the possibility of criminal violations of the Racketeering Influenced and Corrupt Organizations (RICO) Act.

Ultimately, a DOJ task force abandoned the perjury investigation against the CEOs, reasoning that it would be difficult to prove the executives had deliberately lied, given that they had testified that they did not "believe" smoking was addictive. The task force turned its attention to other potential illegalities: false statements, tax violations, and conspiracy to deceive the government and trial courts.[31] At one point, the task force apparently considered indicting company lawyers for conspiring to use attorney-client privilege to protect illegal activities. Although many expected the DOJ to issue criminal indictments on at least some of these charges, despite more than five years of investigation no charges were ever filed. In a separate move, in late 1999, the civil division, at the direction of Bill Clinton, filed a suit against the companies to recover Medicare and Medicaid costs and penalties for civil violations under the RICO Act.[32]

§

The run of bad news for the companies was just beginning. In 1988, Merrell Williams went to work as a paralegal for the Louisville law firm of Wyatt, Tarrant & Combs. A down-on-his-luck former drama professor, Williams was an accident waiting to happen for the tobacco industry. He would emerge at the end of the twentieth century having done more damage to Big Tobacco than perhaps any other person. Brown & Williamson had retained Wyatt to review and sort thousands of internal documents related to the liability actions against them. Williams was charged with classifying and filing these documents from 1988 until 1992, when he was laid off. But during this period, shocked by what he was reading, he began to take documents home. He would sneak them out past the security guards, tucked in his pants, in a corset, or sometimes simply in his briefcase.[33] He then photocopied them and returned the originals to the office. In three-plus years, Williams accumulated more than 4,000 pages of documents, containing some of the most damaging revelations ever to emerge about the tobacco industry's internal workings.

In 1990, while still working at the firm, Williams contacted Richard Daynard, an antitobacco activist and attorney. Daynard suggested that Williams call former *Washington Post* reporter Morton Mintz, who had covered tobacco issues for many years and had been one of the few jour-nalists covering the *Cipollone* trial. Mintz reviewed some of the documents and considered writing a book, but after consulting with lawyers about civil and criminal liability associated with using stolen materials, he decided to return them to Williams.[34]

A lifelong smoker, Williams underwent quintuple bypass surgery in 1993; later that year he informed Wyatt through an attorney that he had in his possession some of the documents he had worked with while at the firm, threatening to sue but at the same time offering to return the docu-ments in exchange for compensation for his physical and psychological in-juries. A Wyatt attorney responded that Brown & Williamson did not settle smoking and health claims. Wyatt, Tarrant & Combs then filed a suit accusing Williams of stealing the documents and breaching the confiden-tiality agreement he had signed upon taking his position. The circuit court in Kentucky issued an order prohibiting any distribution or discussion of the documents.

For more than a year, Williams and the documents—the latter hidden in a friend's apartment in Florida—stood in legal limbo. But in early 1994, he contacted liability lawyer Don Barrett, who had tried a well-known tobacco case in Mississippi, *Horton v. American Tobacco*, which had resulted in a hung jury and accusations of industry jury tampering.[35] Barrett arranged a meeting with his colleague Richard Scruggs, who was then considering lia-bility litigation on behalf of the state of Mississippi with state Attorney General Michael Moore. After a series of meetings with Scruggs, who even-tually offered him legal support and financial assistance, Williams finally agreed to turn over to him the entire set of stolen papers. The attorneys had them flown from Florida back to Mississippi. Scruggs and Attorney General Moore then hand-delivered a full set to Henry Waxman—a shrewd legal maneuver since members of Congress are protected from subpoena and other court orders under the Speech or Debate Clause of the Constitution.

Reporters at ABC were apparently among the first to receive Brown & Williamson documents from Williams's stolen archive, but given the pending libel suit against the network, they were required by company lawyers to return them. Walt Bogdanich, who well understood their significance, was appalled to be barred from reporting them, but the lawyers prevailed. This was a telling example of how the libel suit chilled coverage of the story.[36]

The industry worked diligently to keep the documents under wraps. Brown & Williamson lawyers used every legal means to prevent any further release. But with several sets now in circulation, they could not contain the toxic spill. Philip Hilts, who had been covering tobacco issues for the *New York Times,* was the first reporter to write about the Brown & Williamson documents, which he received from "a government official." On May 7, 1994, he published an article that appeared on the front page of the *Times* entitled, "Tobacco Company Was Silent on Hazards." Hilts focused on a 1963 memo by Brown & Williamson general counsel Addison Yeaman, written shortly before the release of the surgeon general's report, in which Yeaman wrote, "we are, then, in the business of selling nicotine, an addictive drug effective in the release of stress mechanisms."[37] Yeaman would go on to direct the Council for Tobacco Research. According to Hilts, the documents revealed that "the executives of the . . . Brown & Williamson Tobacco Corporation chose to remain silent, to keep their research results secret, to stop work on a safer cigarette and to pursue a legal and public relations strategy of admitting nothing."[38]

Shortly after Hilts's first article appeared, a package of Brown & Williamson documents with the return address of only "Mr. Butts" came by Federal Express to Stanton Glantz of the University of California at San Francisco (UCSF), a leading figure in the antitobacco crusade. Not only did these documents make for good journalistic copy, they would provide a new foundation for grassroots advocacy and the pursuit of tobacco liability litigation. Glantz spent the next year reading the materials and evaluating their significance. Again, Brown & Williamson sued to have the materials returned, but the California court ruled in favor of UCSF. By June 1995, UCSF had placed the full set of documents on the Internet, where they remain available today. The "Cigarette Papers," as Glantz would name them, had crossed into the public domain.

In July 1995, Glantz and colleagues published five peer-reviewed articles in *JAMA* detailing key aspects of the Brown & Williamson documents. These articles described the industry's extensive knowledge about nicotine and addiction and about environmental tobacco smoke and about how Brown & Williamson sought to protect itself from liability action by maintaining legal authority over all research activities.[39] Glantz and colleagues emphasized the striking contradictions between the industry's public denials of the harms of smoking and the internal documents' frank discussions of these harms.

The Cigarette Papers proved that for three decades the company's public statements had radically diverged from its internal activities and practices. Since the 1960s, Brown & Williamson documents had noted the likely carcinogenic effects of smoking, the addictive properties of nicotine, and the potential for harm generated by environmental tobacco smoke. Attempts to produce a safer product were repeatedly scuttled by legal counsel eager to avoid tacit public admission of the existing product's dangers. The industry's own research program, which focused on the "inadequacy" of scientific claims regarding the harms of smoking, was explicitly designed to serve the tobacco companies' public relations needs. Glantz concluded:

> The documents showing lawyers steering scientists away from particular research avenues are inconsistent with the company's purported disbelief in the causation and addiction claims; if the company had been genuinely unconvinced by the causation and addiction hypotheses, then it should have had no concern that new research would provide ammunition for the enemy. Quite the contrary, the documents show that B&W and BAT recognized more than 30 years ago that nicotine is addictive and that tobacco smoke is "biologically active" (e.g., carcinogenic).[40]

The Cigarette Papers radically altered the debate about tobacco. Although other internal industry documents had emerged over the previous years—notably in *Cipollone*—the Brown & Williamson documents presented the most comprehensive look at industry activities that had yet become available. According to Hilts: "These documents are historic in the sense that they probably are the single most important pieces of paper in the history of tobacco versus public health—partly because of their timing, partly because of what they will mean in court cases, partly because they put everybody onto it."[41] Now the industry's critics could know what in the past they had only surmised.

From this point forward, the regulatory and legal case against the tobacco companies would be based on their knowledge and behavior in the years when the risks of cigarette smoking were becoming scientifically explicit. The Brown & Williamson documents provided, for example, additional justification for Kessler's attempt to gain FDA regulatory authority over cigarettes. As one of Glantz's *JAMA* articles concluded, "The documents reveal an intention on the part of B&W and its corporate parent to affect the function of the body with nicotine." The words were chosen to address the heart of Kessler's jurisdictional claim.[42]

As for the legal attack against the companies, tobacco liability cases had always turned on the simple but important question of corporate versus individual responsibility. The companies had defended themselves by claiming, first, that the scientific knowledge of tobacco's harms was shaky, and second, that individuals made informed decisions about whether or not they wished to smoke, which precluded them from holding the companies accountable for any harms they might suffer. The Brown & Williamson documents poured acid on these historic defenses. They revealed a set of strategic debates within the industry about how to deal with the growing knowledge of the harms of smoking; how to continue to successfully market cigarettes in a new environment; and the scientific characteristics of nicotine and addiction.

Williams and Scruggs had each pushed the margins of law and ethics in their efforts to get these documents into the public domain. There is little question that Williams violated both the law and the subsequent restraining order. Scruggs may well have crossed his profession's ethical boundaries by accepting allegedly stolen documents while he was preparing suits against the companies.[43] Yet the social benefits of their actions can hardly be overestimated. They had conspired to break a remarkable conspiracy. To Brown & Williamson, Williams was a petty criminal who had committed an outrageous, immoral act and belonged in jail. To the tobacco-control advocates, he was a hero who, at considerable personal risk, had exposed a decades-long cover-up of great public importance. In one last effort to bring Williams and the reporters who had publicized their documents to justice, Brown & Williamson sent subpoenas to Congressmen Henry Waxman and Ron Wyden (D-OR) as well as to six journalists, including Hilts at the *New York Times* and John Schwartz at the *Washington Post,* demanding return of the documents on the ground that their release violated the Kentucky court order against Williams.

Higher courts quashed these subpoenas. The ones against Waxman and Wyden were dismissed under the Speech or Debate Clause of the U.S. Constitution, which protects congressional investigation from liability. Claims against the media also failed when courts upheld First Amendment protections for news sources; other courts also cited the important public interest served by the free flow of information.[44] Ultimately, Judge Harold Greene, of the Federal District Court for the District of Columbia, declared:

> This is a seemingly arcane dispute over subpoenas and motions to quash them. But what is involved at bottom is not arcane at all: it is a dispute over documents which may reveal that the Brown and Williamson tobacco company concealed for decades that it knew its products to be both hazardous and addictive. The subpoenas are the means by which the company is seeking to intimidate, and in a sense to punish both Dr. Williams, the discoverer of evidence of this possible concealment, and the national legislators who are seeking to investigate the subject further and bring the results to the attention of Congress and the public.

"There are," Greene wrote, "several rules, even constitutional doctrines, that stand in the way of so high-handed a course of conduct, and one so patently crafted to harass those who would reveal facts. . . ." He went on to suggest that the industry's intensive interest in the documents' recovery might be that they "represent the proverbial 'smoking gun' evidencing the company's allegedly long-held and long-suppressed knowledge that its product constitutes a serious health hazard."[45] The ruling was a stinging blow to the companies. The documents were out. And no matter how shady or even illegal Williams's taking them was, no one claimed they were anything but authentic. Although Williams remained in legal jeopardy—

like the other principal whistle-blowers—the importance of these revelations is what ultimately kept him out of jail.

In retrospect, the documents might very well have remained locked within the fortress of Big Tobacco; so much of what we have come to know about the history of the tobacco industry might have remained cloaked by attorney-client privilege. Williams—vilified and celebrated—is a figure of genuine significance in the history of the cigarette. At one time, he was willing to sell the documents back to the law firm from which they were taken. Of the many strategic errors of the tobacco wars, Brown & Williamson's decision to scorn Williams was one of the most disastrous.

§

Nor was Williams the company's only demon. A Brown & Williamson senior research scientist, Jeffrey Wigand, also stepped forward, and soon there was a small chorus of former tobacco employees blowing whistles in unison. Wigand, a biochemist, was Brown & Williamson's head of research and development, studying things like fire safety, ignition propensity, and tobacco additives, from 1989 until he was fired in 1993. He had specialized in approaches to developing safer cigarettes and had been frustrated to find his efforts repeatedly blocked. Despite his dismissal, Wigand honored his confidentiality agreement when deposed by the DOJ in its investigation into the industry's efforts to suppress fire-safe cigarettes. At the time, he denied any wrongdoing on the part of the company. Wigand, however, would soon abrogate his severance agreement.

In early 1994, Wigand was recruited by Lowell Bergman, a producer at CBS's *60 Minutes,* for advice on a piece about fire-safe cigarettes. Among Wigand's assorted projects at Brown & Williamson had been to develop a self-extinguishing cigarette. By the late 1970s, it had become clear that cigarettes led to as many as 30 percent of all fire-related deaths, as well as billions in property damages. Although the industry remained united in opposing fire-safe products, asserting that such cigarettes were unacceptable to consumers, it nonetheless conducted research on how to produce a cigarette that would reduce the risk of fires. At the same time, the industry worked concertedly to deflect attention from the issue by offering support to organizations of firefighters and fire-safety advocates.[46]

Wigand also became a principal informant in the FDA investigation, describing to Kessler's team how the industry enhanced nicotine delivery through the use of ammonia-based compounds, and how different types of tobacco, with varying nicotine content, were blended to assure addictive levels. And he tipped off the FDA to the industry's use of genetically engineered plants to heighten nicotine content.[47]

William Farone, a former Philip Morris chemist, also assisted the FDA in its investigation. Farone had been a director of scientific research at Lever Brothers before coming in 1976 to work at Philip Morris's Richmond laboratories, where he was soon promoted to director of applied research. In this capacity, Farone reported to Thomas Osdene, who directed the company's biological research programs. Farone would request experiments, which Osdene would then have conducted at Philip Morris's European laboratory called INBIFO. This procedure was intended to keep certain projects secret and beyond the reach of American litigation.[48]

Farone was fired by Philip Morris in December 1983. A decade later, he was contacted by Kessler's FDA investigators. "It was Cigarettes 101," explained Mitch Zeller, who directed the inquiry for Kessler. "He was more of a teacher than anything else, very patiently explaining the fundamentals of how you make a cigarette."[49] It was Farone, code named "Philip," who clued the FDA researchers into the fact that Merits, though low in tar, were high in nicotine. Concerned about the legal consequences of breaching his confidentiality agreement, Farone frequently reminded investigators as he led them through the intricacies of cigarette production that the information he was providing was generally available in the literature.[50] Nonetheless, he provided crucial help in discrediting industry claims of naïveté about the cigarette's addictive properties.

Farone had watched the Waxman hearings in April 1994 with surprise and outrage. His entire research program at Philip Morris had centered on two scientific realities: that cigarettes caused cancer and that they were addictive.[51] Hearing the CEOs' flat denials in the face of what he had thought was a principled effort to rectify these twin problems moved Farone closer to a public role. He soon became a public whistle-blower and advocate for federally regulated, less harmful products, which he asserted the companies could readily produce.[52]

Two other former Philip Morris scientists also entered the public spotlight. Victor DeNoble and Paul Mele told Waxman's subcommittee that Philip Morris had pulled the plug on their research into the addictive nature of nicotine. They had shown how the addictive qualities of nicotine could be enhanced through the addition of acetaldehyde to the point where laboratory rats would forgo food and water for nicotine, once addicted. Other research conducted by DeNoble and Mele centered on the development of nicotine analogs that might reduce the cardiac risks of smoking. Both programs were summarily halted by Philip Morris in 1983, at the very time that Edell was filing suit in *Cipollone*. In 1984, the two scientists were ordered to destroy the animals and disband the lab. Offered jobs in a Philip Morris factory, they quit.[53]

In January 1983, DeNoble and Mele had submitted a paper describing their findings to *Psychopharmacology*. The paper, entitled "Nicotine as a Positive Reinforcer in Rats," was withdrawn prior to publication as executives and lawyers became anxious about the legal implications of internal research explicitly confirming the addictive properties of nicotine. Eventually, the paper found its way to Kessler, for whom it constituted clear proof that the industry had both conducted extensive addiction research and suppressed the results.

Lowell Bergman realized that in Wigand he had a potentially major story for *60 Minutes*. But Wigand, like Williams and the other whistle-blowers, had significant concerns about his personal legal vulnerabilities if he talked. It had been risky for him to talk to Kessler, but at least those interviews had been conducted in secret, and in their early conversations Wigand refused to discuss his own experiences. Now, Bergman wanted him to go public with his claims against the company. Over recent decades, the industry had developed precise, typically lifelong confidentiality agreements designed to ensure that any current or former employees who were tempted to tell tales of work inside Big Tobacco would face severe consequences for doing so.[54] Bergman helped Wigand get an attorney to advise him about possible liabilities should the companies claim that he violated his agreement. Still worried about possible criminal violations, Wigand was referred to none other than Richard Scruggs, who agreed to represent him free of charge.

The evolving interests of the plaintiffs' bar, tobacco litigation, and the whistle-blowers were thus converging to create a powerful challenge to the industry. Having successfully brought Williams and his box of documents in from the cold, Scruggs would now become Wigand's main protector as well. For Scruggs, who was busily laying the framework of a massive set of suits against the industry to recover state Medicaid costs, it was a win-win. He did warn Wigand, at considerable length, about the legal and personal attacks that Brown & Williamson was likely to bring against him. "These are tough choices for you and your wife," he wrote to Wigand. "Given the magnitude of this decision, I cannot make a recommendation about whether you should act or risk inaction. I can only assure you of my commitment to [protect] and/or defend you to the full extent of my abilities, whichever decision you both make."[55] After intensive negotiations, CBS, in a somewhat unusual move, agreed to indemnify Wigand for any legal costs arising from his acting as their informant.[56]

In August 1995, Wigand finally sat for an on-camera interview with Mike Wallace. Just before he went on camera, Bergman offered Wigand a handwritten note promising not to air the interview without his permission. Bergman later explained that this was but a courtesy and that Wigand did not have veto power over the segment. Working with whistle-blowers like Wigand required an unusual combination of hand-holding and support, as well as a deep commitment to getting the story into the public domain. In the interview, Wigand leveled a number of charges against his former employer. Especially significant was his allegation that Thomas Sandefur's testimony before the Waxman committee was a perjury. "I believe he perjured himself because I watched those testimonies very carefully," he told Wallace. According to Wigand, Sandefur had once described cigarettes to him as "a delivery system for nicotine." He now explained publicly what he had earlier told FDA investigators about ammonia and "impact boosting." "There's extensive use of this technology which is called ammonia chemistry that allows for nicotine to be more rapidly absorbed in the lung and therefore affect the brain and central nervous system," he told Wallace. Wigand went on to note that when he worked for Brown & Williamson, his scientific reports were edited by legal counsel to ensure that they were "sanitized" of any references to the hazards of cigarettes. "The lawyers intervene and then they purge documents. And every time there was a reference to the words 'less hazardous' or 'safer'" the lawyers would excise it. Wigand reported that in a personal conversation with Sandefur he was told, "I don't want to hear any more discussion about a safer cigarette. . . . We pursue a safer cigarette, it would put us under extreme exposure with every other product. I don't want to hear about it any more."[57]

Wigand also charged that additives in tobacco were known carcinogens, and that when he apprised Sandefur of the risks of coumarin and other additives, he was told they could not be removed. Wallace asked: "In other words, what you're charging Sandefur with and Brown & Williamson with is ignoring health considerations consciously?" "Most certainly," replied Wigand. Later in the interview, he claimed that in the last year he and his family had received death threats and that he had started to carry a handgun.[58]

§

As Bergman moved ahead with the Wigand piece, ABC surprised the broadcast industry by suddenly agreeing to settle its suit with Philip Morris and even to offer a public apology. The settlement shocked ABC's news division as well as outside journalists. Proving libel is no simple matter; Philip Morris and R.J. Reynolds would need to demonstrate that ABC had shown a "reckless disregard for the truth" or engaged in "conscious falsehood" by using the word *spiked.* All ABC would need to demonstrate in order to be exonerated was that the broadcast was "substantially true." And many observers believed it was. On the eve of the trial, ABC's outside attorneys had appeared confident of success. In two mock trials staged for the defense, ABC had emerged victorious.[59] An ABC lawyer wrote to a potential witness:

> We are hard at work preparing to defend the libel suit. . . . I am pleased to be able to report that the course of pretrial discovery, despite strenuous efforts by Philip Morris to stonewall, amply confirms the accuracy and fairness of the broadcast. . . . Although we have taken on Big Tobacco in Marlboro Country, we are confident of victory as any prudent trial lawyers should be.[60]

The depositions turned on the word *spike* and evidence that outside suppliers produced nicotine extract for the tobacco industry. The news division was eager to see the case proceed. New revelations about the manufacture of cigarettes were likely to come out in the course of the trial, reporters believed, and would not only substantiate claims in the report but lead to additional support for regulating the product. ABC's legal team had requested and ultimately received thousands of industry documents explicating the complex processes by which tobacco is turned into cigarettes, the character of nicotine, and the state of industry knowledge.

But as the trial lawyers confidently prepared this defense, other lawyers inside ABC were negotiating a settlement with Philip Morris. As the case moved toward trial, it became clear that the public airing of this dispute would be damaging not only to the tobacco companies but to the network. *Day One* had been forced to turn over notes, video tape, and research on which the piece had been based. These would inevitably make it look like the reporters had manipulated the story, even as they charged that the companies manipulated nicotine. Both industries apparently saw a trial as a threat to the image of their respective products. With so much at stake, a negotiated settlement began to look prudent to both parties. In addition to filing suit against ABC, Philip Morris had reportedly threatened to pull its advertising for brands like Kraft Foods and Miller Beer, which amounted to more than $100 million a year.[61] It is not surprising that ABC blinked first.

In August 1995, ABC offered a public apology to Philip Morris and R.J. Reynolds. According to the agreement, the network would apologize twice, first on *Monday Night Football* and again on *Day One*. The carefully worded statement said: "We now agree that we should not have reported that Philip Morris and Reynolds add significant amounts of nicotine from outside sources. We apologize to our audience, Philip Morris and Reynolds." ABC also paid legal expenses of some $15 million to the tobacco companies. Sources inside the news division at ABC reported widespread dismay that company executives had failed to stand behind the story.[62]

Many saw the apology as an example of powerful corporate interests trumping journalistic practice.[63] It soon became clear that executives at Walt Disney Company, on the verge of acquiring ABC, wanted the case settled before the purchase went into effect. The apology and legal fees were dwarfed by the billions at risk in open court. ABC continued, despite the apology, to insist that the premise of the story—that tobacco companies do meticulously control the level of nicotine in cigarettes to maintain users' dependence—stood up to challenge. But this assertion was merely a whisper in the context of their public apology and the legal settlement. Bogdanich and Martin refused to sign the settlement. Although ABC renewed his contract, Bogdanich soon left to take a position at *60 Minutes*.[64]

The settlement required ABC's lawyers to return thousands of documents from the tobacco companies that had been produced in the discovery process. No reporters were provided access to these materials. Waxman requested that the industry voluntarily release these documents, but to no avail. Antitobacco advocates sharply attacked ABC and parent company Capital Cities for "caving" to the industry. "This lawsuit was never about libel," said Jane Kirtley, executive director of the Reporters Committee for Freedom of the Press. "It was about intimidation and discouraging other news organizations from covering them."[65] And indeed, there was data to suggest that the broadcast media began to shy away from tobacco reporting. According to Andrew Tyndall, editor of the *Tyndall Report*, a media-watch newsletter, "In the first six months of 1994, before Philip Morris sued ABC for libel, the three broadcast networks devoted 177 minutes to the tobacco story. In the second half of 1994, after the lawsuit was filed that May, the coverage dropped to 43 minutes." He concluded, "There definitely was a chilling effect of the lawsuit."[66]

Gloating in a rare public victory, Philip Morris took out full page ads in newspapers and magazines reprinting the ABC statement and declaring "Apology Accepted."[67] The ad continued, "As for the group of people who eagerly embraced the 'spiking' allegation to serve their ongoing crusade against the tobacco industry—we stand ready to accept their apologies as well." But as more evidence became available, it became increasingly clear that Bogdanich had, in fact, broken a major story.

The chilling wind from the ABC settlement blew through "Black Rock," the granite skyscraper that housed the legal and financial headquarters of CBS. Certainly, Lowell Bergman, Mike Wallace, and *60 Minutes* executive producer Don Hewitt were convinced that the Wigand interview was a blockbuster. When Hewitt saw a rough cut of the piece in early September

1995, he apparently told Bergman it was "Pulitzer Prize" material.[68] But when the final piece went to CBS corporate lawyers in October, they decided to kill it. The settlement of the *Day One* suit weighed heavily on discussions at CBS. Executives feared that a lawsuit might easily cost billions. Any case would likely be tried in tobacco-friendly Kentucky, where there were no caps on damage awards. According to some reports, people at CBS talked about whether the story was worth "betting the company."[69] Laurence Tisch, CEO of CBS and father of Andrew Tisch, CEO of Lorillard—who had testified at the Waxman hearings—denied any involvement in the decision. But among the revelations in the *60 Minutes* segment was that the younger Tisch was among the seven CEOs being investigated by the DOJ for possible perjury violations.

In its decision to cancel the broadcast, CBS cited the risk of being accused of "tortious interference," the claim that its producers had acted illegally in encouraging Wigand to break his confidentiality agreement with Brown & Williamson. Hewitt, Bergman, and Wallace contended that the network had not been forthright with them in pulling the piece. "I think we were deceived and lied to. I think that more is going on here than we even know now," fumed an indignant Bergman. Hewitt said in a speech at the National Press Club,

> We have a story we think is solid. We don't think anybody could sue us for libel. There are some twists and turns, and if you get in front of a jury in some states where the people on that jury are all related to people who work for the tobacco companies, look out. We may opt out of the line of fire. That doesn't make me proud, but it's not my money. I don't have 15 billion. That's Larry Tisch.[70]

Wallace, who years earlier had been a pitchman for Philip Morris, expressed disappointment but defended CBS, saying that "The ABC lawsuit did not chill us as journalists from doing the story. It did chill the lawyers who with due diligence had to say, 'We don't want to, in effect, risk putting the company out of business.'. . . They proved in the ABC suit that they [the tobacco industry] will go to the wall."[71]

Most First Amendment experts argued that threats of suit for tortious interference were weak and unlikely to cause significant liability for CBS.

An analysis of the case at the *New York Times* concluded, "Without putting up a fight, CBS has managed to create an ugly precedent. 'Tortious interference with contract' has now been added to the legal armory of enemies of the press without so much as a single decision endorsing it." James Goodale, the general counsel for the *New York Times* during the Pentagon Papers case, concluded in the *New York Law Journal* that it would have been very difficult, if the story were true, for CBS to lose a suit for broadcasting the Wigand piece. Calling the hypothetical trial a "slam dunk win" for CBS, Goodale noted, "Once the court is required to determine whether the publication of embargoed facts is in the public interest, the case is over."[72] According to some media critics, CBS's lack of fortitude was likely to strengthen the confidentiality agreements that had long stymied the flow of information and reporting on the tobacco industry, at great public cost. As Goodale explained, "CBS has now cultivated the impression that a company can bring and win an interference suit against the press. This will surely encourage corporations to require secrecy agreements of their employees, encourage judges to consider such suits seriously and encourage the public to believe that the suits are legitimate."[73] Daniel Schorr, who had helped to bring the Pentagon Papers to light while a reporter for CBS in the 1970s, expressed regret about the network's weakness in the face of legal threat:

> The tobacco industry . . . has apparently settled on the threat of lawsuit as a key weapon in its defense against an increasingly unfavorable press. The weapon turns out to be particularly potent in a period of network acquisition where decisions are made under the influence of money managers anxious to dispel any cloud on the financial horizon. The news managers submit, gracefully or less so.[74]

At the time they decided to kill the *60 Minutes* story, CBS executives were in the final stages of negotiating a $5.4 billion merger with Westinghouse. Just as with ABC and Disney, pending litigation was considered a problem. Some observers believed this was the key factor in CBS's decision. "The CBS and ABC experiences are dismaying for what they portend," wrote *New York Times* media critic Walter Goodman, "The reporters' job is to weigh the price of courage. The probability in this time of big-money takeovers and bottom-line pressures on news departments is that journalistic daring will be declared a debit by the powers that live by corporate balance sheets." The tobacco companies had used the threat of litigation to make a powerful statement that they would use every available method to silence critics and cool the media.

Despite the networks' public embarrassment over the ABC settlement and the CBS decision to pull the Wigand piece, the ironic reality was that the tobacco companies had lost the battle. A coherent account of industry activity with regard to tobacco and nicotine was emerging, supplied by a group of former employees who threatened to turn the industry inside-out. Someone at CBS leaked Wigand's story to the *New York Daily News*. Three months later, the *Wall Street Journal* obtained and published transcripts of the CBS interview. Now, with the threat of legal action much reduced, in an act of little courage, *60 Minutes* ran a revised version of its original story.[75]

Brown & Williamson responded to the publicity by suing Wigand for breach of contract. The company also assembled a five-hundred-page brief accusing him of all manner of personal moral turpitude and fraud. By this time, however, no one in the press was prepared to take a tobacco company at face value. The *Wall Street Journal* systematically ran through the claims against Wigand and concluded that "a close look at the [document], and independent research by this newspaper into its key claims, indicates that many of the serious allegations against Mr. Wigand are backed by scant or contradictory evidence. Some of the charges . . . are demonstrably untrue."[76] The suit was in all likelihood meant to send a message to would-be whistle-blowers that there would be real consequences for any who chose to follow Wigand's lead.

That such a message was even necessary, however, reflected critical changes in the moral climate of cigarette production and promotion. For decades, the industry had maintained an impregnable firewall around its internal research strategies and promotional tactics. But now, with its ongoing denials of the danger and addictiveness of smoking collapsing in the face of overwhelming evidence, the industry began to face new moral quandaries. As the older generation of industry executives and researchers retired, they were replaced by younger men and women—often, like Wigand and Farone, hired to develop safer products—who were not well schooled in a fortressed industry's complex cultural and psychological processes of collective denial. The scientists who volunteered industry knowledge to Kessler and the media held different values. In their eyes, the very nature of science as a process of determining the "truth" had been violated by industry statements contradicting or disparaging their work. Farone, for example, would insist that he could no longer tolerate the industry denials and suppression of his specific research findings about the addictive qualities of nicotine and the analogs he investigated. Whistle-blowing and the investigative media represented important new developments in the consumer society. One could not exist without the other.

These whistle-blowers typically exposed themselves to considerable risk. They understood that coming forward could lead to litigation, economic ruin, or even prison. Wigand, as we saw, told *60 Minutes* that he and his family had received several death threats. At the very least, blowing the whistle would lead to retributive public exposé of their personal and professional lives. Williams's alcoholism and Wigand's marital discord became subject to public scrutiny. It was critical to the industry to discredit not only the information but the source.

At the same time, however, whistle-blowers enjoyed the eager support of the media, regulators, and plaintiffs' lawyers. There were important rewards for coming forward, not the least of which was the notion of taking moral action against the industry's malice. And there was the fame they got from exposing industry deception and fraud. Wigand's coming out would ultimately be celebrated in a popular movie—*The Insider*—starring Russell Crowe in the lead role, with Christopher Plummer playing Mike Wallace and Al Pacino as Bergman. Although the industry would portray them as disgruntled employees with axes to grind—and certainly they were—the whistle-blowers' accounts of the internal workings of tobacco research and production would be consistently sustained by the documents. The cover-up had been undone.

With Williams's and Wigand's revelations, the outlines of Kessler's regulatory initiative were in place. Nicotine was addictive, and the industry deliberately designed and manufactured cigarettes to enhance their addictiveness. Kessler now documented a second critical assertion: the tobacco industry promoted cigarettes to children, who would become addicted before they were mature enough to make an "informed choice" about the risks of smoking. For Kessler, these two elements were linked, and they added up to a powerful refutation of the traditional industry position that smoking constituted a consensual behavior for adults who assume the risks. Kessler's research had sucked the volition out of smoking.

The tobacco companies had long considered young smokers critically important in the marketing of cigarettes. Now that the risks of smoking had become undeniable, appealing to youth became more necessary than ever. Without young smokers, eventually there would be no smokers. Kessler quoted from industry documents that offered a sophisticated psychology of the new smoker:

> Brands tailored for the beginning smoker should emphasize the desirable psychological effects of smoking, also suggesting the desirable physical effects to be expected later. Happily, then, it should be possible to aim a cigarette promotion at the beginning smoker.
>
> The adolescent seeks to display his new urge for independence with a symbol, and cigarettes are such a symbol . . .
>
> The fragile, developing self-image of the young person needs all of the support and enhancement it can get. Smoking may appear to enhance that self-image in a variety of ways. This self-image enhancement effect has traditionally been a strong promotional theme for cigarette brands.[77]

During the years of Kessler's investigation, R.J. Reynolds's Joe Camel campaign embodied the logic of these internal memoranda. The combination of these documents and Joe Camel's mug plastered on billboards and in magazine ads betrayed yet another public hypocrisy—if not fraud—on the part of the industry: its avid interest in promoting cigarettes to children.

Joe Camel, the ultracool cartoon "spokesbeast" for R.J. Reynolds, made his U.S. debut in 1987. Soon, his face was everywhere: in newspapers and magazines, on billboards and posters, and on all manner of apparel and products in the form of decals and logos. Joe Camel was just the sort of slightly older figure whom young boys idolize: he was aggressively independent, fun-loving, and eager to flout authority. Unlike his chief rival the Marlboro Man, a lone cowboy with a horse and cattle under the big sky, Joe Camel was an urbanite. Whether wearing shades and playing pool at a nightclub or out for the night in formal wear, he was the ultimate party animal, often fronting his camel band, known as "Hard Pack." He was never seen without a cigarette dangling from his elongated snout. From the inception of this campaign, few observers doubted that Joe Camel was designed to appeal to young (perhaps very young) smokers.

In the late 1970s, executives at R.J. Reynolds had faced a business dilemma that threatened the very future of their company. The years since the release of the first surgeon general's report in 1964 had been difficult times for the tobacco industry in general. At R.J. Reynolds, however, there were particular problems.[78] The company's most successful brands, Winston and Salem, appealed primarily to older smokers; they were projected to face steeply declining sales as their principal consumers aged. Camel, once the flagship of R.J. Reynolds, was also an old and failing brand. One of the nation's most popular and heavily advertised brands at mid-century, Camel had declined significantly over the decades until, by 1984, it commanded only 4.4 percent of the U.S. cigarette market.[79] And prospects remained discouraging. In 1986, the brand's greatest popularity was among smokers over sixty-five, of whom 44 percent chose Camel; but they were among the least popular of all brands among smokers seventeen to twenty-four, only 2.7 percent of whom preferred Camel. Camel's packaging and pitch had become badly dated.

There was one additional aspect to the problem: the average age at which smokers started smoking had declined over the last decade until by 1985 it was around sixteen.[80] Beyond the simple fact that they live longer, young smokers were desirable for two reasons: the first brand one smokes is likely to be the brand one keeps for life, and the younger someone starts smoking, the less likely they are to be able to quit. Now, however, cigarette companies were forced to focus on a segment of the population that was legally off-limits. Though officially unavailable for solicitation and sales, these "replacement smokers," as the industry called them, were desperately needed to buy the cigarettes no longer being purchased by smokers who quit or died off.[81] The future of R.J. Reynolds rested on the illegal buying decisions of teenagers. And these teenagers weren't buying enough R.J. Reynolds product.

R.J. Reynolds also understood that soliciting underage smokers was not only illegal, but also socially anathema. As the Joe Camel campaign splashed across billboards and magazines throughout the country, company executives circulated memos instructing employees to avoid all mention of the "youth market." Terms, such as *new smoker, pre-smoker,* and *beginning smoker* were stricken from the corporate vocabulary. The target of the campaign was the "younger adult smoker."[82] Nonetheless, R.J. Reynolds's interest in underage smokers was explicit in its marketing research.[83] Its demographic analyses collected data on children as young as twelve.[84] A 1981 memo cautioned researchers to tally all underage smokers in surveys as "age 18."[85]

Smokers' lifelong loyalty to their first brand gave rise to an inescapable logic. If, as was increasingly the case, smokers chose that first brand in their early teens (or younger), and R.J. Reynolds wanted access to beginning smokers, then it had to have a campaign that appealed to children in their early teens. While the industry typically claimed that it was peer pressure, not advertising, that created new smokers, the company now set out to create new smokers—specifically, Camel smokers—through advertising. In a presentation to the board of directors, C. A. Tucker, vice president for marketing, emphasized "the growing importance of the young adult in the cigarette business," defined as fourteen- to twenty-four-year-olds; these individuals, he explained, "represent tomorrow's cigarette business."[86]

Directly contradicting publicly stated tobacco industry positions that advertising was exclusively aimed at existing smokers, Reynolds argued in its internal memoranda that first-brand choice should be its key goal:

> Strong performance among FUBYAS [First Usual Brand Young Adult Smokers] is critical to long term share in the total smoker market for both brands and companies. . . . [a]lthough switching can be important in the near term market, loyalty and thus FUB smokers are the driving force over the long term.[87]

By age eighteen, however, most smokers had already started and were committed to their first brand. To capture the true "FUB smoker," R.J.

Reynolds had to go deeper into the youth market. Given the success of Marlboro in this market, the campaign to win young smokers would need to be aggressive, ubiquitous, and appeal especially to the needs and desires of preadolescents and adolescents. Enter Joe Camel.

Despite public denials, advertising experts at R.J. Reynolds took into explicit consideration the developmental needs of adolescents. Joe Camel was originally introduced in a French youth magazine called *Pilote* in 1974.[88] In the early 1980s, executives began to consider recruiting the "French Camel" to work in the United States.[89] From the first trial ads in the mid-1980s, Joe met this group of young and future smokers on their own social and psychological terrain. An early assessment of the "French" camel as an advertising vehicle praised it as a "smash," noting that "*it's about as young as you can get.*"[90] Market testing in the United States prior to the major campaign confirmed Joe's appeal and projected impact on the youth market.[91] "These ads were well received due to the fun/humor aspects of the cartoons," explained the ad agency researchers, who also noted, as a potential "drawback," that "they may be more appealing to an even younger age group." Company executives were unperturbed by this warning and soon made a full commitment to the development of the campaign. In July 1985, a "French Camel" T-shirt promotion drew a particularly strong response; redemption of coupons for the shirts ran three times higher than other typical promotion offers.[92]

In public, R.J. Reynolds vigorously insisted that the Joe Camel campaign was directed solely to adults and further that the company had no interest whatsoever in persuading youngsters to start smoking. In a series of informational ads published widely in newspapers and magazines just prior to Joe's introduction, R.J. Reynolds explained: "First of all, we don't want young people to smoke. And we're running ads aimed specifically at young people advising them that we think smoking is strictly for adults." Perhaps the ad's copywriters appreciated the irony, given the research that demonstrated smoking appealed to kids precisely as a way of appearing more "adult." R.J. Reynolds also asserted that kids have little interest in advertising: "Research shows that among all the factors that can influence a young person to start smoking, advertising is insignificant. Kids just don't pay attention to cigarette ads, and that's exactly as it should be."[93] Finally, the company insisted that the cause of teen smoking was peer pressure. But as company documents make clear, peer pressure is precisely what the advertising was designed to exploit. "Advertising will be developed," wrote one researcher, "with the objective of convincing target smokers that by selecting CAMEL as their usual brand they will enhance their acceptance among their peers."[94]

> Advertising will rely on clearly aspirational appeals (the me I want to be versus the me I am) to provide the motivation for target smokers to select CAMEL.
>
> Aspiration to be perceived as cool/a member of the in-group is one of the strongest influences affecting the behavior of younger adult smokers.
>
> This approach will capitalize on the ubiquitous nature of Marlboro by repositioning it as the epitome of conformity, versus CAMEL the smoke of the cool/in group.[95]

And if the overt message of these irreverent ads did not hit the mark, perhaps a more subliminal message would. Observers of the campaign often noted the essentially phallic characteristics of Joe's face, including his "rather testicular chin." Barbara Lippert, a well-known commentator on advertising, wrote, "If they wanted to do a penis, they could at least have done a good-looking one."[96] Harvard University cultural studies scholar Marjorie Garber suggested that Joe Camel as phallus was a classic case of "displacement upward." "It's as plain as the nose on your face."[97] Given that the campaign was initially pitched to young men, Joe Camel's macho and occasionally sexist character was a crucial aspect of the advertisements.[98]

Traditional advertising constituted only one element of the campaign; R.J. Reynolds spent nearly half its marketing budget on promotions and premiums. "Camel cash," for example, could be traded for a wide range of merchandise, all bearing enough logos to turn individuals into walking billboards for the brand. These promotional items—T-shirts, hats, lighters, beach coolers, and other gear—proved a critical and enormously popular element of the Joe Camel campaign. "The new catalogue [of promotional items] represents a veritable Disneyland of fantasy life styles, like Club Camel and Camel after hours, all accompanied by appropriate Camel tchotchkes," explained the *New York Times*.[99]

Even as the advertising industry circled the wagons around its First Amendment rights, many called for the end of the Joe Camel campaign. The aggressiveness of these ads and their obvious appeal to kids raised the specter of federal oversight and regulation of the advertising industry as a whole. For R.J. Reynolds, however, the campaign was a life-or-death affair. If the company could attract young smokers, its future would be secure. If antitobacco advocates could prevent smoking among children, the future of the industry was bleak. But at the same time, the battle for the young smoker exposed the industry to new and more aggressive assault.

Joe's success in attracting younger smokers was always double edged. The campaign drove the industry into new and marginal territory within the culture of American capitalism. By exposing the industry's aggressiveness and its critical need for new, even underage smokers, R.J. Reynolds had drawn public indignation and new accusations of illegal practices. Try, though the company did, to deny that it sought young smokers, Joe Camel, in his bright cartoon garb, spoke for himself.

The dilemma in which Big Tobacco found itself had been decades in the making. The strategy of denying that tobacco was harmful and addictive, while offering crucial short-term benefits, had in the long run caused a massive loss of credibility. In this atmosphere, the tobacco executives' further assurances—that their advertising was not pitched to children, that they made cigarettes only for adults—could not be sustained in the long face of Joe Camel.

In August 1996, following an intensive investigation and a year of public comment on proposed regulations, David Kessler announced that the FDA would regulate nicotine-containing tobacco products as medical devices, restrict youth access to tobacco products, and restrict tobacco advertising that might appeal to children. The FDA based its claim of jurisdiction on its finding that nicotine in cigarettes was a drug within the meaning of the 1938 Food, Drug, and Cosmetic Act, which defined *drugs* as "articles (other than food) intended to affect the structure or function of the body."[100] Kessler and his team believed they could conclusively show not only that nicotine met this definition, but that the tobacco industry explicitly "intended" the nicotine in cigarettes to have this effect. Cigarettes were therefore a "drug delivery system" meriting oversight under the FDA's mandate to regulate medical devices. If Kessler had sought to bring tobacco products under the drug mandate, he would have had to require the tobacco companies to show that they were both safe and effective. Since they clearly were not, the only alternative would have been to require their complete withdrawal from the market. Kessler knew that this was not a viable political option for the agency. Rather, he argued, by regulating cigarettes as a "device" for the delivery of nicotine, he could devise approaches to reduce the public health impact of smoking.

The FDA's approval of Nicorette chewing gum in 1984, used as a "replacement therapy" to assist in smoking cessation, underscored nicotine's addictive properties. Other pharmacotherapies were also available. Transdermal patches, inhalers, and nasal sprays, all laced with nicotine, offered smokers new opportunities for the treatment of nicotine addiction. Kessler found himself in the curious position of regulating these products but having no jurisdiction over the product they sought to replace.[101]

In marshalling evidence to support his new initiative, Kessler carefully reviewed the results of the agency's investigation, as well as much that had been learned as a result of the Cigarette Papers and the industry whistleblowers, all of which helped sustain his case for regulatory authority. First, his research within the FDA had demonstrated that as levels of tar had continued to decline over the last decade, nicotine had climbed by nearly 10 percent across the industry. The highest increases had come in the cigarettes lowest in tars. "It seemed unlikely," noted Kessler, "that the delivery of nicotine could increase independently of the delivery of tar unless the manufacturers had made deliberate design decisions." His research team analyzed the nicotine content of low-tar brands like Merit and discovered that those lowest in tars were actually highest in nicotine. "This," Kessler wrote, "suggested that the manufacturers were compensating for the effects of filtration and ventilation, the principal variables in design used to reduce the delivery of tar, by using high-nicotine tobacco blends in their lowest-tar products."[102]

Review of company patents confirmed the industry's interest in controlling nicotine delivery. One patent that the FDA recovered explained, "maintaining the nicotine content at a sufficiently high level to provide the desired physiological activity, taste, and odor . . . can thus be seen to be a

How mild can a cigarette be?

DOCTORS REPORT

In a recent test of hundreds of people who smoked only Camels for 30 days, noted throat specialists, making weekly examinations, reported

"NOT ONE SINGLE CASE OF THROAT IRRITATION DUE TO SMOKING CAMELS!"

SMOKERS REPORT

"I MADE MY OWN PERSONAL 30-DAY TEST! NOW I KNOW...CAMELS ARE THE MILDEST, BEST-TASTING CIGARETTE I EVER SMOKED!"

Sylvia Mac Neill
SECRETARY

According to a Nationwide survey:

More Doctors smoke Camels
than any other cigarette

Doctors smoke for pleasure, too! And when three leading independent research organizations asked 113,597 doctors what cigarette they smoked, the brand named most was Camel.

CAMEL

Ads such as the one above were explicitly designed to allay rising concerns about the health impacts of smoking. The idea of a "30-day" test—conducted both by a doctor on a series of patients and by a "secretary"—implied that individual judgment on the part of clinicians and patients could supplant findings based upon the study of smoking in large populations. "Mildness" became a popular euphemism to suggest a product free of serious risk. "Irritation" was widely associated with cancer-causing toxins.

These Chesterfield advertisements coincided with news of the epidemiological studies linking smoking to lung cancer that appeared beginning in 1950. Arthur Godfrey, who regularly pitched Chesterfields on his televised variety show, promised "No adverse effects to the nose, throat, and sinuses from smoking Chesterfield." Godfrey survived the removal of a lung tumor in 1959 but succumbed to emphysema in 1983.

Prominent Hollywood stars were used in 1950s ads to reassure smokers about the health effects of smoking. Advertisements frequently took on an aura of science, sustained by celebrity hype. Frederic March promised that new L&M Filters were "Just what the doctor ordered." And Marlene Dietrich claimed that "scientific tests prove Lucky Strike milder."

Credit: Courtesy of the James Lind Library

The epidemiological studies of Richard Doll (right) in Great Britain and Ernst Wynder (below) in the United States would offer crucial evidence that smoking causes lung cancer. These studies, as well as others that followed, would become the basis for understanding important causal relationships of health and disease in populations.

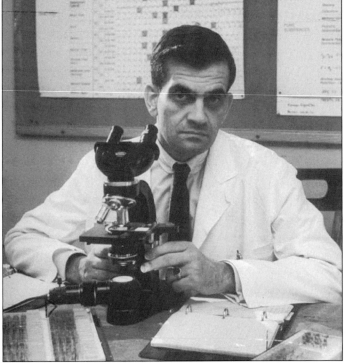

Credit: Time-Life/Alfred Eisenstaedt, 1957

A Frank Statement

to Cigarette Smokers

RECENT REPORTS on experiments with mice have given wide publicity to a theory that cigarette smoking is in some way linked with lung cancer in human beings.

Although conducted by doctors of professional standing, these experiments are not regarded as conclusive in the field of cancer research. However, we do not believe that any serious medical research, even though its results are inconclusive should be disregarded or lightly dismissed.

At the same time, we feel it is in the public interest to call attention to the fact that eminent doctors and research scientists have publicly questioned the claimed significance of these experiments.

Distinguished authorities point out:

1. That medical research of recent years indicates many possible causes of lung cancer.

2. That there is no agreement among the authorities regarding what the cause is.

3. That there is no proof that cigarette smoking is one of the causes.

4. That statistics purporting to link cigarette smoking with the disease could apply with equal force to any one of many other aspects of modern life. Indeed the validity of the statistics themselves is questioned by numerous scientists.

We accept an interest in people's health as a basic responsibility, paramount to every other consideration in our business.

We believe the products we make are not injurious to health.

We always have and always will cooperate closely with those whose task it is to safeguard the public health.

For more than 300 years tobacco has given solace, relaxation, and enjoyment to mankind. At one time or another during those years critics have held it responsible for practically every disease of the human body. One by one these charges have been abandoned for lack of evidence.

Regardless of the record of the past, the fact that cigarette smoking today should even be suspected as a cause of a serious disease is a matter of deep concern to us.

Many people have asked us what we are doing to meet the public's concern aroused by the recent reports. Here is the answer:

1. We are pledging aid and assistance to the research effort into all phases of tobacco use and health. This joint financial aid will of course be in addition to what is already being contributed by individual companies.

2. For this purpose we are establishing a joint industry group consisting initially of the undersigned. This group will be known as TOBACCO INDUSTRY RESEARCH COMMITTEE.

3. In charge of the research activities of the Committee will be a scientist of unimpeachable integrity and national repute. In addition there will be an Advisory Board of scientists disinterested in the cigarette industry. A group of distinguished men from medicine, science, and education will be invited to serve on this Board. These scientists will advise the Committee on its research activities.

This statement is being issued because we believe the people are entitled to know where we stand on this matter and what we intend to do about it.

TOBACCO INDUSTRY RESEARCH COMMITTEE

5400 EMPIRE STATE BUILDING, NEW YORK 1, N. Y.

SPONSORS:

THE AMERICAN TOBACCO COMPANY, INC.
Paul M. Hahn, President

BENSON & HEDGES
Joseph F. Cullman, Jr., President

BRIGHT BELT WAREHOUSE ASSOCIATION
F. S. Royster, President

BROWN & WILLIAMSON TOBACCO CORPORATION
Timothy V. Hartnett, President

BURLEY AUCTION WAREHOUSE ASSOCIATION
Albert Clay, President

BURLEY TOBACCO GROWERS COOPERATIVE ASSOCIATION
John W. Jones, President

LARUS & BROTHER COMPANY, INC.
W. T. Reed, Jr., President

P. LORILLARD COMPANY
Herbert A. Kent, Chairman

MARYLAND TOBACCO GROWERS ASSOCIATION
Samuel C. Linton, General Manager

PHILIP MORRIS & CO., LTD., INC.
O. Parker McComas, President

R. J. REYNOLDS TOBACCO COMPANY
E. A. Darr, President

STEPHANO BROTHERS, INC.
C. S. Stephano, D'Sc., Director of Research

TOBACCO ASSOCIATES, INC.
(An organization of flue-cured tobacco growers)
J. B. Hutson, President

UNITED STATES TOBACCO COMPANY
J. W. Peterson, President

The "Frank Statement" was drafted by the public relations firm of Hill & Knowlton on behalf of the tobacco industry. It appeared in 448 American newspapers on January 4, 1954. It assured the public that "We accept an interest in people's health as a basic responsibility, paramount to every other consideration in our business." In addition, it announced the formation of the Tobacco Industry Research Committee to undertake the "research effort into all phases of tobacco use and health."

The first Scientific Advisory Board of the Tobacco Industry Research Committee was hand picked by Hill & Knowlton executives with the assistance of industry scientists. (Pictured, left to right: McKeen Cattell, Paul Kotin, Clarence Cook Little, Stanley Reimann, Leon Jacobson, and Kenneth Merrill Lynch. Note: Cattell is holding a cigarette.)

Surgeon General Luther Terry announced the findings of his Advisory Committee on Smoking and Health on January 11, 1964, in a nationally televised press conference.

The new findings about the health effects of smoking had powerful implications for the production and marketing of cigarettes. Marlboro cigarettes were first introduced in the late 1920s as a woman's brand with the slogan "Mild as May." In 1954, they were radically repackaged and reengineered as a filter cigarette that would appeal to men.

The introduction of the "new" Marlboro, with the now legendary red and white chevron, drew on the full range of marketing tools in the industry's increasing sophisticated kit. Early Marlboro Men all sported this tattoo, creating a new "brotherhood" of rugged male smokers of filter cigarettes.

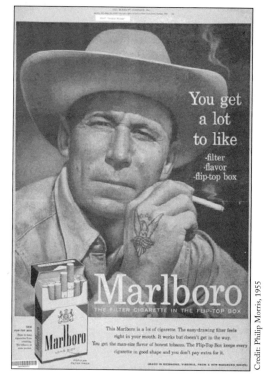

These four ads offer a cigarette history of brands smoked by Rose Cipollone, who sued the companies in 1983 following her diagnosis and treatment for lung cancer. The ads reflect the characteristic trade-offs faced by smokers as new knowledge of the harms of smoking emerged. Cipollone would switch to filters and to brands claiming reduced risks.

These ads became the archetypes of cigarette promotion in the age of known risks. Built upon images both broad and elastic in symbolic meaning, ad copy all but disappeared. The Joe Camel campaign, explicitly designed to compete with Marlboro for new, younger smokers, drew fire for its obvious appeal to youth.

Credit: AP/John Duricka, 1994

This photo from the congressional hearings before the Waxman Committee proved to be a historic public humiliation for the tobacco industry. At these hearings, the CEOs collectively claimed under oath that they "did not believe" that smoking caused cancer and was addictive. These assertions, coming some three decades after the first surgeon general's report, were widely seen as destroying any remaining credibility on the part of the companies. Within a year, all these men would be replaced.

Former Surgeon General C. Everett Koop and FDA Commissioner David Kessler expressed concerns about the "Global Tobacco Settlement" that emerged from negotiations with the attorneys general following their collective suits against the companies. Kessler and Koop aggressively pursued a health agenda on smoking during their terms in office.

Credit: AP/Susan Walsh, 1997

Credit: AP/Rogelio Solis, 1997

Mississippi Attorney General Michael Moore led the states' legal assault on the industry. Pictured here with attorneys Ron Motley and Richard Scruggs, experienced members of the plaintiffs bar, they led the massive legal attack that would culminate in the $246 billion payments to the states. Ultimately, less than 5 percent of these funds would be used to support tobacco-control efforts.

Miami attorney Stanley Rosenblatt had unusual success in bringing two historic class action cases against the industry to trial. *Broin v. Philip Morris*, brought on behalf of flight attendants, would be settled for $300 million. *Engle v. R.J. Reynolds* resulted in a finding of $145 billion for the plaintiffs; this award would ultimately be overturned by the Florida Supreme Court, although the findings against the companies for fraud and conspiracy would be upheld. Rosenblatt is pictured here with expert witness Julius B. Richmond, former surgeon

Credit: AP/Al Diaz, 1997

general, who testified extensively in both trials. Richmond's 1979 surgeon general's report presented the then "overwhelming" scientific evidence of the multiple harms of cigarette use.

Data showing that physicians were among the earliest groups to quit smoking offered a potent message to consumers about the harms of cigarette use.

100,000 doctors have quit smoking cigarettes.

(Maybe they know something you don't.)

U.S. DEPARTMENT OF HEALTH EDUCATION AND WELFARE • Public Health Service

We all share the same air.

Thank you for not smoking.
YOUR ╪ LUNG ASSOCIATION
The 'Christmas Seal' People.®
We care about every breath you take.

The recognition of the harms of cigarette smoke for nonsmokers radically reconfigured public health campaigns to control tobacco.

"COME OUT SLOWLY SIR,
WITH YOUR CIGARETTE ABOVE
YOUR HEAD."

"THE SMELL OF
CIGARETTE SMOKE ANNOYS ME.
BUT NOT NEARLY AS MUCH AS THE
GOVERNMENT
TELLING ME WHAT TO DO."

Tobacco companies sought to combat a rising tide of public restrictions on smoking with a smoker's rights movement that appealed to libertarian values and hostility to big government. "We believe that the answer to most smoking issues lies in accommodation," explained these advertisements, "in finding ways in which smokers and non-smokers can coexist peacefully." Although RJR promised "together, we can work it out," the campaign never generated significant public support.

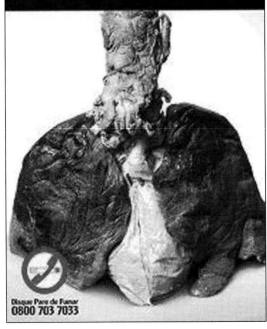

WARNING
CIGARETTES CAUSE MOUTH DISEASES

Cigarette smoke causes oral cancer, gum diseases and tooth loss.

Health Canada

Although the health warning labels in the United States have not been modified since 1984 (four rotating labels on the side of the package), a number of countries have devised pictorial package warnings that have been shown to reduce consumption.

FUMAR CAUSA CÂNCER DE PULMÃO.

Disque Pare de Fumar
0800 703 7033

As smoking began to decline in Western, developed nations, the tobacco industry pushed aggressively to expand into markets in Asia, Africa, and eastern Europe (among others). Western brands were often viewed as possessing special status. Above, Marlboro advertising in Phnom Penh, Cambodia. Left, an Indonesian cigarette vendor in Jakarta.

Credit: John Kaplan, 1993

These children represent the future of the multinational tobacco industry. Recruiting young smokers remains an essential goal of the tobacco industry. In the early twenty-first century, there are more cigarette smokers than ever before. Above, Sergei Mayorov, an eight-year-old street child in St. Petersburg, who insists on smoking Marlboros. Right, street children in Shenzhen, China.

Credit: TimeLife/Forrest Anderson, 1995

significant problem in the tobacco art."[103] Subsequent research had revealed Brown & Williamson's efforts to genetically engineer new varieties of tobacco with double the typical levels of nicotine. Industry blending handbooks described how chemical additives, such as ammonia, could be used to "liberate free nicotine" from the blend, with associated increases, according to smokers, in "impact" and "satisfaction."

The specific policies that Kessler proposed centered on preventing children from becoming addicted. Noting that over 80 percent of smokers begin regular use before they turned eighteen, Kessler reasoned that the most effective approach to this "pediatric disease" would be interventions to assure that children never smoke. His rules prohibited sales to anyone under eighteen years of age, required retailers to check for identification, and banned vending machines, which had been shown to be a major vehicle for underage smokers to obtain cigarettes. The rules also forbade free samples and "kiddie packs" of small numbers of cigarettes. Recognizing the importance of advertising, Kessler called for restrictions on promotional items pitched at kids, restrictions on billboard placement near schools and playgrounds, and text-only, black-and-white tobacco advertisements. These rules would eliminate Joe Camel. Finally, the rules called for a major national educational program directed at youth. Research had shown that although children understood that cigarettes are addictive, they tended to discount the idea that they themselves were vulnerable to the addiction. "This new FDA regulation presents a historical opportunity," the commissioner concluded, "giving the United States a chance to reduce the consumption of a product that kills more Americans each year than die from any other preventable cause. The approach is focused in the right place: sparing children and adolescents a lifetime of addiction to tobacco." [104]

§

Kessler, with the aid of Vice President Al Gore, persuaded President Clinton to back the initiative. During the 1996 presidential race, the tobacco issue had worked to Clinton's benefit.[105] Republican presidential nominee Robert Dole told reporters, "To some people, smoking is addictive; to others, they can take it or leave it." On NBC's *Today Show,* he told Katie Couric, "There is a mixed view among scientists and doctors about whether it is addictive or not. I'm not certain it's addictive." Dole went on to dig an even deeper hole for himself by saying, "We know it's not good for kids. But a lot of things aren't good . . . some would say milk's not good." Although Dole told Couric that "I haven't any idea whether I've had money directed to my campaign by tobacco companies. I'm not in their pocket," reporters quickly revealed that Dole had taken $477,000 in tobacco industry contributions and flown on its corporate jets thirty-eight times. Former Surgeon General Koop commented that Dole was "either exposed by his abysmal lack of knowledge of nicotine addiction or his blind support of the tobacco industry."[106]

The episode was kept alive in the media by a heckler in a cigarette costume, dubbed Buttman, who began to appear at all of Dole's scheduled appearances. The Dole tobacco statements exacerbated the underlying perceptions about Dole's advanced age and his ties to special interests. Clinton's campaign, exacting their advantage, aired spots showing young kids lighting up. "One will die from the habit," noted the narrator. "Bob Dole or Bill Clinton—who is really protecting our children?" Although Clinton had initially been cautious about supporting Kessler's initiative, fearing that it might alienate voters in tobacco-growing states, ultimately the issue—with Dole's help—played into his hands.

The emergence of tobacco in a presidential campaign was yet another indicator of the cigarette's dramatic fall from favor. Association with the tobacco companies and their best-known product were now a liability for a politician. The traditional arguments of freedom of choice, assumption of risk, and scientific uncertainty had begun to collapse under the weight of successive public revelations. The industry and its supporters had been delegitimated in the culture *and* the polity.

§

The regulations issued by the FDA would not go unchallenged. The tobacco industry, built on youth, unfettered promotion, and nicotine, had successfully resisted regulation for a century. From a federal perspective, four decades after the critical studies linking cigarettes to lung cancer, tobacco was all but unregulated. Now, the FDA rules threatened the very fundamentals of the industry's historic ability to promote and sustain the use of cigarettes in American society.

As soon as the FDA issued its rules on tobacco, the industry sued in North Carolina district court, claiming that the FDA did not have jurisdiction over tobacco. Only Congress, the companies argued, had the authority to regulate tobacco. Moreover, they contended that cigarettes did not meet the criteria of either a drug or a drug-delivery device. Since tobacco products were not intended or promoted to affect the function or structure of the body, according to the industry, they could not be regulated on those grounds.

In April 1997, Judge William L. Osteen, Sr., who had grown up on a tobacco farm and had been appointed to the court by President George Bush, ruled that the FDA could in fact "impose access restrictions and labeling requirements." He also asserted, however, that the agency did not have the authority to limit advertising to youth. The decision was immediately appealed by both sides to the U.S. Circuit Court of Appeals for the Fourth Circuit, which heard the case in August 1997. Before a decision could be issued, however, one of three judges on the panel died. As a result, it was reargued in June 1998, and by a 2–1 decision, the FDA rules were struck down. The case then moved to the Supreme Court, where it was heard in December 1999.

The Supreme Court proceedings were largely shaped by the historical idiosyncrasies of the cigarette and its regulatory history. Cigarettes did not fit the therapeutic focus of traditional FDA regulation. Justice Sandra Day O'Connor asked Solicitor General Seth Waxman, "Is it the position of the government that the use of tobacco is safe and effective?" Richard Cooper, a former FDA general counsel who represented the industry, went on to argue that the FDA could not assert regulatory authority over a product "if it doesn't purport to have a health benefit."[107] Cooper called the FDA's assertion of jurisdiction over tobacco "lawless." The FDA had never asserted this authority in the past, he pointed out, and Congress had never given it.

In March 2000, the Supreme Court issued its decision, ruling by a 5–4 margin that the FDA did not have jurisdiction to regulate tobacco. The majority opinion, written by O'Connor and joined by Justices Rehnquist, Scalia, Kennedy, and Thomas, noted that Congress had enacted six statutes regulating tobacco and that it had on several occasions considered and rejected legislation that would have explicitly given the FDA authority over cigarettes. Even as the court directly conceded the powerful public health effects of tobacco products, it nonetheless concluded that only Congress could establish jurisdiction. The decision took what O'Connor called a "holistic" approach to discerning congressional intent, broadly assessing the entire history and purpose of federal tobacco legislation rather than making a close reading of the FDA's definitional claims to authority.[108] The majority noted, somewhat ironically, that "Congress' actions in this area have evidenced a clear intent to preclude a meaningful policy-making role for any administrative agency." This had been precisely the quandary confronted by the FDA. "It is evident that Congress has ratified the FDA's previous, long-held position that it lacks jurisdiction to regulate tobacco products as customarily marketed," the decision concluded. Finally, the Court expressed concern that a finding of FDA jurisdiction would also give it the discretion to ban cigarettes entirely, a move of radical impact and significance.

Justice Breyer, joined by Stevens, Souter, and Ginsburg, argued in dissent that tobacco did fit within the statutory language of the Food, Drug, and Cosmetic Act "read literally." "Second, the statute's basic purpose—the protection of public health—supports the inclusion of cigarettes within its scope." "Unregulated tobacco use," Breyer went on, "causes more than 400,000 people to die each year from tobacco-related illnesses, such as cancer, respiratory illnesses and heart disease. Indeed, tobacco products kill more people in this country every year than AIDS, car accidents, alcohol, homicides, illegal drugs, suicides, and fires, combined." According to the dissent, the "majority's conclusion is counter-intuitive."[109]

It was a striking defeat. Kessler had come within a single vote of achieving the most dramatic public health intervention in the history of the cigarette, yet from a regulatory perspective, the FDA and the federal government remained at square one. Kessler had made a strategic decision to assert jurisdiction—something none of his predecessors had even considered—without any additional legislative authority. He assumed on the basis of critical legal readings of his mandate that the authority was already his. Moreover, he surely realized that following the Republican takeover of the Congress in 1994, no comprehensive new legislation would pass. Nowhere was the political shift in Congress more immediately evident than in the change of command in the House Subcommittee on Health and the Environment, where the chair passed from Henry Waxman to Virginia Republican Thomas Bliley, one of the tobacco companies' most reliable supporters. Newt Gingrich, the architect of the Congressional Republicans' "Contract for America," had called Kessler a "bully" and a "thug."[110]

Following the Court's decision, President Clinton, who had backed Kessler's initiative, urged Congress to support FDA regulation of tobacco. But with a Republican Congress and a strong antiregulatory environment, there was no reason to expect any forward movement. Some 80 percent of political funding from the tobacco industry was routed to Republican candidates.[111] Waxman filed a bill to give the FDA the requested authority, but it never came to a vote. The Republicans "love the tobacco companies," Waxman explained.[112] Republican Congressman J. C. Watts countered that the FDA should be busy enough without adding tobacco regulation to its plate. "The FDA is supposed to be aiding the development and implementation of vaccines and life-saving medicines" Watts noted. "Do we still have diseases that need cures? The FDA seems to be interested in doing everything except what they are responsible for."[113]

No doubt Kessler's tobacco initiative helped expand public knowledge of cigarette production, addiction, and harm. In this instance, as in most of the failed attempts to bring tobacco to heel, whatever social benefits had accrued came from the process rather than the outcome. Kessler, Waxman, the investigative journalists, and the band of whistle-blowers had failed to attain regulatory authority over the tobacco industry. But they had dramatically reframed the essential social and cultural questions of tobacco use. Moreover, they had illuminated the fundamental moral questions underlying the production and promotion of tobacco products. The antitobacco forces—armed with remarkable new ammunition supplied by tobacco company informants—would now return to the arena of liability litigation.

§

The tobacco executives' explicit, on-record, under-oath denials of any knowledge of harm or addictiveness stood in sharp relief to growing mountains of documents. For years, the industry had defended itself by clinging to notions of scientific uncertainty and the voluntary assumption of "alleged" risks. Even after these positions had been clearly identified as self-interested and evasive, they left the industry in a plausible, if marginal, space to continue to aggressively market and promote its product while fending off liability attacks. Now, with the dramatic revelations contained in the documents and the former scientists' and executives' public statements, the fiction that this was an industry acting legitimately to produce a legitimate product grew ever harder to maintain. Industry spokespersons and other supporters of tobacco were always quick to remind the public that the cigarette was a legal product. But from a social and cultural perspective, the makers of that product had come under the kind of legal and moral scrutiny that they had scrupulously avoided for four decades. As the social and political status of the industry deteriorated, a number of institutions took actions to reduce the influence of the companies. Some universities, pension funds, and state governments divested their holdings in tobacco stocks. And a number of universities developed new policies to ban the acceptance of tobacco research funding—acknowledgment that the industry had historically used such grants to gain status and legitimacy, while distorting scientific process.[114]

With the closeted world of tobacco production, research, and promotion opened up for review, essential moral questions about the industry and its executives came to the fore. Journalists and others began to explicitly ask, "How do they live with themselves?" Roger Rosenblatt posed precisely this question to a group of top executives at Philip Morris in early 1994.[115] The company leaders insisted that they were trying to do the right thing and that they felt a deep moral and social responsibility about their business and the effects of cigarette smoking. They were personally hurt by the attacks being leveled against them. "Anybody would feel hurt if somebody says you are a merchant of death and you shouldn't be able to look yourself in the mirror in the morning," said Philip Morris Senior Vice President Steven C. Parrish. "I wish they wouldn't say things like that." The executives who spoke with Rosenblatt relied principally on the industry's traditional defenses: we produce a legal product; everyone is aware that it may be risky; we don't promote smoking to children; there are many risks in the world; freedom of choice is a fundamental social and political value; we make important contributions to the economy and the social good. Parrish told Rosenblatt, "I feel good about what I do, both in how I go about my job and what my role in the company is, so I try not to let it bother me."[116] The corporate culture of Big Tobacco had created a set of powerful rationalizations for denying the harms produced by tobacco and sustaining the financial success of the industry. These were essential psychological protections for those who worked in the industry.

Rosenblatt concluded that the executives who spoke with him were sincere in their convictions. They had a positive moral image of themselves. As Rosenblatt explained, "I felt the presence of the company within the person. In the end, I felt that I was speaking with more company than person, or perhaps to a person who could no longer distinguish the two. In this situation, in which the company has effectively absorbed its employees in its moral universe, the more responsible employees are the company and thus are to blame."[117] Many within the industry expressed moral indignation at what they saw as unrelenting and unjust attacks. This may help to explain why the Wigands and Farones were so rare.

The moral question that had by this time emerged so clearly was greeted by two opposing cultural reactions: outrage and cynicism. On the one hand, the tobacco executives' hypocrisy in claiming that they did not believe smoking is addictive was trumpeted in the press as one more example of powerful corporate interests disregarding the public well-being. Waxman's triumph had been in publicly eliciting self-interested pronouncements that so clearly contradicted both science and common sense. On the other hand, a certain world-weary cynicism in the face of scandal had become commonplace in American culture. Self-interest and deceit in the exercise of power were, after all, not so new. After Watergate, Vietnam, and a range of other personal and political scandals, morally tormented whistleblowers and revelations from secret documents had a familiar sound. The widely documented decline in public trust in institutions, from the presidency to the corporation, offered a corrosive climate for accusations and exposé. Increasingly, accusations that the tobacco companies had lied were greeted with cynical anticipation: well, of course they lied.

To watch someone that you love very much die a slow miserable death, suffocating day by day, is a very unpleasant thing. And to know exactly what caused it. And then when you hear the denials of the cigarette companies that they had never caused the illness of death of a single American citizen, having sat there and watched my mother suffocating. Having the doctors tell me and describe for me exactly what caused it. How it caused it and what it was doing to her.

It makes you very angry. At least it made me very angry. And when I get angry, I try to get even, if it is legitimate to do so.[1]

RON MOTLEY, 1998

In retrospect, you know it's easier to say this now than maybe in 1994 but, in retrospect, it was the—the biggest challenge, the biggest legal challenge in history. . . . Nobody has ever beaten the tobacco industry before. We felt like we had a chance. We also knew if we won, we might just do more good than any lawyer had ever done in history. Might save more lives than most doctors have ever saved in history. So I mean, why not do that? Why not be a part of that? And as the movement grew through the years I became more and more convinced we were going to be successful.[2]

MIKE MOORE, 1998

Their dream became unconditional surrender by the enemy, with huge reparations—or nothing. It was a case of retributive justice run amok. And, irony of ironies, the cunning, monolithic enemy was able to claim itself victimized by a cadre of unforgiving control freaks and health fascists.[3]

RICHARD KLUGER, CA. 2001

CHAPTER 12

The Trials of Big Tobacco

NORMA BROIN WAS LOOKING for a lawyer. Broin had served as a flight attendant for American Airlines for fifteen years. A thirty-six-year-old mother of two and a devout Mormon, she had never smoked a cigarette, but in 1989 she was diagnosed with lung cancer and had to have part of her lung surgically removed. She attributed the cancer to her many hours of flying in smoke-filled airline cabins. Armed with substantial new data on the risks of secondhand smoke as well as specific studies demonstrating the occupational risk to flight attendants, she decided to sue. Lawyers later described her as "the perfect plaintiff."[4]

Broin contacted Patty Young, an activist flight attendant known worldwide in the profession for insisting on the need for protection from exposure to cigarette smoke on flights. With Young's help, Broin was eventually referred to Miami attorney Stanley Rosenblatt, who agreed to take the case.[5] Rosenblatt had never tried a tobacco case. He had, however, successfully defended physician Peter Rosier, who had committed a mercy killing of his wife, who was dying of lung cancer.[6] Rosenblatt was well-versed in the nature of tobacco-related disease and death.[7] When he filed *Broin v. Philip Morris*, friends and colleagues told him he was "out of his mind."[8] It was a class action suit seeking some $5 billion on behalf of 60,000 flight attendants who suffered illnesses caused by occupational exposure to secondhand smoke.

The *Broin* case offered two critical innovations in the ongoing efforts to seek legal redress from Big Tobacco. First, because the case involved nonsmoking flight attendants, it disrupted the traditional industry defense of knowledgeable assumption of risk. As Marc Edell had discovered, the notion of individual responsibility for the decision to smoke was an almost impossible legal hurdle. But the *Broin* case could not be defended on the traditional grounds of plaintiffs being aware of the risks: as Columbia University Law School Professor John Coffee noted, "There is no reason for the jury to agree that these flight attendants assented to whatever risks tobacco posed."[9] Second, by consolidating claims in a class-action litigation, Rosenblatt raised the stakes significantly. Class-action cases dramatically increased the potential rewards for plaintiffs' attorneys and would eventually attract new talent and resources to tobacco litigation. Such litigation would evolve from a mechanism for compensating victims into a critical tool for social policy. If regulation could not be achieved through legislation, perhaps it could be driven by a group of lawyers seeking social justice, public health, and unprecedented paydays.

David Kessler's failed effort to bring tobacco under the FDA's jurisdiction powerfully demonstrated the difficulty of limiting the promotion and sale of cigarettes at the end of the twentieth century. Despite the decline in public acceptance of cigarettes, despite the emergence of internal documents demonstrating industry knowledge and manipulation of the product's addictive quality, and despite the growing recognition—personified in the Joe Camel campaign—that cigarettes were deliberately targeted to children, the industry remained all but unregulated. The industry had brilliantly managed the two major federal "regulations"—package labeling and the advertising ban—to protect its interests. Despite its monumental problems, Big Tobacco had been remarkably effective in resisting serious public health initiatives.

We now know a good deal about how this goal was achieved: a careful mixture of reassurance, half-truths, innovative public relations, disinformation, and deception. The industry had expended unprecedented resources on political lobbying to secure its interests in legislation. Many liked to point out that cigarettes—had they been invented in the second half of the twentieth century—could never be introduced as a consumer product because of any number of government regulations. But since it had eluded these regulatory regimes as they were created, the cigarette was grandfathered to a unique status in American consumer culture.

Litigation, however, remained the industry's great vulnerability. Following the *Cipollone* verdict and the failure to secure a payout from the tobacco industry in similar suits, the plaintiffs' bar viewed tobacco liability litigation with considerable skepticism. The industry went to great lengths to ensure that the costs of such suits did not justify the substantial—even overwhelming—financial risks. Nonetheless, given the potential payoff and the public's growing indignation against corporate malfeasance, some attorneys sought a chance at the elusive gold ring.

§

Before his death in 1987, Nathan Horton, an African-American carpenter in Holmes Country, Mississippi, decided to sue the American Tobacco Company. Horton had started smoking as a child and was a committed Pall Mall smoker throughout high school. Once he joined the Navy, in 1955, and could buy discounted cigarettes at the military exchange, he quickly became a two-pack-a-day smoker and remained so until he was diagnosed with lung cancer in 1986. On Horton's behalf, Don Barrett, a local personal injury attorney (who would later become involved in helping the Brown & Williamson whistle-blower Merrell Williams), sought compensatory and punitive damages from American Tobacco for more than $10 million, claiming breach of warranty as well as "grossly negligent conduct." In its basic structure and arguments, *Horton v. American Tobacco* was much like *Cipollone*. So too was the defense, which relied on assumption of risk while denying that cigarettes had been proven harmful. The *Horton* case ended in a mistrial; the jury deadlocked. Following the trial, Barrett would accuse the defendants of jury tampering, but the charges were never proven. On retrial in Oxford, Mississippi, in 1990, the jury found liability on the part of American Tobacco but awarded no damages. The single big victory repeatedly predicted by activist law professor Richard Daynard had once again failed to materialize. Barrett would try again, this time with a client, Anderson Smith, who had died in 1986 of cancer and emphysema, after spending most of his life in a mental hospital. No jury, reasoned Barrett, would find Smith blameworthy. Barrett received assistance from Richard Scruggs, his local colleague, who was then best known for asbestos litigation but would soon also become involved with Williams. Smith's case, known as *Wilks*, was Scruggs's first exposure to tobacco litigation. Despite an impassioned closing argument from Barrett, the jury would find in favor of American Tobacco after just two hours' deliberation.[10] Barrett and the other plaintiffs' attorneys began to rethink their basic strategy.

Beginning in the 1990s, a group of experienced tort lawyers began to reexamine the potential for actions against the tobacco companies. Edell's success in securing incriminating internal documents through discovery in *Cipollone* had piqued the interest of trial lawyers.[11] But it had also shown the difficulty of overcoming the industry's standard defenses. These lawyers now sought strategies that would address the inherent weaknesses in cases like *Cipollone* and *Horton*.

Between 1994 and 1997, more lawsuits were filed against tobacco firms than in the previous thirty years. The nightmare of industry lawyers and their clients had come true. The irony in this new spate of gigantic and innovative suits was that the companies' longstanding strategy of denying the harms of smoking had made them increasingly vulnerable to the very suits they sought to prevent. For each year they worked to deny the dangers of their product, their legal risks grew geometrically. Tobacco liability was the ultimate self-fulfilling prophecy.[12]

§

Broin v. Philip Morris marked the first successful effort to file and bring a class-action case against a cigarette manufacturer to trial—no small feat given the defendants' "scorched earth" legal tactics.[13] Stanley Rosenblatt, a fierce litigator, and his wife Susan Rosenblatt, appellate expert and brief author, combined to take on an army of seasoned tobacco attorneys. The odds against them were daunting. Daynard would later remark that their effort "was universally viewed at the time as financial suicide."[14] Still, a class-action suit was free of certain crippling weaknesses.

Suits by individuals, like *Cipollone* and *Horton*, had failed for several reasons. First, there were the perennial problems of statistical arguments linking smoking to disease in any single person. Even if smoking increased one's *chances* of getting lung cancer, it was not difficult for the defense to find experts willing to assert their skepticism about causality in any given case. Then would come the intensive focus on the plaintiff's *decision* to smoke, and to *con-*

tinue smoking. Any case brought by a single smoker would fall before the defense argument that smoking was a deliberate action. Even as juries had little sympathy for the companies, they had next to none for smokers who willingly took up an increasingly stigmatized behavior that was known to be dangerous. But perhaps most significantly, juries resisted the notion of large awards to individual smokers. Why should Rose Cipollone's heirs win the lottery, or Nathan Horton's? Even as plaintiffs' lawyers argued that it was time for the industry to take responsibility for the massive death toll from cigarettes, jurors saw an important inequity in enriching a few individual smokers or their survivors. If pursuing the industry meant rewarding these smokers and their lawyers, the litigation movement would gather little support.[15]

Class-action litigation, in which a large number of plaintiffs would aggregate their claims, offered a response to these concerns. The history of such suits provided a more equitable solution to the problem than simply enriching a small group of plaintiffs at the companies' expense. An amendment to the Federal Rules of Procedure in 1966 permitting "common question class action" meant that in addition to traditional compensatory and punitive damages, the courts could require "injunctive relief," mandating that an industry or institution modify its practices.[16] A series of such decisions in the 1970s and 1980s—ranging from faulty medical devices like the Dalkon Shield to toxins like Agent Orange and industrial disasters like the Bhopal gas leak—served as important precedents for tobacco litigation.[17]

Mass torts offered other advantages as well. By directing the court's attention to a large class of injured smokers, such cases would reduce the focus on individual behavior and diagnosis. The "class" marked an important indicator of the social harms of tobacco. Moreover, legal teams could share the high costs of discovery, pretrial briefing, and other procedures. Their pooled resources could begin to match the highly compensated corporate firms representing the companies. Finally, in theory, class actions reduced the burdens of joining a suit for those who had possibly been injured, ensuring a more equitable distribution of the rewards. As U.S. Senior District Judge Jack B. Weinstein, who had presided over a number of historic class-action suits, would argue: "The main advantage of such mass actions—as I have observed them—is that one litigation protects the rights of many. Persons who would otherwise have claims that are too small to warrant the attention of entrepreneurial lawyers or who simply do not know that their rights have been violated can be protected."[18] Given these advantages, some eager attorneys began to envision a massive class action that would once and for all resolve both the many claims against the companies and set forth a new regime for the regulation of the tobacco industry and its dangerous product. They would achieve through the courts what the legislatures had so abysmally failed to accomplish.[19]

§

In 1992, as the Rosenblatts prepared the *Broin* class action, the EPA released its report declaring secondhand smoke a human carcinogen. Nonetheless, the industry would argue—as it had done for more than a decade—that these assessments were based on "junk science." It would take six years of arduous legal wrangling to get *Broin v. Philip Morris* to trial. The case was originally dismissed by the trial judge, but this decision was reversed by the state's Third District Court of Appeal, which sent the case back to the district court in Dade County, where it had originated. The case was eventually tried over five months in 1997—by which time the industry strategy of denial of harms was in tatters. The old arguments of "not proven," calls for more research, and repeated assertions of skepticism were not only out of touch with scientific and cultural realities but, by this time, without moral credibility. In a series of depositions with industry CEOs, Rosenblatt elicited a remarkable array of industry dissembling.[20]

William Campbell, president and CEO of Philip Morris:

Have Surgeon Generals of the United States concluded that cigarette
  smoking causes cancer?
  A. Yes.

Why don't you accept their conclusions? I mean, you don't have a scientific background, so what I want to know is, what information do you
  have, what literature have you received, or in-house memos, that cause
  you to conclude they are wrong?
  A. I have not concluded they are wrong. I said that it has not been proven.

Andrew H. Tisch, chairman and CEO, Lorillard Tobacco Company:

As far as you're concerned, Mr. Tisch, as the chairman and chief executive officer of Lorillard, this warning on the package which says that smoking causes lung cancer, heart disease and emphysema is inaccurate? You don't believe it's true?
A. That's correct.

Because if you believed it were true, in good conscience you wouldn't sell this to Americans, would you, or foreigners for that matter?
A. That's correct.

Would you prefer that your children not smoke at 18 than that they smoke, or are you entirely neutral on that subject?
A. I would prefer that they not smoke.

Bennett LeBow, CEO, the Liggett Group:

If there was not this lawsuit, and if—if—you know, you and I were friends, and we were just talking, and I said, you know, "You're in this business, and I'm very anti-smoking. I can get together for you, any time you ask, 20 leading authorities in the world on the issue of whether or not cigarette smoke causes lung cancer, heart disease, emphysema and other diseases, and you can have as long as you want to question them because I would really like you to be convinced that cigarettes are dangerous, would you avail yourself of that opportunity?
A. No.

Why not?
A. I have no interest.

You never read a Surgeon General's report dealing with the issue of smoking and health, correct?
A. No, correct.

If I mention to you a report that got a lot of attention, of the Environmental Protection Agency, relating to smoke and health, does that ring a bell to you?

A. I read something about it in the newspapers, yes.

Do you remember even generally what you read?
A. There was some claim about second-hand smoke, you know, causing various diseases.

All right.
A. That was the claim.

You never read it?
A. Never read it.

And I assume you don't have any knowledge on the subject.
A. I have no knowledge.

No knowledge?
A. No.

And basically, no interest in acquiring any knowledge?
A. That is correct.

As I understand your position, generally, that kind of issue is somebody else's battle, and you're going to do your thing, as long as it is legal to do it.
A. That is correct.

And make as much money as you can while you're doing it?
A. I'm a businessman.

On the issue of nicotine addiction, James Morgan, president of Philip Morris, said, "I want Gummi Bears. I like Gummi Bears and I eat Gummi Bears, I don't like it when I don't eat my Gummi Bears, but I'm not addicted to them." According to Andrew Schindler, CEO of R.J. Reynolds, cigarettes were "no more addictive than carrots." "Carrot addiction?" asked Rosenblatt. "Yes," responded Schindler. "There's British research on carrots."[21]

But as the trial proceeded, the CEOs began to subtly shift their position and concede—for the first time—that, in fact, cigarettes *might* pose risks. Smoking "might be" harmful: "My view is that cigarette smoking is a risk factor for those diseases and it may cause those diseases. I do not know if it does or doesn't, in that sense. I believe that maybe it's a risk factor," said Schindler. James Morgan said cigarette smoking "may possibly cause cancer."[22] But the companies still insisted that this connection was unproven and debatable.

Before the defense had completed presenting its case in October 1997, a settlement was reached. The industry agreed to pay $300 million to establish a research institute "to sponsor scientific and medical research for the early detection, prevention, treatment and cure of diseases and medical conditions caused from exposure to tobacco smoke."[23] Individual flight attendants' cases against the tobacco companies were permitted to proceed under a streamlined approach in which attendants with certain diseases known to be associated with exposure, such as lung cancer and chronic emphysema, were not required to demonstrate the causal relationship at trial. *Broin* marked the first time the industry had ever settled a case.[24]

§

As *Broin* moved forward, other attorneys were plotting new strategies for a legal assault on the tobacco industry. In late 1994, Don Barrett was among a prominent group of plaintiffs' attorneys gathered in New Orleans at the invitation of Wendell Gauthier, a prominent local lawyer. With the Kessler initiative heating up and new secret documents flooding in, the time now seemed right for a massive legal attack. The gathering included such tort luminaries as Melvin Belli (who had first sued Big Tobacco in the 1950s); John Coale, known for his work on the Bhopal class action; and Ron Motley, the legal nemesis of the asbestos industry.

Nearly everyone present had a friend or acquaintance, a relative or a loved one, who had succumbed to a smoking-related death. Gauthier had conceived the idea of a massive national class-action suit on behalf of addicted smokers after his close friend and legal associate Peter Castano had died of lung cancer at the age of forty-seven in 1993.[25] Ron Motley's mother had recently died of emphysema—a long and painful death. The group not only understood the *cause* of such deaths, they possessed a powerful sense of indignation against the companies—and the desire and the wherewithal to act on this anger. The epidemiology of smoking mortality had fueled a populist plaintiffs' bar, eager to engage in courtroom combat with the attorneys of Big Tobacco.[26]

Following the *Day One* broadcast and Kessler's nicotine initiative, Gauthier decided he now had an argument to derail the traditional assumption of risk defense offered up by the companies. In a case called *Castano v. American Tobacco,* he sought to represent some 45 million American smokers, claiming that the companies had knowingly and intentionally addicted them to nicotine. A class-action suit of this grandiose dimension would require the collaborative effort of a committed—and well-heeled—group of lawyers. Gauthier successfully recruited some sixty firms, each of which put $100,000 toward the effort.

§

When this elite subset of the plaintiffs' bar came to tobacco, they had a powerful model in their successful litigation in the 1970s and 1980s against major asbestos producers, which ultimately drove those companies into bankruptcy. This litigation offered a training ground for going after tobacco. Critical questions in these cases centered on what the asbestos manufacturers knew and when they knew it, as well as the development of medical consensus regarding the harms of asbestos. The companies would contend that they had no way of knowing that asbestos installers and others exposed to their product were at risk.[27] To rebut such claims, the plaintiffs' lawyers became expert in conducting discovery and recruiting and preparing expert witnesses.

Tirelessly inventive in his pursuit of industry documents and medical records, Ron Motley of Charleston, South Carolina, acquired a "virtual landslide" of incriminating materials that became the foundation for his assault on the asbestos industry.[28] Motley eventually came into possession, through discovery, of a 1947 report by W. C. L. Hemeon, the head engineer of the Industrial Hygiene Foundation of America. Hemeon reported that 20 percent of the workforce at two major facilities had developed asbestosis, and warned that current safety standards regarding asbestos dust would not adequately protect workers. The document all but destroyed the industry's "we could not have known" defense. Motley said of the document, "It's not just a smoking gun; it's a stick of dynamite with a burning fuse."[29] Through these litigations, Motley became impressively familiar with respiratory disease as well as the industry strategy of attributing disease to tobacco use rather than occupational exposure to asbestos.

Motley and Richard Scruggs had both enjoyed a series of remarkable and lucrative victories against asbestos manufacturers and users in the early 1980s. They had collaborated in 1993 in trying a major suit that consolidated some seven thousand individual asbestos cases. Ultimately, after hundreds of cases, with thousands of additional claims pending, Johns-Manville and other manufacturers were forced to declare bankruptcy. The courts established a compensation fund for victims. Motley's and Scruggs's asbestos work not only confirmed their strategy, it provided the critical financial resources they would need for a massive legal strike against tobacco.[30]

§

While *Castano* was failing to achieve certification as a class in several venues, Stanley and Susan Rosenblatt, lawyers for the *Broin* case, pushed yet another major class action up the legal mountain. They filed a suit, *Engle v. R.J. Reynolds,* on behalf of addicted smokers across the nation. The Third Circuit Court of Appeals, however, limited the suit to Florida smokers. Eventually, it was estimated that the class might include as many as seven hundred thousand sick Florida smokers and their heirs. The judge in the case, Robert Kaye, who had also presided over *Broin,* decided that the massive action should be tried in three phases.

The first phase centered on whether the companies were responsible for tobacco-related diseases. In July 1999, the jurors returned a verdict on this question, concluding that the companies were liable for making a defective product causing lung cancer, emphysema, and other serious illnesses; that the companies had committed fraud, misrepresentation, and breach of expressed and implied warranties; and that they were liable for punitive damages.[31] At trial, the industry had insisted that there was still no scientific proof of smoking's relationship to these diseases, and that smokers were fully aware of the potential risks. But the tension between these two arguments could no longer be sustained. Moreover, in a class-action litigation like this one, it was far more difficult for the industry to shift the focus to the decisions of an individual smoker. Rosenblatt's arguments were simple and brutally direct: the companies produce a deadly and addictive product, and they have misrepresented its risks—which they well understood—to their customers.

The second phase of the trial centered on the compensatory damages to the three "representatives" of the class: Mary Farnan, Frank Amodeo, and Angie Della Vecchia, each of whom had developed smoking-related cancers. Using principles of comparative fault, the jury determined their total damages to be nearly $13 million. Finally, in phase three, the jury heard evidence for punitive damages, ultimately awarding the class just under $145 billion, the largest such award in legal history.[32] (The companies would appeal all three verdicts.) The *Engle* trial went on for two years, making it the longest trial in the history of civil litigation. It would be the first class action against the tobacco industry to go to verdict. According to Rosenblatt, the jury "got the big picture. . . . They got the history of this industry, and they said to the American people, 'We see through these people. They're liars. They do terrible things.'"[33] Claiming that a massive verdict might bankrupt the companies, which would be required to post bond during appeal, the industry successfully lobbied the Florida state legislature to cap appeal bonds at $100 million per defendant.[34] Ultimately, in July 2006, the Florida Supreme Court would overturn the massive punitive damages award and decertify the class. At the same time, however, the court upheld the jury's findings in Phase I, clearing the way for new individual suits in which plaintiffs would not need to demonstrate that cigarettes are defective, unreasonably dangerous, addictive, and the cause of many deadly diseases. The court argued *"res judicata"*: these issues have been judged.[35]

§

As the Rosenblatts worked away in isolation, a group of trial lawyers began to explore other, novel approaches to a mass litigation against the companies. The plan to seek recovery of state Medicaid costs for smoking-related diseases was hatched in Mississippi. The idea first occurred to attorney Mike Lewis after he visited Jackie Thompson, his secretary's mother, who was dying of lung cancer at age forty-nine at Baptist Central Hospital in Memphis, Tennessee. During her long illness, which included a heart attack and triple bypass surgery, Thompson's insurance had run out, and she ended up on Medicaid; her medical costs soon exceeded $1 million. On the way back to his office in Clarksdale, Mississippi, Lewis developed the scheme of states suing the tobacco companies for their costs in caring for patients like Thompson. He decided to try this idea out on his law school friend, Attorney General Michael Moore. Moore was interested and urged Lewis to consult another former classmate, Richard Scruggs, who was at the time assisting Don Barrett in *Wilks*. With Moore's support, Lewis recruited Scruggs and Barrett to this new approach.[36]

The concept of the Mississippi legal action brought tobacco litigation to bear on what was by then a well-known problem: the growing expenses associated with smoking-related diseases. In the aftermath of the first surgeon general's report, it had become possible to assess not only the prevalence of tobacco-caused diseases, but their costs. The introduction in 1965 of Medicare and Medicaid meant that a significant portion of these costs was borne by the federal and state governments. By 1990, estimates of the price tag for smoking-related diseases approached $2 billion annually.[37] Moore and Lewis soon calculated that tobacco use resulted in $70 to $100 million a year in Medicaid costs in Mississippi alone.[38] In the summer of 1993, Moore, together with Lewis, Scruggs, Barrett, and Ron Motley, began to explore the possibility of a state suit against tobacco. Mississippi's claims would center on the notion of indemnity: the costs of treating smokers should be shifted from the state to the companies.

There was no question that the legal assault on Big Tobacco carried a huge financial risk.[39] Moore, Scruggs, Barrett, and Motley carefully fashioned an agreement about how they would divide the costs associated with bringing the suit (as well as the fees, should they win). Scruggs was in for 25 percent; Motley 22.5; Barrett and Lewis would each put up 10 percent; and other firms ultimately put up the rest. They agreed to work without a contingency contract to avoid criticism from state legislators. Moore would ask the court for attorneys' fees only if the state won the case. Originally they estimated that bringing the suit would cost more than $5 million; ultimately, their expenses would approach three times that.[40]

On May 23, 1994, after a year of planning, Moore filed suit against the major tobacco companies, their wholesalers, trade associations, and public relations firms on behalf of the state of Mississippi. At a press conference, he explained, "This lawsuit is premised on a simple notion: You caused the health crisis, you pay for it. The free ride is over. It's time these billionaire tobacco companies start paying what they rightfully owe to the Mississippi taxpayers." The state suit steered clear of the principal pitfall of the individual suits. The plaintiffs wronged by the industry's actions were the taxpayers, not smokers seeking to "blame" the companies for their own demise. As Barrett exclaimed, "The State of Mississippi has never smoked a cigarette."[41] Barrett's frustrations following the *Horton* and *Wilks* cases made him especially enthusiastic about the Medicaid suit. In an individual case, the companies could always raise questions about specific causality. But a suit to recover medical costs across an entire state made population-based data more relevant.

The Mississippi team consulted widely within academic law and the plaintiffs' bar. Harvard Law Professor Laurence Tribe, who had argued *Cipollone* before the U.S. Supreme Court, agreed to assist them pro bono.[42] In addition to the idea of indemnification, the Mississippi team added the notion of tobacco as a "public nuisance."[43] According to this legal theory, the industry could be held accountable for "the economic by-products of its enterprise."[44] Just like an industrial polluter, the tobacco companies should be responsible for cleaning up their mess. Additionally, the state would seek injunctive relief through prevention programs to protect young people from becoming smokers. Using so-called equitable theories of recovery, the state sought restitution by arguing that its costs for treating tobacco-related diseases constituted the "unjust enrichment" of the companies. In a shrewd maneuver, Moore and Scruggs decided to file the case in chancery court, where it would be heard by a single judge rather than a jury.[45]

Governor Kirk Fordice, a Republican whose reelection had been generously supported by the tobacco industry, actively sought to derail the case. In 1996, he filed a petition with the Mississippi Supreme Court arguing that the attorney general, as the governor's lawyer, could not bring such a suit without his explicit authorization. Further, Fordice claimed that since the Medicaid program was under his authority, such a suit was unlawful without his support. The court eventually refused to adjudicate this dispute, and the case proceeded toward trial.[46]

The industry greeted the Mississippi suit with a mixture of alarm and contempt. Clearly, the suit was based on innovative and untried legal theory; at the same time, the state had actively participated in the sale of cigarettes through licensing and taxation, and had benefited from these revenues. On what grounds could it now seek restitution? Moreover, the industry would assert that it was inappropriate for the state to seek to avoid the clearly defined criteria of product liability. The industry petitioned to turn the Medicaid case into a "subrogation action" in which each Medicaid recipient would be independently assessed for diagnosis, cause of disease, and costs. It sought, in other words, to return to the arena of individual plaintiffs claims, which it could subject to the traditional defense. Scruggs responded, "There are not enough courts, judges, juries, or lawyers in the state of Mississippi—probably in the United States—to conduct" the thousands of trials needed. "If you send us to Circuit Court for individual trials and force the State to stand in the shoes of the smoker, you are saying we have no remedy at all for the health care costs that this enterprise has inflicted on the State of Mississippi."[47] Throughout the trial, the industry's legal team pursued the traditional strategies of defending an individual tort case. The Mississippi state team, by contrast, had worked meticulously to demonstrate that the legal issues and theories of their case were decidedly different.[48]

§

Moore and Scruggs understood that recruiting other states—if possible, all the states—to file similar suits against the companies would radically augment their advantage, even if local conditions and state law did not favor success in a particular state. Backed by a growing coterie of seasoned tort lawyers, they lobbied their colleagues from the state attorneys general's offices to file suits as well, in an effort to turn their suit into a nationwide legal onslaught on the industry. The ambitious and charismatic Moore frequently touted the historical significance of the Mississippi case. "This is probably the most important public health litigation ever in history," he contended. "It has the potential to save more lives than anything that's ever been done."[49] Minnesota filed in August 1994, and West Virginia, Florida, and Massachusetts in 1995. For attorneys general, there was little to lose. Even if the suits were ultimately dismissed, the litigation made a strong political statement against tobacco. All the suits were filed on a contingency basis, with outside counsel—in most instances a combination of Scruggs, Motley, and local state firms—taking on the substantial financial risks; the more states filing, the greater the economies in preparing and trying the cases. Between the time that Moore filed Mississippi's case in May 1994 and the spring of 1997, more than thirty states joined the cause.[50] Attorneys general in states that had not signed on began to see that there could be significant political costs in remaining on the sidelines.[51]

Bennett LeBow, CEO of the Liggett Group, settled with five states and the *Castano* group in March 1997. LeBow was hardly a traditional tobacco executive. A leveraged buyout entrepreneur, he had no long-standing interest in tobacco; rather, he bought and sold companies. At the time, he was eager to acquire R.J. Reynolds. If Liggett were free of liability risk, the value of the company would rise; further, he hoped that any tobacco interests he might acquire would be subject to his agreement.[52] The team of Barrett, Moore, Scruggs, and Motley exacted important concessions from LeBow, who was convinced that a deal would give Liggett important advantages over its competitors. The LeBow deal was both with the *Castano* group and five of the six attorneys general who had filed state cases—Mississippi, Florida, Massachusetts, West Virginia, and Louisiana. The *Castano* action, however, would soon be decertified by the Fifth Circuit Court of Appeals, nullifying this part of the deal.[53]

Ultimately, LeBow signed a second agreement in which, in exchange for immunity from the state claims, he agreed to turn over internal documents not only from Liggett, but from joint industry ventures like the Committee of Counsel—a move the other companies would try to block. LeBow also agreed to acknowledge publicly that smoking causes cancer and is addictive. Further, he conceded that the companies had knowingly marketed to children. In terms of money and documents, the Liggett settlement proved negligible, but it broke the tight alliance the industry had maintained for nearly half a century. The so-called Gentleman's Agreement on the health issue had been irrevocably breached. LeBow explained, "They can criticize my strategy all they want, but I have a settlement and they don't." LeBow's decision marked a historic setback for the tobacco industry's legal interests.

Mississippi Attorney General Mike Moore confidently claimed, "I've been a prosecutor all my life. I know what happens when one of the five turns state's evidence. We've got the goods on 98 percent of the industry by turning the little guy."[54] Whether LeBow had achieved some moral epiphany—as he now suggested—or was simply trying to save his second-tier tobacco business (Liggett controlled just 2 percent of the U.S. market), his action forced the major tobacco producers to reevaluate their defense. In LeBow, the antitobacco forces had found the ultimate whistle-blower. What could be more impressive than a CEO offering up new documentation of illegal activities, a long-standing commitment to denial of risk; and a research program focused on understanding, maintaining, and enhancing the product's addictive properties? LeBow reveled in his new role.

§

Minnesota refused the deal. Attorney General Hubert "Skip" Humphrey III was eager to see his case litigated. Unlike the other attorneys general, who had hired the national legal teams of Scruggs and Motley, Humphrey selected the distinguished Minneapolis firm of Robins, Kaplan, Miller & Ciresi. The team was directed by seasoned trial lawyer Michael Ciresi, who had developed an impressive reputation with major victories against A. H. Robins in Dalkon Shield litigation and had little interest in the larger consortium of plaintiffs' lawyers tying together the other states' litigation. Minnesota would be the only state represented by a single firm. The state added consumer fraud to its claims and also sought recovery of BlueCross BlueShield health insurance expenditures.[55]

Ciresi's team believed that the Merrell Williams documents were but a small sampling of the industry archive. They requested an index of industry documents used in previous litigations. After repeated motions, the industry admitted such a list existed but insisted that it was privileged as attorney-client communication. Ultimately, the judge required that the list be produced. With this in hand, the Robins/Kaplan team pursued the most aggressive discovery in the history of tobacco litigation. They filed motion after motion seeking memos, reports, and letters, repeatedly challenging claims of attorney-client privilege that had protected such materials in earlier cases. Eventually, they pulled in more than 30 million pages of documents from industry files. Ciresi utilized the state's "long-arm" statute to bring British American Tobacco into the litigation. British American Tobacco, the owner of Brown & Williamson, claimed it had no activity in the

United States, but the court eventually ruled—based on extensive research by Ciresi's partner Roberta Walburn—that there were extensive connections that discovery would demonstrate.

Ciresi and Walburn offered considerable evidence of systematic destruction of documents. In one document, Thomas Osdene, Philip Morris's director of research, had written:

> Ship all documents to Cologne . . .
> Keep in Cologne
> OK to phone and telex (these will be destroyed) . . .
> We will monitor in person every 2–3 months.
> If important letters have to be sent please send to home—I will act on them and destroy.[56]

Osdene would invoke the Fifth Amendment more than one hundred times in his videotaped deposition, which was shown at the trial over the objections of industry counsel.[57]

Ultimately, Judge Kenneth J. Fitzpatrick ruled that Philip Morris had engaged "in an egregious attempt to hide information" and ordered the company to "respond to discovery requests properly."[58] In a major victory for the state, he found that lawyers had reviewed industry materials for the very purpose of claiming privilege. Four decades of legal mastery over the industry records were now unraveling. Special Master Mark W. Gehan was requested to review the documents for which the industry claimed privilege. Spot-checking hundreds of documents, he overruled these claims on the basis of what is known as the crime-fraud exception, designed "to ensure that the 'seal of secrecy' between lawyer and client does not extend to communications from the *lawyer* to the client made by the lawyer for the purpose of giving advice for the commission of a fraud or crime."[59] This ruling opened literally millions of pages of internal memoranda and correspondence to public scrutiny.[60]

It did something else as well. Gehan, in effect, charged that industry lawyers had abused the doctrine of attorney-client privilege, committing ethical and possibly criminal violations. His ruling implicated the attorneys as not "representing" the legal interests of their clients but as full-fledged participants in a decades-long conspiracy.[61] Attorney control over science—explicitly to shield research from exposure in litigation—had been widely utilized within the industry since the 1950s. As Brown & Williamson attorney J. Kendrick Wells noted in 1979, "Continued Law Department control is essential for the best argument for privilege."[62] On another occasion, Wells urged, "direct lawyer involvement is needed in all activities pertaining to smoking and health" in order to utilize attorney-client privilege.[63] The Ciresi team had argued "that counsel for the tobacco industry advised the industry to conceal documents and research harmful to the industry by depositing documents with counsel, by routing correspondence through the industry counsel, by naming damning research projects as 'special projects' purportedly ordered by counsel, etc., to cover potentially dangerous materials under a blanket of attorney-client privilege protection, and Plaintiffs wish to tear this blanket away."[64] The meticulous, time-consuming, eye-wearying process of discovery in Minnesota would—in large measure—create the massive record that is now available to the public. The Ciresi team, having built its case on discovery, left behind an unprecedented archive of the industry's internal workings.[65]

§

With the newly available documents, individual litigations gained new prospects for success. The revelations of the early 1990s had the effect of disrupting traditional views of individual responsibility. In August 1996, plaintiffs' attorney Woody Wilner broke the four-decade industry record of "never paying a penny" when his client, lung cancer victim Grady Carter, was awarded $750,000 in damages from Brown & Williamson. Carter had smoked for forty-four years before his diagnosis in 1991. Wilner had fought successfully to bring the Williams documents into the case. In addition, he had obtained a "case management order" that placed strict limits on pretrial motions used by the industry to make litigation slow and costly for the plaintiffs.[66]

Wilner would lose two cases following *Carter*, but then won again in 1998 in the case of Roland Maddox, who had died a year earlier after smoking Lucky Strikes for fifty years. The jury awarded Maddox's family $500,000 in compensatory damages and $450,000 in punitive damages. "We are disappointed that the jurors did not find that Mr. Maddox was personally responsible for the choices that he made," remarked Brown &

Williamson attorney John Nyhan.[67] A Florida appeals court would strike down the *Carter* verdict, ruling that the case had been filed six days after the expiration of the statute of limitations, but the Florida Supreme Court reinstated the judgment in November 2000. Grady Carter received $1.1 million (his award plus interest) from Brown & Williamson in 2001.[68]

In another individual smoker's case in 1999, San Francisco trial lawyer Madelyn Chaber won a $51 million verdict (reduced by the judge to $26.5 million) for Patricia Henley, who had smoked Marlboros for thirty-five years before being diagnosed with lung cancer. Chaber, like a number of other attorneys willing to take on tobacco plaintiffs, had done asbestos lit-igation. Wilner helped her move to tobacco cases by opening his files; Chaber also benefited from discovery in the state suits. "You kill for any one document like this," she said. "We had thousands."[69] In 2004, Philip Morris was ordered to pay Henley $16.7 million ($9 million punitive, $1.5 million compensatory, and $6.2 million in interest)—the first time the in-dustry had ever paid punitive damages.[70]

In 2001, a Los Angeles jury awarded Richard Boeken, a lung cancer vic-tim who had smoked two packs of Marlboros a day for more than three decades, a $3 billion award, the largest punitive damage award ever in in-dividual tobacco litigation and one of the largest jury awards in history. Al-though it was reduced on appeal to $50 million, Philip Morris turned to the U.S. Supreme Court, arguing that the Federal Cigarette Labeling and Advertising Act preempts such claims and that the award was "unconstitu-tionally excessive." The Court refused to hear the case in March 2006, leav-ing the company owing Boeken's survivors $5.4 million in compensatory damages, $50 million in punitive damages, and $26 million in interest.[71] These victories were stunning, but they never generated the snowball effect that the lawyers sought, and that the industry feared.

§

In the state cases, secret negotiations of a "global settlement agreement" between company executives and the attorneys general (all except Min-nesota's Humphrey) began in earnest in April 1997. Such "peace talks" were entirely unprecedented in the history of the tobacco wars. But with thirty state suits hanging over them and others likely, the tobacco com-panies were unusually vulnerable. Defeat in at least some of these suits seemed inevitable. With a hostile media offering new revelations and with thousands of damaging documents coming to light in court, the industry's defenses had eroded significantly. No longer could the companies claim that scientific proof of the dangers of smoking was in doubt; their own in-house studies said otherwise. And now their legal adversaries had the resources and power of the state governments backed by the most successful and aggressive attorneys in the liability field. With Liggett having settled, and its CEO having agreed to cooperate with plaintiffs, some suggested that antitobacco forces were positioned to land a disabling or even life-threatening blow. On Wall Street, investment analysts sounded new calls of caution. The liability assault—once considered the quixotic dream of Professor Daynard—substantially suppressed the value of tobacco stocks.[72]

The talks revealed a radical change in industry strategy. Following the Waxman hearings of 1994, every one of the CEOs who had denied the risks and addictiveness of cigarettes before Congress had been replaced. A new breed of CEOs, eager to move past the high pitch of passions in the tobacco wars and to relegitmate and stabilize their industry, had taken over.

While the more experienced soldiers in the tobacco wars expressed concerns about the negotiations, the attorneys general, relative newcomers to the battlefield, did not bring decades of wounds to the talks.[73] Nor, however, did they have much experience with their foe. For them, the uncertainties of the courtroom set the context for negotiations. The strength of their cases and the likelihood of success varied significantly from state to state. Few could predict with confidence what would happen before an unsympathetic judge or a jury that included smokers. They also understood that the companies would mount an aggressive defense based on the notion that the states had profited handsomely from tobacco through taxes.[74] A high-profile loss in a tobacco suit could mean political and ultimately electoral disaster for an attorney general. While antitobacco advocates were used to such defeats, the attorneys general were not. It was the essential uncertainty on both sides that brought plaintiffs and defendants together for settlement talks.

For the liability lawyers, a settlement would, by its very nature, constitute a victory. Negotiation was their métier, and they were extremely well-versed in high stakes wrangling to avoid litigating cases; a settlement was a far more efficient way to earn their contingency fees than rolling the dice in diverse and potentially hostile courtrooms. Scruggs, Motley, and the other plaintiffs' attorneys now divided up their firms' resources between preparing cases and aggressively seeking a negotiated settlement. Given the funds at stake, an unprecedented legal payday was in the offing.[75]

On June 20, 1997, Attorney General Moore, surrounded by colleagues from other states, announced with much fanfare the "global settlement" with the tobacco industry. The companies had agreed to pay $365.5 billion over the next quarter century to compensate the states for medical costs, smoking cessation programs, and other health care initiatives. The industry agreed that if youth smoking did not fall significantly, it would submit to FDA regulation of nicotine. The companies also acceded to stronger warning labels and new restrictions on advertising and promotion. In return, the industry would be freed from class-action suits and have its other litigation costs capped. Punitive damage awards for past misconduct would be banned. Moore called the agreement "the most historic public health achievement in history."[76]

The proposed settlement went far beyond the authority of those at the negotiating table; they had traded that which was not theirs to give. The Global Settlement, as they called it, would require an act of Congress; it now crossed from the realm of litigation to legislation. Although many would suggest the settlement required congressional "approval," this was a misnomer. It required a major—complex—piece of congressional legislation. At the time of Moore's announcement, this was anything but a done deal.

In the secret negotiations, the industry revealed its concept of the future of cigarette marketing. Tobacco executives apparently saw potential in the introduction of "less hazardous products" that would be subject to FDA evaluation (which might have promotional value). After years of stonewalling, they sought to find a way of admitting the risks of smoking while securing the market for a new, legitimated, and regulated product. In exchange for stronger regulation of advertising, youth sales restrictions, and other limits, the industry would be free to promote cigarettes in other, unregulated markets around the world.[77]

While awaiting congressional action on the Global Settlement, those states with pending court dates moved forward to settle their cases. Clearly, the industry did not want to try these cases at the same time as it was lobbying for a comprehensive settlement through federal legislation. On July 3, 1997, Moore announced the settlement of the Mississippi Medicaid suit days before it was to go to trial. The industry agreed to pay $3.36 billion. With this settlement, Brown & Williamson reluctantly dropped its ongoing suit against Williams and Scruggs for their respective acts of spiriting away the documents and bringing them to public scrutiny. In August, Scruggs agreed to pay Williams $1.8 million as compensation for his controversial role in "assisting" the litigation.[78] Settlements with Florida ($11.3 billion) and Texas ($15.3 billion) followed.

These agreements signaled the companies' eagerness to see through a national settlement. Further, they showed just how vulnerable the companies were to disclosures and the attendant publicity. Witness testimony and the mountains of corporate documents placed in evidence in the Minnesota trial had brought daily revelations of the companies' internal activities. After more than four months of trial, with the defense about to present its case, the companies settled for $6.1 billion, including an additional $469 million for BlueCross BlueShield. For many tobacco control advocates, giving up litigation at that point seemed like an unnecessary and potentially catastrophic concession.[79]

§

The battle over the Global Settlement fractured the public health community, a diverse collection of advocates with an eclectic range of approaches and theories regarding tobacco control. Matthew Myers, the well-known attorney and public interest lobbyist, now vice president of the National Center for Tobacco-Free Kids, was invited by the attorneys general to represent "the public health community" in the negotiations. But it quickly became apparent that there was no consensus about specific public health goals. As Myers observed, "We were a public health community—really a bundle of individuals—who never had to cope with hard, hard choices and competing values. We had all been able to operate at the level of broad rhetoric, because we had never before come close to achieving *any* of our most ambitious objectives."[80] Myers saw a remarkable opportunity to exact unprecedented concessions from the industry. But these would require compromise.

For some of the most seasoned tobacco-control advocates, the very idea of negotiating with the tobacco industry was anathema. The principle successes of tobacco control had come from the grassroots local initiatives and hand-to-hand combat. There could be no "civil discourse" with an industry they deemed not only dishonest but fundamentally immoral. If the industry sought relief from the litigation that now depressed its stock value, that was precisely the time *not* to negotiate. From this perspective, no one had the authority to make concessions on behalf of public health.[81] As Stanton Glantz would later explain, "The fundamental reality of tobacco is that the way to beat them is to beat them. I have never found a single instance anywhere, anywhere, where a compromise with the industry served the public health."[82] Glantz's perspective emphasized an "incremental radicalism," a step-by-step process to ultimately defeat the companies. Myers offered "global pragmatism," which permitted strategic concessions for ultimate gains. Their respective world views reflected critical differences in approach and strategy for public health. In Glantz's view, to give up the right of litigation, one of the antitobacco movement's few credible weapons, on the eve of a significant—perhaps knockout—victory, seemed ludicrous. The movement's more significant guerilla fighters refused to participate in a negotiated settlement.

Years of bitterness could not easily be forgotten. To sit around a table negotiating "compromises" seemed unthinkable to people who had steadfastly been committed to the destruction of antagonists whom they had come to view as fundamentally evil. Some movement leaders believed the negotiations conducted by attorneys general with little public health experience and their high-rolling trial lawyers eager to cut a deal might accomplish nothing except pull the companies back from the brink of obliteration. Their view was that anything the companies might agree to was a sham, and to negotiate with Big Tobacco was to "dance with the devil."[83] Their moral definition of tobacco control precluded pragmatic compromise. Now that the companies were in mortal danger, any agreement would be a sell-out.

Ultimately, the proposed Global Settlement Agreement brought to light an intense social and political debate about the role of litigation in the tobacco wars and in public health generally. Some advocates saw litigation as incremental, inefficient, and inappropriate. Any genuine public health policy to reduce tobacco use could only come from Congress. Others saw the history of congressional legislation as powerfully shaped, if not corrupted, by industry interests and largesse, and viewed the courts as the critical venue for public health reform.

Glantz was especially skeptical of the legal and moral appropriateness of removing a citizen's right to sue. "It will undermine the vital role of tort liability in restraining corporate wrongdoing: If tobacco companies can get away with murder, then this will set a precedent for other companies that harm people or pollute the environment to escape accountability. And it will violate basic tenets of justice . . . to sacrifice a person's right to recover damages against the tobacco industry without fair compensation." Glantz noted presciently that "the tobacco companies will simply pass these costs through to their victims, leaving management and investors untouched. . . . The likelihood that industry officials and lawyers will face criminal prosecution drops."[84] To critics, like Glantz, it appeared that just as litigation had finally emerged as a critical threat to the industry, Myers and a group of come-lately attorneys general were willing to protect the industry from what it most feared, in return for regulation that could be enacted anyway without a "settlement." Myers, said Glantz, was a "fool." "The tobacco control community now has a real opportunity to end the tobacco industry in this century. If that opportunity is lost it will be because the National Center for Tobacco-Free Kids lost it for us."[85] Myers responded, "I continue to believe that I can do more in the room than outside."[86]

Myers's role as the sole representative of "public health" in the negotiations would ultimately alienate many allies, who would be critical to the settlement's success. FDA Commissioner David Kessler, former Surgeon General C. Everett Koop, and Congressman Henry Waxman were outraged to find themselves out of the loop. In retrospect, it is impossible to disentangle their personal and political objections. But it was nonetheless clear that many in the public health "community" saw Myers as a traitor. "In negotiating with the industry," Glantz wrote, Myers "chose to ignore a consensus among public health groups not to enter a deal with the industry."[87]

The wounds opened by the proposed settlement would not soon heal. Myers was subjected to intensive and sometimes personal criticism. "I view him as a tragic figure," said Glantz. "He's spent the last 15 years working on this issue and he's going to go down in history as the guy who allows the industry to slime off the hook again."[88] The patriarch of consumer activism, Ralph Nader, opined that "the role of the National Center in the negotiations is doing serious damage to the public interest and imperiling decades of work by committed public health advocates to curb the ravages of the tobacco corporations."[89] Waxman also attacked the settlement, noting, "This is a Faustian bargain. We don't pay polluters not to pollute, and we shouldn't offer immunity and regulatory relief to get them to stop addicting our children."[90] Critics of the settlement argued that Congress did not need to grant *any* concessions in passing tough regulatory restrictions. "Why do you need a settlement? Why do you need to give the industry immunity?" asked Kessler. Nader worried about the precedent set by offering an industry relief from liability risks. The threat of litigation, he pointed out, was a powerful brake on all sorts of industry activities.[91]

Koop and Kessler, at Waxman's urging, agreed to cochair a committee to review the Global Settlement. Five days after the deal was announced, their group pronounced their opposition to the agreement in its current form. In September 1997, President Clinton, who had closely followed the negotiations through intermediaries, released a statement of five broad principles upon which to structure regulatory legislation. He read the statement at a White House ceremony attended by Koop and Kessler.[92] Clinton's principles cut a middle path between supporters of the Global Settlement Agreement and its increasingly vocal opponents. They cleverly avoided the most contentious issues, especially regarding relief from litigation. Supporters of the settlement eventually concluded that the White House had abandoned them.[93]

Kessler, who had so aggressively sought FDA jurisdiction, feared that weak FDA oversight would only relegitmate the industry after it had been marginalized and stigmatized. This was the downside of regulation: it recognized the industry as a legitimate corporate citizen.[94] Under the settlement regime, tobacco use might even increase. "Once everything is resolved," Kessler argued. "and everyone declares, 'peace now, peace forever,' everyone goes home." He had come to believe that the companies had to be fundamentally destabilized—or disbanded—for public health initiatives to succeed.[95]

§

In Congress, a bipartisan coalition of legislators began for the first time to push for serious regulation of tobacco. Now, the industry found itself on familiar ground. It had more than a half-century of experience in influencing federal regulatory initiatives and in 1995 had set a new record (since broken) by disbursing $4.1 million in congressional campaign contributions.[96] It soon unleashed a characteristically impressive lobbying engine in the halls of Congress. No expense would be spared in the attempt to shape the coming legislation. The tobacco companies signed up former Maine Senator George Mitchell to lead their lobbying efforts; he was joined by former Texas Governor Ann Richards, former Republican National Committee Chairman Haley Barbour, and former Republic Majority Leader Howard Baker.[97] Recruiting Mitchell was but one indication of the power the companies could invest in the federal legislative process. But many were aghast to see him take this role. "How can George Mitchell," asked Maureen Dowd in the *New York Times*, "be both a statesman working against death in Northern Ireland and a shill for death in America?"[98]

Under the leadership of John McCain, Republican Senator from Arizona, the attorneys general's proposed settlement underwent significant revision. The McCain bill surprised the Republican leadership in its aggressive approach to tobacco control, including higher taxes on tobacco to increase prices, FDA regulation of nicotine, and strong look-back provisions for the reduction of teen smoking. The proposed legislation raised the tobacco company penalties to be paid to the states and the federal government from the attorneys general's proposed $385 billion to over $500 billion. In return, the industry would receive relief from litigation.[99] Given the widely recognized shift in the litigation environment, such provisions were central to the industry's support of the legislation.

In April 1998, McCain's bill to codify and expand the negotiated Global Settlement Agreement was voted out of the Senate Commerce Committee for consideration by the full Senate and was immediately met by sharp attack from all sides. It drew the fire of tobacco farmers, those trial lawyers not involved in the settlement, and antitrust experts. Although Clinton claimed to support the deal, he did so at arm's length, refusing to expend much political capital to see it through.[100] Public health advocates decried the preemption of further litigation. As the public health provisions and dollar costs of the bill rose, the industry became increasingly alienated. The McCain bill was caught in the cross fire of public health advocates and industry lobbyists.

Critics of the legislation tended to focus on the provisions banning class-action suits and capping punitive damages. In the past, Congress had acted to limit liability among companies producing products in the public interest, such as vaccine manufacturers. Why, asked critics, would such unusual protections be offered to a hypocritical and socially deviant industry?[101] Other opponents of the legislation focused on what they saw as the industry's ultimate goals in seeking such protections. Glantz, for example, suggested that the "dirty little secret" of the proposed deal was that it would free U.S. tobacco companies to recoup their domestic losses abroad. Despite the name "global settlement," the deal imposed no limits on marketing outside the United States. "The real thing this deal does is clear the decks for international expansion," explained Glantz.[102] In China alone, 70 million people had started smoking since 1987; clearly, any loss in sales in the United States could be many times compensated for by recruiting new smokers in non-Western societies.[103]

Ultimately, the companies came full circle and worked to kill the legislation. Congressional Republicans, who at first had expressed provisional support, now labeled it an "$800 billion tax increase." The companies deployed unprecedented resources to bring down the legislation. In addition to devoting a record $35.5 million to lobbying in 1997, a 23 percent increase over what it spent in 1996, the companies also sponsored a massive public relations effort labeling the legislation as a new tax targeted at working people.[104] Now, the industry was back in its element, sponsoring a full-tilt media blitz to reframe the debate as being about taxes and "big government." It spent $40 million on radio and television ads over a two-month period in 1998 to recast the bill as a grab for massive new taxes.[105]

"Washington has gone cuckoo again," one ad noted, as a cuckoo clock exploded. "Washington wants to raise the price of cigarettes so high there'll be a black market in cigarettes with unregulated access to kids."[106] The media campaign provided Republicans with cover—much to McCain's chagrin—to kill the bill. Among other tactics, they loaded it up with amendments irrelevant to tobacco, and then opposed it on the ground that it was no longer a tobacco bill. The industry could no longer get whatever it wanted from Congress, but it still had the power to kill what it did not want.

For Matt Myers, this spectacle represented the wasting of an unprecedented opportunity for tobacco control. He bitterly concluded: "What we lost [in the McCain Bill] was staggering. The June 1997 settlement, as improved by Senator McCain, wouldn't have solved the problem. But it would have made a great difference. If we believed our own rhetoric over the years, this legislation would have saved tens of thousands of lives."[107] But the antitobacco movement had never considered compromise as an element in its emerging ethos. Attorneys general, steeped in the give and take of politics, and liability lawyers, experienced in the brass knuckles of legal negotiation, had hammered out a deal, with public health advocates largely on the sidelines. Underlying the failure of the McCain bill was the fact that throughout the debate the public took little interest in tobacco legislation.[108]

Many who saw the defeat of the Global Settlement Agreement as a lost opportunity attributed its demise to personal arrogance and political rigidity. But it seems just as likely that deeper structural flaws in the negotiating process and the subsequent politics are to blame. A deal privately negotiated between attorneys general, tobacco executives, and trial lawyers was not likely to be sustained in the highly public legislative arena. Moreover, although there were intensive pressures in the negotiations to reach a "compromise," it is less than surprising that these pressures quickly evaporated when the deal reached Congress.

With the state suits pending and unprecedented regulatory legislation being debated in Washington, some tobacco activists had predicted the beginning of the end of Big Tobacco. They greatly underestimated the continuing power of the tobacco industry to protect its interests. When the McCain bill failed, the momentum in the tobacco wars shifted back to the industry. In August 1998, as we have seen, the Fourth Circuit Court of Appeals overturned an earlier district court ruling supporting FDA regulation. Although it had been clear from the outset that FDA regulation would ultimately be decided by the Supreme Court or additional legislation, the decision nevertheless marked a critical setback for efforts to bring tobacco under regulatory authority.

The debates about the McCain bill had brought into sharp relief the contrast between the tobacco CEOs' worldviews and those of the leaders of the public health community, so loosely configured. The CEOs believed they had shown remarkable flexibility and candor in the negotiating process, seeking to find "common ground" through historic concessions. In return, they sought legitimacy for their industry, relief from legal assault, and a modicum of respect. For them, the Global Settlement grew out of a series of critical *business* decisions, reached through complex assessment of what might best assure their industry's future profitability. Steven Goldstone of R.J. Reynolds, who had promoted the "peace talks," explained, "I finally saw that there wasn't a chance in hell of any resolution to this problem in the near future. . . . I know these guys love to put this in moral terms, but if they can't convince Congress to ban this product, we don't have any choice but to sell it. As far as I am concerned, the day after any bill passes, we'll be selling cigarettes."[109] Geoffrey Bible of Philip Morris remarked:

There's an interesting question you should ask the public health people. What do you think smokers would do if they didn't smoke? You get some pleasure from it, and you also get some other beneficial things, such as stress relief. Nobody knows what you'd turn to if you didn't smoke. Maybe you'd beat your wife. Maybe you'd drive cars fast. Who knows what the hell you'd do.[110]

To public health advocates, the idea of "common ground" and "negotiation" with the tobacco industry was a corruption of their core moral values and political identity. Kessler later explained, "I don't want to live in peace with these guys. . . . If they cared at all for the public health, they wouldn't be in business in the first place."[111] For those who had spent their careers in public health, the very idea of a "conventional business" producing such a dangerous product—especially given the industry's deceitful history—was a contradiction in terms.

§

The tobacco companies weathered the media and tort disasters of the 1990s, the efforts to promote more aggressive regulation, and the attempt to pass comprehensive public health legislation. Richard Scruggs explained, "The industry has the cards. They stopped legislation. They stopped the FDA. They have the momentum."[112] He and others now looked back to the failure of federal legislation with considerable regret and even bitterness, blaming the intransigence of antitobacco forces. "I think history will reflect that June 20 [1997] was a golden opportunity for major reform," noted Washington State Attorney General Christine Gregoire.[113] Following the collapse of the McCain bill, the companies and the attorneys general retreated to fashion a new agreement to settle the cases.

The tobacco companies had learned much from their experiment with a negotiated settlement. They now understood that opening the process to all litigants, let alone public health advocates, was decidedly against their interests. The final settlement negotiations brought together only eight of some forty attorneys general with unresolved cases. These eight negotiated a $200 billion cash settlement with modest provisions for marketing and advertising restrictions. The new agreement was offered to all the states—with a critical seven-day limit for them to sign on. This time limit offered almost no opportunity for public health critics to mount an effective response. It also placed overwhelming economic and political pressure on attorneys general to join in the settlement. For a state to reject billions of dollars to take a chance with a judge and jury constituted too great a political risk for any elected official. Even those critical of the new agreement offered their consent. "If the deal is so good," noted Glantz, "they wouldn't mind putting it out there and letting people take pot shots at it."[114] Although Glantz and others continued to support state-by-state litigation to resolve the suits, arguing that the states that had negotiated individual settlements had achieved more, the pressures bringing the attorneys general into the "master settlement" were intense.[115]

The new Master Settlement Agreement (MSA) was a pale reflection of the earlier proposal. All provisions requiring congressional approval, such as FDA regulation, were dropped, as were mandates for stronger package warnings, tighter enforcement on sales to youth, stronger public smoking bans, and look-back provisions to reduce youth smoking. The MSA, announced on November 16, 1998, consisted of three major terms. First, it required the five major tobacco companies to pay $206 billion to forty-six states over twenty-five years.[116] The four states that had already settled their suits, Mississippi, Florida, Texas, and Minnesota, added another $40 billion to this total. Second, the industry agreed to fund a national foundation devoted to public health and the reduction of smoking. Finally, there were modest restrictions on advertising and promotion; Joe Camel and other cartoon characters would be prohibited. Critics found nothing to celebrate in these provisions. Richard Daynard noted that the restriction on cartoon advertising was an example of "closing the barn door only after the camel has escaped."[117] R.J. Reynolds had agreed more than a year before to withdraw the Joe Camel campaign. Unlike the earlier agreement, which had banned both human and animal figures from tobacco ads, the new proposal only banned cartoons; Ralph Nader pointed out that the settlement "left the Marlboro Man in the saddle."[118]

Right away, public health officials roundly attacked the new settlement. For one thing, there were no guarantees that the money paid by the companies to the states would go to antitobacco programs. In many states, it became clear that these funds would simply be a windfall to governors and legislators with little interest in battling tobacco. The money itself, moreover, was inadequate to cover the costs of smoking-related disease. In California, for example, UCSF health economist Dorothy Rice estimated the costs for just one year at $8.7 billion, but the state was to receive just $500 million. "It's a terrible deal," she concluded.[119]

Public health critics identified a chain of loopholes that weakened various provisions. On a range of issues, from targeting young smokers to sponsorship of sporting events, public health advocates read the agreement with skepticism and often outrage. For example, while the industry conceded to a ban on billboards (already in effect in some states), smaller signs—up to fourteen square feet—were protected. As antitobacco activists well-understood, the industry was both resilient and creative in finding

433

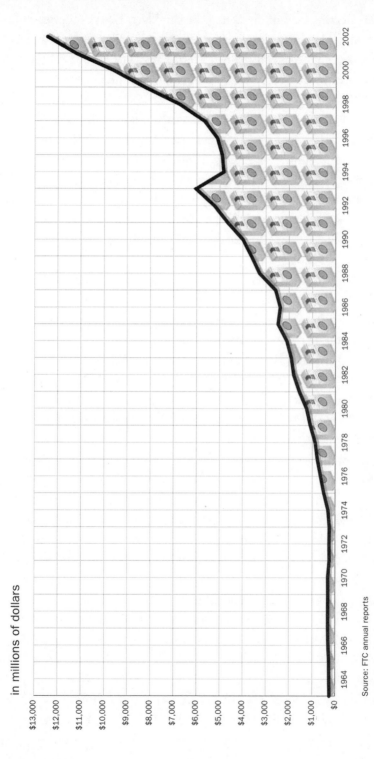

in millions of dollars

Source: FTC annual reports

CHART 6   Cigarette industry advertising and promotion expenditures, 1963–2002

new and effective ways of marketing their product. Even as they ended the use of billboards and promotional paraphernalia, like T-shirts and hats, they dramatically expanded their marketing budgets. From $7.4 billion in 1998, the year of the settlement, promotional spending reached $11.4 billion in 2001.[120]

The settlement preempted any future litigation brought by any "settling states subdivisions (political or otherwise, including, but not limited to municipalities, counties, parishes, villages, unincorporated districts, and hospital districts), public entities, public instrumentalities, and public educational institutions."[121] This preemption did not apply to individual and class-action suits, but it eliminated a wide range of legal vulnerabilities for the industry. Tobacco stocks rallied at the endorsement of the agreement by the forty-six states.

§

The MSA, for all intents and purposes, was principally a new excise tax on cigarettes. Following the agreement, the four principal tobacco companies—Philip Morris, R.J. Reynolds, Brown & Williamson, and Lorillard—raised their prices more than 45 cents per pack. The costs of the settlement, as predicted, were passed on to consumers. Although higher taxes had long had been recognized as one of the most effective mechanisms for reducing smoking, by the mid-1990s state and federal excise taxes were one-third lower in real dollars than they had been at their peak three decades earlier.[122] The federal cigarette tax of 24 cents in 1997 was about half of the 8 cents imposed by Congress in 1951. Since several economic studies had shown that youth smoking was especially sensitive to price, taxes could be a powerful tool in reducing teen smoking and, ultimately, overall smoking prevalence (since adults rarely became new smokers). Most estimates—confirmed by industry assessments—suggested that a 10 percent price increase would reduce demand by at least 4 percent and perhaps as much as 12 percent.[123] This elasticity of demand was well understood within the industry. When Philip Morris reduced the price of Marlboros by 40 cents per pack on April 2, 1993—Marlboro Friday—the other companies immediately followed. So, too, did a sharp increase in the prevalence of youth smoking. By the end of the year, Philip Morris had raised its market share to nearly 47 percent.[124] The MSA "tax" has apparently had a significant impact on youth smoking. Since it went into effect, smoking rates among American adolescents have reached their lowest point in nearly three decades, with approximately 23 percent of teens reporting that they had smoked in the last thirty days.[125]

When the agreement was signed, the attorneys general had noted their states' commitment to reserve some of the new money for tobacco control efforts. The CDC established guidelines recommending that at least 20 percent of the settlement funds go to tobacco prevention and cessation programs. But only a handful of states met this benchmark. By 2005, the states had received nearly $41 billion, according to the National Conference of State Legislatures, but only about 4 percent of it had gone toward tobacco-control efforts.[126] And strikingly, in the wake of the settlement, some states that had developed successful antitobacco programs now found these campaigns being shortchanged.[127] The tobacco settlement funds had been used to balance state budgets.

As critics of the MSA feared, the deal had made the states dependent on tobacco revenues. This had the ironic result of raising concerns within state governments about costly tort litigation against the companies. When they signed the MSA, the states became partners with the tobacco industry; significant revenues now depended on the industry's success and stability. "There's no doubt that the largest financial stakeholder in the industry is our state governments," said Tommy Paine, executive vice president for external affairs at R.J. Reynolds. "Some would say that whole issue has a fair amount of irony associated with it."[128] According to Daynard, "Under the agreement, there's a multi-state permanent lobby for business-as-usual."[129]

Adding insult to the injury suffered by tobacco-control advocates, a number of states sold bonds against future tobacco funds. This process, known as securitization, has resulted in the discounting of revenues from the settlement. The states get immediate cash by selling bonds to be covered by future receipts from the settlement. This approach, now utilized by almost half the states, has further increased their dependence on future tobacco revenues. Glantz offered a pessimistic assessment of the long-range impact of the MSA: "Probably the tobacco industry will win in the long run, largely because of the securitization of the money putting pressure on states to keep consumption up to get their bonds paid off."[130]

Legal threats to the industry have, thus, become threats to the states' cash flow. In instances where the companies might be forced to post bonds while appealing adverse judgments in class-action litigation, attorneys general have worked to get caps legislated. In Illinois, where Philip Morris lost a class-action suit with a judgment of $10.1 billion, more than thirty attorneys general filed an amicus brief warning that bankruptcy to the company would cause dire harm to the states. It was a remarkable turnabout to have the attorneys general *defending* the industry and its economic well-being.[131]

As prices rose following the adoption of the MSA, sales of discount "no name" cigarettes began to climb. As a result, the companies invoked a clause in the agreement allowing them to reduce annual payments to the states if their market share fell below certain levels. The three largest companies, Philip Morris, R.J. Reynolds, and Lorillard, claimed they were owed rebates of as much as 18 percent of recent payments.[132] In March 2006, as a result of declining domestic sales, Philip Morris announced that it expected to withhold $1.2 billion from its annual payment to the states.[133] Payments to the Public Education Fund ended after 2003, when the collective market share of the major companies fell below 99.05 percent. The principal funding of the American Legacy Foundation, the not-for-profit organization established by the MSA, also required that the major companies maintain a 99.05 percent share of the U.S. cigarette market. Legacy was to receive payments of $300 million a year through 2003 and $32 million a year through 2008. When these payments stopped, Legacy could not maintain its full program of public service campaigns and research grants.

Legacy had developed the "truth" campaign, dedicated to informing young consumers about the harms of smoking and issues of corporate responsibility. One ad showed teenagers piling up body bags, representing the twelve hundred who die daily in the United States from tobacco-related diseases. Another Emmy-winning spot, shown during the 2004 Super Bowl, satirized the companies' sales pitch by offering "Shards o' Glass" freeze pops with the slogan, "Yes, it's gravely harmful, but you'll love it!"[134] Evidence suggested that adolescents in particular were influenced by hard-hitting, edgy ads that directed attention at corporate impropriety.[135] But unlike the antitobacco ads aired for free through the Fairness Doctrine between 1968 and 1970, the American Legacy Foundation purchased its ads with MSA funds. After March 2003, when the foundation received its final $300 million payment from the industry, there were limited funds to support the "truth" campaign.[136]

§

The postmortems on the MSA reflected the dashed hopes of the attorneys general, public health officials, and grassroots activists. When the state suits were first filed in the mid-1990s, there had been ambitious talk about "toppling" the tobacco industry. Given the spate of revelations and the growing archive of incriminating documents, it appeared that radical changes were on the horizon: FDA regulation of nicotine; severe marketing and advertising restrictions; massive funding for smoking cessation; and the possibility of a bankrupt industry in receivership. After years of watching the industry derail all serious policy interventions, public health advocates thought the momentum had finally shifted their way. But in the aftermath of the MSA, the attorneys general changed from aggressive public health advocates to defenders of the very industry they had once sought to destroy. According to Mike Moore, the states were guilty of "moral treason. . . . I really believed we were making a difference in this country, and I think we did." But, he said, "we could have made a much larger impact if the states had been true to the cause."[137] Moore's legal ally Scruggs agreed, noting that "the perverse result of what we did was essentially put the states in bed with the tobacco companies. . . . What we did was give the states a financial incentive for tobacco sales. I don't like it at all. . . . The tobacco guys are sitting there laughing at us."[138]

To those who had referred to the settlement negotiations as "dancing with the devil," it appeared in retrospect that the devil had won. "Let's give the devil his due," noted John R. Seffrin, chief executive officer of the American Cancer Society. "They've been a step ahead of us most of the way through this journey. They predicted in advance that this would happen."[139] The attorneys general, with little public health experience and little knowledge of the industry and its strategies, had been outwitted. Their settlements brought billions in cash to their respective states but had minimal public health impact. Frank J. Vandall, a law professor at Emory University, explained, "Some people have said this has worked out as if the tobacco companies designed it. Well, the tobacco companies did design it.

They spent millions and millions of dollars over 50 years lobbying the legislators and the people of America. And now it's paying off." Matt Myers, who once thought the "global settlement" promised substantive public health gains, was forced to admit that the MSA was a debacle: "The tobacco companies counted on the greed and shortsightedness of politicians when they handed them millions of unexpected dollars, and they were right."[140] The MSA proved to be one of the industry's most surprising victories in its long history of combat with the public health forces.

§

To many observers, the state suits and the settlement that resulted typified the growing and objectionable trend of legislation through litigation. After all, the initial "global" settlement agreement had been hammered out by a group of industry lawyers, trial lawyers, the attorneys general and their staffs, and a lone "representative" of the public health "community." This was anything but a process of advice and consent conducted by the duly elected representatives of the people. Not surprisingly, the outcome was skewed by the particular participants' interests. The attorneys general secured revenues for their states; the trial lawyers secured astronomical fees; the industry secured relief from potentially bankrupting litigation; and public health got the short end. The failures of the MSA have been used to sustain traditional arguments against using the courts for regulatory interventions.[141]

The bonanza for the trial lawyers elicited widespread indignation. They were given $1.25 billion initially, with subsequent annual payments of $500 million for twenty-five years. Their firms would receive millions in contingency fees allocated according to a complex formula for work in their respective cases. Many observers argued that litigation was a grossly inefficient way of, in effect, raising cigarette taxes.[142] But the torrent of public resentment about these fees overlooked the fact that without such contingency arrangements, the massive assault on the tobacco industry could not have happened. The firms had invested tens of millions in extremely high-risk litigation.[143]

By definition, tort litigation centers on the compensation of parties injured through fraud, negligence, misrepresentation, and other misdeeds. But in the second half of the twentieth century, litigation began to serve other critical roles as well. It facilitated new forms of corporate exposé by forcing industries to open their records regarding their understanding of the risks of their products, their decisions regarding disclosure, and their marketing practices. These were areas where traditional rule-based regulatory mechanisms often failed to produce timely public knowledge.[144] Nowhere were these regulatory failures as significant as with the tobacco industry.

The political and cultural hostility to tort litigation tended to obscure the fact that conventional legislative routes to regulation of tobacco had been rendered virtually inaccessible by the industry's powerful influence over Congress and state legislatures. Attempts to regulate the tobacco industry had usually—when they yielded any results at all—ended in legislation that protected the industry from regulation. The resort to litigation grew out of these long-standing failures of political and regulatory efforts. During the 1980s and 1990s, prior to the state litigation, tobacco taxes had actually been declining in real terms. After the 1984 legislation requiring rotating warning labels, Congress had been all but silent on any serious tobacco legislation. Even in the aftermath of the Waxman hearings and the FDA findings, it was clear that no new public health legislation to reduce tobacco use would emerge from Congress.

The courts were, therefore, a critical venue not only for injured smokers but for anyone hoping to advance public health policies regarding smoking. Tobacco litigation—even when plaintiffs lost—had a major impact on the larger social and political debates about cigarette smoking, the industry, and responsibility for harm.[145] The failures of the MSA show the limitations of public policy litigation, but these failures are not necessarily inherent in the process.

To view litigation and legislation as mutually incompatible is to misrepresent their complex historical relationship. The question was never legislation *or* litigation.[146] Any successful strategy would need to employ both approaches. The legal battles over tobacco, for example, influenced deeper cultural and political contests about smoking in American society. Slowly, but with increasing severity, the industry's traditional legal defenses, centering on individual responsibility and assumption of risk, came under scrutiny in the courtroom. The decline in the social status of smoking, the recognition that secondhand smoke harmed nonsmokers, the heightened recognition of the addictive properties of nicotine, and the revelations of industry targeting of children, all led to a fundamental reconsideration of the "imposition" of harms.

But perhaps the most significant change was the public recognition of the industry's extensive knowledge of the harms of its product, and its concerted efforts to obscure these facts through scientific disinformation and aggressive marketing. Without the lawsuits, the documents proving these charges would most certainly have remained in the industry's legal vaults. The emergence of a massive archival record demonstrating industry knowledge, action, and intent had created unprecedented legal vulnerabilities. The debate over legislation versus litigation fails to recognize the importance of bringing this history into the open. In this fundamental respect, the *history* of the cigarette served to define and shape the contemporary policy debates about how to best limit its manifold harms. Without the litigation, this history could not be known and so could not inform any legislative effort.

For all the significant political objections to judicial activism and the public disparagement of trial lawyers, it seems important to recognize that the legal process serves certain social ends that the legislative process is poorly structured to address. The courts possess a highly articulated set of procedures for the production and evaluation of evidence on behalf of the public adjudication of responsibility for harms. Demonstrating these harms, within institutional structures that are relatively insulated from the pressures of political and economic interests, serves a critical social good. It is because they brought such facts into public view that the courts have offered such a crucial civic arena for pursuing the control of tobacco.

§

By the end of the twentieth century, American society witnessed radical changes in cigarette consumption. In the years following the MSA, tobacco sales fell by more than 20 percent, reaching a level not seen since 1950.[147] The percentage of adult smokers was about half what it had been at the time of the release of the first surgeon general's report. Despite the striking fall in consumption, more than 50 million Americans—more than one in five adults—continue to smoke regularly. More than 70 percent of these smokers say they want to quit, but even with the development of nicotine replacement technologies (patch, nasal sprays, gum) and other pharmacologic agents now available to assist in quitting, fewer than one in ten smokers currently succeed at the end of one year. Cessation rates are considerably lower among smokers who attempt to quit without counseling or treatment.[148] Unlike the situation in the middle of the twentieth century, when cigarette consumption crossed all socioeconomic segments, today smoking is highly stratified by class and education. And smokers who are less well-off are far less likely to quit. Such data is not surprising given the substantial social science and behavioral research showing that successful quitting is intimately connected to education, strong and supportive social networks, and access to health care.[149] The clinical and behavioral techniques for helping people quit are limited; further reductions in smoking will require a combination of policy and clinical innovation as well as access to services.[150] By any standards, nicotine dependence is a powerful biological and cultural process, difficult to break, with a high likelihood of relapse.

Despite the impressive reductions in consumption, cigarette smoking remains an enormous risk to health and well-being in this new century. Smoking is—by far—the most significant preventable cause of death in the United States, resulting in more than 430,000 deaths each year from heart disease, emphysema, stroke, and lung cancer, among other causes. Lung cancer is not only a stigmatized disease; it is also the most prevalent cancer in the United States, accounting for some 160,000 deaths annually. The new techniques of molecular genetics have been applied to lung cancer, addiction, and other diseases, indicating the possible role of heredity in susceptibility to these diseases. But the reality remains that cigarette smoking is a prominent risk for many diseases in addition to lung cancer; as a result, the behavioral-environmental dimensions of smoking overwhelm the significance of specific vulnerabilities. From both a clinical and public health perspective, the prevention of smoking will undoubtedly remain the single best way of avoiding its potentially devastating and multiple effects. Even if we could know, for example, that we are not at high risk for lung cancer due to genetics, it would also be clear that this chromosomal good luck does not protect us from emphysema, cardiovascular disease, and more than a hundred other tobacco-related diseases.[151] As a result, the genetic basis of lung cancer is a more interesting and important question for the scientific researcher than it is for the smoker. The idea that cancer is a "genetic" disease—long trumpeted by the tobacco industry—is both a truism and a fallacy. It flies in the face of overwhelming evidence that disease is inevitably a complex amalgam of individual susceptibilities and exposures to social determinants.[152]

Given the proclivity to hold smokers accountable for their plight, lung cancer has attracted little research funding. In 2005, $1,829 was spent in federal funding per lung cancer death; for each breast cancer death, federal funding came to $23,474. And yet there are currently four times as many lung cancer deaths each year. Over the last twenty-five years, the five-year survival rate for lung cancer has only inched forward from 13 to 15 percent. Smokers who become ill with lung cancer and other diseases have been noted to internalize the stigma and blame that may be heaped upon them.[153] The recent deaths of ABC news anchor Peter Jennings and of Dana Reeve have drawn renewed attention to lung cancer advocacy, research, and treatment. [154]

§

The failure of the McCain bill and other proposals to regulate tobacco was a powerful reminder that calls for congressional action are likely to go unheeded. Legislative action would require the development of political will that public health measures have largely failed to generate. It is difficult, for example, to name a single piece of major public health legislation since 1995. But public health has rarely generated a serious and effective constituency, except in moments of crisis. Given the long history of tobacco use, it proved impossible to frame cigarette smoking as a crisis. Certainly, by the end of the century, there was little public support for the tobacco industry. After the CEOs' shameless denials at the Waxman hearings, the industry was widely perceived as both dishonest and greedy. But the resulting moral indignation did not lead to effective regulation. It was possible to condemn the industry and simultaneously resist further regulatory action. This was the essential dilemma of public health and tobacco at the end of the century.

There are powerful cultural values that account for the resilience of the cigarette. Tobacco use continues to be widely viewed as the responsibility of the individual smoker. Even as the tobacco-control movement has worked to contest this view—by emphasizing the addictiveness of nicotine and the aggressive pitch to children—common cultural logic continues to assert that smoking is a matter of individual control. This view takes tobacco regulation off any list of political priorities. At the same time, efforts to bring Big Tobacco under regulatory mandates are viewed with considerable skepticism in a polity hostile to big government, big taxes, and Big Brother. Cigarette use, in this view, is an area where government pursuit of social goals must yield to the individual's right to disregard health and well-being.[155] The stigmatization of the smoker, which occurred in the last decades of the twentieth century had the effect of further eroding the political will to regulate tobacco.

Because they are attributed to individuals, large and concrete risks, like smoking, are perceived far more benignly than are smaller but more dramatic risks. Because the effects of tobacco are slow—and iterative—and produce diseases that have other causes and explanations, often later in life, they seldom arouse fear commensurate with their impact.[156] If, for example, we were to identify an infectious organism that caused lung cancer, heart disease, and emphysema in a substantial number of people who were exposed, one can only imagine the level of concern and political action that would result. But we have an industry that produces such an "agent" with a warning label printed on the side of every package.

As a culture, we seek to insist—despite much powerful evidence to the contrary—that smoking remains a simple question of individual agency, personal fortitude, and the exercise of free will. Certainly, if it involves imposing risks on others, its public use should be legally curtailed. As a result, there has been much support for restrictions, increasingly universal, prohibiting smoking in public places. But at the same time, there has been an ongoing insistence that smoking remains an aspect of personal agency, beyond the ken of regulatory interest. This view is widely held because it protects our larger sense of individual control and agency. Smokers, who are easy to stigmatize and condemn, assure our sense of a world in which individuals do make decisions, exercise agency, and control their destinies. Keeping smoking essentially unregulated assists us in a larger cultural denial of forces over which we may have little control. In this sense, we need the cigarette and the smoker to make sense of our world. And the tobacco industry is willing and eager to assist in the assertion of the logic of individual responsibility. Take, for example, the recent major advertising campaign sponsored by Philip Morris known as "Quit Assist." These widely viewed television spots and pamphlets—often perceived as counterintuitive—contend that Philip Morris, the nation's biggest producer of cigarettes, is eager to support efforts to restrict youth smoking and aid those who wish to quit. Not only do such public relations efforts attempt to demonstrate that the company now is a "responsible corporate citizen," the campaign also seeks to underscore the claim that smoking is simply a matter of adult "choice."[157] These ads have been shown to have little or no effect on quitting, but they are quite effective in shoring up the industry's principal defense of cigarette smoking as an individual responsibility. If Philip Morris is offering to help you quit—and you don't—who should be held accountable?[158]

Resisting the blandishments of the companies and the addictiveness of nicotine is one cultural test of our discipline, independence, and individualism.[159] This cultural idiom—central to the way we think about vulnerability, health, and disease—continues to shape the history of the cigarette in our time. But as the last century has shown, this orientation to the cigarette is a product of time and culture, subject to change. That said, it is powerful and resilient, and vast corporate interests seek to reify these values.

Our insistence on personal responsibility may be a double-edged sword. It may encourage a heightened sense of individual control over health but also alienate and distance those who become ill. I cite a common scenario: "I have a friend in the hospital with lung cancer." First question: "Did he smoke?" "Two packs a day—tried to quit and failed." A shrug of the shoulders: "What did he expect?" This quick and commonplace response reveals the nearly instantaneous mechanism by which we identify the smoker as the one responsible for his sorry fate. By doing so, we dissociate ourselves from the complex forces—economic, corporate, cultural, and biological— that have brought such smokers to their plight. Shall we consider smokers ignorant and stupid for maintaining an "unnecessary behavior" that has clearly been defined as highly dangerous, *or* shall we recognize the power of advertising and cultural conventions, as well as the biological and psychological qualities of addiction that constrain individual choice?

Calls for public responsibility need not erode our expectations of individual responsibility. It would be far easier and more appropriate to consider smoking truly an individual choice if, for example, cigarettes were subject to a serious and effective regulation. Setting individual versus social responsibility creates a false dichotomy that has served the tobacco industry's interests.

This is not to suggest that smokers are absolved of accountability. To the contrary, most investigators of addictive behaviors confirm that individual motivation and acceptance of responsibility are critical to cessation and recovery. But we should not allow the industry to use calls for individual responsibility to secure a free ride at the expense of smokers and society. Indeed, the very notion that responsibility can be allocated *either* to smokers *or* the industry misrepresents a deep historical reality about the interconnectedness of culture, behavior, and commerce in the last century.

§

By the early years of the new century, the legal assault on Big Tobacco that once looked so promising had been all but repelled. The industry had secured new allies by providing a steady flow of state revenues. Now state governors and attorneys general would help the companies fight off litigation. In the last decade of the twentieth century, many tobacco-control advocates had dared to envision a broken and bankrupt industry, with jail terms for executives whose perjuries were the least of their crimes. To the contrary, the industry emerged on the other side of the decade decidedly intact, ready to do business profitably at home and abroad.

V

GLOBALIZATION

A good cigarette is an easy and early luxury for a man after he breaks through the barrier of poverty. . . . We know that more smoke signals a burgeoning economy. Where there's smoke, there's a market for many American products.[1]

GEORGE WEISSMAN, 1962
CEO, PHILIP MORRIS

I was with some Vietnamese recently, and some of them were smoking two cigarettes at the same time. That's the kind of customers we need![2]

SENATOR JESSE HELMS, 1996

The last thing we should expect the WHO to be doing is to prioritize smoking—namely, a voluntary health risk the clinical effects of which tend to emerge after the age at which people in poorer countries can expect to die.[3]

ROGER SCRUTON, 2000

I'll tell you why I like the cigarette business. It cost a penny to make. Sell it for a dollar. It's addictive. And there's a fantastic brand loyalty.[4]

WARREN BUFFETT, 1988

CHAPTER 13

Exporting an Epidemic

ALMOST ALL OF US have watched someone trying to escape a nicotine addiction, or gone through it ourselves. It is a struggle that sometimes ends in triumph, more often in defeat, but many have nonetheless accomplished it over the last few decades. In the United States, the proportion of smokers in the adult population has fallen from a high of 46 percent in 1950 to 21 percent in 2004.[5] The wide diffusion of knowledge about the risks of smoking and a cultural climate increasingly antithetical to smoking have meant that many teenagers who might well have taken up cigarettes in the past no longer do so. The public rejection of cigarettes is possibly unique: there may be no other instance in modern history in which a popular and addictive behavior was so fundamentally transformed in the public eye, or in which so many have quit or resisted such an intensively promoted and marketed legal product.[6]

The unprecedented number of smokers giving up cigarettes has reconfirmed what scientists and physicians so ably demonstrated at mid-century. As tobacco use in the United States declined sharply starting in the late 1960s, rates of lung cancer and heart disease have now begun to fall.[7] These data show that it is possible to modify even the riskiest, most addictive behaviors, given the requisite scientific knowledge, cultural transformations, and personal motivation.[8] But when we look at current cigarette use, we see that the success of tobacco control is decidedly limited. The poor and poorly educated are disproportionately represented among remaining smokers.[9] And there are a number of studies indicating that those who continue smoking today may well be more deeply addicted and smoke more cigarettes than smokers in the past.[10]

One of the most disturbing ironies of twentieth century public health is that it was the relative success in reducing tobacco use in the developed world that spurred the sharp increases in cigarette use in developing nations. As Western markets grew increasingly vulnerable to state regulation and a rising antitobacco movement, the multinational tobacco companies began to look covetously at new, untapped markets abroad; first in the developing world and then, following the fall of the iron curtain, in eastern Europe.[11] These markets offered an opportunity to more than offset the losses (from quitting, prevention, and deaths) the industry experienced in the industrialized West.[12]

The dramatic fall in American consumption of cigarettes set the stage for the intensive push into new markets. Between 1975 and 1994, overall cigarette sales in the United States declined by more than 20 percent (from 607.2 to 485 billion cigarettes). During the same period, production of American cigarettes rose by 11 percent.[13] As a result, the ratio of exported cigarettes rose sharply during this period, and opening new markets became a critical element in the industry's growth. Cigarette exports from Philip Morris, R.J. Reynolds, and Brown & Williamson would more than triple between 1975 and 1994, from about 50 billion to 220 billion. This remarkable transformation in the markets for American cigarettes resulted from an opening of world commerce that included changes in world trade regulations, efforts by the companies to open new markets, and interventions on behalf of industry by the U.S. government. Buck Duke's vision of a truly global market for the cigarette has at last been realized.[14] This historical change in tobacco markets from national to transnational has profound implications for world health.[15]

We stand on the threshold of a global pandemic of tobacco-related diseases that is nothing short of colossal. The cigarette will cause far more deaths in this new century than in the last, irrespective of innovative and effective clinical and public health interventions in the future.[16] At no moment in human history has tobacco presented such a dire and imminent risk to human health as it does today. In 2000, 12 percent of adult deaths glob-

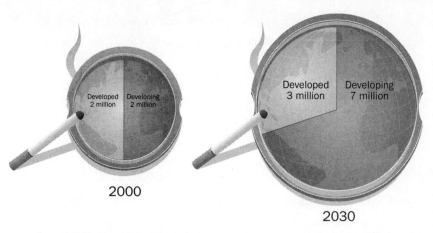

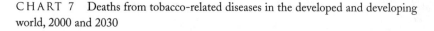

2000

2030

Source: Judith Mackay and Michael Eriksen, *The Tobacco Atlas* (Geneva: World Health Organization, 2002).

CHART 7   Deaths from tobacco-related diseases in the developed and developing world, 2000 and 2030

ally—four million deaths—were associated with cigarette smoking.[17] This ratio is projected to double by 2020, to nearly one quarter of all adult deaths. The largest increases will be among women: although nearly half of all adult men in the developing countries are smokers, only about 11 percent of adult women smoke.[18] Each day, 80,000 to 100,000 individuals become new smokers; most of these are children and adolescents, mostly in the developing world. While tobacco-related deaths are now evenly divided between the industrialized and developing nations, this ratio will not long endure. Of the world's 1.1 billion current smokers, 80 percent live in low- or middle-income countries with nearly 40 percent of the total number of smokers in the world living in East Asian countries and 20 percent living in former Soviet Bloc countries. By 2030, developing nations will claim 70 percent of the world's overall tobacco mortality, exacerbating the health disparities between the developed and the developing world.[19] One hundred million Chinese men currently younger than twenty-nine will die from smoking.

§

The international commerce in tobacco is one of the great ironies of globalization. On one hand, globalization has led to the conviction that traditional barriers to trade and commerce should be reduced to encourage development and growth. Worldwide transportation and communication have led to new forms of cosmopolitan and homogenized cultures. As President Bill Clinton noted in his 2000 State of the Union address:

> To realize the full possibilities of this economy, we must reach beyond our own borders, to shape the revolution that is tearing down barriers and building new networks among nations and individuals, and economies and cultures: globalization. It's the central reality of our time.[20]

On the other hand, globalization is seen as consolidating market economies at the expense of indigenous practices, health, and local environments. As a result, it is increasingly recognized as a rising force in shaping new patterns of disease. Shifts in trade and markets, the diffusion of new media and cultural contacts, and the migration of services, peoples, and goods are rapidly changing how individuals get sick and die.[21]

The global movement of cigarettes illuminates current dilemmas about trade, commerce, and equity in the new global economy. Although many industrialized nations over the last century have evolved regulatory frameworks to address the risks associated with the diffusion of consumer products and markets, such structures are rare in the developing world, and international controls are even more unusual. Even in the industrialized nations, tobacco regulation lagged far behind other forms of consumer protection. It is impossible to say whether this pattern will be repeated in the developing world; one can only note that in most of the world, the tobacco industry maintains strong corporate ties to national governments that typically have little or no history of product regulation.

§

No one has followed globalization more closely or better understood its implications than the tobacco companies. The industry has long been committed to the notion of the "global smoker" and "global brands." As Philip Morris executive Hugh Cullman explained in a 1977 report to the company: "Since 1959, Philip Morris has built a substantial commitment in the developing countries. We have invested more in the developing world than we have recovered. We have been investing for the future."[22] With growing regulatory concerns in the United States and a declining ability to subvert scientific realities, the American tobacco companies moved to expand their international operations.

U.S. and International Cigarette Production, in Billions

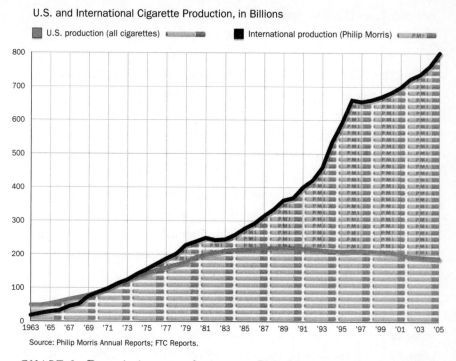

Source: Philip Morris Annual Reports; FTC Reports.

CHART 8   Domestic cigarette production versus Philip Morris international production

The industry secured powerful governmental support for these efforts. U.S. federal trade representatives, for example, repeating the mantra of open markets, worked assiduously through the 1970s and 1980s to expand opportunities for American tobacco companies abroad by attacking high tariffs and bans on tobacco imports.[23] To industry analysts, this was a classic win-win proposition. They would gain new markets; developing countries would reap the joint rewards of culture and trade. As a tobacco industry executive explained in 1982:

Demographically, the population explosion in many underdeveloped countries ensures a large potential market for cigarettes. Culturally, demand will increase with the continuing emancipation of women and the linkage in the minds of many consumers of smoking manufactured cigarettes with modernization, sophistication, wealth, and success—a connection encouraged by much of the advertising for cigarettes throughout the world. Politically, increased cigarette sales can bring benefits to the government of an underdeveloped country that are hard to resist.[24]

By 1984, Marlboro was China's fourth largest advertiser. As it worked to pierce the world's biggest cigarette market, Rene Scull, vice president of Philip Morris Asia, explained in 1985: "No discussion of the tobacco industry in the year 2000 would be complete without addressing what may be the most important feature on the landscape, the Chinese market. In every respect, China confounds the imagination."[25]

Like many developing nations, China has a state-run tobacco monopoly. Begun by Duke's British American Tobacco in the late nineteenth century, the company was nationalized by the Communists following World War II. By the mid-1990s, the China National Tobacco Company was producing some 1.7 trillion cigarettes a year (approximately one-third of the world's total), with modest technical support for joint ventures from the multinationals eager to get a foot in this giant door. The national government gets some 12 percent of its overall revenues from cigarette sales. China is caught between the immediate financial benefits of tobacco revenues and the devastating long-term health impacts that will inevitably result from the some 350 million Chinese currently addicted.[26]

The rise of smoking in China, where per capita consumption of cigarettes more than doubled between 1965 and 1990, mirrors what happened some forty years earlier in the United States. Today, the Chinese market for cigarettes is overwhelmingly male, with over 60 percent of men being regular smokers versus only 7 percent of women. Such ratios have historically been read within the industry as opportunities. Public health has a less benign outlook. According to studies conducted by the Chinese health ministry in collaboration with British epidemiologist Richard Peto, tobacco-related diseases caused more than five hundred thousand deaths in 1996; by 2025 this number would jump to two million (nearly one-third of all deaths occurring between the ages of thirty-five and sixty-nine). Peto noted that when he was invited to Beijing to explain his findings, "my message was very simple: If the Chinese smoke like Americans, they'll die like Americans."[27]

Beyond devising economic and policy strategies, tobacco companies carefully research the cultural significance of multinational products in order to learn how best to break into new markets. Often it is necessary to negotiate a shift from traditional indigenous uses of tobacco to the homogenized and modern product. Using marketing approaches like those it employed in the United States in the early twentieth century, the industry first seeks to kindle interest in cigarettes. As one executive explained in a trade journal in 1998:

> Globalization has its limits. In India, for instance, around 80 percent of the population uses traditional tobacco products such as bidis or chewing tobacco. . . . [But for] how long will these markets resist the attraction of global trends? In one or two generations, the sons and grandsons of today's Indians may not want to smoke bidis or chew pan masala. . . . Global brands are one way to accelerate this process.

In India and elsewhere, where limits on public smoking and advertising are modest, tobacco companies can travel back to a time when there was little opposition to their most aggressive marketing ploys. With the explicit goal of transitioning people from indigenous smoking practices in favor of worldwide brands, the companies utilize well-worked strategies to promote consumption, including sports sponsorship, rock concerts, fashion shows, and free samples. Where regulatory mechanisms exist, the tobacco companies have found them relatively easy to subvert. Empty cigarette packages offer free admission to discos. In Malaysia, R.J. Reynolds employs "brand stretching" to turn Salem Power Station into a prominent record store. In Vietnam, where ads are prohibited, the red and white Marlboro chevron appears widely. The use of tobacco brands in these related contexts "has no relation to cigarettes, absolutely," an R.J. Reynolds spokesman explained. "It was a trademark diversification program."[28] The tobacco companies bring a century of marketing savvy, intelligence, and doublespeak to their promotional efforts in these developing nations.[29]

Just at the moment that the cigarette was losing its glamour, sophistication, and sexual allure in the West, the companies sought to recreate these connotations of smoking in developing countries. *Marketing News* exclaimed in 1991: "Western models and lifestyles create glamorous standards to emulate, and Asian smokers can't get enough."[30] Western brands, in particular, came to be viewed as a mark of social status, cosmopolitanism, and affluence. Western cigarettes offered smokers new social prominence. Such meanings are not inherent in cigarettes; they are explicitly constructed by promotion and marketing. It was an irony not lost on multinational tobacco companies that even as they resisted regulatory initiatives as paternalistic and imperialistic, they aggressively promoted Western cultural idioms. Their campaigns to bring cigarettes to new peoples and places met with considerable success. The industry celebrated the identification of these new markets. As Burson-Marsteller, a Philip Morris public relations firm, explained:

> In any event, despite the lingering tobacco liability cases and the drop in cigarette consumption in the United States, the tobacco companies themselves have never been healthier. First, foreign consumption of American cigarettes continues to grow dramatically, because of the falling value of the dollar, a reduction in tariff and non-tariff barriers to cigarettes and the image of American cigarettes as the best in terms of quality and character. Japan is now importing U.S. cigarettes, and China shows great potential.[31]

As one journalist noted, "Americanization" has become a well-recognized social process worldwide:

> Even in countries where the American government is disliked, there is a reverence for American things. . . . I came upon 17-year-old Daniel Fuqs, who was leaning against an iron fence. . . . He was wearing Levi's and loosely laced Nikes, and smoking a Marlboro: "We like American cigarettes, American music, American clothing. The poorer Brazilian kids can't afford Nikes or Reeboks, so instead they buy baseball caps with the names of American teams. Anything to tie yourself to America. We resent American imperialism, but there is no other way.[32]

American advertising icons are found everywhere. "The red-and-white Marlboro chevron is as familiar as Coca-Cola signs in nations with large numbers of smokers, like the Philippines, where the entire city of Manila smells like an all-night poker game."[33]

A critical aspect of market development in non-Western nations involves creating interest among women and children in smoking. As Gregory Connolly, former head of the Massachusetts Tobacco Control Program, noted, "When the multinational companies penetrate a new country, they not only sell U.S. cigarettes but they transform the entire market ... they transform how tobacco is presented, how it's advertised, how it's promoted. And the result is the creation of new demand, especially among women and young people."[34] In many cultures, tobacco use, including cigarette smoking, has traditionally been a male behavior. The spread of smoking among both sexes in the United States required deep changes in attitudes about gender equality as well as a steadfast effort by the cigarette industry to erase any differences in social convention. Overcoming social mores against women smoking marked a central element of establishing the salience of the cigarette. But as the prevalence of smoking among women approached that among men, so did the prevalence of the resulting diseases. In the United States, for example, rates of lung cancer eclipsed breast cancer in the mid-1980s, following the major increases in women smokers in the middle years of the twentieth century.[35]

As it looks to the developing world, the multinational tobacco industry consciously seeks to recreate its history in the West by aggressively marketing the association of cigarette smoking with modernity and gender equality. In once again making smoking a symbol of women's rights, the industry had taken a powerful, if outdated, set of meanings for its product and deployed it in a new global context.[36] The association of cigarette use with independence and modernity has proved very effective in recruiting women smokers, especially in countries where little public information is available about the health risks of smoking. The tobacco companies have also attracted women smokers—girls, actually—with specific women's brands, light blends, and plenty of free samples. These strategies, refined through decades of test-marketing in the West, are now reengineered to suit new populations.[37] Further, the industry has placed antitobacco advocates in the position of seeming to resist equal status for women because they support maintaining restrictions on women smoking. Serving women's health has been made to appear as if it opposes their freedom.[38]

The other crucial component of building a market is the appeal to youth. American and other multinational companies have used popular music, discos, and nightclubs to turn Western cigarette brands into status symbols among teenagers. Smoking is promoted at discos and nightclubs, on clothing and "gear," all linking brands to youth culture. Marlboro T-shirts in children's sizes may be found in Kiev and Kenya.[39] Not coincidentally, smoking starts at younger and younger ages worldwide. According to the WHO, 250 million children alive today will ultimately die of smoking-related diseases.

In the United Nations Convention on the Rights of the Child, which came into force in 1990, it was determined that:

> [s]tates have a duty to take all necessary legislative and regulatory measures to protect children from tobacco and ensure that the interests of children take precedence over those of the tobacco industry.

But children are not only at risk to become smokers; they are also vulnerable to the smoke exhaled by adults. Because a single adult smoker in a household exposes all the children living there, a majority of the world's children have significant exposure to environmental tobacco smoke. WHO estimates that worldwide some 700 million children live in homes with regular adult smokers.[40] Any assessment of the global impact of tobacco use must include not only the enormous health effects on smokers, but the now well-documented consequences for nonsmokers as well.[41]

§

As the risks of tobacco were better understood and regulated in the West, multinationals began to target nations where regulations were weaker. The laws tended to be especially weak in nations that were significantly dependent on tobacco revenues and those with less stable governments. Even countries that have tried to restrict tobacco sales have been frustrated by the combination of emerging free-trade agreements and the companies' aggressive efforts to expand into new markets. And the companies have brought to the developing world their long experience in turning regulation on its head. From its century-long experience in Western nations, the industry knew that aggressive marketing of tobacco prior to any regulatory intervention assured important market opportunities that, given the addictive qualities of the product, would be difficult to reverse once initiated. It became crucial to the industry to gain a foothold in expanding markets before control efforts could get organized. Moreover, in societies where infectious disease and violent trauma remain significant causes of death, the risks of smoking could be portrayed as small and distant. Indeed, it took an era of sustained good health in the West to fully expose the long-term harms of cigarette smoking.

Securing these new markets has not always been easy. The multinational companies met opposition from domestic tobacco growers and manufacturers as well as health ministries. Many countries, like China, had state-operated tobacco monopolies that were traditionally protected from competition by high tariffs or outright bans on imported cigarettes. Gaining access to these markets would require a cooperative effort. In 1981, the three largest producers of American cigarettes, Philip Morris, R.J. Reynolds, and Brown & Williamson joined together to form the Cigarette Export Association (CEA), a not-for-profit trade association whose mission was "to improve the competitive position" of U.S.-made cigarettes in foreign markets. Section 301 of the Trade Act of 1974 directed American industries who believed their products were subject to illegal trade restrictions to bring their claims to the U.S. Trade Representative (USTR), and in 1985 the CEA began to petition the USTR to open restricted markets to American cigarettes.[42]

According to Clayton Yeutter, who served as the U.S. trade representative from 1985 to 1989, the claim that bans on U.S. tobacco products were devised to protect public health was plain hypocrisy. In the countries with the highest trade barriers, Yeutter argued, governments were knee-deep in the production and sale of their own cigarettes. "I have no problem with Japan or Korea putting up genuine health restrictions," explained Yeutter, "But that's not what these governments were doing. They were restricting trade, and it was just blatant." With U.S. annual trade deficits climbing steeply ($123 billion in 1984), the tobacco companies' demands for help in opening markets received sympathetic attention in the Reagan White House. George Griffin, commercial counselor at the U.S. Embassy in Seoul, articulated the administration's view in a letter to Matthew Winokur, the public affairs manager at Philip Morris Asia, in 1986:

Dear Matt . . .

I want to emphasize that the embassy and the various U.S. government agencies in Washington will keep the interests of Philip Morris
and the other American cigarette manufacturers in the forefront of our
daily concerns.[43]

In the instance of cigarettes, however, it proved difficult to distinguish
restraints on trade from the genuine assertion of public health interests.
State-run cigarette monopolies actually had the effect of limiting consumption. Their cigarettes tended to be high in tar, but they were harsh
to smoke and weakly advertised and promoted. With no competition,
these industries were often inefficient, and cigarettes were often very expensive. If these monopolies were ended, it was well recognized that the
ensuing competition for smokers would lead to an overall increase in
consumption and ultimately in serious diseases. Although the International Monetary Fund and the World Bank generally advocated that
state-owned monopolies be disbanded on economic grounds, these agencies did not evaluate how breaking up state tobacco monopolies might
affect public health.[44]

In 1985, advised by a committee of representatives from the Departments of State, Agriculture, Commerce, Labor, and the Treasury, Yeutter
undertook tobacco trade initiatives against Japan, Taiwan, South Korea,
and Thailand. No advisor from the Department of Health and Human
Services was consulted. Tobacco company representatives were invited to
the trade negotiations and brought several former Reagan administration
officials to negotiate on their behalf: R.J. Reynolds hired former National
Security Adviser Richard Allen; Philip Morris hired former White
House aide Michael Deaver, who was later convicted of lying to Congress
about his lobbying activities. The following year, Japan agreed to abandon
its 26 percent tariff on American cigarettes—what one Japanese newspaper called a "blood offering"—in order to buy time on other trade issues.
Taiwan and South Korea quickly followed suit, lowering their tariffs on
imported cigarettes and easing other restrictions on the distribution of
American tobacco products.

Within two years, overall consumption of cigarettes had risen in these
countries by more than 10 percent. Following Japan's elimination of tariffs,

its imports of cigarettes increased by a factor of three in 1987. The overall rise in consumption was especially dramatic among women. In 1986, about 8.6 percent of Japanese adult women smoked; by 1991, this figure stood at 18.2 percent. Cigarettes jumped from the fortieth most advertised product in Japan to the second. Seoul opened its market in 1988. American tobacco companies spent $25 million on advertising in South Korea in 1988 (up from zero in 1986) and within a year controlled 6 percent of the market.[45] In Taiwan, two years after its tariffs were dropped, market share of American brands had gone from 1 percent to 20 percent.[46] Owen C. Smith, a Philip Morris executive and president of the CEA, remarked that "in international trade terms, it's really very rare that the issues are so clear cut and blatant. . . . These countries were sitting with published laws which on their face discriminated against American products. It was an untenable situation. . . . These were, frankly, open and shut cases."[47]

According to one widely cited study, U.S. cigarette exports to the Asian nations climbed by more than 600 percent in the period following the opening to U.S. trade.[48] Yeutter, who had been tapped to become the secretary of agriculture in 1989, expressed enthusiasm for the successes his office had achieved in opening these markets. He explained at a press conference in 1990: "I just saw the figures on tobacco exports here a few days ago and, my, have they turned out to be a marvelous success story."[49] After leaving government in 1991, Yeutter joined the Board of British American Tobacco.

The success in accessing these new markets would have long-term health implications for these countries.[50] As a result of the USTR's efforts, it appeared that there would be little substantive resistance to the expansion of American tobacco into Asia. Dependence on U.S. trade offered these nations little opportunity to fashion effective health arguments. And that was precisely the way the tobacco industry hoped to frame the discussion: it was strictly a question of trade, not health.

But while three of the four countries targeted by the USTR quickly lowered their tariffs, Thailand refused to succumb to U.S. demands. At the time, Thailand had a $2 billion trade surplus with the United States, generated by exports of textiles, electronics, processed food, and jewelry. The Thai health ministry denounced the American action as "tobacco colonization," spurring protests by a growing group of antismoking activists. Within the Thai government, there was an intense internal dispute about how to respond to the U.S. trade intervention. While the ministry of finance, fearing trade sanctions, strongly supported opening the tobacco market, a coalition of antitobacco forces, citing the significant public health benefits, sought to maintain the import exclusions. A potent alliance between public health forces and the tobacco monopoly in Thailand pressured the government to resist the U.S. action. The Thai government ultimately held that trade restrictions were critical to its ongoing efforts to limit tobacco use.[51]

By 1989, Carla Hills had succeeded Yeutter as USTR, and she followed in his footsteps. Hills took up the tobacco companies' claims against Thailand, arguing that the government's import ban was merely intended to protect the state-run tobacco monopoly from competition. Rather than immediately invoke trade sanctions as the United States had threatened, Hills, apparently concerned that overly aggressive U.S. policies to open the Thai market might backfire elsewhere, opted to file a complaint to the General Agreement on Tariffs and Trade (GATT). It was the first time the GATT dispute resolution procedures had been invoked for tobacco products. Although the tobacco industry protested Hills's decision, it turned out to be a shrewd defense of their interests.[52]

Critics have contended that the GATT process is poorly suited to evaluating the relationships between trade practices and public health. GATT panels are typically made up of lawyers, economists, and judges with little experience in epidemiology or medicine. The burden of proof to demonstrate that prevailing restrictions on trade are "necessary" rests entirely on the country whose trade policies are under question. Thus, Thailand was required to demonstrate to the GATT panel that its tariffs were both "necessary" to achieve a critical public health goal *and* the "least restrictive" approach to attaining that goal. Further, if Thailand could satisfy these two requirements, there was a third: it must prove that the restriction would effectively meet the stated public health goal. This three-pronged standard, as interpreted by the panel, would prove nearly impossible to meet under any circumstances.[53]

In the deliberations that followed, the Thai government claimed that its restrictions on tobacco imports were justified under Article XX(b) of the

GATT, which allowed exceptions to open trade where national health and environmental concerns might be threatened. Thailand argued that its import restrictions supported the public health goals of reducing tobacco-related diseases. Further, the Thai government contended that chemicals and additives in U.S. cigarettes might make these products more dangerous than those manufactured domestically.[54] At the dispute hearing, Thailand denied the U.S. contention that its goal was to protect its market for domestic tobacco. According to the ministry of finance, cigarette imports would actually add some 800 million baht ($30 million) per year to the economy. The government had opted to forgo these profits in favor of its larger public health agenda.[55]

The United States argued that Thailand could pursue its public health goals without imposing a ban on imports and that the Thais had other motives for restricting trade. Citing data that domestic production and consumption of tobacco had risen despite their public health campaign, the United States contended that Article XX(b) was a fig leaf to protect the Thai tobacco monopoly. Opening the Thai market would merely shift some consumption to competitive imports. It would not cause an overall increase in the use of cigarettes; that was happening already. The United States rejected the notion that Thailand had no effective strategies for meeting its public health goals other than restrictive trade practices.[56]

At the urging of the Thailand government, the GATT panel requested that the World Health Organization offer its assessment of the case in regard to public health. WHO expressed serious concerns about the impact of marketing Western cigarettes, their particular appeal to women and youth, and mistaken perceptions that these brands are safer than domestic cigarettes. Its representatives noted the substantial progress tobacco control groups had already made in Thailand, especially in legislation banning advertising and other forms of promotion. According to their presentation to the panel, these impressive, but poorly financed, public health interventions would be "unable to compete with the marketing budgets" of multinational tobacco companies. The result, they argued, would be an overall increase in consumption and ultimately in tobacco-related morbidity and mortality. The United States challenged the WHO presentation, questioning the representatives' competence "to address the health consequences of opening the market for cigarettes," and requested that the panel restrict the issues that WHO could address to the health effects of cigarettes.[57]

Ultimately, the panel refused to accept the argument that competition between imported and domestic cigarettes would necessarily lead to an increase in the total sales. It ordered Thailand to open its market to foreign tobacco. The final report from the Dispute Resolution Body, issued in November 1990, explained:

> There were various measures consistent with the General Agreement which were reasonably available to Thailand to control the quality and quantity of cigarettes smoked which, taken together, could achieve the health policy goals that the Thai government pursues by restricting the importation of cigarettes inconsistently with Article XI:1. The Panel found therefore that Thailand's practice of permitting the sale of domestic cigarettes while not permitting the importation of foreign cigarettes was an inconsistency with the General Agreement not "necessary" within the meaning of Article XX(b).[58]

In other words, so long as the panel could imagine alternative approaches to tobacco control that would achieve the public health goals, trade restrictions under Article XX(b) were not permitted.

But in a victory for the Thai government, the panel did rule that warning labels, nondiscriminatory bans on direct and indirect advertising, and bans on smoking in public places were all consistent with GATT. While acknowledging that tobacco posed an important risk to health, the panel concluded nonetheless that tobacco trade restrictions violated GATT. Although GATT rulings are not specifically considered to be precedent setting, the decision left little doubt that at least for the time being, cigarettes would be treated as a "conventional product."[59]

A number of legal observers have offered important critiques of this particular approach of GATT dispute resolution panels. Such a broad interpretation of *necessary* restrictions creates an unattainable standard and violates the national democratic processes and the authority of local constituents to legislate policies.[60] "An international organization such as the World Trade Organization [WTO (which succeeded GATT in 1994)] should employ a deferential standard of review with respect to certain national decisions and policy choices," wrote international trade law expert Thomas J. Schoenbaum. "If *necessary* were replaced with *arbitrary* or *unjustified* trade discrimination the outcome of the Thai dispute might have been radically different."[61] It was beyond the purview of the GATT panel, however, to assess whether less restrictive measures were "reasonably available" to Thailand under prevailing political and social conditions. And the very character of the GATT provisions made it virtually inconceivable that some alternative would not be theoretically available. As a result, the "necessary" requirement of GATT and subsequent trade agreements created an insurmountable condition for health-related trade restrictions.

With this decision in hand, the U.S. government vigorously promoted the tobacco industry's positions on the selling of cigarettes. It insisted, for example, that in seeking new markets, the companies were exclusively interested in getting existing smokers to switch to new brands, not recruiting new smokers. As the CEA explained, "U.S. companies simply want a level playing field on which to compete."[62] Opening markets to imported cigarettes would simply present existing smokers with new "choices." This argument mirrored traditional industry justifications for advertising as merely encouraging smokers to switch brands. Nonetheless, as the WHO presentation in Geneva noted and as virtually any economist would predict, there was much evidence that countries forced to lower their trade barriers saw cigarette consumption rise dramatically.[63]

The 1990 ruling illuminated a growing conflict between two powerful trends: the liberalization of trade and a rising international movement committed to the control of tobacco and the reduction of tobacco-related diseases. As a result of the GATT ruling and subsequent trade agreements in which tobacco is regarded as a "conventional good," all restrictions on tobacco trade have become increasingly vulnerable. From this perspective, commerce in tobacco products was just as desirable as commerce in textiles, clothes, cars, or computers. Under the GATT ruling it was clear that developing nations could not bar their gates to tobacco. Opening restricted markets to foreign companies intensified competition, stimulated marketing and advertising, reduced prices, and spurred demand. The health toll would inevitably follow.

The GATT ruling caused considerable anger among tobacco-control advocates and helped to generate a grassroots Asian antismoking movement. According to Judith Mackay, director of the Asian Tobacco Consultancy, an advocacy group based in Hong Kong, the American trade actions "united people in Asia in outrage. And Thailand was the key."[64] Some observers compared U.S. policy to the opium wars of the nineteenth century. David Yen, a businessman who founded the John Tung Foundation, a nonprofit antismoking group in Taiwan, noted, "America has given us so many good things over the years. . . . we think it's a pity that with so many wonderful products to sell, you have insisted on pushing disease instead."[65] The Thai government redoubled its antismoking efforts, expanding its existing ad ban, adding provisions restricting sales to youth, prohibiting free samples, and requiring the disclosure of ingredients and additives. Further legislation banned smoking in public places.[66]

In the long run, the Thai case prompted new and innovative approaches to global tobacco control and forced antitobacco advocates to take a clear position on the relationship of trade to public health. Without a new, multilateral approach to tobacco trade, it was clear that the WTO and other trade agreements would dramatically expand the marketing and consumption of tobacco, especially in nations where regulatory regimes had yet to be constructed. In the ongoing tobacco wars, the GATT decision marked a major victory for the tobacco industry, putting many new territories within easy reach of transnational corporations. As CEO James W. Johnston explained in R.J. Reynolds's 1993 *Annual Report*, "Today, Reynolds has access to 90 percent of the world's markets; a decade ago, only 40 percent. Opportunities have never been better."[67]

§

Health advocates in the United States and abroad, meanwhile, blasted the hypocrisy of the Reagan and Bush administrations for working to reduce cigarette consumption at home while opening new markets abroad. A succession of U.S. Trade Representatives held that they were required by law to act on any legally sound complaints that showed U.S. products to be impeded. At the same time, however, they sought to exclude the Department of Health and Human Services, and any other health interests in the government, from any involvement in making trade policy. In 1988, the Inter-agency Committee on Smoking and Health attempted to hold a meeting on tobacco trade policies. Surgeon General Koop invited representatives from the Departments of State, Commerce, and Agriculture. But after the White House and Congress objected, the meeting was called off. The USTR maintained that these were strictly questions of trade, not public health, and Koop's committee had no authority in this realm.[68] Meanwhile, the tobacco lobby secured the support of some twenty-eight senators who signed a letter urging the expansion of foreign cigarette trade.

Vice President Dan Quayle candidly expressed U.S. policy on the matter in 1990:

> Tobacco exports should be expanded aggressively because Americans are smoking less. . . . We're not going to back away from what public health officials say and what reports say. But on the other hand, we're not going to deny a country our export from our country because of that policy.[69]

Quayle's comments simply made explicit what was already clear: the Bush administration would support trade regardless of the public health implications. "We do not see why the U.S. should necessarily set the global public health agenda," said Adam Bryan-Brown, an R.J. Reynolds spokesperson. Trade representatives and industry executives alike continued to argue that opening new markets merely created new competition among brands, not new smokers.[70]

In 1990, the General Accounting Office (GAO) investigated the USTR's policies regarding the export of American tobacco products and concluded that there was a discrepancy between the USTR's actions to open new markets and U.S. health policies regarding domestic and international tobacco control. The GAO also documented that the Department of Health and Human Services was given no role whatsoever in the formulation of trade policy, even on issues that carried significant public health concerns.[71] Surgeon General Koop drew attention to these contradictions in the early 1990s:

> The inconsistency between U.S. tobacco trade policy and U.S. health policy increasingly is obvious and denounced in the international health

community. . . . At a time when we are pleading with foreign governments to stop the export of cocaine, it is the height of hypocrisy for the
U.S. to export tobacco.

Koop later decried the role the government had played in expanding tobacco markets. "I think the most shameful thing this country did was to export disease, disability and death by selling our cigarettes to the world. . . .
What the companies did was shocking, but even more appalling was the
fact that our government helped make it possible."[72]

§

The companies had a long and successful history of opposing tobacco control initiatives in the developing countries. Their strategy included establishing ties to agricultural and finance ministers in developing nations,
emphasizing the economic significance of tobacco, creating resentment
about the "imposition" of controls, and attempting to shift authority over
tobacco from the WHO to more sympathetic agencies, specifically within
the United Nations. These massive and well-financed campaigns took full
advantage of the industry's lobbying and public relations expertise, honed
through its long history of fighting regulations in developed nations, to
derail the recommendations of health ministries. The tobacco companies
fomented opposition, secretly funded "independent," third-party groups
representing local and international leaf growers, and infiltrated UN group
processes.[73]

Industry representatives repeatedly castigated WHO efforts at tobacco
control as paternalistic and intrusive. While WHO sought to develop
transnational regulatory initiatives, the multinational companies insisted
that tobacco policies must be handled at the discretion of individual governments. As British American Tobacco asserted in 1982:

As far as smoking and health issues are concerned, it must be up to individual governments, which have, of course, sovereign rights over their
policies, to state how they wish such matters to be handled. . . . Commercial, marketing and regulatory practices vary widely from country to
country. We believe that to attempt to impose practices which suit one

country on other countries with very different cultural, economic and social circumstances would be irrelevant, impertinent and do little service to the cause of North-South understanding.[74]

The companies constantly reiterated their basic premise that smoking was a matter of individual choice. Third world governments did not need paternalistic public health crusaders determining tobacco policies for their citizens. Management consultant George A. Dalley argued in a private 1984 memo that

> Philip Morris should be unapologetic about its advertising and promotion activity in the third world. There is something patronizing about the WHO approach to smoking and health in the third world. WHO assumes that people must be saved from demon tobacco by their governments; that they can't be trusted to make personal decisions about whether or not to smoke. People in the West, despite increased government intervention, make these decisions all the time, and third world leaders generally resent the implication that they and their people must be protected. Since smoking is often associated with increased affluence, there is the further resentment that part of the lifestyle towards which people in the third world are striving is, by some arbitrary judgment, being made unattainable. Thus nationalism and aspiration for development and a higher standard of living will lead third world governments to resist the efforts of the do-gooders from WHO to impose a smokeless society upon them.[75]

Going a step further, Dalley described how the industry vigorously sought to invent a new image as a responsible and progressive participant in international commerce and development:

> WHO pins the blame on the multimillion dollar tobacco companies for promoting smoking and views with alarm the development of new markets by international corporations such as Philip Morris.
> In this context, Philip Morris needs to be involved in the international debate on the impact of smoking on health and in efforts to defend its ability

to market product in new, developing markets. But beyond this, I believe it would be useful for the company to raise its profile as a responsible international corporate citizen. There is an existing opportunity for the leadership of the company to identify Philip Morris with issues of paramount concern to the so-called Third World, such as the impact of current economic trends in the industrialized world upon the future of their own development, the international debt crisis, trade, the arms race and others. . . .[76]

These leadership initiatives never strayed far from the primary goal of weakening tobacco-control efforts. To coincide with the World Health Conference on Tobacco OR Health held in Argentina in 1992, for example, Philip Morris operatives planned a publicity campaign to refocus public attention on AIDS. A letter from a local British American Tobacco representative to the executives organizing this campaign makes the company's intentions clear:

Please find enclosed herewith draft with the actions to be developed in conjunction with PM [Philip Morris] in orther [sic] to weaken the 8th World Conference on Tobacco or Health. . . .

AIDS CAMPAIGN PROPOSAL

The object will be to scatter the public attention payed [sic] to the Conference and refer it to the AIDS subject, bearing in mind that nowadays Argentina is quite concerned and threatened with AIDS than any other epidemic disease.

Being the disease of the century and a preventive disease, AIDS should be 'public enemy No. 1' because of its terminal consequences at every age.

Facing the AIDS increasing importance in the world and in Argentina we believe this disease to be the sole matter capable of eclipsing the conference.[77]

By the early 1990s, it had become apparent that the considerable progress international health efforts had made in improving life expectancy through disease prevention and better nutrition might be completely undone by cigarettes. In response to this threat, WHO began to direct new attention to the health impacts of tobacco. In 1995, the World Health Assembly, WHO's governing body, began an inquiry into the possibility of an international treaty on tobacco control. The investigation assessed strategies for developing international standards of tobacco control; ways to assist national governments in developing domestic legislation; and the need for an international mechanism to counter the influence of the multinational industry. In May 1996, the World Health Assembly unanimously passed a resolution calling for the director-general to develop a framework convention (a form of multilateral treaty) for tobacco control under Article 19 of the 1948 WHO constitution, which states that WHO "shall have the authority to adopt conventions and agreements with respect to any matter within the competence of the organization."[78]

The idea of such a treaty marked the return of international law, after almost a century of neglect, to matters of public health. International health diplomacy and protocols date back to the mid-nineteenth century. In 1851, the first International Sanitary Conference was held to develop approaches to stem the ongoing epidemics of smallpox, cholera, and yellow fever, which posed a major impediment to international commerce. The initiatives developed from the Sanitary Conference were intended to harmonize public health protocols among European nations and establish international standards for disease surveillance. In this period prior to the development of modern therapeutic regimes, public health was widely regarded as a critical element of international diplomacy and trade.[79]

WHO was established in 1948 with a sweeping mandate: "the attainment by all peoples of the highest level of health," with *health* ambitiously defined as "a state of complete physical, mental, and social well-being, and not merely the absence of disease or infirmity." The WHO charter explicitly included a treaty-making authority, and it was envisioned that this function would be central to the organization's programs. But as of the early 1990s, this capacity had never been deployed. World health initiatives came to center on control of infectious disease: delivery of immunizations and antibiotics, and access to primary health care.[80] This priority was not surprising given that in the immediate postwar period, new antibiotics, vaccines, and other measures appeared to offer unparalleled opportunities to stop infectious disease in its tracks. When the organization invoked its legislative powers, it was generally to support efforts to eradicate infectious diseases through International Sanitary Regulations (later renamed International Health Regulations), which mandate that nations report cases of yellow fever, cholera, and the plague. These legal initiatives, though important, were not in sync with the changing landscape of international health and the rise of chronic noninfectious diseases like cancer and heart disease in the third world, formerly of concern only for wealthier countries. This health transition would ultimately force WHO to confront tobacco. Historically, public health had not had the tools to prevent the chronic diseases associated with tobacco use, but now these noncommunicable diseases were among the most prominent causes of disability and death.[81]

§

The notion of developing an international treaty for tobacco control was first broached in the early 1990s by Ruth Roemer and Allyn Taylor, American legal scholars with strong interests in health and international law. Roemer had extensive experience in tobacco-control issues, and Taylor had fashioned an important argument concerning the need for additional capacity in international public health law. Having floated the idea with WHO staff and tobacco-control advocacy groups, Taylor and Roemer were asked to develop a more fully articulated proposal in 1995.[82] Their manuscript apparently met with mixed reactions in WHO's upper echelons. Some considered it unrealistic, impractical, and overly ambitious, and preferred a nonbinding "code of conduct" to an international treaty. But Derek Yach, the new WHO chief of the Policy Coordination Committee and executive director of noncommunicable diseases and mental health, became a powerful advocate for developing a binding multilateral agreement.

Yach was a physician and public health authority whose tobacco control efforts had met with considerable success in his native South Africa. In the early 1980s, he had written an account of health and economic impacts of smoking in South Africa that the Medical Research Council, where Yach worked, refused to publish, fearing industry retribution. Yach submitted it to the *South African Medical Journal*, where it appeared in 1982. By 1988, he had assisted in the preparation of a special tobacco issue of that journal—an important breakthrough in national antitobacco efforts and a major influence on South Africa's turn to a more proactive tobacco control policy. Between 1993 and 2000, cigarette consumption in South Africa would decline by 20 percent. Yach knew from this early work that tobacco control required the integration of multiple disciplines: "You need the right combination of science, evidence, and politics to succeed," he said in a 2003 interview. "If you have one without the other, you don't see action."[83]

At WHO, Yach sought to bring "best practices"—often modeled on U.S. grassroots activities—to the Tobacco Free Initiative. He was especially influenced by the state initiatives in California and Massachusetts, the two leading U.S. programs, where aggressive antitobacco advertisements were coupled with school-based education, workplace bans, and cessation programs.[84] Further, a number of countries developed national tobacco-control programs that confirmed the efficacy of such interventions on a mass scale. In Poland, for example, under the leadership of physician Witold Zatonski, smoking rates among men dropped from over 60 percent in the late 1970s to 40 percent in 2000. Zatonski credited the Massachusetts program as his model.[85] In Thailand, where Greg Connolly also provided advice and expertise, new public health initiatives—motivated in part by the U.S. trade actions—led to a reduction in rates of smoking from over 26 percent of adults to 20.5 percent between 1992 and 1999.[86] Nations as diverse as Uganda and Ireland passed smoke-free workplace laws despite corporate opposition.[87] Antitobacco activists, public health officials, and nongovernmental tobacco-control organizations now made up an active international network galvanizing activities in countries around the globe.

As this community's influence grew, support for a formal treaty grew as well.[88] With the election of Gro Harlem Brundtland, former prime minister of Norway, to the director-generalship in 1998, WHO became considerably bolder, especially in efforts directed at noncommunicable diseases and the politics of public health. As Brundtland explained in 2002, "I needed to move the global health agenda much more closely to the development debate, on to the tables of prime ministers and development and finance ministers, not just the health ministers."[89]

In addition to dedicating WHO to an "evidence-based" approach that would evaluate public health initiatives for "efficacy," Brundtland brought a reformist agenda to an organization widely regarded as being in disarray. Richard Smith, editor of the *British Medical Journal,* had described WHO as "top heavy," "over centralized," and "smelling of corruption."[90] Extensive cronyism had compromised its technical expertise. Brundtland had to reform WHO's administration at the same time that she refocused its resources on the systemic, chronic diseases now increasingly significant in the developing world. She possessed a deep commitment to the authority of scientific and medical expertise and was not afraid to tackle health issues where commerce and public health might collide.[91] Tobacco control soon rose to the top of her priorities. In 1999, following the approval of the World Health Assembly, formal negotiations began to develop a Framework Convention on Tobacco Control (FCTC). Brundtland established a working group to assist in drafting the treaty. At each step, the likelihood of some agreement seemed increasingly feasible, especially given the strong commitment of the upper echelons of WHO administration.[92]

A framework convention is a complex multilateral agreement that enunciates core principles and policies. These approaches would then be implemented by national legislation and policy initiatives among those who ratify the framework and become "party" to the convention. Most framework conventions of the late twentieth century dealt with environmental issues that were outside the control of individual nations. Climate change, ozone depletion, and environmental pollution—addressed in the Kyoto, Montreal, and Barcelona Conventions—were all problems that required collective policies among nations. As a result, these agreements were fashioned to assign collective responsibilities for mitigating these shared burdens.[93] A central issue of the FCTC was whether tobacco could justify this collective approach. The multinational tobacco companies and their allies contended that tobacco restrictions did not meet this international criterion for common action and should be dealt with exclusively on a nation-by-nation basis. In response, the treaty's advocates directed attention to supranational issues, such as the relationship of taxation to cigarette smuggling, and the "leakage" advertising between nations with strict controls and those without restrictions. Unilateral attempts by nations to control tobacco use were likely to fail, given the companies' aggressive multinational marketing efforts and the WTO's insistence on treating tobacco as a "conventional" product. Tobacco, treaty advocates argued, constituted a risk that could be mitigated only through international collaboration.[94]

§

The drafting of the convention by the Intergovernmental Negotiating Body (which met six times between 2000 and 2003) took many complex turns. Among the most contentious issues were how binding the advertising and other promotional restrictions should be. American negotiators took the position that such restrictions were unconstitutional. Another concern was that the new treaty would conflict with existing trade agreements, raising questions about the legitimacy of regulatory restrictions, such as those on advertising and promotion. A number of delegations sought language to clarify that the framework convention would take precedence; the United States, Germany, and Japan opposed this measure. With the support of Philip Morris, the U.S. negotiators worked to assure that trade agreements would have priority. The American representatives also objected to a proposed system for tracking and tracing cigarette packages in order to combat smuggling, an important source of profit for the industry because such cigarettes go untaxed.[95]

As negotiations continued through the change of U.S. presidential administrations in 2001, the chief U.S. negotiator involved in the process, Assistant Surgeon General Thomas Novotny, a career civil servant and a Public Health Service expert on tobacco control, found himself under serious pressure to weaken previously held positions supporting tobacco control. White House representatives had demanded that he now oppose limitations on terms like *low-tar* and *lights* that the National Cancer Institute had previously deemed to misrepresent the risks of cigarettes. The Bush administration pushed him to demand that the agreement permit any nation to "opt out" of any particular protocol, a proposal that would have rendered the convention meaningless.[96] Administration officials also instructed him to oppose key provisions on taxation and advertising, to argue that controls on exposures to secondhand smoke must be voluntary, and to oppose restrictions on public smoking that were already widely accepted in the United States. "The positions that we had developed, which were headed in the right direction, we had to reverse in midstream, almost in mid-sentence," he later explained. "It was horrible. I felt devastated."[97]

Novotny resigned, joining a small but growing contingent of individuals who had bravely stood up to the powerful interests of Big Tobacco and their allies in government.

Congressman Henry Waxman, a major supporter of stronger restrictions on the industry and a close observer of the FCTC process, accused the Bush administration of undertaking "a breathtaking reversal in U.S. policy—going from global leader on tobacco control to pulling back and advocating the industry's positions." Waxman wrote directly to Bush, asserting, "I have received evidence that the U.S. is seeking to undermine world efforts to negotiate an international agreement to reduce tobacco use."[98] Although the United States eventually voted in the World Health Assembly to support the treaty, there was little doubt that the Bush administration had worked hard to undermine it.[99]

As the convention-building process went forward at WHO, the major tobacco companies took additional countermeasures. Philip Morris hired a public relations firm, Mongoven, Biscoe & Duchin (MBD), to evaluate their liabilities and offer strategies as the framework convention process moved forward in the late 1990s. MBD had achieved fame during the Nestlé boycott in the 1980s by helping Nestlé respond to international sanctions while continuing to aggressively market its controversial infant formulas throughout the world. Following in the historic footsteps of Hill & Knowlton, MBD now offered to play a vital role in fighting off tobacco regulations. Eager to get the full attention of management, MBD's sales pitch to Philip Morris stressed the high stakes for the industry:

> As currently proposed and drafted, the framework convention will provide the means to eradicate the tobacco business worldwide. To shape an agreement into an acceptable program to safeguard minors would require a long-term (five to seven years) strategy involving considerable money, resources and executive commitment. . . . WHO is in the fight with substantial resources, unshakeable determination and powerful allies. It also has all the emotional issues on its side—health, children, women, the poor and a host of others.[100]

As a result of these concerns, MBD proposed approaches for influencing the process in the industry's interest.

> Examination of the draft text will help Philip Morris anticipate the potential protocols that the framework convention will create. The history of framework conventions shows that successful weakening of the language of an article in the framework convention can be easily undermined by the protocol process. The potential protocols are more important to the company in the long-term than the framework convention itself.[101]

Therefore, Philip Morris should remain an engaged participant in the process so as to co-opt and weaken the treaty:

> Aside from delaying the adoption of a convention the company is best served by participating in the development of the agreement. It would be in the company's best interest to have the treaty focus entirely on protecting children and leaving adult choice protected.[102]

Philip Morris's strategy should be to inhibit consensus and disrupt the negotiations:

> Keeping in mind the need to make any treaty more costly than no treaty, proposals can be surfaced which assist many developing countries but which seriously harm others. Resolution of such issues is time consuming and often embittering. . . . The vast majority of the countries participating in the code development process are motivated solely by self-interest and the assumption of that principle should underlie every strategy the company adopts.[103]

As MBD recognized, self-interest was a motivation with which the tobacco industry's executive elite could easily identify.

Much of the documentation WHO used in its investigation of the industry came from the litigation in the United States. The availability of these internal memoranda, reports, and letters revealed not only industry strategy for the promotion and marketing of cigarettes, but also the intensity

and scope of its efforts to undermine international tobacco control initiatives. The U.S. litigation had, in this way, served the interests of international efforts for tobacco control. With these materials in hand,
Brundtland's resolve to push ahead with the FCTC was redoubled.[104]

§

The final version of the FCTC closely followed the format of other recent
international environmental agreements. A lengthy preamble expressed the
particular concerns that gave rise to the treaty:

- The dramatic increase in worldwide tobacco consumption;
- The escalation in smoking and other forms of tobacco consumption
  by children and adolescents;
- The impact of all forms of advertising, promotion, and sponsorship
  aimed at encouraging tobacco use.

The framework seeks to bring all nations into a shared tobacco-regulatory
regime that sets stringent universal standards of control. These standards
are minimums: signatories are invited to pursue additional restrictions.
"Nothing in these instruments shall prevent a party from imposing stricter
requirements that are consistent with the provisions and are in accordance
with international law."[105] The convention explicitly drew upon the public
health initiatives that had over recent decades been shown to have a positive impact on the prevention and reduction of cigarette use. Among the
measures the convention endorses are:

- Taxes: To reduce demand, taxes ought to be raised to both cover
  tobacco-related health costs, as well as increase the price of cigarettes,
  keeping in mind the importance of price to underage customers.
  Duty-free sales ought to be reduced or banned.
- Disclosure: Tobacco manufacturers shall be required to disclose
  ingredients.
- Labeling: Health warnings must cover at least 30 percent of cigarette
  packaging.
- Terms such as *light*, *low-tar*, and *mild* are considered misleading and
  ought not appear on tobacco products. These terms were banned in a

previous draft; it is now at the discretion of each country whether to ban them.

- Education: Each country must promote and strengthen public awareness of tobacco control issues, using all available communication tools.
- Public Restrictions: Countries ought to develop national laws and encourage regions and municipalities to develop laws to protect non-smokers from smoke in public places, including workplaces, public transportation, and restaurants.
- Advertising: Each country ought to enact a comprehensive ban on tobacco advertising, sponsorship and promotion, including cross-border advertising.
- Cessation: Each country shall take effective measures to promote tobacco cessation and ensure adequate treatment for tobacco dependence.
- Smuggling: As an antismuggling measure, each cigarette pack must be marked to show both the exporting and importing countries.
- Youth: To reduce sales to minors, each country must prohibit the distribution of free tobacco products, as well as the sale of individual cigarettes or small packs of cigarettes, both of which increase affordability. Tobacco products may not be sold in any place where they are directly accessible to minors (vending machines, store shelves). Candy, snacks, and toys that resemble tobacco products (i.e., candy cigarettes) may not be manufactured or sold. All vendors must ask for proof of age for tobacco purchases.
- Litigation: Countries are encouraged to consider tobacco litigation to recover damages.

These provisions are both general and modest. The model of the framework convention recognizes that nations are more likely to ratify treaties setting out broadly shared principles than those containing specific mechanisms of implementation and enforcement. Nonetheless, the FCTC offers an important consensual basis for the development of more aggressive and significant protocols that might ultimately provide a balancing force against the current global-trade regime.[106]

The ultimate test for the FCTC will be in the collision with the free-trade regimes of the World Trade Organization. After considerable debate during the drafting process, the final text is silent on the inevitable conflicts between public health restrictions and trade liberalization. In their original 1995 proposal, Taylor and Roemer contended that according to the Vienna Convention on the Law of Treaties, an international tobacco-control treaty would supersede the WTO since subsequent multilateral agreements take precedence over previous international accords. Although a joint study of the WHO and WTO, issued during FCTC negotiations, asserted that the WTO recognized human health as "important to the highest degree," this recognition has yet to be put to any concrete test.[107]

Even the WTO was forced to admit that the sale of tobacco products entails many market failures and inefficiencies. In the developing world, there is inadequate information and education about the health risks of tobacco use or its highly addictive qualities. And the harms imposed on nonsmokers add still more social costs. Nonetheless, tobacco use is defined nearly everywhere as a "lifestyle" issue and an essentially voluntary behavior. This view remains largely unchallenged in the administration of WTO, the North American Free Trade Agreement (NAFTA), and other important trade agreements.[108] In Canada, for example, tobacco companies cited NAFTA in their successful efforts to scuttle a law requiring plain packaging of cigarettes. Philip Morris claimed that proposals to remove *light* and *mild* from packaging violated NAFTA and WTO rules on Technical Barriers to Trade and Intellectual Property because such restrictions could be interpreted as eroding trademarks.[109] The WTO negotiations on corporate services (under the General Agreement on Trade in Services) has the potential to sharply curtail the ability of governments to protect their citizens from commerce in tobacco products.[110]

Under the WTO—as under GATT—anyone advocating restrictions faces a heavy burden to demonstrate scientifically not just the health impact of a dangerous product like the cigarette, but also the efficacy of any proposed regulations. Anticipating possible free-trade objections, WHO worked to ensure that the protocols of the FCTC would be based on scientific evidence of their effectiveness.[111] Although the FCTC did not explicitly urge that tobacco be excluded from free-trade agreements, this was nonetheless the implicit motivation underlying its development. "It would be anomalous for the nations of the world to identify tobacco control as a major global health priority," explained one legal scholar, "justifying several years of multilateral negotiations, only to conclude that tobacco products should in fact be subject to the normal trade rules."[112] According to this view, it was crucial that dangerous products, like cigarettes, be treated as an exception in trade agreements: "This distinction between a beneficial product and a harmful one essentially turns the traditional presumption in favor of free trade on its head with respect to tobacco."[113]

§

Although the final version of the treaty was derided as "feeble" and "meaningless," Derek Yach emphasized the procedural success of establishing a framework. "We will not achieve this goal if the Framework Convention is too stringent, contradicting fundamental political and legal realities in each country, and requiring too much from the first stage of a multistage process. . . . A framework convention cannot go further than the political will of the negotiators at a given time. This process will continue to unfold and mature after the adoption of the Convention."[114] The FCTC, in other words, establishes only the basic foundation for subsequent efforts. Even following its ratification, tobacco control and regulation will face formidable obstacles throughout the world. As Yach recently noted in a series of pointed questions:

How do we move fast from adoption to ratification and full implementation of the FCTC? You need to push daily and weekly for countries to act.

How do we interact with tobacco companies and the investment community as new products are developed?

How do we access funding for governments and NGOs that already exists but is not being requested?

How do we popularize the next era of tobacco control measures needed to move faster ahead: from plain packaging to tax financed health promotion programs to locally effective counter marketing?

How do we work with farmers in poor countries and have them be advocates for tobacco control?

We need to find ways to get the rate of decline to reach 5–10% per year,
not the feeble 1–2% it is in some countries today.[115]

The FCTC would offer a procedural basis for systematically addressing
these questions, but Yach's formulation explicitly recognizes that tobacco
control will achieve no dramatic, precipitous victory.

§

On May 21, 2003, the 192 member nations of WHO unanimously adopted
the FCTC, WHO's first-ever multilateral treaty. Brundtland noted,
"Today, we are acting to save billions of lives and protect people's health for
generations to come. This is a historic moment in global public health,
demonstrating the international will to tackle a threat to health head on."
Matthew Myers, president of the Campaign for Tobacco-Free Kids, went
even further, claiming, "This treaty is the closest thing we have to a vaccine
against tobacco-caused death in the developing world."[116] After more than
a half-century, the organization had exercised its mandate for promoting
public health law through its treaty-making power.

These long-standing advocates of the treaty were not the only ones expressing support. Tommy Thompson, the U.S. Secretary of Health and
Human Services, said, "This is an outstanding day when you can stand up
and make a step forward for public health." Although the United States
was reluctant to support the treaty over the years of negotiations—indeed,
the U.S. vote had been uncertain the night before—Thompson now was
effusive in his praise and eager to remind the assembly that the United
States was a world leader at home in antismoking efforts. Even Philip
Morris seemed eager to show that it had turned over a new tobacco leaf
and become a "responsible corporate citizen." Mark Berlind, associate
general counsel for the company, said, "What we hope and expect is that
this treaty can be a catalyst in every country that signs on for meaningful
and effective treatment of tobacco." Since the FCTC would require the
ratification of forty countries to take effect, such posturing had little immediate cost.

§

The apparent unity masked ongoing and intense conflicts about the marketing and use of tobacco products.[117] The critiques were drafted even before the waiters had cleared away the wine glasses from the closing reception. First, the industry argued that the FCTC imposed Western ideas of health on the rest of the world. Martin Broughton, chairman of British American Tobacco, had complained in 2000 that the FCTC was a "developed world obsession being foisted on the developing world,"[118] and he and his allies now took up this attack again. Under the Brundtland directorship, they charged, WHO had strayed from its essential mission of protecting individuals in poorer nations from the principal threats to health—which in their view meant communicable diseases. This argument was perhaps most effectively voiced by the British philosopher Roger Scruton, who wrote an extensive criticism of the FCTC in 2000. "It cannot be the function of a health bureaucracy," he wrote, "to cure us of such self-imposed risks," a category that included rugby, football, cycling, and horseback riding as well as smoking. For Scruton, tobacco use was not a health problem but simply a question of "lifestyle" outside the purview of medicine, public health, and certainly regulation. His assault on WHO offered a sophisticated amalgam of old saws and nouveau, anti-PC chic.

> By a semantic trick, Mrs. Brundtland and her team have been able to classify as a dangerous disease what is in fact, a voluntary activity and a source of pleasure, the risk of which falls entirely on the smoker. . . . Big tobacco is an easily demonized opponent, and one currently as defenceless as a chained and baited bear.[119]

Scruton's attack on the FCTC could not have been more forceful if he were working for the tobacco industry itself. And it soon came to light that this supposedly independent intellectual was in the employ of Japan Tobacco, one of the world's largest producers and exporters. In an e-mail to his handlers leaked to the *Guardian*, Scruton had sought a bump in salary: "We think we give good value for money in a business largely conducted by shysters and sharks."[120] No doubt he was the best philosopher Big Tobacco could buy. Scruton quickly learned that taking tobacco money on the sly could have repercussions for a professional pundit. The *Financial Times* and *Wall Street Journal* both severed their ties with him after his financial arrangements were made public. But his activities were in no way unusual. The tobacco companies have a long history of acquiring the services of intellectuals and cultural elites as part of their long-term strategy to influence public discourse and debate.[121] In any event, in the industry's concerted effort to disrupt the FCTC, Scruton was a bit player.

British American Tobacco, in a statement rife with historical irony, sought to portray the FCTC as an act of Western colonialism:

> A clumsy pursuit of global standards can become a form of moral and cultural imperialism, based on assumptions that "west is best." Imposing western priorities, or "global solutions" that force the values and priorities of any one country on another, can become a new form of colonialism.[122]

In another instance, British American Tobacco based its opposition to the FCTC on its "respect for cultural diversity":

> Our perspective on doing business throughout the world is based on long held respect for cultural diversity. . . . We do not believe in "one size fits all." In business operations, and in issues surrounding foreign investment, development, the environment, labour standards or appropriate regulation, we believe that local self-determination is vital. National governments and citizens are best placed to define national priorities, and the actions that will work in their societies. . . . Calls for global regulations and standards, however reasonable they may seem to western eyes, can risk alienating emerging nations and damaging their competitiveness. If globalization is to bring widespread benefits, the views of the few should not be imposed on the majority.[123]

The tobacco industry had now honed its new arguments for the defense of the realm. After nearly half a century, the tobacco industry had finally abandoned its traditional justification of "no proof." To maintain a protected social space for an increasingly stigmatized product and behavior, the companies now justified the continued unfettered promotion of tobacco products throughout the world by affecting a posture of democratically minded concern for individual autonomy:

- We have no interest in recruiting new smokers; only in getting current smokers to switch brands;
- Smoking is for adults only; we have no interest in underage smoking. To the contrary, we will work diligently to restrict smoking to adults. When children do become smokers, it is generally a result of peer pressure;
- Advertising and marketing of tobacco products is exclusively for encouraging adult smokers to switch brands;
- We know that smoking is a "risk behavior," and that in some instances may lead to disease;
- There is a significant, if not overwhelming, uncertainty about the risks of smoking to nonsmokers;
- Smoking is a voluntary behavior; anyone can quit, although for some it may be difficult.

These universal half-truths—refined over decades—form the basis for the aggressive marketing of tobacco across the globe. The future of the industry today is based on the effective assertion of this new theme: "responsibly marketing a dangerous product."

Recent studies have shown that historians and astrologers are about equally successful in predicting the future. It is difficult to assess what impact the Framework Convention for Tobacco Control is likely to have. But it has already cleared some important obstacles, and it at least offers the potential for the nations of the world to consolidate a range of antitobacco policies, and so advance the cause of reducing tobacco-related sickness and death in the years ahead. It marks a growing recognition that in many crucial instances public health must take on powerful transnational corporate interests. The ultimate test of the framework convention will be in the negotiation of binding protocols following the treaty's entry into force, which occurred in 2005.[124] The first meeting of the Conference of Parties, which took place in February 2006, initiated this process. As of this writing, 140 countries have become party to the convention. In this respect, the U.S. failure to ratify the FCTC is consistent with the failure to ratify other important conventions and the emerging ethos of American unilateralism. President Bush—Secretary Thompson's effusive public endorsement notwithstanding—has not forwarded the treaty to the Senate for consideration.

The framework convention has the capacity to expose the hypocrisy and exploitation associated with tobacco promotion around the world. The industry's assertion that harms deemed unacceptable in the affluent West are tolerated in the developing world smacks of a dubious moral calculus. It implies that people in India or Egypt really don't object to dying of cancer as long as they were spared from TB or cholera. Common sense suggests the fundamental flaw in this logic. The FCTC also reveals long-standing tensions at WHO—and indeed at the heart of modern public health—between biological and technical approaches to disease and the sociopolitical interventions often required for prevention and health promotion. This is another false dichotomy: all public health engages both the technical and the political. One of the great appeals of biotechnology is that it appeared to free public health from the most difficult sociopolitical questions. Global tobacco control, however, makes gene modification seem simple. And the tobacco wars are a persistent reminder of the powerful economic and political forces arrayed near the trenches. The problems of reducing tobacco-related diseases are radically different from those associated with assuring the provision of vaccines and medication, and they force the public health community to confront its critical limitations in strategy, capacity, and resources.

Is tobacco control merely a luxury for affluent nations that have brought acute infectious diseases under control? The notion that national and international public health programs must address communicable diseases *before* tackling noncommunicable diseases is highly suspect. It is typically based on the misconception that wealthy nations are affected by systemic, chronic diseases whereas poorer nations remain exclusively under the burden of infectious disease. Today, in the *developing* world, noncommunicable diseases have become the leading cause of morbidity and mortality. If the global burden of disease is to be reduced, public health strategists will need to resist the traditional division of communicable and noncommunicable diseases, partly because they share many risk factors in common. The risks of tobacco exacerbate the risks of infection and poverty, and vice versa.[125]

The long latency of tobacco-related diseases remains a major obstacle to regulation and behavior change. Moreover, the slow development of symptoms and health effects have the effect of blocking political initiatives for tobacco control. Politicians and public health officials typically need to demonstrate short-range returns to secure investment or popular support. In the case of tobacco regulation, the health benefits are often two or three decades in the future. Yet the costs in lost agricultural, manufacturing, and tax revenues are quickly and concretely apparent.[126]

It has been conservatively estimated that 100 million people around the world died from tobacco related diseases in the twentieth century. Through the first half of that century, the health risks of smoking had yet to be scientifically demonstrated. In this century, in which we have known tobacco's health effects from the first day, the death toll is predicted to be one billion.[127]

This is a pandemic. But it is different from pandemics that most historians, public health officials, and physicians are familiar with. It is unlike the plague that swept medieval Europe, the flu of 1918, or the HIV disease currently devastating sub-Saharan Africa. The difference is that the agent—the cause of disease—is a popular and aggressively marketed legal product, the lifeline of one of the most successful multinational industries of the last hundred years, and a source of revenues to farmers, workers, and governments throughout the world. Not only individual smokers, but nation states too, suffer from tobacco dependence. For such an epidemic, there will be no magic bullets.

Never in human history has a product been so popular, so profitable, and so deadly. In the twentieth century, we came to understand—in ways both rational and scientific—tobacco's character. But we are only now learning how difficult and complex it will be to mitigate its harms in the face of powerful corporate interests deeply committed to the diffusion of their product and the profits it secures. We must confront a well-known, but often avoided, reality: that public health must engage economy and

In millions

■ If consumption remains constant

■ If the proportion of young adults taking up smoking halves by 2020

□ If adult consumption halves by 2020

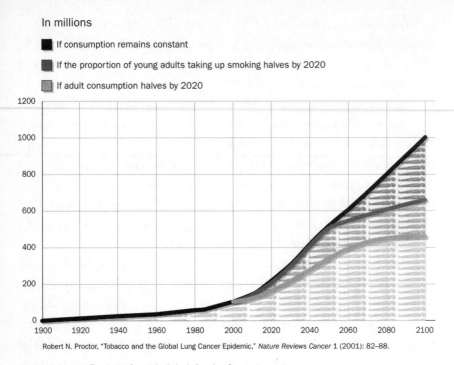

Robert N. Proctor, "Tobacco and the Global Lung Cancer Epidemic," *Nature Reviews Cancer* 1 (2001): 82–88.

CHART 9   Projected total global deaths from cigarettes

politics at the same time it deploys science and medicine. The FCTC marks a contemporary approach—modest and limited, but an approach nonetheless—to public health innovation in the face of an unprecedented, commodity-driven pandemic.

If we are to ultimately develop effective programs to address the epidemiological rise of noncommunicable diseases, we must first understand the social nature of risks and their movement across the globe. Just like infectious pathogens, risk factors for noncommunicable diseases move across the planet in ways that are neither random nor idiosyncratic. Like infectious diseases in the past, they follow the routes of trade and commerce. They move from less vulnerable populations to those more vulnerable, from more highly-regulated polities to less-regulated ones, from more affluent regions to those less well-off, from the literate to the nonliterate, and from nations where cultural cues constrict the risk, to those whose cultures tend to expand it. In the case of tobacco, the movement of risk has been carefully orchestrated, and it is profoundly affecting the global burden of disease; new regions continue to be invaded by this on-going plague of cigarettes—the result of calculated and documented corporate practices, often supported by national governments.

It is, of course, the long-standing position of the tobacco industry that smoking is a voluntary behavior, engaged in by consenting adults who now are well aware of—and *assume*—what risks are attributed to the industry's product. So long as we accept the premise that the *risks* of smoking are *assumed* by individuals who are exercising their *rights,* there is indeed no case for an international tobacco control regime. These classic notions of individual responsibility and freedom are central to the multinationals' ability to promote tobacco use throughout the world. Such arguments, as we have seen, were employed repeatedly in the United States as the risks of tobacco use became known; as long as tobacco was viewed as a risk of individuals, rather than populations and societies, it would remain weakly regulated. We *want* to believe (and the industry wants us to believe) that smoking is a voluntary behavior and that citizens with fortitude can simply quit. And this view is reinforced because people *do* quit all the time.

But we cannot let the fact that some are able to quit blind us to a more complex reality about risk behaviors and their promotion. The tobacco industry's position belies the history of the movement of tobacco's harms around the world. Tobacco use is aggressively promoted and marketed; a vast majority of smokers throughout the world begin as children; smokers become addicted to nicotine, a powerful drug; this addiction is reinforced by marketing, promotion, and powerful cultural symbols; and nonsmokers (again, especially children) are harmed by the tobacco smoke of adults (who became addicted as children). There is a deep cultural and psychological pressure, sustained by the multinational industry, to reject this view of the tobacco trade.

Today, it is commonly understood that cigarette smoking constitutes an important risk to health, that smokers are vulnerable to many significant diseases and death. But the processes by which we determine, measure, and assess risks like smoking are complex and subject to culture, psychology, and politics. Most of these methods offer a uniform and objectified evaluation of risks as a determinant object. There are real advantages in this approach in that it permits us to enumerate and compare disparate risks (e.g., the risk of dying in a traffic accident versus an airplane crash). But risks also have social and cultural attributes that may subvert any single metric.

Risk culture is often shaped by powerful externalities. In the rise of the cigarette, we see the powerful role played by the world wars of the twentieth century. In both wars, the prospect of immediate and violent death overwhelmed any concerns about the health risks of smoking—or worries about its propriety. It took an era of sustained good health in the West to fully expose the cigarette's most serious, long-term harms. By the same token, the risks of smoking may be portrayed as relatively small in societies (or communities) where infectious disease and violent trauma remain significant killers. Much of this book, then, is about the historical process of determining what kind of a risk it is to smoke cigarettes. This is not a simple matter of calculation but a question that draws on a range of disciplines, methods, and theories in historically and culturally specific ways.

What is the risk?
How is it known? And by what methods?
How can it be modified, reduced, or eliminated?
Can it be tolerated? And under what conditions?
Who bears the responsibility for the risks we face?

While the industry is eager to depict the FCTC as an act of Western paternalism toward the developing world, one may as easily read the framework as an attempt to use moral suasion in the service of preventing disease and to construct a world order that reduces the toll a rogue industry takes on human health. Ultimately, international health is based on assumptions of equity and justice: the right to a life free of preventable and treatable disease; the essential injustice that those less well-off and less well educated do not gain the opportunities provided by attainable levels of good health.[128] "There is," noted Brundtland, "an increasing consensus for ethical norms, standards, and codes of rules common to all regions and cultures of the world."[129] If we permit the shift of the burden of tobacco-related disease to continue unchecked, we violate this basic standard of equality.

A century from now, historians will no doubt chronicle the history of the FCTC and assess its impact. Perhaps they will see it as a feeble and belated gesture at averting one of the worst epidemics in human history, exacerbated by the liberalization of trade in dangerous products. Yet if globalization facilitates the mass marketing of tobacco products throughout the world and a rise in overall consumption, perhaps it also holds the possibility of new and innovative arrangements in public health. Perhaps the next century's historians will look back at the FCTC as a breakthrough for public health and the collective action of enlightened states: the beginning of new forms of global governance in an age of civil societies committed to health, equity, and social justice. As historians know too well, only time will tell.

There is no reason for complacency about the dangers . . . of acquiring and propagating bacteria and viruses for biological weapons. But the dangers should be seen in the perspective of other threats to human life. In 1995, the last year for which official statistics are available, the number of people killed by tobacco in the United States was 502,000, of whom 214,000 were aged between thirty-five and sixty-nine. On average, each of these could have expected to live twenty-three years longer. In view of these alarming numbers, it seems to me that the still-prospering to-bacco industry poses a proven threat to health and life that is many thousand times greater than the potential of bio-terrorism.[1]

M. F. PERUTZ, 2000

Epilogue
The Crime of the Century

SHORTLY AFTER I had begun work on this book, I got a call from
an attorney at Shook, Hardy & Bacon, stalwart defender of the tobacco
industry, asking if he could pay me a brief visit. I had already grown suspicious of the industry's lawyers and their arguments, but they were eager to
hear what I was up to, and I was equally eager to hear about their cases. The
fellow soon appeared at my medical school office with four or five other attorneys in tow, all from elite firms like Arnold & Porter and Jones Day.

They wanted to know whether there had been a controversy about
smoking and health in the 1950s. Were any scientists and physicians genuinely skeptical of the epidemiological studies linking smoking to lung
cancer? My answer was that of course there was a controversy, and of
course there were skeptics. It would be difficult to identify a significant
finding in medicine and science that did not attract some degree of skepticism. The lawyers seemed quite pleased with this response.

But I went on to explain two additional facts. First, although there truly
were skeptics, even a handful who were not associated with the industry, they
were a rare breed, and very few had done any original research on smoking
and health. Second, the industry had worked diligently to foment the controversy. Without these efforts, the harms of smoking would have been uniformly accepted by medical science long before the 1964 surgeon general's
report—which, I pointed out, the industry had also sought to trash. The perception of ongoing, heated debate about the relationship of cigarettes and
disease had largely been a product of the industry's intensive public relations
efforts in the 1950s and after. Any professional historian, I said, who had
thoroughly pursued the relevant published and unpublished sources would

place the "debates" about the harms of smoking into this context. Suddenly my visitors were not so happy with me. I never saw them again.

I also heard from plaintiffs' lawyers, including the redoubtable Richard Daynard, who was always anxious to hear what I'd dug up from the archives. The eternal activist-optimist, Daynard would explain to me that the plaintiff attorneys he was advising were about to break through and finally expose the Big Lie, inflicting untold damage on Big Tobacco. I would often reply that in American health culture, where there was such a strong emphasis on individual responsibility and agency, such a victory would be difficult if not impossible. Nonetheless, my sympathies, and my research, began increasingly to sustain Daynard's hopes. Research on nicotine addiction, secondhand smoke, and the Joe Camel campaign all eroded the industry claim—central to its litigation strategy—that the harms of smoking were self-inflicted by choice. Even more importantly, industry documents now offered a paper trail of industry intent and deceit leading right into the CEOs' offices. Perhaps Daynard would turn out to be right.

Daynard would send plaintiffs lawyers to see me, and we would pick each others' brains about the history of the industry and the rise of scientific knowledge. Don Davis, who worked with Don Barrett on *Horton*, visited several times, and Woody Wilner, who represented Grady Carter and several other smokers in successful individual suits, came by to trade footnotes. There was also always a question about my possible availability to testify in a trial on behalf of a plaintiff. Each time I respectfully declined. Certainly, my research confirmed that the industry had conspired over many decades to deny and obscure the deadly risks of its product. The archival record was replete with evidence of corporate malfeasance and deceit that I believed would disrupt the industry's traditional blame-the-victim defense.

But I had no interest in becoming an expert witness. I was pleased to exchange research notes with the likes of Daynard, Davis, and Wilner. My research and my commitments to public health led me to sympathize with their cause. And I had come to believe that in the face of failed attempts at substantive legislative controls, litigation offered an important strategy for reducing the harms of smoking. But I saw no reason why a historian's perspective would carry much weight in a courtroom, where the combat scarcely resembles the staid academic debates I had become accustomed to. It would be best for me to present my work not in the adversarial context of tort litigation, but in the form of a book, where I could lay out my arguments in detail. I did not want my scholarship to be dismissed as "advocacy." The lawyers could use my work as they saw fit. I did not want to become a combatant in the tobacco wars; I much preferred my role as a war correspondent and military historian.

As the litigation heated up in the mid–1990s, I continued to believe that my inclination to avoid the courtroom was correct. Yet I saw that tobacco industry defense counsel were increasingly calling historians as witnesses. Typically, these historians would testify on two questions with which I had become quite familiar: the scientific debates prior to the surgeon general's report, and the idea of "common knowledge," the argument that, despite industry denials, everyone knew tobacco was harmful. I read these testimonies with considerable interest—and professional disgust at the way they radically distorted the historical record. The historians offering these accounts had little or no background in the period in question, had done no work in the history of medicine or public health, and had no specific credentials to undertake research into the questions at hand. Some were even fairly distinguished in their particular fields. Lacy Ford, a well-known historian of early nineteenth-century southern proslavery radicalism, testified on behalf of the industry about public knowledge of tobacco science and the mass media in the 1950s, a subject and a period on which he had published no research at all. It seemed to me that it would not be difficult for plaintiffs' attorneys to discredit such testimony. These industry witnesses had so selectively evaluated the evidence that their claims of widespread public understanding of the harms of smoking could be easily rebutted on cross-examination. Ford, for example, had not examined the massive industry promotion and advertising campaigns of the period in which he supposedly evaluated public knowledge of tobacco's harms.[2]

As the collective cases brought by the state attorneys general got going, Ron Motley came to see me. He was, as virtually everyone has described, highly intelligent, persuasive, and charismatic. I was very impressed, even in this early stage of the litigation, by his knowledge of tobacco science and his command of the industry documents.[3] But despite his generous appeal, I declined Motley's offer to participate as an expert witness. I was aware of these cases' legal and historical importance, but I worried about the loss of control over my work, the autonomy that historians so value to assure that their accounts of the past reflect complexity, subtlety, and nuance. I knew, generally, there is no room in the courtroom to qualify an argument offered on behalf of an adversary.

So when the Department of Justice contacted me in 2000, I invited the attorney to my office but had no intention of changing my now well-rehearsed position. But in 2002, an attorney from the DOJ came back for another visit. Stephen Brody, recently appointed deputy director of the To-bacco Litigation Team, was unlike the other attorneys I had met. Soft-spoken and equipped with a nearly photographic memory, he precisely laid out the basis of the government's case against the major companies. The DOJ had begun investigating the tobacco industry for possible criminal vi-olations shortly after the Waxman hearings in 1994, but a grand jury that heard testimony on perjury and other possible violations did not return any indictments. Nonetheless, Bill Clinton had announced in his State of the Union Address in 1999 that the DOJ would begin civil litigation against the companies to recover federal spending on tobacco-related diseases. The department's initial filing later that year sought to recover Medicare funds but added civil Racketeering Influenced and Corrupt Organizations Act violations, for which the government could seek remedies to restrain un-lawful activities on the part of the companies. Judge Gladys Kessler, who would hear the case in federal district court, ruled that the government could not recover Medicare costs but permitted the RICO action to pro-ceed.[4] Although the RICO statute, passed in the early 1970s, had been de-signed to combat organized crime, it had been successfully used to force legal businesses that had engaged in racketeering and fraud to "disgorge" il-legally gotten profits.[5] The case against the companies, *United States v. Philip Morris*, would seek to recover an estimated $280 billion, the amount of industry profit the government estimated had come from illegal promo-tion and sales to minors over four decades.[6] It was the largest civil litigation in the history of American law. As Brody explained it, the case would turn on the government's ability to demonstrate that the industry had collec-tively participated as an "enterprise"—a conspiracy—to suppress and deny the known harms of smoking. He wanted to know what I had learned on this question.

I spent more than an hour reviewing my research in the John Hill man-uscripts at the Wisconsin Historical Society, which document in such detail the fateful December 1953 meeting of the industry executives at the Plaza Hotel. I explained my ongoing research into the evolution of medical and scientific knowledge about the harms of smoking and the industry's campaign to disrupt this consensus. Unlike so many of the attorneys with whom I had met, Brody seemed especially eager to hear my historical analysis of the emerging medical science, the evolution of the concept of proof in medical research, and the nature of the industry's response.

Brody came armed with several filings in the case, expert statements by historians that the defense had submitted to the court. Unlike the materials I had read in previous cases, however, two of these statements were written by relatively distinguished colleagues in my small field of the history of medicine, Peter English and Kenneth Ludmerer, both of whom were not only expert historians but also practicing physicians. Brody invited me to read their statements before we talked further about my potential role as an expert in the case.[7]

I was, quite simply, astounded by their "expert statements." First, I did not know that either one, both of whom I knew fairly well, had done any research on tobacco issues. Neither had ever published anything about cigarette smoking. They were certainly well aware of my own work, and I would have been pleased to discuss my findings with them. But more importantly, I was appalled by what they had written. I found their statements to be poorly researched, inaccurate in their historical assessments, and highly selective in the questions they raised. By asking narrow questions and responding to them with narrow research, they provided precisely the cover the industry sought.

"I have concluded, based upon my review of the literature, that there was no credible scientific evidence linking cigarette smoking to lung cancer or any life-threatening disease before 1950," explained Ludmerer in his expert statement. Focusing on those scientists who were skeptical about the relationship of smoking and cancer, Ludmerer wrote that "these medical specialists were reluctant to accept causation when medical science had yet to identify anything in tobacco smoke that could account for its alleged cancer-causing activity."[8] But as Ludmerer knew, a number of carcinogens had already been isolated in smoke. They had been identified in industry laboratories as well, but Ludmerer had never looked at any industry documents. It turned out that since 1988, he had frequently served as a witness and consultant to the industry. Deposed in the *Engle* case he was asked:

Let me make sure I understand. You have not reviewed even one single
piece of internal research the tobacco industry did at any time; is that
correct?

A. That is correct.[9]

In his DOJ statement, Ludmerer concluded that following the surgeon
general's report of 1964 "not everyone embraced the Report." This was certainly true. He continued, "Merely because a consensus had developed does
not mean that people cannot legitimately disagree." True again. But I was
shocked to see someone of Ludmerer's stature offering up such misleading
"opinions" on behalf of the industry in such an important litigation. As historian Robert Proctor, who worked for the government on the DOJ case
and appeared as an expert for plaintiffs in other tobacco litigation, would
conclude, Ludmerer's work on behalf of the industry bordered on "historical
malpractice."[10] The industry "used to control the science," commented
Proctor, "and now they're trying to control the history." Ludmerer would
later explain, "I gave the standard account of how we came to know cigarette
smoking causes lung cancer."[11] In a deposition, when asked by a plaintiff's
attorney, "So, as you sit here today in 1998, does cigarette smoking—in your
opinion as a medical doctor, does cigarette smoking cause lung cancer?"
Ludmerer replied, "I do not have an expert opinion on causation."[12]

Later, Steve Brody explained to me that if the DOJ failed to rebut Ludmerer and English's testimony with its own experts, the judge might be
persuaded that medical historians accept the notion that there was no medical consensus and that the industry claims of "not proven" were legitimate.
Although nearing the completion of this book, I put it aside to participate
in the case. Over the next two years, I centered my attention on several
questions central to the case. First, I prepared an expert statement to rebut
Ludmerer's and English's conclusions about the tobacco controversy and its
resolution, focusing on the evolution of medical and scientific knowledge
and the development of consensus regarding the harms of smoking. Second, I examined what the industry knew and when it knew it. As we have
seen, company scientists like Claude Teague, Alan Rodgman, Helmut
Wakeham, and Thomas Osdene had documented the carcinogenic properties of tobacco smoke and reported their findings internally but were never
allowed to publish them. At the same time, I reviewed what the industry

was saying publicly in its masterfully dishonest spin campaign. I had never doubted that there was once a substantial controversy about smoking and health—in the 1950s and beyond—but I asked the questions that I believe any professional historian would ask: What was the nature of the controversy? What interests were represented? How had these interests worked to shape the debate? Where Ludmerer and English had been highly selective in the materials they reviewed and the questions they asked, I sought to be as comprehensive as possible.

After preparing my expert statement, I spent some fourteen hours over two days in August 2003 being deposed in the case by Douglas Smith, an attorney at Kirkland & Ellis. In the breaks between the questioning, Smith assured me that he wasn't doing much work in tobacco litigation at the time. He told me he had enjoyed reading my work. I couldn't tell whether he was trying to soften me up or seeking moral absolution. In my deposition, he asked me about my relationship with Ken Ludmerer, pointing out that Ludmerer was currently president of the American Association for the History of Medicine (AAHM). Was this a prestigious organization? I assured Smith that if he could come up with $70 a year for dues, the AAHM would welcome him as a member.

Judge Gladys Kessler, who presided over the trial, had ordered that all direct testimonies must be submitted in writing prior to a witness appearing in court. This would speed the trial, which was expected to be long and complex. As a result, expert witnesses like myself would appear for our cross-examinations, but would not have the typical courtroom opportunity to lay out in detail our qualifications and opinions with the help of friendly counsel. There was, however, one exception in this ruling. If a witness had a chart, or "demonstrative," as part of their direct testimony, they would have up to an hour to explain it in the courtroom. I had prepared a simple chart of three overlapping rings as part of my description of the genesis of new medical and scientific knowledge. One circle represented clinical knowledge, another experimental knowledge, and the third, population-based knowledge. Under questioning from Brody, I was able to show how each of these areas had contributed to the development of new knowledge regarding the causes of disease in a series of examples ranging from James Lind's investigations of scurvy in the eighteenth century to John Snow's research on cholera in the nineteenth, to more recent work on HIV. Finally,

I showed how emerging knowledge linking smoking to lung cancer in the late 1940s and early 1950s had drawn on each of the three domains. This was a crucial part of my testimony since the industry would argue that during the 1950s and 1960s there was "no proof" that tobacco caused disease. As Ludmerer had claimed in his statement, "They [the scientists] held out for a higher standard of proof, one requiring experimental proof of causation." I was eager to show that this so-called "experimental" standard—constructed by the industry and now sustained by its historical experts—was apocryphal. Contrary to Ludmerer's assertion, there was never a single gold standard for proof of causality in medicine. Moreover, epidemiologic findings and population-based assessments had been used for centuries in evaluating causality. This was a question of considerable importance. Throughout the history of medicine, important public health actions have been taken on the basis of emerging clinical, population-based, and experimental evidence. Should John Snow have left the handle on the Broad Street Pump for thirty years until the organism causing cholera was identified under a microscope? Even then, questions about the organism's virulence and infectivity would remain unsettled. Did it make sense to attempt to protect the blood supply prior to the identification of the human immunodeficiency virus? Does the doubt of a few scientists that HIV is the cause of AIDS mean that we should wait for "proof"? I wanted to show that the industry claims of "not proven" were explicitly designed to serve the companies' financial interests with reckless disregard for the health of their patrons and that this approach—"doubt is our product"—cost millions of lives.

My testimony focused on the state of knowledge in medicine in the 1950s and 1960s, the character of industry denials, and the intensive public relations activity in the area of industry-sponsored research—all critical themes of this book. I understood that my claims would be subject to aggressive and hostile questions from the industry defense counsel. On the night before my court appearance, I met with Steve Brody to review some of the questions likely to come up in my cross-examination. Just before I was about to return to my hotel room, Sharon Eubanks, the DOJ attorney who was directing the tobacco litigation team, stopped in to greet me. She asked me if I understood what would happen during the cross-examination. I assured her that I realized that the industry lawyers would try to make me look as bad as possible. "No," she responded. "That's not it. They want to destroy you and leave you in a pool of blood."

The next day, I faced my principal interrogator, David Bernick of Kirkland & Ellis, for the first time. A notoriously fierce defense attorney, Bernick exhibited contempt and disdain for me and my testimony. He sought to establish several basic points. First, he spent a good deal of time on questions about my qualifications and interests in the case. He questioned my credentials (not an MD) and asserted that I was an advocate eager to destroy the industry and seek the prohibition of tobacco (positions I had never taken). I was there not as a historical expert, Bernick argued, but as a partisan activist against the companies. Second, Bernick hoped to show that my research had been inadequate and one-sided in that I had ignored the genuine and intense scientific controversy regarding smoking and disease in the 1950s. He would ask long and involved questions, all but testifying himself; at the end he would demand a yes or no answer from me. Was Harold Stewart, an NIH pathologist, a skeptic? Yes. Was his position unreasonable? It's a simple yes or no question, he would exclaim. No. Bernick brandished such exchanges as if they proved his case and destroyed my testimony. I found my time on the stand highly frustrating.

His questions centered on the notion that there was indeed a substantial and legitimate scientific controversy, and that the government's contention of industry conspiracy was therefore moot. How could there be a conspiracy to deny "knowledge" that was not definitively known? Finally, Bernick attempted to rehabilitate the idea that the industry had been a good actor by sponsoring important peer-reviewed scientific research. We sparred on each of these points at considerable length. Hadn't the industry sponsored scientific research to answer these very questions? Didn't the industry want "good science"? Yes, I answered, as long as it was not relevant to smoking and health.

As I had anticipated, the courtroom was not the best forum for me to fully explain my conclusions. After my first day on the stand, I had returned to my room to check the online media coverage of the trial. To my disappointment, there wasn't much. But one brief article from the Reuters news service noted that I had been forced to "concede" that there had been a controversy. Of course there had been a controversy; the point of my testimony was that it had been fundamentally shaped by the PR campaign of the industry. I was, however, pleased to read that I had been "unapologetic" in my assessment that the tobacco companies were a "rogue" industry.[13]

In a brief redirect, at the end of a second grueling day on the stand, Brody asked me why I considered tobacco a "rogue" industry. I explained that when an industry knows it is producing a dangerous and deadly product but denies these harms for decades, all the while vigorously promoting the product, it is well outside the boundaries of American corporate practice. On this note, much relieved and a bit bruised, I was permitted to leave the stand.

During the fifth month of the trial, the federal appeals court ruled by a 2–1 margin that the $280 billion being sought by the government was not "forward looking" as required by the statute. Any relief sought by the government must "prevent and restrain" future misconduct, and according to the court, the disgorgement of four decades' worth of illegal profits did not meet this criterion.[14] But the case continued, and the government devised new remedies that were designed to meet the standards established by the appeals court. These included prohibitions on marketing targeted to youth, the elimination of the terminology of *light* cigarettes, and the dismissal of certain senior managers from the companies. In addition, the government proposed a national cessation program, estimated to cost $5.2 billion per year over twenty-five years. The total cost, projected by physician Michael Fiore, a well-known expert on cessation programs, came to $130 billion.[15] At the trial, Fiore presented testimony that showed that this program could reduce the number of smokers in the United States by some 33 million.

In the final days of the trial, however, Bush political appointees at the Department of Justice ordered the trial team to reduce the government's request for a cessation remedy to approximately $10 billion. Several expert witnesses then came forward to say that the government had asked them to soften their testimony in the remedies phase of the trial. Eubanks and Brody, according to the *New York Times,* had strongly resisted the demands of the senior attorneys at the DOJ. In a memo quoted in the *Times,* they argued that "we do not want politics to be perceived as the underlying motivation, and that is certainly a risk if we make adjustments in our remedies presentation that are not based on evidence."[16] Judge Kessler immediately noted the sudden shift in the government's position: "perhaps it suggests that additional influences have been brought to bear on what the government's case is."[17] As Fiore would conclude in an article in the *New England Journal of Medicine,* "If there is a valid reason for the abandonment of the $130 billion smoking cessation remedy, the Justice Department has failed to articulate it in a convincing manner. As a result, attention has focused on political influence rather than on the compelling portrayal of tobacco-industry crimes presented by the tobacco-team attorneys."[18] Although fifty Democratic Senators and Congressmen, including Henry Waxman, requested an investigation by the DOJ's Office of Professional Responsibility, it seemed unlikely that the government's position would change.[19] There had always been a good deal of skepticism about the Bush administration's commitment to prosecute the case. Public health groups quickly requested that Judge Kessler make them "parties" to the case since their interests were "no longer being adequately represented by the government."[20] She granted their motion over the objections of the defense.[21]

In August 2006, Judge Kessler issued her decision in the case, finding that the tobacco industry had violated the racketeering statutes. Although there had been other adverse decisions for the companies in litigation, the monumental scope of the Kessler decision, its precision and scope, was unprecedented. According to Judge Kessler, the industry had engaged in a fifty-year conspiracy, lying to the American public about their product and its dire consequences for health. "Put more colloquially and less legalistically," Judge Kessler explained in her 1,683 page opinion, "over the course of 50 years, defendants lied, misrepresented, and deceived the American public, including smokers and the young people they avidly sought as 'replacement smokers,' about the devastating health effects of smoking and environmental tobacco smoke." The companies "suppressed research, they destroyed documents, they manipulated the use of nicotine so as to increase and perpetuate addiction . . . and they abused the legal system in order to achieve their goal—to make money with little if any regard for individual illness or suffering, soaring health care costs, or the integrity of the legal system."[22] Judge Kessler's decision was a model of reasoned historical and legal analysis.

At the same time, however, despite her judicial excoriation of the companies, Judge Kessler explained in her ruling that the appeals court had left her with few, if any, remedies to address the massive deceptions and frauds that she so closely documented. Although she ordered the companies to cease and desist in their use of misleading terms like *light*, *low tar*, and *mild* (which the defendants immediately appealed), she did not offer extensive and costly remedies, such as the national cessation program proposed by the government. The force of her findings and her lack of available legal remedies illuminate the central problem with the appeals court decision: it is as if a court had determined that a major crime had been committed, but it could not punish the perpetrator or, for that matter, even restrain its future illegal behavior. It remains to be seen if the Supreme Court (or the Appeals Court) will review the limitations that have tied Judge Kessler's hands. Nonetheless, it is critically significant that a federal court has now conclusively found that the industry engaged in a racketeering conspiracy to defraud the American public about the mortal dangers of their product, and that it continues to do so.

Wall Street celebrated the Kessler decision as a green light for Big Tobacco. But it is possible that this partying is premature. Kessler's decision (and the recent Florida Supreme Court ruling in *Engle*) may well open the door to a new wave of litigation based upon the findings in these historic legal cases. These rulings may make it less difficult for new plaintiffs to individually and collectively bring claims against the companies. Litigation remains a looming vulnerability for the industry despite the self-interested claims of Wall Street "analysts" who do the companies' bidding in the media.[23]

That said, there are no easy victories for the forces of public health in the tobacco wars, and the perpetual prediction of a knockout blow that radically reforms business as usual in the tobacco industry is certainly not in the immediate offing. *United States v. Philip Morris* has become—at least for the time being—yet another example of how the promise of tobacco control keeps getting turned upside down.

At times, as I watched the trial unfold, I felt that Eubanks, Brody, and their small team of DOJ career attorneys were all that stood between the tobacco industry and the future global pandemic. If the industry could remove this last major legal obstacle, it would cross over into a new era in which the threat of litigation had been all but removed. If the tobacco companies could win this case, they would have gotten away with the crime of the century. And perhaps they have.

Time and again, the tobacco industry has proven remarkably successful in devising new ways to resist public health regulations and promote its product. The industry is here to stay, and no historian is likely to fundamentally alter how it does business, in the United States or around the globe. But understanding the history of cigarettes may be a small but important element in the process of building societies and cultures that know their dangers and have strategies for their control. It seems to me that *United States v. Philip Morris* is an example of how we might recover a "usable past" that serves the public good.[24] And it is equally critical that this past not be purchased and subverted by the interests of the industry. At one time, I worried that serving as an expert witness might be perceived as compromising the integrity and persuasiveness of this book. I have put this concern to rest. Historians are hardly exempt from the common duty to contribute to public life and civil society. It seems to me now, after the hopes and disappointments of the courtroom battle, that we have a role to play in determining the future of the tobacco pandemic. If we occasionally cross the boundary between analysis and advocacy, so be it. The stakes are high, and there is much work yet to do.

REFERENCES

Introduction

1. Douglas Martin, "Douglas Leigh, the Man Who Lit Up Broadway, Dies at 92," *New York Times*, December 16, 1999; Dudley Dalton, "Big Electric Signs Costly to Erect," *New York Times*, June 30, 1963; and Douglas Leigh, "Times Square Camel Billboard Contract," October 8, 1953, Bates No. 500161833/1837, http://legacy.library.ucsf.edu/tid/hbr31d00.

2. Doug Stewart, "Times Square Reborn," *Smithsonian*, February 1998, 34–45.

3. Natalie Jaffe, "Billboard Gives Up Smoking Camels," *New York Times*, January 4, 1966.

4. According to Gallup polls, 45 percent of American adults smoked in 1954, 40 percent in 1963, 42 percent in 1971, and 43 percent in 1973. Rick Blizzard, *U. S. Smoking Habits Have Come a Long Way, Baby*, October 19, 2004, http://www.galluppoll.com.

5. See Ronald Bayer and James Colgrove, "Children and Bystanders First: The Ethics and Politics of Tobacco Control in the United States," in *Unfiltered: Conflicts over Tobacco Policy and Public Health*, eds. Eric A. Feldman and Ronald Bayer (Cambridge, MA: Harvard University Press, 2004), 8–37.

6. U.S. Department of Health and Human Services, *Reducing the Health Consequences of Smoking: 25 Years of Progress: A Report of the Surgeon General* (Rockville, MD: Public Health Service, Centers for Disease Control, 1989), i.

7. C. A. Tucker, "Presentation to RJR B of D—9/30/74: Marketing Plans," September 30, 1974, Document ID 50142 1310 at the *Mangini v. RJR* case, Exhibit 1, UCSF archives, http://galen.library.ucsf.edu/tobacco/mangini.

8. Seth Moskowitz to R. Sanders, C. Pennell, and H. MacFarlane, "Times Square Camel Billboard Publicity Proposal," March 22, 1989, Bates No. 506867504/7508, http://legacy.library.ucsf.edu/tid/hvf44d00.

9. "Camel Times Square Billboard Fact Sheet," Bates No. 507090288, http://legacy.library.ucsf.edu/tid/tfj34d00.

10. Federal Trade Commission, *Complaint in the Matter of R.J. Reynolds Tobacco Company*. Washington, DC, 1997, http://www.ftc.gov/os/1997/05/d9285cmp.pdf; and "Old Joe Must Go," *Advertising Age*, January 13, 1992, 16.

11. Joseph R. DiFranza et al., "RJR Nabisco's Cartoon Camel Promotes Camel Cigarettes to Children," *JAMA* 266, no. 22 (1991): 3149–3153.

12. Paul M. Fischer, Meyer P. Schwartz, Jr., John W. Richards, Adam O. Goldstein, and Tina H. Rojas, "Brand Logo Recognition by Children Aged 3 to 6 Years: Mickey Mouse and Old Joe the Camel," *JAMA* 266, no. 22 (1991): 3145-3148; "Camels for Kids," *Time*, December 23, 1991; Kathleen Deveny, "Joe Camel Is Also Pied Piper, Research Finds," *Wall Street Journal*, December 11, 1991; Walecia Konrad, "I'd Toddle a Mile for a Camel," *Business Week*, December 23, 1991; and "Camels That Kill," *New York Times*, January 15, 1991.

13. "Joe Camel Billboard Ends Broadway Run," August 12, 1994; and Peggy Carter, "Camel Times Square Billboard: Response to *New York Times*," August 11, 1994, Bates No. 512724244/4245, http://legacy.library.ucsf.edu/tid/cje33d00.

14. "Hooked on Tobacco: The Teen Epidemic," *Consumer Reports*, March 1995, 144.

15. Barry Meier, "Lost Horizons: The Billboard Prepares to Give Up Smoking," *New York Times*, April 19, 1999.

16. The *Mangini* case was among a group of cases in the early 1990s in which the tobacco industry lost or settled for the first time.

17. Dennis L. Breo, "Kicking Butts—AMA, Joe Camel, and the 'Black-Flag' War on Tobacco," *JAMA* 270, no.16 (1993): 1962.

18. David Margolick, "At the Bar: Joe Camel Takes His Lumps at the Hands of a California Lawyer," *New York Times*, June 17, 1994.

19. Jim Doyle, "Joe Camel Is History in California: Tobacco Firm Settles Suit—S.F. to Share in $10 Million," *San Francisco Chronicle*, September 9, 1997.

20. Robert N. Proctor, "Tobacco and the Global Lung Cancer Epidemic," *Nature Reviews Cancer*, no. 1 (2001): 82–88; and World Health Organization, *The Tobacco Atlas* (Geneva: WHO, 2002).

Chapter 1

1. William K. Boyd, *The Story of Durham* (Durham, NC: Duke University Press, 1925), 76.

2. Oscar Wilde, *The Picture of Dorian Gray* (London: Ward, Lock, 1891).

3. Johannes Wilbert, "Tobacco and Shamanism in South America," in *Psychoactive Plants of the World*, eds. Richard Evans Schultes and Robert F. Raffauf (New Haven, CT: Yale University Press, 1987), 1–19; and Jordan Goodman, *Tobacco in History: The Cultures of Dependence* (New York: Routledge, 1993), 3–5.

4. Goodman, 25. Experiential assessment of tobacco's use must be historically and contextually specific, but this should not deny the physiological characteristics of use.

5. Wilbert, 16–19.

6. Ibid.

7. Ibid., 133.

8. Wilhelm Heinrich Posselt and C. L. Reimann, "Chemische Untersuchungen Des Tabaks Und Darstellung Des Eigentümlichen Princeps Dieser Planze," *Magazin für Pharmazie und die dahin einschlagenden Wissenschaften* 24–25 (1828–1829); and Goodman.

9. Goodman, 167.

10. Ibid., 51–55.

11. Alfred W. Crosby, *The Columbian Exchange: Biological and Cultural Consequences of 1492*, vol. 2 (Westport, CT: Greenwood Publishing, 1972), 66, 68.

12. Allan Kulikoff, *Tobacco and Slaves: The Development of Southern Cultures in the Chesapeake, 1680–1800* (Chapel Hill: University of North Carolina Press, 1986); and Edmund S. Morgan, *American Slavery, American Freedom: The Ordeal of Colonial Virginia* (New York: W. W. Norton, 1975).

13. King James I, *Counterblaste to Tobacco* (London: Robert Barker, 1604).

14. Goodman, 60.

15. Other European countries also consumed tobacco in large volume, following distinct consumption patterns (Goodman, 61–67).

16. On colonial tobacco agriculture, I have relied on T. H. Breen, *Tobacco Culture: The Mentality of the Great Tidewater Planters on the Eve of Revolution* (Princeton, NJ: Princeton University Press, 1985). See also, Fernando Ortiz, *Cuban Counterpoint: Tobacco and Sugar* (New York: Knopf, 1947).

17. As T. H. Breen explained: "And it was precisely because tobacco mattered in Virginia society so very much that it became in the eye of major producers a measure of self, a source of meaningful social identity, as well as a means to maintain a high standard of living" (71).

18. Ibid., 46–53.

19. Ibid.

20. Ibid., 21–23, 41; and Rhys Isaac, *The Transformation of Virginia, 1740–1790* (Chapel Hill: University of North Carolina Press, 1982).

21. Edmund S. Morgan, *American Slavery, American Freedom: The Ordeal of Colonial Virginia* (New York: W. W. Norton, 1975), 110.

22. Ibid., 114.

23. Gloria L. Main, *Tobacco Colony: Life in Early Maryland, 1650–1720* (Princeton, NJ: Princeton University Press, 1982), 9.

24. Kulikoff, 40.

25. Breen, 27, 32.

26. Morgan.

27. Robert Sobel, *They Satisfy: The Cigarette in American Life* (Garden City, NY: Anchor Books, 1978), 15–16.

28. Goodman, 195; Sobel; and Robert K. Heimann, *Tobacco and Americans* (New York: McGraw-Hill, 1960), 131–133, 169–173, 272–273.

29. John van Willigen and Susan C. Eastwood, *Tobacco Culture: Farming Kentucky's Burley Belt* (Lexington: University Press of Kentucky, 1998), 12.

30. Nannie M. Tilley, *The Bright-Tobacco Industry, 1860–1929* (Chapel Hill: University of North Carolina Press, 1948), 64.

31. Goodman, 98–99; and B. C. Akehurst and Edward M. Brecher, *Licit and Illicit Drugs* (Boston: Little, Brown, 1972), 277.

32. Charles Dickens, *American Notes and Pictures from Italy* (London: Chapman & Hall, 1874), 130–131; Heimann, 117–119; Iain Gately, *Tobacco: A Cultural History of How an Exotic Plant Seduced Civilization* (New York: Grove Press, 2001), 173–176.

33. G. Cabrera Infante, *Holy Smoke* (New York: Harper & Row, 1985); Morton Keller, *The Art and Politics of Thomas Nast* (New York: Oxford University Press, 1968).

34. Sobel, 19; Heimann, 203–211.

35. Sobel, 19.

36. Cassandra Tate, *Cigarette Wars: The Triumph of "The Little White Slaver"* (New York: Oxford University Press, 1999), 7.

37. Robert Franklin Durden, *The Dukes of Durham, 1865–1929* (Durham, NC: Duke University Press, 1975).

38. Roberts, 259, 260.

39. Tate, 15.

40. Richard B. Tennant, *The American Cigarette Industry* (New Haven, CT: Yale University Press, 1950), 17–18. Bonsack initially failed to receive a patent. Albert Hook from Rochester, New York, a competitor, had already received a patent for a similar, if inferior, machine in 1876, and Charles and William Emery, principals of Goodwin & Company from New York, patented another prototype in 1879. In 1880, Bonsack's father arranged to purchase Hook's original patent, clearing the way for his son's successful application. In September, the Bonsack Cigarette Making Machine received its much coveted registration from the U.S. Patent Office. A year later, the younger Bonsack was still working to improve his machine, updating the patent. See B. W. C. Roberts and Richard F. Knapp, "Paving the Way for the Tobacco Trust: From Hand Rolling to Mechanized Cigarette Production by W. Duke, Sons and Company," *North Carolina Historical Review* 69 (1992): 268–269.

41. Brooke Hindle, *Emulation and Invention* (New York: New York University Press, 1981).

42. Tennant, 18.

43. Roberts, 271.

44. Ibid., 272.

45. Heimann, 213.

510 References

46. Patrick Reynolds and Tom Shachtman, *The Gilded Leaf: Triumph, Tragedy, and Tobacco: Three Generations of the R. J. Reynolds Family and Fortune* (Boston: Little, Brown, 1989), 37.

47. David F. Noble, *America by Design: Science, Technology, and the Rise of Corporate Capitalism* (New York: Knopf, 1977), 87.

48. Durden, 42.

49. "The Plight of the Cigar," *Current Opinion* (1924): 98–99. In a 1924 opinion piece, it was noted that "for the last dozen years, unnoticed by the general public, the cigar has been falling into comparative disuse." Noting that ten cigarettes were produced for every cigar, the author went on to mention, "The triumph of the cigarette over the cigar has been the triumph of machinery over handicraft." On the larger social process of modernization see, Richard D. Brown, *Modernization: The Transformation of American Life, 1600–1865* (New York: Hill & Wang, 1976).

50. E. H. Mathewson, *The Culture of Flue-Cured Tobacco* (Washington, DC: U.S. Department of Agriculture, 1913).

51. Sobel, 64–71.

52. Thomas Park Hughes, *American Genesis: A Century of Invention and Technological Enthusiasm, 1870–1970* (New York: Viking, 1989), 4.

53. Thomas K. McGraw, "Rethinking the Trust Question," in *Regulation in Perspective: Historical Essays*, ed. Thomas K. McGraw (Cambridge, MA: Harvard University Press, 1981), 1–55.

54. Neil Harris, "The Drama of Consumer Desire," in *Yankee Enterprise: The Rise of the American System of Manufactures*, eds. Otto Mayr and Robert C. Post (Washington, DC: Smithsonian Institute Press, 1981), 189–230.

55. Patrick G. Porter, "Advertising in the Early Cigarette Industry: W. Duke, Sons & Company of Durham," *North Carolina Historical Review* 69, no. 1 (1971): 31–43; Tilley, 558–559; Roberts, 264–266; and Tate, 25.

56. Jackson Lears, *Fables of Abundance: A Cultural History of Advertising in America* (New York: Basic Books, 1994); Robert Jay, *The Trade Card in Nineteenth-Century America* (Columbia, MO: University of Missouri Press, 1987); Paul Martin, *Popular Collecting and the Everyday Self: The Reinvention of Museums?* (New York: Leicester University Press, 1999); and Stephen H. Riggins, *The Socialness of Things: Essays on the Socio-Semiotics of Objects*, eds. Thomas A. Sebeok, Roland Posner, and Alain Rey (New York: Mouton de Gruyter, 1994).

57. "Prizes for Ill-Doing," *New York Times*, December 25, 1888.

58. Porter, 39.

59. Neil H. Borden, "The Effect of Advertising on the Demand for Tobacco Products—Cigarettes," *The Economic Effects of Advertising* (Chicago: Richard D. Irwin, 1944), 207–249.

60. Porter, 41.

61. McGraw, 1–24; and Tennant, 24–25.

62. Alfred D. Chandler, Jr., "American Tobacco: Managing Mass Production and Distribution of Packaged Products," in *The Visible Hand* (Cambridge, MA: Belknap Press, 1977), 382–390; and Naomi R. Lamoreaux, *The Great Merger Movement in American Business, 1895–1904* (New York: Cambridge University Press, 1985).

63. Lamoreaux, 157.

64. Durden, 56.

65. Malcolm R. Burns, "Economics of Scale in Tobacco Manufacture, 1897–1910," *Journal of Economic History* 43, no. 2 (1983): 465–466.

66. Chandler, 382.

67. Ibid., 390.

68. Tracy Campbell, *The Politics of Despair: Power and Resistance in the Tobacco Wars* (Lexington: University Press of Kentucky, 1993).

69. Chandler, 386.

70. Olivier Zunz, *Making America Corporate, 1870–1920* (Chicago: University of Chicago Press, 1990).

71. Robert Wiebe, *The Search for Order, 1877–1920* (New York: Hill and Wang, 1967).

72. Durden, 73.

73. Ibid., 74.

74. James A. Thomas, *Trailing Trade a Million Miles* (Durham, NC: Duke University Press, 1931); Durden, 77–80; and Tennant, 32.

75. Lamoreaux, 182.

76. Chandler, 389–390; Patricia A. Cooper, *Once a Cigar Maker: Men, Woman, and Work Culture in American Cigar Factories, 1900–1919* (Urbana: University of Illinois Press, 1987).

77. Lamoreaux, 182; and Tennant, 28–37.

78. Tennant, 39.

79. Albert Charles Muhse, "The Disintegration of the Tobacco Combination," *Political Science Quarterly* 28, no. 2 (1913): 249–278.

80. Morton Keller, *Regulating a New Economy* (Cambridge, MA: Harvard University Press, 1990), 25–26.

81. Lamoreaux, 159.

82. Ibid.

83. McGraw, 38.

84. U.S. Supreme Court, *U.S. v. American Tobacco Co.*, 221 U.S. 106, 182 (1911).

85. Keller.

86. Muhse, 276; and William H. Nicholls, *Price Policies in the Cigarette Industry* (Nashville: Vanderbilt University Press, 1951).

87. Tennant, 64. See also Maurice Corina, *Trust in Tobacco: The Anglo-American Struggle for Power* (New York: St. Martin's, 1975), 128.

88. Louis D. Brandeis, "An Illegal Trust Legalized," *World To-Day* (1911): 1440–1441.

89. Ellis W. Hawley, *The New Deal and the Problem of Monopoly: A Study in Economic Ambivalence* (New York: Fordham University Press, 1966).

90. "III: Cigarettes," *Fortune*, June 1935, 68.

91. Centers for Disease Control, "Total and Per Capita Manufactured Cigarette Consumption and Percentage Change in Per Capita Consumption—United States, United States Department of Agriculture, 1900–1995," http://www.cdc.gov/tobacco/research_data/economics/consump1.htm.

Chapter 2

1. From a poster, described in Gordon L. Dillow, "The Hundred-Year War Against the Cigarette," American Heritage Magazine, February–March 1981, 103.

2. Nannie M. Tilley, *The R.J. Reynolds Tobacco Company* (Chapel Hill: University of North Carolina Press, 1985), 223.

3. "Fighting the Tobacco Trust," *New York Times*, March 17, 1893.

4. Robert Sobel, *They Satisfy: The Cigarette in American Life* (Garden City, NY: Anchor Books, 1978), 144; Jack S. Blocker, *Alcohol, Reform, and Society: The Liquor Issue in Social Context* (Westport, CT: Greenwood, 1979); and Thomas R. Pegram, *Battling Demon Rum: The Struggle for a Dry America, 1800–1933* (Chicago: Ivan R. Dee, 1998).

5. Allan M. Brandt and Paul Rozin, eds., *Morality and Health* (New York: Routledge, 1997); and James A. Morone. *Hellfire Nation: The Politics of Sin in American History* (New Haven: Yale University Press, 2003).

6. Neil Harris, "The Drama of Consumer Desire," in *Yankee Enterprise: The Rise of the American System of Manufactures,* eds. Otto Mayr and Robert C. Post (Washington, DC: Smithsonian Institute Press, 1981), 191.

7. See T. J. Jackson Lears, *No Place of Grace: Antimodernism and the Transformation of American Culture, 1880–1920* (New York: Pantheon, 1981).

8. Vida Milholland, "Tobacco: An Enemy of American Progress," reprint of a radio address (New York: Radio Station WHAP, [after 1926?]), p. 3, from the Harvey Washington Wiley Papers, ca. 1854–1944, Library of Congress.

9. Editorial, *New York Times,* January 29, 1884.

10. Cassandra Tate, *Cigarette Wars: The Triumph of "the Little White Slaver"* (New York: Oxford University Press, 1998), 39.

11. Milholland, "Tobacco: An Enemy of American Progress," p. 6. See Henry Ford, *The Case Against the Little White Slaver,* vols. I–IV (Detroit: Henry Ford, 1916).

12. Quoted in Allan L. Benson, "Smokes for Women." *Good Housekeeping,* August 1929, 190.

13. "A City's War Against Cigarets," *Independent,* November 8, 1915.

14. "Killing the Cigaret Habit," *Literary Digest,* December 6, 1913, 1118.

15. "Smokers' Palates Painted in Court," *New York Times,* January 22, 1914.

16. "Cures Women of Smoking," *New York Times,* March 14, 1914.

17. "Rush For Cigarette Cure," *New York Times,* January 29, 1914.

18. Review of *Habits That Handicap: The Menace of Opium, Alcohol, and Tobacco, and the Remedy,* by Charles Barnes Towns, *New York Times,* August 22, 1915.

19. Charles B. Towns, "The Injury of Tobacco and Its Relation to Other Drug Habits," *Century,* March 1912, 766–772; and Charles B. Towns, "Women and Tobacco," *Delaware State Medical Journal* 7 (1916): 3–5. For a profile of Towns, see William L. White, *Slaying the Dragon: The History of Addiction Treatment and Recovery in America* (Bloomington, IL: Chestnut Hills Systems, 1998), 84–87.

20. Twyman Abbott, "The Rights of the Nonsmoker," *Outlook* (1910): 763–767.

21. "Form Non-Smokers' League," *New York Times,* May 10, 1910.

22. "To Smoke or Not to Smoke," *New York Times,* August 21, 1913.

23. Anti-Smoke, letter to the editor, *New York Times,* August 29, 1913.

24. "Refuges for Non-Smokers," *Literary Digest,* November 22, 1924, 28.

25. "A Restriction Entirely Commendable," *New York Times,* October 22, 1913.

26. "72,000 Smokers Petition," *New York Times,* October 12, 1913.

27. Richard B. Tennant, *The American Cigarette Industry* (New Haven: Yale University Press, 1950), 140.

28. "May Deprive Navy of Its Cigarettes," *New York Times,* November 24, 1907.

29. Cassandra Tate, "In the 1800s, Antismoking Was Still a Burning Issue." *Smithsonian* 20, no.4 (1989): 116. See also Grant Showerman, "Smith, Smoke and the War." *New Republic,* February 23, 1918, 109–110; and Gordon L. Dillow, "Thank You for Not Smoking: The Hundred-Year War Against the Cigarette." *American Heritage,* February–March 1981, 95–107.

30. G. K. Chesterton, "The Nightmare of Dr. Saleeby," *Living Age,* February 10, 1917, 374–375.

31. Sobel, 84.

32. Tate, 76–92.

33. Walter Duranty, "Help Heartens French," *New York Times,* May 27, 1918.

34. Edwin L. James, "War Department Will Issue Tobacco Rations," *New York Times,* May 23, 1918.

35. "They've Had a Lot of Tobacco," *New York Times,* May 24, 1918; and "$30,000 For Navy Smokes," *New York Times,* March 1, 1918.

36. Edith Nilsson Lowe, "Cigarettes for Soldiers," *New York Times,* March 17, 1918.

37. "Girls Raise Tobacco Fund," *New York Times,* April 26, 1918.

38. Edwin L. James, "War Department Will Issue Tobacco Rations," *New York Times,* May 23, 1918.

39. "Makings for the Front," *New York Times,* April 12, 1918.

40. "And War Is Indeed Terrible," *New York Times,* April 5, 1918.

41. "What It Would Cost to Place a Ban on Tobacco," *Current Opinion* 67, no. 62 (1919).

42. Carl Avery Werner, "The Triumph of the Cigarette," *American Mercury,* December 1925, 415–421.

43. Fullerton L. Waldo, *America at the Front* (New York: E. P. Dutton, 1918), 155.

44. Alexander Woollcott, *The Command Is Forward: Tales of the A. E. F. Battlefields as They Appeared in the Stars and Stripes* (New York: Century, 1919), 74.

45. Sobel, 84.

46. E. Alexander Powell, *The Army Behind the Army.* (New York: Charles Scribner's Sons, 1919), 159.

47. See James D. Norris, "Advertising and the Transformation of American Society, 1865–1920," in *Contributions in Economics and Economic History* (New York: Greenwood, 1990).

48. Sobel, 75; and Nannie M. Tilley, *The R.J. Reynolds Tobacco Company* (Chapel Hill: University of North Carolina Press, 1985), 611.

49. Sobel, 77.

50. Norris, 138.

51. Richard Kluger, *Ashes to Ashes* (New York: Knopf, 1996), 58.

52. Discontinued brands included Turkish-Fatima, Murad, Mecca, Mogul, Virginia Bright, Sunshine, Home Run, King Bee, and Sweet Caporals.

53. See William E. Leuchtenburg, *The Perils of Prosperity: 1914–1932* (Chicago: University of Chicago Press, 1958); Lizabeth Cohen, *Making a New Deal: Industrial Workers in Chicago, 1919–1939* (New York: Cambridge University Press, 1990); and Robert Wiebe, *The Search for Order, 1877–1920* (New York: Hill & Wang, 1967).

54. See Jennifer D. Keene, "Doughboys, the Great War, and the Remaking of America," in *War/Society/Culture,* ed. Michael Fellman (Baltimore: Johns Hopkins University Press, 2001), for a discussion of the nationalizing of American culture during World War I.

55. T. S. Eliot, *Collected Poems, 1909–1935* (London: Faber & Faber, 1936), 17. The original year of publication for the poem was 1917.

56. Alfred E. Parker, "Training for Athletics and Health," *Hygeia,* June 1933, 537.

57. "Women and the Weed," *Literary Digest,* December 19, 1925, 31–32.

58. "Jail For Smoking Mother," *New York Times,* October 18, 1904.

59. "No Public Smoking by Women Now," *New York Times,* January 21, 1908.

60. "Arrested for Smoking," *New York Times,* January 23, 1908.

61. Tate, 101–102; "No Public Smoking by Women Now"; "Smoking by Women Called Deplorable," *New York Times,* January 23, 1908; "Women Mustn't Smoke," *New York Times,* January 22, 1908; and "Mayor Lets Women Smoke," *New York Times,* February 4, 1908.

62. Michael Schudson, *Advertising, the Uneasy Persuasion* (New York: Basic Books, 1985).

63. A. E. Hamilton, "Killing Lady Nicotine," *North American Review* 225, no. 842 (April 1928): 465–468.

64. "Women War-Workers Fight for Privileges, Including Smoking," *Literary Digest,* June 28, 1919, 76.

65. Benson, 40–41.

66. L. Ames Brown, "Is a Tobacco Crusade Coming?" *Atlantic Monthly,* October 1920, 447.

67. "Argument on Anticigaret Measure Waged Earnestly on Second Day in House," *Salt Lake Tribune,* February 16, 1921; and John C. Burnham. "American Physicians and Tobacco Use: Two Surgeons General, 1929 and 1964," *Bulletin of the History of Medicine* 63, no. 1 (Spring 1989): 1–31.

68. "Cigarette Bill Is Still Under Discussion," *Deseret News,* February 16, 1921.

69. "Cigarette Measure Is Discussed in Senate," *Deseret News,* February 3, 1921.

70. "Senator Southwick Tells Why He Desires Passage of Anticigaret Measure," *Salt Lake Tribune,* February 3, 1921.

71. Senator Reed Smoot of Utah, speaking for the Extension of Food and Drugs Act to Tobacco and Tobacco Products in the United States Senate, 71st Cong., 1st sess., *Congressional Record* (June 10, 1929).

72. "Anticigaret Bill Put under Fire," *Salt Lake Tribune,* February 10, 1921.

73. On the historical rise of a consumer culture, see especially Jackson Lears, *Fables of Abundance: A Cultural History of Advertising in America* (New York: Basic Books, 1994); Roland Marchand, *Advertising the American Dream: Making Way for Modernity* (Berkeley: University of California Press, 1985); Richard Wightman Fox and T. J. Jackson Lears, eds., *The Culture of Consumption: Critical Essays in American History 1880–1980* (New York: Pantheon Books, 1983); Lawrence B. Glickman, ed., *Consumer Society in American History: A Reader* (Ithaca, NY: Cornell University Press, 1999); Stuart Ewen and Elizabeth Ewen, *Channels of Desire: Mass Images and the Shaping of American Consciousness* (New York: McGraw Hill, 1982); and Charles McGovern, Susan Strasser, and Matthias Judt, eds., *Getting and Spending: European and American Consumer Societies in the Twentieth Century* (New York: Cambridge University Press, 1998).

74. M. V. O'Shea, *Tobacco and Mental Efficiency* (New York: Macmillan, 1923).

75. "Must Lady Nicotine Follow John Barleycorn?" *Literary Digest,* March 15, 1919, 19–20.

76. "Preparing to Save Tobacco," *New York Times,* October 11, 1919.

77. "Shall Tobacco Follow Alcohol?" *Independent,* April 12, 1919, 50.

78. Sinclair Lewis, *Arrowsmith* (New York: Harcourt, Brace, 1925).

79. Benson, 192.

80. Ibid., 193.

81. "How Parents Handle the Smoking Problem," *Parents Magazine,* April 1935, 18.

82. Alice Payne Hackett, *Wellesley: Part of the American Story,* American College and University Series, vol. 3 (New York: E. P. Dutton, 1949), 218; and "5 College Bar Girls from Football Dance; Wellesley Upholds Off-Campus Smoking Ban," *New York Times,* November 19, 1925.

83. "Scolded for Smoking, Two Quit Wellesley; New Woman Has No Chance, Freshmen Say," *New York Times,* October 30, 1922.

84. Hackett, 241.

85. "Smoking Co-Eds Penalized," *New York Times,* March 15, 1930.

86. Paula S. Fass, *The Damned and the Beautiful: American Youth in the 1920s* (New York: Oxford University Press, 1977), 277.

87. Fass, 294.

88. "Women and the Weed," *Literary Digest,* December 19, 1925, 31–32; and Cornelia Meigs, *What Makes a College? A History of Bryn Mawr* (New York: Macmillan, 1956).

89. Fass, 298. The dean was from the University of Minnesota.

90. "Smoking Co-Eds," *Literary Digest,* May 15, 1937.

91. Ibid.

92. "I," *New York Times,* March 1, 1922.

93. "Girls Ban Jazz, Petting, Cigarettes," *New York Times,* February 18, 1922.

94. "Is Cigarette Advertising Teaching Women to Smoke?" *Printers' Ink,* April 17, 1919, 53–56.

95. William K. Anderson, "Will They Force Us to It?" *Christian Century,* December 18, 1929, 1577.

96. Benson, 194.

97. Marguerite Harrison, "Sorority of Smoke on Wheels," *New York Times,* July 22, 1922.

98. "Few Hotels Have Rules Against Women Smokers," *New York Times,* March 16, 1919.

99. Fass, 3.

100. Opponents identified the advertising onslaught as principally responsible for the striking increase in the popularity of the cigarette. The Methodist Episcopal Church's Board of Temperance, Prohibition, and Public Morals urged a moratorium on cigarette advertising, noting "the number of tobacco users would probably increase by half in five years." The board urged regulatory oversight that would "force the Tobacco Trust to eliminate from their advertising fraudulent

claims as to the virtues and effects of their commodity." But such calls for restrictions on advertising only indicated just how distant opponents had become from the central forces driving the new consumer culture. See Frances Warfield, "Lost Cause: A Portrait of Lucy Page Gaston," *Outlook and Independent,* February 20, 1930, 244–247, 275–276; and "Seeks Check by Law on Cigarette Ads," *New York Times,* February 3, 1930.

101. Werner, 421.

Chapter 3

1. "Smoking by Women Called Deplorable," *New York Times,* January 23, 1908.
2. Frederick Lewis Allen, *Only Yesterday* (New York: Harper and Row, 1931), 90–91.
3. Michael Schudson, *Advertising, the Uneasy Persuasion: Its Dubious Impact on American Society* (New York: Basic Books, 1984).
4. Mrs. Elton Fulmer, *Century Magazine* 116, no. 2 (May 1928): 254.
5. "The American Tobacco Co.," *Fortune,* December 1936, 97.
6. Albert Davis Lasker, *The Lasker Story, as He Told It* (Chicago: Advertising Publications, 1963), 5.
7. George H. Allen, "Albert Davis Lasker," *Advertising and Selling,* October 13, 1932, 36.
8. Robert Sobel, *They Satisfy: The Cigarette in American Life* (Garden City, NY: Anchor Books, 1978), 80.
9. Hill, quoted in J. W. George, "Lucky Strike Campaign Starts Fight over Radio Censorship," *Advertising & Selling,* December 26, 1928, 65.
10. Jackson Lears, *Fables of Abundance: A Cultural History of Advertising in America* (New York: Basic Books, 1994); M. N. Gardner and A. M. Brandt, "'The Doctors' Choice Is America's Choice': The Physician in U.S. Cigarette Advertisements, 1930–1953," *American Journal of Public Health* 96, no. 2 (2006): 222–32; and Nancy Tomes, *The Gospel of Germs: Men, Women, and the Microbe in American Life* (Cambridge, MA: Harvard University Press, 1998).
11. Stephen Fox, *The Mirror Makers: A History of American Advertising and Its Creators* (New York: William Morrow, 1984), 115.
12. Allen, 21.
13. Roland Marchand, *Advertising the American Dream: Making Way for Modernity* (Berkeley: University of California Press, 1985), 21–22.
14. Quoted in Sobel, 101.
15. Philip Wagner, "Cigarettes vs. Candy," *New Republic,* February 13, 1929, 343–345.
16. Lasker, a titan in the history of tobacco sales and promotion, would during the 1930s develop a second identity as a medical philanthropist. He and his wife Mary directed their considerable largesse to cancer research and the prolongation of life, a telling irony in the history of this product. (See Allen, 21–22, 36–37.)
17. Warren Susman, "'Personality' and the Making of Twentieth-Century Culture," in *New Directions in American Intellectual History,* eds. John Higham and Paul Conkin (Baltimore: Johns Hopkins University Press, 1979), 212–226.
18. Marchand, 96–97; 99–101.
19. Ibid., 97–98.
20. Sobel, 101.
21. Fox, 116.
22. Wagner, 344.
23. Ibid.
24. Kenneth M. Goode, "Lucky Strike Advertising Tosses Bombs Among the Bonbons," *Advertising & Selling,* November 14, 1928, 19–20.

25. George, 23.

26. Goode, 20.

27. Keller, 32–33.

28. Marchand, 100–103.

29. Philip Wagner, 343–345.

30. Frank Presbrey, *The History and Development of Advertising* (Garden City, NY: Doubleday, 1929), 593. Other front-runners were Coca-Cola, which spent $5 million; Procter and Gamble, which spent $4 million on Ivory Soap; Wrigley's, which spent $3 million; and Campbell's Soup, which spent $2.5 million.

31. Quoted in Presbrey, 598.

32. Otis A. Pease, *The Responsibilities of American Advertising; Private Control and Public Influence, 1920–1940* (New Haven, CT: Yale University Press, 1958).

33. Lord & Thomas, *Altruism in Advertising* (Chicago, New York: Lord & Thomas, 1911), 12.

34. Walter Dill Scott, *The Psychology of Advertising* (New York: Dodd, Mead, 1931), i.

35. Peter B. B. Andrews, "The Cigarette Market, Past and Future," *Advertising and Selling*, January 16, 1936, 27.

36. See Marchand and Lears.

37. Carl A. Naether, *Advertising to Women* (New York: Prentice Hall, 1928), 234.

38. Harry M. Wootten, "Cigarettes' High Ceiling," *Printers' Ink*, February 1941, 5.

39. "The American Tobacco Co.," 100.

40. Robert Littell, "Cigarette Ad Fact and Fiction," *Reader's Digest*, July 1942, 5–8; and Stuart Chase, "Blindfolded You Know the Difference," *New Republic*, August 8, 1928, 296–298.

41. Chase, 297.

42. Robert Littell, "Cigarette Ad Fact and Fiction," *Reader's Digest*, July 1942, 8.

43. E. Ruth Pyrtle, "A Call to Action," *NEA Journal*, 19, no. 4 (1930): 117.

44. Albert T. Poffenberger, *Psychology in Advertising* (New York: A.W. Shaw, 1925), 61.

45. Neil Harris, "The Drama of Consumer Desire," in *Yankee Enterprise: The Rise of the American System of Manufactures*, eds. Otto Mayr and Robert C. Post (Washington, DC: Smithsonian Institute Press, 1981), 189–230.

46. Obituary, *New York Times*, March 10, 1995.

47. Richard S. Tedlow, *Keeping the Corporate Image: Public Relations and Business, 1900–1950* (Greenwich, CT: JAI, 1979), 43.

48. Tedlow, 43.

49. Upon reviewing the Edward Bernays papers at the Library of Congress, I was impressed not only by the details of his publicity campaigns, but also by the recognition of seeing what had to be secret, internal documentation of his many interventions on behalf of American Tobacco. Why would Bernays maintain such scrupulous records of his hidden efforts? The answer, it seems, is that only such documentation could effectively demonstrate his success. This accounts for the many scrapbooks, memos, and ghostwritten letters that reveal the instrumental activities behind a coherent and powerful initiative to generate media.

50. Edward Bernays to George Washington Hill, February 7, 1929, Edward Bernays Manuscript Collection [Bernays collection], Box 56, Folder 2, Library of Congress.

51. Edward L. Bernays, *Biography of an Idea: Memoirs of Public Relations Counsel Edward L. Bernays* (New York: Simon and Schuster, 1965), 383. See also Larry Tye, *The Father of Spin: Edward L. Bernays & the Birth of Public Relations* (New York: Crown, 1998). On the history of public relations, see Richard S. Tedlow. "Keeping the Corporate Image: Public Relations and Business, 1900–1950," in *Keeping the Corporate Image: Public Relations and Business, 1900–1950* (Greenwich, CT: JAI, 1979), 27–51; Richard S. Tedlow, *New and Improved: The Story of Mass Marketing in America* (New York: Basic Books, 1990); Stuart Ewen, *PR!: A Social History of Spin* (New York: Basic Books, 1996).

52. Bernays collection, Box 86, Folder 1.

53. Ibid., Box 89, Folder 5.

54. Bernays, 386.

55. Ibid., 383.

56. Ibid., 386.

57. Memorandum, "System Outline for Easter Smokers," Bernays collection, Box 84.

58. "Easter Sun Finds the Past in Shadow at Modern Parade." *New York Times,* April 1, 1929.

59. Bernays, 387.

60. Ibid., 390.

61. Ibid., 391.

62. Bernays collection, Box 86, Folder 4 (1929–1930).

63. See Richard Klein, *Cigarettes Are Sublime* (Durham, NC: Duke University Press, 1993), 53–55, 114–115, 162–180, 200–201, 575, 645, 776; and Harris Lewine, *Good-Bye to All That* (New York: McGraw Hill, 1970).

64. Giles Playfair, "Smoke Without Fire," *Atlantic Monthly,* April 1948, 96.

65. Raymond Fernand Loewy, *Never Leave Well Enough Alone: The Personal Record of an Industrial Designer* (New York: Simon and Schuster, 1951), 148. See also Stephen Bayley, *The Lucky Strike Packet by Raymond Loewy,* ed. Volker Fischer (Frankfurt am Main: Verlag form, 1998).

66. Loewy, 149.

67. "The American Tobacco Co.," 156; R.J. Reynolds, "Turning the Light of Truth on False and Misleading Statements in Recent Cigarette Advertising," 1930, Bates Nos. ATX05 0240005–0240008, http://tobaccodocuments.org/atc/71000389.html.

68. "$57,000,000 Worth of Whizz and Whoozle," Fortune, August 1938, 30.

69. Nannie M. Tilley, *The R.J. Reynolds Tobacco Company* (Chapel Hill: University of North Carolina Press, 1985), 330.

70. "$57,000,000 Worth of Whizz and Whoozle," 30.

71. Ibid.

72. Lizabeth Cohen, *Making a New Deal: Industrial Workers in Chicago, 1919–1939* (New York: Cambridge University Press, 1990).

73. Carl Avery Werner, "The Triumph of the Cigarette," *American Mercury,* December 1925, 416.

74. "VI: Cigarettes," *Fortune,* April 1936, 218.

75. Ibid.

76. Peter B. B. Andrews, "Cigarette Advertising and the 1935 Sales Race," *Advertising and Selling,* February 14, 1935, 28, 72.

77. See Frank Presbrey, *The History and Development of Advertising* (Garden City, NY: Doubleday, 1929).

78. "The American Tobacco Co.," 154.

79. "Cigarette Rumor," *Business Week,* July 23, 1936, 22.

80. See Reavis Cox, *Competition in the American Tobacco Industry, 1911–1932: A Study of the Effects of the Partition of the American Tobacco Company by the United States Supreme Court* (New York: Columbia University Press, 1933).

81. In 1942, the three leading companies were convicted of conspiracy to monopolize under the provisions of the Sherman Act; this ruling was upheld by the Supreme Court in 1946, but sanctions and fines were minimal. Richard B. Tennant, *The American Cigarette Industry* (New Haven, CT: Yale University Press, 1950), 317–387; and Ellis W. Hawley, *The New Deal and the Problem of Monopoly: A Study in Economic Ambivalence* (New York: Fordham University Press, 1966).

82. Edward G. Connelly, "The Ups and Downs of Tobacco," *Advertising and Selling,* November 12, 1930, 20.

83. Neil H. Borden, "The Effect of Advertising on the Demand for Tobacco Products—Cigarettes," *The Economic Effects of Advertising* (Chicago: Richard D. Irwin, 1944), 248.

84. "Philip Morris & Co.," *Fortune,* March 1936, 106.

85. Borden, 234–235.

86. Gene Borio, *Tobacco Timeline,* Accessed July 4, 2006. Available from http://www.tobacco .org/resources/history/Tobacco_History.html.

87. "The Old Gold Contest," *Fortune,* July 1937, 50.

88. Ibid., 49–50, 136, 138, 140.

89. On the rise of radio advertising, see Russell Sanjek, *American Popular Music and Its Business: The First Four Hundred Years, vol. III: From 1900 to 1984* (New York: Oxford University Press, 1988); Arnold Shaw, *Let's Dance: Popular Music in the 1930s,* ed. Bill Willard (New York: Oxford University Press, 1998); Susan J. Douglas, *Listening in Radio and the American Imagination* (New York: Times Books, 1999); Paul Starr, *The Creation of the Media: Political Origins of Modern Communications* (New York: Basic Books, 2004); and Ben Gross, *I Looked and I Listened: Informal Recollections of Radio and TV* (New York: Random House, 1954).

90. "Philip Morris & Co.," 114.

91. Ibid., 119.

92. "More Cigarets?" *Time,* March 26, 1945, 86–87.

93. "The American Tobacco Co.," 98.

94. Ibid.

95. Harry M. Wootten, "Cigarettes' High Ceiling," *Printer's Ink Monthly,* February 1941, 5.

96. Emil Bogen, "The Composition of Cigarets and Cigaret Smoke," *JAMA* 93, no. 15 (1929): 1110–1114.

97. "A Whiff from the Pipe: The Uses and Abuses of the Tobacco Plant," *New York Times,* March 10, 1889.

98. Quoted in Lears, 183. The year of the original ad was 1929.

99. Walter B. Hayward, "Why We Smoke—We Like It," *New York Times Magazine,* May 18, 1947, 20, 53–54.

100. Henner Hess, "The Other Prohibition: The Cigarette Crisis in Post-War Germany," *Crime, Law and Social Change* 25, no. 1 (1996): 43–61.

Chapter 4

1. *Saturday Evening Post,* October 16, 1937.

2. *Ladies' Home Journal,* February 1947.

3. "Nothing Can Be Said in Favor of Smoking," *In Fact* 4, no. 10 (1942): 23.

4. Bernard DeVoto, "Doctors Along the Boardwalk," in *The Easy Chair* (Boston: Houghton Mifflin Company, 1947), 85–102.

5. John C. Burnham, "American Medicine's Golden Age: What Happened to It?" *Science* 215, no. 4539: 1474–1479.

6. R.J. Reynolds, "According to a Recent Nationwide Survey: More Doctors Smoke Camels Than Any Other Cigarette!" 1946, Bates No. 502470717, http://legacy.library.ucsf.edu/tid/ bwj88d00. R.J. Reynolds established a "Medical Relations Division" under the direction of A. Grant Clarke, from the William Esty Agency, to solicit support of physicians in their Camel campaigns. See M. N. Gardner and A. M. Brandt, "'The Doctors' Choice Is America's Choice': The Physician in U.S. Cigarette Advertisements, 1930–1953," *American Journal of Public Health* 96, no. 2 (2006): 222–232.

7. Leonid S. Snegireff and Olive M. Lombard, "Survey of Smoking Habits of Massachusetts Physicians," *New England Journal of Medicine* 250, no. 24 (1954): 1042–1045; and "The Physician and Tobacco," *Southwestern Medicine,* December 1955, 589–590.

8. "Cigaret Smoking Causes Lung Cancer," *NEA Journal* 35, no. 2 (1946).

9. "Camels, Cows and Tobacco," *Literary Digest,* July 7, 1923, 31.

10. "Cigarettes Killed Him: At Least Coroner Messemer Has Reason to Think So," *New York Times,* August 10, 1887.

11. "Cigarette Smoking Killed Him," *New York Times,* September 27, 1890.

12. R. Kissling, "The Chemistry of Tobacco," *Scientific American Supplement,* November 25, 1905, 24999; and Johannes Wilbert, "Tobacco and Shamanism in South America," *Psychoactive Plants of the World,* eds. Richard Evans Schultes and Robert F. Raffauf (New Haven, CT: Yale University Press, 1987).

13. J. Hilton Thompson, "Carbon Monoxide Poisoning by the Inhalation of Cigarette Smoke," *Lancet* 163, no. 4197 (1904): 395.

14. "Harmless Smoking," *Harper's Weekly,* August 3, 1912.

15. D. H. Kress, "The Cigarette as Related to Moral Reform," *Interstate Medical Journal* 23, no. 6 (1916): 485–489.

16. Kress, 485.

17. "Cigarette Smoking Among Boys," *Pilgrim's Scrip,* November 1910, 140–141.

18. See Allan M. Brandt and Paul Rozin, eds., *Morality and Health* (New York: Routledge, 1997).

19. Thomas Warrington Gosling, "Tobacco and Scholarship," *School Review* (1913): 691–693.

20. Josephine Baker, "What Price Tobacco," *Ladies' Home Journal,* November 27, 1926, 27.

21. Charles J. Aldrich, "The Deleterious Effect of Tobacco upon the Undeveloped Nervous System," *Dietetic and Hygienic Gazette* 20, no. 4 (1904): 202.

22. "Tobacco as the Great Producer of Degenerates," *Current Literature,* August 1907, 217.

23. Charles B. Towns, "The Injury of Tobacco and Its Relation to Other Drug Habits," *Century,* March 1912, 766–772.

24. William A. McKeever, "The Cigarette Boy," *Education,* November 1907, 154–160.

25. "Cigarette Smoking Among Boys," 140–141.

26. "Incidents and Effects of Smoking," *Harper's Weekly,* February 27, 1904, 314.

27. "Tobacco and Physical Health," *New York Times,* April 30, 1891.

28. "School Coaches Express Opinions on Smoking by the Athlete," *Hygeia,* April 1934, 375.

29. George L. Meylan, "The Effects of Smoking on College Students," *Popular Science Monthly,* August 1910, 169–178.

30. J. Rosslyn Earp, "The Smoking Habit and Mental Efficiency," *Lancet* 207, no. 5360 (1926): 1018–1020.

31. M. P. R., "Tobacco and Mental Efficiency," *American Journal of Public Health* 13, no. 9 (1923): 763–764.

32. Bruce Fink, "Smoking and Scholarship Again," *School and Society,* August 20, 1921, 87–89. See also M. V. O'Shea, *Tobacco and Mental Efficiency* (New York: Macmillan, 1923).

33. William Frederick Bigelow, "To Smoke or Not to Smoke," *Good Housekeeping,* April 1926, 4.

34. Edward W. Bok, *The Americanization of Edward Bok: The Autobiography of a Dutch Boy Fifty Years After* (New York: Charles Scribner & Sons, 1922).

35. H. S. Diehl, "The Physique of Smokers as Compared to Non-Smokers: A Study of University Freshmen," *Minnesota Medicine* 12 (1929): 424–427.

36. Ibid.

37. Harry Burke, "Women Cigarette Fiends," *Ladies' Home Journal,* June 22, 1922, 19.

38. Charles B. Towns, "Women and Tobacco," *Delaware State Medical Journal* 7 (1916): 4.

39. Daniel Kevles, *In the Name of Eugenics: Genetics and the Uses of Human Heredity* (Cambridge, MA: Harvard University Press, 1998); and Donald K. Pickens, *Eugenics and the Progressives* (Nashville, TN: Vanderbilt University Press, 1968).

40. Rosalind Rosenberg, *Beyond Separate Spheres* (New Haven, CT: Yale University Press, 1982); and Rosalind Rosenberg, *Divided Lives* (New York: Hill & Wang, 1992).

41. Towns, 4.

42. Bertha Van Hoosen, "Should Women Smoke?" *Medical Woman's Journal* 34 (1927): 227.

43. J. F. Denton, "Research on Tobacco," *Journal of the Florida Medical Association* 10, no. 4 (1924): 269–270.

44. Alexander M. Campbell, "Excessive Cigarette Smoking in Women and Its Effect upon Their Reproductive Efficiency," *Journal of the Michigan State Medical Society* 34, no. 3 (1935): 146.

45. Robert A. Hatcher and Hilda Crosby, "The Elimination of Nicotin in the Milk," *Journal of Pharmacology and Experimental Therapeutics* 32, no. 1 (1927): 1–6 (quotation from p. 6).

46. H. Harris Perlman, Arthur M. Danneberg, and Nathan Sokoloff. "The Excretion of Nicotine in Breast Milk and Urine from Cigaret Smoking," *JAMA* 120, no. 13 (1942): 1003–1009.

47. William Benbow Thompson, "Nicotine in Breast Milk," *American Journal of Obstetrics and Gynecology* 26 (November 1933): 666.

48. "Infant Mortality in Relation to Smoking by Mothers," *Hygeia,* June 1934, 564.

49. F. J. Schoeneck, "Cigarette Smoking in Pregnancy," *New York State Journal of Medicine* 41, no. 5 (1941): 1948. Research conducted later in the century would ultimately confirm not only the impact of smoking on lactation, but a wide range of risks to mothers, fetuses, and children. See, for example, Alicia Dermer. "Smoking, Tobacco Exposure Through Breast Milk, and SIDS," *JAMA* 274, no. 3 (1995): 214–215; Hillary Sandra Klonoff-Cohen, Sharon Leigh Edelstein, Ellen Schneider Lefkowitz, Indu P. Srinivasan, David Kaegi, Jae Chun Chang, and Karen J. Wiley, "The Effect of Passive Smoking and Tobacco Exposure Through Breast Milk on Sudden Infant Death Syndrome," *JAMA* 273, no. 10 (1995): 795–798; and "Transfer of Drugs and Other Chemicals into Human Milk," *Pediatrics* 108, no. 3 (2001): 776–789.

50. Josephine Baker, "What Price Tobacco," *Ladies' Home Journal,* November 27, 1926, 223.

51. Ibid., 27.

52. Wiley was quoted in "Are Cigarettes Harmful?" *Good Housekeeping,* February 1981, 253. For more on Wiley, see Oscar Edward Anderson, *The Health of a Nation: Harvey W. Wiley and the Fight for Pure Food* (Chicago: University of Chicago Press, 1958).

53. Nicholas Kopeloff, "The Tobacco Habit," *New Republic,* September 5, 1923, 44. See also Carl Avery Werner, "The Triumph of the Cigarette," *American Mercury,* December 1925, 415–421.

54. "Cigarette Tar in Cancer," *Scientific American,* April 1933, 246.

55. "Makes Chemical Analysis of Cigarets," *Hygeia,* December 1929, 1215.

56. W. A. Bloedorn, "The Barbarous Custom of Smoking," *Medical Record* 97 (1920): 188.

57. Gardner and Brandt.

58. Baker, 223.

59. William H. Burnham, "The Effect of Tobacco on Mental Efficiency," *Pedagogical Seminary* 24, no. 3 (1917): 297, 317.

60. On the historical question of scientific objectivity, see Lorraine Daston and Peter Galison, "The Image of Objectivity," *Representations* 40 (1992): 81–128.

61. See, for example, Alvan R. Feinstein, *Clinical Judgment* (Baltimore: Williams & Wilkins, 1967).

62. See "Effect of Tobacco on the Heart," *Scientific American,* December 11, 1915, 523.

63. "Tobacco Pains," *American Journal of Surgery* 1, no. 5 (1926): 296–297; Harlow Brooks, "The Tobacco Heart," *New York Medical Journal* 10, no. 2 (1915): 830–837; W. E. Dixon, "The Tobacco Habit," *Lancet* 210, no. 5434 (1927): 881–886; and Charles J. Aldrich, "The Deleterious Effect of Tobacco upon the Undeveloped Nervous System," *Dietetic and Hygienic Gazette* 20, no. 4 (1904): 199–202.

64. See Robert Abbe, "The Tobacco Habit," *Medical Record* 89, no. 5 (1916): 177–180; and Robert Abbe, "Effect of Smoking on the Circulation," *New York Medical Journal* 10, no. 5 (1915): 896.

65. Robert Maris, "The Facts About Smoking," *Hygeia,* October 1944, 740–741; and Grace M. Roth, John B. McDonald, and Charles Sheard, "The Effect of Smoking Cigarets," *JAMA* 125, no. 11 (1944): 761–763.

66. A. Behrend and C. H. Thienes, "The Development of Tolerance to Nicotine by Rats," *Journal of Pharmacology and Experimental Therapeutics* 48 (1933): 317–325.

67. Floyd De Eds and Robert H. Wilson, "III. Effect of Nicotine-Containing Diets on the Estrus Cycle." *Journal of Pharmacology and Experimental Therapeutics* 59, no. 3 (March 1937): 260–263.

68. J. M. Essenberg, Justin V. Schwind, and Anne R. Patras, "The Effects of Nicotine and Cigarette Smoke on Pregnant Female Albino Rats and Their Offspring," *Journal of Laboratory and Clinical Medicine* 25, no. 4 (1940): 716.

69. Ibid., 715.

70. A. H. Roffo, "Tobacco-Induced Carcinoma in Rabbits," *Bulletin of the Institute of Experimental Medicine for Cancer Research & Treatment* 7, no. 24 (1930); and A. H. Roffo and L. B. Smith, "Tobacco as a Carcinogenic Agent," *Deutsche Medezinische Wochenschrift* 63 (1937): 1267–1271. For more on Roffo, see Robert N. Proctor, "Angel H. Roffo: The Forgotten Father of Experimental Tobacco Carcinogenesis," *Bulletin of the World Health Organization* 84, no. 6 (2006): 494–496.

71. Rowland V. Long and William A. Wolff, "The Effect of Tobacco on Estrus, Pregnancy, Fetal Growth, and Lactation," *North Carolina Medical Journal* 9, no. 10 (1948): 522. On animal models, see Angela N. H. Creager, *The Life of a Virus: Tobacco Mosaic Virus as an Experimental Model, 1930–1965* (Chicago: University of Chicago Press, 2002); and Karen Rader, *Making Mice: Standardizing Animals for American Biomedical Research* (Princeton, NJ: Princeton University Press, 2004).

72. On the broader question of proof and science, see, among others, Ludwik Fleck, *Genesis and Development of a Scientific Fact,* eds. Thaddeus J. Trenn and Robert K. Merton, tr. Fred Bradly and Thaddeus J. Trenn (Chicago: University of Chicago Press, 1979); Steven Shapin, *A Social History of Truth: Civility and Science in Seventeenth-Century England* (Chicago: University of Chicago Press, 1994); Mary Poovey, *A History of the Modern Fact: Problems of Knowledge in the Sciences of Wealth and Society* (Chicago: University of Chicago Press, 1998); and Bruno Latour and Steve Woolgar, *Laboratory Life: The Construction of Scientific Facts* (Princeton, NJ: Princeton University Press, 1986).

73. Macfarlane Burnet, *The Natural History of Infectious Disease* (London: Cambridge University Press, 1972); Harry Filmore Dowling, *Fighting Infection: Conquests of the Twentieth Century* (Cambridge, MA: Harvard University Press, 1977); and Charles-Edward Amory Winslow, *The Conquest of Epidemic Disease: A Chapter in the History of Ideas* (Madison: University of Wisconsin Press, 1943).

74. K. Codell Carter, "Koch's Postulates in Relation to the Work of Jacob Henle and Edwin Klebs," *Medical History* 29, no. 4 (1985): 353–374; and Bernard Dixon, *Beyond the Magic Bullet* (New York: Harper & Row, 1978).

75. Rene J. DuBos and Jean DuBos, *The White Plague: Tuberculosis, Man and Society* (Boston: Little, Brown, 1952): 88.

76. G. M. Cochran, P. W. Ewald, and K. D. Cochran, "Infectious Causation of Disease: An Evolutionary Perspective." *Perspectives in Biology and Medicine* 43, no. 3 (2000): 406–448; M. C. Sutter, "Assigning Causation in Disease: Beyond Koch's Postulates," *Perspectives in Biology and Medicine* 39, no. 4 (1996): 581–592; Alfred S. Evans, "Causation and Disease: The Henle-Koch Postulates Revisited," *Yale Journal of Biology and Medicine* 49, no. 2 (1976): 175–195; and Richard F. Shope, "Koch's Postulates and a Viral Cause of Human Cancer," *Cancer Research* 20, no. 8 (1960): 1119–1120.

77. James J. Walsh, "Cigarettes and Pathology," *Commonweal* (1937): 665.

78. The figures are from the United Nations, *Statistical Yearbook 1948* (New York: UN Statistical Office, 1949), 52–60, and *Statistical Yearbook 1973* (New York: UN Publications, 1974), 80–85.

In all these cases, life expectancy rate trends for women were comparable but always a few years higher than for men. On the epidemiologic transition, see especially, A. R. Omran, "The Epidemiologic Transition: A Theory of Population Change," *Millbank Memorial Fund Quarterly* 49, no. 4 (1971): 509–538; and John C. Caldwell, "Toward a Restatement of Demographic Transition Theory," *Population and Development Review* 2, no. 3/4 (1976): 321–366.

79. On this debate, see Jerome Cornfield, William Haenszel, E. Cuyler Hammond, Abraham M. Lilienfeld, Michael B. Shimkin, and Ernst L. Wynder, "Smoking and Lung Cancer: Recent Evidence and Discussion of Some Questions," *Journal of the National Cancer Institute* 22, no. 1 (1959): 173–203; and Milton B. Rosenblatt, "Relation of Smoking to Lung Cancer" [presentation before the Society of the New York Medical College], March 16, 1954, Bates No. 501876160/6183, http://legacy.library.ucsf.edu/tid/gjw29d00.

80. On scurvy, see James Lind, *An Essay on the Most Effectual Means on Preserving the Health of Seamen in the Royal Navy* (London: D. Wilson, 1779). On cholera, see John Snow, *On the Mode of Communication of Cholera* (London: John Churchill, 1849); and Peter Vinten-Johansen, Howard Brody, Nigel Paneth, Stephen Rachman, and Michael Rip, *Cholera, Chloroform, and the Science of Medicine: A Life of John Snow* (Oxford: Oxford University Press, 2003). On pellagra, see Alan Kraut, *Goldberger's War: The Life and Work of a Public Health Crusader* (New York: Hill & Wang, 2003); Joseph Goldberger, C. H. Waring, and W. F. Tanner, "Pellagra Prevention by Diet Among Institutional Inmates." *Public Health Reports* 38, no. 41 (1923): 2361–2368; Joseph Goldberger, "Considerations on Pellagra," *Public Health Reports* 29 (1914): 1683–1686; and Daphne A. Roe, *A Plague of Corn: The Social History of Pellagra* (Ithaca, NY: Cornell University Press, 1973).

81. Herbert L. Lombard and Carl R. Doering, "Cancer Studies in Massachusetts. 2. Habits, Characteristics and Environment of Individuals with and Without Cancer," *New England Journal of Medicine* 196, no. 10 (1928): 481–487.

82. Ibid., 486.

83. Ibid., 487.

84. Morton Keller, *The Life Insurance Enterprise, 1855–1910: A Study in the Limits of Corporate Power* (Cambridge, MA: Harvard University Press, 1963).

85. Robert N. Proctor, *Cancer Wars: How Politics Shapes What We Know and Don't Know About Cancer* (New York: HarperCollins, 1996), 21–24.

86. Frederick L. Hoffman, "Cancer and Smoking Habits," *Annals of Surgery* 93, no. 1 (1931): 50–67.

87. Frederick L. Hoffman, America Prudential Insurance Company, Company Pacific Mutual Life Insurance, and Company John Hancock Mutual Life Insurance, *San Francisco Cancer Survey, 1st–9th (Final) Preliminary Reports* (Newark, NJ: Prudential Press, 1924–1934).

88. Ibid. (1931), 56.

89. Ibid., 62.

90. Ibid., 65.

91. Ibid., 65–66.

92. Raymond Pearl, "Tobacco Smoking and Longevity," *Science* 87, no. 2253 (1938): 216–217.

93. Ibid., 216.

94. F. H. Müller, "Abuse of Tobacco and Carcinoma of the Lungs," *JAMA (Zeitschrift fur Krebsforschung, Berlin)* (1939): 1372. The ideology of the Third Reich, with its deep commitments to bodily purity and race hygiene, attracted considerable attention to the toxic effects of tobacco. The work of Müller, which utilized rudimentary epidemiological techniques, drew attention in the United States in the period just prior to the war. Subsequent work within Nazi science confirmed the harms of smoking, but these investigations had little impact following the war, when they would be viewed as tainted by their political and cultural origins. I have relied on Robert N. Proctor's *The Nazi War on Cancer* (Princeton, NJ: Princeton University Press, 1999) for my assessment of German tobacco science. See also Robert N. Proctor, "Nazi Medicine and Public Health Policy," *Dimensions* 10, no. 2 (1996): 29–34; and E. Schairer and E. Schöniger, "Lung Cancer and Tobacco Consumption," *Inter-*

national Journal of Epidemiology 30, no. 1 (2001): 24–27 (with commentaries by Richard Doll (30–31); Robert N. Proctor (31–34); and Susanne Zimmermann, Matthais Egger, and Uwe Hossfeld (35–37).

95. Alton Ochsner and Michael DeBakey, "Symposium on Cancer: Primary Pulmonary Malignancy, Treatment by Total Pneumonectomy: Analysis of 79 Collected Cases and Presentation of 7 Personal Cases," *Surgery, Gynecology and Obstetrics* 68 (1939): 435–451.

96. Burnham, 18; Evarts A. Graham to Alton Ochsner, October 29, 1940, Evarts A. Graham Papers, Washington University School of Medicine Library Archives, St. Louis, MO. "You, in my opinion, have presented better evidence in favor of the effects of cigarette smoking as an etiological factor in bronchogenic carcinoma than anybody else. My facetious remarks about the silk stockings should not be taken too seriously. On the other hand, I think that there are still some things about bronchogenic carcinoma which are difficult to explain on the basis of cigarette smoking."

97. Later, Ochsner and DeBakey, in 1941, graphically posed the cigarette-cancer hypothesis when they compared the rising curves of cigarette consumption and the growing prevalence of cancer of the lung.

98. Fritz Lickint, *Tabak and Organismus: Handbuch der Gesamten Tabakkunde* (Stuttgart: Hippokrates, 1939).

99. It was widely noted that randomization could be achieved experimentally only under certain clear conditions that did not place experimental subjects or controls under undue risk. A. B. Hill, "The Clinical Trial," *New England Journal of Medicine* 247, no. 4 (1952): 113–119.

100. Evarts A. Graham, "Remarks on the Aetiology of Bronchogenic Carcinoma," *Lancet* 263, no. 6826 (1954): 1305–1308.

Chapter 5

1. Alton Ochsner, *Smoking and Cancer: A Doctor's Report* (New York: Julian Messner, 1954), viii.

2. Tobacco Industry Research Committee, *A Scientific Perspective on the Cigarette Controversy*, 1954, Bates No. 961008152/8172, http://legacy.library.ucsf.edu/tid/wye21a00.

3. E. Cuyler Hammond, "Cause and Effect," *The Biological Effects of Tobacco*, ed. Ernest Wynder (Boston: Little, Brown, 1955), 193–194.

4. Peter D. Olch, "Evarts A. Graham: Pivotal Figure in American Surgery," *Perspectives in Biology and Medicine* 26, no. 3 (1983): 472–485; Arthur E. Baue, "Evarts A. Graham and the First Pneumonectomy," *JAMA* 251, no. 2 (1984): 261–264; Carl E. Lischer, "Evarts A. Graham (1883–1957), Surgeon and Educator," *American Journal of Surgery* 133, no. 6 (1977): 733–736; and C. Barber Mueller, *Evarts A. Graham: The Life, Lives, and Times of the Surgical Spirit of St. Louis* (Hamilton, Ontario: B. C. Decker, 2002).

5. Evarts A. Graham to Alton Ochsner, October 28, 1940, Box 69, Folder 494, Evarts A. Graham Papers, Washington University School of Medicine Library Archives, St. Louis, MO [Graham Papers].

6. Evarts A. Graham to Alton Ochsner, February 18, 1949, Box 69, Folder 494, Graham Papers.

7. Ernst L. Wynder, "Tobacco and Health: A Review of the History and Some Suggestions," *Public Health Reports* 103, no. 1 (1988): 8–18; Ernst L. Wynder, "Tobacco as a Cause of Lung Cancer: Some Reflections," *American Journal of Epidemiology* 146, no. 9 (1997): 687–694; and Ernst Wynder to Evarts A. Graham, July 16, 1949, Box 103, Folder 762, Graham Papers.

8. Ernst L. Wynder and Evarts A. Graham, "Tobacco Smoking as a Possible Etiologic Factor in Bronchiogenic Carcinoma: A Study of 684 Proved Cases," *JAMA* 143, no. 4 (1950): 334.

9. For example, see Ernst Wynder to Evarts A. Graham, July 17, 1949, Box 103, Folder 762, Graham Papers; and Evarts A. Graham to Ernst Wynder, July 25, 1949, Box 103, Folder 762, Graham Papers.

10. Wynder and Graham (1950), 331.

11. David Lilienfeld, personal communication to author, April 17, 1996. The State Institute was later renamed Roswell Park Memorial Institute. Levin also had an article linking cigarettes to

lung cancer in the same *JAMA* issue where the Wynder and Graham article appeared. See Morton L. Levin, "Cancer and Tobacco Smoking: A Preliminary Report," *JAMA* 143, no. 4 (1950): 336–338.

12. Wynder and Graham (1950), 334.

13. Ibid.

14. Ernest L. Wynder to Evarts A. Graham, August 27, 1949, Box 103, Folder 762, Graham Papers. In this letter, Graham discusses visits to Denver, Salt Lake City, and San Francisco.

15. Evarts A. Graham to Dickinson W. Richards, October 5, 1949, Box 103, Folder 762, Graham Papers.

16. N. Fields and S. Chapman, "Chasing Ernst L. Wynder: 40 Years of Philip Morris' Efforts to Influence a Leading Scientist," *Journal of Epidemiology and Community Health* 57, no. 8 (2003): 571–578; "Wynder, Ernest L(udwig)," *Current Biography Yearbook* (1974): 448–450; and Richard Doll, "Ernst Wynder, 1923–1999," *American Journal of Public Health* 89, no. 12 (1999): 1798–1799.

17. Evarts A. Graham to Alton Ochsner, February 18, 1949, Box 69, Folder 494, Graham Papers.

18. See Charles Webster, "Tobacco Smoking Addiction: A Challenge to the National Health Service," *British Journal of Addiction* 79, no. 7 (1984): 7–16.

19. "Obituary: Sir Austin Bradford Hill, 1897–1991," *Journal of the Royal Statistical Society* 154, no. 3 (1991): 482–485.

20. Austin Bradford Hill, *Principles of Medical Statistics* (London: Lancet, 1937).

21. Ibid.

22. See Harry M. Marks, *The Progress of Experiment: Science and Therapeutic Reform in the United States, 1900–1990* (New York: Cambridge University Press, 1997).

23. Medical Research Council, Streptomycin in Tuberculosis Trials Committee, "Streptomycin Treatment of Pulmonary Tuberculosis," *British Medical Journal* 2 (1948): 769–783; Austin Bradford Hill, *Principles of Medical Statistics* (London: Lancet, 1937); and A. B. Hill, "The Clinical Trial," *New England Journal of Medicine* 247, no. 4 (1952): 113–119.

24. Richard Doll, "Conversation with Sir Richard Doll (Journal Interview 29)," *British Journal of Addiction* 86, no. 4 (1991): 367–368.

25. Robert A. Aronowitz, *Making Sense of Illness: Science, Society, and Disease* (New York: Cambridge University Press, 1998): 111–144. See also William G. Rothstein, *Public Health and the Risk Factor: A History of an Uneven Medical Revolution* (Rochester, NY: University of Rochester Press, 2003).

26. Doll, 368.

27. Ibid.

28. Ibid., 369.

29. Raymond Pearl, "Tobacco Smoking and Longevity," *Science* 87, no. 2253 (1938): 216–217.

30. See Marks, 139–148.

31. Richard Doll and Austin Bradford Hill, "Smoking and Carcinoma of the Lung: Preliminary Report," *British Medical Journal* 224 (1950): 742–743, 747.

32. Ibid., 745.

33. Ibid., 747.

34. Ibid., 741.

35. Doll, 370.

36. Doll and Hill (1950), 747.

37. See Evarts A. Graham to Alton Ochsner, December 21, 1950, Box 69, Folder 464, Graham Papers; Ernst Wynder to Evarts A. Graham, July 11, 1951, Box 103, Folder 762, Graham Papers; Evarts A. Graham to A. Bradford Hill, January 5, 1951, Box 45, Folder 354, Graham Papers; A. Bradford Hill to Evarts A. Graham, January 19, 1951, Box 45, Folder 354, Graham Papers; and Evarts A. Graham to A. Bradford Hill, February 13, 1951, Box 45, Folder 354, Graham Papers.

38. Mervyn Susser, "Judgment and Causal Inference: Criteria in Epidemiologic Studies," *American Journal of Epidemiology* 105, no. 1 (1977): 1–15; and Abraham M. Lilienfeld and David E. Lilienfeld, "Epidemiology and the Public Health Movement: A Historical Perspective," *Journal of Public Health Policy* 3, no. 2 (1982): 140–149.

39. Levin, 336–338; R Schrek, et al., "Tobacco Smoking as an Etiologic Factor in Disease I Cancer," *Cancer Research* 10, no. 1 (1950): 49–58; C. A. Mills and M. M. Porter, "Tobacco Smoking Habits and Cancer of the Mouth and Respiratory System," *Cancer Research* 10, no. 9 (1950): 539–542; and D. A. Sadowsky, A. G. Gilliam, and J. Cornfield, "The Statistical Association Between Smoking and Carcinoma of the Lung," *Journal of the National Cancer Institute* 13, no. 5 (1953): 1237–1258.

40. R. Doll, A. B. Hill, P. G. Gray, and E. A. Parr, "Lung Cancer Mortality and the Length of Cigarette Ends: An International Comparison," *British Medical Journal* 1 (1959): 322–325.

41. Sadowsky et al., 1254.

42. J. Berkson, "The Statistical Study of the Association Between Smoking and Lung Cancer," *Mayo Clinic Proceedings* 30 (1955): 319–348; and J. Berkson, "Smoking and Lung Cancer: Some Observations on Two Recent Reports," *Journal of the American Statistical Association* 53, no. 281 (1958): 28–38. Berkson would argue that the American Cancer Society study was also affected by selection bias. But he had erroneously compared never-smokers with the overall lung cancer rate. See Jonathan M. Samet, "Reflections: Testifying in the Minnesota Tobacco Lawsuit," *Tobacco Control* 8, no. 1 (1999): 101–105.

43. R. A. Fisher, letter to the editor, *British Medical Journal* 2 (1957): 43; and R. A. Fisher, "Cigarettes, Cancer, and Statistics," *Centenary Review* 2 (1958): 151–166.

44. Paul D. Stolley, "When Genius Errs: R. A. Fisher and the Lung Cancer Controversy," *American Journal of Epidemiology* 133, no. 5 (1991): 416–436.

45. Ernst Wynder to Evarts A. Graham, July 11, 1951, Box 103, Folder 762, Graham Papers.

46. Richard Doll and A. Bradford Hill, "The Mortality of Doctors in Relation to Their Smoking Habits: A Preliminary Report," *British Medical Journal* 228 (1954): 1451–1455.

47. Richard Doll and A. Bradford Hill, "Lung Cancer and Other Causes of Death in Relation to Smoking: A Second Report on the Mortality of British Doctors," *British Medical Journal* 230 (1956): 1071–1081.

48. Doll and Hill (1954), 1455.

49. Graham to Ochsner, December 21, 1950, Box 69, Folder 264, Graham Papers.

50. E. Cuyler Hammond and Daniel Horn, "Tobacco and Lung Cancer," in *Proceedings of the National Cancer Conference, Volume II* (American Cancer Society, National Cancer Institute and American Association for Cancer Research, 1953), 871–875; E. Cuyler Hammond, Daniel Horn, Lawrence Garfinkel, Constance L. Parcy, and Craig Leonard. "The Relationship Between Human Smoking Habits and Death Rates," *JAMA* 155, no. 15 (1954): 1316–1928; and E. Cuyler Hammond and Daniel Horn, "Smoking and Death Rates—Report on Forty-Four Months of Follow-up of 187,783 Men," *JAMA* 251, no. 21 (1958): 1294–1308.

51. E. Cuyler Hammond to Evarts A. Graham, March 26, 1954, Box 3, Folder 26, Graham Papers.

52. Evarts A. Graham to Alton Ochsner, September 15, 1954, Box 69, Folder 464, Graham Papers.

53. Hammond to Graham, 1954.

54. Hammond et al., "Smoking, Cancer and Heart Disease," *New England Journal of Medicine* 251, no. 14 (1954): 583–584; and R. W. Buechley, R. M. Drake, and L. Breslow, "Relationship of Amount of Cigarette Smoking to Coronary Heart Disease Mortality Rates in Men." *Circulation* 18, no. 6 (1958): 1085–1090.

55. E. Cuyler Hammond to the ACS Board of Directors, "Results of Smoking Study," June 16, 1954, Box 3, Folder 26, Graham Papers.

56. E. Cuyler Hammond, "Classics in Oncology: Remarks on Smoking Evidence and Ethics," *CA-A Cancer Journal for Clinicians* 38, no. 1 (1988): 59.

57. The National Cancer Institute also conducted an extensive prospective study using U.S. veterans. See Harold F. Dorn, "Tobacco Consumption and Mortality from Cancer and Other Disease," *Public Health Reports* 74, no. 7 (1959): 581–593; and Harold A. Kahn, "The Dorn Study of Smoking and Mortality Among U. S. Veterans: Report on Eight and One-Half Years of Observation," *Epidemiological Approaches to the Study of Cancer and Other Chronic Diseases* (Bethesda, MD: U.S. Department of Health, Education, and Welfare, Public Health Service, 1966), 1–125.

58. They also considered confounders. See Ernest L. Wynder and Evarts A. Graham, "Etiologic Factors in Bronchiogenic Carcinoma with Special Reference to Industrial Exposures," *Archives of Industrial Hygiene and Occupational Health* 4, no. 3 (1951): 221–235; and Ernest L. Wynder to Evarts A. Graham, November 22, 1950, Box 103, Folder 762, Graham Papers.

59. Ernest L. Wynder, "Neoplastic Diseases," *The Biologic Effects of Tobacco*, ed. Ernest L. Wynder (Boston: Little, Brown, 1955), 126; and Ernst L. Wynder, Evarts A. Graham, and Adele B. Croninger, "Experimental Production of Carcinoma with Cigarette Tar," *Cancer Research* 13, no. 12 (1953): 855–864.

60. A. H. Roffo, "Tobacco as a Carcinogenic Agent," *Deutsche Medizinische Wochenschrift* 63 (1937): 1267–1271; and A. H. Roffo, "Tobacco-Induced Carcinoma in Rabbits," *Bulletin of the Institute of Experimental Medicine for Cancer Research & Treatment* 7, no. 24 (1930).

61. Ernst L. Wynder, Evarts A. Graham, and Adele B. Croninger, "Experimental Production of Carcinoma with Cigarette Tar," *Cancer Research* 13, no. 12 (1953): 855–864.

62. Evarts A. Graham to Charles S. Cameron, January 7, 1954, Box 3, Folder 26, Graham Papers.

63. Ernest L. Wynder to Evarts A. Graham, June 28, 1954, Box 103, Folder 762, Graham Papers.

64. Ernest L. Wynder to Evarts A. Graham, August 25, 1954, Box 103, Folder 762, Graham Papers.

65. Evarts A. Graham to Alton Ochsner, September 15, 1954, Box 69, Folder 464, Graham Papers.

66. On the history of statistical thinking, see especially Marks, *The Progress of Experiment*; Lorraine J. Daston, Lorenz Krüger, and Michael Heidelberger, eds., *The Probabilistic Revolution* (Cambridge, MA: MIT Press, 1987); and Theodore M. Porter, *Trust in Numbers: The Pursuit of Objectivity in Science and Public Life* (Princeton, NJ: Princeton University Press, 1995).

67. A. Bradford Hill, "The Clinical Trial," *New England Journal of Medicine* 247, no. 4 (1952): 113–119.

68. Peter Vinten-Johansen et al., *Cholera, Chloroform, and the Science of Medicine: A Life of John Snow* (Oxford: Oxford University Press, 2003); John M. Eyler, *Victorian Social Medicine: The Ideas and Methods of William Farr* (Baltimore: Johns Hopkins University Press, 1979); Christopher Hamlin, *Public Health and Social Justice in the Age of Chadwick: Britain, 1800–1854* (New York: Cambridge University Press, 1998); and Barbara Gutmann Rosenkrantz, *Public Health and the State: Changing Views in Massachusetts, 1842–1936* (Cambridge, MA: Harvard University Press, 1972).

69. Rene DuBos, *Mirage of Health: Utopias, Progress and Biological Change* (New York: Harper & Brothers Publishing, 1959); Thomas D. Brock, *Robert Koch, a Life in Medicine and Bacteriology* (New York: Springer-Verlag, 1988); and K. Codell Carter, *The Rise of Causal Concepts of Disease: Case Histories* (Burlington, VT: Ashgate, 2003).

70. See William G. Rothstein, *Public Health and the Risk Factor: A History of an Uneven Medical Revolution* (Rochester, NY: University of Rochester Press, 2003); and Robert A. Aronowitz, *Making Sense of Illness: Science, Society, and Disease* (New York: Cambridge University Press, 1998).

71. Jerome Cornfield, "Statistical Relationships and Proof in Medicine," *American Statistician* 8, no. 5 (1954): 21. See also Evarts A. Graham, "Remarks on the Aetiology of Bronchogenic Carcinoma," *Lancet* 263, no. 6826 (1954): 1305–1308. Graham mentions here what a human experiment would require.

72. Quoted in A. Bradford Hill, "Observation and Experiment," *New England Journal of Medicine* 248, no. 24 (1953): 1000.

73. Ibid., 999.

74. Ibid., 1000. See also Carl V. Phillips and Karen J. Goodman, "The Missed Lessons of Sir Austin Bradford Hill," *Epidemiologic Perspectives and Innovations* 1, no. 3 (2004).

75. Major Greenwood, "Is the Statistical Method of Any Value in Medical Research?" *Lancet* 204, no. 5265 (1924): 153–158; and A. Hardy, and M. E. Magnello, "Statistical Methods in Epidemiology: Karl Pearson, Ronald Ross, Major Greenwood, and Austin Bradford Hill, 1900–1945," *Sozial und Präventivmedizin* 47, no. 2 (2002): 80–89.

76. Sir Richard Doll, "Proof of Causality: Deduction from Epidemiological Observation," *Perspectives in Biology and Medicine* 45, no. 4 (2002): 500.

77. This is a position often voiced among historians working on behalf of the tobacco industry in litigation. See, for example, the expert statement of Kenneth Ludmerer, *U.S. v. Philip Morris, et al.*, Washington, DC: United States District Court (D.C. Cir.), 2002.

78. On the history of epidemiological approaches, see Mervyn Susser, "Epidemiology in the United States after World War II: The Evolution of Technique," *Epidemiologic Reviews* 7 (1985): 147–177; Mervyn Susser, *Causal Thinking in the Health Sciences* (New York: Oxford University Press, 1973); Mervyn Susser, "Judgment and Causal Inference: Criteria in Epidemiologic Studies," *American Journal of Epidemiology* 105, no. 1 (1977): 1–15; Sander Greenland, ed., *Evolution of Epidemiologic Ideas: Annotated Readings on Concepts and Methods* (Newton Lower Falls, MA: Epidemiology Resources, 1987).

79. Carl V. Weller, "Causal Factors in Cancer of the Lung," *American Lecture Series,* ed. J. Arthur Myers (Springfield, IL: Charles C. Thomas, 1955), 99.

80. Ibid., 99–100.

81. Ibid., 100.

82. Charles S. Cameron to Evarts A. Graham, February 13, 1952, Box 3, Folder 26, Graham papers.

83. Charles S. Cameron, "Lung Cancer and Smoking—What We Really Know," *Atlantic Monthly,* January 1956, 74.

84. Ibid., 75.

85. Leonid S. Snegireff and Olive M. Lombard, "Smoking Habits of Massachusetts Physicians: Five-Year Follow-up Study (1954–1959)," *New England Journal of Medicine* 261, no. 12 (1959): 603–604.

86. Evarts A. Graham, foreword to *Smoking and Cancer: A Doctor's Report,* by Alton Ochsner (New York: Julian Messner, 1954), vii–viii.

87. Daniel Horn, Charles S. Cameron, and David Kipnis, "Survey of Medical Opinions Towards Smoking," August 1, 1955, attached to a letter from Cameron to the physicians and scientists who participated in the Survey on Medical Opinion Towards Smoking, September 7, 1955, Box 3, Folder 25, Graham Papers, p. 11.

88. Evarts A. Graham to Alton Ochsner, February 14, 1957, Box 69, Folder 494, Graham Papers.

89. Alton Ochsner to Evarts A. Graham, February 19, 1957, Box 69, Folder 484, Graham Papers.

Chapter 6

1. "Smoke Group" [confidential memo], March 1, 1957, Bates No. 650312917/2930, http://legacy.library.ucsf.edu/tid/gln93f00.

2. "The Controversial Princess," *Time,* April 11, 1960, 104–112.

3. Alan Rodgman, "The Smoking and Health Problem—a Critical and Objective Appraisal," 1962, Bates No. 504822847/2852, http://legacy.library.ucsf.edu/tid/zhm55d00.

4. James Patterson, *The Dread Disease: Cancer and American Culture* (Cambridge, MA: Harvard University Press, 1987).

5. Robert N. Proctor, *Cancer Wars: How Politics Shapes What We Know and Don't Know About Cancer* (New York: HarperCollins, 1996): 101–132.

6. Roy Norr, "Smokers Are Getting Scared!" *Christian Herald,* October 1952, 19–20, 89–92.

7. Roy Norr, "Cancer by the Carton," *Reader's Digest,* December 1952, 7–8.

8. "Beyond Any Doubt," *Time,* November 30, 1953, 60–61.

9. Ibid. See also "Smoking a Cause of Cancer," *Consumer's Research Bulletin,* August 1953, 24–25; "Cigarette Hangover," *Time,* November 9, 1953, 100; "Cigarettes and Cancer," *Scholastic,* October 14, 1953, 18; "Cigarettes and Cancer," *Newsweek,* November 3, 1952, 102; "Fresh Hope but Hard Reality: Cubebs or Coffin Nails," *Life,* December 21, 1953, 10; and "Smoking & Cancer," *Time,* December 22, 1952, 34.

10. Godfrey quotation is from National Better Business Bureau, "Chesterfield Copy Theme Condemned as Misleading," February 1953, Bates No. 1003080053/0056, http://legacy.library.ucsf.edu/tid/xff38e00. For a typical advertisement featuring Arthur Godfrey, see http://tobaccodocuments.org/pollay_ads/Ches09.07.html.

11. R.J. Reynolds, "How Mild Can a Cigarette Be?" July 1949, Bates No. 502471375, http://legacy.library.ucsf.edu/tid/nfj88d00.

12. R.J. Reynolds, "Not One Single Case of Throat Irritation Due to Smoking Camels! Noted Throat Specialists Report on 30-Day Test of Camel Smokers . . . ," January 1949, Bates No. 502598158, http://legacy.library.ucsf.edu/tid/flr78d00.

13. R.J. Reynolds, "30-Day Smoking Test Proves Camels Mildness!" November 20, 4, 6, 7; December 1948; January 1949, Bates No. 502597957, http://legacy.library.ucsf.edu/tid/obs78d00.

14. National Better Business Bureau.

15. Val Adams, "Surgeons Remove Godfrey's Cancer," *New York Times,* May 1, 1959; and Albin Krebs, "Arthur Godfrey, Television and Radio Star, Dies at 79," *New York Times,* March 17, 1983.

16. Paul Hahn, American Tobacco, "Smoking & Lung Cancer—No Proof," 1953, Bates Nos. 02025–29, http://tobaccodocuments.org/ness/6746.html. Individual tobacco companies had funded research through entities such as the Damon Runyon Fund; records indicate that there is good reason to doubt the independence of this research. See John H. Teeter to H. B. Parmele, May 17, 1956, Bates No. 01182882, http://legacy.library.ucsf.edu/tid/nku71e00; and Tommy Ross, "Some Notes on the Damon Runyon Memorial Fund for Cancer Research," October 19, 1950, Bates No. 950152715/2717, http://legacy.library.ucsf.edu/tid/tcn54f00.

17. American Tobacco, "Press Release," November 26, 1953, Bates Nos. 02025–29, http://tobaccodocuments.org/ness/6746.html.

18. The meeting was attended by Paul M. Hahn, president of American Tobacco; E. A. Darr, president of R.J. Reynolds; William J. Halley, president of Lorillard; Timothy V. Hartnett, president of B&W; O. Parker McComas, president of Philip Morris; Joseph F. Cullman, Jr., president of Benson and Hedges; J. B. Hutson, president of Tobacco Associates, Inc.; and J. Whitney Peterson, president of U.S. Tobacco. Only Liggett declined. On the 1939 price-fixing conviction, see William H. Nicholls, *Price Policies in the Cigarette Industry* (Nashville: Vanderbilt University Press, 1951): 337–423; see also Aviva L. Brandt, "Anti-Trust Action Against Tobacco Industry," *Associated Press,* October 20, 1998; and Philip J. Hilts, *Smokescreen: The Truth Behind the Tobacco Industry Cover-Up* (Reading, MA: Addison-Wesley, 1996), 4.

19. Timothy V. Hartnett, "Memorandum from T. V. Harnett," December 15, 1953, Bates Nos. 1005039779/9783, http://legacy.library.ucsf.edu/tid/gvp34e00.

20. See "Draft of Proposals for Cigarette Makers for Discussion by Hill & Knowlton, Inc., Planning Committee Monday Evening, December 21, 1953," December 21, 1953, WHS–John W. Hill Papers, Box 8, November–December 1953, Wisconsin Historical Society, Madison, WI [WHS–John W. Hill Papers]; and Bert C. Goss, Hill & Knowlton, "Background Material on the Cigarette Industry Client," December 15, 1953, Bates No. TIOK0034094/4098, http://legacy.library.ucsf.edu/tid/ufu91f00.

21. Quoted in Karen S. Miller, *The Voice of Business: Hill & Knowlton and Postwar Public Relations* (Chapel Hill: University of North Carolina Press, 1999), 4. See also Miller, 1–5, 128–129; and Scott M. Cutlip, *The Unseen Power: Public Relations, A History* (Hillsdale, NJ: Lawrence Erlbaum Associates, 1994).

22. John W. Hill to R. C. McMath, "(Re: Leahy diet)," December 3, 1953, WHS–John W. Hill Papers, Box 8, November–December 1953; and John W. Hill to R. E. McMath, "(Re: Leahy diet)," December 11, 1953, WHS–John W. Hill Papers, Box 8, November–December 1953.

23. Edwin Dakin and Hill & Knowlton, "Forwarding Memorandum: To Members of the Planning Committee," December 15, 1953, Bates No. 98721562/1571, http://tobaccodocuments.org/ness/3793.html; and WHS–John W. Hill Papers, Box 110, Folder 2.

24. Hill & Knowlton had worked on similar industry collaborations before, most notably with the steel industry. See Miller, 91–120.

25. H. R. Hanmer, "Luncheon Meeting," November 5, 1953, Representatives of Industry, Yale Club. November 5, 1953, Bates No. 950167334/7335, http://legacy.library.ucsf.edu/tid/bqh54f00. Hanmer also reported that Clarke had been allotted "ample funds" from R.J. Reynolds to fund such an effort.

26. John W. Hill, [Re: Revisions to White Paper by Mr. Hanmer], December 30, 1953, WHS–John W. Hill Papers, Box 8, November–December 1953, http://tobaccodocuments.org/ness/5306.html.

27. On the speed of Hill & Knowlton's work, see Hill & Knowlton, "Talks With Research Directors for Cigarette Companies," December 16, 1953, WHS–John W. Hill Papers, Box 111, Folder 5, http://tobaccodocuments.org/ness/27662.html; Hill & Knowlton, "Letter of Transmittal to Manufacturers," December 22, 1953, WHS–John W. Hill Papers, Box 110, Folder 2; Hill & Knowlton and Cigarette Research and Information Committee, "A Frank Statement to the Public by the Makers of Cigarettes," December 22, 1953, WHS–John W. Hill Papers, Box 110; http://tobaccodocuments.org/ness/4601.html; and "Conference Report: Tobacco Industry Research Committee," December 29, 1953, WHS–John W. Hill Papers, Box 108, Folder 12, http://tobaccodocuments.org/ness/4715.html.

28. "Draft of Proposals for Cigarette Makers for Discussion by Hill & Knowlton, Inc., Planning Committee, Monday, Evening, December 21, 1953"; and Hill & Knowlton, "Preliminary Recommendations for Cigarette Manufacturers," December 24, 1953, http://legacy.library.ucsf.edu/tid/bbz34f00; WHS–John W. Hill Papers, Box 108, Folder 12.

29. In subsequent years, this would be referred to as the Gentleman's Agreement. See "Written Direct Testimony of Jeffrey E. Harris, MD, PhD," U.S. Department of Justice, Civil Division, *U.S. v. Philip Morris et al.*, October 4, 2004, http://www.usdoj.gov/civil/cases/tobacco2/Writtend%20Direct%20of%20Dr.%20Jeffrey%20E.%20Harris.pdf.

30. Hill & Knowlton, "Report of Conversation Between Carl Thompson and Judge Barnes," December 31, 1953, WHS–John W. Hill Papers, Box 8, November–December 1953, http://tobaccodocuments.org/ness/3796.html.

31. Carl Thompson to J. W. Hill, B. C. Goss, R. W. Darrow, T. Hoyt, and L. Zahn, "Meeting with Representatives of TIRC Members, Thursday, June 7, 1956," June 12, 1956, WHS–John W. Hill Papers, Box 109, Folder 3, http://tobaccodocuments.org/ness/4637.html.

32. Tobacco Industry Research Committee, "A Frank Statement to Cigarette Smokers," January 4, 1954, Bates No. 86017454, http://legacy.library.ucsf.edu/tid/qxp91e00.

33. Ibid.

34. E. C. K. Read and Hill & Knowlton to J. W. Hill, "Tobacco Industry Research Committee," January 4, 1954, WHS–John W. Hill Papers, Box 110, Folder 10, http://tobaccodocuments.org/ness/3637.html.

35. "Tobacco Industry Takes Look, Too," *Cleveland News,* January 5, 1954.

36. Leslie Gould, "Tobacco Firms Take the Right Step to Squash Lung-Cancer Scare," *New York Journal-American,* January 6, 1954.

37. "Blowing Away the Smoke," *Jersey Journal,* January 5, 1954.

38. Ernest L. Wynder to Evarts A. Graham, November 18, 1953, Box 103, Folder 762, Graham Papers.

39. Evarts A. Graham to Ernest L. Wynder, February 16, 1953, Box 103, Folder 762, Graham papers.

40. Alton Ochsner to Evarts A. Graham, January 26, 1954, Box 69, Folder 464, Graham Papers.

41. Alton Ochsner, *Smoking and Cancer: A Doctor's Report* (New York: Julian Messner, 1954), 72.

42. Covington and Burling (inferred author), "Public Relations in the Field of Smoking and Health," January 1963, Bates Nos. ATX110005290-303, http://legacy.library.ucsf.edu/tid/zcw51a00.

43. John W. Hill, Richard W. Darrow, Carl Thompson, W. T. Hoyt, Hill & Knowlton, "Smoking, Health and Statistics: The Story of the Tobacco Accounts," February 26, 1962, Bates No. 98721513/1551, http://legacy.library.ucsf.edu/tid/ksn33c00 [Tobacco Accounts].

44. As Brown & Williamson's public relations consultant John V. Blalock explained, Hoyt was "without question . . . the administrative head" of the TIRC. Stanton Glantz, *Cigarette Papers* (Berkeley: University of California Press, 1996), 40. On Hoyt's retirement, see Robert F. Gertenbach, "Deposition of Robert F. Gertenbach" [deposition of Gertenbach in the Matter of Broin], August 1, 1994, Bates Nos. CTRMN000001-268, http://tobaccodocuments.org/ctr/CTRMN000001–0268.html.

45. Hill & Knowlton, "Press Release" [Hartnett named TIRC chairman], July 1, 1954, Bates Nos. CTR11310600–1, http://tobaccodocuments.org/ctr/11310600–1.html.

46. "Report of Visit to University of Chicago and Michael Reese Hospital by Irwin Tucker, Grant Clarke and H. R. Hanmer, Members of the Technical Committee, Subject: Scientific Director for TIRC," February 1954, Bates No. 961007789/7799, http://legacy.library.ucsf.edu/tid/jdr94f00.

47. H. R. Hanmer, "Report of Visit to Washington DC, Houston, and Galveston, Texas by Irwin Tucker, Grant Clarke and H. R. Hanmer, Members of the Technical Committee," March 1, 1954, Bates No. 950168374/8382, http://legacy.library.ucsf.edu/tid/hjm31a00.

48. W. T. Hoyt, "A Brief History of the Council for Tobacco Research—U. S. A., Inc. (CTR) Originally Tobacco Industry Research Committee (TIRC)," 1984, Bates No. 515847269/7336, http://legacy.library.ucsf.edu/tid/tpg3aa00. See also Proctor, *Cancer Wars.*

49. Paul M. Hahn to T. V. Hartnett, February 4, 1954, http://tobaccodocuments.org/ness/3775.html. Stewart, Cattell, and Wilhelm Hueper turned down the position. R. H. Rigdon, the other possible candidate, was interested, but the industry decided not to offer the position to him. See Industry Technical Committee, "Confidential Report on Meeting," March 24, 1954, Bates No. 961010516/0517, http://legacy.library.ucsf.edu/tid/qsq94f00.

50. O. Parker McComas, "Appointment of Scientific Director and Scientific Advisory Board Meeting, May 17, 1954," May 26, 1954, WHS–John W. Hill Papers, Box 111, Folder 9, http://tobaccodocuments.org/ness/3906.html.

51. "Expert on Cancer Gives Kindly Nod to Cigarette," *New York Times,* February 25, 1954.

52. Hill & Knowlton, "Tobacco Industry Research Committee Press Conference (condensed)," June 15, 1954, WHS–John W. Hill Papers, Box 110, http://legacy.library.ucsf.edu/tid/ryd6aa00.

53. Tobacco Industry Research Committee, "Confidential Report—Tobacco Industry Research Committee Meeting," October 19, 1954, Bates Nos. CTRMN007295–7, http://tobaccodocuments.org/ctr/CTRMN007295–7297.html.

54. "Dr. Little Accepts Birth Control Post," *New York Times,* January 24, 1936.

55. "Dr. Little Decries Materialistic Aim," *New York Times,* June 5, 1936.

56. "Sees a Super-Race Evolved by Science: Dr. C. C. Little Tells Ithacans Laws to Weed Out Misfits Are 'Just around the Corner,'" *New York Times,* August 25, 1932.

57. George D. Snell, "Clarence Cook Little: October 6, 1888–December 22, 1971," in *Biographical Memoirs* (Washington, DC: National Academy of Sciences, 1975), 241–263.

58. "Lists Three Evils in Our Colleges," *New York Times,* July 28, 1931.

59. "Trials of Faculties Urged in Colleges," *New York Times,* July 29, 1931.

60. Richard Kluger, *Ashes to Ashes* (New York: Knopf, 1996), 141.

61. In both Michigan and Maine, Little had maintained a laboratory and conducted research during the summers, keeping a hand in research even as he focused on administration.

62. "To Finance Dr. Little in Studies of Cancer: Five Wealthy Detroiters Provide for Research by Retiring Head of Michigan," *New York Times,* May 8, 1929.

63. The Bar Harbor fire of 1947 destroyed almost the entire laboratory along with some 60,000 mice. Laboratories around the world that had been supplied with strains of mice by the Jackson Laboratories now contributed to replenishing the lab with descendents of the mice first bred there, and Little worked assiduously to raise the funds to rebuild. See "A Hundred Thousand Mice," *New York Times,* November 1, 1947; and "Mice, Cancer and Men," *New York Times,* November 1, 1948.

64. Patterson, 173.

65. "Cancer Cure Seen Job for One Person," *New York Times,* October 28, 1950.

66. Clarence Cook Little, *1957 Report of the Scientific Director,* June 30, 1957. Bates No. 501773418/3466, http://legacy.library.ucsf.edu/tid/fof39d00.

67. Evarts A. Graham to A. Bradford Hill, August 9, 1956, Box 45, Folder 354, Graham Papers.

68. "$82,000 Is Granted to Study Smoking," *New York Times,* November 8, 1954.

69. Clarence Cook Little, "Guest Editorial: Smoking and Lung Cancer," *Cancer Research* 16, no. 3 (1956): 184.

70. Clarence Cook Little, "Press Conference of the Tobacco Industry Research Committee," June 15, 1954, Bates Nos. 11310464–500, http://legacy.library.ucsf.edu/tid/vyd6aa00.

71. See, for example, Colin Talley, Howard I. Kushner, and Claire E. Sterk, "Lung Cancer, Chronic Disease Epidemiology, and Medicine, 1948–1964," *Journal of the History of Medicine and Allied Sciences* 59, no. 3 (2004): 329–374; Mark Parascandola, "Skepticism, Statistical Methods, and the Cigarette: A Historical Analysis of a Methodological Debate," *Perspectives in Biology and Medicine* 47, no. 2 (2004): 244–261; and Kenneth Ludmerer, expert statement and deposition, *U.S. v. Philip Morris, et al.* For a thorough rebuttal of this position, see especially Robert N. Proctor, "Tobacco and Health," Expert Report, *United States v. Philip Morris et al.,* 2002.

72. E. Cuyler Hammond, "Epidemiological Studies on Smoking in Relation to Lung Cancer," *Unio Internationalis Contra Cancrum; VI Congres international Contre Le Cancer* 8, no. 1 (1954): 90. On Hammond's skepticism regarding the retrospective studies, see E. Cuyler Hammond and Daniel Horn, "Tobacco and Lung Cancer," in *Proceedings of the National Cancer Conference, Volume II* (American Cancer Society, National Cancer Institute and American Association for Cancer Research, 1952), 871–875. His statements were reported in the general press as well. See Robert K. Plumb, "Study on Smoking and Cancer Is Set," *New York Times,* October 20, 1954. Hammond is quoted here as saying that the evidence of "a possible cause-and-effect relationship between smoking and lung cancer" was "overwhelming."

73. See also discussion in chapter 7 on consensus statements emerging in the late 1950s and early 1960s, and Proctor's "Tobacco & Health," his expert report, *United States v. Philip Morris, et al.,* 2002.

74. For a longer discussion of Hueper, see especially Robert Proctor, *Cancer Wars.*

75. See Hoyt, *Brief History* and Glantz, *Cigarette Papers,* 33–40.

76. "Report on Meeting of Scientific Advisory Board Charleston, S.C,. February 14–15, 1958," February 19, 1958, Bates No. 950259598/9602, http://legacy.library.ucsf.edu/tid/naz34f00. See also "Report on Meeting of Scientific Advisory Board, New York, N.Y., May 10–11, 1958," May 13, 1958, Bates No. 961003439/3443, http://legacy.library.ucsf.edu/tid/kpr94f00; and "Confidential Report, Tobacco Industry Research Committee Meeting, May 8, 1958," May 8, 1958, Bates No. 980314235/4242, http://legacy.library.ucsf.edu/tid/uhm85f00.

77. Oscar Auerbach et al., "Changes in the Bronchial Epithelium in Relation to Smoking and Cancer of the Lung: A Report of Progress," *New England Journal of Medicine* 256, no. 3 (1957): 104. Auerbach would present additional confirmatory findings in 1961 and 1979. See Oscar Auerbach et al., "Changes in the Bronchial Epithelium in Relation to Cigarette Smoking and in Relation to Lung Cancer," *New England Journal of Medicine* 265, no. 6 (1961): 253–267; and Oscar Auerbach, E. Cuyler Hammond, and Lawrence Garfinkel, "Changes in the Bronchial Epithelium in Relation to Cigarette Smoking, 1955–1960 vs. 1970–1977," *New England Journal of*

Medicine 300, no. 8 (1979): 381–386. In subsequent research, Auerbach would expose beagles to smoke, producing similar changes in the lung tissue. E. C. Hammond, O. Auerbach, D. Kirman, and L. Garfinkel, "Effects of Cigarette Smoking on Dogs," *Archives of Environmental Health* 21, no. 6 (1970): 740–753; and O. Auerbach, E. C. Hammond, D. Kirman, and L. Garfinkel, "Effects of Cigarette Smoking on Dogs. II. Pulmonary Neoplasms," *Archives of Environmental Health* 21, no. 6 (1970): 754–768. See also Nicholas Wade, "Premature Puff for Smoking Beagles," *Nature*, April 30, 1971, 544–545; and Kluger, *Ashes to Ashes*, 350–358.

78. "Confidential Report, Scientific Advisory Board Meeting, May 11, 1957," May 11, 1957, Bates No. 950261352/1355, http://legacy.library.ucsf.edu/tid/nny34f00.

79. O. Parker McComas, "Memorandum to T. V. Hartnett," July 15, 1957, Bates No. 70123537.

80. Earl Newsom & Company, Research Department, "Annual Reports of the Council for Tobacco Research," December 21, 1972, Bates No. MNAT00515749/5762, http://legacy.library.ucsf.edu/tid/hah70a00.

81. A. W. Spears, "Confidential. . . . Brief Review of the Organizations Contributing to Research into Tobacco," June 24, 1974, Bates No. 01421596/1600, http://legacy.library.ucsf.edu/tid/lmf20e00.

82. Donald Cooley, "Smoke Without Fear," *True Magazine*, 1954, Bates No. 11310873/0908, http://tobaccodocuments.org/landman/11310873-0908.html; for Tobacco Industry Research Committee involvement with Cooley's article, see T. V. Hartnett, "Report of Activities Through July 31, 1954," July 31, 1954, Bates No. 82106817/6841, http://legacy.library.ucsf.edu/tid/bwc34c00; Hill & Knowlton, "MEMORANDUM TO: Tobacco Industry Research Committee, October 8, 1954," Bates No. 01139591/9647, http://legacy.library.ucsf.edu/tid/evh50e00; and Carl Thompson, Conference with Cooley, November 17, 1954, WHS–John W. Hill Papers, Box 111, Folder 2, http://tobaccodocuments.org/ness/3545.html.

83. Clarence Cook Little, [speech], May 26, 1962, Bates No. HT0137037/7044, http://legacy.library.ucsf.edu/tid/nqx1aa00.

84. Richard W. Darrow and Hill & Knowlton to C. Thompson, "Jim Payne Project," March 17, 1955, WHS–John W. Hill Papers, Box 111, Folder 3, http://tobaccodocuments.org/ness/3585.html.

85. Harry Haller to J. W. Hill, B. C. Goss, B. Littin, White and Battersby, "Moves to Counter Anti-Tobacco Blasts," May 12, 1954, WHS–John W. Hill Papers, Box 111, Folder 1, http://tobaccodocuments.org/ness/3456.html.

86. John W. Hill to C. C. Little, July 15, 1954, WHS–John W. Hill Papers, Box 111, Folder 9, http://tobaccodocuments.org/ness/3898.html.

87. W. T. Hoyt to W. F. Rienhoff, "(Re: Ochsner book)," November 5, 1954, WHS–John W. Hill Papers, Box 111, Folder 9, http://tobaccodocuments.org/ness/3886.html.

88. Stephen Klaidman, "Blowing Smoke," in *Health in the Headlines: The Stories Behind the Stories* (New York: Oxford University Press, 1991), 182–228.

89. Tobacco Information Committee, "Tobacco and Health," January–February 1958, Bates No. MNAT00515648/5651, http://legacy.library.ucsf.edu/tid/utg70a00, p. 1.

90. Tobacco Industry Research Committee, "Confidential Report Tobacco Industry Research Committee Meeting, Council for Tobacco Research," April 28, 1955, Bates Nos. CTRMN003816–35, http://legacy.library.ucsf.edu/tid/toq30a00, p. 11.

91. Hill & Knowlton, "Report on TIRC Booklet—A Scientific Perspective on the Cigarette Controversy," May 3, 1954, Bates Nos. BBAT003814–50, http://tobaccodocuments.org/ness/10362.html.

92. Tobacco Industry Research Committee, *A Scientific Perspective on the Cigarette Controversy*, March 1954, Bates No. 961008152/8172, http://legacy.library.ucsf.edu/tid/wye21a00, p. 4.

93. Joseph Garland, "A Scientific Perspective," *New England Journal of Medicine* 250, no. 21 (1954): 923.

94. Garland, 924.

95. Paul M. Hahn, [reaction to the Frank Statement], March 9, 1954, Bates No. 11309945/9945, http://legacy.library.ucsf.edu/tid/dnd6aa00.

96. John W. Hill, "Edward R. Murrow program *See It Now*," December 1, 1954, http://tobaccodocuments.org/ness/3634.html.

97. See also Fred Friendly and Edward R. Murrow, "Cigarette and Lung Cancer—Part I," *See It Now*, CBS-TV, 1955; Friendly and Murrow, "Cigarettes and Lung Cancer—Part II," *See It Now*, CBS-TV, 1955; "Tobacco Industry Research Committee Information Activities, August and September, 1954," October 7, 1954, Bates No. 92438596/8599, http://legacy.library.ucsf.edu/tid/dyb09c00; and "Edward R. Murrow, Broadcaster and Ex-Chief of U.S.I.A., Dies," *New York Times*, April 28, 1965.

98. Hill & Knowlton to T. V. Hartnett, "Report of Activities Through July 31, 1954," July 31, 1954, Bates No. 82106817/6841, http://legacy.library.ucsf.edu/tid/bwc34c00, p. 10.

99. Ibid., 11–12.

100. John W. Hill, "Smoking, Health and Statistics: the Story of the Tobacco Accounts."

101. Hill et al., Tobacco Accounts, Bates No. 98721532.

102. See Letter from John W. Hill to T. V. Hartnett, "Edward R. Murrow Program 'See It Now,'" December 1, 1954, WHS–John W. Hill Papers, Box 9, Folder 10; letter from Carl Thompson to John W. Hill, "For Personal Use: Re: Some Current TIRC Projects," September 9, 1954, WHS–John W. Hill Papers, Box 111, Folder 2; and letter from Carl Thompson to John W. Hill and others, "Meeting with Representatives of TIRC Members, Thursday, June 7, 1956," 1956, WHS–John W. Hill Papers, Box 109, Folder 3.

103. Rene DuBos, *Mirage of Health: Utopias, Progress and Biological Chance* (New York: Harper & Brothers, 1959).

104. "Draft of proposals for cigarette makers for discussion by Hill & Knowlton, Inc. Planning Committee Monday Evening, December 21, 1953," December 21, 1953, WHS–John W. Hill Papers, Box 8, November–December 1953.

105. John W. Hill to B. C. Goss, "Re: Public Opinion Research Job should be done by the Industry-Wide-Committee," January 8, 1954, Bates Nos. 000854–5, WHS–John W. Hill Papers, Box 8, January 1954, http://tobaccodocuments.org/ness/27566.html.

106. John W. Hill, "Program Projects," January 15, 1954, Bates No. 1005104309/4313, http://legacy.library.ucsf.edu/tid/jbf91a00.

107. Tobacco Information Committee, *Tobacco and Health*, January/February 1958, Bates No. MNAT00515648/5651, http://legacy.library.ucsf.edu/tid/utg70a00.

108. Hill et al., Tobacco Accounts, Bates No. 98721530.

109. Philip Morris, "Another Frank Statement to Smokers," January 1959, Bates Nos. 1002607695–7, http://legacy.library.ucsf.edu/tid/cov74e00.

110. There is no clear documentation that this second "Frank Statement" ever appeared in print. However, its existence in the industry files indicates its continued use of the idea of "not enough research."

111. Hill et al., Tobacco Accounts, Bates No. 98721548.

112. Claude E. Teague, "Survey of Cancer Research with Emphasis upon Possible Carcinogens in Tobacco," February 2, 1953, Bates Nos. 501932947–68.

113. George Weissman, "Public Relations and Cigarette Marketing," March 30, 1954, Bates No. 2022239339/9343, http://legacy.library.ucsf.edu/tid/ipp53e00; R. N. DuPuis, [letter to George Weissman re: NATD speech], March 31, 1954, Bates No. 1002366507, http://tobaccodocuments.org/pm/1002366507.html. See also American Tobacco, Press Release, February 23, 1955, Bates No. 950206999/7002, http://legacy.library.ucsf.edu/tid/jvu44f00; Hill & Knowlton, "Tobacco and Health Studies Cover Wide Range of Research," May 17, 1955, Bates No. 950207788/7791, http://legacy.library.ucsf.edu/tid/djo31a00.

114. Richard Kluger, Interview with Charles J. Kensler, June 12, 1989, Bates No. 96746611/6617, http://legacy.library.ucsf.edu/tid/ufw44c00.

115. Alan Rodgman, "The Analysis of Cigarette Smoke Condensate. I. The Isolation and/or Identification of Polycyclic Aromatic Hydrocarbons in Camel Cigarette Smoke Condensate," September 1956, Bates No. 501008279, http://tobaccodocuments.org/rjr/501008241-8293.html [The Analysis of Cigarette Smoke Condensate].

116. "R.J. Reynolds Research and Development Activities Fact Team Memorandum Volume III," December 31, 1985, Bates Nos. 515873805–929, http://tobaccodocuments.org/ness/37102.html.

117. Rodgman, The Analysis of Cigarette Smoke Condensate, Bates No. 501008280.

118. Alan Rodgman, "The Optimum Composition of Tobacco and Its Smoke," November 2, 1959, Bates Nos. TIOK0034800–3, http://tobaccodocuments.org/ti/TIOK0034800–4803.html.

119. Richard Kluger, *Ashes to Ashes*, 196–197; and Kluger, Interview with Charles J. Kensler.

120. R. N. DuPuis, "Confidential Memo to George Weissman and Parker McComas," March 31, 1954, Bates No. 2022239347, http://legacy.library.ucsf.edu/tid/etx74e00.

121. Helmut Wakeham, "An Opinion on Cigarette Smoking and Cancer," September 22, 1959, Bates No. 2065388779/8780, http://legacy.library.ucsf.edu/tid/bay43a00.

122. Helmut Wakeham, "Tobacco and Health—R&D Approach: Presentation to R&D Committee at Meeting Held in New York Office," November 15, 1961, Bates No. 2023193305/3328, http://legacy.library.ucsf.edu/tid/uxc85e00, p. 21.

123. Hill & Knowlton, "New Evidence Shows Complexities of Lung Cancer, Scientist Says," September 27, 1960, Bates No. 500518873/8875, http://legacy.library.ucsf.edu/tid/nqh79d00.

124. H. R. Bentley, D. G. I. Felton, and W. W. Reid, "Report on Visit to U.S.A. and Canada, April 17–May 12, 1958," Bates No. TINY0003106/3116, http://legacy.library.ucsf.edu/tid/fmt22f00.

125. Hill et al., Tobacco Accounts, Bates No. 98721549.

126. Joseph Lelyveld, "Cigarette Makers Prosper Despite Debate on Hazards," *New York Times*, November 29, 1963.

127. Ernest L. Wynder, "An Appraisal of the Smoking–Lung-Cancer Issue," *New England Journal of Medicine* 264, no. 24 (1961): 1239.

128. Ibid., 1240.

129. Clarence C. Little, "Some Phases of the Problem of Smoking and Lung Cancer," *New England Journal of Medicine* 264, no. 24 (1961): 1241.

130. Ibid., 1245.

131. Joseph Garland, "The Great Debate," *New England Journal of Medicine* 264, no. 24 (1961): 1266.

132. Ibid.

133. Joseph Garland, "Cancer of the Lung," *New England Journal of Medicine* 249, no. 11 (1953): 465.

Chapter 7

1. Speech, National Conference on Smoking and Youth, June 10, 1964, quoted in "Health Service Opens Campaign on Smoking," *Los Angeles Times*, June 11, 1964.

2. Addison Yeaman, "Implications of Battelle Hippo I & II and the Griffith Filter," July 17, 1963, Bates No. 2074459290/9294, http://legacy.library.ucsf.edu/tid/ari52c00.

3. Thomas Whiteside, *Selling Death: Cigarette Advertising and Public Health* (New York: Liveright, 1971), 31.

4. Brown & Williamson, "Smoking and Health Proposal," 1969, Bates No. 690010951/0959, http://legacy.library.ucsf.edu/tid/rgy93f00.

5. See Barbara Gutmann Rosenkrantz, *Public Health and the State: Changing Views in Massachusetts, 1842–1936* (Cambridge, MA: Harvard University Press, 1972); and Judith Walzer Leavitt, *The Healthiest City: Milwaukee and the Politics of Health Reform* (Princeton, NJ: Princeton University Press, 1982).

6. See Rene DuBos, *Mirage of Health: Utopias, Progress and Biological Change* (New York: Harper & Brothers Publishing, 1959); A. R. Omran, "The Epidemiologic Transition: A Theory

of the Epidemiology of Population Change," *Milbank Memorial Fund Quarterly* 49, no. 4 (1971): 509–538; and Walsh McDermott, "Medicine: The Public Good and One's Own," *Perspectives in Biology and Medicine* 21, no. 2 (1978): 167–187.

7. James H. Cassedy, *Charles V. Chapin and the Public Health Movement* (Cambridge, MA: Harvard University Press, 1962); and Judith W. Leavitt, *Typhoid Mary: Captive to the Public's Health* (Boston: Beacon, 1996).

8. Allan M. Brandt and Martha Gardner, "Antagonism and Accommodation: Interpreting the Relationship Between Public Health and Medicine in the United States During the 20th Century," *American Journal of Public Health* 90, no. 5 (2000): 707–715. See also Rosenkrantz; Paul Starr, *The Social Transformation of American Medicine* (New York: Basic Books, 1982); and Institute of Medicine, Committee for the Study of the Future of Public Health, *The Future of Public Health* (Washington, DC: National Academy Press, 1988).

9. Frank M. Strong et al., "Smoking and Health: Joint Report of the Study Group on Smoking and Health," *Science* 125, no. 3258 (1957): 1129–1133.

10. Strong, 1129.

11. Leroy E. Burney, "For Release in P.M. Newspapers," July 12, 1957, Bates No. TIMN0110057/0058, http://legacy.library.ucsf.edu/tid/kkk92f00.

12. Brandt and Gardner, 707–715.

13. Lewis C. Robbins, "Position Statement of Surgeon General on Smoking and Cancer" (Washington, DC: Public Health Service, Cancer Control Program, 1956). See also Dennis L. Breo, "The Unsung Public Health Hero Who Helped Launch the War on Tobacco," *JAMA* 264, no. 12 (1990): 1597–1598.

14. Jerome Cornfield, William Haenszel, E. Cuyler Hammond, Abraham M. Lilienfeld, Michael B. Shimkin, and Ernst L. Wynder, "Smoking and Lung Cancer: Recent Evidence and Discussion of Some Questions," *Journal of the National Cancer Institute* 22, no. 1 (1959): 198.

15. Ibid., 173.

16. Ibid.; and Strong, 1129.

17. L. E. Burney, "Smoking and Lung Cancer: A Statement of the Public Health Service," *JAMA* 71, no. 13 (1959): 1835–1836.

18. W. L. Laurence, "Science in Review: Controversy on Lung Cancer and Smoking Flares Up Again over the Statistics," *New York Times*, December 6, 1959.

19. See L. E. Burney, "Policy over Politics: The First Statement on Smoking and Health by the Surgeon General of the United States Public Health Service," *New York State Journal of Medicine* 83, no. 13 (1983): 1253. See also Mark Parascandola, "Cigarettes and the U.S. Public Health Service in the 1950s," *American Journal of Public Health* 91, no. 2 (2001): 196–205.

20. John H. Talbott, "Smoking and Lung Cancer," *JAMA* 171, no. 15: 2104. Historian Jon M. Harkness has recently published an extensive analysis of the Talbott editorial, which was drafted within the surgeon general's office (but without Burney's approval) by Deputy Surgeon General John Porterfield. See Harkness, "The U.S. Public Health Service and Smoking in the 1950s: The Tale of Two More Statements," *Journal of the History of Medicine and Allied Sciences* (advance access on September 15, 2006): 1–42. Although Harkness draws the conclusion that the editorial reflected ambivalence about the evidence linking smoking to lung cancer, it seems more likely that it reflected the very significant trepidation within the Public Health Service about treading on the professional prerogatives of the medical profession and the AMA. By the time of Burney's 1959 statement, there was no longer significant debate within the PHS about the importance and consistency of the epidemiological findings; the debate centered on what the surgeon general should do about these findings. Harkness, like other historians who have worked as experts on behalf of the tobacco industry in litigation, does not explore the role of the industry in shaping the scientific debate. It is particularly striking that in such a deeply researched (and speculative) article, he fails to note, for example, that Little and other executives at the TIRC had met with Porterfield and corresponded with him and others in the PHS in the

year before the editorial. See, for example, "Report on Meeting of Scientific Advisory Board Charleston, S.C., February 14–15, 1958," February 19, 1958, Bates No. 950259598/9602, http://legacy.library.ucsf.edu/tid/naz34f00; Clarence C. Little, "Letter to John D. Porterfield," May 22, 1958, Bates No. 1005039304/9305, http://legacy.library.ucsf.edu/tid/jht74e00; John D. Porterfield, "Letter to C. C. Little," June 4, 1958, Bates No. 1005039293, http://legacy .library.ucsf.edu/tid/hht74e00; Joseph F. Cullman, III, "Letter to Timothy Hartnett," June 9, 1958, Bates No. 1002607482, http://legacy.library.ucsf.edu/tid/uiu74e00; and R. C. Hockett, "Visit to Dr. H. R. Heller and Dr. Burroughs Mider at the National Cancer Institute on June 10, 1958," June 16, 1958, Bates No. 1005039331/9333, http://legacy.library.ucsf.edu/tid/sap94e00.

21. British Medical Research Council, "Tobacco Smoking and Cancer of the Lung: Statement of British Medical Research Council," June 29, 1957 (statement was printed in the *British Medical Journal* and *Lancet*); World Health Organization, "Epidemiology of Cancer of the Lung; Report of a Study Group," *WHO Technical Reports* (1960): 192; and Royal College of Physicians of London, *Smoking and Health: Summary and Report of the Royal College of Physicians of London on Smoking in Relation to Cancer of the Lung and Other Diseases* (New York: Pitman Publishing, 1962) [Royal College: *Smoking and Health*].

22. Royal College: *Smoking and Health*, 1.

23. Ibid., 27.

24. See also Virginia Berridge, "Science and Policy: The Case of Postwar British Smoking Policy," in *Ashes to Ashes: The History of Smoking and Health*, eds. Stephen Lock, Lois Reynolds, and E. M. Tansey (Atlanta, GA: Editions Rodpi B.V., 1998), 143–163.

25. Royal College: *Smoking and Health*.

26. "Differ on Effects of Heavy Smoking; Cancer Report and Reply," *New York Times*, July 13, 1957.

27. Stefan Timmermans and Marc Berg, *The Gold Standard: The Challenge of Evidence-Based Medicine and Standardization in Health Care* (Philadelphia: Temple University Press, 2003).

28. Surgeon General's Advisory Committee on Smoking and Health, *Smoking and Health: Report of the Advisory Committee to the Surgeon General of the Public Health Service* (Washington, DC: U.S. Department of Health, Education, and Welfare, Public Health Service, 1964), 7 [Surgeon General: *Smoking and Health*].

29. "Transcript of the President's News Conference on Foreign and Domestic Matters," *New York Times*, May 24, 1962. For a description of the press conference, see A. Lee Fritschler, *Smoking and Politics: Policy Making and the Federal Bureaucracy* (Upper Saddle River, NJ: Prentice Hall, 1989), 39–40.

30. Fritschler, 40–41; M. B. Neuberger, *Smoke Screen: Tobacco and the Public Welfare* (Upper Saddle River, NJ: Prentice Hall, 1963), 62–64.

31. Richard Pearson, "Dr. Luther Terry, Former Surgeon General, Dies," *Washington Post*, March 31, 1985.

32. In 1958, the TIRC was renamed the Council for Tobacco Research (CTR), with its PR functions detailed to the newly created Tobacco Institute.

33. Clark MacGregor to Surgeon General Luther Terry, November 9, 1962, Washington, DC: National Archives Record Group 90, Surgeon General's Advisory Committee on Smoking and Health.

34. Three members of the committee smoked cigarettes, and two others occasionally smoked pipes or cigars. "Press Conference by Surgeon General's Committee on Smoking and Health," January 11, 1964, Bates No. 690000011, http://legacy.library.ucsf.edu/tid/kag33f00.

35. Surgeon General: *Smoking and Health*, 9; and A. Lee Fritschler, *Smoking and Politics: Policy Making and the Federal Bureaucracy* (Upper Saddle River, NJ: Prentice Hall, 1989), 44; Kluger, *Ashes to Ashes* (New York: Knopf, 1996), 221–223, 242–262.

36. Robert C. Hockett, "Memorandum for the Files: Surgeon General's Committee," August 13, 1962, Bates No. 11308722/8722, http://legacy.library.ucsf.edu/tid/quc6aa00.

37. Clarence Cook Little, "Suggested Scientists," 1962, Bates No. 980197925/7927; Richard Kluger, Interview with Leonard M. Schuman, July 15, 1988, http://tobaccodocuments.org/ness/76600.123.html; and Kluger, *Ashes to Ashes*, 242–246.

38. W. T. Hoyt, "Memorandum for the Files," September 28, 1962, Bates No. 11308689/8690, http://legacy.library.ucsf.edu/tid/otc6aa00.

39. Luther L. Terry, "The Surgeon General's First Report on Smoking and Health: A Challenge to the Medical Profession," *New York State Journal of Medicine* 83, no. 13 (1983): 1254.

40. Ibid., 1254–1255.

41. Surgeon General's Advisory Committee on Smoking and Health, "The Nature, Purpose and Suggested Formulation of the Study of the Health Effects of Smoking, Phase I," 1962, Washington, DC: National Archives Record Group 90.

42. Surgeon General's Advisory Committee on Smoking and Health, "Minutes of Meeting on the Nature, Purpose and Suggested Formulation of the Study of Health Effects of Smoking, Phase I," 1962, Washington, DC: National Archives Record Group 90.

43. Peter Hamill, "Letter to Leonard Schuman," 1963, Washington, DC: National Archives Record Group 90.

44. "Oral History of Stanhope Bayne-Jones," Stanhope Bayne-Jones Papers, 1870–1969, p. 1127, Washington, DC: National Library of Medicine.

45. U.S. Public Health Service, "Criteria for Judgment," in Surgeon General: *Smoking and Health*. On meta-analysis, see G. V. Glass, "Primary, Secondary, and Meta-analysis," *Educational Researcher* 5 (1976): 3–8; J. A. Hall, L. Tickle-Degnen, R. Rosenthal, and F. Mosteller, "Hypotheses and Problems in Research Synthesis," in *The Handbook of Research Synthesis*, eds. H. Cooper and L. V. Hedges (New York: Russell Sage Foundation, 1994); and L. V. Hedges and I. Olkin, *Statistical Methods for Meta-Analysis* (San Diego: Academic Press, 1985).

46. J. Berkson and T. Hoyt, [Re: Payment schedule], August 6, 1966, Bates No. 11330791/0791, http://legacy.library.ucsf.edu/tid/yrp6aa00; and W. T. Hoyt, [Re: Consulting job with CTR], July 29, 1966, Bates No. 11330476/0476, http://legacy.library.ucsf.edu/tid/glp6aa00.

47. Surgeon General: *Smoking and Health*; and "The Smoking Report," *New York Times*, January 12, 1964.

48. Clarence C. Little, "Memorandum for the Files: Conference with Drs. Hamill and Bayne-Jones, January 15, 1963," 1963, Bates No. 11309627/9629, http://tobaccodocuments.org/ctr/11309627–9629.html; Clarence C. Little, "Memorandum for the Files: Conference with Dr. Hundley, January 16, 1963," 1963, Bates No. 11309630, http://tobaccodocuments.org/ctr/11309630–9630.html.

49. Clarence Cook Little, "Memorandum for the Files: Telephone Conversation with Dr. Hamill, Initiated by CCL, 10:45 A.M., December 10, 1962," 1962, Bates No. 11308649/8650, http://legacy.library.ucsf.edu/tid/osc6aa00.

50. Peter Hamill, "Letter to C.C. Little," November 30, 1962, Bates No. 92525958/5959, http://legacy.library.ucsf.edu/tid/qnh54a00.

51. Clarence Cook Little, "Memorandum for the Files: Telephone Conversation with Dr. Hamill, Initiated by CCL, 10:45 A.M., December 10, 1962," 1962, Bates No. 11308649/8650, http://legacy.library.ucsf.edu/tid/osc6aa00.

52. Peter Hamill, "Visit with Dr. C. C. Little, TIRC, NYC, November 19th and 20th," 1962, Bates No. 70102841/2843, http://legacy.library.ucsf.edu/tid/clj59c00.

53. Peter Hamill, "Visit with Dr. C. C. Little, TIRC, NYC, November 19th and 20th," 1962, Bates No. 70102841/2843, http://legacy.library.ucsf.edu/tid/clj59c00.

54. Stanhope Bayne-Jones, "Oral History of Stanhope Bayne-Jones," Stanhope Bayne-Jones Papers, 1870–1969.

55. Richard Kluger, Interview with Peter V. Hamill, September 8, 1988, http://legacy.library.ucsf.edu/tid/prw56c00.

56. Clarence Cook Little, "Confidential Memorandum: Meeting with Dr. Peter V. V. Hamill on April 29," 1964, Bates No. HK0441013/1014, http://legacy.library.ucsf.edu/tid/dfx10a00.

57. Surgeon General: *Smoking and Health*, 21.

58. Ibid.

59. Ibid., 182, 183, 183–184, 185.

60. Austin Bradford Hill, "The Environment and Disease: Association or Causation?" *Proceedings of the Royal Society of Medicine* 58 (1965): 295–300; and Mervyn Susser, "Epidemiology in the United States After World War II: The Evolution of Technique," *Epidemiologic Reviews* 7 (1985): 147–177.

61. Richard Kluger, Interview with Leonard M. Schuman, 1988, http://tobacco documents.org/ness/76600.123.html; Lester Breslow, "Some Sequels to the Surgeon General's Report on Smoking and Health: Thirty Years Later," *Annual Epidemiology* 6 (1996): 372–375; Luther L. Terry, "The Surgeon General's First Report on Smoking and Health: A Challenge to the Medical Profession," *New York State Journal of Medicine* 83, no. 13 (1983): 1254–1255; and Leonard M. Schuman, "The Origins of the Report of the Advisory Committee on Smoking and Health to the Surgeon General," *Journal of Public Health Policy* 2, no. 1 (1981): 19–27.

62. "Press Conference by Surgeon General's Committee on Smoking and Health," January 11, 1964, Bates No. 690000019, http://legacy.library.ucsf.edu/tid/kag33f00.

63. Surgeon General Luther Terry, Interview by Hugh Downs, *Today Show*, NBC, January 13, 1964.

64. Mark Ross, "Why I Am Still Smoking 25 a Day," *Daily Express*, January 13, 1964.

65. Louis F. Fieser, "Letter to Members of the Committee on Smoking and Health," 1965, William Cochran Papers, Harvard University Archives, Cambridge, MA [Cochran Papers].

66. Louis F. Fieser, "Letter to William Cochran," 1965, Cochran Papers.

67. As quoted in Clarence Cook Little, *Report of the Scientific Director, 1963–64*, 1963, Bates No. 946007710/7782, http://legacy.library.ucsf.edu/tid/xwy85f00.

68. See Stephen Klaidman, *Health in the Headlines: The Stories Behind the Stories* (New York: Oxford University Press, 1991), 182–228.

69. Stanley Joel Reiser, "Smoking and Health: Congress and Causality," in *Knowledge and Power*, ed. Sanford A. Lakoff (New York: Free Press/Macmillan, 1966), 301.

70. Austin Bradford Hill, "The Environment and Disease: Association or Causation?" *Proceedings of the Royal Society of Medicine* 58 (1965): 300.

71. See Fritschler, 89.

72. R. K. Heimann, "TIRC Meeting January 29, 1964," January 31, 1964, Bates No. 966000481/0484, http://legacy.library.ucsf.edu/tid/xxl21a00.

73. Addison Yeaman, "Implications of Battelle Hippo I & II and the Griffith Filter," July 17, 1963, Bates No. 2074459290/9294, http://legacy.library.ucsf.edu/tid/ari52c00.

74. Ibid., 2.

75. Ibid.

76. J. S. Dowdell, "Public Opinion—Smoking and Health," August 10, 1967, Bates No. 500006192/6194, http://legacy.library.ucsf.edu/tid/yni99d00.

77. William Kloepfer, "Memorandum" [planning for future institute projects], April 15, 1968, Bates No. TIMN0252389/2391, http://legacy.library.ucsf.edu/tid/vne72f00.

78. Helmut Wakeham, [letter to Earle C. Clements re: problems of the tobacco industry], May 26, 1970, Bates No. 87657726/7727, http://legacy.library.ucsf.edu/tid/btp91e00.

79. Helmut Wakeham. "'Best' Program for C.T.R." [memo to Joseph F. Cullman, III], December 8, 1970, Bates No. CTRMN045348/5350, http://legacy.library.ucsf.edu/tid/cst30a00.

80. Stanton A. Glantz, *The Cigarette Papers* (Berkeley: University of California Press, 1996), 290.

81. Kluger, *Ashes to Ashes*, 362–363; and Richard Kluger, Interview with Freddy Homburger, May 10, 1988, Bates No. 82131011/1017, http://legacy.library.ucsf.edu/tid/tiq34c00.

82. George Weissman, "Surgeon General's Report" [letter to Joseph F. Cullman III], January 29, 1964, Bates No. 1005038559/8561, http://legacy.library.ucsf.edu/tid/ctv74e00.

83. Carl Thompson, "Tobacco and Health Research Procedural Memo," October 18, 1968, Bates No. TIMN0071488/1491, http://legacy.library.ucsf.edu/tid/upv92f00.

84. "Tobacco Industry's Peak Year: 523 Billion Cigarettes Smoked," *New York Times*, January 1, 1964; "Cigarette Sales Decline Sharply," *New York Times*, June 30, 1964; "Has the Smoking Scare Ended?" *U.S News & World Report*, October 18, 1965; and *Total and Per Capita Manufactured Cigarette Consumption* and Percentage Change in Per Capita Consumption—United States, United States Department of Agriculture, 1900–1995* (Centers for Disease Control—National Center For Chronic Disease Prevention and Health Promotion), 2005, available from http://www.cdc.gov/tobacco/research_data/economics/consump1.htm.

85. See [report re: talks by Surgeon General Luther Terry in Miami Beach, Sunday, Nov 29], November 29, 1964, Bates Nos. TIMN0114118–21, http://tobaccodocuments.org/ahf/TIMN0114118–4121.html.

86. John Parascandola, "The Surgeons General and Smoking," *Public Health Reports* 112 (1997): 440–442.

87. D. F. Thompson, "Understanding Financial Conflicts of Interest," *New England Journal of Medicine* 329, no. 8 (1993): 573–576.

88. James Q. Wilson, *The Politics of Regulation* (New York: Basic Books, 1980); and James T. Patterson, *Grand Expectations: The United States, 1945–1974* (New York: Oxford University Press, 1996). On the general topic of science advising and political regulation, see Sheila Jasanoff, *The Fifth Branch: Science Advisors as Policymakers* (Cambridge, MA: Harvard University Press, 1990).

Chapter 8

1. "Hearing of the Senate Commerce Committee," March 29, 1965, Bates No. 501944403.

2. Thomas Whiteside to FDA Commissioner Charles C. Edwards, quoted in Thomas Whiteside, *Selling Death: Cigarette Advertising and Public Health* (New York: Liveright, 1971), 135.

3. S. Bayne-Jones, Oral History Memoir, National Library of Medicine, Bethesda, Maryland, 1108.

4. It was a frequent claim on the part of the industry and the Tobacco Institute that as a result of the "controversy," there was widespread "common knowledge" of the "alleged" harms of the product. This claim would be argued in litigation in order to justify the industry position that individuals had "assumed" the risks of smoking. See, for example, the discussion in Richard A. Wegman, "Cigarettes and Health: A Legal Analysis," *Cornell Law Quarterly* 51, no. 4 (1966): 699–705.

5. David Kessler, *A Question of Intent: A Great American Battle with a Deadly Industry* (New York: Public Affairs, 2001), 6–7; Martha A. Derthick, *Up in Smoke: From Legislation to Litigation in Tobacco Politics* (Washington, DC: Congressional Quarterly Press, 2002), 52–55; and A. Lee Fritschler, *Smoking and Politics: Policy Making and the Federal Bureaucracy* (Upper Saddle River, NJ: Prentice Hall, 1989), 32–34.

6. Michael Schudson, *Advertising, the Uneasy Persuasion: Its Dubious Impact on American Society* (New York: Basic Books, 1984).

7. Roland Marchand, *Advertising the American Dream: Making Way for Modernity* (Berkeley: University of California Press, 1985).

8. "Cigarette Concern Stops 'Health' Ads," *New York Times*, January 24, 1930; and "The FTC and Cigarettes," *New Republic*, August 17, 1942.

9. M. N. Gardner and A. M. Brandt, "'The Doctors' Choice Is America's Choice': The Physician in U.S. Cigarette Advertisements, 1930–1953," *American Journal of Public Health* 96, no. 2 (2006): 222–232.

10. "'Guide' Published on Cigarette Ads," *New York Times,* September 22, 1955.

11. R. W. Pollay and T. Dewhirst, "The Dark Side of Marketing Seemingly 'Light' Cigarettes: Successful Images and Failed Fact," *Tobacco Control* 11 (Suppl 1) (2002): I20.

12. Claude E. Teague, "Survey of Cancer Research with Emphasis upon Possible Carcinogens in Tobacco," February 2, 1953, Bates No. 501932947/2968, http://legacy.library.ucsf.edu/tid/lvs29d00.

13. W. L. Dunn and Myron Johnston, "Market Potential of a Health Cigarette," June 1966, Bates No. 1000338644/8671, http://legacy.library.ucsf.edu/tid/bdw67e00.

14. Edwin Dakin, Hill & Knowlton, "Forwarding Memorandum: To Members of the Planning Committee," December 15, 1953, Bates No. 98721562/1571, http://tobaccodocuments.org/ness/3793.html; Pollay and Dewhirst, I18–I30; Bert C. Goss, Hill & Knowlton, "Background Material on the Cigarette Industry Client," December 15, 1953, Bates No. TIOK0034094/4098, http://legacy.library.ucsf.edu/tid/ufu91f00; and Lippincott & Margulies, "Development of a Positioning Statement for a New Filter Cigarette, Code Name—HRH," September 1963, Bates No. 990197077/7148, http://legacy.library.ucsf.edu/tid/ahl70a00.

15. Lisa Rosner, ed., *The Technological Fix, Hagley Perspectives on Business and Culture* (New York: Routledge, 2004).

16. Hugh Cullman, Interview by R. C. Hottelet, *CBS Evening News,* January 11, 1964.

17. "Richards Calls 'Digest' Cigaret Article 'Unfair,'" *Advertising Age,* June 30, 1958, 1.

18. Richard Kluger, *Ashes to Ashes* (New York: Knopf, 1996), 170.

19. Representative John A. Blatnik, "Making Cigarette Ads Tell the Truth," *Harper's Magazine,* August 1958, 45–49.

20. Representative John A. Blatnik, "False and Misleading Advertising (Filter-Tip Cigarettes)," House Committee on Government Operations, 1958.

21. Blatnik, "Making Cigarette Ads Tell the Truth," 45–49.

22. M. B. Neuberger, *Smoke Screen: Tobacco and the Public Welfare* (Upper Saddle River, NJ: Prentice Hall, 1963), 57.

23. Clarence Cook Little, [letter to Timothy V. Hartnett re: increased filter consumption], January 30,1959, http://legacy.library.ucsf.edu/tid/otf1aa00.

24. "Filtered for Safety," *Time,* July 29, 1957, 28.

25. Clarence Cook Little to Henry R. Luce, August 3, 1957, Bates No. 1005039176/9177, http://legacy.library.ucsf.edu/tid/ccp94e00.

26. Henry R. Luce to Clarence Cook Little, August 9, 1957, Bates No. 1005039186/9188, http://legacy.library.ucsf.edu/tid/atv74e00.

27. "Tobacco: End of the Tar Derby," *Time,* February 15, 1960, 93.

28. Robert Alden, "Advertising: Shift in the Cigarette Industry Stirs a New Dispute," *New York Times,* February 8, 1960.

29. A. Lee Fritschler, *Smoking and Politics: Policy Making and the Federal Bureaucracy* (Upper Saddle River, NJ: Prentice Hall, 1989), 69–71; and Walter Sullivan, "Cigarettes Peril Health, U. S. Report Concludes; 'Remedial Action' Urged," *New York Times,* January 12, 1964.

30. "FTC Tries to Kick the Habit," *Business Week,* January 25, 1964, 28.

31. Ibid.; "To Smoke—or Not to Smoke? The Individual Ponders the U.S. Health Report—and the Industry Reels from Tough FTC Proposals," *Newsweek,* January 27,1964, 70–73; and "Tobacco: The Washington Hearings on Cigarette Labeling," *Time,* March 27, 1964, 79–80.

32. Beginning in the early years of the New Deal, a tobacco price-support program was undertaken to stabilize tobacco prices for farmers under the provisions of the Agricultural Adjustment Administration. The program was comprised of two principal provisions: first, quotas that limited tobacco growing to those holding specific rights to do so; and second, guarantees of a minimum price to farmers within the quota system. This program, by reducing the acreage committed to farming tobacco, had the desired effect of raising prices and the overall economic well-being of the

farmers.See Anthony J. Badger, *Prosperity Road: The New Deal, Tobacco, and North Carolina* (Chapel Hill: University of North Carolina Press, 1980). On the history and culture of twentieth-century tobacco agriculture, see also Pete Daniel, *Breaking the Bond: The Transformation of Cotton, Tobacco, and Rice Cultures Since 1880* (Chicago: University of Illinois Press, 1985); and Peter Benson, "To Not Be Sorry: Moral Life in North Carolina Tobacco Country," Harvard University PhD dissertation, 2007.

33. David G. Altman et al., "Tobacco Farming and Public Health: Attitudes of the General Public and Farmers," *Journal of Social Issues* 53, no. 1 (1997): 113–128; A. Lee Fritschler, *Smoking and Politics: Policy Making and the Federal Bureaucracy* (Upper Saddle River, NJ: Prentice Hall, 1989); H. M. Sapolsky, "The Political Obstacles to the Control of Cigarette Smoking in the United States," *Journal of Health Politics, Policy, and Law* 5, no. 2 (1980): 277–290; "Tobacco Farmers Protest Tax with 'Tea Party,'" *New York Times,* June 10, 1994; and Henry West et al., "Tobacco Bill Will Aid Farmers," *Lexington Herald-Leader,* May 17, 2004.

34. See especially Howard Wolinsky and Tom Brune, *The Serpent on the Staff: The Unhealthy Politics of the American Medical Association* (New York: Jeremy P. Tarcher/Putnam, 1994). Relevant industry memoranda include: Helmut Wakeham, "AMA Education and Research Foundation Fund—Tobacco and Health Committee," December 9, 1965, Bates No. 680911531/1532, http://legacy.library.ucsf.edu/tid/fgk93f00; William Kloepfer, "Report on Meeting at AMA Re: ERF Tobacco Program," September 3, 1971, Bates No. 680911522/1524, http://legacy .library.ucsf.edu/tid/bgk93f00.

35. On the history of the AMA-ERF scientific efforts, see Kluger, *Ashes to Ashes*, 360–362.

36. F. J. L. Blasingame, "Full Text of AMA Letter of Testimony to F.T.C.," *JAMA* 188, no. 1 (1964): 31.

37. Drew Pearson and Jack Anderson, *The Case Against Congress: A Compelling Indictment of Corruption on Capitol Hill* (New York: Simon & Schuster, 1968), 329–330.

38. "Congress Urged to Act as FTC Hits Cigarets," *Advertising Age,* June 29, 1964, 59.

39. Richard A. Wegman, "Cigarettes and Health: A Legal Analysis," *Cornell Law Quarterly* 51, no. 4 (1966): 678–759.

40. E. A. Darr, [letter to Paul Hahn re: TIRC], July 30, 1957, Bates No. 961000327/0328, http://legacy.library.ucsf.edu/tid/ags94f00.

41. Carl Thompson, "Meeting with Representatives of TIRC Members, Thursday, June 7, 1956," June 12, 1956, http://tobaccodocuments.org/ness/4637.html.

42. Covington & Burling, "Confidential Report Prepared by TI Outside Counsel Reflecting TI Outside Counsel's Advice and Thoughts Regarding Industry Strategy," January 1963, Bates Nos. MNATPRIV00024887-900, http://tobaccodocuments.org/bliley_atc/MNATPRIV00024887–4900.html.

43. Philip J. Rogers and Geoffrey F. Todd, "Report on Policy Aspects of the Smoking and Health Situation in the U.S.A.," October 1964, Bates No. 2048925980/6014; http://legacy.library .ucsf.edu/tid/prq74e00, 6.

44. Ibid., 3.

45. Ibid., 8.

46. Elizabeth Brenner Drew, "The Quiet Victory of the Cigarette Lobby: How It Found the Best Filter yet—Congress," *Atlantic Monthly,* September 1965, 76–80.

47. Three other legal subcommittees reported to this group. One centered attention on medical–legal issues, CTR oversight, and congressional analysis, as well as "making certain that no assurances of any kind relating to the safety of smoking are given by any manufacturers (e.g., in advertisements)." The industry sought to walk a fine line between denying the medical harms of smoking and, at the same time, avoiding any guarantees of safety. Another committee centered its attention on the FTC and its evolving regulatory proposals, and a third on litigation.

48. Frederick P. Haas, "Re: Summary of Meeting of Executives of Various Tobacco Companies," February 20, 1964, Bates Nos. LG2000133-8, http://tobaccodocuments.org/youth/FtToLIG19640220.me.html.

49. Rogers and Todd.

50. "Re: Meetings of January 17, 20, 1964," January 23, 1964, Bates Nos. LG2008157-64, http://tobaccodocuments.org/youth/AmToLIG19640123.Me.html (emphasis added).

51. "Caution: Cigarette Smoking May Be Hazardous to Your Health," *Consumer Reports*, October 1965, 488–491.

52. D. R. Hardy and S. Hardy, "When to Warn—Why—and How," April 20, 1970, Bates Nos. 502083233–60, http://tobaccodocuments.org/rjr/502083233–3260_D1.html.

53. Emerson Foote, *Smoking and Health Newsletter*, July–August 1965, Bates No. 1005036558/6565, http://legacy.library.ucsf.edu/tid/cun94e00, 2.

54. "Biographical Sketch of Earle C. Clements," 1973, Bates No. 521044984, http://legacy .library.ucsf.edu/tid/hjl24f00.

55. Drew, 77.

56. Michael Pertschuk, *The Giant Killers* (New York: W.W. Norton, 1986), 34.

57. Jonathan Kwitny, "Defending the Weed: How Embattled Group Uses Tact, Calculation to Blunt Its Opposition Tobacco Institute Manages Cigaret Firms' Strategy," *Wall Street Journal,* January 24, 1972.

58. Robert A. Caro, *The Years of Lyndon Johnson: Master of the Senate*, vol. 3 (New York: Knopf, 2002), 624, 630–631.

59. Drew, 76–80; Oren Harris to P. R. Dixon, August 19, 1964, Bates No. 680534985/4986, http://legacy.library.ucsf./tid/iyl93ff00; and William McGaffin, "Smoking: Politics and Pressures," *Chicago Daily News,* February 15, 1965.

60. Pertschuk, 37.

61. "Re: Meetings of January 17, 20, 1964," January 23, 1964, Bates Nos. LG2008157-64, http://tobaccodocuments.org/youth/amtolig19640123.me.html.

62. "Cigarette Controls: A Sick Joke So Far," *Consumer Reports,* February 1968, 98.

63. Kluger, *Ashes to Ashes*, 289; and William McGaffin, "Smoking: Politics and Pressures," *Chicago Daily News,* February 15, 1965.

64. "8 Congressmen Ask Cigarette Bill Veto," *New York Times,* July 17, 1965.

65. Pertschuk, 33.

66. Ibid.

67. "Cigarettes vs. F.T.C.," *New York Times,* July 9, 1965.

68. Drew, 76.

69. D. S. Greenberg, "Tobacco: After Publicity Surge, Surgeon General's Report Seems to Have Little Enduring Effect," *Science* 145, no. 3636 (1964): 1021.

70. "Cigarette Controls: A Sick Joke So Far."

71. Beyond the above sources, see also Dan Cordtz, "Cigarets and Health: Congress Likely to Vote a Mild Law Requiring Warnings on Packages," *Wall Street Journal,* March 22, 1965; Edward Schneier, "The Politics of Tobacco," *Nation,* September 22, 1969, 274–279; and "New Label Bill Worse Than None," *Sarasota Herald Tribune,* July 16, 1965.

72. "Surgeon General Asks Stronger Smoking Warning," *New York Times,* April 17, 1969; "F. T. C. Demands Cigarette Ads Include 'Clear' Danger Warning," *New York Times,* July 2, 1971.

73. Pertschuk, 50–81.

74. "Cigarette Manufacturers Adopt New Code," *Christian Century,* May 13, 1964; and "F. P. Haas to Mr. Toms, Mr. Harrington, and Mr. Horan, Re: Meetings at Covington & Burling with Regard to the Code and F.T.C. Problems," May 8, 1964, Bates Nos. LG2008142-50, http:// tobaccodocuments.org/ness/34703.html.

75. "Text of Cigarette Industry's New Code," *New York Times,* April 28, 1964.

76. Richard W. Pollay, "Promises, Promises: Self-Regulation of U.S. Cigarette Broadcast Advertising in the 1960s," *Tobacco Control* 3, no. 2 (1994): 134–44; and J. W. Richards, Jr., J. B. Tye,

and P. M. Fischer, "The Tobacco Industry's Code of Advertising in the United States: Myth and Reality," *Tobacco Control* 5, no. 4 (1996): 295–311.

77. "Report of Proceedings, Committee on Interstate and Foreign Commerce, U.S. House of Representatives," June 10, 1969, Bates No. 968219048/9238, 11, http://legacy.library.ucsf.edu/tid/auwx94f00.

78. Ibid., 13.

79. Ibid., 17.

80. Ibid., 20.

81. Ibid., 25.

82. Christopher Lydon, "A Foe of Smoking Tells of TV Study," *New York Times*, June 9, 1969; Stanley Cohen, "NAB Cigaret Code Met Plenty of Resistance, Testimony Reveals," *Advertising Age*, June 16, 1969, 93.

83. Sam Blum, "An Ode to the Cigarette Code," *Harper's Magazine*, March 1966, 60–63.

84. Ibid.

85. After David Ogilvy retired in 1973, Ogilvy & Mather began accepting tobacco industry accounts.

86. John Horn, "Cigarettes: Hard Look at TV Ads," *New York Herald Tribune*, April 16, 1964.

87. John D. Morris, "Cigarette Code on Ads Dropped," *New York Times*, November 13, 1970.

88. Leo Burnett, "The Marlboro Story: How One of America's Most Popular Filter Cigarettes Got That Way" [as advertised in the *New Yorker*], November 15, 1958, Bates No. 2045214247/4249, http://legacy.library.ucsf.edu/tid/dvp65e00; and Kluger, *Ashes to Ashes*, 73–74.

89. Kluger, *Ashes to Ashes*, 179.

90. Philip Morris, "Marlboro Copy History, 1982," Bates No. 2080847898/7912, http://legacy.library.ucsf.edu/tid/alr20c00; N. Hafez and P. M. Ling, "How Philip Morris Built Marlboro into a Global Brand for Young Adults: Implications for International Tobacco Control," *Tobacco Control* 14, no. 4 (2005): 262–71; and Kluger, *Ashes to Ashes*, 179–180.

91. Leo Burnett to Roger Greene, January 7, 1955, Bates No. 2040320959/0961, http://legacy.library.ucsf.edu/tid/brp93e00.

92. Ibid.

93. Burnett, *The Marlboro Story*.

94. Philip Morris, "Marlboro Copy History."

95. Leo Burnett to Roger Greene, January 7, 1955, Bates No. 2040320959/0961, http://legacy.library.ucsf.edu/tid/brp93e00.

96. Michael E. Starr, "The Marlboro Man: Cigarette Smoking and Masculinity in America," *Journal of Popular Culture* 17, no. 4 (1984): 45.

97. Elizabeth B. Drew, "The Cigarette Companies Would Rather Fight Than Switch," *New York Times Magazine*, May 4, 1969.

98. For illustrations of industry involvement in the production and distribution of the article, see "J. V. Blalock to A. Y. Yeaman, E. P. Finch, and J. W. Burgard, Re: Stanley Frank Article," March 28, 1967, Bates No. 690012994; J. V. Blalock, "Re: B&W, Joseph Field, Stanley Frank, and *True Magazine*," 1968, Bates No. 690012567/2569; and J. V. Blalock to R. Spangler, January 17, 1968, Bates No. TO12656.

99. Stanley Frank, "To Smoke or Not to Smoke: That Is Still the Question," *True Magazine* 1968, Bates No. 680241037/1044, http://legacy.library.ucsf.edu/tid/ydv08c00.

100. Elizabeth Drew, "The Truth About . . . True's Article on Smoking," *Consumer Reports*, June 1968, 336–339.

101. See Donald Cooley, "Smoke Without Fear," 1954, Bates Nos. 11310873–908, http://tobaccodocuments.org/landman/11310873–0908.html; and Bert C. Goss to J. W. Hill, B. Littin, W. T. Hoyt, and R. W. Darrow, "Editorial Tour Idea," June 8, 1954, John W. Hill Papers, Wisconsin Historical Society, Box 111, Folder 1, http://tobaccodocuments.org/ness/3467.html.

102. Drew, "The Truth About . . . True's Article on Smoking."

103. Jonathan Kwitny, "Defending the Weed; How Embattled Group Uses Tact, Calculation to Blunt Its Opposition Tobacco Institute Manages Cigaret Firms' Strategy," *Wall Street Journal,* January 24, 1972.

104. Rogers and Todd, 32.

105. "Cigarette Controls: A Sick Joke So Far."

106. Ibid.; U.S. Federal Trade Commission, *Report to Congress Pursuant to the Federal Cigarette Labeling and Advertising Act, 1966* (Washington, DC: Federal Trade Commission, 1967), 29.

107. "Cigarette Controls: A Sick Joke So Far."

108. Matthew L. Myers et al., *Staff Report on the Cigarette Advertising Investigation* (Washington, DC: Federal Trade Commission, 1981), 20.

109. Ibid.

110. "Cigarette Controls: A Sick Joke So Far."

111. Norman I. Silber, *Test and Protest: The Influence of Consumers Union* (Teaneck, NJ: Holmes & Meier, 1983).

112. Thomas Whiteside, *Selling Death: Cigarette Advertising and Public Health* (New York: Liveright, 1971), 55.

113. Drew, "The Cigarette Companies Would Rather Fight Than Switch."

114. Whiteside, 56–57. See also Pamela Pennock, "Televising Sin: Efforts to Restrict the Televised Advertisement of Cigarettes and Alcohol in the United States, 1950s to 1980s," *Historical Journal of Film, Radio, and Television* 25, no. 4 (2005), 619–636.

115. Whiteside, 68–69.

116. Ibid., 71.

117. Ibid., 70.

118. Richard Kluger, "How Goes the War on Smoking?" *Medical News,* February 14, 1969, 46. Yul Brynner would later film a similar ad before his death from lung cancer. See"The Late Yul Brynner in Anti-Smoking Ads," *New York Times,* February 20, 1986.

119. Kenneth E. Warner, *Selling Smoke: Cigarette Advertising and Public Health* (Washington, DC: APHA Health Policy Monograph Series, 1986), 26.

120. Joseph A. Page, "The Law Professor Behind ASH, Soup, Pump and Crash," *New York Times,* August 23, 1970.

121. R. R. Millhiser to P. D. Smith, "Subject: Anti-Cigarette Commercials," February 20, 1969, Bates No. 2012550207, http://tobaccodocuments.org/bliley_pm/22805.html.

122. John D. Morris, "F.C.C., in 6–1 Vote, Seeks Ban on Broadcast Cigarette Ads," *New York Times,* February 6, 1969.

123. Drew, "The Cigarette Companies Would Rather Fight Than Switch."

124. "New Medium for the Message," *Consumer Reports,* May 1976, 277–279; and Pertschuk, 38–39.

125. "Worldwide Increase in Smoking Found by Health Service," *New York Times,* January 8, 1972.

126. Jack Gould, "Networks Look for Lean Season," *New York Times,* November 16, 1970.

127. Kenneth E. Warner, "The Effects of the Anti-Smoking Campaign on Cigarette Consumption," *American Journal of Public Health* 67, no. 7 (1977): 645–650; and Whiteside.

128. Whiteside, 120.

129. Ibid., 120–121.

130. Ibid., 122.

131. John D. Morris, "Senate Opposes TV Cigarette Ads," *New York Times,* December 13, 1969.

132. "Agency Ruled Able to Curb Cigarettes That Are High-Tar," *New York Times,* April 25, 1975.

133. Colman McCarthy, "Cigarettes and Politics," *Washington Post,* May 23, 1975.

134. Horace Kornegay, "Remarks at Annual Meeting of the Tobacco Institute," January 29, 1976, Bates No. TIMN0067698/7714, http://legacy.library.ucsf.edu/tid/mox92f00.

135. Richard Doll, "In Memoriam: Ernst Wynder, 1923–1999," *American Journal of Public Health* 89, no. 12 (1999): 1798–1799; Richard Kluger, Interview with Ernest L. Wynder, April 1, 1991, Bates No. 83724553/4567, http://legacy.library.ucsf.edu/tid/mso34c00; and Richard Kluger, Interview with Dietrich Hoffman, May 31, 1991, Bates No. 96746924/6928, http://legacy .library.ucsf.edu/tid/qsw44c00.

136. Mark Parascandola, "Science, Industry, and Tobacco Harm Reduction: A Case Study of Tobacco Industry Scientists; Involvement in the National Cancer Institute's Smoking and Health Program," *Public Health Reports* 120, no. 3 (2005): 338–349.

137. Victor Cohn, "Some Cigarettes Now 'Tolerable,' Doctor Says," *Washington Post*, August 10, 1978.

138. U.S. Public Health Service, Office on Smoking and Health, *Smoking and Health: A Report of the Surgeon General* (Washington, DC: U.S. Department of Health, Education, and Welfare, Public Health Service, 1979).

139. A. Fairchild and J. Colgrove, "Out of the Ashes: The Life, Death, and Rebirth of the 'Safer' Cigarette in the United States," *American Journal of Public Health* 94, no. 2 (2004): 192–204. See also Kluger, *Ashes to Ashes*, 428–434; Richard Kluger, "Gio B. Gori" [background and published works], April 4, 1989, Bates No. 96746917/6923, http://legacy.library.ucsf.edu/tid/ psw44c00; and Richard Kluger, "Gio B. Gori: Questions and Answers," March 1989, Bates No. 2015002615/2620, http://legacy.library.ucsf.edu/tid/gnk68e00. For more on Gori and his relationship with the industry, see Murray Senkus, "Meeting with Dr. G. Gori Deputy Director, Division of Cancer Cause and Prevention National Cancer Institute, May 12, 1978," May 17, 1978, Bates No. 2074658529/8531, http://legacy.library.ucsf.edu/tid/drj66c00; Murray Senkus to Gio Gori, March 17, 1973, Bates No. 501990170/0171, http://legacy.library.ucsf.edu/tid/bmn29d00; I. W. Hughes to Gio B. Gori, March 28, 1972, Bates No. TIFL0539459/9460, http://legacy .library.ucsf.edu/tid/tex02f00; I. W. Hughes to Gio Gori, May 31, 1973, Bates No. 680143028, http://legacy.library.ucsf.edu/tid/eou04f00; Murray Senkus to Gio B. Gori, March 17, 1973, Bates No. 955018146/8147, http://legacy.library.ucsf.edu/tid/htt41a00; R. B. Seligman, "Meeting with Gio Gori—July 20, 1977, National Cancer Institute," July 21, 1977, Bates No. 1005072118/2122, http://legacy.library.ucsf.edu/tid/ttt38e00; and I. W. Hughes, "Meeting with Gio Gori—January 18, 1972," January 21, 1972, Bates No. 680231771/1775, http://legacy.library.ucsf.edu/tid/owq04f00.

140. Jonathan Kwitny, "Defending the Weed: How Embattled Group Uses Tact, Calculation to Blunt Its Opposition Tobacco Institute Manages Cigaret Firms' Strategy," *Wall Street Journal*, January 24, 1972.

141. Maxwell Associates, "The Tobacco Conference from June 5–June 11, 1975," June 5, 1975, Bates Nos. 03801841–92, http://tobaccodocuments.org/lor/03801841–1892.html.

142. A. Lee Fritschler, *Smoking and Politics: Policy Making and the Federal Bureaucracy* (Upper Saddle River, NJ: Prentice Hall, 1989).

143. See, among others, Morton Keller, *Regulating a New Economy* (Cambridge, MA: Harvard University Press, 1990); Gabriel Kolko, *The Triumph of Conservatism: A Reinterpretation of American History, 1900–1916* (New York: Free Press of Glencoe, 1963); and James Q. Wilson, *The Politics of Regulation* (New York: Basic Books, 1980).

144. On the limits of tobacco regulation, see especially Jonathan Franzen, "Sifting the Ashes," in *How to Be Alone* (New York: Farrar, Straus and Giroux, 2002), 143–163.

145. Kwitny.

Chapter 9

1. Steve Martin, *Let's Get Small*, Warner Brothers, 1977.

2. David Carrig "Phone Merger Talks," *USA Today*, April 18, 1996.

3. Emily Post, "The Etiquette of Smoking," *Good Housekeeping*, September 1940, 37. On the history of manners and their social significance, see Norbert Elias, *History of Manners*, trans. Ed-

mund Jephcott (New York: Urizen Books, 1978); and John F. Kasson, *Rudeness and Civility: Manners in Nineteenth-Century Urban America* (New York: Hill & Wang, 1991).

4. Kenneth E. Warner, "The Effects of the Anti-Smoking Campaign on Cigarette Consumption," *American Journal of Public Health* 67, no. 7 (1977): 648.

5. Allan M. Brandt and Paul Rozin, eds., *Morality and Health* (New York: Routledge, 1997). See the special volume on "Risk," *Daedalus* 119, no. 4 (1990).

6. John H. Knowles, "The Responsibility of the Individual," *Daedalus* 106 (1977): 57–80.

7. Thomas Whiteside, *Selling Death: Cigarette Advertising and Public Health* (New York: Liveright, 1971).

8. Howard M. Leichter, *Free to Be Foolish: Politics and Health Promotion in the United States and Great Britain* (Princeton, NJ: Princeton University Press, 1991).

9. Allan M. Brandt, "Blow Some My Way: Passive Smoking, Risk, and American Culture," in *The History of Smoking and Health,* eds. Lois Reynolds, E. M. Tansey, and Steven Lock (Amsterdam: Rodopi, 1998), 164–191; Ronald Bayer and James Colgrove, "Children and Bystanders First: The Ethics and Politics of Tobacco Control in the United States," in *Unfiltered: Conflicts over Tobacco Policy and Public Health,* eds. Eric A. Feldman and Ronald Bayer (Cambridge, MA: Harvard University Press, 2004), 8–37.

10. Ronald Bayer and James Colgrove, "Science, Politics, and Ideology in the Campaign against Environmental Tobacco Smoke," *American Journal of Public Health* 92, no. 6 (2002): 949–954.

11. "The Right Not to Smoke," *New York Times,* May 5, 1978.

12. Constance A. Nathanson, *Analysis of U.S. Tobacco Control Movement: A Final Report to the Association of Schools of Public Health and the Centers for Disease Control and Prevention* (Baltimore: Johns Hopkins University Press, 1997), 31. See also Ronald J. Troyer and Gerald E. Markowitz, *Cigarettes: The Battle over Smoking* (New Brunswick, NJ: Rutgers University Press, 1984).

13. On common sense assessments, see James Surowiecki, *The Wisdom of Crowds* (New York: Doubleday, 2004).

14. U.S. Department of Health and Human Services, *The Health Consequences of Involuntary Smoking: A Report of the Surgeon General* (Washington, DC: GPO, 1986) [*Involuntary Smoking*]; United States Environmental Protection Agency, *Respiratory Health Effects of Passive Smoking: Lung Cancer and Other Disorders* (Washington, DC: U. S. Dept. of Health and Human Services, 1993); National Research Council Committee on Passive Smoking, *Environmental Tobacco Smoke: Measuring Exposures and Assessing Health Effects* (Washington, DC: National Academy Press, 1986).

15. Robert Gottlieb, *Forcing the Spring: The Transformation of the American Environmental Movement* (Washington, DC: Island, 2005); Caroline Merchant, ed., *The Columbia Guide to American Environmental History* (New York, NY: Columbia University Press, 2005), 174–191; and Lewis S. Warren, ed., *American Environmental History* (Malden, MA: Blackwell Publishers, 2003).

16. P. H. Abelson, "A Damaging Source of Air Pollution," *Science* 158, no. 808 (1967): 1527.

17. Frederic Speer, "Tobacco and the Nonsmoker: A Study of Subjective Symptoms," *Archives of Environmental Health* 16, no. 3 (1968): 443.

18. Ibid., 445.

19. T. Hirayama, "Non-Smoking Wives of Heavy Smokers Have a Higher Risk of Lung Cancer: A Study from Japan," *British Medical Journal (Clin Res Ed)* 282, no. 6259 (1981): 183–185.

20. D. Trichopoulos, A. Kalandidi, L. Sparros, and B. MacMahon, "Lung Cancer and Passive Smoking," *International Journal of Cancer* 27, no. 1 (1981): 3.

21. Ibid.

22. J. L. Repace and A. H. Lowrey, "Indoor Air Pollution, Tobacco Smoke, and Public Health," *Science* 208, no. 4443 (1980): 464–472.

23. Richard Kluger, *Ashes to Ashes* (New York: Knopf, 1996), 493.

24. John D. Spengler and Ken Sexton, "Indoor Air Pollution: A Public Health Perspective," *Science* 221, no. 4605 (1983): 9–17.

25. Jonathan E. Fielding and Kenneth J. Phenow, "Health Effects of Involuntary Smoking," *New England Journal of Medicine* 319, no. 22 (1988): 1452–1460. The article reported eighteen studies since 1981—three prospective and fifteen case-control.

26. John Banzhaf, "'Please Put Your Cigarette Out; the Smoke Is Killing Me!'" *Today's Health,* April 1972, 38–41. See also Joseph A. Page, "The Law Professor Behind ASH, Soup, Pump and Crash," *New York Times,* August 23, 1970; and Nathanson, 72–73.

27. Banzhaf, 39.

28. Ibid.

29. Constance A. Nathanson, "Social Movements as Catalysts for Policy Change: The Case of Smoking and Guns," *Journal of Health Politics, Policy and Law* 24, no. 3 (1999): 421–488.

30. Nathanson, *Analysis of U.S. Tobacco Control Movement,* 74.

31. A. Lee Fritschler, *Smoking and Politics: Policy Making and the Federal Bureaucracy* (Upper Saddle River, NJ: Prentice Hall, 1989), 116–117.

32. Nathanson, *Analysis of U.S. Tobacco Control Movement*; Mark Wolfson, *The Fight Against Big Tobacco: The Movement, the State, and the Public's Health* (New York: Aldine de Gruyter, 2001).

33. "Enforcement of Ban on Smoking in Minnesota Is No Easy Matter," *New York Times,* September 9, 1979.

34. No relation to the author.

35. Theodore H. Tsoukalas, Jennifer K. Ibrahim, and Stanton A. Glantz, "Shifting Tides: Minnesota Tobacco Politics," *Tobacco Control Policy Making: United States* (San Francisco: Center for Tobacco Control Research and Education, University of California, 2003).

36. Ibid.

37. Douglas E. Kneeland, "Antismoking Drive Keeps Gaining, but Impetus Seems to Have Slowed," *New York Times,* January 26, 1979.

38. Richard Martin, "Pressure Rises to Go Smokeless," *Insight,* May 19, 1986, 8.

39. John K. Iglehart, "Health Policy Report: The Campaign Against Smoking Gains Momentum," *New England Journal of Medicine* 314, no. 16 (1986): 1059–1064; and Ruth A. Behrens, "Reducing Smoking at the Workplace" [Washington Business Group on Health Worksite Wellness Series], October 1985, Bates No. 2045964535/4570, http://legacy.library.ucsf.edu/tid/rkc03e00.

40. Behrens.

41. Iglehart.

42. The Roper Organization, Inc., "A Study of Public Attitudes Toward Cigarette Smoking and the Tobacco Industry in 1978, Vol. I," May 1978, Bates No. 966071061/1341: 1073, http://legacy.library.ucsf.edu/tid/jdc70a00.

43. Ibid.

44. Ibid.

45. Ibid., 1067.

46. Ibid., 1068.

47. Ibid., 1069.

48. Ibid.

49. J. L. Steinfeld, "Women and Children Last? Attitudes Toward Cigarette Smoking and Nonsmokers' Rights, 1971," *New York State Journal Medicine* 83, no. 13 (1983): 1257–1258.

50. U.S. Department of Health and Human Services, Office of the Surgeon General, *The Health Consequences of Smoking: A Report of the Surgeon General, 1972* (Washington, DC: GPO, 1972).

51. *Involuntary Smoking*; and National Research Council Committee on Passive Smoking, *Environmental Tobacco Smoke: Measuring Exposures and Assessing Health Effects* (Washington, DC: National Academy Press, 1986) [*Environmental Tobacco Smoke*].

52. Irvin Molotsky, "Surgeon General, Citing Risks, Urges Smoke-Free Workplace," *New York Times,* December 17, 1986.

53. *Involuntary Smoking*; *Environmental Tobacco Smoke,* 28–31.

54. *Involuntary Smoking*; *Environmental Tobacco Smoke.*

55. S. L. Temko, "The Tobacco Institute, Inc. Minutes of Meeting of the Executive Committee December 10, 1987 New York, New York," 1987, Bates Nos. TIMN0014390-3. See also A. D. C. Turner, "Managing the ETS Issue—Report by ETS Issue Management Group," June 18, 1987, Bates Nos. 620805325–53, http://tobaccodocuments.org/landman/1458482.html; and "Indoor Air Quality Alternative Strategy," http://tobaccodocuments.org/landman/137830.html.

56. Philip Morris, "Indoor Air Quality Alternative Strategy," March 21, 1986, Bates No. 2025858759, http://legacy.library.ucsf.edu/tid/vrr85e00.

57. John P. Rupp, "Privileged & Confidential Attorney Work Product: Letter from John Rupp (C&B) to Sharon Boyse (BATCo) Explaining Setup, Function of Center for Indoor Air Research (CIAR)," March 12, 1993, Bates Nos. 87803009–13, http://tobaccodocuments.org/landman/87803009–3013.html.

58. "Remarks by William Murray, Vice Chairman of the Board, Philip Morris Companies Inc., at the 1989 Philip Morris Legal Conference, Ritz-Carlton Hotel, Naples, Florida," April 4, 1989, Bates No. 2023265282/5295, http://legacy.library.ucsf.edu/tid/qpi46e00. See also Turner.

59. D. E. Barnes and L. A. Bero, "Why Review Articles on the Health Effects of Passive Smoking Reach Different Conclusions," *JAMA* 279, no. 19 (1998): 1566–1570.

60. John C. Luik, "Pandora's Box: The Dangers of Politically Corrupted Science for Democratic Public Policy," *Bostonia,* Winter 1994, 50–60.

61. Don Colburn, "Smoke Gets in Your Eyes Leading Scientists Examine Effects of Sidestream Fumes," *Washington Post,* February 5, 1986. See also Philip Witorsch, "ETS and Cardiorespiratory Disorders" [testimony before the National Academies of Science], January 29, 1986, Bates Nos. TI2995 1555–833: 1725, http://tobaccodocuments.org/nysa_ti_m2/TI29951555.html.

62. Colburn.

63. "Government Health Officials Involved in Efforts to Censor Dissenting Scientific Viewpoints. The Tobacco Institute Demands Cabinet-Level Investigation, Accuses Officials of Abusing Science for Political Ends," December 11, 1986, Bates No. 2501052381/2382, http://legacy.library.ucsf.edu/tid/btw19e00; Tobacco Institute, "Tobacco Smoke and the Nonsmoker: Scientific Integrity at the Crossroads," 1986, Bates No. 980237045/7101, http://legacy.library.ucsf.edu/tid/lrp90c00.

64. Charles Rosenberg, "Banishing Risk: Continuity and Change in the Moral Management of Disease," in *Morality and Health,* eds. Allan M. Brandt and Paul Rozin (New York: Routledge, 1997): 35–52.

65. R. B. Seligman, "Memorandum from Philip Morris Employee to Philip Morris Counsel and Philip Morris Employee Containing Information Requested by Philip Morris Counsel Regarding Joint Defense Research," November 17, 1978, Bates Nos. 1003718428–32, http://tobaccodocuments.org/landman/1003718428–8432.html.

66. "Project Down Under Conference Notes," 1987, Bates Nos. 2021502102–34, http://tobaccodocuments.org/landman/23693.html.

67. Ibid., Bates No. 2021502112.

68. Ibid., Bates No. 2021502128.

69. Ibid., Bates No. 2021502117.

70. Ibid., Bates No. 2021502114.

71. Ibid., Bates No. 2021502110.

72. Ibid.

73. R. Seitz, "Memorandum Concerning Meeting with Dr. Walter Spitzer and His Group Studying the Effects of Passive Exposure to Tobacco Smoke on 880830 and 880831," September 9, 1988, Bates No. 2023552141/2146, http://tobaccodocuments.org/landman/172490.html.

74. Project Down Under Conference Notes, Bates No. 2021502116.

75. B. Samuels and S. A. Glantz, "The Politics of Local Tobacco Control." *JAMA* 266, no. 15 (1991): 2110–2117.

76. Ward Sinclair, "Massive New U.S. Report Blasts Cigarette Smoking; Antismoking Drive Growing in America," *Washington Post,* January 12, 1979.

77. Ibid.

78. Stanley S. Scott, "Smokers Get a Raw Deal," *New York Times,* April 29, 1985.

79. Philip Morris, "Tapgram: The Winners," June 1987, Bates Nos. TIMN0418364-9, http://tobaccodocuments.org/ti/TIMN0418364–8369.html.

80. "Both Sides in Cigarette Fight Hold National Essay Contests." *New York Times,* November 5, 1986.

81. *Great American Smoker's Kit*, 1986, Bates No. 2024274461/4470: 4463, http://legacy .library.ucsf.edu/tid/irh04e00.

82. Ibid., Bates No. 2024274465.

83. Michael S. Givel and Stanton A. Glantz, "Tobacco Lobby Political Influence on U.S. State Legislatures in the 1990s," *Tobacco Control* 10, no. 2 (2001): 129.

84. Peter D. Jacobson, Jeffrey Wasserman, and Krisiana Raube, "The Politics of Antismoking Legislation," *Journal of Health Politics, Policy and Law* 18, no. 4 (1993): 787–819: 803.

85. "Smoking and Health Initiatives—P.M. International," March 1985, Bates No. 2023268366/8374, http://tobaccodocuments.org/landman/178716.html.

86. R.J. Reynolds, "Introduction to the SOSAS Recommended Action Programs," October 1, 1978, Bates Nos. 500009897–920, http://tobaccodocuments.org/landman/500009897–9920.html.

87. Sarah Booth Conroy, "Fired Up over Philip Morris," *Washington Post,* November 10, 1989.

88. Peter D. Jacobson and Soheil Soliman, "Co-Opting the Health and Human Rights Movement," *Journal of Law, Medicine & Ethics* 30, no. 4 (2002): 705–715; and M. Teresa Cardador, Anna R. Hazan, and Stanton A. Glantz, "Tobacco Industry Smokers' Rights Publications: A Content Analysis," *American Journal of Public Health* 85, no. 9 (1995): 1212–1217.

89. See Monique E. Muggli, Jean L. Forster, Richard D. Hurt, and James L. Repace, "The Smoke You Don't See: Uncovering Tobacco Industry Scientific Strategies Aimed Against Environmental Tobacco Smoke Policies," *American Journal of Public Health* 91, no. 9 (2001): 1419–1423; and David Garne, "Environmental Tobacco Smoke Research Published in the Journal *Indoor and Built Environment* and Associations with the Tobacco Industry," *Lancet* 365, no. 9461 (2005): 804–806.

90. William Kloepfer, "Report on Public Smoking Issue, Executive Committee," April 10, 1985, Bates No. TIMN0013710/3723, http://legacy.library.ucsf.edu/tid/owo03f00.

91. Susan Stuntz, Jeff Ross, and Lisa Osborne, "Corporate Contacts Re: Workplace Smoking," April 15, 1986, Bates No. 85544385/4435, http://legacy.library.ucsf.edu/tid/kuu31e00.

92. This approach was supported, for example, in R.J. Reynolds advertisements.

93. Judith Martin (pseud. Miss Manners), "Non-Smoker's Behavior Was Publicly Offensive," *Toronto Star,* August 23, 1991.

94. Judith Martin (pseud. Miss Manners), "Where There's Smoke, There's Ire," *Washington Post,* December 1, 1985.

95. Ibid.

96. Judith Martin (pseud. Miss Manners), "Wait Until Course Is Over Before Trying to Date Prof," *Toronto Star,* March 17, 1989.

97. Trish Hall, "Smoking of Cigarettes Seems to Be Becoming a Lower-Class Habit," *Wall Street Journal,* June 25, 1985.

98. See "'No Smoking' in Translation," *New York Times,* June 30, 1996.

99. Morris D. Rosenberg, "Fearless Traveler: Speaking of the Fair," *Washington Post,* August 15, 1982.

100. Editorial, *Washington Post,* June 17, 1977.

101. James Ott, "Carriers Strongly Oppose CAB Smoking Restrictions," *Aviation Week and Space Technology,* August 20, 1979.

102. Norman A. Adler, "Airliners Devoid of Unpolluted Air," *New York Times,* July 1, 1983.

103. Mitchell Smyth, "Hey, Weed Addicts! Here's Your Smoking Salon in the Sky," *Toronto Star,* September 30, 1995.

104. Scott Thurston, "Support Growing for Smoking Ban on Overseas Flights: Attendants Stepping to Forefront of Battle," *Atlanta Journal-Constitution,* March 12, 1994.

105. Douglas B. Feaver, "Smoking on Airliners Off, Then On," *Washington Post,* June 1, 1984; and Irvin Molotsky, "No-Smoking Rule Is On and Off Again," *New York Times,* June 1, 1984.

106. A. L. Holm and R. M. Davis, "Clearing the Airways: Advocacy and Regulation for Smoke-Free Airlines," *Tobacco Control* 13 (Suppl 1) (2004): 30–36.

107. "Senate Weighs Ban of Flight Smoking," *New York Times,* September 14, 1989.

108. Dan Morgan, "Airline Smoking Ban Takes Off in Senate," *Washington Post,* September 8, 1989.

109. The Tobacco Institute, "Passport to Smokers' Rights," April 1990, Bates Nos. TI10030648–718, http://tobaccodocuments.org/nysa_indexed/TI10030648.html.

110. *Respiratory Health Effects of Passive Smoking: Lung Cancer and Other Disorders* (Washington, DC: Environmental Protection Agency, 1992); and Warren E. Leary, "U.S. Ties Secondhand Smoke to Cancer," *New York Times,* January 8, 1993. See also Michelle Murphy, *Sick Building Syndrome and the Problem of Uncertainty: Environmental Politics, Technoscience, and Women Workers* (Durham, NC: Duke University Press, 2006).

111. Leary; and Timothy Noah, "EPA Declares 'Passive' Smoke a Human Carcinogen," *Wall Street Journal,* January 6, 1993.

112. Noah.

113. T. Humber, "ETS Media Strategy," February 1993, Bates No. 2023920090/0101, http://legacy.library.ucsf.edu/tid/sav88e00; and T. Humber, "Memo to Ellen Merlo and Victor Han on ETS," February 1993, Bates No. 2023920074/0089, http://legacy.library.ucsf.edu/tid/mpf34e00.

114. E. K. Ong and S. A. Glantz, "Constructing 'Sound Science' and 'Good Epidemiology': Tobacco, Lawyers, and Public Relations Firms," *American Journal of Public Health* 91, no. 11 (2001): 1749–1757.

115. Ellen Merlo, "Our Preemption Strategy," October 24, 1994, Bates No. 2040236685, http://tobaccodocuments.org/landman/157850.html.

116. Kathleen Sylvester, "The Tobacco Industry Will Walk a Mile to Stop an Anti-Smoking Law," *Governing,* May 1989, 37.

117. Michael Siegel et al., "Preemption in Tobacco Control: Review of an Emerging Public Health Problem," *JAMA* 278, no. 10 (1997): 858.

118. Ibid.

119. Sylvester, 34–40.

120. Daniel M. Weintraub, "Controversial Tobacco Bill Passes Test," *Los Angeles Times,* June 14, 1990.

121. Siegel et al., 858–63. See also M. L. Nixon, L. Mahmoud, and S. A. Glantz, "Tobacco Industry Litigation to Deter Local Public Health Ordinances: The Industry Usually Loses in Court," *Tobacco Control* 13 (2004): 65–73.

122. Hall.

123. Paul K. Edwards, *The Southern Urban Negro as a Consumer* (1932; College Park, MD: McGrath Publishing, 1969); Sarah S. Lochlann Jain, "'Come up to the Kool Taste': African American Upward Mobility and the Semiotics of Smoking Menthols." *Public Culture* 15, no. 2 (2003): 295–322; Philip Morris, "A Pilot Look at the Attitudes of Negro Smokers Toward Menthol Cigarettes," September 1968, Bates No. 1002483819/3830, http://tobaccodocuments.org/landman/ 178106.html; and Robert E. Weems, Jr., *Desegregating the Dollar* (New York: New York University Press, 1998).

124. Gehrmann Holland, "A Study of Ethnic Markets," September 1969, Bates Nos. 501989230–469, http://tobaccodocuments.org/landman/501989230–9469.html; A. P. Gaspar, "Re: Black Market Analysis," December 2, 1977, Bates Nos. 500384796–7, http://beta.tobacco documents.org/landman/187904.html.

125. "Sales of Philip Morris Cigarettes Drop 48%," *The White Sentinel,* October 1956, 2.

126. "Discussion Paper: Total Minority Marketing Plan," September 7, 1984, Bates No. 531000141/0144, http://legacy.library.ucsf.edu/tid/dmf41f00.

127. "An Uproar over Billboards in Poor Areas," *New York Times,* May 1, 1989.

128. Ibid.; and Ben Wildavsky, "Tilting at Billboards" *New Republic,* August 20, 1990, 19–20.

129. Gaspar.

130. E. D. Balbach, R. J. Gasior, and E. M. Barbeau, "R.J. Reynolds' Targeting of African Americans: 1988–2000," *American Journal of Public Health* 93, no. 5 (2003): 822–827.

131. "Dr. Sullivan's Unfiltered Anger," *New York Times,* January 21, 1990. See also Marlene Cimons, "New Cigarette Condemned by Health Secretary Marketing: Louis Sullivan Says the Promotion Campaign for a New R.J. Reynolds Brand Targeted to Blacks Is 'Slick and Sinister' and Promotes a 'Culture of Cancer,'" *Los Angeles Times,* January 19, 1990; Rick Christie, "RJR Unit Blasted for New Cigarette Aimed at Blacks," *Wall Street Journal,* January 19, 1990; and Philip J. Hilts, "Health Chief Assails Reynolds Co. for Ads That Target Blacks," *New York Times,* January 19, 1990.

132. Lockhart Pettus, "Uptown Cigarette Damage Assessment Study: A Proposal to Conduct a Nationwide Research Study Among Black Cigarette Smokers to Assess RJR's Image and Its Viability of Introducing a Menthol Cigarette Targeted to Blacks," January 31, 1990, Bates No. 2505557826/7859, http://legacy.library.ucsf.edu/tid/rii19c00.

133. "An Uproar over Billboards in Poor Areas."

134. V. B. Yerger, and R. E. Malone, "African American Leadership Groups: Smoking with the Enemy," *Tobacco Control* 11, no. 4 (2002): 336–345.

135. Bob Herbert, "Tobacco Dollars," *New York Times,* November 28, 1993.

136. Subsequent research would continue to explore the possibility of genetic differences. See Sandra Blakeslee, "Black Smokers' Higher Risk of Cancer May Be Genetic," *New York Times,* April 13, 1994; C. A. Haiman, D. O. Stram, L. R. Wilkens, M. C. Pike, L. N. Kolonel, B. E. Henderson, and L. Le Marchand, "Ethnic and Racial Differences in the Smoking-Related Risk of Lung Cancer," *New England Journal of Medicine* 354, no. 4 (2006): 333–342; and N. Risch, "Dissecting Racial and Ethnic Differences," *New England Journal of Medicine* 354, no. 4 (2006): 408–411.

137. Stanton A. Glantz, "Achieving a Smokefree Society," *Circulation* 76, no. 4 (1987): 749. See also "Top Secret Operation Rainmaker," March 20, 1990, Bates No. 2048302227/2230, http:// legacy.library.ucsf.edu/tid/wos65e00; and R. Ferguson and M. Waugh, "Social-Political Context of Cigarette Sales in the U.S.," May 25, 1987, Bates No. 2050864094, http://tobaccodocuments .org/landman/138246.html.

138. D. Durden, "Memorandum Prepared by RJR Employee Transmitted to RJR Employee, RJR Managerial Employees, and RJR In-House Legal Counsel for the Purpose of Providing Confidential Information in Order to Assist in the Rendering of Legal Advice Concerning Smoking and Health Issue," December 22, 1978, Bates Nos. 500869538–62, http://tobaccodocuments .org/bliley_rjr/500869538–9562.html.

139. Ibid.

140. Robert A. Kagan and Jerome H. Skolnick, "Banning Smoking: Compliance Without Enforcement," *Smoking Policy: Law, Politics, and Culture,* ed. Robert L. Rabin and Stephen D. Sugarman (New York: Oxford University Press, 1993), 69–94; Timothy F. Kirn, "More 'No Smoking' Signs Seen in Hospitals," *JAMA* 259, no. 19 (1988): 2814; and Stephen N. Kales, "Smoking Restrictions at Boston-Area Hospitals, 1990–1992," *Chest* 104, no. 5 (1993): 1589–1591. See also Simon Chapman, "Great Expectorations! The Decline of Public Spitting: Lessons for Passive Smoking?" *British Medical Journal* 311, no. 7021 (December 1995): 1685–1686.

141. Glantz, "Achieving a Smokefree Society."

Chapter 10

1. "Why One Smokes," 1969, Bates No. 1003287836/7848, http://legacy.library.ucsf.edu/tid/ pds74e00.

2. Claude E. Teague, R.J. Reynolds, "Research Planning Memorandum on the Nature of the Tobacco Business and the Crucial Role of Nicotine Therein," April 14, 1972, Bates Nos. TINY0003015–24.

3. Tracy Schroth, "At Last, Edell Sees Light at End of Tobacco Tunnel," *New Jersey Law Journal* (1992): 1; Daniel Leduc, "Back Fire: Lawyer Marc Edell Took on the Tobacco Industry and Won—for a While," *Philadelphia Inquirer,* March 14, 1993; and Morton Mintz, "Winning Lawyer Hasn't Quit Fight Against Tobacco Firms," *Washington Post,* June 19, 1988.

4. Richard Kluger, Interview with Marc Z. Edell, May 17, 1989, Bates No. 83724497/4510, http://legacy.library.ucsf.edu/tid/xbo34c00; Marc Edell, "Cigarette Litigation: The Second Wave," *Tort and Insurance Law* 22, no. 1 (1986): 90–103; and Schroth.

5. Richard A. Wegman, "Cigarettes and Health: A Legal Analysis," *Cornell Law Quarterly* 51, no. 4 (1966): 697.

6. Testimony of Clarence Cook Little, *Green v. American Tobacco,* November 25, 1964, 1136–1204; Testimony of Clarence Cook Little, *Lartigue v. R.J. Reynolds,* October 5, 1960, 2713–2775; Testimony of Clarence Cook Little, *Lartigue v. R.J. Reynolds,* October 6, 1960, 2777–2912.

7. See, for example, the testimony of Sheldon Sommers in *Cipollone* and in *Rogers v. R.J. Reynolds* (1985), and of James Glenn in *Cipollone* and *Minnesota v. Philip Morris* (1998).

8. Richard A. Wegman, "Cigarettes and Health: A Legal Analysis," *Cornell Law Quarterly* 51, no. 4 (1966): 704.

9. Ibid., 699–705; Donald W. Garner, "Cigarette Dependency and Civil Liability: A Modest Proposal," *Southern California Law Review* 53, no. 5 (1980): 1423–1465; and Robert L. Rabin, "A Sociolegal History of Tobacco Tort Litigation," *Stanford Law Review* 44, no. 4 (1992): 853–878.

10. Wegman, 699.

11. Ibid., 700.

12. Gary T. Schwartz, "Tobacco Liability in the Courts," *Smoking Policy: Law, Politics and Culture,* ed. Robert L. Rabin and Stephen D. Sugarman (New York: Oxford University Press, 1993), 154. See also James R. Hackney, Jr., "The Intellectual Origins of American Strict Products Liability: A Case Study in American Pragmatic Instrumentalism," *American Journal of Legal History* 39, no. 4 (1994): 443–509.

13. Quoted in G. Edward White, *Tort Law in America: An Intellectual History* (New York: Oxford University Press, 2003), 109.

14. White, 109.

15. Quoted in Daniel Givelber, "Cigarette Law," *Indiana Law Journal* 73, no. 3 (1998): 873.

16. Wegman, 707.

17. On the expansion of torts, see White. On the exemption of tobacco, see Daniel Givelber, "Cigarette Law," *Indiana Law Journal* 73, no. 3 (1998): 867–902.

18. D. R. Hardy and S. Hardy, "When to Warn—Why—and How," April 20, 1970, Bates No. 502083249, http://tobaccodocuments.org/rjr/502083233–3260_D1.html.

19. U.S. Federal Trade Commission, *Report to Congress Pursuant to the Federal Cigarette Labeling and Advertising Act, 1966* (Washington, DC: Federal Trade Commission, 1967), 4; and D. R. Hardy, "When to Warn—Why—and How," ed. S. Hardy, 1970, Bates Nos. 502083233–60.

20. Wegman, 723.

21. Donald W. Garner, "Cigarette Dependency and Civil Liability: A Modest Proposal," *Southern California Law Review* 53, no. 5 (1980): 1423–1465.

22. Marc Edell, "Cigarette Litigation: The Second Wave," *Tort and Insurance Law* 22, no. 1 (1986): 90.

23. Lisa A. Bero et al. "Lawyer Control of the Tobacco Industry's External Research Program: The Brown and Williamson Documents." *JAMA* 274, no. 3 (1995): 241–247.

24. Edell (1986): 92.

25. U.S. Department of Health and Human Services, Office on Smoking and Health, *The Health Consequences of Smoking for Women: A Report of the Surgeon General* (Washington, DC: U.S. Department of Health and Human Services, 1980), 18–20 [*Health Consequences of Smoking for Women*].

26. "Deposition of Rose DeFrancesco Cipollone in *Cipollone v. Liggett*," 1984: 271.5, http://tobaccodocuments.org/datta/CIPOLLONER012684.html.

27. Recent research on women and nicotine addition suggests that women have poorer outcomes in cessation attempts than do men. Kenneth A. Perkins, "Smoking Cessation in Women," *CNS Drugs* 15, no. 5 (2001): 391–411.

28. Quoted in Lorillard, "Case Before U.S. District Court for the District of New Jersey: A Smoker vs. Tobacco Manufacturers, A 'Talking' Paper," 1986, Bates Nos. 92346718/6730, 92346721, http://legacy.library.ucsf.edu/tid/grp20e00.

29. *Health Consequences of Smoking for Women*, 20.

30. Hal Weinstein, Leo Burnett Company, "How an Agency Builds a Brand—The Virginia Slims Story," October 28, 1969, Bates No. 2045080272/0291, http://legacy.library.ucsf.edu/tid/soc65e00; and B. A. Toll and P. M. Ling, "The Virginia Slims Identity Crisis: An Inside Look at Tobacco Industry Marketing to Women," *Tobacco Control* 14, no. 3 (2005): 172–180.

31. Richard Kluger, *Ashes to Ashes* (New York: Knopf, 1996), 647. On targeting women in tobacco ads, see Jean Kilbourne, *Deadly Persuasion: Why Women and Girls Must Fight the Addictive Power of Advertising* (New York: Free Press, 1999).

32. Quoted in Lorillard, "Case Before U.S. District Court for the District of New Jersey."

33. Philip Morris, "The Low-Tar Cigarette with a Recessed Tip" [print advertisement], 1972.

34. Quoted in Lorillard, "Case Before U.S. District Court for the District of New Jersey."

35. U.S. Department of Health and Human Services, *Risks Associated with Smoking Cigarettes with Low Machine-Measured Yields of Tar and Nicotine*, ed. Donald R. Shopland (Washington, DC: 2001); N. L. Benowitz et al., "Smokers of Low-Yield Cigarettes Do Not Consume Less Nicotine," *New England Journal of Medicine* 309, no. 3 (1983): 139–142; Murray E. Jarvik,

"Working Meeting: Research Needs on Low Yield Cigarettes," June 1980, Bates No. TIMN0112484/2486, http://legacy.library.ucsf.edu/tid/wdj92f00; H. Wakeham, "Trends of Tar and Nicotine Deliveries over the Last Five Years," March 24, 1961, Bates No. 1000861953, http://legacy.library.ucsf.edu/tid/hnt74e00; and R. W. Pollay and T. Dewhirst, "The Dark Side of Marketing Seemingly 'Light' Cigarettes: Successful Images and Failed Fact," *Tobacco Control* 11 (Suppl 1): i18–i31.

36. "Deposition of Rose DeFrancesco Cipollone in *Cipollone v. Liggett*," 1984: 276.

37. U.S. Department of Health and Human Services, *Reducing the Health Consequences of Smoking: 25 Years of Progress: A Report of the Surgeon General* (Rockville, MD: Public Health Service, Centers for Disease Control, 1989).

38. Joseph Kelner and Robert S. Kelner, "The Tobacco Industry and 'Cipollone,'" *New York Law Journal* (1992): 3.

39. Morton Mintz, "Cigarette Trial Breaks New Ground; Firms Compelled to Open Their Files," *Washington Post,* March 27, 1988.

40. *Cipollone v. Liggett Group, Inc., et al.*, 789 F.2d 181 (1986).

41. Mintz, "Cigarette Trial Breaks New Ground; Firms Compelled to Open Their Files."

42. Morton Mintz, "Tobacco Firms' Attorneys Reconnoiter After Setbacks," *Washington Post,* May 1, 1988.

43. Morton Mintz, "Cigarette Suppressed, Court Told; Researcher Says Liggett Held Back Safer Product," *Washington Post,* February 12, 1988. "The European tobacco industry has agreed that smoking is harmful and is hard at work to develop 'less hazardous' products. Development and marketing of such cigarettes by European firms will put great pressure on Philip Morris International to do likewise. . . . Once International markets a 'less hazardous' cigarette, her American counterpart will be able to do no less." H. Wakeham, "Presentation to Philip Morris Board/Revised Draft," October 15, 1973, Bates No. 2022886158/6160, http://legacy.library.ucsf.edu/tid/gic78e00.

44. Morton Mintz, "Documents on Tobacco Are Opened," *Washington Post,* July 19, 1985.

45. Morton Mintz, "Supreme Court Allows Release of Evidence in Cigarette Suit," *Washington Post,* December 8, 1987.

46. R. A. Daynard and Laurie Morin, "The Cipollone Documents: Following the Paper Trail to Tobacco Industry Liability," *Trial* (1988): 50.

47. Donald Janson, "A 'Bulldog' Battles Tobacco Industry," *New York Times,* June 12, 1988,

48. H. B. Parmele, Lorillard, [letter to A. Riefner], 1946, Bates No. 94701389/1390, http://legacy.library.ucsf.edu/tid/ase44a00.

49. Trial Testimony of Jeffrey E. Harris, MD, PhD, *Cipollone v. Liggett Group, Inc., et al.*, 1988 U.S. Dist. LEXIS 16709: 12595 (1988).

50. Arthur D. Little, "L & M—A Perspective Review," March 15, 1961, Bates No. 2021382496/2498; *Cipollone*, http://legacy.library.ucsf.edu/tid/ffn23e00.

51. "Notes on Conference," May 1955, Bates No. 91799298/9319, http://legacy.library.ucsf.edu/tid/kxx98c00.

52. Morton Mintz, "Pact Barring Cancer Study Disclosed," *Washington Post,* May 21, 1988.

53. Ibid.

54. H. Wakeham, "Why Are We All Here?" February 17, 1971, Bates No. 85868088/8099, http://legacy.library.ucsf.edu/tid/gyd70e00.

55. F. Panzer and H. R. Kornegay, "The Roper Proposal," May 1, 1972, Bates No. TIOK0000424/0427, http://legacy.library.ucsf.edu/tid/rdv91f00.

56. Alix M. Freedman and Laurie P. Cohen, "Smoke and Mirrors: How Cigarette Makers Keep Health Question 'Open' Year After Year," *Wall Street Journal,* February 11, 1993. See also Lisa A. Bero et al., "Lawyer Control of the Tobacco Industry's External Research Program: The Brown and Williamson Documents," *JAMA* 274, no. 3 (1995): 241–247; Philip J. Hilts,

Smokescreen: The Truth Behind the Tobacco Industry Cover-Up (Reading, MA: Addison-Wesley, 1996).

57. R. B. Seligman, "Memorandum from Philip Morris Employee to Philip Morris Counsel and Philip Morris Employee Containing Information Requested by Philip Morris Counsel Regarding Joint Defense Research," 1978, Bates Nos. 1003718428–32, http://tobaccodocuments.org/landman/1003718428–8432.html

58. In 1992, in another of Edell's tobacco cases, *Haines v. Liggett,* Judge Sarokin ruled that the tobacco industry may be "the king of concealment and disinformation." He would be removed from the case in September 1992 when the federal court of appeals ruled that he had failed to maintain the appearance of impartiality. But the industry documents detailing the activities of the CTR, previously "privileged," would emerge as a result of his ruling in the case. See "Judge Orders Files Opened on Cigarettes," *Washington Post,* February 8, 1992; Charles Strum, "Ruling in Tobacco Case Tests Boundaries of Judicial Bias," *New York Times,* September 20, 1992; "Outline of Presentation Issues," October 30, 1992, Bates Nos. 2048924986–5018, http://tobaccodocuments.org/bliley_pm/27616.html.

59. Morton Mintz, "Cigarette Ads Said Full of 'Health' Cues," *Washington Post,* March 10, 1988.

60. Trial testimony of Jerome Herbert Jaffe, March 2, 1988 [P.M.], 3703.

61. Trial testimony of Jerome Herbert Jaffe, March 2, 1988 [P.M.], 3705.

62. Morton Mintz, "Expert Cites Dependencies of Smokers: Tobacco Is Addictive, Psychiatrist Testifies," *Washington Post,* March 4, 1988.

63. Trial testimony of Jerome Herbert Jaffe, March 2, 1988 [P.M.], 3720.

64. "Trial testimony of Jerome Herbert Jaffe, March 3, 1988 [A.M.], *Cipollone v. Liggett,*"March 3, 1988, 3777, http://legacy.library.ucsf.edu/tid/jmz75a00.

65. Trial testimony of Jerome Herbert Jaffe, March 3, 1988 [A.M.], 3804.

66. Harold H. Kassarjian and Joel B. Cohen, "Cognitive Dissonance and Consumer Behavior: Reactions to the Surgeon General's Report on Smoking and Health," *California Management Review* (1965): 55–64; Trial Testimony of Joel B. Cohen, Ph.D., March 9, 10, 11, 15, 16, 1988, *Cipollone v. Liggett*; Howard Leventhal and Paul D. Cleary, "The Smoking Problem: A Review of the Research and Theory in Behavioral Risk Modification," *Psychological Bulletin* 88, no. 2 (1980): 370–405. On risk perception and smoking, see especially Paul Slovic, ed., *Smoking: Risk, Perception & Policy* (Thousand Oaks, CA: Sage Publications, 2001); W. Kip Viscusi, *Smoking: Making the Risky Decision* (New York: Oxford University Press, 1992); Thomas C. Schelling, *Choice and Consequence* (Cambridge, MA: Harvard University Press, 1984).

67. Shook, Hardy & Bacon, "The *Cipollone* Case," August 31, 1988, Bates No. 2022885364/5386, http://legacy.library.ucsf.edu/tid/gfh12a00.

68. Allan M. Brandt, "From Nicotine to Nicotrol: Addiction, Cigarettes, and American Culture," in *Altering American Consciousness: The History of Alcohol and Drug Use in the United States, 1800–2000,* eds. Sarah W. Tracy and Caroline Jean Acker (Amherst, MA: University of Massachusetts Press, 2004), 383–402.

69. C. Everett Koop, *Koop: The Memoirs of America's Family Doctor* (New York: Random House, 1991).

70. Surgeon General's Advisory Committee on Smoking and Health, *Smoking and Health: Report of the Advisory Committee to the Surgeon General of the Public Health Service* (Washington, DC: U.S. Department of Health, Education, and Welfare, Public Health Service, 1964), 350, 351.

71. U.S. Department of Health and Human Services, *The Health Consequences of Smoking: Nicotine Addiction: A Report of the Surgeon General* (Washington, DC: GPO, 1988).

72. On the history of addiction, see especially Sarah W. Tracy and Caroline Jean Acker, eds., *Altering American Consciousness: The History of Alcohol and Drug Use in the United States,*

1800–2000 (Amherst, MA: University of Massachusetts Press, 2004); David T. Courtwright, *Forces of Habit: Drugs and the Making of the Modern World* (Cambridge, MA: Harvard University Press, 2001); Roy Porter and Mikulás Teich, eds., *Drugs and Narcotics in History* (New York: Cambridge University Press, 1995).

73. U.S. Department of Health and Human Services, *Reducing the Health Consequences of Smoking: 25 Years of Progress, A Report of the Surgeon General* (Washington, DC: GPO, 1989): 285.

74. "Potential Rebuttals to the Surgeon General's Report on Tobacco and Addiction," 1988, Bates No. 2021255011/5012, http://legacy.library.ucsf.edu/tid/oom24e00.

75. David Newman (Host), *Open Line Detroit*, Detroit: WXYT-AM Radio, January 11, 1989.

76. Ed Bean, "Surgeon General's Stature Is Likely to Add Force to Report on Smoking as Addiction," *Wall Street Journal*, May 13, 1988.

77. P. M. Sirridge, Shook, Hardy & Bacon, "Re: July, 1983 Discussed Memorandum," July 23, 1983, Bates No. 2046754726, http://tobaccodocuments.org/landman/3801.html.

78. P. M. Sirridge, Shook, Hardy & Bacon, "Re: July, 1983 Discussed Memorandum," July 23, 1983, Bates Nos. 2046754720–31: 2046754727–8, http://tobaccodocuments.org/landman/3801.html.

79. P. M. Sirridge, Shook, Hardy & Bacon, "Re: July, 1983 Discussed Memorandum," July 23, 1983, Bates No. 2046754727, http://tobaccodocuments.org/landman/3801.html. An industry attorney noted, "Shook, Hardy reminds us, I'm told, that the entire matter of addiction is the most potent weapon a prosecuting attorney can have in a lung cancer/cigarette case. We can't defend continued smoking as 'free choice' if the person was 'addicted.'" P. Knopick, "Memo Re: Natl Institute of Drug Abuse Desire to Have Addictive Added to Cigarette Warnings," September 9, 1980, Bates Nos. TIMN0107822–3, http://tobaccodocuments.org/ti/TIMN0107822–7823.html.

80. P. M. Sirridge, Shook, Hardy & Bacon, "Re: July, 1983 Discussed Memorandum," July 23, 1983, Bates No. 2046754731, http://tobaccodocuments.org/landman/3801.html.

81. C. E. Teague, Reynolds R. "Research Planning Memorandum on the Nature of the Tobacco Business and the Crucial Role of Nicotine Therein, Exhibit # 10031," April 14, 1972, Bates No. TINY0003021.

82. J. L. Charles and P. Morris, "Nicotine Receptor Program—University of Rochester," March 18, 1980, Bates No. 85873828/3829, http://legacy.library.ucsf.edu/tid/ifd70e00.

83. W. L. Dunn, "Motives and Incentives in Cigarette Smoking," 1972, Bates No. 91788938/8955, http://legacy.library.ucsf.edu/tid/unb60e00.

84. Morton Mintz, "Risk Estimated by Ex-Official of Tobacco Industry," *Washington Post*, April 20, 1988.

85. "Plaintiffs' Conduct as a Defense to Claims Against Cigarette Manufacturers," *Harvard Law Review* 99, no. 4 (1986): 810.

86. Morton Mintz, "Tobacco Firms Open Defense in N.J. Trial," *Washington Post*, April 8, 1988.

87. Amy Singer, "They Didn't Really Blame the Cigarette Makers," *American Lawyer*, September 1988, 31.

88. Michael T. Kaufman, "Joseph F. Cullman 3rd, Who Made Philip Morris a Tobacco Power, Dies at 92," *New York Times*, May 1, 2004; and Richard Kluger, *Ashes to Ashes* (New York: Knopf, 1996).

89. Trial testimony of Joseph Frederick Cullman, III, February 24, 1988 [A.M.], *Cipollone v. Liggett*, February 24, 1988, http://legacy.library.ucsf.edu/tid/cea85a00: 2928.

90. H. Lee Sarokin, "Exhibit I. Antonio Cipollone, Individually and as Executor of the Estate of Rose D. Cipollone v. Liggett Group, Inc., Philip Morris Incorporated, and Lorillard, Inc. Opinion," 1988, Bates No. 506894860/4893, http://legacy.library.ucsf.edu/tid/job44d00.

91. Morton Mintz, "Closing Arguments Begin in Four-Month-Old Tobacco Product-Liability Trial," *Washington Post*, June 2, 1988.

92. Singer, 31.

93. *Cipollone v. Liggett Group, Inc. et al.*, 1988 U.S. Dist. LEXIS 16709: 12595 (1988).

94. Morton Mintz, "Smoker-Death Trial Ends with Plea for Punitive Damages," *Washington Post*, June 7, 1988.

95. Singer, 31.

96. Donald Janson, "Cigarette Maker Assessed Damages in Smoker's Death," *New York Times*, June 14, 1988.

97. Ibid.

98. Myron Levin, "Anti-Smoking Group May Resort to Racketeering Law," *Los Angeles Times*, June 15, 1988.

99. *Cipollone v. Liggett Group, Inc., et al.*, 893 F.2d 541 (1990).

100. John Riley, "Award Struck Down in Smoker's Death," *Newsday*, January 6, 1990.

101. Ibid.

102. Linda Greenhouse, "Court Hears Debate on Suits Against Makers of Cigarettes," *New York Times*, October 9, 1991.

103. "No Immunity for Coffin Nails," *New York Times*, January 12, 1992.

104. Ibid.

105. *Cipollone v. Liggett Group, Inc. et al.*, 505 U.S. 504 (1992).

106. "Preemption Doctrine After *Cipollone*," *Harvard Law Review* 106, no. 4 (1993): 967.

107. Joseph Kelner and Robert S. Kelner, "The Tobacco Industry and 'Cipollone,'" *New York Law Journal*, August 25, 1992, 3.

108. Laurie P. Cohen, "Broader Suits over Cigarettes May Be Possible," *Wall Street Journal*, January 8, 1990.

109. Alison Frankel, "Was Budd Larner Another Smoking Victim?" *New Jersey Law Journal*, July 12, 1993, 7.

110. Ibid.

111. Richard A. Daynard, "The Third Wave of Tobacco Products Liability Cases," *Trial*, November 1994, 34.

112. Graham E. Kelder, Jr., and Richard A. Daynard, "Judicial Approaches to Tobacco Control: The Third Wave of Tobacco Litigation as a Tobacco Control Mechanism," *Journal of Social Issues* 53, no. 1 (1997): 172.

113. Quoted in Leduc.

Chapter 11

1. *Nicotine and Cigarettes: Hearing of the House Energy and Commerce Committee, Subcommittee on Health and the Environment*, April 14, 1994, available from http://www.pbs.org/wgbh/pages/frontline/shows/settlement/timelines/april94.html.

2. Ibid.

3. Ibid.

4. David Kessler, *A Question of Intent: A Great American Battle with a Deadly Industry* (New York: Public Affairs, 2001), 393.

5. Alix M. Freedman and Suein L. Hwang, "Leaders of the Pact: How Seven Individuals with Diverse Motives Halted Tobacco's Wars," *Wall Street Journal*, July 11, 1997. See also Dan Zegart, *Civil Warriors: The Legal Siege of the Tobacco Companies* (New York: Delacorte, 2000), 100–112.

6. "Smoke Screen," *Day One*, ABC, February 28, 1994.

7. Ibid.

8. W. L. Dunn, "Motives and Incentives in Cigarette Smoking," 1972, Bates No. 91788938/8955, http://legacy.library.ucsf.edu/tid/unb60e00.

9. Kessler, 130. For a history of the FDA, see Philip J. Hilts, *Protecting America's Health: The FDA, Business, and One Hundred Years of Regulation* (New York: Knopf, 2003).

10. Philip J. Hilts, *Smokescreen: The Truth Behind the Tobacco Industry Cover-Up* (Reading, MA: Addison-Wesley, 1996), 116–118; and Michael York, [letter to Benjamin Wittes of Legal Times], January 11, 1996, Bates No. 2048325599/5608, http://legacy.library.ucsf.edu/tid/abd37c00.

11. Dunn, 1972.

12. "Smoke Screen," *Day One*.

13. David Kessler, [letter to Scott Ballin, Coalition on Smoking OR Health], February 25, 1994, Bates No. 980290781/0783, http://legacy.library.ucsf.edu/tid/cen85f00.

14. Marlene Cimons, "Tobacco Industry Fights Spiraling Efforts to Snuff It Out," *Los Angeles Times*, March 26, 1994.

15. Kessler, 161.

16. Kessler, 167–168.

17. Kessler, 162.

18. Chester Atkins, Henry A. Waxman, Bob Whittaker, Richard J. Durbin, Fortney H. Stark, [letter from members of Congress to FDA Commissioner Frank E. Young About Premier], October 11, 1988, Bates No. 506921052/1053, http://legacy.library.ucsf.edu/tid/dly34d00; Michael Waldholz, "Influential Congressman Presses FDA to Decide Status of New RJR Cigarette," *Wall Street Journal*, December 5, 1988; Kessler, 28–29; Michael J. McCarthy, "RJR's Premier Is Off—But Not Running," *Wall Street Journal*, December 12, 1988; and Betsy Morris and Peter Waldman, "The Death of Premier," *Wall Street Journal*, March 10, 1989.

19. Philip Morris, "Philip Morris Developments: The Denicotinized Tobacco Story," 1999, Bates No. 2078425524/5540, http://legacy.library.ucsf.edu/tid/xap75c00.

20. Kessler, 161.

21. Jill Zuckman, "Tobacco Executives at Hearing; Nicotine Focus of House Unit," *Boston Globe*, April 15, 1994.

22. Earl Lane, "Never Say Die: Tobacco Bosses Visit Congress, Defend Smoking," *Newsday*, April 15, 1994.

23. Zuckman, "Tobacco Executives at Hearing; Nicotine Focus of House Unit"; Philip J. Hilts, "Tobacco Chiefs Say Cigarettes Aren't Addictive," *New York Times*, April 15, 1994; "Executives Deny Spiking Cigarettes: House Panel Hears One Equate a Cigarette with a Cup of Coffee," *St. Louis Post-Dispatch*, April 15, 1994; "Tobacco Firms Are Ordered to Provide Nicotine Research," *Baltimore Sun*, April 15, 1994; "Defending Tobacco: 'We Do Not Do Anything to Hook Smokers,'" *Atlanta Constitution*, April 15, 1994; Mike Brown, "The Chief Executive Officers . . . " *Courier-Journal*, April 15, 1994; Earl Lane, "Never Say Die: Tobacco Bosses Visit Congress, Defend Smoking," *Newsday*, April 15, 1994; Jeff Nesmith, "America's Tobacco Chiefs Face Critics in Congress," *Atlanta Constitution*, April 15, 1994; and Michael Wines, "Makers of Laws and Tobacco Joust at Capitol," *New York Times*, April 15, 1994.

24. Lane.

25. Waxman et al.

26. U.S. Department of Health and Human Services, *The Health Consequences of Smoking: Nicotine Addiction: A Report of the Surgeon General* (Washington, DC: GPO, 1988).

27. "Blowing Smoke," *Baltimore Sun*, April 16, 1994.

28. "Blowing Smoke at Congress," *New York Times*, April 17, 1994.

29. Hilts, 124.

30. Martin Meehan to Janet Reno, December 14, 1994, http://legacy.library.ucsf.edu/tid/qzv70f00.

31. Barry Meier and David Johnston, "How Inquiry into Tobacco Lost Its Steam: Criminal Case Ran out of Time and Energy," *New York Times*, September 26, 1999.

32. "First Amended Complaint for Damages and Injunctive and Declaratory Relief (*U.S. v. Philip Morris, et al.*)," ed. United States Department of Justice, Washington, DC: United

States District Court (D.C. Cir.), 2001; President William Clinton, State of the Union Address, 1999.

33. On Merrell Williams, see especially Orey. See also Glantz's *Cigarette Papers,* Zegart's *Civil Warriors,* and Pringle's *Cornered.*

34. Orey, 173–175.

35. Ibid., 133–143.

36. Steve Weinberg, "Smoking Guns: ABC, Philip Morris and the Infamous Apology," *Columbia Journalism Review,* November/December 1995, 29–37.

37. Addison Yeaman, "Implications of Battelle Hippo I & II and the Griffith Filter," July 17, 1963, Bates No. 2074459290/9294, http://legacy.library.ucsf.edu/tid/ari52c00.

38. Philip J. Hilts, "Tobacco Company Was Silent on Hazards," *New York Times,* May 7, 1994.

39. Lisa A. Bero et al., "Lawyer Control of the Tobacco Industry's External Research Program: The Brown and Williamson Documents," *JAMA* 274, no. 3 (1995): 241–247; and Deborah E. Barnes et al., "Environmental Tobacco Smoke: The Brown and Williamson Documents," *JAMA* 274, no. 3 (1995): 248–253.

40. Stanton A. Glantz et al., "Looking Through a Keyhole at the Tobacco Industry: The Brown and Williamson Documents," *JAMA* 274, no. 3 (1995): 219–224.

41. "Philip Hilts: The Interview," *Frontline,* WGBH, 1999, http://www2.pbs.org/wgbh/pages/frontline/smoke/interviews/hilts1.html.

42. Glantz et al.

43. Orey, 198–203, 338.

44. Laurie McGinley, "Judge Quashes Subpoenas Granted to Tobacco Firm," *Wall Street Journal,* June 7, 1994.

45. *Maddox v. Williams,* 855 F. Supp. 406 (1994).

46. M. Gunja et al., "The Case for Fire Safe Cigarettes Made Through Industry Documents," *Tobacco Control* 11, no. 4 (2002): 346–353. Philip Morris had sponsored research in the 1980s to develop a self-extinguishing cigarette known as Project Hamlet (to burn or not to burn), but nonetheless decided against moving forward. B. N. Leistikow, D. C. Martin, and C. E. Milano, "Fire Injuries, Disasters, and Costs from Cigarettes and Cigarette Lights: A Global Overview," *Preventive Medicine* 31, no. 2 (2000): 91–99; and Andrew McGuire, "How the Tobacco Industry Continues to Keep the Home Fires Burning," *Tobacco Control* 11, no. 4 (1999): 67–69.

47. Kessler, 186–87.

48. John Schwartz, "Reengineering the Cigarette," *Washington Post,* January 31, 1999.

49. Ibid.

50. Kessler, 116.

51. Schwartz.

52. Ibid.

53. Zegart, 59–77.

54. Kessler, 82, 116, 139.

55. Orey, 305.

56. "Smoke in the Eye: Why Did CBS and ABC Back Off from Exposes on the Tobacco Industry?" *Frontline,* WGBH, 1999, http://www.pbs.org/wgbh/pages/frontline/smoke.

57. Mike Wallace, "Interview With Jeffrey Wigand, PhD," *60 Minutes,* CBS, 1996.

58. Ibid.

59. Verne Gay, "Where There's Smoke . . . /When It Comes to Fighting Tobacco Wars, TV Isn't Butting Out Yet," *Newsday,* March 31, 1996.

60. Weinberg.

61. Ibid. See also Jeff Cohen and Norman Solomon, "The Wrong Smoke Signals from ABC News," *Newsday,* August 28, 1995.

62. Weinberg.

63. See Gay, "Where There's Smoke . . . "

64. Peter Johnson, "ABC's Tobacco Muckraker Says He's Leaving Network," *USA Today*, April 3, 1996.

65. Rita Ciolli, "ABC Libel Deal: Chilling Effect?" *Newsday*, August 23, 1995.

66. Jane Hall, "ABC News Steps Up to the Plate Again," *Los Angeles Times*, March 21, 1996.

67. "Apology Accepted" [advertisement], *New York Times*, August 25, 1995.

68. "Smoke in the Eye: Why Did CBS and ABC Back Off from Exposés on the Tobacco Industry?"

69. Lawrence K. Grossman, "CBS, 60 Minutes, and the Unseen Interview," *Columbia Journalism Review*, January/February 1996, 39.

70. Bill Carter, "'60 Minutes' Ordered to Pull Interview in Tobacco Report," *New York Times*, November 9, 1995.

71. Ibid.

72. James C. Goodale, "'60 Minutes' v. CBS and Vice Versa," *New York Law Journal*, December 1, 1995, 3.

73. Ibid.

74. Daniel Schorr, "Money Managers Take the Bite out of News," *Christian Science Monitor*, December 1, 1995.

75. Alix M. Freedman, "The Deposition: Cigarette Defector Says CEO Lied to Congress About View of Nicotine," *Wall Street Journal*, January 25, 1996.

76. Suein L. Hwang and Milo Geyelin, "Getting Personal: Brown & Williamson Has 500-Page Dossier Attacking Chief Critic," *Wall Street Journal*, February 1, 1996.

77. Claude E. Teague, "Research Planning Memorandum on Some Thoughts About New Brands of Cigarettes for the Youth Market," February 2, 1973, Bates No. 502987407/7418, http://legacy.library.ucsf.edu/tid/edy62d00, quoted in Jeffrey Goldberg, "Next Target: Nicotine," *New York Times Magazine*, August 4, 1996, 22–27, 36, 44, 47.

78. Frank V. Tursi, Susan E. White, and Steve McQuilkin, *Lost Empire: The Fall of R.J. Reynolds Tobacco Company* (Winston-Salem: Winston-Salem Journal, 2000).

79. H. T. Hughes, "Cigarette Market Share History," February 26, 1985, Bates No. 555007431/7439, http://legacy.library.ucsf.edu/tid/dzz13f00.

80. *Preventing Tobacco Use Among Young People: A Report of the Surgeon General*, (Atlanta, GA: U.S. Department of Health and Human Services, Centers for Disease Control and Prevention, National Center for Chronic Disease Prevention and Health Promotion, Office on Smoking and Health, 1994).

81. Diane S. Burrows, "Younger Adult Smokers: Strategies and Opportunities," February 29, 1984, Bates No. 505458066/8160, http://legacy.library.ucsf.edu/tid/bot15d00.

82. Ibid.

83. Ibid.

84. Jack Wolf, R.J. Reynolds, "Teenage Smoking—Incidence and Consumption," March 25, 1982, Bates No. 503419308/9308, http://legacy.library.ucsf.edu/tid/xfy52d00.

85. Doug Levy and Melanie Wells, "Papers: RJR Did Court Teens: Critics Say Tobacco Firm Lied About Marketing Aim," *USA Today*, January 15, 1998.

86. C. A. Tucker, "1975 Marketing Plans Presentation—Hilton Head, September 30, 1974," September 30, 1974, Bates No. 501421310/1335, http://legacy.library.ucsf.edu/tid/rpx62d00.

87. "Are Younger Adult Smokers Important?" Bates No. 502035180/5286, http://legacy.library.ucsf.edu/tid/mhy52d00.

88. Patrick J. Coughlin and Frank J. Janecek, Jr., *Executive Summary a Review of R.J. Reynolds' Internal Documents Produced in* Mangini v. R.J. Reynolds Tobacco Co., *Civil No. 939359—the Case That Rid California and the American Landscape of Joe Camel (*New York: Milberg Weiss Bershad & Schulman LLP, 1998).

89. E. A. Horrigan, R.J. Reynolds, "Subject: Funny Camel Poster," August 3, 1981, Bates No. 503906210, http://legacy.library.ucsf.edu/tid/rys75d00.

90. Dana Blackmar, "French Camel Filter Ad," February 7, 1974, Bates No. 502303940, http://legacy.library.ucsf.edu/tid/oal19d00.

91. Joel B. Cohen, "Playing to Win: Marketing and Public Policy at Odds over Joe Camel," *Journal of Public Policy and Marketing* 19, no. 2 (2000): 155–167. See also John E. Calfee, "The Historical Significance of Joe Camel," *Journal of Public Policy and Marketing* 19, no. 2 (2000): 168–182.

92. E. C. Leary, "CAMEL April Sampling/Free French CAMEL T-Shirt Test Premium Response Evaluation," July 2, 1985, Bates No. 505320278/0280, http://legacy.library.ucsf.edu/tid/nek25d00.

93. "We Don't Advertise to Children," [half-page advertisement], *New York Times*, June 19, 1984.

94. Rick T. Caulfield, "RE: Camel New Advertising Campaign Development," March 12, 1986, Bates No. 503969238/9242, http://legacy.library.ucsf.edu/tid/pil75d00.

95. Ibid., 4.

96. Barbara Lippert, "Old Joe, New Image: A Macho Mascot, Filtered Through the Sands of Time," *Chicago Tribune*, November 18, 1988.

97. Marjorie Garber, "Joe Camel, an X-Rated Smoke," *New York Times*, March 20, 1992.

98. Claude E. Teague, "Research Planning Memorandum on Some Thoughts About New Brands of Cigarettes for the Youth Market," February 2, 1973, Bates No. 502987407/7418; and *Mangini*, http://legacy.library.ucsf.edu/tid/edy62d00.

99. Stuart Elliott, "Adoring or Abhorring the Camel," *New York Times*, July 29, 1992.

100. Federal Food, Drug, and Cosmetic Act of 1938, Pub. L. No. 75–717, 52 Stat. 1040, (1938).

101. Kenneth E. Warner, Clar C. Peck, Raymond L. Woosley, Jack E. Henningfield, and John Slade, "Treatment of Tobacco Dependence: Innovative Regulatory Approaches to Reduce Death and Disease," *Food and Drug Law Journal* 53 (Suppl) (1998): 1–8.

102. David A. Kessler et al., "The Food and Drug Administration's Regulation of Tobacco Products," *New England Journal of Medicine* 335, no. 3 (1996): 988–994.

103. Ibid., 989.

104. Ibid., 993.

105. Glenn Frankel, "Dole's Link to Big Tobacco Aged in Years of Dealmaking," *Washington Post*, May 18, 1996.

106. "Mr. Dole's Smoke Rings," *New York Times*, July 4, 1996.

107. Kessler, 382.

108. Thomas W. Kirby, "Giving Agencies Less Deference; Tobacco Decision Looked Broadly for Congress' Intent," *Legal Times*, March 27, 2000, 66.

109. *Food and Drug Administration, et al. v. Brown and Williamson Tobacco Corporation, et al.*, 529 U.S. 120 (2000).

110. David E. Rosenbaum, "Everyone Wants to Do Something About Tobacco, but Few Agree on What," *New York Times*, March 11, 1998.

111. *Open Secrets: Tobacco Long-Term Contribution Trends*, available from http://www.opensecrets.org/industries/indus.asp?Ind=A02, accessed June 30, 2006.

112. Adam Clymer, "Clinton Urges Giving F.D.A. Oversight of Tobacco," *New York Times*, March 26, 2000.

113. Ibid.

114. N. Wander and R. E. Malone, "Selling Off or Selling Out? Medical Schools and Ethical Leadership in Tobacco Stock Divestment," *Academic Medicine* 79, no. 11 (2004): 1017–1026; L. Fisher, "Divestment in the Tobacco Industry," *Cancer Causes and Control* 11, no. 4 (2000): 381–382; Ruth Malone, *Secret Papers Show Tobacco Company Tried to Preserve Financial Ties with Academic*

Medicine [Internet newsletter], University of California, San Francisco, October 25, 2004; Frank Phillips, "Dukakis Will Seek Tobacco Divestment," *Boston Globe*, May 29, 1990; Frank Philips, "Harvard Divests of Tobacco Firms' Stock," *Boston Globe*, May 23, 1990; and "Group Urges Divestment of Tobacco Stocks," *New York Times*, May 27, 1990. Rather than divesting, some religious groups have used shareholder responsibility proxies to challenge industry policies. See M. H. Crosby, "Religious Challenge by Shareholder Actions: Changing the Behaviour of Tobacco Companies and Their Allies," *British Medical Journal* 321, no. 7257 (2000): 375–377. On bans on research funds, see Alan Blum, "Ethics of Tobacco-Funded Research in U.S. Medical Schools," *Tobacco Control* 1, no. 3 (1992): 244–245; D. E. Barnes and L. A. Bero, "Industry-Funded Research and Conflict of Interest: An Analysis of Research Sponsored by the Tobacco Industry Through the Center for Indoor Air Research," *Journal of Health Politics, Policy, and Law* 21, no. 3 (1996): 515–542.

115. Roger Rosenblatt, "How Do Tobacco Executives Live with Themselves?" *The New York Times Magazine*, March 20, 1994, 34.

116. Ibid., 39

117. Ibid., 73-74.

Chapter 12

1. *Frontline: Inside the Tobacco Deal*, WGBH, 1998, http://www.pbs.org/wgbh/pages/frontline/shows/settlement/interviews/motley.html.

2. Ibid.

3. Quoted in Michael Pertschuk, *Smoke in Their Eyes: Lessons in Movement Leadership from the Tobacco Wars* (Nashville, TN: Vanderbilt University Press, 2001), 279.

4. Mark Hansen, "Second-Hand Smoke Suit," *American Bar Association Journal*, February 1992, 26; and Glenn Collins, "Trial Near in New Legal Tack in Tobacco War," *New York Times*, May 30, 1997.

5. Sheryl Stolberg, "2 Women in Vanguard of Anti-Smoking Battle," *Los Angeles Times*, February 21, 1996.

6. Terri Somers, "The Billion Dollar Mitzvah Religious Faith and a Passion for the Cause Led Stanley Rosenblatt to Take on Big Tobacco," *Sun-Sentinel*, October 8, 2000.

7. Stanley M. Rosenblatt, *Murder of Mercy: Euthanasia on Trial* (Amherst, NY: Prometheus Books, 1992).

8. Myron Levin, "Tobacco Firms to Settle Flight Attendants' Suit," *Los Angeles Times*, October 11, 1997; and John Schwartz, "Secondhand Smoke Trial Ends in Deal: Tobacco Firms' Settlement Includes $300 Million for Research Foundation," *Washington Post*, October 11, 1997.

9. Collins.

10. I have relied heavily on Michael Orey's excellent *Assuming the Risk: The Mavericks, the Lawyers, and the Whistle-Blowers Who Beat Big Tobacco* (New York: Little, Brown, 1999) for my assessment of the emergence of state litigation. See also Benjamin Weiser, "Tobacco's Trials," *Washington Post*, December 8, 1996.

11. Peter Pringle, *Cornered: Big Tobacco at the Bar of Justice* (New York: Henry Holt, 1998), 40–41; and Dan Zegart, *Civil Warriors: The Legal Siege of the Tobacco Companies* (New York: Delacorte Press, 2000), 86.

12. Robert K. Merton, *Social Theory and Social Structure* (New York: Free Press, 1949).

13. Zegart, 85.

14. R. A. Daynard, "How Did We Get Here?" *Tobacco Control* 13 (Suppl 1) (2004): i3.

15. Graham E. Kelder, Jr., and Richard A. Daynard, "Judicial Approaches to Tobacco Control: The Third Wave of Tobacco Litigation as a Tobacco Control Mechanism," *Journal of Social Issues* 53, no. 1 (1997): 169–186; "Editorials on Tobacco . . . Smokers Chose Their Fate," *Los Angeles Daily Journal* 104, no. 93 (1991): 6; and Philip J. Hilts, "Lawsuits Against Tobacco Companies May Be Consolidated," *New York Times*, November 6, 1994.

16. Kenneth W. Dam, "Class Actions: Efficiency, Compensation, Deterrence, and Conflict of Interest," *Journal of Legal Studies* 4, no. 1 (1975): 47–73. For a history of class actions, see Harry Kalven, Jr., and Maurice Rosenfield, "The Contemporary Function of the Class Suit," *University of Chicago Law Review* 8, no. 3 (1941): 684–721.

17. Peter H. Schuck, *Agent Orange on Trial: Mass Toxic Disasters in the Courts* (Cambridge, MA: Belknap Press of Harvard University Press, 1986); Sheila Jasanoff, ed., *Learning from Disaster: Risk Management After Bhopal, Law in Social Context* (Philadelphia: University of Pennsylvania Press, 1994); Mary F. Hawkins, *Unshielded: The Human Cost of the Dalkon Shield* (Toronto: University of Toronto Press, 1997); and Morton Mintz, *At Any Cost: Corporate Greed, Women, and the Dalkon Shield* (New York: Pantheon Books, 1985).

18. Jack B. Weinstein, "Compensating Large Numbers of People for Inflicted Harms" [keynote address], *Duke Journal of Comparative and International Law* 11, no. 1 (2001): 165–178. See also Jack B. Weinstein, "Ethical Dilemmas in Mass Tort Litigation," *Northwestern Law Review* 88, no. 2 (1993–1994): 469–568; and Jack B. Weinstein, "Restatement of Torts and the Courts, the Symposium: The John W. Wade Conference on the Third Restatement of Torts," *Vanderbilt Law Review* 54, no. 3 (2001): 1439–1446.

19. See especially Lynn Mather, "Theorizing About Trial Courts: Lawyers, Policymaking, and Tobacco Litigation," *Law & Social Inquiry* 23, no. 4 (1998): 897–940; and John C. Coffee, Jr., "Class Wars: The Dilemma of the Mass Tort Class Action," *Columbia Law Review* 95, no. 6 (1995): 1343–1465.

20. All quotes taken from Michael Janofsky, "On Cigarettes, Health and Lawyers," *New York Times,* December 6, 1993.

21. Carrick Mollenkamp et al., *People vs. Big Tobacco: How the States Took on the Cigarettte Giants* (New York: Bloomberg Press, 1998), 14.

22. "Tobacco Executives Still Claim Smoking Not Killer, Paper Says," *Houston Chronicle,* April 21, 1997.

23. *FAMRI—Flight Attendant Medical Research Institute Mission Statement,* accessed February 28, 2006, available from http://www.famri.org/mission_statement/index.php.

24. Levin; and Schwartz.

25. Weiser.

26. John Coale and another *Castano* lawyer, Russ Herman, also had parents with smoking-related diseases. See Saundra Torry, "Liability Lawyers Trying to Smoke Out Tobacco Industry," *Washington Post,* May 30, 1994.

27. Paul Brodeur, *Outrageous Misconduct* (New York: Pantheon, 1985).

28. Ibid., 143. For more on Motley, see Dan Zegart, *Civil Warriors: The Legal Siege of the Tobacco Companies* (New York: Delacorte, 2000).

29. Brodeur, 143–144.

30. Marianna S. Smith, "Resolving Asbestos Claims: The Manville Personal Injury Settlement Trust," *Law and Contemporary Problems* 53, no. 4 (1990): 27–36. See also Brodeur and Zegart.

31. Barry Meier, "Tobacco Industry Loses First Phase of Broad Lawsuit; Jury Finds a Conspiracy to Hide Effects of Smoking," *New York Times,* July 8, 1999; and Stanley M. Rosenblatt, personal communication with the author, April 14, 2003.

32. Gordon Fairclough and Milo Geyelin, "Tobacco Companies Rail Against Verdict, Plan to Appeal $144.87 Billion Award," *Wall Street Journal,* July 17, 2000.

33. R. Davis, "A $145bn Verdict and a "Roar of Moral Outrage," *British Medical Journal* 321, no. 7257 (2000): 322.

34. F. Charatan, "Florida Jury Finds Tobacco Companies Guilty of Fraud," *British Medical Journal* 319, no. 7203 (1999): 143; Richard A. Daynard, "The Engle Verdicts and Tobacco Litigation," *British Medical Journal* 321, no. 3 (2000): 312–313; M. Larkin, "Tobacco Industry Giants Scorched in Florida Lawsuit," *Lancet* 354, no. 9174 (1999): 231; Myron Levin, "Court Throws Out $144.8-Billion Award Against Tobacco Industry," *Los Angeles Times,* May 22, 2003; Barry Meier, "Tobacco

Industry Loses First Phase of Broad Lawsuit: Jury Finds a Conspiracy to Hide Effects of Smoking"; "Smokers Win First Class-Action Suit Against Tobacco," *St. Louis Post-Dispatch*, July 8, 1999; and Richard Willing, "Smokers' Suit Could Have Far-Reaching Implications," *USA Today*, July 6, 1999.

35. *Engle v. Liggett Group, Inc.*, No. SC03–1856, Supreme Court of Florida, 2006 Fla. Lexis 1480, July 6, 2006. [The appeal of *Engle v. R.J. Reynolds* is known as *Engle v. Liggett*.]

36. Mollenkamp et al.

37. M. Coller, G. W. Harrison, and M. M. McInnes, "Evaluating the Tobacco Settlement Damage Awards: Too Much or Not Enough?" *American Journal of Public Health* 92, no. 6 (2002): 984–989.

38. Pringle, 30.

39. "Billion-Dollar Legal Fees," *New York Times*, February 11, 1998; and "Mining the Torts," *Forbes*, July 7, 1997, 44.

40. Orey, 265.

41. Michael Janofsky, "Mississippi Seeks Damages from Tobacco Companies," *New York Times*, May 24, 1994; Junda Woo, "Mississippi Wants Tobacco Firms to Pay Its Cost of Treating Welfare Recipients," *Wall Street Journal*, May 24, 1994; and Mollenkamp et al., 29.

42. Orey, 268.

43. Ibid., 270.

44. Pringle, 31.

45. Mollenkamp et al.

46. Pringle.

47. Orey, 281.

48. Ibid., 282.

49. Kevin Sack, "Tobacco Industry's Dogged Nemesis," *New York Times*, April 6, 1997.

50. Tobacco Control Resource Center, Inc., "State Suit Summary," *The State Tobacco Information Center*, http://stic.neu.edu/summary.htm.

51. For more on the Mississippi story, see Christopher Caldwell, "The Pair from Pascagoula," *Weekly Standard*, August 11, 1997, 24; Myron Levin, "Moore Scores Again Against Big Tobacco," *Los Angeles Times*, July 4, 1997; Barry Meier, "Acting Alone, Mississippi Settles Suit with 4 Tobacco Companies," *New York Times*, July 4, 1997; and Doug Levy and Peter Eisler, "The Tobacco Warrior: How Mike Moore's Fight Against Cigarettes Fired Up His Future," *USA Today*, July 16, 1997.

52. There is extensive newspaper coverage of the deal: Glenn Collins, "An Entrepreneur's High-Stakes Move," *New York Times*, March 21, 1997; Alix M. Freedman and Suein L. Hwang, "Leaders of the Pact: How Seven Individuals with Diverse Motives Halted Tobacco's Wars," *Wall Street Journal*, July 11, 1997; Milo Geyelin and Suein Hwang, "Liggett to Settle 22 States' Tobacco Suits," *Wall Street Journal*, March 21, 1997; Myron Levin, "Under Oath, Liggett Owner Says Cigarettes Are Addictive," *Los Angeles Times*, July 22, 1997; John Schwartz, "A Maverick's Complaint: Liggett's LeBow Broke Tobacco's Ranks, but He Says the States Broke a Deal," *Washington Post*, July 24, 1997; and Mollenkamp et al.

53. Weiser.

54. Sack.

55. The most comprehensive account of the Minnesota lawsuit is Deborah C. Rybak et al., *Smoked: The Inside Story of the Minnesota Tobacco Trial* (Minneapolis, MN: MSP Communications, 1998). Other sources include: Michael V. Ciresi, "Decades of Deceit: Document Discovery in the Minnesota Tobacco Litigation," *William Mitchell Law Review* 25, no. 2 (1999): 477–566; Andy Czajkowski, "Money Isn't Enough," *Washington Post*, March 28, 1998; Hubert H. Humphrey, "The Decision to Reject the June, 1997 National Settlement Proposal and Proceed to Trial," *William Mitchell Law Review* 25 (1999): 397–405; "No Deal," *Philadelphia Enquirer*, November 18, 1998; Jonathan M. Samet, "Reflections: Testifying in the Minnesota Tobacco Lawsuit," *Tobacco Control* 8, no. 1 (1999): 101–105.

56. Pringle, 210; Thomas Osdene, "Memo," Bates No. 1000130803, http://legacy.library.ucsf .edu/tid/iyu53e00.

57. David Phelps, "Tobacco Scientist's Video Causes Stir on Both Sides; Company Memos to Push Case," *Star Tribune,* February 18, 1998.

58. Pringle, 211.

59. Mark W. Gehan, *Report of Special Master: Findings of Fact, Conclusions of Law and Recommendations,* 1997, 38, http://www.tobacco.neu.edu/bix/BOEKENBox/MN%20Crime%20Fraud %20Background/2%20Report%20of%20Special%20Master%2020091097.pdf. See also Ciresi.

60. Stanton A. Glantz, *The Cigarette Papers* (Berkeley: University of California Press, 1996), 288–327.

61. Ibid.

62. J. Kendrick Wells III, "Southampton Smoking and Health Material," June 15, 1979, Bates No. 680585391/5392, http://legacy.library.ucsf.edu/tid/hfy95a00.

63. J. Kendrick Wells III, Brown and Williamson, "Conference with BAT Legal on U.S. Products Liability Litigation," June 12, 1984, Bates No. 685092972/2974, http://legacy.library .ucsf.edu/tid/lgx95a00.

64. Ciresi, 477–566.

65. Rybak et al.

66. Glenn Collins, "Marketplace: Is That a Crack in the Tobacco Industry's Legal Wall, or a Shadow?" *New York Times,* August 13, 1996.

67. Barry Meier, "Cigarette Maker Is Liable in Smoker's Death," *New York Times,* June 11, 1998.

68. Barry Meier, "Florida Court Voids Verdict Against Tobacco Company," *New York Times,* June 23, 1998; Thomas C. Tobin, "Ex-Smoker Savors Tobacco Win," *St. Petersburg Times,* July 16, 2001; and *Carter v. Brown & Williamson Tobacco Corp.,* 778 So. 2d (Fla. 2000).

69. Harriet Chiang, "Madelyn Chaber, Godmother of Tobacco Suits," *San Francisco Chronicle,* November 20, 2002.

70. Myron Levin, "High Court Turns Away Philip Morris," *Los Angeles Times,* March 22, 2005; Bob Egelko, "Tobacco Damages Upheld; Philip Morris Must Pay $10.5 Million," *San Francisco Chronicle,* March 22, 2005. In a subsequent individual smoker's case in 2000, Chaber won an award of $21.7 million.

71. Myron Levin, "Philip Morris Vows to Appeal Judgment to U.S. High Court," *Los Angeles Times,* August 12, 2005; Myron Levin and Dalondo Moultrie, "L.A. Jury Awards $3 Billion to Smoker," *Los Angeles Times,* June 7, 2001; and Myron Levin, "Widow's Legal Battle with Philip Morris Ends," *Los Angeles Times,* March 21, 2006.

72. Patricia Lopez Baden, "State Tobacco Stock to Be Sold over 3 Years," *Star Tribune,* September 3, 1998; Barnaby J. Feder, "Cigarette Makers in a $368 Billion Accord to Curb Lawsuits and Curtail Marketing: Companies' Cost Would Be Great. But So Is Their Outlook for Profit," *New York Times,* June 21, 1997; Alisa Gravitz, "Big Tobacco Going Way of Its Customers," *USA Today,* April 9, 1997; Constance L. Hays, "Tobacco Stocks Recoup After Legislation Fizzles," *New York Times,* June 19, 1998; and Larry Light, Irene Kunii, and Carol Matlack, "Smoke Alarms at RJR," *Business Week,* November 16, 1998, 75.

73. Michael Pertschuk, "Making Deals with the Devil: Beware of Big Tobacco's Tricks," *Washington Post,* May 11, 1997.

74. Richard Kluger, *Ashes to Ashes* (New York: Knopf, 1996).

75. "Billion-Dollar Legal Fees," *New York Times,* February 11, 1998; "Greed Breeds Bad Case of Eye-Popping Legal Fees," *USA Today,* December 9, 1997; John Kennedy, "Lawyer Fees Ignite Spat in Tobacco Deal," *Orlando Sentinel,* August 29, 1997; and George F. Will, "The Tobacco Melee," *Washington Post,* February 15, 1998.

76. Barry Meier, "Cigarette Makers in a $368 Billion Accord to Curb Lawsuits and Curtail Marketing: Impact on Health: Hazy," *New York Times,* June 21, 1997; Stuart Elliot, "Industry Still

Has Many Weapons Available," *New York Times,* June 21, 1997; and "A Worrisome Tobacco Deal," *New York Times,* June 21, 1997.

77. I have relied heavily on Michael Pertschuk, *Smoke in Their Eyes: Lessons in Movement Leadership from the Tobacco Wars* (Nashville, TN: Vanderbilt University Press, 2001) for my assessment of public health advocacy and the McCain bill. Pertschuk, a major figure in the development of tobacco control advocacy, offers an excellent "insider's" view of the split in public health forces, who frequently consulted him during the debate.

78. Orey, 365.

79. David Phelps and Melissa Levy, "$7 Billion Deal: Minnesota, Industry Settle Suit Before Jury Starts Deliberations," *Star Tribune,* May 9, 1998.

80. Pertschuk, 37–38.

81. Ibid., 48.

82. Ibid., 50.

83. Ibid.

84. Ibid., 98.

85. Ibid., 99, quoting *Corporate Crime Reporter,* May 5, 1997.

86. Ibid., 100.

87. Ibid., 97.

88. Ibid., 101, quoting Sheryl Gay Stolberg, "Beleaguered Tobacco Foe Holds Key to Talks," *New York Times,* June 4, 1997.

89. Ibid., 107, quoting statement issued on May 2, 1997.

90. Ibid., 133, quoting Henry A. Waxman, "The Tobacco Settlement; Don't Sign It; on Balance, a Bad Deal for Public Health," *Washington Post,* June 29, 1997.

91. Ibid., 135, quoting Michael Siegel.

92. See Ibid., 173.

93. Martha A. Derthick, *Up in Smoke: From Legislation to Litigation in Tobacco Politics* (Washington, DC: Congressional Quarterly Press, 2002), 84, 143.

94. Pertschuk, 191.

95. Ibid.; and David Kessler, *A Question of Intent: A Great American Battle with a Deadly Industry* (New York: Public Affairs, 2001).

96. "Spat over Tobacco Money Spotlights Big Donors," *USA Today,* July 10, 1996.

97. Bill McAllister, "Heavy Hitters in the High-Stakes Tobacco Fight Arena," *Washington Post,* June 4, 1998.

98. Jill Abramson and Barry Meier, "Tobacco Braced for Costly Fight," *New York Times,* December 15, 1997; and Maureen Dowd, "Integrity Clearance Sale," *New York Times,* December 20, 1997.

99. David E. Rosenbaum, "Senate Is Offered Sweeping Measure to Fight Smoking," *New York Times,* March 31, 1998.

100. Derthick.

101. Susan B. Garland, "What May Stub Out the Settlement," *Business Week,* September 8, 1997, 83.

102. "World Anti-Smoking Activists Decry U.S. Deal in Tobacco Suits," *Tampa Tribune,* August 28, 1997. See also Judith Mackay et al., "Statement of International Tobacco Control Advocates on U.S. Tobacco Litigation Settlement Discussions," 1997, http://legacy.library.ucsf.edu/tid/pbq63c00.

103. "Progress Against Tobacco," *Christian Science Monitor,* August 28, 1997.

104. Dean T. Jamison, Andrew Creese, and Thomson Prentice, "Combating the Tobacco Epidemic," *The World Health Report 1999* (Geneva: World Health Organization, 1999), 65–79.

105. Howard Kurtz, "The Democrat Who Switched and Fought: Former Gore Confidant Formulated Tobacco Industry's Effective Ad Blitz," *Washington Post,* June 19, 1998; and Kirk Victor, "McCain Gets Hit by Friendly Fire," *National Journal,* May 2, 1998, 994–995.

106. The tobacco industry ran a similar, ultimately unsuccessful campaign in California in 1988. See E. D. Balbach, M. P. Traynor, and S. A. Glantz, "The Implementation of California's Tobacco Tax Initiative: The Critical Role of Outsider Strategies in Protecting Proposition 99," *Journal of Health Politics, Policy, and Law* 25, no. 4 (2000): 689–715; and M. E. Begay, M. Traynor, and S. A. Glantz, "The Tobacco Industry, State Politics, and Tobacco Education in California," *American Journal of Public Health* 83, no. 9 (1993): 1214–1221.

107. Pertschuk, 248.

108. Robert J. Blendon and J. T. Young, "The Public and the Comprehensive Tobacco Bill," *JAMA* 280, no. 14 (1998): 1279–1284.

109. Jeffrey Goldberg, "Big Tobacco's Endgame," *New York Times Magazine,* June 21, 1998, 38, 62.

110. Ibid., 39.

111. Ibid., 36.

112. Barry Meiers, "Court Rejects FDA Authority over Tobacco," *New York Times,* August 15, 1998.

113. Ibid.

114. Eric Brazil, "Tobacco Firms Are 'Getting Off Cheap,'" *San Francisco Examiner,* November 12, 1998.

115. Allan M. Brandt and Julius B. Richmond, "Settling Short on Tobacco: Let the Trials Begin," *JAMA* 278, no. 12 (1997): 1028.

116. Brown & Williamson Tobacco Corporation, Lorillard Tobacco Company, Philip Morris Incorporated, R.J. Reynolds Tobacco Company, Commonwealth Tobacco, and Liggett & Myers. The Liggett Group, the last tobacco manufacturer to sign on, was released from its previous settlements with a number of states and will not have to contribute to the settlement fund unless its sales rise more than 25 percent over current levels.

117. Richard A. Daynard, *The Emperor's Fig Leaf: Draft Summary of AG Tobacco Deal Contains Few New Public Health Provisions and Lacks Many Critical Industry Concessions,* 1998, accessed June 27, 2006, from http://www.tobacco.neu.edu/tobacco_control/resources/msa/analysis_of_draft.htm.

118. Ralph Nader, "Perspective on the Tobacco Settlement: Marlboro Man Still in the Saddle," *Los Angeles Times,* November 24, 1998.

119. Brazil.

120. F. A. Sloan, C. A. Mathews, and J. G. Trogdon, "Impacts of the Master Settlement Agreement on the Tobacco Industry," *Tobacco Control* 13, no. 4 (2004): 356–361.

121. "Master Settlement Agreement, 1998," accessed July 2, 2006, at http://www.naag.org/tobac/cigmsa.rtf.

122. Kenneth E. Warner, "Cigarette Taxation: Doing Good by Doing Well," *Journal of Public Health Policy* 5, no. 3 (1984): 312–319; E. M. Lewitt and D. Coate, "The Potential for Using Excise Taxes to Reduce Smoking," *Journal of Health Economics* 1, no. 2 (1982): 121–145; and F. J. Chaloupka et al., "Tax, Price and Cigarette Smoking: Evidence from the Tobacco Documents and Implications for Tobacco Company Marketing Strategies," *Tobacco Control* 11 (Suppl 1) (2002): i62–i72.

123. M. Grossman and F. J. Chaloupka, "Cigarette Taxes: The Straw to Break the Camel's Back," *Public Health Reports* 112, no. 4 (1997): 290–297.

124. Chaloupka et al., "The Effects of Excise Taxes and Regulations on Cigarette Smoking," *Journal of Health Economics* 10, no. 1 (1991): 43–64; M. H. Showalter, "The Effect of Cigarette Taxes on Cigarette Consumption," *American Journal of Public Health* 88, no. 7 (1998): 1118–1119; K. J. Meier and M. J. Licari, "The Effect of Cigarette Taxes on Cigarette Consumption, 1955 through 1994," *American Journal of Public Health* 87, no. 7 (1997): 1126–1130; and Jonathan Gruber, "Youth Smoking in the U.S.: Prices and Policies" [Working Paper 7506], National Bureau of Economics Research (2000).

125. After declines since 1997, in 2006 the CDC reported that teen smoking rates had "plateaued." Centers for Disease Control and Prevention, National Youth Risk Behavior Survey, June 9, 2006.

126. Myron Levin, "States' Tobacco Settlement Has Failed to Clear the Air," *Los Angeles Times,* November 9, 2003.

127. H. K. Koh et al., "The First Decade of the Massachusetts Tobacco Control Program," *Public Health Reports* 120, no. 5 (2005): 482–495.

128. Levin, "States' Tobacco Settlement Has Failed to Clear the Air."

129. Richard A. Daynard, e-mail to Smokescreen mailing list, November 10, 1998.

130. Steven A. Schroeder, "Tobacco Control in the Wake of the 1998 Master Settlement Agreement," *New England Journal of Medicine* 350, no. 3 (2004): 293–301.

131. Daniel Gross, "Cigarette Burns: State Governments Learn the Cost of Their Addiction to Tobacco Revenues," *Slate,* April 3, 2003. *Price* was later overturned by the Illinois Supreme Court.

132. Dean Foust, "The High Cost of Nicotine Withdrawal," *Business Week,* May 23, 2005.

133. Vanessa O'Connell, "Big Tobacco Seeks $1.2 Billion Cut in Payments to States," *Wall Street Journal,* March 8, 2006.

134. Seth Stevenson, "How to Get Teens Not to Smoke: Prey on Their Insecurity," *Slate,* March 7, 2005.

135. M. C. Farrelly et al., "Evidence of a Dose-Response Relationship Between 'Truth' Anti-Smoking Ads and Youth Smoking Prevalence," *American Journal of Public Health* 95, no. 3 (2005): 425–431; and Lois Biener, et al., "Impact of Smoking Cessation Aids and Mass Media Among Recent Quitters," *American Journal of Preventive Medicine* 30, no. 3 (2006): 217–224. See also Cheryl Healton, "Who's Afraid of the Truth?" *American Journal of Public Health* 91, no. 4 (2001): 554–558.

136. The American Legacy Foundation, "The Truth," accessed July 5, 2006, at http://www.protectthetruth.org.

137. Myron Levin, "States' Tobacco Settlement Has Failed to Clear the Air."

138. Thomas Farragher, "Up in Smoke/First of Two Parts; Little of $246b Deal Fights Tobacco," *Boston Globe,* August 9, 2001.

139. Ibid.

140. Ibid.

141. Derthick; P. D. Jacobson and K. E. Warner, "Litigation and Public Health Policy Making: The Case of Tobacco Control," *Journal of Health Politics, Policy, and Law* 24, no. 4 (1999): 769–804; W. Kip Viscusi, ed., *Regulation Through Litigation* (Washington, DC: Brookings Institution, 2002); and Larry O. Gostin, *Public Health Law: Power, Duty, Restraint* (Berkeley: University of California Press, 2000).

142. Kenneth W. Dam, "Class Actions: Efficiency, Compensation, Deterrence, and Conflict of Interest," *Journal of Legal Studies* 4, no. 1 (1975): 47–73.

143. "The Tobacco Litigation and Attorneys' Fees," *Fordham Law Review* 67, no. 6 (1999): 2827–2858.

144. Jon D. Hanson and Kyle D. Logue, "The Costs of Cigarettes: The Economic Case for Ex Post Incentive-Based Regulation," *Yale Law Journal* 107, no. 5 (1998): 1163–1362.

145. Brandt and Richmond.

146. On the debates about litigation and policy, see especially Lynn Mather, "Theorizing About Trial Courts: Lawyers, Policymaking, and Tobacco Litigation," *Law & Social Inquiry* 23, no. 4 (1998): 897–940; Peter D. Jacobson and Soheil Soliman, "Litigation as Public Health Policy: Theory or Reality?" *Journal of Law, Medicine & Ethics* 30, no. 2 (2002): 224–238; and Peter D. Jacobson and Kenneth E. Warner, "Litigation and Public Health Policy Making: The Case of Tobacco Control," *Journal of Health Politics, Policy and Law* 24, no. 4 (1999): 769–804.

147. National Association of Attorneys General, "Cigarette Sales in U.S. Reach Historic 55-Year Low," press release, March 8, 2006.

148. N. A. Rigotti, "Clinical Practice. Treatment of Tobacco Use and Dependence," *New England Journal of Medicine* 346, no. 7 (2002): 506–512; and S. Zhu, T. Melcer, J. Sun, B. Rosbrook, and J. P. Pierce, "Smoking Cessation with and without Assistance: A Population-Based Analysis," *American Journal of Preventive Medicine* 18, no. 4 (2000): 305–311.

149. E. M. Barbeau, A. Leavy-Sperounis, and E. D. Balbach, "Smoking, Social Class, and Gender: What Can Public Health Learn from the Tobacco Industry About Disparities in Smoking?" *Tobacco Control* 13, no. 2 (2004): 115–120; P. M. Lantz et al., "Socioeconomic Disparities in Health Change in a Longitudinal Study of U.S. Adults: The Role of Health-Risk Behaviors," *Social Science and Medicine* 53, no. 1 (2001): 29–40; D. A. Lawlor et al., "Smoking and Ill Health: Does Lay Epidemiology Explain the Failure of Smoking Cessation Programs Among Deprived Populations?" *American Journal of Public Health* 93, no. 2 (2003): 266–270; and *Clinical Practice Guideline: Treating Tobacco Use and Dependence,* ed. Michael C. Fiore (Washington, DC: U.S. Department of Health and Human Services, 2000).

150. On recent policy debates, see especially the work of economist Kenneth Warner, "The Effects of the Anti-Smoking Campaign on Cigarette Consumption," *American Journal of Public Health* 67, no. 7 (1977), 645–650; "Health and Economic Implications of a Tobacco-Free Society," *JAMA* 258, no. 15 (1987): 2080–2086; "The Economics of Tobacco: Myths and Realities," *Tobacco Control* 9, no. 1 (2000): 78–89. See also Stephen L. Isaacs and Steven A. Schroeder, "Where the Public Good Prevailed: Government's Public-Health Successes," *American Prospect,* June 4, 2001, http://www.prospect.org/web/printfriendly-view.ww?id=5737; K. Michael Cummings, "Programs and Policies to Discourage the Use of Tobacco Products," *Oncogene* 21, no. 48 (2002): 7349–7364; and John B. McKinlay and Lisa D. Marceau, "Upstream Healthy Public Policy: Lessons from the Battle of Tobacco," *International Journal of Health Services* 20, no. 1 (2000): 49–69.

151. U.S. Department of Health and Human Services, *The Health Consequences of Smoking: A Report of the Surgeon General* (Washington, DC: U.S. Department of Health and Human Services, Centers for Disease Control and Prevention, National Center for Chronic Disease Prevention and Health Promotion, Office on Smoking and Health, 2004).

152. H. Ahsan and D. C. Thomas, "Lung Cancer Etiology: Independent and Joint Effects of Genetics, Tobacco, and Arsenic," *JAMA* 292, no. 24 (2004): 3026–3029; N. Risch, "Dissecting Racial and Ethnic Differences," *New England Journal of Medicine* 354, no. 4 (2006): 408–411; and R. Bayer, and J. Stuber, "Tobacco Control, Stigma, and Public Health: Rethinking the Relations," *American Journal of Public Health* 96, no. 1 (2006): 47–50.

153. A. Chapple, S. Ziebland, and A. McPherson, "Stigma, Shame, and Blame Experienced by Patients with Lung Cancer: Qualitative Study," *British Medical Journal* 328, no. 7454 (2004): 1470–1474.

154. Carey Goldberg, "Changing the Face of Lung Cancer," *Boston Globe,* September 26, 2005; Virginia Anderson, "Blame, Shame Overshadow Real Plight of Lung Cancer Sufferers: There's Still No Clear Way to Catch It Early," *Atlanta Journal-Constitution,* August 16, 2005.

155. Howard M. Leichter, *Free to Be Foolish* (Princeton, NJ: Princeton University Press, 1991), 134–142.

156. Cass R. Sunstein, *Laws of Fear: Beyond the Precautionary Principle* (New York: Cambridge University Press, 2005); Cass R. Sunstein, *Risk and Reason: Safety, Law and the Environment* (New York: Cambridge University Press, 2002); and Paul Slovic, *The Perception of Risk* (Sterling, VA: Earthscan Publications, 2000).

157. Philip Morris USA Web site, http://www.pmusa.com.

158. Lois Biener, "Anti-Tobacco Advertisements by Massachusetts and Philip Morris: What Teenagers Think," *Tobacco Control* 11 (Suppl 2) (2002): ii43–ii46; P. A. McDaniel, E. A. Smith, and R. E. Malone, "Philip Morris's Project Sunrise: Weakening Tobacco Control by Working with It," *Tobacco Control* 15, no. 3 (2006): 215–223; and Krueger's posts on "Tobacco On Trial," http://www.tobacco-on-trial.com.

159. Allan M. Brandt, "Behavior, Disease, and Health in Twentieth Century America: The Moral Valence of Individual Risk," *Morality and Health,* eds. Allan M. Brandt and Paul Rozin (New York: Routledge, 1997), 53–77. See also James A. Morone, *Hellfire Nation: The Politics of Sin in American* History (New Haven, CT: Yale University Press, 2003); Dan E. Beauchamp, *The Health of the Republic: Epidemics, Medicine, and Moralism as Challenges to Democracy* (Philadelphia: Temple University Press, 1988); and Dan Wikler, "Personal and Social Responsibility for Health," *Public Health, Ethics, and Equity,* eds. Fabienne Peter, Amartya Sen, and Sudhir Anand (Oxford: Oxford University Press, 2005).

Chapter 13

1. Robert J. Cole, "Record Export Sales Forecast for U.S. Cigarette Producers," *New York Times,* November 7, 1962.

2. David E. Sanger, "For Helms, His Home State Is Source of Foreign Policy," *New York Times,* April 2, 1996.

3. Roger Scruton, *WHO, What and Why? Trans-National Government, Legitimacy and the World Health Organization* (London: Institute of Economic Affairs, 2000).

4. Quoted in Bryan Burrough and John Helyar, *Barbarians at the Gate: The Fall of RJR Nabisco* (New York: HarperCollins, 1990), 218.

5. "Cigarette Smoking Among Adults—United States, 2004," *Morbidity and Mortality Weekly Report* 54, no. 44 (2005).

6. Centers for Disease Control, "Smoking Prevalence Among U.S. Adults, 2002," accessed March 26, 2004, at http://www.cdc.gov/tobacco/research_data/adults_prev/prevali.htm.

7. A. Jemal et al., "Cancer Statistics, 2006," *CA: A Cancer Journal for Clinicians* 56, no. 2 (2006): 106–130.

8. Spencer Rich, "Cigarette-Related Deaths Decline," *Washington Post,* August 27, 1993; and A. J. Alberg and J. M. Samet, "Epidemiology of Lung Cancer," *Chest* 123 (1 Suppl) (2003): 21S–49S.

9. "Cigarette Smoking Among Adults—United States, 2000," *Morbidity and Mortality Weekly Report* 51, no. 29 (2002): 642–645.

10. B. L. Nordstrom et al., "Predictors of Continued Smoking over 25 Years of Follow-up in the Normative Aging Study," *American Journal of Public Health* 90, no. 3 (2000): 404–406.

11. For a comparative assessment of Western regulatory approaches, see Donley T. Studlar, *Tobacco Control: Comparative Politics in the United States and Canada* (Toronto: Broadview, 2002).

12. Carl E. Bartecchi, Thomas D. MacKenzie, and Robert W. Schrier, "The Global Tobacco Epidemic," *Scientific American,* May 1995, 44–51; Susan Headden, "The Marlboro Man Lives!" *U.S. News & World Report,* September 21, 1998; Jane Perlez, "Fenced In at Home, Marlboro Man Looks Abroad," *New York Times,* June 24, 1997; and Paul Klebnikov, "Opiate of the Masses," *Forbes,* April 11, 1994, 74–75.

13. U.S. Department of Agriculture, *Tobacco Situation and Outlook Report* (Washington, DC: U.S. Department of Agriculture, 1995).

14. Robert Franklin Durden, *The Dukes of Durham, 1865–1929* (Durham, NC: Duke University Press, 1975), 73.

15. F. J. Chaloupka and A. Laixuthai, "U.S. Trade Policy and Cigarette Smoking in Asia" [Working Paper W5543], National Bureau of Economic Research (1996); and P. Jha et al., "Estimates of Global and Regional Smoking Prevalence in 1995, by Age and Sex," *American Journal of Public Health* 92, no. 6 (2002): 1002–1006.

16. Judith Mackay, Michael Eriksen, and Omar Shafey, *The Tobacco Atlas,* 2nd ed. (Atlanta, GA: American Cancer Society, 2006); and Robert N. Proctor, "Tobacco and the Global Lung Cancer Epidemic," *Nature Reviews Cancer* 1, no. 1 (2001): 82–88.

17. Majid Ezzati and Alan D. Lopez, "Estimates of Global Mortality Attributable to Smoking in 2000," *Lancet* 362, no. 9387 (2003): 847–852.

18. Nancy J. Kaufman and Mimi Nichter, "The Marketing of Tobacco to Women: Global Perspectives," *Women and the Tobacco Epidemic: Challenges for the 21st Century,* eds. Jonathan M. Samet and Soon-Young Yoon (Geneva: World Health Organization, 2001), 69–98.

19. Bo-Qi Liu et al., "Emerging Tobacco Hazards in China: 1. Retrospective Proportional Mortality Study of One Million Deaths," *British Medical Journal* 317, no. 7170 (1998): 1411–1422; World Health Organization, *Making a Difference* (Geneva: World Health Report, 1999); Kenneth E. Warner, "Tobacco," *Foreign Policy* (May/June 2002): 20–28; and Glenn Frankel and Steven Mufson, "Vast China Market Key to Smoking Disputes," *Washington Post,* November 20, 1996. On changing cultural norms in China, see Matthew Kohrmann, "Should I Quit? Tobacco, Fraught Identity, and the Risks of Govermentality in Urban China," *Urban Anthropology* 33, no. 2 (2004): 211–245.

20. President William Clinton, State of the Union Address, 2000.

21. Gill Walt, "Globalisation of International Health," *Lancet* 351, no. 9100 (1998): 434–437; and David P. Fidler, "International Law and Global Public Health," *Kansas Law Review* 48, no. 1 (1999).

22. Hugh Cullman, "Partners in Progress: A Report on Philip Morris in the Developing Countries" (New York: Corporate Affairs Department, Philip Morris), 1977, Bates No. 2015006022/6039, http://legacy.library.ucsf.edu/tid/ksk68e00.

23. Chaloupka; Brown & Williamson, "Priority 3: Expand and Grow Internationally," 1987, Bates No. 635616578/6597; Robert Weissman and Ross Hammond, "International Tobacco Sales," *Foreign Policy in Focus* 3, no. 17 (2000); Clyde H. Farnsworth, "Section 301 Is Polished as U.S. Trade Weapon," *New York Times,* August 27, 1985; Clyde H. Farnsworth, "Trade Pact Set with Taiwan," *New York Times,* December 9, 1986; United States General Accounting Office, *Trade and Health Issues: Dichotomy Between U.S. Tobacco Export Policy and Antismoking Initiatives,* (1990) [*Trade and Health Issues: Dichotomy*]; Clyde H. Farnsworth, "Freer World Trade Falls Victim to Its Own Success," *New York Times,* October 27, 1990; United States General Accounting Office, *International Trade: Advertising and Promoting U.S. Cigarettes in Selected Asian Countries,* (1992).

24. "DRAFT: 1982 Analysis: Tobacco Sales in Developing Countries," 1982, Bates No. 2025038090/8097, http://legacy.library.ucsf.edu/tid/vpb81f00.

25. Ibid.; Rene Scull, "Bright Future Predicted for Asia Pacific," *World Tobacco* 94 (1986): 35; and Stan Sesser, "Opium War Redux," *New Yorker,* September 13, 1993, 77–89.

26. Jonathan Watts, "China Promises to Dash Hopes of Tobacco Industry Giants," *Lancet* 363, no. 9402 (2004): 50; D. Yach, "Injecting Greater Urgency into Global Tobacco Control," *Tobacco Control* 14, no. 3 (2005): 145–148; and Wu Zhong, "China: A Smoker's Paradise." *Asia Times,* July 11, 2006.

27. Glenn Frankel and Steven Mufson, "Vast China Market Key to Smoking Disputes," *Washington Post,* November 20, 1996; Bo-Qi Liu et al.; A. D. Lopez, "Counting the Dead in China: Measuring Tobacco's Impact in the Developing World," *British Medical Journal* 317, no. 7170 (1998): 1399–1400; and Shi-Ru Niu et al., "Emerging Tobacco Hazards in China: 2. Early Mortality Results from a Prospective Study," *British Medical Journal* 317, no. 7170 (1998): 1423–1424.

28. Headden.

29. Derek Yach and Douglas Bettcher, "Globalisation of Tobacco Industry Influence and New Global Responses," *Tobacco Control* 9, no. 2 (2000): 207.

30. Mike Levin, "U.S. Tobacco Firms Push Eagerly into Asian Market," *Marketing News,* January 21, 1991, 2.

31. Burson-Marsteller, "Position Paper, First Draft: The Effect of Product Liability Litigation on Tobacco Industry Stocks," 1988, Bates No. 2021269356/9374, http://legacy.library.ucsf.edu/

tid/mih48d00. For more on the tobacco industry's interest in international markets, see Mike Levin, "U.S. Tobacco Firms Push Eagerly into Asian Market"; Sesser; and Philip Shenon, "Asia's Having One Huge Nicotine Fit," *New York Times*, May 15, 1994.

32. William Ecenbarger, "We Are the World: The Americanization of Everywhere," *Plain Dealer*, August 15, 1993.

33. Ibid.

34. Glenn Frankel, "U.S. Aided Cigarette Firms in Conquests Across Asia," *Washington Post*, November 17, 1996.

35. P. Jha et al.; "U.S. Mortality Public Use Data Tapes 1960–1999," *U.S. Mortality Volumes 1930–1959* (National Center for Health Statistics, Centers for Disease Control and Prevention, 2002).

36. Kaufman and Nichter.

37. Ibid.

38. "Women's Cigarette Market," Bates No. 500734972/5015; G. N. Connolly, "Worldwide Expansion of Transnational Tobacco Industry," *Journal of the National Cancer Institute* 12 (1992): 29–35; Katherine Deland, Karen Lewis, and Allyn L. Taylor, "Developing a Public Policy Response to the Tobacco Industry's Targeting of Women and Girls: The Role of the WHO Framework Convention on Tobacco Control," *Journal of the American Medical Women's Association* 55, no. 5 (2000): 316–320; Virginia Ernster et al., "Women and Tobacco: Moving from Policy to Action," *Bulletin of the World Health Organization* 78, no. 7 (2000): 891–901; and Kaufman and Nichter; R. Richmond, "You've Come a Long Way Baby: Women and the Tobacco Epidemic," *Addiction* 98, no. 5 (2003): 553–557.

39. Headden.

40. World Health Organization, *Tobacco and the Rights of the Child* (Geneva: World Health Organization, 2001).

41. Ron Scherer and Howard LaFranchi, "Taking Tobacco out of Mouth of Babes," *Christian Science Monitor*, March 17, 1999; Connolly; Ernest Beck and Gordon Fairclough, "BAT Aims to Open Stores with Luckies-Logo Theme—Hip Urban Outlets Would Carry 'American Original' Items Including Clothing, Candy," *Wall Street Journal*, October 27, 2000; Sesser; World Conference on Tobacco OR Health, "WHO Chief Warns Tough Times Ahead for Global Tobacco Control Treaty," press release, April 8, 2003; United Nations General Assembly, "Convention on the Rights of the Child," September 2, 1990; Centers for Disease Control and Prevention, *The Health Consequences of Involuntary Exposure to Tobacco Smoke: A Report of the Surgeon General* (Atlanta, GA: U.S. Department of Health and Human Services, 2006).

42. Clyde H. Farnsworth, "Enforcing Reagan's New Trade Policy," *New York Times*, November 24, 1985; Clyde H. Farnsworth, "Section 301 Is Polished as U.S. Trade Weapon," *New York Times*, August 27, 1985; Louis Uchitelle, "A Crowbar for Carla Hills," *New York Times*, June 10, 1990; Peter Schmeisser, "Pushing Cigarettes Overseas," *New York Times Magazine*, July 10, 1988; "U.S. Delays Thai Action," *New York Times*, May 26, 1990; Sesser; Glenn Frankel, "U.S. Aided Cigarette Firms in Conquests Across Asia"; and Robert Weissman, *International Trade Agreements and Tobacco Control: Threats to Public Health and the Case for Excluding Tobacco from Trade Agreements* (Washington, DC: Essential Action, 2003).

43. Frankel.

44. Philip J. Hilts, "Health Dept. Softens Stance on Cigarette Exports," *New York Times*, May 18, 1990; Philip J. Hilts, "Thailand's Cigarette Ban Upset," *New York Times*, October 4, 1990; Daniel R. Seely, "Death by the Pack for the Third World," *New York Times*, October 30, 1990; Paul Taylor, "GATT: U.S. and Thailand in Brief Harmony Amid Discord," *Financial Times*, December 6, 1990; Chaloupka and Laixuthai; Sesser; John Bloom, *Public Health, International Trade, and the Framework Convention on Tobacco Control* (Washington, DC: American Cancer Society

and Campaign for Tobacco-Free Kids, 2001); and Joy de Beyer and Linda Waverley Brigden, *Tobacco Control Policy: Strategies, Successes and Setbacks* (Geneva: World Bank, 2003).

45. Frankel; Chaloupka and Laixuthai; Anna White and Robert Weissman, "The Hand-off to Big Tobacco: IMF Support for Privatization of State-Owned Tobacco Enterprises," *Multinational Monitor* 23, no. 9 (2002).

46. Frankel.

47. Ibid.

48. Chaloupka and Laixuthai.

49. Frankel.

50. "Thailand Lifts Cigarette Ban," *New York Times,* October 10, 1990; Sesser; S. Haman, "Thailand: Victories and Defeats in the Long War," *Tobacco Control* 12, no. 1 (2003): 8; Taylor; Philip J. Hilts, "Thailand's Cigarette Ban Upset," *New York Times,* October 4, 1990; Chantornvong and McCargo, "Political Economy of Tobacco Control in Thailand," *Tobacco Control* 10, no. 1 (2001): 48–54; and Frankel.

51. Glenn Frankel, "Thailand Resists U.S. Brand Assault," *Washington Post,* November 18, 1996.

52. Joseph N. Eckhardt, "Balancing Interests in Free Trade and Health: How the WHO's Framework Convention on Tobacco Control Can Withstand WTO Scrutiny," *Duke Journal of Comparative and International Law* 12, no. 1 (2002): 197–230; GATT, *Thailand—Restrictions on Importation of and Internal Taxes on Cigarettes* (1990).

53. Thomas Schoenbaum, "WTO Dispute Settlement: Praise and Suggestions for Reform," *International and Comparative Law Quarterly* 47 (1998): 647–658; Ira S. Shapiro, "Treating Cigarettes as an Exception to the Trade Rule," *SAIS Review* 22, no. 1 (2002): 87–96; and Weissman.

54. *Thailand—Restrictions on Importation of and Internal Taxes on Cigarettes.*

55. Ibid.; and Bloom.

56. *Thailand—Restrictions on Importation of and Internal Taxes on Cigarettes;* and Bloom.

57. *Thailand—Restrictions on Importation of and Internal Taxes on Cigarettes;* Bloom; Carlos Correa, "Implementing National Public Health Policies in the Framework of WTO Agreements," *Journal of World Trade* 34, no. 5 (2000): 113; and Ron Scherer, "World Cracks Down on Big Tobacco," *Christian Science Monitor,* May 22, 2003.

58. *Thailand—Restrictions on Importation of and Internal Taxes on Cigarettes.*

59. Weissman.

60. Schoenbaum.

61. Correa, 94; and Schoenbaum.

62. "Global Tobacco Trade: U.S. Policy and American Cigarettes," Bates Nos. TI02861448–99, 1457, http://tobaccodocuments.org/nysa_ti_s4/TI02861448.html.

63. *Thailand—Restrictions on Importation of and Internal Taxes on Cigarettes;* and A. Taylor et al., "The Impact of Trade Liberalization on Tobacco Consumption," in *Tobacco Control in Developing Countries,* eds. Prabhat Jha and Frank Chaloupka (Oxford: Oxford University Press, 2000).

64. Frankel, "Thailand Resists U.S. Brand Assault."

65. Ibid.

66. Ibid.; S. Chantornvong and D. McCargo, "Political Economy of Tobacco Control in Thailand," *Tobacco Control* 10, no. 1 (2001): 48–54; Haman; P. Vateesatokit, B. Hughes, and B. Ritthphakdee, "Thailand: Winning Battles, but the War's Far from Over," *Tobacco Control* 9, no. 2 (2000): 122–127; and Global Analysis Project, "Political Economy of Tobacco Control in Low-Income and Middle-Income Countries: Lessons from Thailand and Zimbabwe," *Bulletin of the World Health Organization* 78, no. 7 (2000): 913–919.

67. Philip Shenon, "Asia's Having One Huge Nicotine Fit," *New York Times,* May 15, 1994.

68. Robert Pear, "Embassy Asks Trade Caution," *New York Times,* May 16, 1989; Frankel, "U.S. Aided Cigarette Firms in Conquests across Asia."

69. Sesser, 85.

70. Sesser; Richard Kluger, *Ashes to Ashes* (New York: Knopf, 1996), 714; and Headden.

71. Frankel, "U.S. Aided Cigarette Firms in Conquests Across Asia"; and *Trade and Health Issues: Dichotomy.*

72. Kluger, 713.

73. M. E. Muggli and R. D. Hurt, "Tobacco Industry Strategies to Undermine the 8th World Conference on Tobacco or Health," *Tobacco Control* 12 (2003): 195–202.

74. British American Tobacco, "Statement on BAT Industries' Tobacco Interests in Developing Countries," 1982, Bates No. 2501021383/1385, http://legacy.library.ucsf.edu/tid/agx19e00.

75. G. A. Dalley, "The World Health Organization's Campaign on Smoking and Health: Some Thoughts on a Corporate Response" [memo to Donald S. Harris, Philip Morris], 1984, Bates No. 2023272993/2996, http://legacy.library.ucsf.edu/tid/xyv36e00.

76. Monique E. Muggli et al., "The Smoke You Don't See: Uncovering Tobacco Industry Scientific Strategies Aimed Against Environmental Tobacco Smoke Policies," *American Journal of Public Health* (2001): 1419–1423; British American Tobacco, "Statement on BAT Industries' Tobacco Interests in Developing Countries"; Jorge R. Basso, "8th World Conference on Tobacco OR Health" [letter from Jorge R. Basso Dastugue of BATCo. to Sharon Boyse of BATCo.], 1992, Bates No. 300504295/4298, http://www.library.ucsf.edu/tobacco/batco/html/14400/14454; and George A. Dalley, "The World Health Organization's Campaign on Smoking and Health: Some Thoughts on a Corporate Response" [memo to Donald S. Harris, Philip Morris], 1984, Bates No. 2023272993/2996.

77. "8th World Conference on Tobacco OR Health."

78. Ruth Roemer, Allyn Taylor, and Jean Lariviere, "Origins of the WHO Framework Convention for Tobacco Control," *American Journal of Public Health* 95, no. 6 (2005): 936–938; and Ruth Roemer and Allyn L. Taylor.

79. David P. Fidler, "The Future of the World Health Organization: What Role for International Law?" *Vanderbilt Journal of Transnational Law* 31, no. 1079 (1998); and Fidler, "International Law and Global Public Health."

80. Allyn Lise Taylor, "Making the World Health Organization Work: A Legal Framework for Universal Access to the Conditions for Health," *American Journal of Law and Medicine* 18, no. 4 (1992): 301–346; and Michelle Forrest, "Using the Power of the World Health Organization: The International Health Regulations and the Future of International Health Law," *Columbia Journal of Law and Social Problems* 33 (1999–2000): 153–179.

81. *International Strategy for Tobacco Control* (Geneva: World Health Organization, Programme on Substance Abuse, 1996), 38 [*International Strategy for Tobacco Control*]; and Christopher J. Murray and Alan D. Lopez, "Evidence-Based Health Policy—Lessons from the Global Burden of Disease Study," *Science* 274, no. 5288 (1996): 740–743.

82. Weissman, 26; also cited as the "later in time" rule in Taylor, 350; Vienna Convention on the Law of Treaties, 1969; and Roemer, Taylor, and Lariviere, 936–938.

83. Mia Malan and Rosemary Leaver, "Political Change in South Africa: New Tobacco Control and Public Health Policies," in *Tobacco Control Policy: Strategies, Successes and Setbacks,* eds. Joy de Beyer and Linda Waverley (Washington, DC: World Bank, 2003), 121–153.

84. Roddey Reid, *Globalizing Tobacco Control: Anti-Smoking Campaigns in California, France, and Japan* (Bloomington: Indiana University Press, 2005); and Stephen Smith, "Global War on Smoking Uses Bay State Battle Plan," *Boston Globe,* June 26, 2002. For more on state antitobacco campaigns, see H. K. Koh et al., "The First Decade of the Massachusetts Tobacco Control Program," *Public Health Reports* 120, no. 5 (2005): 482–495; Stanton A. Glantz and Edith D. Balbach, *Tobacco War: Inside the California Battles* (Berkeley: University of California Press, 2000); and John P. Pierce et al., "Has the California Tobacco Control Program Reduced Smoking?" *JAMA* 280, no. 10 (1998): 893–899.

85. Stephen Smith, "Global War on Smoking Uses Bay State Battle Plan," *Boston Globe*, June 26, 2002; and Witold Zatonski, "Democracy and Health: Tobacco Control in Poland," in *Tobacco Control Policy: Strategies, Successes and Setbacks.*

86. Prakit Vateesatokit, "Tailoring Tobacco Control Efforts to the Country: The Example of Thailand," in *Tobacco Control Policy: Strategies, Successes and Setbacks*, 154–178.

87. F. Howell, "Smoke-Free Bars in Ireland: A Runaway Success," in *Tobacco Control* 14, no. 2 (2005): 73–74.

88. Roemer, Taylor, and Lariviere, 936–938.

89. Gavin Yamey, "WHO in 2002: Interview with Gro Brundtland," *British Medical Journal* 325 (2002): 1355–1358.

90. Richard Smith, "The WHO: Change or Die," *British Medical Journal* 310 (1995): 543–544.

91. Ibid.; R. Horton, "WHO: The Casualties and Compromises of Renewal," *Lancet* 359, no. 9317 (2002): 1605–1611; and Yamey, 1355.

92. Henry J. Waxman, "The Future of the Global Tobacco Treaty Negotiations," *New England Journal of Medicine* 346, no. 12 (2002).

93. *International Strategy for Tobacco Control.*

94. *The Framework Convention on Tobacco Control: A Primer* (World Health Organization, 2003); Jeff Collin, Kelley Lee, and Karen Bissell, "The Framework Convention on Tobacco Control: The Politics of Global Health Governance," *Third World Quarterly—Journal of Emerging Areas* 23, no. 2 (2002): 265–282; David P. Fidler, *World Health Organization's Framework Convention for Tobacco Control*, March 28, 2003, American Society of International Law, http://www.asil.org/insights/insigh100.htm; *International Strategy for Tobacco Control*; and David Satcher, "Why We Need an International Agreement on Tobacco Control," *American Journal of Public Health* 91, no. 2 (2001): 191–193.

95. Sabin Russell, "Ex-Clinton Official Rips White House on Tobacco Treaty," *San Francisco Chronicle*, February 13, 2003; "U.S. Accused of Hampering Tobacco Control Talks," *Nation's Health* 32, no. 4 (2002); Alison Langley, "Anti-Tobacco Pact Gains Despite Firms' Lobbying," *Washington Post*, May 30, 2003; and Marc Kaufman, "U.S. Seeks to Alter Anti-Tobacco Treaty; 'Reservations' Clause Sought as Way Out of Some Provisions," *Washington Post*, April 30, 2003.

96. Kaufman; Clare Kapp, "Who Chief Endorses Diluted Antitobacco Text," *Lancet* 361, no. 9354 (2003): 315; and Kapp, "Tobacco-Control Treaty Language Approved Despite Objections," *Lancet* 361, no. 9360 (2003): 839–840.

97. Russell; Barry Yeoman, "Secondhand Diplomacy," *Mother Jones*, March/April 2003, 15–16; and "U.S. Accused of Hampering Tobacco Control Talks."

98. Henry J. Waxman, Letter to President George W. Bush, August 2, 2001, accessed August 12, 2003, at http://www.house.gov/reform/min/pdfs/pdf_inves/pdf_tobacco_control_let_bush.pdf.

99. Marc Kaufman, "Negotiator in Global Tobacco Talks Quits; Official Said to Chafe at Softer U.S. Stands," *Washington Post*, August 2, 2001; Waxman; "About-Face on Tobacco Pact," *New York Times*, May 24, 2003; and Marc Kaufman, "U.S. Signs Tobacco Control Treaty," *Washington Post*, May 12, 2004.

100. Mongoven, Biscoe & Duchin, Inc, "An Analysis of the International Framework Convention Process: Executive Summary—the WHO Tobacco Control Convention," 1997, Bates No. 2074292077/2082, http://legacy.library.ucsf.edu/tid/wqp87d00.

101. Ibid., 33.

102. Ibid., 3.

103. Ibid., 33. See also Stacy M. Carter, "Mongoven, Biscoe & Duchin: Destroying Tobacco Control Activism from the Inside," *Tobacco Control* 11, no. 2 (2002): 112–118.

104. Committee of Experts on Tobacco Industry Documents, *Tobacco Company Strategies to Undermine Tobacco Control Activities at the World Health Organization* (Geneva: WHO, 2000). The WHO committee of experts comprises Thomas Zeltner, MD, director of the Swiss Federal

Office of Public Health; former FDA Commissioner David A. Kessler, MD; Anke Martiny, PhD, a former member of the German Parliament; and Fazel Randera, MD, inspector general of intelligence for South Africa and a former member of that country's Truth and Reconciliation Commission.

105. WHO Framework Convention on Tobacco Control, Art. 2 (2003).

106. Ibid.

107. World Health Organization, *WTO Agreements & Public Health* (Geneva: World Trade Organization, 2002).

108. Ibid.; Eckhardt; Neil Collishaw, Cynthia Callard, and Michelle Swenarchuk, "Trade Agreements and Tobacco Control: How WTO Agreements May Stand in the Way of Reducing Tobacco Use," *Development Bulletin* 54 (2000): 11–14; and Shapiro.

109. Bloom, 200; Cynthia Callard, Neil Collishaw, and Michelle Swenarchuk, *An Introduction to International Trade Agreements and Their Impact on Public Measures to Reduce Tobacco Use* (Ottawa: Physicians for a Smoke-Free Canada, 2001); Sinclair, 2000; and General Agreement on Trade and Services.

110. World Health Organization, *WTO Agreements & Public Health* (Geneva: World Trade Organization, 2002); Eckhardt; Collishaw, Callard, Swenarchuk, "Trade Agreements and Tobacco Control: How WTO Agreements May Stand in the Way of Reducing Tobacco Use"; and Shapiro.

111. World Health Organization, *WTO Agreements & Public Health*; Derek Yach, "Tobacco Control: From Concern for the Lung to Global Political Action," *Thorax* 56, no. 4 (2001): 247–248; D. Yach and D. Bettcher, "The Globalization of Public Health, I: Threats and Opportunities," *American Journal of Public Health* 88, no. 5 (1998): 735–738; Yach and Bettcher, "The Globalization of Public Health, II: The Convergence of Self-Interest and Altruism," *American Journal of Public Health* 88, no 5 (1998): 738–741; and Gavin Yamey, "Why Does the World Still Need the WHO?" *British Medical Journal* 325, no. 7375 (2002): 1294–1298.

112. Shapiro, 93.

113. Ibid., 89.

114. Derek Yach, "WHO Framework Convention on Tobacco Control," *Lancet* 361, no. 9357 (2003): 611–612.

115. Derek Yach, Message from Dr. Derek Yach, 2003, available from http://www.procor.org/discussion/displaymsg.asp?ref=1287&cate=ProCOR+Dialogue.

116. "WHO Adopts Strict Tobacco Control Plan," *Hotels*, July 1, 2003, 60; "World Cracks Down on Big Tobacco," *Christian Science Monitor*, May 22, 2003.

117. Alison Langley, "World Health Meeting Approves Treaty to Discourage Smoking," *New York Times*, May 22, 2003; and Ron Scherer, "World Cracks Down on Big Tobacco," *Christian Science Monitor*, May 22, 2003.

118. British American Tobacco, *1999 Annual Review* (2000).

119. Roger Scruton, "WHO, What and Why? Trans-National Government, Legitimacy and the World Health Organization," 2000, Bates No. 2084588179/8238.

120. Kevin Maguire and Julian Borger, "Scruton in Media Plot to Push Sale of Cigarettes," *Guardian*, January 1, 2002.

121. Maguire and Borger; Alexander Stille, "Advocating Tobacco, on the Payroll of Tobacco," *New York Times*, March 23, 2002; and Sophie Scruton, "Memo to Quentin Browell, Japan Tobacco," 2002, http://www.ash.org.uk/html/conduct/pdfs/scruton.pdf. On efforts of the tobacco industry to influence cultural and academic discussion of tobacco, see Philip Morris, "Chronology and Development of Project Cosmic," 1988, Bates No. 2023919844/9846, http://legacy.library.ucsf.edu/tid/rbv88e00; and Robert N. Proctor, "Should Medical Historians Be Working for the Tobacco Industry?" *Lancet* 363, no. 9410 (2004): 1174–1175.

122. "Globalisation and Business Integrity," British American Tobacco Web site, http://www.bat.com/oneweb/sites/uk__3mnfen.nsf/0/0c8b098b3046982a80256bf400019871?OpenDocument.

123. Ibid.

124. Derek Yach, "Injecting Greater Urgency into Global Tobacco Control," *Tobacco Control* 14, no. 3 (2005): 145–148.

125. Christopher J. L. Murray and Alan D. Lopez, "Evidence-Based Health Policy—Lessons from the Global Burden of Disease Study," *Science* 274, no. 5288 (1996): 740–743.

126. Howard Barnum, "The Economic Burden of the Global Trade in Tobacco," *Tobacco Control* 3 (1994): 358–361.

127. Judith Mackay, Michael Eriksen, and Omar Shafey, *The Tobacco Atlas*, 2nd ed. (Atlanta, GA: American Cancer Society, 2006).

128. Norman Daniels, *Just Health Care* (New York: Cambridge University Press, 1985).

129. G. H. Brundtland, 1998. See also Derek Yach and Douglas Bettcher, "The Globalization of Public Health, I: Threats and Opportunities," *American Journal of Public Health* 88, no. 5 (1998): 735–738; and Derek Yach and Douglas Bettcher, "The Globalization of Public Health, II: The Convergence of Self-Interest and Altruism," *American Journal of Public Health* 88, no. 5 (1998): 738–741.

Epilogue

1. "The Threat of Biological Weapons," *New York Review of Books,* April 13, 2000.

2. "Trial Testimony of Lacy K. Ford, Ph.D.," *Jones v. R.J. Reynolds Tobacco Co.* (2000); and "Deposition of Lacy K. Ford, Ph.D.," *Engle v. R.J. Reynolds Tobacco Co.,* 1999.

3. Dan Zegart, *Civil Warriors: The Legal Siege on the Tobacco Industry* (New York: Delacorte, 2000).

4. Order, *United States v. Philip Morris, et al.,* November 28, 2000 [116 F.Supp. 2d 131 (D.D.C. 2000)].

5. Stasia Mosesso, "Up in Smoke: How the Proximate Cause Battle Extinguished the Tobacco War," *Notre Dame Law Review* 76, no. 1 (2000): 257–340.

6. *Litigation Against Tobacco Companies,* Civil Division, U.S. Department of Justice, 1999–2006 (available from http://www.usdoj.gov/civil/cases/tobacco2).

7. "Expert Statement of Theodore Wilson," *United States v. Philip Morris, et al.* (2002); and "Expert Statement of Peter English," *United States v. Philip Morris, et al.* (2002).

8. "Expert Statement of Kenneth Ludmerer," *United States v. Philip Morris, et al.* (2002), 3, 5.

9. "Deposition of Kenneth Ludmerer, M.D.," *Engle v. R.J. Reynolds Tobacco Co.* (1998).

10. Robert N. Proctor, "'Everyone Knew But No One Had Proof': Tobacco Industry Use of Medical History Expertise in US Courts, 1990–2002," *Tobacco Control* 15 (Suppl 4) (2006): iv117–iv125; Robert N. Proctor, "Should Medical Historians Be Working for the Tobacco Industry?" *Lancet* 363, no. 9410 (2004): 1174–1175; Louis M. Kyriakoudes, "Historians' Testimony on 'Common Knowledge' of the Risks of Tobacco Use: A Review and Analysis of Experts Testifying on Behalf of Cigarette Manufacturers in Civil Litigation," *Tobacco Control* 15 (Suppl 4) (2006): iv107-iv116; and Robert N. Proctor, "Tobacco and Health," Expert Report, *United States v. Philip Morris, et al.,* 2002.

11. Patricia Cohen, "History for Hire in Industry Lawsuits," *New York Times,* June 14, 2003.

12. "Deposition of Kenneth Ludmerer, M.D.," *Engle v. R.J. Reynolds Tobacco Co.* (1998), 9.

13. Peter Kaplan, "U.S. Trial Raises History of Smoking-Cancer Link," *Reuters News Service,* September 27, 2004.

14. *United States v. Philip Morris, et al.,* No. 04–5252 (D.C. Cir. 2005).

15. "Trial Testimony of Michael Fiore," *United States v. Philip Morris, et al.* (2005).

16. Eric Lichtblau, "Lawyers Fought U.S. Move to Curb Tobacco Penalty," *New York Times,* June 16, 2005.

17. Eric Lichtblau, "Political Leanings Were Always Factor in Tobacco Suit," *New York Times,* June 19, 2005.

18. M. C. Fiore, P. A. Keller, and T. B. Baker, "The Justice Department's Case Against the Tobacco Companies," *New England Journal of Medicine* 353, no. 10 (2005): 972–975.

19. Henry A. Waxman, Letter to DOJ Inspector General Glenn A. Fine, June 8, 2005 (available from http://democrats.reform.house.gov/Documents/20050609182600–65485.pdf); Brian Blackstone and Vanessa O'Connell, "Judge in Federal Tobacco Case Urges Sides to Settle," *Wall Street Journal*, June 21, 2005; and Michael Janofsky and David Johnston, "Award Limit in Tobacco Case Sets Off a Strenuous Protest," *New York Times*, June 9, 2005.

20. Motion to Intervene by the Tobacco-Free Kids Action Fund, American Cancer Society, American Heart Association, Americans for Nonsmokers' Rights, and National African American Tobacco Prevention Network, *United States v. Philip Morris, et al.*, No. 99–2496 (Gk) (D.C. Cir. 2005); filed June 29, 2005.

21. Gladys Kessler, *United States v. Philip Morris, et al.*, No. 99–2496 (Gk) (D.C. Cir. 2005); Campaign for Tobacco-Free Kids, *Special Reports: Department of Justice Civil Lawsuit* (2006), available from http://www.tobaccofreekids.org/reports/doj.

22. *United States v. Philip Morris, et al.* U.S. Dist LEXIS 57757 (D.C. Cir. 2006): 1500–1501 (available from http://www.dcd.uscourts.gov/opinions/district-court–2006.html). Vanessa O'Connell, "From the Ashes of Defeat—a Recent Court Ruling Forces Cigarette Makers to Revamp Marketing of Their Products," *Wall Street Journal*, August 21, 2006; and Philip Shenon, "U.S. Judge Sets New Limits on Marketing of Cigarettes," *New York Times*, August 18, 2006.

23. In a recent ruling, Federal District Court Judge Jack B. Weinstein certified a national class action in a civil RICO litigation contending that consumers were defrauded by industry claims for "light cigarettes." According to Weinstein, there was "substantial evidence" that the tobacco companies knew that these cigarettes were at least as dangerous as regular products. The suit asks for $200 billion for perhaps as many as 60 million "light" cigarette smokers. *Schwab v. Philip Morris USA, Inc.*, No. 04-CV–1945 (JBW), United States District Court for the Eastern District of New York, 2006 U.S. Dist. LEXIS 73211, September 25, 2006 (available from http://www.tobacco-on-trial.com/files/20060925schwabmemo.pdf).

24. Allan M. Brandt, "From Analysis to Advocacy: Crossing Boundaries as a Historian of Health Policy," in *Locating Medical History: The Stories and Their Meanings,* eds. Frank Huisman and John Harley Warner (Baltimore: Johns Hopkins University Press, 2004), 460–484. See also Rosemary A. Stevens, Charles E. Rosenberg, and Lawton R. Burns, eds. *History and Health Policy in the United States* (New Brunswick, NJ: Rutgers University Press, 2006).

NOTE ON SOURCES

There is a remarkable array of source material to support the investigation of cigarette use in history. A number of writers have made substantial contributions on which I relied heavily in this book. Most significantly, Richard Kluger's *Ashes to Ashes* (Knopf, 1996) remains an indispensable source for anyone interested in the history of tobacco in the twentieth century. The book, filled with telling detail, is based on hundreds of interviews with prominent tobacco industry figures and public health advocates. Kluger generously donated his research files to Yale University, where they can be utilized by other researchers. Notes from his many interviews are available online. In addition to Kluger's, there are several other important books that critically informed my own work. These include Richard Tennant's *The American Cigarette Industry* (Yale University Press, 1950); the important work of Nannie E. Tilley on the rise of the tobacco industry, *The Bright Tobacco Industry, 1860–1929* (University of North Carolina Press, 1948); and the highly readable, brief *They Satisfy,* by business historian Richard Sobel (Anchor Books, 1978). I have also found Jordan Goodman's *Tobacco and History* (Routledge, 1993) as well as his recent, two-volume encyclopedia, *Tobacco in History and Culture* (Thomson Gale, 2005) to be extremely useful.

There are several scholars whose work has significantly shaped the field over recent decades, and I have repeatedly relied on their findings and their insights. In particular, economist Kenneth Warner has made critical contributions over several decades to understanding the relationship between public policies to reduce smoking and their efficacy. Epidemiologists Richard Peto and Jonathan Samet have done groundbreaking work that follows in the tradition of Doll and Hill, illuminating the morbidity and mortality associated with smoking in the United States and around the world. Anyone seeking to understand the evolution of the contemporary tobacco pandemic and strategies for its control should consult their voluminous and critically important work.

A number of recent books are especially helpful in grounding an understanding of tobacco politics and regulation. A. Lee Fritschler's *Smoking and Politics* (1969; 4th ed. Prentice Hall, 1989) is a classic assessment of the obstacles to regulation. More recently, there have been a number of especially valuable accounts of tobacco litigation: these include Michael Orey's *Assuming the Risk* (Little, Brown, 1999), Peter Pringle's *Cornered: Big Tobacco at the Bar of Justice* (Henry Holt, 1998), and Dan Zegart's *Civil Warriors* (Delacorte, 2000). Michael Pertschuk, a leading figure in the efforts to regulate tobacco use, has written *Smoke in Their Eyes: Lessons in Movement Leadership from the Tobacco Wars* (Vanderbilt University Press, 2001), a particularly useful insider's assessment of the disputes associated with tobacco legislation at the end of the century.

Former FDA Commissioner David Kessler's account of his efforts to bring tobacco under his agency's regulatory aegis is brilliantly narrated in his *A Question of Intent* (Public Affairs, 2001). I have also found Robert Rabin and Stephen Sugarman's two edited volumes, *Smoking Policy* (Oxford University Press, 1993) and *Regulating Tobacco* (Oxford University Press, 2001) to be especially valuable.

Several books written in the 1990s are based substantially on the emergence of previously secret tobacco documents into the public realm. Stanton Glantz and colleagues produced the *Cigarette Papers* (University of California Press, 1996), a critically important review of the Brown &

Williamson documents recovered by Merrell Williams. Glantz is responsible for a remarkable body of advocacy-oriented research that I have utilized in this book. And *New York Times* reporter Philip Hilts's *Smokescreen* (Addison-Wesley, 1996) expertly narrates the Williams saga and evaluates the significance of these materials.

In addition to Hilts's path-breaking journalism, I have relied heavily on the critical work of a number of other journalists. It would be difficult to overstate the importance of a small band of journalists who brilliantly covered the tobacco story, especially over the last three decades. These include Morton Mintz of the *Washington Post*, whose coverage of the *Cipollone* trial was crucial to getting the full story of industry activity into the public media; Milo Geyelin and Alix Freedman at the *Wall Street Journal;* Jonathan Schwartz and Glenn Frankel at the *Washington Post;* Barry Meier and Michael Janofsky at the *New York Times;* and Myron Levin at the *Los Angeles Times.* This remarkable group of reporters has produced the kind of civic journalism that is critical to the democratic process. Broadcast journalists like Walt Bogdanich and Lowell Bergman also made crucial contributions to public knowledge.

In the course of my historical investigations on the history of tobacco, I have utilized a number important archival collections, including those of Harvard University (William Cochran); the Countway Library of Medicine, Harvard Medical School (McKeen Cattell); the University of Maine (C. C. Little); Washington University, St. Louis (Evarts Graham); the Wisconsin Historical Society (Bruce Barton, John W. Hill, Robert Lasch, M. V. O'Shea); the Alan Mason Chesney Medical Archives at the Johns Hopkins Medical Institutions (Lewis Robbins); the University of Pennsylvania (Luther Terry); the University of Washington, Seattle (Warren Magnuson); the Library of Congress (Edward Bernays, Harvey W. Wiley); Yale University (Chester Bliss, Lester Savage); Duke University (the John W. Hartman Center for Sales, Advertising and Marketing History); the Smithsonian (N. W. Ayer Collection, the Warshaw Collection of Business Americana); the National Library of Medicine (Stanhope Bayne-Jones); and the National Archives (the Surgeon General's Advisory Committee).

This book is heavily based on the tobacco archives that emerged as a result of litigation since the 1980s. Without the brilliant work of a series of plaintiffs' attorneys, the history of the cigarette would largely remain in the locked vaults of the tobacco industry. Now, literally millions of letters, memoranda, and research reports are all available online and downloadable. Taken together, the tobacco archives are in many ways the single most impressive example of the power of the Internet and how it might shape historical research in the future. At the same time, however, this record of the tobacco industry represents the most unusual of all archives. There is no industry that is so fundamentally open to scrutiny. I strongly invite my readers to even briefly experiment using these materials. One quickly finds that there is hardly any aspect of modern American life that is not part of these collections, starting from law and politics, to media, to constitutional rights, to PR; it is literally a few clicks to an unprecedented body of archival materials. Certainly, these tobacco archives could easily support intensive research on many questions only tangentially related to the cigarette. The Web sites involved have excellent information about conducting searches and strategies for effective use. Among the main Web sites are: Tobacco Documents Online (http://www.tobaccodocuments.org), which was set up by Michael Tacelovsky in 1999, and the Legacy Tobacco Documents Library (http://legacy.library.ucsf.edu), which was established at the University of California, San Francisco, in 1994. Both of these Web sites are grant supported, primarily by the National Cancer Institute and the American Legacy Foundation, respectively.

In addition, a number of individuals, expert in the use of the archives, have created links to documents of particular importance. I have relied in a number of instances on the exceptional research of Anne Landman, who has identified and annotated a large number of important industry documents. In addition to the online archives of tobacco industry documents, there are extensive online resources to support cigarette-related research. In particular, there is a remarkable depository of tobacco news as a result of the critical efforts of Gene Borio, who began an electronic bulletin board in 1995, extensively culling tobacco news from around the world. This site is now To-bacco.org, which is maintained by Borio and colleague Michael Tacelovsky. Researchers are much in their debt.

As I worked on this book, the combination of discovery in tobacco litigation and the Internet revolution radically reconfigured both the sources and the process of investigation. Unlike some historical inquiries where one hunts a spare trail of extant sources, the history of tobacco is replete with literally millions of documents and thousands of important publications from federal reports, research science, and the public media. The character of these materials, coupled with their sheer volume, raises critical questions about the nature of historical scholarship in the twenty-first century.

ACKNOWLEDGMENTS

Over the many years that I worked on this book, I repeatedly found that within the worlds of the academy, medicine, and public health, there is a deep reservoir of generosity, collegiality, and critical engagement. I consider myself exceptionally fortunate to have been able to draw upon the expertise of my colleagues and to have made so many new friends in the course of writing this book. The process of work on this project was unusual in the quality of the many personal relationships that grew out of the research, the ideas, and the important policy questions that have arisen. There is no way to repay the many debts that I have incurred, but I certainly hope my friends and colleagues understand the depth of my gratitude, and my sense of humility in the face of their extensive contributions to this work.

A number of my students provided excellent research support at various stages of the project. These gifted and enthusiastic students not only found sources and materials, they provided important ideas and critiques. I am enormously grateful to: Conevery Bolton Valenčius, Nicholas King, Jeremy Greene, Lara Freidenfelds, Stuart Strickland, David Greenes, Carolyn Frank, Scott Podolsky, David Jones, Deborah Levine, and Gary Negbaur. At an early stage of the project, Christian Warren not only provided excellent research support, but helped me conceptualize central themes and debates.

My colleagues and friends at the University of North Carolina have provided support and guidance long after my brief tenure there. These include Gail Henderson, Myron Cohen, Sue Estroff, Don Madison, Larry Churchill (now at Vanderbilt), and especially William Leuchtenburg, whose work has profoundly shaped my own. Historian Robert Proctor of Stanford University, a fellow student of the cigarette, has been a constant sounding board; he is a model for me of the possibilities of collegiality, academic courage, and social advocacy. To my great benefit, he meticulously read and critiqued the complete manuscript.

My colleagues in the Department of the History of Science at Harvard listened patiently over the years, and several read fragments—and more—on demand. In particular, I have greatly benefited from the many generous interventions of Peter Galison, Charles Rosenberg, Barbara Rosenkrantz, Peter Buck, and Mario Biagioli. Sophie Wadsworth brought a generous and kind poet's eye to my often awkward prose. And Jude Lajoie excelled in providing administrative backing. My colleague and friend at the Harvard Graduate School of Education, Robert Selman, consistently provided both good counsel and moral support. Matthew Miller of the Harvard School of Public Health read the entire manuscript, providing crucial input about the nature of causal inference, and great personal support throughout. And both Robert Aronowitz and David Barnes, now at the University of Pennsylvania, each provided expert advice and loyal support as I worked through essential questions in the book.

At the Department of Social Medicine, I have been in the unusual situation of relying on senior mentors on a daily basis. Julius B. Richmond, Leon Eisenberg, and Rashi Fein have all offered consistently sage advice over more than two decades. In different ways they each have offered a critical role model of committed scholarship that I have worked to follow. Arthur Kleinman and Byron Good provided an excellent environment for my research as well as an ongoing tutorial on the nature of cultural meaning and change. And Helena Martins and Christine Moreira offered crucial administrative support. Abigail Henderson ably assisted in the preparation of the manuscript. The expert editing skills of Stephen Scher greatly improved the final product. I am very grateful to Alison Fillmore of Vervaine Design Studio for her excellent work on the charts.

I have had the benefit of working in great libraries and archives throughout the United States and abroad. At the Countway Library of Medicine, the remarkable reference and archival skills of Richard Wolfe and Thomas Horrocks proved indispensable.

Early on in my research, John Pinney and Thomas Schelling at the Institute for the Study of Smoking Behavior and Policy provided both intellectual and research support. Several foundations provided crucial backing in the form of fellowships and grants. These include the Rockefeller Foundation for the Humanities, the Charles E. Culpeper Foundation, the Burroughs Wellcome Fund, and the Flight Attendants Medical Research Institute. I was especially honored to be named a Dr. William Cahan Distinguished Professor by FAMRI. This award supported the final stages of my research and writing.

William Frucht of Basic Books has been greatly patient and supportive in shepherding this sometimes unwieldy project to press. I am enormously grateful for his ongoing encouragement and confidence in this book, as well as for his exceptional editing skills. He has made this a much better and (believe it or not) shorter book.

Wynne Lundblad's research and editorial skills proved essential to the completion of this work. Her intelligence, unlimited energy, and great kindness helped the project to clear major hurdles. And her steadfast dedication to the work consistently reminded me of the larger purpose of the book.

Over a number of years Martha Gardner has brought her many historical skills and insights to this project. She has provided outstanding research, editing, and ideas with great generosity and commitment. During the course of our work together, we became both colleagues and collaborators. I have come to rely on her excellent judgment and true friendship.

A book like this inevitably creates a shortage of time and energy. My greatest debts are to my wife Shelly Greenfield and my sons, Daniel and Jacob. Without the love and unconditional commitment of my family, this book would not have been possible. No doubt, they will be greatly pleased and relieved to see it in this final form.

This book is ultimately about agency and responsibility. As a result, I feel compelled to take responsibility for any errors, omissions, or other faults, large and small.

AMB
Boston, Massachusetts
2006

INDEX